THE DOCTRINE OF
THE WORD OF GOD

CHURCH DOGMATICS

BY

KARL BARTH

VOLUME I

FIRST HALF-VOLUME

THE DOCTRINE OF
THE WORD OF GOD

THE DOCTRINE OF
THE WORD OF GOD

(Prolegomena to Church Dogmatics, being Vol. I, Part I)

BY

KARL BARTH, D.Theol., D.D.(Glas.)

AUTHORISED TRANSLATION BY

G. T. THOMSON
D.D.(Edin.), M.A., B.A.(Oxon.), B.D., B.Litt., S.S.T.P.
EDINBURGH UNIVERSITY

EDINBURGH : T. & T. CLARK, 38 GEORGE STREET

PRINTED IN GREAT BRITAIN BY
MORRISON AND GIBB LIMITED

FOR

T. & T. CLARK, EDINBURGH

NEW YORK : CHARLES SCRIBNER'S SONS

SBN 567 09011 6

FIRST PRINTED 1936
LATEST REPRINT . . . 1969

NOTE BY THE TRANSLATOR

KARL BARTH accepted my offer to translate without hesitation. It was necessary to await this second edition. Translation work on it has been delayed for about twelve months by circumstances over which human beings have no control. Now it is finished. I have done my best. I think the English makes sense. I know that many " Fachleute " will be grateful for it, if it is good enough. It should be read slowly and digested ; the " difficulty " will vanish, and the reward be great. Barth's text is characteristically full of marks of e m p h a s i s. These, together with authors' names when first mentioned in a context, are given effect to by s p a c i n g t h e t y p e. The device, common in German books, is retained in the translation. In the " Dogmatik" it is a valuable aid to the argument. The student is assured that the eye soon becomes used to picking out the s p a c i n g s on a page. No other device could be used, without either causing a confusion of signs or producing an ugly page. The original is undoubtedly the greatest treatise on the Trinity since the Reformation, by one whose faith has been put to the touch and come out the stronger ; I have read nothing like it except Martin Luther and John Calvin. May Karl Barth in our day and generation, like John Calvin in his, continue to fear God always, but man never !

My chief acknowledgments are : first and last to my Publishers ; to my wife, for valuable assistance ; to my colleague Dr. G. D. Henderson, for translating the passage in Dutch from Bavinck ; and—incomparably most of all—to the unparalleled kindness of the Very Rev. H. R. Mackintosh, D.D., of Edinburgh University, who crowned his encouragement of the work by reading the whole of it in typescript. The magnitude and the thoroughgoing nature of this service some may guess at, I alone can judge. It reduces to silence. But the value of it to readers will be inestimable. I am responsible for any errors which remain.

I wish to acknowledge the carefulness of the typist, Miss Young, of the Gregg School, Aberdeen.

Note by the Translator

Karl Barth has meant much to myself spiritually, and I consider his work to be a vital and much-needed challenge to all theology, as well as to that of our own Reformed Church and his. I therefore feel that I cannot better signalise the close of a humble effort to second that challenge, than by invoking the Triune Name, praying that His Word in our time may have free course and multiply, for His own glory and the saving of many.

In nomine Patris et Filii et Spiritus sancti. AMEN.

G. T. T.

Christmas, 1934.

AUTHOR'S FOREWORD

HUMAN affairs—even those we think we can control—invariably take a different course from the one planned. *Hominum confusione?* *Dei providentia?* No doubt also and no doubt decisively *Dei providentia*, but no doubt in such a way that on the other, or human side, all is *confusio* primarily and *per se*, many plans are not carried out at all, and practically all are carried out differently from their planning at the time.

When, five years ago, I published " The Doctrine of the Word of God " as volume I of a *Christian Dogmatics in Outline*, I thought then—all sorts of not unusable preliminary work was in my hands— that I should and could supply the whole of what I thereby promised within the time which has now elapsed. It fell out otherwise. The first volume, when it lay before me in print, showed me too clearly (whatever the experience of others may be, more clearly than a MS. lying in a cupboard could possibly have shown me), how much I myself had still to learn historically and materially ; the opposition which the book met, at least among colleagues, was too general and vehement, and the displacements which intervened meanwhile in the theological, ecclesiastical, and general situation gave me too much to think about—in the meantime Anselm of Canterbury also had to have his book !—to let me just listen to the gradually increasing chorus of friendly or even ironical demands, as to where my " second volume " was, and simply continue writing on the level and in the strain of my beginning in 1927. This, of course, first became clear to me when the four thousand copies of the book printed as volume I were sold out, and I was faced with the task of first of all working at a new edition of the first part. My experience of twelve years ago in re-editing the *Römerbrief* was repeated. I could and I wanted to say the same thing as before ; but now I could no longer say it in the way in which I had said it before. What else was left me, except to begin at the beginning and, true, to say the same thing over again, but the same thing over again in quite a different way ? And so I must now delight my readers, or perhaps even annoy them in part, by the fact that, instead of the new book they expected, I am first of all setting before them a second time merely the old one made new. I trust some may believe me when I say that, at least from my point of view, all this perforce took a course so contrary to plan by the pressure of outward and inward necessities ! And I trust some may even appreciate my good sense in letting myself be held up and led aside in this not exactly usual fashion.

The alteration which I have made consists in the first place, formally, in the very much greater explicitness which I thought should be given to the exposition. This is shown visibly by the fact that, to start with, for all the not inconsiderably larger size of the book and in spite of some severe suppressions, I have achieved only half the material promised in the first sketch of it, and so can only present a first half-volume. What can I do ? During the five years every problem has assumed for me a very much richer, more mobile, and more difficult aspect. I had to make more extensive soundings and lay broader foundations. And now I still venture to hope that with it all everything has actually become simpler and clearer.

The external growth of the book is also connected with my desire to give more space to indicating Biblical and theological presuppositions, the connections with the history of theology and the polemical relations of my statements. All these things I have condensed into the subparagraphs in small print, and have so regulated the dogmatic exposition that it can be read connectedly, especially by non-theologians, by skipping these *excursûs* if necessary. Ought I, on the other hand, to have to request the dainty among the theologians, not to confine their reading to the *excursûs?* At a pinch the text can be understood (but really only at a pinch) even without the *excursûs*, but not the *excursûs* without the text. If I have mostly reproduced *in extenso* the passages adduced from the Bible, the Fathers, and theologians, this was done not only out of consideration for the many, who might not have the books used handy, but because I wished to give all readers an opportunity, more directly than would have been possible by mere references, to hear the very voices which rang in my ears as I wrought out my own text, which guided, taught, or stimulated me, and by which I wish to be measured by my readers. I by no means suggest that these voices had said the same thing as myself, but rather that what needs must be said and listened to in Dogmatics to-day is better understood, in fact, in the last resort, only fully understood, when we join in listening to these voices so far as Bible passages are concerned, as to the real ground text, upon which everything else and everything of one's own can only be a commentary, listening to it right through everything else and of one's own. Should any one find cause to miss the citation of this or that authority which has importance for him, let him at least reflect that the principle of selection in a dogmatics must be different from that in an historical exposition in the narrower sense. Yet even so I have not systematically pursued even the antitheses implicitly or explicitly contested by me, even those of my special and direct adversaries and critics of to-day, but, pursuing my own way, I have taken up those which in any sense have made an impression on me, and taken them up at the point at which it appeared to me materially serviceable for the raising or even merely for the illumination of problems.

The facts as to the change in content introduced between the first and this second edition the reader may gather from the book itself. I may content myself here with some general observations.

When the word " Church " replaces the word " Christian " in the title of the book, that means firstly that with regard to renouncing the light-hearted use, so much combated by myself, of the great word " Christian " I might proceed with good precedent—but also the material fact, that *a priori* I might point to the circumstance that dogmatics is not a " free " science, but one bound to the sphere of the Church, where and where alone it is possible and sensible. The lament over the general course of my development will undoubtedly at once ring out still more clearly in view of such a visible alteration as this. Some will perceive directly from that what was meant, when in recent years (and, for that matter, in the book itself too) I have frequently with some liveliness spoken against—nay, rather on behalf of—the Church. But be that as it may, in this new edition the lines will be found drawn more sharply in the actual direction indicated by this alteration.

That means, above all, that I think I now have a better understanding of some things (among them my own purposes), in that to the best of my ability I have cut out in this second issue of the book everything that in the first issue might give the slightest appearance of giving to theology a basis, support, or even a mere justification in the way of existential philosophy. " The Word or existence ? " The first edition gave acumen or even stupidity some cause to put this question. I may hope that the answer to it,

at least so far as my purpose is concerned, is now clear. Because
in the former undertaking I can only see a readoption of the line
Schleiermacher-Ritschl-Herrmann, and because in any thinkable
continuation of this line I can only see the plain destruction of
Protestant theology and the Protestant Church, because I can
see no third possibility between play with the *analogia entis*,
legitimate only on Roman Catholic ground, between the greatness
and the misery of a so-called natural knowledge of God in the sense
of the *Vaticanum*, and a Protestant theology self-nourished at
its own source, standing upon its own feet, and finally liberated from
such secular misery, I can therefore only say No here. I regard
the *analogia entis* as the invention of Antichrist, and think that
because of it one can not become Catholic. Whereupon I at
the same time allow myself to regard all other possible reasons for
not becoming Catholic, as shortsighted and lacking in seriousness.

This at once states my attitude to the reproach, which I had
foreseen with the utmost clarity five years ago, and which was
raised at once almost right along the line, in every possible key
from friendly regret to blazing outbursts of anger, that historically,
formally, and materially I am walking in the steps of scholasticism.
It would appear, people said, that Church History does not first
begin for me with the year 1517. I am in a position to quote
Anselm and Thomas also without a sign of horror. There manifestly exists for me what might be called an authoritativeness in
Early Church doctrine. I deal fully and explicitly with the doctrine
of the Trinity and in its place with that of the Virgin Birth. The
last-named alone would obviously have been enough for many
contemporaries to hold me more than suspect of crypto-Catholicism.
What am I to say? Shall I excuse myself by pointing out that
the connection between the Reformation and the Early Church,
Trinitarian and Christological dogma, the concept of dogma in
general and the concept of the Biblical Canon are ultimately not
malicious inventions of mine? Or shall I counter indignation
with indignation, at the presumption which on their side seems to
consider it necessary to ignore or deny those things, which on their
side seems already to consider an epigonous fideism as dogmas,
despisers of which may forthwith be accused of " Catholicising "?
Or shall I—perhaps naming names—ask why not one of the so-called
positive theologians, of whom there are still supposed to be several
in German Universities—they or their predecessors, a good twenty
years ago, ran a pretty vigorous campaign about " the Confession "!

—leaped to my assistance in this matter ?   Or what and what sort
of mention would they have made to-day of Trinity and Virgin
Birth ?   Or shall I merely be astonished at a philistinism which
usually thinks, where it fails to recognise its own ethicism, that it
ought to utter laments over " speculation," which does not notice
that not only the most important, but also the finest and most
interesting problems in dogmatics begin at the point where on this
showing we should have to stop thinking because of the fable of
" unprofitable Scholasticism " or the catchword about the " Greek
thought of the Fathers " ?   Or should I smile at the phonetically
ridiculous talk about *fides quae* and *fides qua*, by which some
obviously think to get rid of all scholastic cares at a blow, by which
they also imagine they can dispose of me most speedily ?   Or
should I rather weep over the constantly increasing barbarism,
tedium, and insignificance of modern Protestantism, which has gone
and lost—apparently along with the Trinity and the Virgin Birth—
an entire third dimension (let us say it once for all, the dimension
of mystery—not to be confused with religiously moral " seriousness ") ;   only to be punished with every possible worthless substitute, only that it might with all the less check relapse into High
Church, German Church, Christian Community, religious socialism,
and similar miserable cliques and sects, only that in the end so-and-
so many of its preachers and faithful people might learn finally how
to discover religious insight in the intoxication of their Nordic
blood and in their political *Führer* (Leader) ?   Whatever the right
thing may be, I can only pass by this objection and the whisper
about my " Catholicising," and in face of the enemy repeat more
emphatically and expressly all that in this respect has been deplored
in my book.   Particularly on this specially contested side I am of
specially good courage and specially sure of my cause.

One remark in closing upon the present theological situation.
In agreement or in opposition this book will be all the better understood, the more it is conceived (as I already said in the Foreword
to the first edition) as being " on its own," the less, that is, it is
conceived as the exponent of a movement, tendency, or school.
Even in this sense it seeks to be " Church."   I may take it as well
known that there exists between Eduard Thurneysen and
myself a theological affinity of long standing, which has always
proved itself something self-evident.   More than that, I am
acquainted, among theological colleagues, ministers, and non-
theologians, with many a man and many a woman, towards whom

I am conscious of being whole-heartedly sympathetic in general outlook. But that is not a school, and particularly of those who are mostly associated with myself as protagonists of the so-called " dialectic theology " or as closely related thereto, I could not for a moment think in such a pronounced way. It will be justice to them as well as to myself, if this book, even in its new form, is not claimed as the dogmatics of the " dialectical theology." The communion, in and for which I have written this book, is the communion of the Church, not a theological "community of work." Of course, there is within the Church an Evangelical theology which is to be affirmed, and a heretical non-theology which is resolutely to be denied. But I rejoice that *in concreto* I am unaware and need not be aware who stands where, and that therefore I serve a cause and not a party, that I indeed fence myself off against a cause but not against another party, in a word, that I do not have to work for or against persons. And so that I am free even towards my apparent and real neighbours, and on earth responsible only to the Church ! What I did want was that I might be understood in this matter by some who would like to see me walking arm in arm with X and Y.

I am not unaware that to undertake a dogmatics of the Evangelical Church to-day, even in itself and apart from the objections specially relevant to it, is exposed to doubts which it cannot prove easy for me to answer. For where at present is the Evangelical Church which wants any one to take her as seriously, to confess her in such a sense, as is the case in this book ? Am I not aware that in the realm of modern Protestantism, Church authority has no desire anything like so clamant as that of being forced to listen to Church doctrine as little as possible ? Am I not aware that even the doctrinal interest existing in the Church of to-day is directed to quite other matters than those dealt with in my main positions ? Am I not aware of the want of connection between what fills the heads and hearts of all to-day and what I seek to expound as stimulating and important in these pages ? Am I not aware how probable it is, that from large circles of those accustomed to take notice of theological work in general the cry will arise afresh, that stones are being offered here instead of bread ? Yes, I am aware of it all, and it might well discourage me to think upon it. I can only reply that I hold myself forbidden to let myself be discouraged by thinking about it. Because I think any one would wait in vain till the day of judgment for an Evangelical

Church that took itself seriously, unless in all humility he was willing to risk being such a Church in his own place and as well as he knew how. Because I think I understand present-day Church government better than it understands itself, when I do not consider its resentment, only too well known to me, against what should have been to it the most important task, but appeal from Church government badly informed to Church government which is to be better informed. Because I am firmly convinced that we cannot reach the clarifications, especially in the broad field of politics, which are necessary to-day and to which theology to-day might have a word to say (as indeed it ought to have a word to say to them !), without having previously reached those comprehensive clarifications, in theology and about theology itself, with which we should be concerned here. Because it is to be expected of the Church and with her of theology a world within the world, as they doubtless are, no less than chemistry or drama !—that she should stick doggedly and particularly to the rhythm of her own relevant concerns, that is, consider carefully what the real needs of the day are, by which she has to direct her programme. Because I have found by experience that ultimately " people " (so highly respected by many Churchmen and theologians !) then and only then take account of us, when, quite untroubled by what " people " expect of us, we do what is actually laid upon u s. Because I believe as a matter of fact that a better Church dogmatics (even apart from all utilitarian ethical applications) might be an ultimately weightier and more solid contribution even to questions and tasks like that of German liberation, than most of the well-meant stuff which so many, even among theologians, think in their dilettantism they should and can supply, with respect to these questions and tasks. For these reasons I hold myself forbidden to let myself be discouraged by such thoughts. For these reasons I venture upon what is really a venture for my feelings also, to proceed in the middle of the year 1932 to a dogmatics and, still more, to a dogmatics of such compass. I was resolved not to omit expressing this, in order to indicate that any comments upon it, in jest or earnest, have been appreciated even by me.

At the publishers' desire I have great pleasure, though without at all binding myself, in informing readers how I think of continuing the start made with this half-volume.

First of all, in a second half-volume of, I suppose, pretty much the same size, the *Prolegomena to Dogmatics* will be brought to a close ; thus, in accordance with the first edition the doctrine of Revelation will, to begin with, have to be finished off and the doctrine of Holy Scripture and the doctrine of Church Proclamation set forth.

The second volume should contain the doctrine of God, the third the doctrine of Creation, the fourth the doctrine of Reconciliation, the fifth the doctrine of Redemption.

Ethics so-called I regard as the doctrine of God's command and do not consider it right to treat it otherwise than as an integral part of dogmatics, or to produce a dogmatics which does not include it. The concept of the command of God in general should in this dogmatics be discussed at the close of the doctrine of God. The commandment of God from the viewpoint of Order will be dealt with at the close of the doctrine of Creation, from the viewpoint of Law at the close of the doctrine of Reconciliation, from the viewpoint of Promise at the close of the doctrine of Redemption.

I need not say that, in order to carry out this plan in the way which now presents itself to me as right, I must count upon many years. And all sensible people will realise that in a matter of such wide prospect I cannot to-day tie myself down to detailed announcements drawn from my preliminary labours ; but I venture to ask them to believe in advance, on the basis of the indications just given, that I know what I am after. " If God will and we are alive " (Jas. 4^{15}).

BERGLI, OBERRIEDEN (CANTON ZÜRICH),
August 1932.

CONTENTS

THE DOCTRINE OF THE WORD OF GOD

CHAPTER I

THE WORD OF GOD AS THE CRITERION OF DOGMATICS

CHAPTER II

THE REVELATION OF GOD

PART I. THE TRIUNE GOD

INTRODUCTION

§ 1

THE TASK OF DOGMATICS

As a theological discipline, dogmatics is the scientific test to which the Christian Church puts herself regarding the language about God which is peculiar to her.

1. THE CHURCH, THEOLOGY, SCIENCE

Dogmatics is a theological discipline. But theology is a function of the Church.

The Church confesses God, by the fact that she speaks of God. She does so first of all through her existence in the action of each individual believer. And she does so in the second place through her special action as a community; in proclamation by preaching and administration of the Sacrament, in worship, in instruction, in her mission work within and without the Church, including loving activity among the sick, the weak, and those in jeopardy. Fortunately the Church's reality does not coincide exactly with her action. But her action does coincide with the fact that alike in her existence in believers and in her communal existence as such, she speaks about God. Her action is " theology," alike in the former, broader sense, and in the latter, narrower sense.

Theology is *de divinitate ratio sive sermo* (Augustine, *De civ. Dei*, VIII 1). Θεολόγος est ὁ τὸν θεὸν ἐκ θεοῦ ἐνώπιον τοῦ θεοῦ εἰς δόξαν αὐτοῦ λέγων (Coccejus, *Summa theol.* 1669 I 1).

But by her very confession of God, the Church also confesses to the humanity and likewise to the responsibility of her action. She is aware of her exposure to fierce temptation in speaking of God, aware also that she has to reckon with God for her speaking. The first, last, and decisive answer to this double compulsion

1

consists in the fact that she finds His grace sufficient, whose strength is mighty in the weak.   Yet in virtue of her very contentment with that, she recognises and undertakes, as an active Church, a further human task, the task of criticising and revising her language about God. This confronts us with the concept of theology in the third, strictest, and proper meaning of the word.

Cf. for this threefold concept of theology J oh. Gerhard, *Loci theol.* 1610 *Prooem.* 4: Theology is—1. *fides et religio Christiana, quae omnibus fidelibus doctis aeque ac indoctis communis est, ut sic theologi dicantur ; 2. functio ministerii Ecclesiastici ;* 3. *accuratior divinorum mysteriorum cognitio, qua ratione theologi dicuntur, qui possunt veritatem divinam solide stabilire, eique oppositam falsitatem potenter destruere.*

Theology as science (as distinguished from the " theology " of the simple testimony of faith and life and from the " theology " of public worship) is the Church taking her measure, in view of the temptation and responsibility just mentioned, which attaches to her language. It would be meaningless without justifying grace, which in this case too can alone make good what man as such invariably makes a mess of ; yet it may have significance as an act of obedience to this very grace, that obedience whereby man in this case too may believe without seeing, that he is doing well for himself.

Early theology is already aware that : . . . *et hominum officio ipso sancto Spiritu largiente in docendis etiam ipsis doctoribus non debere cessare et tamen neque qui plantat esse aliquid neque qui rigat sed Deum qui incrementum dat* (Augustine, *De doctr. christ.* IV 16).

The Church produces theology in this special and peculiar sense, by subjecting herself to a self-test. She faces herself with the question of truth, i.e. she measures her action, her language about God, against her existence as a Church. Thus theology exists in this special and peculiar sense, because before it and apart from it there is, in the the Church, language about God.—Theology follows the language of the Church, so far as, in its question as to the correctness of the Church's procedure therein, it measures it, not by a standard foreign to her, but by her very own source and object. Theology guides the language of the Church, so far as it concretely reminds her that in all circumstances it is fallible human work, which in the matter of relevance or irrelevance lies in the balance, and must be obedience to grace, if it is to be well done. Theology accompanies the language of the Church, so far as it is itself nothing but human " language about God," so far as, with that language, it stands under the judgment that begins with the house of God, and so far as, with it, it lives by the promise given to the Church.

The work in which the Church submits herself to this self-test falls into three circles, which intersect in such a way that the centre of each is also within the circumference of the other two ; but as for a " systematic " centre, the centre of the circle which includes the three, considering what alone can be the centre here, it is better neither to assert nor to construct one. The question of truth, with which theology is throughout concerned, is the question as to the agreement between the language about God peculiar to the Church and the essence of the Church. The criterion of Christian language, in past and future as well as at the present time, is thus the essence of the Church, which is Jesus Christ, God in His gracious approach to man in revelation and reconciliation. Has Christian language its source in Him ? Does it lead to Him ? Does it conform to Him ? None of these questions can be put without the others, but each in all its force must be put independently. Thus as Biblical theology, theology is the question as to the foundation, as practical theology it is the question as to the aim, as dogmatic theology it is the question as to the content, of the language peculiar to the Church.

Church History so-called answers, from the point of view of Christian language about God, to no question that need be put independently, and is therefore not to be regarded as an independent theological discipline. It is the indispensable auxiliary science to exegetical, dogmatic, and practical theology.

Since the Church in putting the question of truth in this triple sense is acting not arbitrarily but relevantly, this self-test of hers acquires the character of a scientific undertaking, which as such ranks independently along with other human undertakings of a like or similar kind, as this special, or theological " science." As to both claims, the claim of theology to be a " science " and her claim to a separate place alongside the other " sciences," these can of course only be upheld practically and with reservations.

To begin with, the vaunted independence of theology over against the other sciences is at least not to be proved as a matter of necessary principle. As for treating the question of the truth of language about God as a special question belonging to a particular faculty, that is a difficulty which it should be our desire to make the best of by acknowledging seriously its actual inevitability, but not to justify on final grounds. Only theological arrogance would dream of arguing here otherwise than practically. It might be that philosophy, or historical science or sociology or psychology or pedagogics, or all of them together, working in the sphere of the Church, would undertake the task of measuring the Church's language about God against her essence as a Church, and thus render a special theology superfluous. In reality theology does not find itself in possession of special keys for special doors ! Neither has it at its disposal a basis of knowledge, which might not straightway be realised in every other science, nor is it aware of an objective area, which is necessarily hidden away from any other science whatsoever. It would have to ignore the factual nature of revelation as an event, the possibility of grace and thereby its own nature, were it to dream of such an assertion. In the same way neither can we possibly admit proof of a fundamental need for the theology of public worship. Jer. 31[34] might be conceived as an accomplished fact ! Philosophy and " secular " science generally really need not be " secular," need not be heathen ; it might be *philosophia christiana.*

Porro si sapientia Deus est, per quem facta sunt omnia sicut divina auctoritas veritasque monstravit, verus philosophus est amator Dei (Augustine, *De civ. Dei*, VIII 1).

To contest this on principle combines despair of the " world " with an over-valuation of the " Christian " world, in a way incompatible either with Christian hope or with Christian humility. Theology as a special science, like the " theology " of public worship as the peculiarly Christian language, can only be justified as a relative necessity, necessary in practice.

Absolute et simpliciter Theologia non est necessaria, ne quidem toti Ecclesiae ; potest enim Deus homines immediate h.e. sine ministerio hominum Theologorum informare et convertere— sed ex hypothesi posita scil. Dei voluntate (Quenstedt, *Theol. did.-pol.* 1685 I cap. 1, sect. 2, qu. 1, ekth. 6).

As a matter of practice the other sciences have not recognised and assumed the task of theology as their own. True, the language of the Church about God has long been criticised from many quarters, and attempts have been made to correct it. But what must be done here is to criticise and revise it from the standpoint of the essence of the Church, of Jesus Christ as her foundation, her end and her content. Practically it is the case (although it does not admit of proof as a necessary matter of principle), that the historian, educationist, and so on, and not least the philosopher himself, for all their goodwill in taking this matter into account, always, within the framework of their own sciences, speak past the problem here confronting them. In other words, they judge the Church's language about God on principles foreign to it, instead of on its own principles, and thus increase instead of diminishing the harm on account of which the Church needs a critical science. And that the more perniciously, when they do it in the name of " theology ! " In practice the services of the philosopher, historian, etc., to the problem here presented can only be indirectly significant, by means of a definite interpretation. Up to date, in practice—in each of the three departments of theological inquiry— philosophy, science of history, psychology, etc., have in a direct sense succeeded only in increasing the self-alienation of the Church, in degenerating and devastating her language about God. But in that interpretation, so the competent experts will at once object, philosophy ceases to be philosophy, history to be history. In practice *philosophia christiana* has never yet taken shape ; if it was *philosophia*, it was not *christiana* ; if it was *christiana*, it was not *philosophia*. If then the interests of the Church are not simply to be neglected, the special function of a scientific theology, corresponding to the special function of public worship, is in practice indispensable. Its task is (a task in practice not neglected by the other sciences) to criticise and revise language about God by the standard of the principle peculiar to the Church. Theology is the science which ultimately sets itself this and only this task, in fact subordinating to this task all other possible tasks in man's investigation of truth.

Non ubique quidquid sciri ab homine potest in rebus humanis . . . huic scientiae tribuens, sed illud tantummodo, quo fides saluberrima, quae ad veram beatitudinem ducit, gignitur, nutritur, defenditur, roboratur (Augustine, *De trin.* XIV 1, 3). *Theologia . . . ita est omnium arbitra et domina, ut de ipsis judicet et ipsa a nulla alia scientia judicetur ; omnes enim aliae disciplinae exigendae sunt ad ejus amussim, ut quicquid habent cum theologia non consonum reiiciatur.* (Fr. Turretini, *Instit. Theol. elenchth.* I 1679 I 6, 7.) Cf. Thomas Aquinas, *S. theol.* I qu. 1, art. 5.

The other sciences too might finally set themselves this and only this task, and subordinate all other tasks to this task. All the sciences at their acme might be theology. The fact that they are not, need neither be complained of nor justified here. In any case it creates a vacuum, which for the Church is intolerable. The separate existence of theology signifies the special measures upon which the Church has been forced to resolve, in view of the actual refusal of the other sciences to do so. An epistemological basis for this cannot be given. From the particular viewpoint of the Church and so of theology this special existence of theology is theoretically quite problematical. Of the efforts made to assign her a place in the system of sciences, theology must say itself that this is too great—and too small—an honour.

The case is also somewhat similar with the question whether theology is a " science " at all. This question is never a vital question for theology. There is no fundamental necessity, there are no inner grounds, to cause it to claim membership of this genus. Rather it has abundant reason to renounce it in every form.

In early Protestant orthodoxy, so far as I am aware, Baier (*Comp. Theol. posit.* 1686 *Prol.* I 15), followed by Buddeus (*Instit. Theol. dogmat.* 1724 I 1, 28), was the first emphatically to call theology a *scientia*. Presumably with reference to Thomas Aquinas (*S. theol.* I *qu.* 1, *art.* 2, 6) they spoke deliberately, in the older school at Leiden (e.g. Waläus, *Loci comm.* 1640 p. 4, Leiden *Synopsis pur. Theol.* 1624 I 9), of *scientia vel sapientia* ; whereas otherwise, so far as I see, the preponderating majority of the older (e.g. Wolleb, *Christ. Theol. Comp.* 1626 *Praecog.*) and younger (e.g. Mastricht, *Theol. theor.-pract.* 1698 I 1, 1) Reformed writers, even the Lutheran Quenstedt (*Theol. did.-pol.* 1685 I *cap.* 1 *sect.* 1 *th.* 28) preferred the concept *doctrina*. J. Gerhard expressly rejected the designation of theology as *scientia* on the following grounds : 1. *Scientiae certitudo ab internis et inhaerentibus principiis, fidei vero ab externis videlicet ab autoritate revelantis pendet.* 2. *Subjectum theologiae est Christus, cujus cognitio scientifico modo haberi nequit, sed ex divina revelatione eam peti oportet.* 3. *Cujusvis scientiae principium est intellectus quando ex principiis apte cognitis ad scientiam conclusionum devenitur. At in theologia intellectus non est principium sed finis.* 4. *Scientiis ratiocinando inventis potest subesse falsum* (*Loci theol.* 1610 *Prooem.* 8). He and later Hollaz (*Ex. Theol. acroam.* 1707 *Prol.* I 1) choose the concept *sapientia*. In the 19th century A. F. C. Vilmar (alone, so far as I know) entered a protest against the name " science " as " in the meantime " too heavily overloaded (*Dogmatik*, 1874 I p. 38. Cf. *Die Theologie der Tatsachen wider die Theologie der Rhetorik*, 4th edn. 1876 p. VI f.). The pathos with which Georg Wobbermin assures us that " theology has the very greatest, i.e. a thoroughly existential interest in ranking as a real science, as a science in the strict, in fact in the strictest sense of the word " (*Richtlinien evang. Theologie*, 1929 p. 25) is excessive. For the ancient and mediæval prehistory of this question cf. G. Söhngen, *Die kathol. Theologie als Wissenschaft und Weisheit* (*Catholica, Vierteljahrschrift für Kontroverstheologie*, April 1932).

If theology lets itself be called and calls itself a " science," it thereby declares that—1. Like all other so-called sciences, it is a human effort after a definite object of knowledge. 2. Like all other sciences, it follows a definite, self-consistent path of knowledge. 3. Like all other sciences, it is in the position of being accountable for this path to itself and to every one—every one who is capable of effort after this object and therefore of following this path. But it would not make the slightest difference to what it has to do, if it had to rank as something other than just a " science." Because it is so ranked and claims so to be ranked, it is by no means obliged to spoil or prejudice itself in its own task, by heeding what " science " means elsewhere. In effecting this, its special task, it must rather completely subordinate and, if necessary, sacrifice every single consideration of what " science " means elsewhere. While remembering the existence of the other sciences, and the respect-compelling fidelity with which many at least of them follow out their axioms and methods, it cannot and must not forget that it too should follow out its own task orderly, that is, with corresponding fidelity. But it cannot allow itself to be taught by them the concrete meaning which that involves in its own case. As regards method it has nothing to learn in their school.

It has not to justify itself before them, least of all by submitting to the claims of any concept of science, whether its general validity is accidental or not.

To the question, what the " science " really is to which theology must adhere completely, Georg Wobbermin replies (*op. cit.* p. 29), most ingenuously, " Striving after the highest possible adequacy and completeness of knowledge, about the reality to which we have access." But what good theology will assign its object to " the reality to which we have access ? " And will a bad theology which does so, really win the recognition it seeks at the hands of the other sciences ?

What it would mean to accommodate oneself to the concept of science in repute and force to-day—and apparently not only to-day—may be made strikingly plain to us in the essay of Heinrich Scholz, " *Wie ist eine evangelische Theologie als Wissenschaft möglich ?* " (*Z.d.Z.* 1931 pp. 8–53). The claims made upon an undertaking which aspires to rank as " science," and also upon theology, are, according to Scholz (*op. cit.* pp. 18–24, 28–48), in an ascending scale as follows : 1. Freedom from contradiction in all the propositions to be constructed by the so-called science in question (" Proposition Postulate "). 2. The unity in its objective sphere (" Coherence Postulate "). 3. All propositions drawn up to be capable of being tested " by any reader or hearer who is sufficiently attentive " (" Controllability Postulate "). 4. Regard to be had to what is physically and biologically impossible ("Congruity Postulate"). 5. Freedom from "any sort of prejudices" ("Independence Postulate"). 6. All propositions to be capable of being broken up into axioms and theorems and susceptible of proof on this basis (this, solemnly, "the supreme claim which can be made on any science"). Scholz is certainly right in guarding against the possibility of the theologian discerning in this conception of science a somewhat arbitrary, modern invention : "Even this concept has a tradition, a great classical tradition, and it is a splendid thing and worth the trouble to side with the high esteem in which it is held" (*op. cit.* p. 51). In addition to its theoretical basis in the history of philosophy since Plato and Aristotle, it has on its side the historical evolution of at least the last two to three hundred years, as well as a practical execution carried out with tolerable uniformity in Berlin, New York, and Tokio. Moreover, it is intended not as a hard and fast, but as a flexible principle, readily admitting of degrees in practical application. There would therefore be no sense in pointing out here its internal difficulties and the hiatuses which occur, in the application of it, perhaps without a break and right into the natural sciences. Yet it is for that reason the concept of science for our time. And this very concept theology can but flatly declare to be unacceptable to it. The very minimum postulate of freedom from contradiction is acceptable by theology only upon the very limited interpretation, by the scientific theorist upon the scarcely tolerable one, that theology will not assert an irremovability in principle of the "contradictions" which it is bound to make good. But the propositions in which it asserts their removal will be propositions concerning the free action of God, and so not propositions that "remove" the contradictions "from the world." The remaining sections of Scholz's law can only remind the theologian that he should know what he is doing when he transgresses them, and that as a theologian he cannot escape the necessity of transgressing them. Not an iota can be yielded here without betraying theology, for any concession here involves surrendering the theme of theology On the other hand, Scholz has replied (*op. cit.* p. 52) to the question whether relevancy or objectivity should not also or even above all be added to the postulates of the concept of science, that so far he has come across no criterion, "with the help of which it could be decided, even only in a single and seriously controversial instance, whether a thought, given beforehand, is relevant in this instance or not." Possibly the theologian better than others will appreciate the weight to be attached to this pronouncement. But he will say that relevancy in this annoyingly indefinite sense is itself the most general expression of the one characteristic rule, to which theology should and must hold.—So that dealings with this concept of science can only consist of the dry declaration that in no circumstances can it be that of theology.

An apparently more harmless because more general definition of the concept of "science" is given by Arthur Titius in his Berlin University address of 26th July 1931 : "*Ist systematische Theologie als Wissenschaft möglich?*" According to Titius, science "is present or thought of as realised, wherever in the realm of knowledge common work exists or is possible. That is only the case where the object behind the knowledge can be made accessible to each with the requisite clarity and can be expounded according to methods which are the same for all" (p. 5 f.). The possibility of this condition being fulfilled by systematic theology Titius sees first of all (p. 11 f.) in the fact that in the thought, recently become prevalent again, of the unity of the world it has a "point of approach" accessible to any one capable of thought ;

secondly (p. 14 f.), in the possibility of the myth of the immediate working of God, as an inner causality of a personal and miraculous nature, in the Christian form of which the theologian beholds " profound truth "—truth which in its " weightiness," etc., even those who reject this myth must acknowledge ; and finally (p. 27 f.) in the psychological, sociological, and moral significance of the Christian religion, which is to be made clear to every one. " Thus theology admits of incorporation with knowing " (p. 30), if only as, in a word, is the case also with historical science and finally also with natural science, it is conceded the opportunity of also making proper use of the " view of essences " (" A kind of intuition, in virtue of which æsthetic elements enter in and contribute their determining value to the process of knowledge " p. 30). On these terms theology does in fact submit to incorporation with knowing. But it is precisely in view of the three considerations which should here justify its place as a science, the idea of unity, the possibility of myth, and the human reference in Christianity, that theologically it can only be described as utterly empty, that theology thus incorporated must be disowned as theology. How can it be otherwise, if the object of theology is to be made accessible with requisite clarity to every one, and expounded according to methods valid for all ? Concept of science notwithstanding, this object of knowledge will never stand this treatment.

If theology allows itself to be called or calls itself a science, it cannot at the same time take over the obligation to submit to measurement by the canons valid for other sciences.

Likewise it cannot justify itself before the other sciences on the score of setting up for discussion on its own side a concept of science which does not exclude but includes a good theology. To put itself in a systematic relationship with the other sciences, theology would have to regard its own special existence as fundamentally necessary. That is exactly what it cannot do. It absolutely cannot regard itself as a member of an ordered cosmos, but only as a stop-gap in an unordered one. How could there possibly be a concept of science common to the stop-gap and to the unordered cosmos ? Upon the antagonism of the will to taking up or not taking up the theme of theology, any attempt of this kind must founder at the start. And this antagonism of the will, at least from the viewpoint of theology, really ceases to be a " problem " soluble by any synthetic construction.

Against the attempts of scientific encyclopedia to include theology as a science, as they have ever and anon been made since the time of S c h l e i e r - m a c h e r, the general objection may be raised that the abnormality of the peculiar status of theology is thereby overlooked and something fundamentally impossible therefore undertaken. The actual result of all such attempts was and will be the disturbing, in fact destructive, surrender of theology to the general concept of science, and the mild inattention with which non-theological science—possibly with a better nose for actualities than theologians who thirst for synthesis—is wont to reply to this particular mode of justifying theology.

Thus even the duty of drafting a better definition of science, regarded as a fundamental act of self-justification, can only be rejected on the part of theology.

There is no other possible way for theology to prove its " scientific nature " than by showing in its work at its task of knowledge—work actually done and determined by its object— what it exactly means by " scientific nature." No science possesses manorial rights to the name of " science," nor is there any theory of science with final authority to give away or to withhold this title. No conventions brought into currency by any general concept of science can claim final respect. To decide whether a person or thing is what he or it claims to be, belongs to the event which from time to time implements or does not implement the claim, not to stipulations, however weighty, regarding the justi- fication or otherwise of such claim. To this event we leave it. Theology has no cause to forbid itself the name of a science. For who knows but it is more of one than many or all of the " sciences " grouped under the above convention ?

The practical interests, however, served by our quiet adherence to the designation of theology as a science, are as follows :

1. By designating itself a " science," theology brings itself into line ; as a human effort after truth, it confesses its solidarity with other efforts of this kind which to-day are united for good and all under this idea ; enters a protest against the conception that it is raised ontologically above these others (which might easily insinuate itself in the designations *doctrina* or *sapientia*, given such emphatic currency by the ancients) ; and reminds itself of the fact that it is only a " science," and so of the " profaneness " with which it too, on its relatively special path, does its work even in the most exalted regions.

2. By refusing simply to abandon the concept of " science " to the others, it also enters its necessary protest (with all due respect to classical tradition) against the admittedly " heathen " general concept of science. It can do neither its own most stalwart repre- sentatives, nor the university, any harm to be reminded, by the proximity of the theologian under the same roof, that the quasi- religious unconditionality of their interpretation of this concept of science is in practice not undisputed, that the tradition beginning with the name of Aristotle is at all events but one among others,

and that, once for all, the Christian Church at least does not have Aristotle for its ancestor.

And 3, in conclusion, theology proves by its inclusion of itself among the " sciences " practically under the same name (in spite of the fundamentally irremovable difference in its understanding of this concept), that it does not take their heathen character so seriously as to separate itself from them in a superior manner under another name ; that rather, in spite of their denial of the theological task and in spite of their concept of science being so intolerable to theology, it reckons them with itself in the Church. It believes in the forgiveness of sins, and not in the final reality of a heathen pantheon. A proof of this faith is not here to the point, but still less is a denial of it. But a denial of it might be the explanation of too clean-cut a distinction between theology and the " sciences."

These are the external—non-fundamental—reasons we have for neglecting this distinction.

2. DOGMATICS AS AN INQUIRY

Dogmatics is the self-test to which the Christian Church puts herself in respect of the content of her peculiar language about God. Our object, the proper content of this language, we call " dogma." This concept as such and also the concept of " dogmatics " as such will be explained in § 7. At this point we must first make the following addition to the contents given.

In designating the proper content of the Church's peculiar language about God as the object of human inquiry or cognitive activity, we presuppose equally its capacity, and its need to serve as an object of human inquiry, and the necessity as well as the possibility of a " science of dogma." Neither proposition, clearly, is obvious, and they require to be established.

1. Dogmatics as an inquiry presupposes the ascertainability by man of the proper content of Christian language about God. It makes this presupposition because it believes, in the Church and with the Church, in Jesus Christ, as the revealing and reconciling approach of God to man. Language about God has the proper content, when it conforms to the essence of the Church, i.e. to Jesus Christ. . . . εἴτε προφητίαν, κατὰ τὴν ἀναλογίαν τῆς πίστεως (Rom. 12⁶). Dogmatics investigates Christian language by raising the question of this conformity. Thus it has not to discover the measure with

which it measures, still less to invent it.   With the Christian Church
it regards and acknowledges it as given (given in its own thoroughly
peculiar way, exactly as the man Jesus Christ is given us, as God
gives Himself to faith in His revelation—but given, and perfect in
itself), standing to its claim without previous discussion, and certain
that there must be a standard, a measure, by which serious measurement can and ought to be made.   Dogmatics presupposes that as
God in Jesus Christ is the essence of the Church, that is, as He has
promised Himself to the Church, He is the truth ; and not merely
in Himself, but (we do k n o w Him, and we know Him o n l y,
in faith in Jesus Christ) also and precisely the truth f o r u s.   So
far as dogmatics receives the measure, by which it measures the
language about God, in J e s u s C h r i s t, in the event of the
d i v i n e action in accordance with the promise given to the·Church,
it is possible for it to be the knowledge of the truth.   What the
proper content of such language about God is or is not, is in itself,
in the light into which we are here drawn, clear in a flash and in
the highest perfection and certainty.   The c o m p l e t i o n of the
knowledge, the event of h u m a n action, the a p p r o p r i a t i o n
corresponding to this adoption, right from the intuitive grasp to
the conceptual formulation in speech, in which the opening up of the
analogia fidei, with the clearness in dogmatics resulting from it
(not first nor only in dogmatics, but also in dogmatics), gains
creaturely form—this is frankly a second item as compared with
the event proceeding from God, made one indeed with it in faith,
but also in faith emphatically to be distinguished from it.   Only,
this second item does not do away with the first.   In, with, and
beneath the human q u e s t i o n dogmatics speaks of the divine
answer.   In i n v e s t i g a t i n g it, it is also a w a r e of it.   In
l e a r n i n g it, it is already t e a c h i n g it.   In human uncertainty,
like any other science, it establishes the most certain truth, which
long ago came to light.   As a s t a t e m e n t o f f a i t h every statement in dogmatics, in view of its peculiar o b j e c t, must be
ventured upon in the certainty that it expresses not human, but
divine truth ; it must not avoid by a hair's breadth the rigour of the
" dogmatic " (as distinguished from the academic reserve of a
philosophical proposition).   The necessary corrective arises out of
the thing itself : " as a s t a t e m e n t o f f a i t h . . . in view of its
o b j e c t ! "   The intractability of faith and its object should and
will see to it that divine certainty cannot become human security.
But it is just intractable faith and its intractable object that make

possible the knowledge with which dogmatics is concerned, namely, as divine, certain knowledge.

ὁ δὲ πνευματικὸς ἀνακρίνει μὲν τὰ πάντα, αὐτὸς δὲ ὑπ' οὐδενὸς ἀνακρίνεται. τίς γὰρ ἔγνω νοῦν Κυρίου, ὃς συμβιβάσει αὐτόν; ἡμεῖς δὲ νοῦν Χριστοῦ ἔχομεν (1 Cor. 2¹⁵ᶠ·). *Viderint, qui Stoicum et Platonicum et dialecticum Christianismum protulerunt. Nobis curiositate opus non est post Christum Jesum nec inquisitione post evangelium* (Tertullian, *De praescr.* 7). *Aliud est, de silvestri cacumine videre patriam pacis et iter ad eam non invenire et frustra conari per invia . . . et aliud tenere viam illuc ducentem curia coelestis imperatoris munitam* Augustine, *Conf.* VII 21, 27). *Civitas Dei . . . habens de rebus quas mente et ratione comprehendit etiamsi parvam . . . tamen certissimam scientiam (De civ. Dei,* XIX 18). *Tolle assertiones, et Christianismum tulisti* (Luther, *De servo arb.* 1525 W. edn. 18, p. 603, l. 28). *Spiritus sanctus non est Scepticus, nec dubia aut opiniones in cordibus nostris scripsit, sed assertiones ipsa vita et omni experientia certiores et firmiores (ib.* p. 605, l. 32). *Veritas periclitari potest, perire non potest. Impugnatur quidem, sed non expugnatur : Quia verbum Domini manet in aeternum* (Comm. on Gal. 1⁷,1535 W. edn. 40¹, p. 115, l. 15). *Sic ego omnino nihil audio contrarium meae doctrinae ; sum enim certus et persuasus per spiritum Christi meam doctrinam de Christiana justitia veram ac certam esse (Comm. on Gal.* 3¹, W. edn. 40¹, p. 323, l. 28). *Haec est ratio, cur nostra Theologia certa sit : Quia rapit nos a nobis et ponit nos extra nos, ut non nitamur viribus, conscientia, sensu, persona, operibus nostris, sed eo nitamur, quod est extra nos, hoc est, promissione et veritate Dei, quae fallere non potest (Comm. on Gal.* 4⁶, W. edn. 40¹, p. 589, l. 25). *Ut certa est cuilibet sano haec sententia : bis quattuor sunt octo . . . ita sint certi nobis et immoti articuli fidei, comminationes et promissiones divinae. . . . Quare illam dubitationem philosophicam seu ἐποχὴν nequaqam admittamus ad doctrinam ecclesiae a Deo traditam . . . Non alenda est hic aut laudanda dubitatio, sed sit fides certa assensio . . .* (Melanchthon, *Loci comm.* 1559 C.R. 21, p. 604 f.).—" The critical interrogation," with which Eberhard Grisebach thinks it compulsory to approach the work of theology, has the value of intensifying the view (frankly, not absolutely new to some theologians) that the propositions of dogmatics have no other certainty than that which the statements of faith acquire in view of their object, and that this object of theirs, no less than the faith, is not at the disposal of the dogmatician. So far as such criticism passes over from the question as to theological certainty to denial of it, it destroys itself and need not be listened to. And theologians of this school may well be asked, how much longer they expect to live upon the repetition of " critical interrogation."

It was obviously in view of this side of the matter (can dogmatics be an inquiry ?) that the orthodox Reformers, by a rather hazardous abbreviation, named theology *doctrina revelata* or *patefacta*. Still, among their successors, we do find the more accurate definition, that theological propositions possess *evidentia* and *certitudo* in view of their *ratio objectiva* (that is, revelation) and the *habitus* (that is, faith) in which we affirm them (Fr. Burmann, *Syn. theol.* 1678 I 2, 60). *ea cognitio est vera, etiamsi non sit adaequata, quia quae de Deo cognoscuntur . . . carent omni mendacio, licet plus in re ipsa sit, quam a nobis intelligi potest* (Coccejus, *Summa theol.* 1669 I 4).

2. As an inquiry dogmatics presupposes that the proper content of Christian language' about God must be known humanly. Christian language must be investigated as to its conformity to Christ. In this conformity it is by no means presented to us obviously or free from difficulties. The finally and adequately given divine answer is the counterpart of the human question which retains its faithfulness throughout unwearied, honest advance, of the cry that is sincere even amid the loftiest attainments, " not as though I had already attained ! " True, dogmatics receives the measure with which it measures in an act of human appropriation. Therefore it must be an inquiry. It knows the light that is perfect in itself, that discovers all in a flash. But it knows it only in the prism of this act, which, however, radically or existentially it may be regarded, is a human act, offering in itself no sort of surety for the correctness of the appropriation in question, being rather fallible and therefore itself in need of criticism and revision, of repeated and ever closer re-testing. The creaturely form which God's revealing action comes to take in dogmatics is therefore not that of knowledge attained in a flash, which it would have to be, to correspond to the divine gift, but a laborious advance from one partial human insight to another, intending but by no means guaranteeing an " advance ! "

Βλέπομεν γὰρ ἄρτι δι᾽ ἐσόπτρου ἐν αἰνίγματι . . . ἄρτι γινώσκω ἐκ μέρους (1 Cor. 13¹²).
And with a like application we may also recall 2 Cor. 4⁷ : Ἔχομεν δὲ τὸν θησαυρὸν τοῦτον ἐν ὀστρακίνοις σκεύεσιν, ἵνα ἡ ὑπερβολὴ τῆς δυνάμεως ᾖ τοῦ Θεοῦ καὶ μὴ ἐξ ἡμῶν. *Diximusne aliquid et sonuimus aliquid dignum Dei ? Imo vero nihil me aliud quam dicere voluisse sentio : si autem dixi, non hoc est, quod dicere volui* (Augustine, *De doctr. christ.* I 6). *Cur non te sentit, Domine Deus, anima mea, si invenit te ? An non invenit, quem invenit esse lucem et veritatem ? . . . An et veritas et lux est, quod vidit, et tamen nondum te vidit, quia vidit te aliquatenus, sed non vidit te, sicuti es ? Domine Deus meus, formator et reformator meus, dic desideranti animae meae, quid aliud es, quam quod vidit, ut pure videat quod desiderat* (Anselm of Canterbury, *Prosl.* 14). *Et ut omne aenigma est sermo obscurus, nodosus, involutus, intellectu difficilis : ita nostra Theologia ratione obiecti est inevidens, complectens mysteria profundissima et in hac mortalitate cognitu difficillima* (Hollaz, *Examen Theol. acroam.* 1707 *Prol.* I 8).

By the very fact that truth in faith is presupposed as the admitted measure of all things, it is decided that it is by no means assumed to be " present." Truth comes, in the faith in which we begin and in the faith in which we cease (and begin all over again) to know. Results of earlier dogmatic work, like our own results, can on principle only be signs of its coming. Results are invariably results of human effort. As such they are a help to, but they are also the object of, fresh human effort. Dogmatics exists only as the *theologia crucis*—that is, in the act of obedience which is certain in faith but for that very reason humble, which is always thrown back on the start and always opening up afresh ; not a triumphant help-yourself without work, nor yet a work that is now and then to be gone through with and has been gone through with. It is always on the narrow way leading from the revelation that happened to the revelation promised.

. . . ἐκ πίστεως εἰς πίστιν (Rom. I¹⁷). Augustine in an important passage evolves the doctrine that *credere* would have to precede *intelligere*, so far as it is the faith caused by the *vox de coelo* (*verbum Dei*). But *credere* would have to follow *intelligere*, so far as it is the faith to be established by the *sermo propheticus* (*verbum meum*), of which Mark 9²² is a case! Faith as faith in God stands on its own feet, and is the basis of knowledge. Faith as man's faith requires knowledge, and is established by it.

Here our way diverges from that of Roman Catholic dogmatics, and here we must also enter a caveat against a definite tendency in the Old Protestant tradition. Dogmatics is the science of Dogma. Only in a subordinate sense and strictly in conjunction with the first sense is it also the science of Dogmas. The task of dogmatics is thus not merely the combination, repetition, and transcription of a number of already present "truths of revelation," once for all expressed and authentically defined as to wording and meaning.

In the Roman Catholic view also there seems to be "a true advance of the teaching Church," in the knowledge and understanding, in the development and application of revealed truth, and in the expression of it (Diekamp, *Kath. Dogmatik*, 6th ed. vol. I 1930 p. 19. Cf. with it the doctrine of Vincent of Lerins on the *profectus religionis*, *Common.* I 22 f.). But by "truth of revelation" we are here to understand the "Apostolic deposit" infallibly set forth by the Church's living teaching staff, consisting of Holy Scripture and the oral Apostolic tradition (Diekamp, *op. cit.* p. 24 f.). This "deposit" is thus identical with a sum of sacred texts. Dogmatics is faced with the task of "mediating a fuller understanding of these truths by inferences" (Diekamp, *op. cit.* p. 76 f.). The presupposition of which is, further, that the "meaning" of these truths (=texts!) to be mediated has already been mediated by the Church's teaching staff and authoritatively proclaimed by them, so that in this task of "understanding" there can be no question of anything more than a transcription in a somewhat higher sense: *Hinc sacrorum quoque dogmatum is sensus perpetuo est retinendus, quem semel declaravit sancta mater Ecclesia, nec unquam ab eo sensu altioris intelligentiae specie et nomine recedendum.* (*Conc. Vatic., Sess. III Constit. de fide cath. c. 4.*)

This only too practicable opinion, by its direct equation, in the dogmas, of divine bestowal and human appropriation, fails to recognise the divine-human character of the Church's essence. The essence of the Church is Jesus Christ, and is therefore irremovably a divine-human Person, the action of God on man, an action in distinction from which human appropriation, as actually attested in the very " dogmas " believed in by the Church, may be termed worthy, respectable, but by no means " infallible," and so not withdrawn from further interrogation as to " whether that is the relation." The concept " truths of revelation," in the sense of Latin propositions given and sealed once for all by divine authority in wording and meaning, is theologically impossible, if it be the case that revelation has its truth in the free decision of God, made once for all in Jesus Christ, and for that very reason and in that way strictly future for us, and must become true in the Church from time to time in the intractable reality of faith. Truth of revelation is the freely acting God, Himself and quite alone. Results of dogmatic work, like the dogmas underlying the creeds, which are venerable results, because gained in the common knowledge of the Church at a definite time, may and should guide our own dogmatic work, but never replace it at any point in virtue of their authority. Moreover, in dogmatics it can never be a question of the mere combination, repetition, and summarising of Biblical doctrine.

Melanchthon seems already to have understood the task in this sense (*Loci comm.* 1559 *C.R.* 21, p. 601). Still more coarsely Heidan (*Corp. Theol. christ.* 1686 *Prol.* 1 f.) taught that Holy Scripture was *non scripta ut systema quoddam, sed historica nobis facta Ecclesiae ab initio mundi ad finem describit.* The task of *Loci communes* then was to present *res S. Scriptura contentas certo et concinno ordine : . . . ut certo methodo res divinas complecti et eas suo ordine collocare possitis et sicut Pharmacopolae solent medicamenta sua certis capsulis distinguere et disponere, ita vos omnia suis quaeque locis digerere possitis.*

The inquiry concerning Biblical doctrine as the basis of our language about God falls upon exegetical theology. It must also be kept continually before the eyes of dogmatics. But the proper basis of Christian language is identical with its proper content, only in God and not for us. Therefore dogmatics as such does not inquire what the Apostles and Prophets have said, but what we ourselves must say " on the basis of the Apostles and Prophets." This task cannot be taken from us, even by the knowledge of the " Scripture basis " which necessarily precedes it.

Although in his work exegesis and dogmatics are continually interwoven, the practical meaning of *Institutio religionis christiana* was, even for C a l v i n, to direct Christian thought and language to its own responsibility in the present.

Even in allowing herself to attest by Scripture (and with divine authority only by Scripture) that her own essence is the measure of her language, the Church recognises the claim upon her to know it herself and therefore also to ask, particularly in view of this basis of all Christian language, with the utter seriousness of one who does not yet know, what Christian language ought to say and should say to-day.

Nam et ego tecum credo et inconcusse credo . . . sed nunc molimur id quod in fidem recepimus, etiam intelligendo scire ac tenere firmissimum (Augustine, *De lib. arb.* I 3, 6 ; cf. 4, 10). *Quod enim hortante ipso quaerimus eodem ipso demonstrante inveniemus, quantum haec in hac vita et a nobis talibus inveniri queunt* (*ib.* II 2, 6).—Anselm of Canterbury's purpose regarding the question raised by his collocutor is *non tam ostendere, quam tecum quaerere* (*Cur Deus homo ?* I 2). His aim in *intellectus fidei* is not to repeat the believer's *legere,* but really *intus legere* Scripture and dogma, without basing upon their authoritative givenness (however certainly this is presupposed !) : . . . *quatenus auctoritate Scripturae penitus nihil in ea* (scil. *meditatione*) *persuaderetur* (*Monol., Prol.*) . . . *ut quod fide teneamus . . . sine Scripturae auctoritate probari possit* (*Ep. de incarn.* 6). For the distinction between dogmatic inquiry and authoritative quotation the well-known, though not quite unobjectionable formula of Anselm again may serve : *remoto Christo . . . quasi nihil sciatur de Christo* (*Cur Deus homo ? Prol.*). *Quaedam disputatio ordinatur ad removendam dubitationem an ita sit; et in tali disputatione theologica maxime utendum est auctoritatibus, quas recipiunt illi, cum quibus disputatur . . . Quaedam vero disputatio est magistralis in scholis non ad removendum errorem, sed ad instruendum auditores, ut inducantur ad intellectum veritatis quam intendit; et tunc oportet rationibus inniti investigantibus veritatis radicem et facientibus scire, quomodo sit verum, quod dicitur* (Thomas Aquinas, *Quodlib.* 4, 18). This side of the content, the necessity under which dogmatics lies to investigate, was clearly present to the Orthodox Lutherans, it being their custom expressly to distinguish theology from Holy Scripture as *ex verbo Dei exstructa* (e.g. J. Gerhard, *Loci Comm.* 1610 *Proem.* 31) *docens . . . ex divina revelatione* (Baier, *Comp. Theol. pos.* 1686 *Prol.* 38) and so on. (So, too, among the Reformed writers, Burmann, *Syn. Theol.* 1678 I 2, 41.)

3. DOGMATICS AS AN ACT OF FAITH

Dogmatics is a part of the work of human knowledge. But this part of the work of human knowledge comes under a special decisive limitation. It demands of course, like all work of human knowledge, the intellectual faculties of attention and concentration, of understanding and judgment. Like all serious work of human knowledge it demands the best will to utilise these faculties and,

2

finally, surrender of the entire personality to such utilisation. But over and above this it presupposes Christian faith, which even in the deepest and purest surrender to this task in itself does not by any means just happen. In fact dogmatics is a function of the Christian Church. The Church tests herself by essaying dogmatics. To the Church is given the promise of the criterion for Christian faith, namely, the revelation of God. The Church can ply dogmatics. Even in the Church dogmatics need not be the work of a special theological science. Yet dogmatics is impossible outside the Church. To be in the Church means to be called upon with others through Jesus Christ. To act in the Church means to act in obedience to this call. This obedience to the call of Christ is faith. In faith the judgment of God is acknowledged and His grace praised. In faith self-testing is necessary in view of responsibility before God. Faith grasps the promise of being " led into all truth " (John 16¹³). Faith knows God. Faith is the determination of human action by the essence of the Church, that is by Jesus Christ, by the gracious approach of God to man. In faith and only in faith is human action related to the essence of the Church, to the revealing and reconciling action of God. Thus dogmatics is only possible as an act of faith, in the determination of human action by listening, and as obedience towards Jesus Christ. Without faith it would lack object and meaning; even in the case of the most adequate technical imitation of what the Church is doing here, even with the most honest intention of " doing what the Church does," it would only be an idle speculation without content of knowledge.

H. Scholz (*Z.d.Z.* 1931 p. 34) asks (expressly with a view to dogmatics) : " Is it possible to construct a form of Christianity, so to construct it, that the sight of this form and absorption in it is worth while, without having to believe oneself in this Christianity for better or for worse, or is it impossible ? " His answer (fortunately only indirect !) runs, " that we are thoroughly confident of evolving, from Platonism, from Aristotelianism, from Leibniz and Kant, the image which should impress any one at all susceptible to such spiritual images, and in such a way that we are for better or for worse neither Platonists nor Aristotelians nor Leibnizians nor Kantians, but what it is our destiny to be."—Our comment is that, so far as by Christianity is understood the Christian view of life and the world as it is a creaturely reality in the history of the spirit parallel to Platonism, Aristotelianism, etc., and by a " form " or " image " of Christianity an exposition of Christianity in this its creatureliness, an exposition evolved in responsibility to the laws of the science of such reality—to that extent the construction of an " impressive " form of Christianity, " without having to believe oneself in this Christianity for better or for worse " is certainly a fair possibility with compensations of its own. But

in dogmatics that is not the point. For " Christianity " we must here insert
" the proper content of language about God, ventured upon in the fear of
God." For " form," " the propositions in which, by inquiry about this
content, we fix our preliminary answers." And in place of the problem
of " impressing " spiritually receptive men, the problem here confronts us
starkly of responsibility to God. This third point asserts that in dogmatics
there is nothing to " construct " outside of the real contraposition of God
and man—and that is just what faith is. And the " proper content " spoken
of, Jesus Christ, does not coincide with creaturely reality. He is revelation,
divine-human reality. If there is such, and if there is knowledge of such—
the Church and, with her, dogmatics presuppose both—then this knowledge
can only be that of faith : in which case we should certainly ask the question,
whether faith were faith, were it not faith " for better or for worse."
Omnis recta cognitio Dei ab obedientia nascitur (Calvin, *Instit.* I 6, 2).
Plato's claim to make us Platonists may be parried without prejudice to an
impressive exposition of Platonism. Christ's claim to our obedience is
identical with the essence of the Church and cannot be got round by any
dogmatics that does not abdicate self and want to become a mere meditation
on the history of the human mind. Dogmatics does not presuppose that it is
" our destiny " to believe in the Christian way, but rather that " our destiny "
not to believe in the Christian way is not the last word for us, and that we
are " not disobedient to the heavenly voice " (Acts 26[19]).

Now faith is not the sort of determination of human action that
man can apply to his action at will, or that, once received, he can
maintain at will. It is rather itself the gracious approach of God
to man, the free personal presence of Jesus Christ in man's action.
Thus we assert that dogmatics presupposes faith, presupposes the
determination of human action through listening, and as obedience
to the essence of the Church ; whence we assert that at every
step and proposition it presupposes the free grace of God, which
may from time to time be given or else refused, as the object and
meaning of this human action. It depends from time to time upon
God and not upon us, whether our hearing is real hearing, our
obedience real obedience, whether our dogmatics is blessed and
hallowed as knowledge of the proper content of Christian language,
or is idle speculation.

From this standpoint we have to deliver judgment upon what was once a
much discussed theme, the demand for rebirth or conversion in the theologian,
which to-day is being debated afresh as the necessity for so-called existentiality
in theological thinking. Urgent warnings that theologising is powerless,
unless the object is related to the person of the theologian, unless the real and
entire theological man is laid claim to, are already to be found in Anselm of
Canterbury : the *credere* that underlies the *intelligere* cannot be a mere
credere id, it must be a *credere in id, quod credi debet* (*Monol.* 76–78).
Rectitudo fidei et intellectus necessarily involves a *rectitudo volendi* (*De Concordia, qu.* III 2 and 6). *Non solum ad intelligendum altiora prohibetur mens*

ascendere sine fide et mandatorum Dei obedientia, sed etiam aliquando, datus intellectus subtrahitur . . . neglecta bona conscientia (Ep. de incarn. 1). *Non est . . . securus transitus a scientia ad sapientiam ; oportet ergo medium ponere, scilicet sanctitatem* (Bonaventura, *In hex.* XIX 3). Against certain so-called " mystical " theologians, whose practical life experience was the opposite of all *theologia negativa,* who knew nothing of the Christian's love unto death and hell, Luther in his younger days wrote the words : *Vivendo, immo moriendo et damnando fit theologus, non intelligendo, legendo aut speculando (Op. in Psalm.* W. edn. 5, p. 163, l. 28) . . . " Doctors of art, medicine, law, philosophy the Pope, Emperors and Universities can make ; but be quite sure, a doctor of Holy Writ will no man make you, save alone the Holy Ghost from heaven, as Christ saith in John 6, ' They must all be taught of God Himself.' Now the Holy Ghost asketh not after red or brown cheeks or ought that's showy, nor yet whether one is young or old, lay or clerical, monastic or secular, virgin or married ; yea, He spake aforetime by an ass against the prophet that rode on him. Would God we were worthy such doctors were given us. . . ." (Luther, *An d. chr. Adel deutsch. Nation v. d. chr. Standes Besserung,* 1520 W. edn. 6, p. 460, l. 28). . . . But even Melanchthon (e.g. *Apol. Conf. Aug., De Justif,* 9 and 37, *C.R.* 27, 430 and 434) was glad to insist, that proper knowledge of salvation was to be gained not by empty speculations, but only *in agone conscientiae et in acie.* The theological meaning of all that was indicated, in the age of orthodoxy, by saying that *Theologia concretive considerata* (theology as a fact as distinguished from its concept) was described as a *habitus* θεόσδοτος *per verbum a Spiritu sancto homini collatus* (J. Gerhard, *Loci theol.* 1610 *prooem.* 31). We know that, *Post lapsum non nascuntur theologi, sed fiunt scil. a Deo docti per verbum scriptum* (Quenstedt, *Theol. did. pol.* 1685 I *cap.* 1, *sect.* 2, *qu.* 2, *ekth.* 2). Thus, real theology is a determination and claim by God acting, which man really encounters. That at this point the danger of centring theological knowledge upon man could become menacing, is shown by the certainly not unambiguous assertion of Anselm of Canterbury : If we care to compare the preaching and hearing of the Word of God with a sowing *(agricultura),* then the *semen,* the Word of God, is *immo non verbum sed sensus qui percipitur per verbum (De Concordia, qu.* III 6). Obviously there is here the threat of an awkward turnover from a divine determining to a human determinateness ; if not expressly to a human performance, as was the opinion of Bonaventura, who understood that *sanctitas* and could give an adequate description of it as a *vita timorata, impolluta, religiosa, aedificatoria (In Hex.* XIX 20 f.). Extend this line of thought, and the *sensus,* the human determinateness, the experience and attitude of the knowing subject might well be exalted into the criterion of theological knowledge. Obviously to avoid this danger the middle and later orthodoxy (e.g. Quenstedt, *op. cit. ekth.* 5 ; Hollaz, *Ex. theol. acroam.* 1707 *Prol.,* 1, 18–21 ; Buddeus, *Instit. theol. dogm.* 1724 I 1, 49 wanted to know how to distinguish between the objective theological *habitus* on the one hand and the faith, or rebirth, of the theologian on the other : *Constat, habitum Theologiae reapse separare posse a fide salvifica* (so Heidan, *Corp. Theol. christ.* 1686 l. 1, p. 3). It need scarcely be remarked that this was not intended in Luther's sense. By this antithesis a suggestion was made of what was far worse, that one was on the way to interpret faith, rebirth, and conversion as already and decisively a human experience and attitude. How little certainty there was about the facts was shown by the idea that the possibility of a theology of unconverted theologians, a theology that lived by the *habitus*, the possibility of a *theologia irregenitorum* such as had to be asserted on the basis of that distinction, had yet to be hedged round by all possible reservations and limitations No wonder pietism once more abandoned this distinction, and urged upon students of theology at least an earnest effort after personal conversion (A. H. Francke, *Method. stud. theol.* 1723 *Cap.* 2). But it was already clear, by the fact that only an effort after it was mentioned, how much a matter of course the conception had meanwhile become, that faith was definitely to be regarded as a determination of human reality. The fact that Rationalism (e.g. G. J. Planck, *Einl. i.d. theol. Wissensch,* 1794 *Bd.* I p. 62 f.), so far as this subjective presupposition is concerned, no longer wished to hold on to the necessity of " Christian religiousness," but only to that of a " religiousness in general," was likewise not exactly an improvement of the situation. And the moment Schleiermacher as a theologian wished only to speak of what was " the inmost motive of my being," out of " an irresistible inner necessity of my nature " (*Reden ub. d. Rel.* 1799 p. 5), " in order to set up his own idea as an object for the rest " (*op. cit.* p. 182), the sense for what Anselm, Luther, and Melanchthon desired, with their claim for *sensus* and *experientia* as the substratum of a proper theology, was utterly lost to view. " That no one is and remains a theologian, no one makes religion or Christianity his vocation for life, if he does not stand in an inner relationship to religion or Christianity, may be taken for granted (as generally speaking no one will profess a definite portion of the spiritual sciences as a vocation, without loving the object of his science) "—such is their concern, translated into the language of 19th-century Liberalism (H. Mulert, *Evangelische Kirchen und theologische Facultäten,* 1930 p. 16 f.). The anthropologising of theology was complete. And now the serious question is whether the same must not be said of what to-day is being demanded in the atmosphere of Kierkegaard, but above all, consciously or unconsciously, in continuation of the pietistic tradition, as the " existential " element in theological thought and language. The circumstance is not without humour ; at the same time it is somewhat suspicious that, following the trend of the time, G. Wobbermin has recently undertaken to interpret his theology (*Wort Gottes und evangelischer Glaube,* 1931 p. 14 f.), which from start to finish is certainly not interested in or oriented by Kierkegaard, as the theology of a " religio-psychological, existential thought." If this " existential element " is sought for in the fact that the propositions of theology would have to be accounts of the human condition, as radically revealed in faith, of the theologian who is actually speaking, if the claim is that their pronouncements would have to be " the cry of a man who, like a Christ-bearer, collapses under the unduly heavy burden of something that had, in any circumstances, to happen now in present-day Germany," if, e.g. the proposition that we are all sinners together, only ceases to be a mere phrase, " if I utter it for a perfectly concrete reason, if it reaches my consciousness in quite definite circumstances, that this hopeless renunciation of mine springs from an egoism . . ., which I share with all my fellowmen " (K. Heim, *Glaube und Denken,* 1931 p. 409), then these are psychologisms and legalities, under the yoke of which we neither must nor should bend. It should then be time to grasp with new comprehension at the pre-pietistic doctrine of the theological *habitus,* in virtue of which the theologian is what he is by the grace of God, quite apart from his greater or less connection with Christ-bearing and without the slightest need for existential screaming and the like. A reaction in this sense, a fresh change over from Christ-bearing to Christ is then at once upon the carpet : " Theological pronouncements are only possible on the basis of the fact that gospel, message, proclamation is there," comes the call to us afresh. A proposition with theological intention " is a proposition really detached from the actual situation of the speaker and deriving its meaning for its hearers solely on the score of this detachment " (K. Fr. Schumann, *Der Gottesgedanke und der Zerfall der Moderne*, 1929 p. 348 f.). And with a sharp polemical touch : " Ἀκοὴ πίστεως, when the promise is grasped, is not to be regarded as an existential decision of faith " (H. M. Müller, *Glaube und Erfahrung bei Luther*, 1929 p. 90). " Where the existential element, by whatever process, is exalted into the object of theology, it is fundamentally the human element that is being served. . . . There is but one alternative : either we understand our own existence as a being in grace, or we expect God's contingent visitation at the real end of this existence " (*op. cit.* p. 187). Such a reaction is certainly opportune and useful. But the original claim of an Anselm, a Luther, and a Melanchthon, in which the old and new doctrine of *theologia regenitorum*, " existential theology," also has its *particula veri*, should not therefore be lost sight of. " God's contingent visitation " touches man's e x i s t e n c e, even although from the side of the end, even although from " without," and so too the gift of its promise through faith is a divine determination of and claim upon the c o n c r e t e being of man, my s e l f. Where this was not the case, theology would turn into an objectless onlooker's wisdom outside the Church. In it knowledge would consist merely in the irresolute form of an imitative and formal participation in the knowledge of the Church and of faith. Where this ceased, the power of knowledge contained in such a theology would also have to cease, as Anselm quite rightly declared. But no theology is at any moment humanly insured or insurable against the danger of becoming such onlooker's wisdom outside the Church, against the danger of becoming atheology. Faith, rebirth, conversion, " existential " thinking (i.e. thinking that proceeds on the basis of existential perplexity) is indeed the indispensable requisite for dogmatic work ; not so far as the intention is to include an experience and attitude to which *I* adjust myself, which *I* put into train, a " Yes, I'll go ! " on the theologian's part, so that his theology would have to be throughout a personal cry, a narrative of his own biographical situation : but so far as thereby is meant the grace of divine predestination, the free gift of the Word and of the Holy Spirit, the act of calling him into the Church which ever and anon the theologian must encounter from the acting God, in order that he may be what he is called and does, what answers to his name.

The Church can and ought to undertake and carry through her self-test on her own responsibility, by human application of human means. But whether in so doing she is acting as the Church and so is discerning God in faith, whether the result of her action is therefore just and weighty criticism or revision, and not a worse devastation of Christian language, does not lie within her province. Obviously the givenness of the special and decisive conditions of dogmatics, the decision from time to time of what is or is not the truth in dogmatics, are matters of divine predestination. Fear of the Lord must ever and anon repeatedly be the beginning of wisdom here. That is the frequently felt difficulty of all theology, but quite uniquely of dogmatic theology.

Cognovi, explicationem dogmatum Ecclesiae propter multas causas opus esse difficillimum et quamquam necessarium est, tamen plenum esse ingentium periculorum (Melanchthon, *Loci comm.* 1559 *C.R.* 21, 602). Indeed it was probably rather more than a monkish trick of style, when Anselm of Canterbury spoke of the *imbecillitas scientiae meae* (*Cur Deus homo* ? I 25), or Bonaventura of the *pauper portiuncula scientiolae nostrae* (*Breviloq., Prooem.*), or when Petrus Lombardus on the first page of his book of Sentences compared his achievement with the widow's mite or the twopence which the Good Samaritan gave to the innkeeper, with the promise to pay him in full later. It is related of Thomas Aquinas, whose *Summa theologica* has notoriously remained a torso, that he answered the demand that he should continue writing : " Reginald, I cannot, because all that I have written appears to me like chaff. My hope from God is that He will soon make an end of my life and teaching " (M. Grabmann, *Das Seelenleben des hl. Thomas v. Aq.*, 1924 p. 51). On the contrary, the other report that, while he was engaged upon the Christological part of that work, Christ appeared to him with the words, " *Bene scripsisti de me, Thoma* ! " may certainly be termed less near to the facts. The title *doctor ecclesiae* with the wearing of the halo Thomas himself rightly reserved for eschatology (*S. theol.* III *qu.* 96, *art.* 6).

As an act of repentance and obedience dogmatics cannot remit its labours, and precisely as such an act it can only take place by trust in the absolutely uncontrollable presence-on-the-spot of the ground both of its reality and of its knowledge, upon God's promised revelation to the Church and upon the power of the faith that grasps the promise. That holds alike for teacher and for pupil in dogmatics, for the authors of works on dogmatics as well as for their readers. Without exception the act of faith (i.e. its basis in divine predestination, the free act of God on man and his work) is the condition which renders dogmatic work possible, by which also it is called in question in deadly earnest.

Paul Althaus finds the problem of theology as a science in the conflict between the " critical attitude " and the " Church connection," both of which were equally necessary to the theologian, but which appeared mutually to endanger one another (*Grundriss d. Dogmatik*, 1929 § 1). This problem dispenses with real dead earnest. As Althaus himself shows, it can be solved by the Left as well as by the Right with comparative ease and friendliness. The older theologians rightly looked for the difficulty of theology and its conquest on a different level : *Non ego te duco, sed ille, de quo loquimur, sine quo nihil possumus, nos ducit, ubicumque viam veritatis teneamus* (Anselm of Canterbury, *Cur Deus homo* ? II 9). *In Theologia . . . datur subiectum plane divinum, quod est . . . omni re prius, ut nullam principiati rationem habere possit, unde . . . fit, ut duas hasce rationes simul contineat, sitque subjectum, de quo agit Theologia et simul etiam ejus principium* (Fr. Turrettini, *Inst. Theol. el.* I 1679 1 qu. 5, 9). *Ille enim solus idoneus est de se testis, qui quod sibi gratum est, docere nos possit et cui nihil gratum esse potest, nisi a se profectum et naturae suae conveniens. Quod quale sit nemo novit nisi ipse. At id quomodo nobis innotescat, nisi nobis ab ipso patefiat et reveletur ?* (Heidan, *Corp. Theol. chr.* 1686 B. I p. 7). *Quemadmodum in spiritualibus nemo mortalium sibi ipse quidquam absque gratiae viribus aut dare aut tribuere, ita multo minus ea largire potest, quae ad theologiae habitum requiruntur* (Buddeus, *Instit. Th. dogm.* 1724 I 1, 51). In his book " *Die Entstehung der chr. Theol. und des kirchl. Dogmas,*" 1927 pp. 54 f., 87 f., Ad. v. Harnack has, in view of past and present, declared that there is and always has been— 1. A ("charismatic") theology from within, in which the theologian, speaking from the " standpoint " of the believer, counts for " his truth " upon its inner power of persuasion, and is never without the consciousness " that only with the aid of God's Spirit can he utter theology, that therefore his work is charismatically conditioned." This kind of theology is founded by Paul, but it can never become either ecclesiastical or scientific theology. It is confession and preaching, and so not constructive of a community. 2. A Theology from without. It " sets the religion in question in the context of the other objects of knowledge and describes its reality and truth according to generally valid historical, psychological and theoretical principles of knowledge." Its Fathers are the apologists of the second century, and it and it alone is constructive of a community, can become ecclesiastical and scientific. " We may deplore this, because the inadequacy of such a theology is obvious ; but no one can alter that and whoever tries to, suffers shipwreck and confuses theology. His task lies in preaching "—It is assuredly fitting to let this testamentary declaration of one who was an honoured teacher even to me, speak itself here for or against itself without comment or contradiction.

And so, humanly speaking, there is no getting over this fundamental difficulty, which, because fundamental, oppresses theology alone among all the sciences, and in theology only dogmatics, no known way of getting round the special and decisive conditions of dogmatics. We may " call up good intentions," but even the best intentions are no help here. And no one can call up the Christian faith which decisively constitutes the theological habitus. Popular shyness of theology (and in theology, of dogmatics in particular) is only too well grounded. Man here always seems to presume too much, and after all his trouble seems yet to remain with empty hands. Here we seem always to have an effort after a useless object with insufficient means. And it belongs far too much to the nature of the case that this seeming should be possible for it to be permanently avoidable by a change of method.

The mystery of *ubi et quando visum est Deo,* Conf. Aug., *Art.* 5 (cf. for the understanding of this passage the references of Hans Engelland,

Melanchthon, 1931 p. 568 f.), has accompanied Christian language about God in general until the present day, and also dogmatics in particular, through all the stages of their history. It cannot be otherwise, nor ever will be in the future.

Humanly speaking we say nothing to lighten this difficulty : we but confess the mystery in which it is grounded, we but repeat the statement that dogmatics is possible only as an act of faith, when we refer to prayer as the attitude apart from which dogmatic work is impossible.

Hoc intelligere quis hominum dabit homini ? quis angelus angelo ? quis angelus homini ? A te petatur, in te quaeratur, ad te pulsetur : sic accipietur, sic invenietur, sic aperietur (Augustine, *Conf.* XIII 38, 53). *Non solum admonendi sunt studiosi venerabilium Litterarum, ut in scripturis sanctis genera locutionum sciant . . . verum etiam, quod est praecipuum et maxime necessarium orent ut intelligant. In eis quippe Litteris, quarum studiosi sunt, legunt quoniam Dominus dat sapientiam et a facie ejus scientia et intellectus a quo et ipsum studium, si pietate praeditum est, acceperunt* (*De Doctr. chr.* III 37). Anselm of Canterbury, *Prosl.* I—we return to this passage in § 6, 4— need only be mentioned here. Thomas Aquinas has prefixed his *Summa theologica* with the following prayer : *Concede mihi quaeso, misericors Deus, quae tibi sunt placita ardenter concupiscere, prudenter investigare, veraciter agnoscere et perfecte implere ad laudem nominis tui.* The purpose with which A. H. Francke acted in an entire section of his instructions for theology, entitled *De Oratione*, was thoroughly relevant. And it will assuredly not be regarded as a mere baroque flourish, when Hollaz allows the treatment of every separate locus to pass over into a " *Suspirium,*" language about God to pass expressly into language to God.

Prayer may be the acknowledgment that for all our intentions (indeed, our intentions to pray too !) nothing has been done. Prayer may be the expression of man's desire for the will of God. Prayer may mean that man (" for better or for worse ! ") gives the verdict for God and against himself. Prayer may be man's answer to the divine hearing of prayer already experienced on the way, the content of the true faith which we ourselves have not actually taken to ourselves. We would not be speaking of real prayer, if we were to say " must " instead of " may." The way from " may " to " must " is according to Rom. 8 $^{26f.}$ itself veiled in the mystery, at the gates of which we stand here. With this indication we are presenting no one with a means, by the use of which he might contemplate success for himself in his work. But it has to be said that we cannot see how this work in particular can succeed otherwise than on the basis of a divine correspondence with this human attitude : " Lord, I believe, help thou mine unbelief ! "

§ 2

THE TASK OF PROLEGOMENA TO DOGMATICS

Prolegomena to Dogmatics is the name we give to the introductory part of Dogmatics, in which it is our business to explain its particular path to knowledge.

1. THE NEED FOR DOGMATIC PROLEGOMENA

Prolegomena to a science, so far as such are necessary and possible, will always consist mainly in reflections and statements as to how knowledge is reached in the science in question. By " prolegomena to Dogmatics " (*praecognita Theologiae*, as many of the ancients still more pregnantly termed them) we understand the attempt to give an explicit account of the particular path to knowledge trodden in dogmatics, we might even say, of the particular point from which in dogmatics we have to see, think, and judge. It is not clear on the face of it that questions on these points will be explicitly raised and answered, that there must therefore be prolegomena to dogmatics. It might even be that the questions are answered simply by the way in which dogmatics treads its path. The presuppositions made might simply be indicated and approved by the application of them. The language itself might mean the saving of any introduction. The absence of or the utmost economy in prolegomena need not be the sign of a naïve attitude ; they might be the sign of a very conscious, well-thought-out, scientific one. And such an attitude need not rest on self-deception ; it may have its legitimate ground in the simplicity of the truth, in the acme of scientific healthiness. *Ab esse ad posse valet consequentia* might be its justification. It makes us think, the fact that at all events the great representatives of Dogmatics in the ancient Church and the Middle Ages were content with the briefest of reflections upon the path as such, which they were to tread.

E.g. in John of Damascus' Ἔκδοσις ἀκριβὴς τῆς ὀρθοδόξου πίστεως we find at the most two introductory chapters, which might be claimed as prolegomena, upon the knowability of God. Peter Lombard begins his

Sentences after a brief prologue without any discussions upon method. In the *Summa theologica* of Thomas Aquinas we find an opening quaestio of ten articles on the idea of *doctrina sacra*, in his *Summa c. gent.* eight introductory sections on faith and knowledge. Among the Reformers, Zwingli in his *Comm. de vera et falsa religione*, 1525, has still adhered to this tradition with a concise treatment of the concept *religio*. His *Fidei ratio* of 1530, after an address to the Emperor, begins straight away with the dogma of the Trinity ; so too his *Fidei christianae expositio* of 1531, destined for the French king, starts by developing the concept of God. Among more recent writers, Ad. Schlatter, *Das christliche Dogma*, 2nd edn. 1923, has almost succeeded in dispensing with prolegomena altogether.

But the phenomenon is susceptible of more than one interpretation. Along with thoughtful relevance there is also occasionally a less thoughtful boastfulness and self-assurance to be adduced in explanation. In forming a theological judgment we must take account of both possibilities and reserve final assertions either way.

Either way I should regard it as over-hasty to see without further ado in the business-like bluntness of these ancients (like E. Brunner, *Theologie und Kirche, Z.d.Z.* 1930 p. 397) the expression of a *theologia gloriae* which fails to recognise its own problematic nature. On the other hand, by designating the former procedure as that of a " classical " age, and the one in favour to-day as that of a " decadent " age, I made myself responsible for a romanticising philosophy of history from which I now wish to resile.

The situation in the Church, which constitutes the area of dogmatic work, is not always the same, but from time to time imposes special conditions on this work. What we are on our guard against now need not have existed always. What was allowed once, may be forbidden us to-day. And we are forbidden to-day to come to the point in dogmatics without giving an express and explicit account of the question as to the way to knowledge. The only question is—and one of decisive importance at that—on what grounds we feel this restriction and so regard dogmatic prolegomena as essential.

Here it is usual to point, and in latter years with fresh zeal, to the change in the general civilised consciousness and conception of the world which set in three centuries or so ago and has been calling theology as such in question ; to the wave of paganism by which Church and theology to-day are threatened, which, so we are told, is specially overwhelming ; to the " radicalism of intellectual thought," said to be significant of our times more than of others, with its total denial of revelation as such.

" Already in the second half of the 17th, but still more in the first half of the 18th century the hesitations, objections, and doubts raised against the Christian doctrines of faith and also against the science of them on the part of naturalists, rationalists of the time, so-called free spirits, had become so many that a short introduction did not cover the ground, and preliminary discussions had to be engaged in before dogmatics were approached " (Carl Daub, *Prolegomena zur Dogmatik*, 1839 p. 3).—" The point to-day is not the way in which God exists, but whether He exists, not what is revealed, but whether there is such a thing as revelation, not rationalistic destructiveness at isolated points, but the doubts cast upon the miracle of revelation as such ; the distinctive mark of all Christian theology, the norm, the concept of revelation, not its contents, and so the problem of intellect and revelation is the issue at stake " (E. Brunner, *Z.d.Z.* 1930 p. 414).

It is this altered situation, so they say, which to-day makes prolegomena to dogmatics necessary. If dogmatics to-day would be " existential " theology and not deteriorate into a " parlous puzzle," then in addition to its first task, of the Church's becoming conscious of the Word of God, a second and different task of theology, which has grown out of the said situation, would have to be recognised and tackled.

E. Brunner (*Die andere Aufgabe der Theologie, Z.d.Z.* 1929 p. 255 f.), to whom I specially refer here, would call this discipline preliminary to dogmatics, not apologetics but " eristics." But is he not making the old apologetic worse than it was, in order merely to be able to move away from it, when he characterises it in the lump as " a feeble, uneasy defensive before an intellectual tribunal, as a self-justification of Christians before a world which has lost confidence in them " (*op. cit.* p. 258) ? Should the difference, say, between Chr. E. Luthardt's *Apologetischen Vorträgen*, 1870 f., and Karl Heim's *Glauben und Denken*, 1931, be any other than that of worse and better, or even simply of old-Frankish and modern ? Would it not be clarifying to accept the name of " apologetics " again without false shame ? Overbeck's " scourge," with which Brunner sees the earlier apologetics chastised, can scarcely be dodged even by an " eristist."

The task of theology would then consist in the " struggle against the self-assurance of the modern spirit," the struggle against " reason's axiom of the final reality of reason," in " wrestling to a fall with this exclusive and therefore anti-Word reason," and in " liberating reason, the intellect, which amid the delusion and loneliness of its own nature, secretly longs for the divine Thou."

With more reserve Karl Heim says (*op. cit.* p. 433) : " In proportion to the special position of service which. . . . knowledge occupies towards life, there falls to Christian philosophy a merely negative task. It must ' unsecure ' man. It must frankly show up in its impossibility everything that man has at any time undertaken, in order to move into a position in reserve where he is secure in face of the question of eternity, which every moment confronts him with afresh."

There is, however, it is held, a " point of connection for the divine message in man," undestroyed by sin, a " questioning after God," natural to man.

E. Brunner understands by the, to him, very important idea of the " point of connection," " that awareness of himself, which man may have as a non-believer and which as such is taken up into belief " (*Theologie und Ontologie, Z.Th.K.* 1931 p. 112).

In connection with this connecting point one would have " to show how through the Word of God the human reason is partly unveiled as a source of error inimical to life, partly fulfilled in its own unachievable search."

E. Brunner, *Z.d.Z.* 1929 pp. 257, 260, 262, 264, 267, 273 f. Cf. also *Z.d.Z.* 1930 pp. 398, 410 ; *Gott und Mensch*, 1930 p. 55 f.

This ground for the necessity of dogmatic prologomena is to be rejected for three reasons :

1. Because the difference presupposed between our own and earlier times cannot be established theologically. Was there ever a time in which theology was not likewise fundamentally faced with a comprehensive negation of the revelation believed in by the Church ?   Had not the ancients and the Middle Ages also, with the full cognizance of Christian theologians, their enlighteners, atheists, and secularists, the forerunners of our specifically modern paganism ? Was not the tactical position of faith in revelation, which presumably is the point in dispute here, more dangerous in a different way during the second half of the 18th century, than to-day ?   And above all, did the host of gods, demons, and miracles, which distinguished the ancient view of the world preceding ours, really constitute an advantage from the Christian standpoint, compared with the de-deification so broadly characteristic of our own world ? Could the educated consciousness before Kant and Copernicus, affording, as it did, more scope than in our case for this and that revelation, for revelation as a whole and in general, seriously ease the situation for the Christian Church and her dogmatics, and so constitute a serious reason for the scantiness of prolegomena among the said ancients ?   And on the other hand, has the modern educated consciousness and view of the world with its particular threat to " all revelation," revelation as a whole and in general, really created for Christian dogmatics a fundamentally more dangerous situation, one in need of security or discussion on quite different lines ?   Both points could be conceded, only if revelation as believed in by the Church were to be regarded

as a special case within the genus " revelation as a whole and in general." But, as by way of preliminary we have simply asserted, this is not the case. Knowledge of the revelation believed in by the Church neither stands nor falls by the general religious possibility, made easy by the ancient and difficult by the recent view of the world. Rather, the discussion between man's reason without faith and the revelation believed in by the Church has been the problem of Christian language in general, and of dogmatics in particular, at all times and with a fundamentally like seriousness. Therefore we cannot be asked to take as tragically as is presupposed by this conception of the necessity for dogmatics, the tragedy of modern godlessness in particular, as if we were faced with something unusual.

2. But the conception is also awkward, in that these very prolegomena are involved in a cross-examination in which the task of dogmatics is forthwith dropped instead of gripped hold of. In dogmatics the Church has to measure her language about God by the measure of her own essence, i.e. the divine revelation. But her language about God is the language of the *per se* faithless and anti-faith reason of man. Thus right along the line dogmatics is the discussion between this reason of man's and the revelation believed in by the Church. But this discussion actually takes place in the sphere of the Church, i.e. its bearings depend, not upon the counter-utterance (Widerspruch) of reason, but upon the utterance (Spruch) of revelation. Its personal interest lies not in exhibiting a " point of connection " with the divine message to man, but purely in the divine message published and apprehended. Moreover, her epistemological question can not run : How is human knowledge of revelation possible? (as if it were a question whether revelation is known ! as if it were to be expected from an investigation of human knowledge that we would see into the possibility of know-ing divine revelation !). But it runs, What is man's real knowledge of divine revelation ? (the presupposition being that revelation creates the needful " point of connection " in man, itself and on its own initiative). Displace this relation, make the contradiction of reason as such the object of investigation and the conquest of it as such its goal, and at once you quit the sphere of the Church ; in fact " another task " is put in the place of the task of dogmatics.

"Eristic theology is distinguished from dogmatic by caring more for the person with whom it speaks about faith, by going more into his objections, and so to that extent speaking more *ad hominem*" (E. Brunner, *Z.d.Z.*

1929 p. 269). As if dogmatics had more to say to angels ! But where there is emphasis upon the intention of talking *ad hominem*, the attitude of theology in general, as well as of dogmatics, is at once endangered.

However it may stand with the legitimacy and the possibility of this second task, in that case the task of dogmatics comes to a dead stop. In that case it does nothing towards answering its own special epistemological question, or establishing its own special scientific nature. With the second form of question, prolegomena to dogmatics would necessarily signify more an extraduction from than an introduction to the work of dogmatics.

It is of course not just the zeal of fresh discovery that has caused E. Brunner, particularly in the 1929 essay, to put the work of dogmatics proper in a thoroughly unpleasant light compared with his own " eristics."

3. But we must also ask whether, with the conception of the need for dogmatic prolegomena here under discussion, the particular desire obviously at the root of it, namely, the " responsibility and up-to-dateness " of theological thinking (E. Brunner, *Z.d.Z.* 1930 p. 397), does not actually come off the loser. Is dogmatics to be saved from becoming a Chinese puzzle, and its certainly desirable connection with its unbelieving contemporaries to be secured to it, by the fact that at the very first step it loses sight of its objective and—authority, please ?—turns to the astounding task of " smashing the axiom of reason ? " (E. Brunner, *Z.d.Z.* 1929 p. 256). We say, No ! Really responsible, up-to-date theological thought, in genuine rapprochement with its contemporaries, will reveal itself to be such even to-day (if by God's grace it is all this !) by refusing to discuss the basis of its ground, questions such as whether God is, whether there is such a thing as revelation, etc., but also, however unjustified in its action, as it is bound to be any way in this matter, by actually achieving its own consummation as thought on this ground and by being thereby actually on the spot, as the witness of faith against unbelief. There is no dispute about the fact that dogmatics too, together with the Christian Church generally, has to speak all along the line as faith opposing unbelief, and that to that extent all along the line her language must be apologetic, polemical. But there has never been any other effective apologetic and polemic of faith against unbelief than the unintended one (impossible to intend ! purely experiential !) which took place when God Himself sided with the witness of faith. All intended apologetic and polemic, on the other hand, has for three reasons invariably and notoriously

been an irresponsible act, not up-to-date and so ineffective as well.

(a) In it obviously faith must take unbelief seriously and itself not quite seriously, and therefore secretly or openly cease to be faith. What unbelief expects of faith is purely the one thing, that it should be an event. It is not in our power to cause this event. But in " discussion " with unbelief faith is certainly not an event. Does not the article on forgiveness of sins already forbid a dialogue in which the unbelief of the partner in the dialogue is taken seriously, i.e. in which he is addressed as a child of the world and is apprehended in his unbelief ? Do we expect in this way even apagogically to be able to instruct him as to the wrongness of his prejudices against faith ?

(b) In all apologetic and polemic for faith that comes forward independently, the feeling is betrayed that dogmatics itself is quite happily situated.

Karl Heim begins the Introduction to his *Glaube und Denken*, 1931, with the amazing statement : " We have sufficient dogmatic textbooks . . . to introduce us excellently to the doctrine of the evangelical Church." Sufficient ! ?   Excellently ! ?

The theologian who indulges in such tricks obviously thinks he has plenty time and authority to turn his back upon any anxiety about dogmatics and, instead of working at the matter itself, to talk with other people about the matter. This confident dispersion of energy is out of place and in the long-run cannot even outwardly gain credence.

(c) An independent eristics at least suggests the risk, that conversely a dogmatics which imagines it has already left behind it the discussion with unbelief in the form of such prolegomena, will let slip the essential knowledge as to the standing menace to all its pronouncements, and of course in Chinese fashion (the building of the Great Wall was admittedly a thoroughly eristic undertaking !) will comport itself like an esoterics, assured *praenumerando*.

So far as even theology is really and effectively apologetic and polemic, it is so because its distinctive work, which can take place nowhere save amid the battle between faith and unbelief, is acknowledged, strengthened, and blessed by God as a witness to faith, but not because of special arrangements by which it can also reveal exclusively to its partner in the debate, only that it either deceived him in alleging that it was negotiating with him on the

basis of common presuppositions, or was not itself on the spot
if it really did so. In either way it will certainly not succeed in
" smashing the axiom of reason," but if at all, then without special
effort and honourably in its own way. Apologetics and polemics
can only be an event, they cannot be a programme.

Yet it holds even for theology, that " we must take care not so to deface
the gospel (not by its own strength but by our powers) that it is quite lost, to
defend it so well that it collapseth. Let us not be anxious, the gospel needeth
not our help, it is sufficiently strong of itself, God alone commandeth it,
whose it is. . . . Therefore 'tis a small wretched thing that this puny breath
should range itself against the sophists : What would this bat accomplish
by its flapping ? Let them go ! 'tis of God's grace an ignorant folk. . . . In
all this there is no better counsel than to preach the gospel ill and continue
sincerely, and ask God to lead and guide us " (Luther, *Sermon vom Glauben
und guten Werken*, 1522 W. edn. 10III, p. 354, l. 15). " Thus conclude we
that of God's Word can be no master or judge or any protector save God
Himself. 'Tis His Word, and as He letteth it go forth without man's service
and counsel, so will He hold and maintain it Himself for man's help and
strength. And whoso for this seeks protection and comfort with men, shall
be abandoned by God and men " (*Fastenpostille*, 1525 W. edn. 17II, p. 108,
l. 26).

The necessity for dogmatic prolegomena, i.e. the necessity for
giving an explicit account of the special path of knowledge to be
trodden by dogmatics, must, to be authoritative, be an inner
necessity, grounded in the thing itself. If it rests upon a conflict
in which faith is involved, then this conflict, to be serious, must
be a conflict of faith with itself. Moreover, the conflict of faith
with unbelief can only be important in the case and form in which
it is a conflict of faith with itself ; because in faith itself unbelief
has somehow reported itself verbally and claims a hearing. Now
this paradoxical fact consists in the circumstance that faith consists
not only and consists not at all, in the first and most important
sense, in conflict with unbelief, but in conflict with itself, i.e. with
a form or forms of faith, in which it recognises itself in form but
not in content—fails so much to recognise itself, that in the forms
for their form's sake it must equally acknowledge faith, Christian
faith, but for their content's sake can only regard this faith as
difference of faith. Difference of faith is faith in which we hear
unbelief express itself in words. When we would descend to the
task of dogmatics we come up against this fact of difference of
faith. For when we would inquire into the essence of the Church,
into Jesus Christ as the norm of the Church's action, we find that
already in understanding this norm, in knowing Jesus Christ as the

3

Lord of the Church, we are so much at one with some, that we can get down with them to the task together, but with others from the start we are not at one in this presupposition (in the way in which we understand it) and so cannot join with them in getting down to dogmatic work. We must make it clear that our understanding of the essence of the Church is by no means the only one in the field, that alongside of our own there are in the field other and strange ways of regarding the essence of the Church, that community with the representatives of these other ways can only be the community of conflict with them, and this for the reason that we can regard the difference, the strangeness in their view, not as a possibility of faith itself, as yet perhaps unknown to us, but only as a possibility opposed to faith, as unbelief ; and yet because of its formal presuppositions we must regard it as a possibility of faith. Such is the paradoxical fact of h e r e s y. By heresy we understand such a form of Christian faith that formally (because it too stands in relation to Jesus Christ, His Church, baptism, Holy Writ, the general Christian confessional formulæ, etc.) we cannot dispute its property of being a form of Christian faith, without yet being in the position to understand what we are doing in acknowledging it as such, because we can only regard its content (the interpretation which it contains of these general presuppositions) as a contradiction of faith.

This paradox in the fact of heresy is very finely brought out in the words of I r e n a e u s : *Similia enim loquentes fidelibus . . . non ᶜolum dissimilia sapiunt, sed et contraria et per omnia plena blasphemiis, per quae interficiunt eos, qui per similitidinem verborum dissimile affectionis eorum in se attrahunt venenum ; sicut quis aquae mixtum gypsum dans pro lacte, seducat per similitudinem coloris, sicut quidam dixit superior nobis de omnibus qui quolibet modo depravant quae sunt Dei, et adulterant veritatem : In Dei lacte gypsum male miscetur (C.o. haer.* III 17, 4).

Just because of this paradox of the fact of heresy this is an important matter of faith, we might even say that unbelief in the form of heresy becomes an important matter for faith, a thing which it certainly is not as pure unbelief. Because in heresy it appears simultaneously as a form of faith, here it becomes serious, and there m a y and there m u s t be conflict, and serious conflict, between faith and heresy.

As a rule in the ancient, the mediæval and to this day in the post-Reformation Church down to Pietism and the Enlightenment, conflict with Jews, pagans, and atheists was purely incidental, pursued with nothing like the same emphasis and zeal as that against heretics. That (even to the mutual obloquy and mutual burning of those far-off days, things certainly not commendable nor even essentially relevant) was sensible, because between Church and heretics they really talked against each other (instead of past each other), i.e. absolutely differently about absolutely the same object.   People took opposite sides to the death, as can only happen when brothers are at feud.   The much-boasted progress from the 17th to the 18th century consisted in the fact that people made up their minds to tolerate one another, i.e. freely and mutually to leave one another to their fate.   Thus for the first time there came a break in the fellowship which hitherto had still always been preserved in conflict.

In the conflict between the Church and heresy, the whole point is work on the thing itself (although undertaken in a quite opposite sense), not talk about the thing, which is condemned from the start to barrenness in results.   The theme is the same : hence the possibility of conflict here.   Certainly it concerns a totally different interpretation of the same theme ; hence the inevitability of conflict here.   So different is the Church's interpretation from that of the heretics that the question threateningly enough arises, whether what is involved on each side is not some quite different theme, whether the opposing difference of belief ought not perhaps to be regarded merely as unbelief.   The dialogue between the Church and the heretics would not be so serious, were it conducted otherwise than in view of this threatening question.   But so long and so far as the dialogue is still being carried on, this question has at least not been decided in the sense that the Church and heretics have nothing to do with one another.   The dialogue that takes place, and perhaps the very keenness of it, are proof of the very opposite.   In this dialogue the Church must tackle heresy on the point that it itself seeks to be the Church.   And heresy can only attack the Church on the ground that the latter is not sufficiently, not truly the Church. Neither can happen without recourse to the general formal presuppositions, however problematical these may have become. Disunited in the content of faith, people yet appeal on both sides to certain general forms of faith, thereby asserting (were it merely by raising the threatening question) a common ground of faith which at least always receives consideration again.   As soon as the Church and heresy should have ceased to meet each other, or to have anything further to say to each other, this bow of peace which undoubtedly spans both, though at a distance, would be broken to bits or at least rendered meaningless.   In the real encounter with heresy, faith is plunged into conflict with itself—because—so long and so far as it is not quit of heresy, so long and so far as the latter rather gets home on it, so long and so far as it must justify itself against heresy—faith cannot avoid treating it as at least faith too, and not merely as unbelief, in spite of the voice of unbelief which it feels it gets out of it.   It must regard it as a possibility of faith, though, of course, one profoundly incomprehensible to it, one which it can only conceive as a possibility of the disturbance and destruction of faith, a possibility which it must avert—but as a possibility of faith in itself, and therefore and to that extent (whence too the need for tremendous caution !) as its own possibility, as a possibility not without but, however unimaginably as such, within the Church.   That is why this conflict is a serious conflict, why the task of giving an explicit account of the path to knowledge to be trodden by dogmatics may and must become an inner necessity based upon the thing itself.

We are faced with the fact of heresy.   Concretely, we are faced with the fact of Roman Catholicism, in the form which it gave itself in the 16th century in the struggle with the Reformation.   And within the organised unities of the Evangelical Churches we are faced with the fact of pietistic-rationalistic Modernism, with its roots in mediæval mysticism and the humanist Renaissance.   The fact of the modern " denial of revelation," etc., is entirely uninteresting compared with this double fact.   For at this point, in its opposition to Roman Catholicism and to Protestant Modernism, evangelical faith is in conflict with itself.   Neither of the two is a sort of irrelevant paganism, that at least is not their intention ; but they meet us, if we take them as they present themselves, as possibilities of faith, our own faith of course, as possibilities within and not without the Church.   And by listening to them, by not resiling from the formal correctness of their claim, we must say that we do not recognise faith and the Church in these two forms, do not recognise them in so full a sense, that the question is inevitable, whether these possibilities are not possibilities of simple unbelief, whether Roman Catholic and Modernist Protestant theologians are not to be regarded according to Matt. 18[17] as " heathens and publicans."   But our encounter with heresies would be no real encounter, we should already be cutting adrift from them again, already be ceasing to listen to them, were we to regard this question as decided.   If they really face us as a fact and if the question is consequently not yet decided, then it turns against us too, and in view of our own understanding of the essence of the Church, in view of our own knowledge of Christ, we are called to purification, to a rendering of our account, to responsibility. Of course the fact that the theology we favour is purely and solely evangelical, we can as little discuss and account for, as the fact that we are baptised and believe. Even with regard to ourselves we can only start from the fact, so far as it is actually given as a fact. But heresies simply force us to make it clear, how far, in what sense, upon what inner ground we stand here and not there, and so understand revelation not in a Catholic nor yet in a modernist but in an evangelical sense.

The view that in the existence of heresies we must emphatically listen to this demand is an ancient one. *Improbatio quippe haereticorum facit eminere quid Ecclesia tua sentiat et quid habeat sana doctrina* (Augustine, *Conf.* VII 19, 25, cf. *De cat. rud.* 24, 44, *De civ. Dei*, XVI 2, 1).—*Ob hoc haereseon non statim divinitus eradicantur auctores, ut probati manifesti fiant, id est : ut unusquisque, quam tenax et fidelis et fixus catholicae fidei sit amator appareat* (Vincent of Lerins, *Common.* I 20, 25, cf. 19, 24).—*Quia perversi homines apostolicam doctrinam et caeteras doctrinas et scripturas pervertunt ad sui ipsorum perditionem . . . ideo necessaria fuit temporibus procedentibus explicatio fidei* (Thomas Aquinas, *S. theol.* II² qu. 1, art. 10).

The purification to which we are called must naturally be a purification in respect of the path of knowledge to be trodden. The paths in fact diverge right from the basis of knowledge. Thus, straightway, with regard to the basis of knowledge we must be at one with ourselves, in view of the varying possibilities. But what the ground of knowledge is, other than just the essence of the Church, is a matter that can itself obviously be so differently interpreted, that everything following from it becomes as different as is the case in every detail between the Church and heresies. To clear up the evangelical view of those seemingly or really identical formal presuppositions on both sides, is the inner need, laid upon us to-day, for dogmatic prolegomena.

Heretical tendencies and even whole heretical Churches (e.g. Marcionite, Donatist, Arian) were, of course, already known to ecclesiastical antiquity and the Middle Ages. But it must be asserted that it was first through and since the Reformation, that heresy became a universally and fundamentally felt problem. Formally there was nothing new, yet materially there was something quite new, in the way in which the evangelical Church of a Luther and a Calvin regarded the Papacy, and in which on the contrary the Catholicism of the 16th and 17th centuries regarded this particular " heresy." That was the time, and the first time, that it was impressed upon the Church, what " difference of faith " is. Thereafter in consequence there are dogmatic prolegomena on all sides. We shall have to find the first traces of them on the evangelical side in the preambles on the Scripture principle which crop up particularly in the Reformed confessions (first in the *Conf. Tetrapol.* 1530, and later with increasing regularity). With the fresh, material knowledge of Christ (regarding the connection between forgiveness of sin and Christian life) which produced the Reformation, there was bound up from the very start, and summarised in the doctrine of the sole normativity of Holy Scripture, a new formal theology, which, it immediately became inevitable, had to be brought to explicit and independent expression, in view of the contradiction facing the thing itself, and in view of the fact that this contradiction was not one of unbelief but one of difference in belief. The growing need in this direction may be gathered from the increase in introductory discussions about the Scripture principle even in the different drafts of Melanchthon's *Loci*. The first example to be claimed of prolegomena that go back to first principles in our sense will of course be the first ten chapters of Calvin's Institutio of 1559. Fundamental formal definitions to repel the evangelical Scripture principle were also needed by the opposing Roman Catholic dogmatics. The first broadly visible step in this direction was the set of definitions at the head of the deliverances of the Council of Trent, upon the value of Church tradition which was to count as equal to, really before, Holy Scripture. The natural result is that prolegomena to Catholic dogmatics since the Vatican decree revolve around the conception of the Church's teaching power centred in the Pope, as the real source of revelation and of the corresponding " Catholic Faith." The task of thus giving an account of the formal presuppositions became still more stringent, and dogmatic prolegomena acquired in a clearly recognisable way more weight and compass, when up popped pietistic-rationalistic Modernism as a third character in the dialogue, particularly active and successful on the evangelical side, but not without cross-connections even on the Catholic. Over against it, although it has neither been expelled from the evangelical churches nor voluntarily gone over to found a counter-church, we draw the line as definitely as over against Catholicism. The faith which is engaged in struggling with doubt about the truth, struggling with the question, Is there a God ? is a different one from the faith in which man asks whether God, whose existence is not a problem, is gracious to him, or whether man must despair of himself. The first is the modernist, the second is the evangelical faith ; and the two can only recognise one another mutually in the complete identity of their formal presuppositions. They are one in Christ and at the same time not at all one in Christ. Modernist faith has felt this as keenly as evangelical or Catholic faith. For which reason the moment it began to evolve its own dogmatics, it also expounded from its own side, in the doctrine of " religion " which is such a feature of the 18th and 19th centuries, its thoroughly characteristic approach to the matter, as it felt it had to understand it. The significance of Schleiermacher consists above all in his having, in his doctrine of Christian piety as the essence of the Church, given this heresy a formal basis which fulfilled the time preceding him, as well as foretold the time succeeding him. He is not the inaugurator, he is the great ripe classic of Modernism, which, if it understands itself, will never let itself be turned away from following him.

2. THE POSSIBILITY OF DOGMATIC PROLEGOMENA

How are dogmatic prolegomena possible ? How can we come to a preliminary understanding as to the path of knowledge to be trodden in dogmatics ? Such an understanding obviously presupposes a point from which this path is visible and comprehensible. What is this point ?

The answer offered theology since the days of the Enlightenment and with fresh urgency to-day, the answer of modernist dogmatics, is this : the Church and faith are to be understood as part of a larger essential context, and dogmatics as part of a larger scientific problem-context, from the general structural laws of which we are to read off its special epistemological conditions, and to recognise its special scientific claims. This problem-context is, however, that of an ontology ; and ever since Descartes that must mean a comprehensively explicated self-interpretation of man's existence, such as will, among other things, also help at the right point to the preliminary understanding of an existence in the Church, i.e. in faith, and so to a preliminary understanding and criterion of theological knowledge.

It was idealist philosophy which at one time led Schleiermacher and De Wette to regard man's existence as a sum of " powers " or " tendencies " or " activities " of man's self-consciousness, and to discover in this at a central point, in the form of " feeling " or " immediate self-consciousness," an original disposition or foundation for the piety which was to be realised in history, and, simultaneously, the principle of knowledge in Christian dogmatics, which was the self-explanation of this definite and historically real piety. Here, too, of course, the presupposed meaning of existence formally and in content, was still far too naïve in view of the real problems of human existence. Hence present-day ontology, taught something better theoretically by Kierkegaard and practically by world-war and revolution, interpets man's being not as secondarily, but as radically " history " and as materially not so much powers, etc., as " inherence in nothingness " (M. Heidegger, *Was ist Metaphysik?* 1929 p. 20). And quite intelligibly, a theology in personal search of a more essential understanding of the New Testament did attempt to interpret existence thus understood as " prior to faith," i.e. to look there for the ontologically existential possibility of the existential occurrence of faith, and by means of its analysis to gain a " preliminary understanding " of Christian language and Christian theology, above all of exegesis (R. Bultmann, *Der Begriff der Offenbarung im NT* 1929 : *Die Geschichtlichkeit des Daseins und der Glaube* Z.Th.K. 1930 p. 339 f.). The homogeneity in method of both the Schleiermacher–De Wette and the Bultmann conception should be clearly noted. " That the beginning of theology takes place in a determination of being, of man . . . is fundamentally a bit of Liberalism. It might have been thought that it would have proved impracticable to undertake for one moment to speak first of man as a believer, apart from God " (Heinrich Barth, *Philosophie, Theologie und Existenzproblem, Z.d.Z.* 1932 p. 113 f.). Cf. G. Wobbermin's commendation of Bultmann (*Richtlinien evangel. Theologie,* 1929 pp. 102, 110 note, 116, 143).

On the basis of this conception, dogmatic prolegomena will clearly consist : First, in showing that practically there is room in a general ontology, or anthropology, for this ontic element too, namely, the essence of the Church, i.e. of faith ; that man's existence is also realisable as believing existence ; Second, in the concretely historical recollection that this special ontic element actually appears as an event, and thereby as the object of an ontic science ; Finally, in drawing up the rules which must arise for this science, and so for the criticism and revision of Christian language, from this ontologico-ontic basis on which it rests.

1. Anthropological possibility.—2. Historico-psychological realisability—3. Method : these are the lines on which the introductions to Schleiermacher's *Der Christliche Glaube* (§ 3–10, § 11–19, § 20–31) and De Wette's *Lehrbuch der christlichen Dogmatik*, 1831 (§ 1–27, § 28–45, § 46–61), are actually drawn up and on which of course the introduction to a dogmatics in Bultmann's sense would also have to be drawn up.

The statements in such prolegomena do not claim to be themselves statements of dogmatic knowledge. The syllable pro- in the word prolegomena is to be translated " previously."

In that case it is held with *Schleiermacher* " that all propositions occurring here cannot themselves be dogmatic as well " (*D. chr. Gl.* § 1, 1).

The statements, then, in such prolegomena present themselves rather, partly as borrowings from metaphysics, anthropology (ethics, according to Schleiermacher), philosophy of religion, and history of religion, partly as pure discussions on methodology. What dogmatic-knowledge is, would then really be fixed *praenumerando* outside dogmatics, and would also be fixable for one who purposes taking no further trouble with dogmatics itself.

The possibility of this solution stands or falls with the answer in the affirmative to the question, whether there really is an essence-context superior to the essence of the Church and so a scientific problem-context superior to dogmatics. Is there an existential potentiality different from the actuality of revelation, on the basis of which the latter can be regarded as an event ? Is there possible something universally human, of which this special thing can be claimed subsequently as the realisation ? Is there an existential ontological prius to this ontic existential thing ? If this presupposition be admitted, prolegomena of the kind are possible. But all through this very presupposition bears not a neutral but an extremely theological character. That the nature of dogmatic knowledge is established outside dogmatics, can only be right in so far as it is actually established outside a definite, in this case Reformed evangelical (also outside Romaan Catholic) dogmatics :

to be more definite, within modernist dogmatics. The assertion of an existentially ontological prius for ontically existential faith, i.e. the definition of faith as a mode of the historical actuality of human existence, is a cardinal proposition of the faith which regards the essence of the Church, which decidedly regards itself, as a determination of man's reality, as piety.

Schleiermacher's assertion, that his introduction is not itself dogmatics, is not tenable. Even his pupil Alex. Schweizer already saw and declared that in it " there is contained by no means a merely introductory interpretation, but the basis of the *Glaubenslehre* itself," and has therefore for himself defined the task of prolegomena by saying that " a special part of doctrine " must " itself be prefixed as fundamental, in which Christian consciousness of faith gives an account of itself, as yet apart from distinctions between the various elements inherent in it " (*Die christliche Glaubenslehre*, 2nd edn. 1877 vol. I p. 92 f.). Now weigh Schleiermacher's assertion against his definitions of the Church which follow shortly after : " a community arising solely through free human actions, which can only continue by such," " a community concerned with piety " (*D. chr. Gl.* § 2, 2 ; § 3, 1). This definition, decisive for all that follows, is clearly the one with significance for Modernism, as it has its source in English Congregationalism (cf. e.g. Arts. 20, 23, 24 of the " platform " of the Savoy Declaration, 1658). It and it only could empower Schleiermacher to open up his foundations with borrowings from ethics ; it therefore thus characterises the propositions borrowed as dogmatic—we say, heretically dogmatic.

We regard this modernist faith as common Christian property, so far as the essence of the Church denotes in fact a determination of human reality. But we cannot regard it as Christian, so far as it interprets the possibility of this reality as a human possibility, so far as it fails to see that such a determination of human reality only proceeds, and is to be perceived as proceeding, from something outside all human possibilities, i.e. from God acting, so far as, instead of trying to explain its own history from itself, it does so from a general capacity or the general historicity of man's existence. If this faith gives way, so does this interpretation of faith, so does the presupposition of an anthropological prius to faith, so too the possibility of prolegomena of this kind.

Heinrich Barth (*op. cit.* p. 105) understands by " existence " " the concrete decision for a possibility which experiences its realisation in this decision," but defines it in opposition to M. Heidegger and R. Bultmann as " connected with something beyond it " (p. 117), namely with " the criterion that transcends it " (p. 108) which " on its part possesses the significance of existence " (p. 109), which is identical with the " idea " of existence (p. 110). This " existence in limitation," H. Barth would, " to use the old scholastic expression—term an ' analogy ' of knowledge of God " (p. 116 f.). The scene of the existence-dialectic thus interpreted is history, and in such

wise that " each historical phase represents something once-for-all and irrepeatable." " One such once-for-all " would then meet us in that element
in history which the theologian means by the " history of revelation," in
which " the truth of existence and with it the meaning and possibility of its
responsibility, shines out in a purely individual and unprecedented manner "
(p. 118 f.).   On these terms the connection between philosophy and theology
is to be defined thus : " Existence-philosophy starts from existence in
general ; since it avails itself only of existence as it finds it for its point of
connection, it should not expect to be able to settle up with the ' new existence '
of Biblical man by a pure extension of thinking.   Hence it is sensible and firmly
rooted in the essence of the existence-problem, to leave the reflective work
upon it to a special science, theology." What " constitutes " this " a
special science, is the positive fact of a definite historical element.
Theology is to that extent a ' positive ' science " (p. 121).   " Theology has
for its object the believing existence of Biblical man and the self-
interpretation of the certainty of his existence deposited in the title-deeds of
Scripture.   To this fact, historical in a special sense, the theologian should
devote his reflection " (p. 122).   It is " the possibility of a sifting and clarifying summary of the items of existential knowledge met with there," which
takes shape particularly in the attempt at a " dogmatics " (p. 122 f.).   Unquestionably we have here to do with a very energetic and impressive attempt
to overcome the anthropological narrowness of Heidegger's existence-philosophy on the basis and by means of the existence-philosophy itself, with a
philosophical outline which is prepared to renounce the validation of an
anthropological prius to faith, and so the tutelage and modification of theology,
which both Heidegger and Bultmann distinctly fail to overcome.   H. Barth's
meaning is as follows : 1. The opposition of the concept of general and special
is not here to imply any attempt to force the special (the problem of special
historical reality) into subsumption under a general concept.   2. The truth of
existence which flashes out in the history of revelation is not to be regarded
as identical with the " general " truth of existence, with which existence
philosophy as such has to do, but as the light which flashes exactly there and
nowhere else   The philosophical (" general ") concept of existence, in short,
offers not knowledge of God, but merely an " analogy " to knowledge of God.
Thus here philosophy neither can nor wishes to regulate and subordinate
dogmatics to its own problem-context, but merely to indicate its " relation "
to dogmatics, which indeed it is in a position to do on the basis of its transcending comprehension.   3. Only in retrospective (from revealed truth) recapitulation, not in anticipation, is the philosophical existence concept to be an
" analogy " to knowledge of God.   In no case is it to be regarded as an instrument of such knowledge.—The wish may well be expressed, that this self-
interpretation of the " critical existence-philosophy " may also in public
discussion be brought to light in a form less liable to misunderstanding, than
has been the case in the essay quoted (cf. e.g. the quoted definition of theology
(p. 122) or the designation of revelation as " one such once-for-all " (p. 119)) ;
for which purpose it might certainly be useful to abandon the categories of
" general " and " special " (positive, historical), which are too much over-
weighted in this respect.   Further, the responsibility for the assertion that in
the transcending knowledge of man's existence we have to do with an
" analogy " to knowledge of God, must continue to be left to the philosopher ;
i.e. this assertion cannot be a theological proposition.   For it is impossible

to see how it could be given a theological basis. As regards the theologian, therefore, a strict warning is appropriate, not to let himself be enticed even by this new use of the "old scholastic expression," into any philosophical certification of his work, i.e. into any further possibility of natural theology. "Prolegomena to dogmatics" cannot be produced even out of "critical existence-philosophy." If the assertion about the "analogy" is really to be regarded as one of recapitulation and not of anticipation, this warning should itself be implicit in the meaning of this philosophy.

As distinct from the conception just reviewed, the point from which it makes sure of its path of knowledge is described in Roman Catholic dogmatics as the reality, beginning with itself and resting on itself, of divine revelation and of the corresponding supernatural faith resting upon it. Dogmatic prolegomena consist here in the finding, that in the form of Holy Scripture, Church tradition, and the living teaching apostolate of the Church infallibly representing and interpreting both, we have the objective principle of knowledge, while in the form of the *fides catholica*, which receives the revelation in what is set before it by the Church, we have the subjective principle of knowledge.

So e.g. Matth. Jos. Scheeben, *Handbuch der kathol. Dogmatik*, vol. I 1874; B. Bartmann, *Lehrbuch der Dogmatik*, 7th edn. vol. I 1928. How changeable this conception can be in individual cases is manifest in the fact that on the one hand Joh. Kuhn's *Einleitung in die katholische Dogmatik* (1846; the Catholicism here, as with J. A. Möhler, is still conceived in rapprochement with idealism!) can consist almost exclusively of a doctrine of faith, while on the other hand the introduction to F. Diekamp's *Katholische Dogmatik*, vol. I 6th edn. 1930, can consist almost as exclusively of a doctrine of the "sources of dogmatics," i.e. of the objective principle of knowledge.

It is self-evident here that these findings are themselves already propositions of faith and in their scientific form propositions in dogmatics. But we can only rate them as propositions of another faith and an alien dogmatics. They take for granted that the essence of the Church, Jesus Christ, no longer the free Lord of their existence, but bound up with the existence of the Church, is finally limited and conditioned by definite concrete formulations of man's understanding of His revelation and of the faith that grasps it. Once more we cannot fail to recognise the common Christian character of this faith, so far as here the conception of God acting, of the fundamental transcendence of all human possibilities, is, at least begins by being, taken seriously as the source of dogmatic knowledge. But once more our community with this faith breaks off, in view of the way in which grace here becomes nature, in which here God's action disappears at once and dissolves into the action of man visited by grace, in which what is outside all human possibility is here at once transformed into a something enclosed within the Church's reality, and the personal act of divine approach into a continuously present and objective relation. Roman Catholic faith believes in this transformation. It can recognise itself and God's revelation again in this continuously present relation between God and man, in this objective revealedness. It affirms an *analogia entis*, the actuality of a likeness in the creature to God even in a fallen world and therewith the possibility of applying the profane " *es gibt* " (there is) even to God and divine things ; just as it is the—of course ontological—presupposition of the transformation, the circumvention and neutralisation of the decisive character of revelation and faith.

Inhorresco in quantum dissimilis ei sum ; inardesco in quantum similis ei sum (Augustine, *Conf.* XI 9, 11). *Id quod in Deo perfecte est, in rebus aliis per quandam deficientem participationem invenitur. . . . Et sic creatura habet quod Dei est ; unde et Deo recte similis dicitur* (Thomas Aquinas, *S.c. gent.* I *c.* 29). Cf. also *Conc. Later.* IV 1215 *De trin.* etc. *cap.* 2 in Denzinger's *Enchiridion Nr.* 432 *ad fin.* and on it E. Przywara, *Religionsphilosophie kath. Theol.* 1926 p. 22 f. and *passim*.

If this faith is not ours, if we know nothing of such transformation and what it presupposes, if the association of the words " there is revelation " is as impossible as the other, " there is faith," then to us too is forbidden the point from which dogmatic knowledge is here gained.

The remaining possibility—on the presupposition of evangelical faith—of making dogmatic knowledge comprehensible is to draw a line on the left by renouncing the presupposition of an existential ontological possibility for the essence of the Church, on the right by renouncing the presupposition of a continuously present inherence of the essence of the Church in a creaturely form, in an " *es gibt.*" On the left we say : the essence of the Church is *actus purus*, divine action beginning with itself, the source and means of its own insight, therefore action unpredictable on an anthropological basis. On the right we say : the essence of the Church is *actus purus*, free action, not a continuously present relation ; grace is an event of personal approach, not a transferred tangible state of the soul. Left and right our first question can only be, how it could be otherwise, if the essence of the Church is identical with Jesus Christ. If that be so, then neither the precedence of an anthropological possibility nor the subsequence of a reality in the

Church can be considered as the point from which to contemplate and to understand the path to dogmatic knowledge, but solely the present instant in which Jesus Christ Himself speaks and is heard, when the light divine is created in our hearts.

λάμπειν ἐν ταῖς καρδίαις ἡμῶν, 2 Cor. 4⁶, compared by Paul with the " Let there be light ! " of Gen. 1³.

It is from the direction of Jesus Christ as the essence of the Church that we may expect free personal decision as to what ought to be the proper content of Christian language, and so also as to what should be the way to knowledge of it, to knowledge of dogma. Like all desire to know dogma itself, all explanation of the trend of this desire can be but a special form of the ready expectation, supported upon the promise, of this decision of the Lord of the Church.

Which means at least the establishment of the insight, self-evident on the basis of Roman Catholic dogmatics and in the end inevitable even in modernist dogmatics, that prolegomena to dogmatics are possible only as a portion of dogmatics itself. The syllable pro- in the word prolegomena is to be understood figuratively ; what is in question is not the things that must be said previously but the things that must be said first.

Our aim being to render an account of the path to knowledge to be trodden by dogmatics, we cannot move to a position lying somewhere apart from this actual path, somewhere above dogmatic work. Such a position apart and above would be making ontology, or anthropology, the basic science of the human possibilities, among which at some point that of faith and the Church also would have to be provided for. We should have to consider any so-called reality of the Church, in which the decision of the Lord of the Church is anticipated, as such a position apart and above. In either case, in the prolegomena to modernist or to Catholic dogmatics, we can, previous to entering upon it, know and say which will be the right way to knowledge. Evangelical dogmatics cannot do that. It can only venture to tread its path, in order on this path —from the start, maybe, as we have already recognised to be necessary, but on this path—to busy itself with the knowledge of the rightness of this path. It knows that no one can enter the closed circle of this business from without, either from a general human possibility or from a reality in the Church. It knows that all its knowledge—even the very knowledge of the rightness of its knowledge—can only be an event, but cannot be certified as right knowledge from a position apart from and above this event. It cannot possibly regard the account of its situation which it has to give in its prolegomena, as an attempt at such certification. Rather this account can only be completed within, although at the beginning of, actual dogmatic work—which, if regarded from any position apart and above, is uncertified work.

We see the possible starting-point of such an account in the circumstance that the Christian Church ventures to speak about God, i.e. ventures to regard its language as language about God. This circumstance in itself, apart from the possible and actual contents of such language, is obviously itself a bit of " language about God." It asserts of God that the Church speaks about Him. This assertion, however intended or however explicable, is as little self-evident, as much in need of explanation as any other assertions, i.e. assertions with content, which the Church ventures to make about God. Like them it requires criticism and revision, inquiry into the right the Church has to make it and the sense in which she makes it. The right she has to make it and the sense in which she makes it is then obviously identical with the norm for measuring what she states, the norm of the remaining content of her language about God. The knowledge of this right and meaning is identical with the knowledge of the rightness of things she knows, of the proper path she has to tread in criticising and revising the things she knows. If there is to be special reflection concerning this path as such—and we have seen that there should be—then it must consist of the question (in itself already the dogmatic question) as to the proper content of the presupposed assertion concerning the language about God to be found in the Church. This assertion possesses a proper content, if connected with a Word of God spoken previously to the Church that speaks about God. If and so far as such a word is spoken by God Himself to the Church, then and only then is there any right or any meaning in speaking in the Church about God. Then and only then is there a criterion—the Word of God Himself is then the criterion—of the rightness of such speaking and therewith a criterion of right criticism and revision of such speaking, a criterion of dogmatics. In the prolegomena to dogmatics, then, we inquire into the word of God as into the criterion of dogmatics. By inquiring into it we, being already on the path, are giving ourselves an account of the path we tread.

Thus understood the theme of the prolegomena to dogmatics

is clearly in essentials none other than that which Old-Protestant theology, in its defence against Catholicism and also, soon after, against the inroads of Modernism, dealt with under the title *De scriptura sacra*. In fact we shall see that the main proposition in the doctrine of the Word of God, which we shall try to evolve in what follows, will materially be none other than that of the authority and normativity of Holy Writ, as the witness to God's revelation and as the presupposition of the Church's proclamation. But in the situation to-day regarding both Catholicism and Modernism, anything there is to say about Holy Writ as the criterion of dogmatics requires a comprehensive explanation of that connection. Therefore what we essay is a doctrine of the Word of God and not merely a doctrine of Holy Scripture—a doctrine of Holy Scripture in the context of a comprehensive doctrine of the Word of God. In developing the locus *De scriptura sacra*, even the Old-Protestants did not in practice finish it off without decisive indications of the contents of Christian language about God, i.e. without anticipating material dogmas (e.g. the doctrine of reconciliation, of the Holy Spirit, of faith, of the Church). We too must make such anticipations and for clearness' sake must extend them still further. The most striking anticipation of this kind will be the discussion of the entire doctrine of the Trinity and essential portions of Christology at this early stage, as constituent parts of the answer to the question as to the Word of God. The question of formal dogma cannot be raised without at this very central point entering upon material dogma, since the supposedly formal dogma is itself in reality extremely material ; only that just here, at the start of the whole task, apart from the stress on its material significance, an assessment should be made of its formal significance, as being the foundation of dogmatic knowledge as such.

THE DOCTRINE OF THE WORD OF GOD

CHAPTER I

THE WORD OF GOD AS THE CRITERION OF DOGMATICS

§ 3

CHURCH PROCLAMATION AS THE MATERIAL
OF DOGMATICS

The language about God to be found in the Church is meant to be proclamation, so far as it is directed towards man in the form of preaching and sacrament, with the claim and in an atmosphere of expectation that in accordance with its commission it has to tell him the Word of God to be heard in faith. So far as, in spite of this claim and this expectation, it is man's word, it becomes the material of dogmatics, i.e. of the investigation into its responsibility, measured by the Word of God which it means to proclaim.

1. LANGUAGE ABOUT GOD AND CHURCH
PROCLAMATION

Not all man's language is language about God. Perhaps it really might and ought to be. In principle we can give no reason for it being otherwise. Because God is the Lord, of whom and to whom we are, because moreover the realities and truths distinct from Him and from ourselves, which normally constitute the concrete cause and object of human language, are from Him and to Him, there really might be and should be no profane language, but, understood in its final relevance, only language about God. As it is, all serious reflection upon human language about God must start from the fact that actually everything is quite otherwise, that it is quite impossible to interpret human language as such as language about God. We know man, i.e. know ourselves, not as man in his original state nor yet as man in the realm of glory. Of the one or the other we should, of course, have to say, All his language is language about God. But such is not our knowledge of ourselves. We know ourselves only as man, met in his fallen, lost and damned state by mercy, man in the realm of grace, man of to-day, between the times of creation and redemption. We stand under the sign of a decision, repeatedly imposed on us, between the profanity and the sanctity of our being, between sin and grace, between a human existence that forgets God, is absolutely neutral towards God, i.e. absolutely in conflict with Him, and the same existence awakened by God in His revelation through faith to existence in the Church, to a hold upon His promise. This divorce is also continually the lot of man's language. It is not identical with the divorce between " worldly " and " religious " language. Religious language is, of course, distinguished outwardly from worldly language in that " God " is its more or less expressed object. Inwardly it is also distinguished by the intention expressly or even tacitly directed towards this object, by the more or less straightforward purpose to speak directly or indirectly about God. But this divorce extends also into the realm of his profane existence. Neither the object nor the intention converts man's language into hallowed language about God, just as on the contrary it need not therefore necessarily be profane, because it lacks this object and intention. This divorce, like that between a believing, religious attitude and an unbelieving, worldly one in general, is only a symptom, and yet in addition never an unambiguous symptom of the real, final divorce between profane and hallowed existence. Still, a necessary symptom. The constantly consummated event of the final divorce, of the event in which God is the actor, casts its shadow before in the event of this preliminary divorce in which man acts.

It cannot then be generally correct to characterise this preliminary divorce as " humanity's split between sacramental possession and profane evacuation " (Paul Tillich, *Relig. Verwirklichung*, 1930 p. 64). Of course it does not necessarily coincide with the divine divorce, and so far as that is the case may indeed be described in this way. But as a symptom of the divine divorce it may be a pointer to its truth and so obviously cannot be exhaustively described in this way. Further, it is no fruit of careful consideration to say generally that from God's point of view the historical Church has no advantage over historical society, that God's act, revelation, is directed equally to society and the Church, that the " invisible community " may be proclaimed and realised, " quite indifferently from the religious or from the cultural side " (P. Tillich, *Kirche und Kultur*, 1924 pp. 10 f., 16 f., 19). Certainly God is not tied to the historical Church, but is free and able of these stones to raise up children to Abraham. But that does not alter the fact that the opposition between Church and society, not in the abstract likeness but precisely in the concrete unlikeness of their members, is a sign of the divine divorce and may be an indication of its truth. Finally, to interpret this opposition as in general " repellent in essence " (*op. cit.* p. 9) and to make it the object of a general " protest " " from the thither side of essential being " (*Relig. Verwirklichung*, p. 46), is not in point, because our position is neither the time of creation nor the time of redemption, and so emphatically not a " thither side of being," but the present between the times, the time of the *regnum gratiae*, in which the symptom of the human divorce, in all the ambiguity of its relativity and preliminary nature, may prove every moment to be extremely essential as an indication of the divine divorce.

Likewise the event in which God acts consists altogether in the fact that men are by God visibly aroused, set apart, and gathered together into being in the visible Church. A visible opposition between " religious " and " worldly," arising within the profane realm, is now established and preserved, not of itself but in this event of divine election, and is thereby marked out as a genuine indication of the opposition between judgment and grace, in which it is not a case of this man or that acting against others, but of God acting on men. Of course it is only in faith that this event is visible as this event, that being in the Church is visible as divine election and sanctification. What is in itself visible is also in this case an event within the profane realm. Its significance may be missed, it may actually even be withdrawn from it again.

" Thereby he of a surety indicateth that the preaching of the Gospel is no external, lasting, abiding doctrine, but is as a travelling patch of rain that runneth about, what it toucheth it toucheth, what it misseth it misseth. But it returneth not, neither doth it stay fast, but the sun and heat come down and lick it up, etc. So it is the experience that in no spot in the world hath the Gospel stayed clean and pure, beyond one man's memory, but so long as they abide that introduced it, it stayeth fast and hath waxed ; if the same were gone, so was it also lightly gone ; there followed at once thereon a pack of rabble spirits and false teachers " (Luther, *Fastenpostille*, 1525 W. edn. vol. XVII[II] p. 179, l. 28).

He who is roused up and gathered into being in the Church has every cause for full certainty of faith : but for security and vaunting no cause, even for a moment.

Why not ? Τὸ φῶς ἐν τῇ σκοτίᾳ φαίνει καὶ ἡ σκοτία αὐτὸ οὐ κατέλαβεν (John 1[5]). So it is with us !

But in spite of this endangerment, interminable as seen from without, man's being in the Church *ubi et quando visum est Deo* is a genuine, concrete event, a visible being in the visible Church. In the same sense there is a human language distinguished genuinely and concretely from other human language as language about God ; certainly not in and for itself, but in virtue of divine confirmation and preservation—divine confirmation and preservation of what genuinely and concretely distinguishes it from other human language. When the essence of the Church, Jesus Christ as the acting Person of God, sanctifies the being of men in the visible area of human happening into being in the Church, then He also sanctifies their language into the language about God which is found in the Church.

Not all the language about God to be found in the public worship of the Church is meant to be proclamation. That it will not be in the first place, where it is addressed as man's language to God. The prayer, singing, and confession of the Church are obviously what they are alleged to be, only when they do their utmost to abstain, on the one hand from the impossible, namely, wishing to proclaim something to God, on the other hand also from the unworthy, namely. wishing by the way to proclaim something to men. It is the answer directed to God of the praise, repentance, and thanks of the man who has experienced a proclamation from Him. It is a sacrifice, the offering of which to God can only signify the attestation of what He has done to man, in which the latter obviously can entertain no designs regarding the other men who may chance to be present with him.

We think of Luther's well-known demand in his sermon at the dedication of the Schlosskirche at Torgau in 1544, " that nothing else should take place therein than that our dear Lord Himself should speak with us through His holy Word, and we again speak with Him through prayer and praise " (W. edn. 49, p. 588, l. 15, cf. p. 592, l. 17 ; p. 594, l. 26). " Thirdly, we have heard God's Word when we also bring for God a common holy smoke or incense, i.e. when with one another we call upon and pray to Him " (p. 599, l. 25).

But there are also other factors in the Church's life in which language about God is directed towards men, but which yet cannot pretend to be proclamation. To these pertains a function which from the beginning has been recognised, in some form or other, as a constitutive element in the life of the Church, the activity of helpful solidarity towards the external needs of human society. This also belongs to man's answer to God. If and because it is the answer of the real man, it must, according to Matt. 5¹⁴, be a shining light among people, in whose society alone after all he is a real man. If God is there for man, as the Church's prayer, praise, and confession declare in answer to the proclamation heard, then this man must also be there for his fellow-men, in association with whom he is alone a real man, as the man for whom God is there. But the special language about God, which is to consist in the action of this man, is primarily and properly language likewise directed to God and not to men. It can neither think of entering into quite superfluous competition with society's necessary efforts of self-help in her straits, nor can it think of proclaiming how God helps, as the demonstration of peculiarly Christian action. " That they may see your good works and glorify your Father in heaven," that it should be a commentary on the proclamation of God's help, is, of course, freely promised it, but it cannot concentrate its designs upon that. It is like prayer, praise, and confession, especially in cases such as Francis of Assisi and Bodelschwingh, always unbounded, unpremeditated, in the final and best sense unpractical language about God. Then and in that way did its light shine.

This was surely overlooked in H. Bär's work, *Weniger Predigt!* 1930, in which he recommends making service to-day in moral and social reform the form of proclamation, " more " than preaching.

Were Church social work as such meant itself to be proclamation, it could only become propaganda, and not very good propaganda at that. Genuine Christian love with its all-too-human action would be shocked at the thought of giving itself out as the proclamation of the love of Christ.

Again, also, Church instruction of youth cannot as such pretend to be proclamation.

Here Gerh. Bohne's book, *Das Wort Gottes und der Unterricht,* 1929, appears to me to lack a certain needful sobriety. Th. Heckel, too, *Zur Methodik des evangelischen Religionsunterrichts,* 1928, surely goes too far when (p. 33) he claims the evangelical teacher as " witness, priest, and herald."

Language about God here, as preparing for the understanding of proclamation, as a sort of technical substructure, means very simply instruction, teaching about what the Church up to date, up to the appearance of this new generation of those called to it, has recognised and confessed as the right faith, making them acquainted with the most important elements in the tradition with which proclamation to-day has to link up. Undoubtedly Church instruction of youth will have to pass over at a definite place, though one not easy to define outwardly, into worship by youth. But that must by no means be to the disadvantage of what it has to effect compared with the latter. As such, instruction of youth has to teach, not to convert, not to " bring to a decision," and to that extent not to proclaim.

Lastly, according to our understanding of the matter, neither can theology as such claim to be proclamation. It too is language about God to men. But proclamation is its presupposition, its raw material and its practical goal, not its content or its task.

Theology reflects upon proclamation. It confronts it as a court of criticism. It is Church instruction of youth on a higher grade, entrusted with the special purpose of testing the coherence of present-day proclamation with the original and prevailing essence of the Church, and of indicating the correct and relevant lines upon which to continue it. Crossings of the boundary into proclamation will be unavoidable here too, and in fact in all disciplines of theology, and here and there will be extremely seasonable, as a reminder of our theme. But, here, too the exceptions prove the rule, that theology as such is not proclamation but science, instruction, and investigation. In a somewhat wider sense also we shall count Church instruction of youth and theology as such among the elements of Church life, in which man answers the proclamation he has heard, in which he tries to take up a position towards it.—All the functions here enumerated have this in common, that they presuppose the proclamation which has taken and ought to take place.

But the language about God to be found in the Church claims itself to be proclamation where it is directed towards men with the definite claim, and in the atmosphere of the definite expectation, that it has to declare the Word of God to them. We at once see that the concept " language about God " comes out here in a quite new light, in fact it acquires a content which threatens to blow it to pieces. All that we have hitherto touched upon as the language about God to be found in the Church, has this in common with this language about God, that whether it is language addressed to God Himself and alone or also to man, it claims unambiguously to be language about God, concerning God, to have God for its object. In the Church's proclamation it is not the concept " language about God " that goes to pieces, but its unambiguity. " To proclaim " of course also means to speak about God. But here in language about God is concealed, as the meaning of this action, proclamation, the intention to speak the word of God Himself.

Παραλαβόντες λόγον ἀκοῆς παρ' ἡμῶν τοῦ Θεοῦ ἐδέξασθε οὐ λόγον ἀνθρώπων, ἀλλὰ καθὼς ἀληθῶς ἐστιν λόγον Θεοῦ (1 Thess. 2¹³). Ὡς ἐκ Θεοῦ κατέναντι Θεοῦ ἐν Χριστῷ λαλοῦμεν (2 Cor. 2¹⁷). Εἴ τις λαλεῖ ὡς λόγια Θεοῦ (1 Pet. 4¹¹). *Praedicatio verbi Dei est verbum Dei* (Conf. Helv. post. 1562 art. 1, 2. According to the German text : " Therefore when still daily the Word of God is proclaimed in the Churches through the preachers who are orderly called, we believe that the Word of God is preached and apprehended by the faithful"). *Idem verbum est, quod et homo praedicat et spiritus sanctus cordi inscribit : Una proprie vocatio, sed*

cuius causa et medium duplex, organicum : homo verbum extus praedicans.
principale : Spiritus sanctus intus illud cordi inscribens (H. Heidegger,
Corp. Theol. 1700 XXI 22, quoted acc. to Heppe, *Die Dogmatik der ev,*
ref. Kirche, 1861 p. 379).

Proclamation is human language in and through which God
Himself speaks, like a king through the mouth of his herald, which
moreover is meant to be heard and apprehended as language in and
through which God Himself speaks, and so heard and apprehended
in faith as the divine decision upon life and death, as the divine
judgment and the divine acquittal, the eternal law and the eternal
gospel both together.

Where human language about God is proclamation, it raises
this claim, it lives in this atmosphere of expectation. With what
right ? Certainly not with the right of logical form or material
content, of religious profundity or personal power, which might
pertain to this human language about God in itself. In and for
all that it is in itself, it can only serve the actual Word of God.
And that divine self-Word does not cease to be itself because it
lets itself be served by human language. But because it permits
this service on its part, It is itself this human language, and
because this human language serves It, It is itself the divine
self-Word.

For the proper explanation of this " is," reference would have to be made
thus early to the Christological " doctrine of the two natures."

Thus if human language claims to be proclamation, that can
only mean that it claims to serve the Word of God, to point to
its having previously been spoken through God Himself. That it
is God's Word, that God sanctifies the human pointer to bear
witness to Himself, this it cannot take to itself. The will on man's
side here brought in question can only be that of accepting a
commission. It goes decisively with what all true prophecy
has discerned, that no man as such can possibly utter the Word
of God. If man's language about God claims to be proclamation,
it claims to be not grace, but the service of grace, the means of
grace. Were the will here questioned the will of man to reach out
beyond himself, to put himself with his word about God in the
place of God, it would be blasphemous rebellion. Therefore it can
have nothing to do with such a claim and expectation. But it has
to do with the fact that the Church has a commission to
serve the Word of God, and that therefore in her there must ever
and anon be found the will to take up this commission. Thus

proclamation is queried, not as to its completeness in form or content—the highest completeness would not make human speech into proclamation nor the most insignificant prevent it from being proclamation—but as to whether it is a service, whether it has a commission.

We might also say, as to whether it is διακονία τοῦ λόγου (Acts 6⁴), *ministerium verbi divini. Potes facere, quicquid infra te est : Quicquid autem* toucheth *dei cultum, nihil fac, nihil loquere, nisi certus sis habere dei verbum et opus . . . quando autem verbum dei* runneth, *tum opera omnia bona sunt* (Luther, *Pred a. 2 Advent*, 1523 W. edn. II p. 209, l. 22). " Beloved, be stedfast until God bid thee, unto sureness and goodness of heart. Yea wert thou wiser and cleverer than Solomon and Daniel, thou shouldest fly as from hell from speaking one single word, except thou shouldest be bidden and called thereto. If God need thee, He will surely call thee. If He call thee not, beloved, let not thy skill tear open thy belly, Thou thinkest very foolishly of the use and piety . . . thou wouldest do, Believe me, none will do good with preaching, except he who is bidden and forced to preach and teach without his will and desire, For we have but one master, our Lord Jesus Christ, who alone teacheth and bringeth forth fruit through His servants, whom He hath called thereto. But whoso teacheth uncalled, teacheth not without harm, both to himself and to the hearers, for that Christ is not with him " (*Festpostille*, 1527 W. edn. 17ᴵᴵ, p. 258, l. 38).

The will which says not Nay but Yea, not so much to the venture of speaking authoritatively about God, as to this commission that is to be taken up, this will is the will to proclamation in the Church. Its inner problem, insoluble because only answered in the divine predestination and in faith, is to decide whether in this respect it is an obedient will.

But what is the function of proclamation in the Church among and along with her other functions ? We saw that not all language about God to be found in the Church is meant to be proclamation. Obviously, therefore, it is not decided whether it might not still be and now and again is so, is so perhaps in a much higher measure than that very language about God which actually makes the claim. Real proclamation of the Word of God cannot be limited by our intention to speak the Word of God. Why should not prayer and active love, instruction and theology, actually now and then be proclamation, and perhaps in a much more real sense ? Given the validity of *ubi et quando visum est Deo*, as it ought to be valid for us, then obviously we at once have a case where on principle No cannot possibly be the reply. And it is indeed not a trivial truth but a trivial question, whether the sacrificial part of our public worship is not actually infinitely more proclamation than the other part which in claim and expectation is dedicated to proclamation, and whether the existence of a Bodelschwingh has not been more of a proclamation than the deliberate proclamation of a thousand preaching parsons. The same question would certainly also have to be asked regarding Church instruction and theology. We shall have to bear in mind as we continue to advance, that for God nothing can exist to prevent Him turning even such language about God into a proclamation of His word to us, which, in its character as hallowed language to be found in the Church, is for us at first partially or completely hidden. That the Church is always visible need not yet mean that we actually see it yet in its real extent, that the dimensions of its area might not very often be quite different from what we think we know them to be. God may very suddenly be pleased to have Abraham blessed by Melchisedek, or Israel by Balaam, or to have him helped by Cyrus. And still more, it could scarcely be denied either that God can speak His Word to man in quite a different way than by the language about Himself to be found in the known Church or the Church freshly to be discovered, and therefore in quite a different way from actual " proclamation." He can found the Church directly and afresh, when and where and as it pleases Him.

Modus vocationis opposite consideratus in externum et internum distinguitur. Ille foris per verbi et sacramentorum administrationem, hic intus per operationem Spiritus sancti peragitur. Non semper Deus utrumque vocationis modum ad hominum conversionem sibi possibilem adhibet, sed quosdam interno tantum Spiritus sancti lumine ac numine absque externo verbi sui ministerio ad se vocat. Qui vocationis modus per se quidem est ad salutem sufficiens, sed rarus admodum, extraordinarius, nobisque incognitus (Syn. pur. Theol. Leiden, 1624 *Disp.* 30, 32–33). This doctrine is not to be confused either with the doctrine of the *ideae Dei potentia nobis semper inexistentes*, represented by A. Heidan (*Corp. Th. chr.* 1686 *Loc.* I p. 8 f.) under the influence of Descartes, or with, e.g., the Quaker doctrine of the *lumen internum*, attacked by Hollaz (*Ex. Th. acr.* 1707 I 1, 9). It too has faith in its mind, but insists that God ought not to be thought of as tied down to the way of the *vocatio ordinaria*, the way of proclamation, as the foundation of faith.

Hence it can never be the case with God's Word that it should be confined to the proclamation of the Church as it already exists from time to time, or to the proclamation of the Church known to us as such, or to the language about God to be found in this Church known to us, which specially claims to be proclamation. Church proclamation itself, in fact, regards itself merely as the service of the Word of God, the means of grace in the hands of an unrestricted God. Hence it cannot be master of the Word, it cannot dream of regarding the Word as confined within its own bounds. But after

we have not only calmly recognised as such all the divine possibilities
to be considered here in a sensible way, but have also as openly as
possible expected them as realities which might at any time eventu-
ate, we have still to remember that the question, What can God
do ?, is different from the question, What is the commission
laid on us through the promise given to the Church ?

*Non pas que Dieu soit attaché à telles aides ou moyens inferieurs, mais pource
qu'il luy plaist nous entretenir soubz telle charge et bride* (*Conf. Gallic.* 1559
art. 25).   The peculiarity of Paul Tillich's teaching seems to me to lie in
the constant confusion of these two questions, which makes it ultimately
uninteresting as a contribution to theological work.   If the first presupposition
of thought is that we imagine that we can as well (or better) think and speak
about the Church from without as from within, without recognising the
obligation of her commission as when bound by it, then to be sure the door is
open for that "radicalism" which "on the basis of the unconditioned"
knows how to deal with the Church and civilisation, the spheres of sacred and
profane, sacrament and nature, Protestantism and the proletariate, possession
and exorcism, and likewise with the symbol of the Word and every other kind
of symbol, in a manner as imperial as it is free of obligations either way,
generally maintaining its point to the end, exactly as we deal with things beneath and not above us.   But if " on the basis of the unconditioned " makes
the same assertion as " on the basis of God," it simply cannot mean on the
basis of the infinite potentiality of God, but only on the basis of the concrete
behest of God, which without coming too close to the all-power of God—
how could it in any case ?—neither demands of us the superior position of
God nor allows us to choose our own possibility, but decides as to our reality,
as a commandment that finds or does not find concrete obedience.   It is
with this commandment of God that the Church is concerned.   And it is upon
the Church's connection with it and with it alone that theology reflects.   A
philosophy of the history of mind may reflect, with all the goodwill in the
world, upon something different and then likewise upon an " unconditioned "
or " thitherward of being " discerned elsewhere than in this commandment.
Only it should not imagine that it has touched the task of theology with even
one finger.   In this sense we must apply to Tillich the sequel to the passage
from the *Conf. Gallic.: En quoi nous détestons tous fantastiques qui voudroyent
bien, entant qu'en eux est, anéantir le ministère et prédication de la parole de
Dieu et de ses Sacraments.*

If the question, what God can do, forces theology to be
humble and candid, the question, what is commanded us, forces
it to concrete obedience.   God may speak to us through Russian
communism or a flute concerto, a blossoming shrub or a dead dog.
We shall do well to listen to Him if He really does so.   But we
shall not be able to say—that would mean that we considered ourselves the prophets and founders of a new Church—that we are
commissioned to spread what we so hear as an independent proclamation.   God may speak to us through a pagan or an atheist, and

in that way give us to understand that the boundary between Church and the profane still and repeatedly takes a course quite different from that which we hitherto thought we saw. But that is not equivalent to saying—once more that could only be said to a prophet—that we should have ourselves to proclaim the pagan and atheist thing we heard. And so, finally, we may very well and rightly suppose that we have heard God's Word in the prayer and loving action, in the youth instruction and in the theology of the Church we know, without our having on our side received a commission to push it all as actual proclamation. However it may stand with those undoubted possibilities of God's outside the Church or in a new Church, with the greater area of the visible Church, perhaps unknown to us, and, within the Church we see, with the unintended but actual proclamation through the other factors in the life of the Church—this is certain, that along with the commission she would fain obey by listening and answering in these other functions as well, this Church we know has a s p e c i a l commission to proclaim, and so not merely to listen and answer but distinctly to s p e a k about, God to and for men, a commission which she would be neglecting were she to seek to proclaim, where and what she had n o commission at all to proclaim to us.

But what is this special commissioned proclamation of the Church, which has to be taken over as a commission to and for men ? We reply first of all with a simple statement :

1. P r e a c h i n g is such proclamation ; i.e. the attempt, essayed by one called thereto in the Church, to express in his own words in the form of an exposition of a portion of the Biblical testimony to revelation, and to make comprehensible to men of his day, the promise of God's revelation, reconciliation and calling, as they are to be expected here and now.

It may be instructive to append the definition given by Karl Fezer (*Das Wort Gottes und die Predigt*, 1925 p. 77 ; cf. the review by Eduard Thurneysen, *Theol. Bl.* 1925 p. 197 f.) : " Preaching is man's attempt by free speech to co-operate in securing that God who grants us His fellowship in the Word of Scripture should be present jointly to a group of other men through the Holy Spirit." (I hear that the formula has meantime received a different shape in Fezer's oral instruction. My purpose in quoting it is not polemical, but with a view to indicating the problems to be assessed here.)

2. A s a c r a m e n t is such proclamation ; i.e. the symbolic act consummated in the community of the Church according to the directions of the Biblical witness to revelation, which accompanies and confirms preaching, an act, the aim of which as such is to attest

the event of God's revelation, reconciliation and calling, which not only fulfils, but already proves the promise.

Cf. the unusually clear and exhaustive definition of the concept "sacrament" in the Heidelberg Catechism, 1563 *qu.* 66: "What are the Sacraments? —They are visible, sacred signs and seals appointed by God, so that through the use of the same He may the better give us to understand the promise of the Gospel ; and seal the fact that for the sake of the one sacrifice of Christ consummated on the Cross He graciously grants us forgiveness of sins and everlasting life."

Such is the aim of the language about God to be found in the Church, if it claims to be proclamation, if it is directed towards men with the claim and in the atmosphere of expectation that it has to tell them the Word of God.   Proclamation in the form of preaching and sacrament may and should be this, because the Church has a commission to make this proclamation.

In attempting to explain the statement thus made, we shall above all have to make the following point clear, that since we do not ourselves issue the commission, but regard ourselves strictly as those commissioned, the givenness as well as the meaning of a commission can be proved in two and only two ways : either by repeating the order received in the form in which we think we have received and heard it.   Or by creating a fact through simply attempting to obey it.   In both cases the answer given to the request for proof is an indirect one, in both cases it is therefore extremely " unsatisfactory " to the questioner.   In both cases the answer consists in a further inquiry ; it is left to the questioner whether, in our handing on what we have heard as an order, or in our attempt to obey this order, he personally cognises or recognises the will of the Giver of the commission and the meaning of this will of His, and therefore the existence of a real commission with a meaning.   Consequently, if we are asked why the language about God to be found in the Church aims in particular at being pro-clamation in the form of preaching and sacrament, i.e. how far she supposes that in this particular action she has her special com-mission to proclaim, we can only give the twofold and each time simple answer : first, that we learn from the Biblical witness to revelation that, over and above the command to believe, love, and hope, and distinct from the command to call in common upon His name, to help the brethren, etc., Jesus Christ has given His Church the commission to proclaim, and to proclaim through preaching and sacrament.   Does He wish His people only to take up their cross and follow Him ?   Does He only intend these other functions of the Church to witness to this following ?   Or does He not rather mean both, since He also and precisely and above all means this, that the very Word of God should be proclaimed in His Church and through His Church ?   And if that is so, is " make disciples of all nations, baptizing them—teaching them ! " (Matt. 28¹⁹ᶠ·), a genuine summary of what is told us by the Biblical documents in regard to this will of His, and has it therefore to stand as His behest to us ?   And secondly ; of course we cannot prove the existence and content of this order by a reference to the convincing excellence of our obedience to it, as if the former would speak for itself in the latter.   For once more the question whether our act is obedience to this order is not decided by the person commissioned, but by the Giver of the commission.   Our language about God may mean to be proclamation in terms of our commission, and therefore preaching and sacrament according to the will and command of the Lord of the Church.   But it is not with our obedience or with the uprightness of our intention to obey that we shall comfort ourselves, but only with the actual behest which we have heard, which in fact must speak for itself if it is to be recognisable by others as such.   And so here also, timidly and reluctantly enough, we shall only be able to ask whether in spite of all concurrent disobedience the Lord's command cannot still join in and speak for itself in what the Church does.

Hence it is only subsequently, *a posteriori*, exegetically, not in the sense of proving the commission existent in the Church, that the following considerations on the subject are in place.   Would the mere thought of God's Word becoming revealed outside the Church so far existing or so far known to us, be possible for one who had not previously been acquainted with real proclamation within the Church ?   Could we appeal to parallel real experiences, say to our having heard the Word of God through the voice of Communism or of some other reality that, as they say, " gets us existentially where we live," if we had not brought a criterion to such hearing and applied it well or ill, on the basis of previous experience of the reality of the Word of God, as it somehow meets us as proclamation in terms of a commission ?   But above all—and this is the real point for us in our present context—would not the Church's life itself precisely lack its distinctive medium, the point of contact with all its other functions, without this function, the function of proclamation ?   We saw indeed that all those other elements are in some sense the answer to the Word of God heard. Assuredly preaching and sacrament may be classed in the category, that they are also the answer to what man has heard ; as assuredly those other elements may also be proclamation and indubitably now and then are so. But as indubitably these answering elements, as we saw, cannot as such claim to be proclamation ; as indubitably they must be faced with an element, which of course is also interpretable as an answer, but which is not only capable of being, and now and then succeeds in being, but is meant to be so, as distinct from the former proclamation—meant to be, because it ought to be meant to be—an element in which the proclamation there presupposed has its proper and peculiar place and position. Assuredly the medium, the point of contact upon which is directed the whole life of the Church including the elements of proclamation, can only be the Word of God Himself, and proclamation will as little claim to push into its place, as would any other of the functions of the Church. But the question is whether the Word of God does not claim to be represented within the realm of man's will to obey, does not demand a definite function in the Church, whether therefore the proclaiming of the Church is not made into a task at least as much as the answering to God's Word, as that might take place in adoration and Church nurture, in instruction and theology. Whether the answer is yes, is not a matter to be inferred ; it is decided by the commission, which must be the source of all real proclamation.

Let us suppose that the commission has been issued and received ; the next thing to be made clear will be that proclamation sensibly enough and actually consists of preaching and sacrament.— This thing which in the form of proclamation should meet the listening and answering in the Church as the representation of God's Word, demands in some sense a setting apart, a special imperative calling of the man who is to function here. Further, what such a man may claim to utter as God's Word in the exercise of proclamation, cannot be the actual Word of God as such, but only the repetition of His promise, repetition of the promise, " Lo, I am with you alway ! " (Matt. 28[20]). Proclamation must mean announcement—announcement, met by the real " I am with you," as the future fulfilment. Further, if this announcement is to be the legitimate repetition not of any promise, but of the one given by God Himself to the Church, then it cannot be arbitrary religious language, it must be language controlled and guided in the form

of a homily, that is, the exposition of Scripture. But if it is
to be a real repetition of this promise, it cannot consist in mere
reading of Scripture, i.e. in repetition and transcription of the
vocabulary of Biblical witness, rather it can only have this as its
presupposition. The concrete meeting of God and man to-day,
the reality of which can, of course, only be created through the
Word of God Himself, must thus have its counterpart in the human
event of proclamation, i.e. the person called must be ready to make
the promise given to the Church comprehensible in his own
words to the men of his time. Calling, promise, exposition of
Scripture, reality—these are the important determinations of the
concept of preaching. If proclamation is preaching in accordance with a commission—the fact that this is so should not be proved,
because it cannot be proved—these concepts are the supplementary explanation of the meaning of preaching.—Proclamation
interpreted solely as preaching would clearly suffer from a sensible
weakness. Preaching is human language in the form of words
thought and expressed by men. The promise as merely preached
is thus in the preacher's mouth as in the hearer's ear a human
work, at best it is an " existential " decision first of all taken by
the preacher and then likewise to be taken by the hearer. Were
it no more than that, how could it be a pointer to the very Word
of God ? Does man's word spoken and apprehended, the more
earnestly it is spoken and apprehended, not as such necessarily
signify a total eclipse of the Word of God which it claims to serve ?
The promise given to the Church and attested in Holy Scripture is
itself obviously no such work of man, in distinction from the
promise preached. It is the Word, as the divine event that happened, as the completed divine act of judging and reconciling grace,
in which a decision is made about man prior to all his decisions,
from which his decisions can alone receive the qualification of
decisions of faith, from which therefore anything that the preacher
and his hearer do in human wise can alone become a pointer to the
very Word of God. If this event is not part of proclamation, how
far is the promise given to the Church really proclaimed, how far
instead of a *ministerium verbi divini* is the Church's proclamation
not rather an insuperable obstacle placed in the path of God's
very Word ? But how is this event to be part of proclamation ?
How is it to come about that proclamation proclaims not only
truth but truth as reality, that is as God's work, and thereby
and not till then unambiguously proclaims grace as grace ? How

5

is that to come about, so far as proclamation ought to be unambiguously identical with preaching ?   We are here faced with the
fundamental difficulty in the task of preaching, beside which we
may with a quiet conscience designate all others child's play.
From this point of view it is quite understandable, if in practice
little importance any way attaches in the Church to the claim and
expectation that preaching has to utter God's Word—it is quite
understandable, if on the one hand Roman Catholic preaching
seems largely to rest satisfied with the level of higher instruction
in religion and morals, and if on the other hand typically neo-
Protestant preaching does not claim to be more than as genuine
and lively an expression as possible of the personal piety of the
speaker in question.   We have still to speak of both evasions.
In view of their root difficulty as the answer to the question how
God's Word can be proclaimed as God's Work, we should straightway have recourse to the no doubt very true and very valid reference
to God Himself, to the Holy Spirit, who will establish as His own
work, in the preacher's mouth and in the hearer's ear, the work
of the faith proclaimed in words of human thought and expression,
and turn the promise preached into the event of the real promise
given to the Church.   This reference to the personal power of God's
very Word amid and in spite of the darkness of the human word
that serves it, is of course the Alpha and the Omega, the *ultima ratio*,
without which not merely the concept of preaching but also the
concept of the Church's proclamation could not be completed at all.
The only question is whether this reference is not represented
in the concept of the proclamation actually enjoined upon the
Church by a second element not identical with preaching as such,
in which proclamation would be precisely what it obviously cannot
be as preaching alone, proclamation of reality, of the promise as
God's work, of the grace of the faith preached and apprehended,
of the decision taken before and beyond all our decisions, which
human speech and hearing designate worship in spirit and in truth.
Of course even this second element in proclamation might only be
man's language about God.   It might claim to be no more than
preaching, in so far as even it could merely announce, i.e. announce
the coming revelation, reconciliation, and calling, and so only be
the repetition of the promise, the means of grace.   Nor could
it claim to be independent proclamation alongside of preaching, it
could only claim to be the confirmation of it, as the seal beneath a
letter confirms its authenitcity but adds nothing to its contents.

makes no other assertion anywhere save under the letter, where it stands for itself. It would have to be co-ordinated with preaching, in the sense that, like preaching itself, it sets forth the promise as such, sets forth on its own part the character of the promise as an event, i.e. as grace, in contrast to all man's personal work on the level of human occurrence. In order to represent this basis of the promise it should not consist in further words ; it would have to be action. But to be proclamation it should as little as preaching be arbitrarily chosen action, but it would have to be action demanded and defined by the Biblical witness. Further it could, as little as preaching, wish itself to supersede the Word of God, and therefore, just as preaching is strictly representative language, it could only be strictly representative action, pretty much as preaching could only be service in the Word of God ; that which in either case is more than a setting forth, a service, or a symbol, is the event whose subject is not the Church but God Himself. And the object which it has to set forth would have to be that very presupposition of preaching, which preaching as such, as language human in thought and in expression, cannot for a moment set forth, for which man's word as such cannot be a symbol, namely, revelation, reconciliation, and calling, which the Church can only believe, hope, and proclaim she has before her, when she has it behind her as the act of divine grace, which she only really expects, when she owes her own origin to it (because it happened once for all in the appearing of Jesus Christ). Promise in the form of an adjunct to preaching, action as distinct from mere speech, conformity to Scripture, representative symbolical connection with the " once-for-all " of revelation—these are the decisive determinations of the concept of sacrament. Moreover, we have not postulated even this concept ; we have expounded it on the presupposition that its content is reality in the life of the Church because of the divine commission, and that to that extent it is before us as a text susceptible of exposition. We can as little speak of a free proof of the necessity of sacrament as of the one necessity for preaching and proclamation in general. Thus in looking back upon what has been said and in reply to the question as to its final proof, we should not omit to point away from the exposition, back to the actual text before us.

But this exposition of the concepts proclamation, preaching, and sacrament requires at the close an express declaration, that evangelical dogmatics expounds these concepts exactly as has been done.

We may here ignore the fact that there is a specifically evangelical-Reformed dogmatics which in this connection has been the spokesman in certain individual details.

This exposition holds good primarily, in view of the superconcept of proclamation, as opposed to modernist dogmatics. Even it is aware of the function here indicated ; but it is not aware of the essential distinctiveness, compared with all other functions of the Church, which belongs to the former when it rests upon a commission to and for men, when as man's language about God it has to serve an actual divine word, spoken from a point irremovably the contrary of all humanity. Modernist thought knows nothing finally about the fact that man in relation to God has constantly to be letting something be said to him, constantly to be listening to something, of which he is constantly not yet aware and which in no circumstances and in no sense he can say to himself. Modernist thought hears man answer without any one having called him. It hears him talk to himself. To it therefore proclamation is a necessary expression of life for the human community called " the Church," an expression in which one man, in the name and for the advancement of a number of other men, drawing from a treasure common to him and to them, gives forth, for the enrichment of this treasure, an interpretation of his own history and present state, as evidence of the reality alive in this group of men.

A doctrinal passage " On service in the divine Word " is not lacking even in Schleiermacher's *Glaubenslehre* (§ 133 f.). But we are at once told that the " divine Word " is nothing else than " the spirit in all men," i.e. of all who are united in the Church (§ 134, 3). Therefore service in this Word is the " act of the community as such " (§ 135, 2) ; in concrete terms, the " relation of the self-active to the receptive " (§ 133, 1) ; or the " influence of the stronger upon the weaker " (§ 133, 2) by means of self-impartation, i.e. " of a self-display with a stimulating effect, in which the emotion of the displayer, taken up by imitation, becomes in the receptively stimulated person taking it up a power which calls forth the same emotion " (§ 133, 1). It embraces the " whole Christian life " and for the sake of good order and the preservation of the common consciousness only requires special " management " (§ 134, 3 ; 135).—We find ourselves nowhere else save at the other, the realistic end of the path idealistically entered upon by Schleiermacher, when a century later, according to P. Tillich, a " fresh sacramental situation " would have to be " created " to save Protestantism (*Relig. Verwirkl.* 1930 p. 166), by " our success in reaching the depths of our own undivided pre-objective being " (*op. cit.* p. 154), and by gaining on that basis an understanding of the fact that there is a mastery over natural things and situations and so among other things over the Word as well, to be experienced in the " historical fate " of reciprocally affecting and being affected, in virtue of which it might become for faith the vehicle of " sacramental mastery " (p. 176). If by " sacramental situation " is here meant the same thing which we call proclamation, and if the way to this "sacramental situation," namely, the historical fate by which it is created, is really the relation between a deepened understanding of self and a deepened understanding of the world and *vice versa*, then we should be forced to conjecture that here too man is thought of as in the long-run conversing purely with himself. And in fact " religious symbols are created in process of religious history " (p. 106). " One has a right to say that, e.g., Christ or Buddha are symbols, so far as the unconditionally transcendent can be viewed in them " (p. 104). " God as Object is a representation of what is ultimately intended in the religious act " (p. 103). "The unconditionally transcendent goes beyond any positing of an essence, even a very high one. So far as such is posited, it is also abrogated again in the religious act. This abrogation, this atheism immanent in the religious act, is the depth of the religious act " (p. 102). " The truth of a symbol rests upon its inner necessity for the symbol-creating consciousness " (p. 103). " At the point at which— apart from all material connections—the soul-part expresses itself, it expresses itself religiously " (p. 94).

For this conception the concepts of language, word, proclamation, preaching, which in themselves might still all point to the contraposition of God and man, must obviously disappear in the general concept of operation or emotion, i.e. into the idea of a general dynamic or even meaningness, inclusive of God and man, which is somehow the vehicle of our existence, collectively and severally, and should somehow—this being where proclamation would be required—be made articulate by us. But in that case Logos, in its isolation as the Word spoken this way and that, of necessity becomes one symbol amid a host of others. " I cannot possibly rate the word so highly," i.e. as the expression of the dynamic or meaningness. The question now in all seriousness becomes : Why do I choose precisely these symbols, precisely language about God, precisely this form of language (actual exposition of the Bible), and precisely these two or seven sacraments ? Are precisely these the truest symbols, if my soul-part ought or wishes to express itself ? Might there not be truer ones than, these ?

The fact that we speak of the Word of God—" in the choice (!) of this symbol lies the spiritual character of the self-impartation of Being Beyond. . . . But it is quite wrong to equate the Word as a symbol of the self-imparta-tion of Being Beyond, with the Word as the physical medium of the self-comprehension and self-impartation of the human spirit, and in this way to mix up God's Word with the word of Scripture or the word of preaching " (P. Tillich, *Rel. Verwirkl.* 1930 p. 48 f. ; cf. p. 60). " Word is not only present where it is spoken and conceived, but Word is also present where it is made visible and acted in powerfully operative symbols. *Verbum* is more than *oratio*. That is what Protestantism has largely forgotten. *Verbum*, the Word of revelation, may (!) be in everything in which spirit expresses itself, even in the silent symbols of art, even in the works of society and law. And therefore a Church must be able to speak in all these forms. They must all become symbols of the Word of revelation. And that means that nothing less than the whole life of society on every side is appointed to be symbolically powerful for God " (*Kirche und Kultur*, 1924 p. 19 f.). Which of the various expressions available for choice has most " symbolic power " to-day ? That is now the solemn question of the *Berneuchener* ; and a " fountain " to be set up in the Church " with running water as an allegory of God's creative life-stream " (*Berneuchener Buch*. 1926 p. 112), coloured window-panes as symbols of the " light from the uncreated Light," and all sorts of cheerful things of a similar kind now have a chance of entering into a not wholly purposeless rivalry with a preaching become less seasonable, ever since, long ago now, the organ was admittedly raised (by Julius Smend) to the dignity of a " second pulpit," which must proclaim " to us in other tongues, above all, in holy accents, the immensity, the inexpressibility in religion and supremely in the Gospel " (quoted according to Herbert Birtner, *Die Probleme der Orgelbewegung* : *Theol. Rundschau*, 1932 p. 66). For the groan becomes general and impossible longer to ignore : " Preaching, pedestalled (!) on the person of the preacher, now stands too much in the foreground " (O. Dibelius, *Das Jahrhundert d. Kirche*, 5th edn. 1928 p. 252). Therefore, " Less preaching ! More action and more different forms of proclamation ! " " The rivalry of other spiritual presentations " has to-day become far too great. " More and more parsons to-day have insufficient time to work up their sermons." " We speak of inspiration in the poet as in the religious orator. But few mortals can be inspired to order." Perhaps even Jesus would have been " increasingly dissatisfied with speaking had He been tied down to public work and public speaking for decades instead of for one year " (!!). (H. Bär, *Weniger Predigt*! 1930 pp. 8 f., 12 f.). And so on !

And beyond all that the final question is surely bound to arise : Why proclamation at all ? Why symbols at all ? Why not rather be silent ? Why not, as the truest word we can utter, give up all special language about God, all dealing with symbols whatsoever ?

" Undoubtedly the highest aim of a theological work would be to discover the point at which reality itself speaks unsymbolically alike of itself and of the unconditioned, to discover the point at which reality itself without a symbol becomes a symbol, at which the opposition between reality and symbol is removed." Would it not be the most powerful expression of what is in us, if we were to omit all expression in favour of " immediate language about things, so far as they impinge on us unconditionally, so far as they stand in the transcendent " (P. Tillich, *Rel. Verwirkl.* p. 108) ?

What has to be said in criticism of this doctrine is said clearly enough by itself. To regard the concept of proclamation along these lines is simply to end in dissolving it. In the long-run proclamation as self-exposition must turn out to be a superfluous and impossible undertaking, and has obviously and extensively so turned out. The distinction between such proclamation and the other functions of the Church cannot be proved to be essential. But do not these other functions, too, thereby become unessential as answers (answers to what ?) ? What is the Church, what should she be, if she is to lack the very medium by which man can really be addressed ? If the truth of her essence is to be that man is alone in his world and with his world ? Is it not plain that there is here a fateful confusion between man at this moment, man of the *regnum gratiae*, and man in his original state or in eternal glory, who, as we saw at the outset, neither does nor will need a special language about God or, therefore, a chance of being addressed about God or, therefore, a Church ? If we are not this man, whence does the modernist doctrine get its legal ground ?

All that evangelical faith cannot here understand in the faith foreign to it on the Left may be compressed into the question in Rom. 10¹⁴. Πῶς οὖν ἐπικαλέσονται εἰς ὃν οὐκ ἐπίστευσαν; πῶς δὲ πιστεύσωσιν οὗ οὐκ ἤκουσαν; πῶς δὲ ἀκούσωσιν χωρὶς κηρύσσοντος; πῶς δὲ κηρύξωσιν ἐὰν μὴ ἀποσταλῶσιν . . . . ἄρα ἡ πίστις ἐξ ἀκοῆς, ἡ δὲ ἀκοὴ διὰ ῥήματος Χριστοῦ.

The other no less serious difference here to be touched upon separates us from Roman Catholic dogmatics. It concerns in the first place, but only in the first place, not the superconcept of proclamation, but the mutual relations of the concepts of preaching and sacrament. Its dogmatics cannot emphasise too strongly the fact that the Church lives from and by the latter means of grace.

The sacraments are the *canales gratiae*, the *vasa medicinae* against sin and death, the *fundamenta et cardines vitae christianae*, the stream that according to Gen. 2¹⁰ flows out of Eden, the seven pillars upon which according to Prov. 9¹ wisdom has built her house, the bond of peace of Eph. 4¹⁶ (H. Hurter, S.J., *Theol. dogm. compend*, 12th edn. 1908 vol. III p. 214). " The activity of the Church at their consummation is the most real revelation and outward confirmation of her mysterious life ; they are the essential content of the Church's worship and therefore the most exquisite means of preserving the visible Church in unity and making it recognisable and distinguishable as the true Church. Reception of them is the most essential sign of the Church's fellowship, their administration the most excellent and sublime activity of her priests." . . . They are " the most concentrated expression and the inmost kernel of the Church's faith and life " (Scheeben-Atzberger, *Handb. d. Kath. Dogm.* vol. IV 1903 p. 463). Cf. also Bartmann, *Lehrb. d. Dogm.* 7th edn. vol. II 1929 p. 207.

But it might seriously be asked whether the superlatives we have to listen to here do not always say too little, when we realise that in these dogmatics preaching, compared with a sacrament taken and celebrated so seriously, receives not only a slighter, but we might almost say no significance. Indeed the fact is not merely that Catholicism over-emphasises the sacrament as Protestantism does oral preaching.

This schematism becomes pure nonsense, when in the pointedness of Klaus Harms (in his 95 Theses of 1817) it elicits the declaration, that the Roman Church keeps to and cultivates " preferably " the sacrament, the Reformed " preferably " the Word, but the Lutheran " more splendidly than either " the sacrament as well as the Word (briefly reproduced again by Max Glage, *Unsere Taufe*, 1931 p. 4). For, in the first place, Lutheran Protestantism as compared with Reformed, even though it only remains to a certain extent in Luther's footsteps, cannot, on the score of its greater emphasis on and preferential treatment of preaching over against sacrament, possibly wish to be detached from the rest and placed in such a superior milieu ; secondly, the importance assigned to sacrament along with and in the greater emphasis on and preferential treatment of preaching in the actual practice of the Reformed Church, the care with which the problem of sacrament was and is actually treated in Reformed dogmatics, cannot possibly be made parallel to what happens to preaching in Catholic dogmatics. The very same will have to be said of modernist Protestant dogmatics. Neither Schleiermacher's nor Troeltsch's valuation of the sacraments—judge them in point of content as we may—can for one moment be compared with what, so far as I can see, happens on principle and as a rule with respect to preaching in Catholic dogmatics.

What preaching encounters here is simply *silentium altissimum*. Roman Catholic dogmatists pass from the treatise on grace or even from that on the Church to that on the sacraments, they develop the doctrine of the sacrament of the priestly *ordo*, they even speak throughout of the teaching office of the Church as if there were no such thing at all as preaching, regarded as an indispensable means of grace to be taken seriously. What interests them in preaching, and naturally can only interest them in passing, are juristic questions like those as to the primary and secondary bearers of legitimate Church doctrine, the necessity of a special *missio canonica* for preaching, and so on.

So, too, in the articles on the " teaching office " in Josef Braun, *Handlexikon d. kath. Dogm.* 1926 p. 185 f., which remains absolutely dumb upon preaching, proclamation, etc. Cf. *C. jur. can. c.* 1327–28.

It ought to be said that in writings of a more practical tendency Catholic theology can discover incidentally lofty and apparently also dogmatically relevant notes to sound on preaching.

Through " Word and sacrament " the priest builds up the mystical body of the Lord, the Church. " Through this Word of preaching and in it Christ mystically extends His life, builds up, expands, lights up, comforts, pardons His Church continually, pursues His work of redemption through every century, feeds our souls on the bread of truth, just as He incorporates all mankind in Himself through the Eucharistic bread. And preaching has no other task then to translate this Word of God into human speech, to expound and to apply it." It works by itself becoming God's Word (Fran z Hettinger, *Timotheus: Briefe an einem jungen Theologen*, 3rd edn. 1909 pp. 45, 48). We should surely know whether such sentences are to be judged merely as the *pia opinio* (or perhaps even as the *propositio temeraria* ?) of an individual—or why in the other event they have no parallels in the manuals of Catholic dogmatics. There is a Homiletics by the same author, entitled *Aphorismen über Predigt und Prediger*, 1888, in which likewise we look in vain for a dogmatic proof of the necessity of preaching.

Such occasional affirmation does not in the least alter the fact that Catholic dogmatics itself and also the standard dogmatic utterances of the Church's teaching office, neither of which is wont to be niggard in expression where a thing is of importance to them, shroud themselves in almost complete darkness on this point.

The strongest expression in favour of preaching, to be found in Denzinger's collection (No. 426), is a concessive sentence in the *Professio fidei Waldensibus praescripta* of 1208, in which it is still actually designated as *valde necessaria et laudabilis*. A relatively noteworthy estimation of preaching is found in the *Praefatio* to the *Catech. Roman.* 1566. But it seems to coincide very closely with the contemporary need of actively warding off Protestantism (*qu.* 5–7 !), and the dogmatic content even in this text is not considerable, at least in regard to the connection between preaching, faith, and grace.

As little can the circumstance that the weekly Sunday sermon is prescribed for the Catholic parish priest, and the fact that the Catholic Church in ancient and modern times has produced more than one outstanding preacher, at all alter the fact that this function even in its exercise is forced into a curious aloofness ; shown externally by the fact that the service of Mass may be complete without it.

The liturgical place of preaching is the so-called pre-Mass (the ancient *missa catechumenorum*), of which to-day the (Latin) reading of the " Gospel " constitutes the organic centre. Pius Bihlmeyer, O.S.B., makes the following notes at the passage in question (*Das vollständige römische Messbuch*, 3rd edn. 1930 p. 533) : " Now Christ speaks to us through His Word or through His miracles and redemptive acts. The same loving, wonder-working Saviour will appear Himself at the holy sacrifice, to complete mysteriously in us (!) what according to the Gospel narrative He has wrought in others (!). In this faith and hope we listen to the Gospel . . . with the Gospel is often (!) included according to ancient usage (!) a sermon in which the holy words of God are more closely explained and expounded as the guide for our life." Note that the approach to this action is constituted by : 1. the *Introitus* with *Kyrie* ; 2. the Christological *Gloria* ; 3. an *Oratio* for the day in question ;

4. the reading of the Epistle ; 5. the *Graduale*, with or without the Tractus and Sequence ; 6. the beautiful prayers : *Munda cor meum ac labia mea, omnipotens Deus, qui labia Isaiae prophetae calculo mundasti ignito ; ita me tua grata miseratione dignare mundare, ut sanctum Evangelium tuum digne valeam nuntiare. Per Christum Dominum nostrum. Amen.—Jube, Domine, benedicere. Dominus sit in corde meo et in labiis meis : ut digne et competenter annuntiem Evangelium suum. Amen.* And upon that reading, with or without sermon, there follows (obviously saying more than Bihlmeyer) : *Per evangelica dicta deleantur nostra delicta ;* and in conclusion the Nicaeno-Constantinopolitan *Credo.* One cannot avoid the impression that this mighty structure stands in no relation to the poverty of its centre to-day (e.g. is it worth while for the sake of a mere Lesson to appeal to Is. 6 ?). Is not the very thing to which everything seems to point here lacking, the sermon as the distinctive and necessary *annuntiatio* (beyond the mere Lesson) ? But actually even the modern form of the Benedictine liturgy does not appear to counteract at all this liturgical anomaly, this non-necessity for the sermon.

Inwardly this aloofness of preaching is shown in the fact that it seems scarcely to want to rise in principle above the level of apologetic instruction and moral exhortation, and as a whole not to claim the character of genuine proclamation, which is somehow equal in seriousness to the solemnisation of sacrament.

Cf. the quotations from Bihlmeyer. *C. jur. can. c.* 1347 I reads as follows regarding the content of preaching : *In sacris concionibus exponenda imprimis sunt, quae fideles credere et facere ad salutem oportet.*

In sharp distinction from sacrament, preaching is not a constitutive element in the concept of the Catholic priesthood.

Except in case of special dispensation, every priest must celebrate his Mass daily ; on the other hand, according to *Trid. Sess. XXIII De Sacr. ordinis, can.* 1, one may quite well be a priest without ever preaching.

That is what cannot possibly be said of the position of sacrament in the theory and practice of the evangelical Churches, with the possible exception of certain sects.

If we would understand this peculiar state of affairs on the Roman Catholic side and also the meaning and importance of the evangelical counter-thesis, we must above all be perfectly clear that Catholicism—in this respect not unlike modernism—sees in this medium of the Church's life, which we have designated by the concept " proclamation," something quite different happen from just proclamation. Proclamation must mean the repetition of the divine promise. On the basis of the Word which God has spoken to His Church, attention is drawn in His Church through men to the Word which God wishes to speak to His Church. The presence of God is consequently God's grace, i.e. His unfathomably free act from time to time in which He acknowledges the attention drawn and thereby fulfils the promise in a twofold sense : by making its repetition, completed by men, a true one, and by keeping faith with the promise proclaimed by the real new coming of His Word. But then the grace of this twofold fulfilment meets man simply in his hearing of the promise and his obedience to it. It meets him in faith alone. This is how the Reformers regarded that event in the midst of the Church's life. They regarded it under the concept of proclamation, i.e. under the concept of the *promissio* repeated by man's act, because they thought they could not otherwise understand the presence of the Holy Spirit among unholy men, than as the grace of the strictly personal free Word of God, which reaches its goal in the equally personal free hearing of man, the hearing of faith, which in its turn can only be regarded as grace. This presupposition is lacking in Roman Catholic dogmatics. It too gives the name of grace to the event in the centre of the Church's life. But by grace it understands not the connection of Word and faith, but the connection between a divine Being as the cause and a divine creaturely Being as the operation. With the proper reservation we may also say that it understands by it not an historical but a physical event. It sees the presence of Jesus Christ in His Church, the mystical unity of the Head with the whole Body, in the fact that from Jesus Christ under definite conditions there proceeds a steady unbroken inflow of divine-human being upon His own people.

At this particular point we can scarcely fail to realise the inner connection between the Roman Catholic and the modernist conceptions. The assertion of a communion between God and man in the form of an operation beyond the contraposition of the divine and human persons, beyond the act of the divine and human decisions, is at least common to both, although we must always remember that this synthetic operation is thought of in modernism as completed from man's side, in Catholicism on the contrary as completed from God's side. But what is the meaning here (and not only here !) of the opposition between " anthropocentric " and " theocentric " theology ? Nevertheless in the disinclination to acknowledge an ultimate necessity for proclamation the two coincide.

Obviously " proclamation " cannot be the designation of this event. Grace neither is and remains here the personal free Word of God, nor is and remains here listening faith. Neither must it be precisely Word on God's side, nor must it be precisely faith in man. Neither need man here listen to an already spoken Word of God, nor need he here wait for one that must first be spoken. Neither must faith here grasp the promise made as made by God, nor must it here wait for a fulfilment still outstanding. Neither is blessedness recognised here in this very grasping and waiting, nor judgment discerned in a situation other than this grasping and waiting. Clearly the only verdict can be that it is all said in a manner partly unsatisfactory, partly superfluous, partly perverted, if grace from the side of the divine Dispenser as well as on the side of the human recipient is an operation, an influence, an action and passion alternating, not essentially or ultimately between Person and person, but materially, between God as the Founder on the one part and the " grounds of being " in man's person on the other.

Protestant polemics is urgently recommended not to use the word " magical " in this connection. There is no sensible definition of the concept of " magic " by which the authentic Catholic conception of that material happening is really touched.—Cf. for the whole Domasus Winzen, O.S.B., *Die Sackramentenlehre der Kirche in ihren Verhältnis zur dialektischen Theologie*, *Catholica*, 1932 p. 19 f.

We are here faced with a fundamental decision. For a man in the position to interpret an operation, an influence of an impersonal character as the grace of Jesus Christ, everything else follows self-evidently. Naturally sacrament must on this presupposition be the one and all ; as an act in distinction from the spoken word, of course, it is suited to be the medium and channel of this influence, once " influence " signifies the thing that takes place in the Church between God and man.

Naturally the meaning of sacrament must then be described as a *causare, continere et conferre gratiam* (*Conc. Florent.* 1438, *Decr. pro Arm. Denz. Nr.* 695), and its power as active *ex opere operato*, i.e. independently of divine decision and human faith—*Si quis dixerit, non dari gratiam per hujusmodi sacramenta semper et omnibus, quantum est ex parte Dei, etiam si rite ea suscipiant, sed aliquando et aliquibus :* A.S. (*Trid. Sess. VII Can. de sacr. in genere can.* 7) S.qu.d., *per ipsa novae legis sacramenta ex opere operato non conferri gratiam, sed solam fidem divinae promissionis ad gratiam consequendam sufficere :* A.S. (*ib. can.* 8).

And naturally preaching must be treated with that peculiar aloofness. Practically it is not essentially necessary here and can only continue alongside the essentially necessary as the preliminary and secondary exposition and inculcation of it.

Certainly even the Catholic Church (e.g. *Cat. Roman., Praef. qu.* 2) is aware of and emphasises the truth that *fides* comes *ex auditu* (Rom. 10[17]), but she regards faith that comes from hearing the Word as merely the preparation for receiving righteousness before God. *Disponuntur autem ad ipsam justitiam dum excitati divina gratia et adiuti, fidem ex auditu concipientes, libere moventur in Deum, credentes, vera esse, quae divinitus revelata et promissa sunt (Trid. Sess. VI, cap. 6).*

It cannot be the means of real sanctifying grace, *gratia gratum faciens*, it can only be the means of a preparatory grace.

When in the doctrine of the so-called " actual " grace dogmatists talk at a definite point about hearing as well, it is only the grace of *illustratio intellectus*, characterised as very preliminary, which is expounded under this viewpoint (M. J. Scheeben, *Hand. der kath. Dogm.* vol. III 1882 new edn. 1925 p. 666 ; B. Bartmann, *Lehrb. der Dogm.* 7th edn. vol. II 1929 p. 15).

The former kind, in fact, would mean the calling to life again of the partly unsatisfying, partly superfluous, partly perverted problematic condition which is inevitable where the issue is the Word and the hearing of it. But it is in these very conditions that Roman Catholic dogmatics refuses to see and understand the event in the centre of the Church's life. Therefore for it preaching cannot have its place anywhere else save on the very outmost margin of the Church's action. Therefore in Roman Catholic practice preaching can only claim to be instruction and exhortation. Further, where one is in the position of regarding the grace of Jesus Christ as a *causare gratiam ex opere operato*, it all happens in a certain order and cannot work otherwise than in this exact order.

But the Reformers did not see themselves in this position. They thought they should regard this grace not as cause and effect but as Word and faith, and for that very reason regard the representative event in the centre of the Church's life as proclamation, as an act concerned with speaking and hearing, indicative of the fact that even in the actual thing proclaimed what is involved is not a material connection but a personal encounter. For them that was the standpoint from which also the mutual relation between preaching and sacrament had to be regulated in a quite definite way. True, they could not and would not assign to sacrament the place which falls to preaching according to Roman Catholic dogmatics. Proclamation of the ground of the promise laid down once for all, and so proclamation in the form of symbolic action, had to be and to remain for them an essential necessity. But this proclamation obviously presupposes that the other is taking place, namely, repetition of the Biblical promise. The former must be for the sake of the latter, and so sacrament for the sake of preaching and not *vice versa*. Therefore not sacrament alone, and not preaching alone, nor yet, to speak meticulously, simply preaching and sacrament in double track, but preaching plus sacrament, plus the visible act that confirms its human language as God's work, is the constitutive element, the visible centre of the Church's life. Regarded *a parte potiori*, but only *a parte potiori*, the evangelical Churches, Lutheran as well as Reformed, may and must be termed Churches of preaching.

" To achieve such faith God hath instituted the office of preaching, given Gospel and sacraments " (*Conf. Aug. art.* 5). " Then the Word brings Christ to the folk and makes Him known in their hearts, a thing they never understood from the sacrament. Therefore 'tis a hard thing for our times that people are all for holding Masses and hasten only to found Masses, and unfortunately the foremost thing, for which Masses are introduced, comes in second, that is preaching " (Luther, *Ausleg. deutsch d. Vaterunsers*, 1519 W. edn. vol. II p. 112, l. 15). " Now to do away with this misuse, the first thing is to know that the Christian community should never come together, except there God's very Word be preached and prayer made. . . . Therefore where God's Word is not preached, 'tis better people should neither sing nor read, nor come together. . . . 'Tis better to leave out all, save the Word. And there is naught better to pursue than the Word. For the whole Scripture sheweth that that same should be compulsory among Christians, and Christ also saith Himself, Luke 10⁴² ' One thing is needful.' For that Mary should sit at Christ's feet and hear His Word daily is the best part to choose, and is never taken away. It is an eternal saying that all else must pass away, however much there is for Martha to do " (*Von Ordnung Gottesdiensts* 1523 W. edn. 12, p. 35, l. 19 and p. 37, l. 29). *Primum vero et summum omnium, in quo omnia pendent alia, est docere verbum dei. Nam verbo docemus, verbo consecramus, verbo ligamus et solvimus, verbo baptisamus, verbo sacrificamus, per verbum de omnibus iudicamus, ut cuicunque verbum cesserimus, huic plane nihil negare possumus, quod ad sacerdotem pertinet* (*De instit. ministris Ecclesiae*, 1523 W. edn. 12, p. 180, l. 5). " . . . Where the preaching chair lies and snores, that it wakes not up nor expounds the words, one may well read and sing in it, but without any understanding " (E. edn. 1, 229, between 1530–34). " Therefore we should know that God hath so ordered that none should come to knowledge of Christ or acquire forgiveness through Him or receive the Holy Spirit without external public means, but hath put such treasure in the oral word or preaching office and will not deliver it in a corner or secretly in the heart, but will have it cried aloud and imparted openly among the people, as Christ enjoineth, ' Go ye into all the world and preach the Gospel to every creature ' " (*Sermon on Matt.* 9¹ᶠ·, W. edn. 29, p. 579, l. 25). *Est itaque Benedicere : praedicare et docere verbum Evangelii, confiteri Christum, et cognitionem ipsius propagare in alios. Et hoc sacerdotale officium est et juge sacrificium Ecclesiae in novo Testamento, quae benedictionem illam distribuit praedicando, administrando sacramenta, absolvendo, consolando et tractando verbum gratiae.* (*Komm. zu Gal.* 3⁹, 1535 W. edn. vol. XL.¹, p. 387, l. 21.) *Ecclesia nihil facere debet, quam recte et pure docere Evangelium atque ita generare liberos* (*zu Gal.* 4²⁷, p. 664, l. 27). " For the very greatest, holiest, most needful, highest service of God, which God hath demanded in the first and second command as the greatest, is to preach God's Word, for the preacher's office is the highest office in the churches, where then public worship is omitted, how can there be there knowledge of God, the teaching of Christ, or the Gospel ? (Melanchthon, *Apologie*, C.R. 28, 220). Calvin called preaching

(*doctrina*) the *anima ecclesiae* (*Instit.* IV 12, 1, cf. *Suppl. Exhort.* 1543 *C.R.*
6, 459) or the *mater ex qua nos Deus generat* (*Comm. Gal.* 4²⁴, *C.R.* 50, 237) and
in his great letter to the Duke of Somerset (Oct. 1548 *C.R.* 13, 70 F.) has
expressly declared that mere readings could not take the place of *prédication
vive*, and that the possibility of excesses on the preacher's part, which in any
case had of course to be reckoned with, should not here constitute a reason for
preventing it : *Tous les dangers quon peult craindre ne doibvent empescher que
l'Esprit de Dieu nayt sa liberte et son cours en ceulx ausquelz il a distribue de ses
graces pour edifier L'Église.* For . . . *de dire que nous puissons avoir dévotion
soit à priére, soit à cérémonie sans y rien entendre c'est une grand moquerie :
combien qu'il se dict communement. Ce n'est pas une chose morte ne brutifve, que
bonne affection envers Dieu : mais est un mouvement vif, procedant du sainct
Esprit quand le cœur est droictement touché, et l'entendement illuminé . . . il n'y
a nulle edification : sinon où il y a doctrine* (*Forme des Prières,* 1542 *Epistre au
Lecteur, C.R.* 6, 165 f.).—In face of this it must simply be described as theological thoughtlessness and caprice for certain Lutherans of the 19th century
(Klaus Harms, Vilmar, Löhe) to have thought they could afford, while
more or less clearly discrediting preaching, once again to proclaim the " altar "
and the " sacrament of the altar " as the centre of the Church's action. In
contrast, listen to the declaration of the quite unobjectionably Lutheran
Hermann Bezzel. " How are Word and Sacrament related to one
another ? . . . The Word has been the first and will remain the first. It
does not say, Heaven and earth shall pass away, but my sacraments shall not
pass away ; but it says, But my words shall not pass away. And just because
with us it is easy for an overvaluation of the sacraments to enter in, for the
reason that a magical effect is expected from them, it is necessary as between
them to consider the sober evangelical concept. The Word is the primary
thing. There is of course Word without sacrament, but never sacrament
without Word. The Word is the first thing. The Word existed before
sacrament was. The Word stands alone, sacrament can never stand alone.
The Word is God's original essence, sacrament is first aroused by our need.
The Word will remain after our need, sacrament will disappear after our need.
This presupposed, I must say that the Word is the audible sacrament and
sacrament is the visible Word. The Word was before sacrament and
exists without sacrament, and will also still exist hereafter " (Johannes
Rupprecht, *Hermann Bezzel als Theologe,* 1925 p. 369).

2. DOGMATICS AND CHURCH PROCLAMATION

The claim with which Church proclamation comes forward and
the atmosphere of expectation with which it is surrounded should
not mislead us as to the fact that it is always and always will be—
man's word. It is also more than that, it is also something quite
different from that. It is, namely, when and where God pleases,
God's own Word. Upon the promise of this divine good pleasure
it makes its venture in obedience. Upon that depends the claim
and the expectation. But proclamation, alike as preaching and as
sacrament, does not cease to be representation, to be man's
service.

" Therefore we also confess that the servants of the Church are God's fellow-workers, as St. Paul calls them . . . yet with this addition and understanding that in it all we ascribe all effect and power to the Lord alone, to whom servants, however, lend this extra service ; for 'tis sure that this power and effect never ought to nor could be bound to any creature at all, save God who imparts it to us of His own free will, to whom He will (*Conf. Helv. prior*, 1536 *art.* 15).

And so far as it is this, it is no unassailable action, insured in its proper meaning, but rather like all human action it is exposed to the question of its responsibility. This question can, of course, be put in such a way that it ought to be dismissed. For instance, as regards content the Church's proclamation may not allow a question as to whether it is in treaty with the peculiarities and interests of a race, people, nation, or state. It cannot permit a question as to its agreement with the demands of this or that scientific or æsthetic culture of the moment. It cannot permit a question as to whether it is making the necessary contribution towards the preservation or perhaps even to the overthrow of this or that form of society or economy. A proclamation which takes up responsibilities in these or similar directions spells treachery to the Church and to Christ Himself. It only gets its due if sooner or later its mouth is stopped by some sort of delicate or brutal godlessness. Far better none at all, than proclamation like that. Just because of its real responsibility Church proclamation must be unconditionally free in every other direction. Its real responsibility arises out of its intention to be proclamation of the Word of God. The very claim with which it comes forward and the very expectation with which it is surrounded also point to the critical authority from whose standpoint alone it must permit itself to be questioned, from whose point of view its fate is settled rightly or wrongly from time to time. And because in proclamation the concern is with the centre of the Church's life, so far as it claims to be the representation of the divine summons to which all other elements in the life of the Church have to respond, we have to assert that as, and while she proclaims, the Church herself generally is questioned from time to time by that critical authority, as to the truth of her existence as a Church.

Est autem Ecclesia congregatio sanctorum, in qua Evangelium recte docetur et recte administrantur sacramenta (*Conf. Aug. art.* 7). Thus *docere Evangelium* and *administrare sacramenta* are carried out on the presupposition of a *rectitudo* presupposed in this action and made the object of effort, of a norm that decides as to the rightness of this action. And this *rectitudo* in teaching and in sacrament decides at the same time whether the Church here and now is really the Church, the *ecclesia*, the *congregatio sanctorum*.

Thus it is on the basis of its actual origin and ground, of the actual essence of the Church, that Church proclamation and with it the Church herself is really attacked and called in question. No other attack that may arise can be anything like so oppressive as this one. According as she is really oppressed here she may and must be of good courage in face of all other attacks. But the oppression of this question will always have a double side, one facing the past and one the future : what was it that claimed to be Christian proclamation yesterday ? and what will the thing be that is going to come forward anew to-morrow with this claim, in the atmosphere of this expectation ? In the centre between this yesterday and to-morrow, coming home to both at once, attacking yesterday's thing subsequently and to-morrow's in advance, criticising yesterday's in order to correct to-morrow's, crops up the question of responsibility now engaging us. Because it is God's service that Church proclamation claims to be, it is God Himself and God alone who here asks, and whom we require to answer. But for that very reason and in that very way the Church is seriously and solidly burdened with this responsibility. Because she can and ought to withdraw from all other responsibilities, this becomes a very burning one. Were it not, were the Church with her proclamation to feel herself secure in God's very face, all these other responsibilities would of course have to become burning ones, it might and of course it would have to be, that every contradiction raised against Church proclamation on the part of state, social, cultural, and similar points of view, without possessing any right in itself would acquire one against the Church, and in its entire non-Churchness become a very necessary criticism of the Church.

The *ad fontes !* cry of the humanists at the beginning of the 16th century was certainly in itself a matter of a historism, theologically easy to see through and definitely to be rejected. The discovery of the free creative individual, in the form in which it spread over all departments with increasing power from the middle of the same century, was certainly in itself nothing else than a bit of newly revived paganism. The judicious way in which the 18th century imagined that it could master the problems of life better than the Church was sufficiently sharply marked to be altogether manifestly a theological error. Church proclamation had assuredly no room for the ideas of eudæmonistic rationalism, to which modern socialism owes its origin and from which it has derived its spiritual look to this day. The new " Humanism " preached to-day in America, the single aim of which is to become the world view of the near future, already betrays, by the perfect way in which it potters along, the fact that, compared with the Church, it is in itself in an extremely subordinate position. And quite as little in the Asiatic crudities of Bolshevist ideology

6

could one see a rival to the proclamation of the Church, a rival which had in the smallest degree developed within her. But that could only have held good and would to-day only hold good, if for " Church " generally were substituted the Church conscious of her own responsibility with regard to her proclamation, sorely oppressed by it, seriously concerned about it. For an unconcerned self-assured Church, immune from attack on her own centre, all these adversaries were and are serious adversaries.

The Church should fear God and not fear the world. But only if and as she fears God need she cease to fear the world. If she fears not God, then it does not help her at all, in fact it only then begins to imperil her, if she fears the world, listens to its contradiction, and considers it in her attitude, undertakes all sorts of responsibilities towards it, however necessary and justified may be the criticism she meets at its hands.

It was the prophetic thinker and preacher Hermann Kutter (1863–1931), who represented in the last generation, with a force like that of no one near him, the knowledge that the realm of God's power is greater than the realm of the Church, and that ever and anon it pleases and has pleased God to meet His Church with warning and comfort right amid the figures and events of the profane world process. Kutter said so, especially in his older books, *Sie müssen* (1903), *Gerechtigkeit* (1905), and *Wir Pfarrer* (1907), especially in view of the Social Democracy of the pre-war period. What Kutter intended as an actual view and interpretation of the signs of the times and not at all as a programme, first became in Leonhard Ragaz the theory, that the Church must take up a position towards socialism as towards a preliminary manifestation of the kingdom of God ; in other words became the particular system of " religious socialism." After the war, P. Tillich, an incomparably more bloodless and abstract thinker than Kutter or Ragaz, both replaced socialism by profane culture in general, and this profaneness, tricked out with the insignia of prophetic significance, he erected generally into a systematic principle over against the Church. On all of which in our context the comment is, that if we assume that in the actual circumstances to-day there is something to be said for the world, and perhaps for Socialism in particular, having a decisive word to say to the Church, then, if the criticism most needed is not to mean the wickedest treachery, the result of this encounter can be none other than that the Church lets herself appeal to herself through that alien non-Church voice, recognising in it the voice of God, lets herself be reminded of the straits, so full of promise, of her special service. Even the greatest, humblest, openest readiness on the Church's part to have something told her by the world might certainly mean that for the first time she is really ceasing to think of taking her special responsibility more seriously, and is once more allowing her energies to be dissipated ; under the delusion that all she has failed in is consciousness of the times, open-mindedness and activity, and fondly imagining that, e.g. a feeling for social needs, a capacity for radical social ideals and purposes, a will to social action could be a substitute for careful concentration upon her own business, hitherto neglected by her. If the point is really the prophetic vision and interpretation of the contradiction that directly or indirectly meets the Church on the part of the world, if therefore it is the " diction " of God which the Church thinks she recognises in this contra-diction, then in any circumstances all that she has to take out of that can only be an injunction to this careful concentration upon her own business, to renewed uneasiness about her fidelity to her commission, and not an invitation to a distracted assumption of alien responsibilities. It is not only sufficient as the outcome of such an encounter between the Church and the world, it is the only possible outcome for her, that in future the Church should take more seriously than in the past the simple question as to the meaning of *recte docere Evangelium, recte adminstrare sacramenta*. It is in this direction that Kutter's doctrine pointed, as distinguished from that of Ragaz and Tillich. Even of him more cannot be said in this connection. It may have been the salutary concentration and impatience of a prophet, it may also have been a philosophy of immediacy that pointed backwards rather than forwards, which caused him to see in all theology nothing but an attempt to make the divine a theory and secular at that, instead of living directly in it. Of Ragaz one may say, without going too closely into him, that he has never carefully or thoroughly come to terms with the attempt to take serious account of the Church's encounter with socialism along these lines, and that probably he is not generally speaking in a position to view it with detachment. For all the respect which we cannot withhold from him, he should not expect to impress us by his nervous attacks (latterly in the work edited by Georg Wünsch, *Reich Gottes, Marxismus, National-sozialismus*, 1931 pp. 1–65). But Tillich has on the one hand remained too incorrigible an historian of the spirit, too much the heir of liberal theological feeling towards the Church (and, apparently, has become increasingly so), and on the other hand has allowed himself systematically to be too much determined and fixed by the pseudo-eschatological " situation " of the years immediately after the War, for his protests against " the supranaturalistic consummation of the dialectical movement in Barth's dogmatics " (*Rel. Verwirklichung*, 1930 p. 20) to arouse my interest. Both of them, Ragaz (*op. cit.* p. 53) and Tillich (*op. cit.* p. 21), regard their action as dynamics, mine as statics. . . . What ought I to say to that ?

But according to the indications of the Parable of the Talents the fear of God which the Church badly needs cannot be inactive, her knowledge of the responsibilities of her proclamation cannot be a theoretical proviso. The attack on her from God's side demands something to correspond on man's side, i.e. human conscientiousness and investigation. Was her proclamation yesterday adequate to her responsibility ? Will it be adequate to it to-morrow ? If the question of the Church is really propounded by God, then it must meet her within in the realm of human possibilities, press upon her and rouse her. With the prayer which is her ultimate response to this attack, a work must be associated as a penultimate, a work of critical revision and investigation of the Church's proclamation in view of the divine verdict, to which she appeals as that which she means to be. In all that the Church can and ought to do here there is absolutely no question of her coming forward with her own verdict in place of this divine verdict or thinking that she can execute this divine verdict. She would not be taking seriously the tribunal of God before which she stands, were she to think she could herself execute it by herself, with anything she does.

The line which needs to be drawn here is evident. Roman Catholic dogmatics wots of an infallibility of the Church, of the Church's teaching office in particular, and of the Roman Pope most particularly, *in definienda doctrina de fide vel moribus (Conf. Vatic. sess. IV, Constit. dogm. de Eccl. Christi*, cap. 4), which permits and commands her to deal with the *doctrina (propositio) ecclesiae* (cf. Bartmann, *Lehrbuch der Dogm.* 7th edn. vol. I 1928 p. 33 f.) as an *infallibilis et divina regula* (Thomas Aquinas, *S. Theol.* II¹, *qu.* 6, *art.* 3). Is *doctrina ecclesiae=divina regula* ? Does not that imply that the Church herself is to judge herself with a divine judgment ? Here we can only repeat our question already put : On this presupposition how far is serious work being put into the Church's proclamation ? On this presupposition how far can we distinguish the trouble taken about it from the transmission, with commentary, of results which were finally made confessional ages ago ? And, if this question cannot be cleared up, how far is there recognition of the fact that the Church's proclamation is being seriously attacked as a human work ? Or if even this ought not to be recognised, with what right and in what spirit ?

The Church can neither absolutely question her proclamation nor absolutely put it right. She can therefore only take pains to see how far it is called in question, and to what extent it ought to be put right. Upon her human work she can, once more, only do a human work of criticism and revision. And because this is so, she will be far from thinking that she wants to or can get rid of the assailability of her proclamation, the unrest prepared for her by God Himself. This work of criticising and revising her proclamation the Church can only undertake in the right spirit, if she knows that the unrest prepared for her is irremovable ; and the result of it, if it is well done, will moreover always be to render her much more acutely conscious of the unrest prepared for her. But this actual human work is obviously enjoined upon her along with the proclamation itself. Over against and alongside of the Church's proclamation there must go a Church theology, especially dogmatics. Theology, and dogmatics in particular, is in contradistinction to all scattered answers to immaterial questions, the Church's concentrated anxiety and concern about her most intimate responsibility. In making her proclamation the raw material of dogmatics, she is doing, apart from the proclamation itself and the prayer that it may be right, the one thing that she badly needs, the only thing she as the Church can do about the obvious centre of her life. For how should not the one thing that she badly needs be involved at the point at which not only the right answers to the divine call

are involved (and they also are certainly to be taken seriously !) in
the same way as in the Church's other functions, but the correct
representation of the divine call itself, and therefore public worship
in this intensified sense of the term ? And how should not a serious
work of reflection upon the background of Biblical exegesis, with
a view to the practice of preaching, be the only thing there is to
do about this one thing (always apart from prayer), nay the only
thing it is practically possible to do ?

How disastrously the Church must misunderstand herself if, on whatever
pretext, she can dream of being able to undertake and carry out anything
serious in the certainly important fields of public worship reform, or social
work, or Christian education or the regulation of her relationship to State and
society, or an international understanding among the Churches, without the
necessary and possible being done simultaneously in regard to the visible
centre of her life.   As if it were patent on the face of it, as if we could confidently count upon it, that *evangelium recte docetur et recte administrantur
sacramenta !*   As if we could confidently leave that to God and meantime
busy ourselves with the circumference of the Church's circle, which has
perhaps been revolving for ever so long round a wrong centre !   As if we could
actually put ourselves in God's hands without a single care as to what happens
at this decisive point !   Once more, how disastrously must the Church misunderstand herself, if she can dream that theology is the business of a few
theorists specially appointed for the purpose, to whom all the rest, as vigor-
ously confident practical men, are to listen incidentally with half an ear,
so that on their side they may make it a title of honour to live " quite untheologically " for the demands of the day (" love ") !   As if these practical
men did not themselves over and over again preach or at least talk and write
and also had their right to do so sincerely questioned !   And as if there could
be anything more practical than to give this question its head ; that is, simply,
to do theological, dogmatic work !   And once more, how disastrously the
Church must misunderstand herself, if she can imagine that theological
reflection is a matter for quiet situations and times which suit and invite
contemplation, a sort of peace-time luxury, to have no time for which is not
only permitted but commanded, should circumstances become really serious
and exciting !   As if there could actually be, particularly for a Church attacked
even externally, a more exacting task than that of making a beginning at
proper inward consolidation, which means, of course, assiduous work at theology !
As if the very undertaking of preaching did not mean that the Church finds
herself permanently in a serious fix !   And as if theology could be properly
practised, otherwise than in direct view of this standing fix !   Let us not be
deceived.   It is, thanks to these perverted ideas about theology and dogmatics
in particular, that there arises and exists for the life of the Church a lasting
and growing deficit for which we cannot expect those specially active in this
department to maintain the needed balances.   The whole Church must
seriously desire a serious theology, if she desires to possess a serious theology.

We have still to weigh the connection between dogmatics and
proclamation from the other side.—When we term the Church's
proclamation the raw material of dogmatics, our meaning is that

Church proclamation is at least also man's language about God. And precisely as man's language is it the concrete problem of dogmatics, the *factum* and *faciendum* to which dogmatics as a science relates. Starting from the question how men spoke about God in the Church yesterday, dogmatics asks how this should be done to-morrow. The question is put primarily and directly to those entrusted with the task of proclamation, indirectly, but not for that reason with less weight, to the Church in general, which as a whole has a corporate responsibility for the proper discharge of this as of all other functions. Only as a matter of order but not of principle, and so too not without the possibility of exceptions, the office of preaching and administration of sacraments, according to the evangelical idea, is attached to the class of theologians in particular. But that means that in matters of the dogmatic question there can be no dispensation in principle even for non-theologians.

The luxury of " quite untheological " thought and language, i.e. taking no part in the dogmatic question, a luxury in which even theologians of all people are wont to indulge themselves gladly and not without being vain about such freedom, can, strictly speaking, really only materialise in the form of secretly quitting the Church for a passing or a permanent period. It is freedom to babble heresy or what makes heretics, that men claim when they think they ought to or can theologise " quite untheologically." There is no room in the Church for this freedom.

The possibility of putting the dogmatic question, the possibility of dogmatic criticism and revision, arises out of the claim with which language about God comes forward in the Church, and out of the atmosphere of expectation with which it is there surrounded. We should have to deny this claim and this expectation, and thereby the Church herself, were we seriously to assume a lack of interest in the dogmatic question. The language about God to be found in the Church claims, as proclamation, to be the Word of God. By this its own peculiar standard it is measured in dogmatics. In the raw material of dogmatics the first object is a series of expressions which, more or less constantly and emphatically, usually make up the spoken matter of proclamation in the whole Church, i.e. on both sides of the divisions in the Church. But here, as everywhere, these expressions acquire their meaning from the associations and contexts in which they are used. In virtue of this varying meaning, language about God becomes from time to time a definite, charac- teristic language. It exists for dogmatics from time to time in a congeries of analogous determinations, and the sense of the dogmatic question will generally be, whether and how far it (i.e. the meaning with which the expressions are used) is appropriate or not to its purpose of serving the Word of God. Yesterday's proclamation, with criticisms of which dogmatics methodically starts out, would therefore consist fundamentally of the sum-total of the attempts at Church proclamation that have occurred up to date, as variously determined by the meaning attached to the expressions in question. Actually it is but a very small fraction of this total which, where dogmatic work is done, can be taken as known and therefore can be made the object of investigation. But even within this known fraction there can be, once more, only some few elements, which stand out representatively from the rest in the series, and with which this work can busy itself. Finally, it could neither be relevant nor profitable for dogmatics to dream of associating itself at all directly with Church preaching as delivered yesterday or the day before or previous to that. Rather, in order to a real demand that the Church test herself concerning this her central function, it will get in touch with that form of yesterday's proclamation, in which we find this function already tested, criticised, and revised, i.e. with the results of the history of dogmatics itself. Precisely in her dogmatics up to date the Church has given an authoritative deliverance on the extent to which, in her own opinion, she regards as proclamation the language about God to be found within her, when measured by the standard of the Word of God. The result is what without sentimentalities we must regard as a necessity, namely, that in dogmatics the main thing decidedly is a debate of dogmaticians with each other ; and naturally by " dogmaticians " are meant not only dogmatic teachers and authors, but simply and generally those of yesterday and to-day who are concerned with and interested in the dogmatic question. Already in these limitations regarding the *factum* presupposed the essentially g y m n a s t i c character of dogmatics is betrayed. For, as a critical retrospect of yesterday, it can only work through examples, and not comprehensively or exhaustively. But this character is also revealed in the *faciendum* striven after. Once more our subject-matter is the series of expressions which constitute the material of all Christian proclamation, which should now, so far as this is seen to be necessary, on the basis of previous criticism, be used in altered connections and contexts and therefore in a new and, we hope, a better sense. But as this revision of the language about God can never affect more than a fraction of its amount to date, so, too, only a fraction of what is to be spoken to-morrow about God in the Church will stand as directly corrected, and even this fraction will only stand as a first correction for the time being. The Church's personal test in respect of her proclamation must be continued to-morrow with the proclamation itself. Thus dogmatic work even on this side will not be able to claim more than a gymnastic character. It is *pars pro toto*. It cannot—at this early stage we may say so— have in view a system of Christian truth. All else apart, that would mean that it had the power to criticise all the Church proclamation ever made, and to put the whole of a corrected Church proclamation finally before the public. That it simply cannot do. Moreover, in view of to-morrow it can only take examples and it can only take these pending better instruction, and certainly not conclusively so or in any other way. In dogmatics, criticism and revision of the language about God should be exercised upon a definite section of the entire world of past and future Church proclamation—there is a lesson to be learned, and in dogmatics even that can really only be the lesson for the needs of next day. Thus dogmatics clearly betrays itself as an affair of sch o ol, where the instruction can in no wise anticipate the reality of life, but can only give the most immediate and most needed guidance for meeting this reality. Church proclamation is the raw material of dogmatics. But it would be a fatal confusion to think of asserting the opposite also, that dogmatics is the raw material of Church proclamation.

> It is a well-known and perhaps unavoidable beginner's mistake in students and licentiates when preaching, to imagine that they must and may con- fidently take the m a t t e r of their preaching from some once treasured College notebook or textbook on dogmatics. Whereas, on the other hand, older preachers are usually far too confident in withdrawing from the jurisdiction of this critical authority.

The ̇ actual thing to be proclaimed we may not and cannot expect to hear from dogmatics. That must be found from time to time in the middle space between the definite text of the Bible in the context of the whole Bible and the community in the definite situation of the varying present. Dogmatics can only be a guide to proper superiority and proper adaptability, proper boldness, and proper caution for the moment, in which all depends on finding the message, on being guided to one's bearings between the other two poles, what must be said under all circumstances, and what may not be said under any circumstances ; in short, on being guided to the act of choosing between the various possibilities in the way in which it is characteristic of this human action, *qua* human action, as of any other action—being guided from the point of view that in this action the main thing ought to be to proclaim the Word of God, and that in this sense it must take the form compatible with the best human knowledge and conscience.

The direct connection between theology, i.e. dogmatics, and the task of Church proclamation has already been expressly represented by Augustine : *ut non solum legendo alios . . . sed et aliis ipsi aperiendo proficiant (De doctr. chr. Prol.* 1, cf. 1, 1). For the instruction of Church teachers there were during the period of the Reformation, in addition to Luther's Larger Catechism, 1529, the Berne Synod, 1532, and the Roman Catechism, 1566. This aim in dogmatics of rendering the theologian *aptum ad instituendum hominem ad salutem* is notably asserted in Old Protestantism precisely by no less than the Lutherans J. Gerhard (*Loci. theol.* 1610 *Prooem.* 26, 31), Quenstedt (*Theol. did. pol.* 1685 *p.* 1, *ch.* 1, sect. 2, qu. 3, ekth. 15), Baier (*Comp. Theol. pos.* 1686 *Prol.* 1, 1), Buddeus (*Instit. theol. dog.* 1724 I 1, 28). Further, it was admittedly none other than Schleiermacher who raised the practical task of Church guidance and leadership right up to the level of the constitutive principle of theological science (*Kurze Darstellung,* 1830 §§ 1–13). In most energetic agreement with him is Vilmar of Marburg: "According as dogmatics removes itself from the sphere of the Church, it ceases to serve salvation and panders to individual vanity in knowledge. Dogmatics should know that as an object which prepares for the spiritual office, it stands in the relation of a school to real life, and that to it also it is said, *Non scholae sed vitae discimus.* The life of the Church stands above dogmatics." In Vilmar we find the remark so characteristic of the conception set forth here, that dogmatics " really contains *gymnasmata* for the Church office and its holders " (*Dogmatik,* part I 1874 p. 59). Good words to counter the idea that dogmatics has material to offer the practising theologian for his sermons and catechisings, were found by Schleiermacher's pupil August Twesten (*Vorlesungen über die Dogm. d. ev.-luth. Kirche,* vol. I 1838 p. 82 f.) : he says it afforded him not an immediate but a mediate advantage, the more important for being mediate, of impressing upon his whole activity the " character of a loftier circumspection." " But as regards his call to teach, quite apart from its beneficent influence upon the depth and range of his religious thinking, it accustoms him to a method of criticism which covers not merely the form, as is usually the case, but also the Christian content of his discourses, and its relation to the highest tasks of practical theology in general " (*op. cit.* p. 85). Finally, this view of dogmatics as a school, its connection with the "conduct of Church instruction," is also significant for the theological work of Albrecht Ritschl (*Unterricht i.d. christl. Rel.* 3rd edn. 1886 § 87, *Rechtfertigung und Versöhnung,* vol. II 4th edn. 1900 pp. 3, 13). ,

By " proclamation of the Word of God " we are to understand withal, primarily and decisively, preaching and the sacraments ; with regard to the latter, which, as *verba visibilia* in actions, belong to a special order, the main thing will likewise be the oral proclamation accompanying them, the " doctrine " of the sacraments which is significant for the meaning of their administration in vogue at the time. But we saw that the task, though not the reality of proclamation, may be reduced and limited to these two concepts, preaching and sacrament. The other, the sacrificial and generally responsive elements in the Church's life, may also be proclamation. And in so far as in these other Church functions also there is language about God through a human channel, they too are liable to be asked to what extent it is properly used. That the *factum* and *faciendum* of the Church's instruction of youth must be included in the sphere of dogmatics, follows at once from the inevitability with which it is bound, from time to time, to pass over from teaching to proclamation. But even in theology itself the dogmatic question cannot continue to be avoided, either by the exegete on the one hand, or by the practical theologian on the other. Not by the exegete, because even his textually ever so faithful exposition of the Bible invariably exhibits a web of Bible material with a wrapping of imported word-connections of his own, and therefore of possibilities of meaning, which web, in order to be presented in the Church as proper proclamation, cannot possibly evade the question as to the legitimacy of this imported element. And the dogmatic question cannot be evaded by the practical theologian, because even the most external question regarding the performance of the Church's service in the present may receive such very varying answers, according to what is judged to be or not to be proper proclamation. Further, prayers and singings in Church cannot be treated as absolutely without dogmatic importance. Liturgy and Hymn-book also claim to be taken seriously, on the score that their contents consist of human words, and that therefore they too may be effective as proclamation—perhaps as very perverted proclamation.

It is a remarkable thing that in the evangelical Churches, when there is a revision of Books of Order or of Praise, every possible authority is usually consulted as being standard, with the sole exception of dogmatic science. The results naturally correspond !

But even in Church social work, which to-day is dragged so much to the fore, really there is not only action but all sorts of language too, and incidentally language which claims to be proclamation : it will be different when dogmatic reflection is behind it, and when this is not the case. But we have further established, that we must reckon with God sometimes speaking to us also through something external to the Church now familiar to us or even now real to us, and to that extent the attention of dogmatics too is not to be limited by the Church walls Of course it will always mean a venture, a deviation from its real line, if it thinks it should really take to do with such an extra-Church proclamation of the Word of God, or if on the contrary instead of, as is its regular office, speaking to the known visible Church, it thinks it should at the same time speak to the world.

It would be senseless to wish to prescribe this to it as a rule ! Dogmatics once for all is not a general gnosis of God and the world.

In doing this the individual dogmatician shoulders the responsibility of a prophet ! It cannot be denied that possibly he may occasionally have to do so. The normal and central fact with which dogmatics has to do is, very simply, the Church's Sunday sermon of yesterday and to-morrow, and so it will continue to be. The Church stands or falls by this function which is enjoined upon her. She has every cause to take dogmatic work very seriously, as the criticism and revision of this her decisive function.

Corresponding to this setting of the problem we have still to interpret or correct what in ancient and recent times has been said about the raw material of dogmatics. Catholics and Protestants, ancients and moderns, give us in all sorts of variants as the raw material of dogmatics, God and divine things, or man in his relation to God, or God's revelation in Christ, or Christian faith, also of course recently, the Christian principle; or the essence of Christianity. In short, the object of Christian language, the Christian subject-matter.

To that no objection can be raised, so far as Christian language becomes the raw material of dogmatics, obviously because it is language about the Christian subject-matter and because, thus indirectly, it is actually also the Christian subject-matter itself. But it is worth while not to lose sight of the indirectness with which alone this can be. The following three points of view should be noted here.

1. The necessity for dogmatics is of a different kind from that for Church proclamation. Proclamation must exist as the execution of the divine behest to the Church. Dogmatics must exist, because proclamation is fallible human work. These are two different things. The relation of proclamation to the Christian subject-matter is obviously a primary one, that of dogmatics a secondary. The datum from which dogmatics starts is neither God, nor revelation, nor faith. This is the datum from which proclamation starts. Certainly even dogmatics may and should be proclamation, in which case it too starts from this datum. But so far as it has a

function of its own which does not coincide with that of proclamation, its datum is a different one, namely the debatable fact that in proclamation by men there is human language about God, revelation, faith—debatable, because it is not self-evident that this is uttered in truth and purity, and because the Church cannot shirk responsibility for the fact that it ought to be uttered in truth and purity. Dogmatics is the servant of preaching, because it raises this question. It tests the " orthodoxy " of contemporary kerygma. As indeed even concrete dogma is nothing but kerygma tested, provisionally purified, and reduced to a definite " correct " formula by the Church. More should not be expected of dogmatics than what it, as dogmatics, can supply. And in dogmatics there is much which is really peculiar to it *qua* dogmatics, that we should not take exception to.

E.g. the *rabies theologorum*, which Melanchthon was so pleased to think he would no longer encounter in heaven.

Its aim is not a positive, stimulating and edifying presentation ; not for a moment does it contemplate an instructive exposition in the same sense as preaching. It deals with God, revelation, faith, only in view of their repercussions in proclamation. In being an exposition, it is also an investigation and a polemic, a criticism and a revision.

Its task is ἐπικόψαι τὰς τῆς πλάνης ὁδούς, ἵνα μίαν ὁδὸν βασιλικὴν ὁδεύσωμεν (Cyril of Jerus., *Catech*. 16, 5). " The Church's definitions of doctrine are only the balustrade which on either side guards against the fall into the abyss, like the buoys which mark off the proper fairway " (Fr. Ad. Philippi, *Kirchl. Glaubenslehre*, 1854 f. vol. II p. 150).

We spare ourselves many an unnecessary disillusionment over the form and results of dogmatics, if we keep this soberly in view.

2. Dogmatics is the servant of Church proclamation. Its relation to the latter may be paralleled by what was called in the ancient Church *Pistis* and *Gnosis* and since Augustine *credere* and *intelligere*, so far as we understand by *Pistis or credere* the simple reproduction and dissemination of its content, which aims at an unreflecting correspondence with the message as heard, and by *Gnosis or intelligere* the scientific investigation of this correspondence. But in this confrontation we must insist upon three provisos, which were not always observed in the ancient Church, and the failure to observe which may still lead to mistakes to-day.

(*a*) As compared with proclamation dogmatics signifies a different mode and function, but by no means a higher degree, of faith or knowledge of faith.

Admittedly it was one of the results of the discussion with ancient Gnosticism that the Church refused to recognise an aristocracy of scientific theologians in her midst. But there is involved here an idea which lies so close at hand that in practice it may become a continual source of temptation.

We must be very clear, that the simplest proclamation of the gospel may in the most unlimited sense be proclamation of the truth, and may with perfect validity communicate this truth to the most unsophisticated hearer, if it be God's will. Dogmatics is not the technique of certain people who are better placed spiritually, the privilege of an esoteric Christianity of getting better possession of the truth than in the form in which God lets it be proclaimed in His Church to the masses. In his efforts to improve what man here does, the dogmatician is not therein better placed, either as a believer or as a knower, than any member of the Church, as regards what God does here.

(b) As compared with Church proclamation, dogmatics cannot have access to a higher, better source of knowledge, to be sought in the supposed fact that in it Christian thought first began, or that in it thought was more adequate, comprehensive and profound than in simple preaching. It is not the case that the attempt to think in human terms about God, revelation, faith, first began in dogmatics ; unquestionably this attempt is already made, undertaken in proclamation itself (so far and so certainly as it is human language) and in listening to proclamation (so far as it is a human act) ; and, moreover, there is absolutely no reason why it should not and might not be made here in the form of an adequate, comprehensive, and profound thought.

Paul Althaus writes : " Theology means the completion of the act of faith in the sphere of thought. Faith ought to overcome the world. Theology is the wrestling to overcome the world of spirits and of thoughts. Theologians thereby achieve reflection . . . as a service to the whole community, and therefore, so to speak, as a service in representative thinking " (*Evangelium und Leben*, 1927 p. 26 f.). In spite of and in face of this detailed definition, would it not be ascribing too much to theology, to make a thing which is promised only to faith as such (which in that case may also be the faith of a " layman ") the goal of its " wrestling " ?

Not to mention the fact that with the introduction of the critical reflexion, which, of course, does distinguish dogmatics from proclamation, a higher norm of knowledge is put in place of that of proclamation. Here naturally we are constantly threatened with the inroad of some kind of philosophy, which will then raise the claim *in concreto* to indicate that source of knowledge. For whence should such critically reflective thought derive its mode and norm, save from man's intellect and therefore *in concreto* from some kind of philosophy? In that case we are bound to have a continual intrusion of the idea, that as certainly as critically reflective thought is the thought of man's reason, and whatever be the complexion of its philosophy, it must be related to the object of the Church's proclamation, and its execution must be determined by its divine object and not by its human origin and essence.

" *Credo ut intelligam* " in Anselm of Canterbury (*Prosl.* 1) means, certainly not the transition from faith to another genus, but an αἰχμαλωτίζειν πᾶν νόημα εἰς τὴν ὑπακοὴν τοῦ Χριστοῦ (2 Cor. 10⁵).

In practice it is not in our power to prevent this inroad of philosophy into dogmatics. Neither is it in our power to give to critically reflective human thought in practice such a relation to the divine object or such a determination in terms of it. But it is, of course, in our power to keep before us the need for such a relation and definition, and therefore to refuse any philosophy this right of irruption, to give the last word not to any immanent regulations of critically reflective thought, not to any longing on the part of man's need for thought, but solely to the needs of the Object here called in question. At least we may be aware that only on one side ought dogmatics to be open and obedient without restrictions, and that it has this one side in common with the proclamation of the Church and not with any kind of philosophy.

(*c*) As compared, therefore, with Church proclamation dogmatics cannot wish to be an end to itself. The relationship is not that God, revelation, faith were given to proclamation, and then apart from that and in some other way to dogmatics as well. But all that is given to the Church, and given not to consider but to proclaim, and even to dogmatics only so far as it is the presupposition of her test of the human work of this proclamation. It is given to the Church as her essence, as her life principle creating and establishing her, but for that very reason not as something existent, which might become the object of an independent theory, gnosis, or speculation, remote from her action, but as the divine action with which the Church herself must actively come to terms. But this human activity of hers is of course primarily proclamation, and anything else than the proper fulfilment of that cannot be the purpose of dogmatics. As a critical theory, gnosis or speculation, it has room and right, only so far as it serves this purpose.

In the opposition between Thomas Aquinas and Duns Scotus ·over the question whether theology is a *scientia speculativa* or *practica*, Old-Protestant dogmatics with increasing decisiveness came down on the side of Duns Scotus. That circumstance, to which we shall return again, is equivocal. It sprang, on the one hand undoubtedly, from the wave of modern religionism then rising and its rejection of further knowledge of the objectivity of God, on the other from a healthy revulsion from an abstract and basically non-Church contemplation and talk about God, from the pure, self-centred theological speculation, in the classical form which it attained in the famous writings of Pseudo-Dionysius, but which subsequently had pretty potent results in the scholasticism of the mediæval monastery, even among orthodox Protestants themselves, and which we still meet to-day in certain sections of Roman Catholic dogmatics. It signifies a recognition of the danger threatening Roman Catholic dogmatics from this side, when B. Bartmann in his text-books add to many (far from all !) of his paragraphs a concluding special section entitled " life values " (that is, of the dogmatic theme in question), although after all the problem should not be so simply soluble as that ! Talk of the practical character of theology might mean the knowledge that the Church is not an Academy, and that there is not even an academic corner in the Church. *Semper cogitandum est, Filium Dei non ob eam causam prodidisse ex arcana sede aeterni Patris, et revelasse doctrinam coelestem, ut seminaria spargeret disputationum, quibus ostendendi ingenii causa luderetur, sed potius ut homines de vera Dei agnitione et omnibus iis quae ad aeternam salutem consequendam necessaria sunt, erudirentur* (M. Chemnitz, *Loci theol. ed.* 1590 *Hypomnemata*, 9).

To sum up : because dogmatics neither signifies a higher Christian possibility of life, nor can substantiate an independent basis of knowledge, nor claim an independent rôle and significance as a theory, therefore the Christian subject-matter does not exist for it in any other way than as it exists in Christian proclamation.

3. The object of Church proclamation, the Christian subject-matter, demands dogmatics so far as the proclamation of it is a responsible act, and so far as dogmatics is precisely the effort to discharge this responsibility regarding the object of proclamation. But it is by no means the case that in dogmatics the Church is so to speak to become the Lord and Judge of the Christian subject-matter, so that the results of dogmatics from time to time would have to rank as a deity, as a law superimposed, so to speak, upor its revelation and upon faith. Dogmatics has to investigate, and now and again to re-establish her findings as to how we are best to speak about God, revelation, faith, so far as human language about these things is to rank as Church proclamation. But it must not imagine it can establish what God, revelation, faith are in

themselves. Alike in its investigations and in its findings it must keep in view that God is in heaven, but itself upon earth, that as compared with any human language and so even with that of the best dogmatics God, His revelation, and faith continue to live their own free life. Though we have repeatedly considered everything and set it right and improved the formulation of it, as is our duty to the Christian subject-matter in respect of man's language about it—and though our results should even be exalted into the Church's confession and dogma, we ought then to say, We are unprofitable servants ! and in no sense to imagine that we have in the very slightest become masters of the subject-matter.

In the well-known introductory words of the so-called Athanasian Creed dogmatics, i.e. dogma, comes forward with the following claim : *Quicunque vult salvus esse, ante omnia opus est, ut teneat catholicam fidem, quam nisi quisque integram inviolatamque servaverit, absque dubio in aeternum peribit.* That goes too far. Such fixation of saving faith in a human theologoumenon which is to that extent always open to attack, has nothing to do with the binding and loosing upon earth with which according to the Gospel (Matt. 16¹⁹, 18¹⁸) there corresponds a being bound or loosed in heaven, because in that way the power to judge, there assigned to the act of obedience involved in apostolic proclamation, is transferred to a formula abstracted from this act, to a sequence of words as such, which as contrasted with the act of obedience mentioned is an instrument with which man masters God, revelation, and faith. We ask : to what extent does this mastery find no place in the Roman Catholic conception of dogmatics and dogma ? No matter ; since according to it dogma is first confessed and proclaimed in part and therefore even dogmatics cannot yet be complete, and since on the other hand it does distinguish between an explicit and an implicit *fides catholica*, even it acknowledges that revelation and saving faith, as contrasted with the law of faith, live their own life which in one way is richer, in another more confined.— On the other hand, we have to remember here the theology of Wilhelm Herrmann. No trait in its construction is more significant than its unwearied fight against the idea of a doctrinal law imposed upon faith. This it is that has given Herrmann's lifework a definitely anti-Catholic impress. In this fight what did he aim at upholding ? The peculiar free life of the Christian subject-matter as against all human findings, all efforts to convert the " on earth " into an " in heaven," all intellectual righteousness by works ? Or solely the mere human claim of a romantic anti-intellectualism, individualism, and a craze for truthfulness ? We must, of course, say that the second is the answer in the foreground, just as the first is the answer in the background. So far as, perhaps, somewhat daringly on purely exegetical grounds, one might say the first, Herrmann's protest will have to be valued as a necessary protest against the *quicunque vult salvus esse*. So far as we must say the second, Protestantism will do well not to identify itself with Herrmann.

But then, neither must we so understand the task of dogmatics regarding proclamation as though it had to prescribe God, revelation, faith to the latter as the content of its preaching. We already saw that what dogmatics can give is not contents but guidance, indications, points of view, basic propositions, and limits, for language correct by human estimate. In this sense it may be called doctrinal law. Yet the very presupposition of it is that preaching gets its contents from a totally different quarter. For that very reason it cannot be Lord and Judge here either. It may, of course, and ought to give counsel in all seriousness, but it neither can nor ought to claim to give orders in the Church.

Here we may apply 2 Cor. 1²⁴ : οὐχ ὅτι κυριεύομεν ὑμῶν τῆς πίστεως, ἀλλὰ συνεργοί ἐσμεν τῆς χαρᾶς ὑμῶν.

Along with the Christian subject-matter itself Church proclamation must also in the last resort remain free, free to receive the behest which it must ever and anon receive from that personal free life of the Christian subject-matter itself. In the Church, it, Church proclamation, and not dogmatics, is in direct touch with God. It must be necessary, and dogmatics only for its sake. By it dogmatics lives, as surely as it lives only in the Church. In it and only so far as God, revelation, faith are its object, in these things, therefore, dogmatics has to seek its raw material.

What Ambrose (*De fide ad Grat.* 1, 5, 42) wrote against a heretical theology, really holds of all theology : *Non in dialectica complacuit Deo salvum facere populum suum. Regnum enim Dei in simplicitate fidei est, non in contentione sermonis.*

7

THE WORD OF GOD IN ITS THREEFOLD FORM

The presupposition which makes proclamation to be proclamation and therewith the Church to be the Church, is the Word of God.   It attests itself in Holy Scripture in the word of the prophets and apostles, to whom it was originally and once for all uttered through God's revelation.

1. THE WORD OF GOD AS PREACHED

We have to speak of the presupposition which makes proclamation proclamation, and therewith the Church the Church.   Indeed from time to time proclamation must become proclamation ; from being an act which, coming forward with the appropriate claim in an atmosphere of appropriate expectation, claims to be and should be proclamation, it must become an act which is proclamation. And because the event of real proclamation is the life-function of the Church which conditions all the rest, we must say that in this same event from time to time the Church herself must become the Church.   Of course proclamation and the Church are also simply and visibly there, exactly as bread and wine at the Lord's Supper are simply and visibly there, or as the distribution, eating, and drinking of bread and wine in the Lord's Supper simply and visibly take place.   But as what they claim to be and should be, as theologically relevant entities, as realities of revelation and faith, they are not simply and visibly there, but as such they have from time to time to come into existence.

The connection with the Lord's Supper is not to be regarded as merely incidental.   What holds of proclamation and the Church in general, cannot be better represented than precisely by the sacrament.   Calvin says of the tree of life in Paradise and of Noah's rainbow : *Non quod arbor praestaret illis immortalitatem . . . aut arcus coercendis aquis foret efficax . . . sed quia notam a verbo Dei insculptam habebant, ut documenta essent testamentorum eius ac sigilla.   Et antea quidem arbor erat arbor, arcus arcus ; ubi inscripta fuerunt verbo Dei, indita est nova forma, ut inciperent esse quod prius non erant (Instit.* IV 14, 18).   And H. Bullinger says of the earthly elements in the sacrament : *Verbo Dei fiunt, quae antea non fuerunt, sacramenta.   Consecrantur enim verbo et sanctificata esse ostenduntur ab eo qui instituit.* Therefore, and to that extent they are called not merely water, bread, and wine, but, without them therefore having altered their nature, the bath of regeneration, the body and blood of the Lord (*Conf. Helv. post.* 1562 *art.* 19, in K. Müller, p. 207, l. 11 f. and 34 f.). It would be very out of place to start back at concepts like *fieri* and *nova forma*, as we find them actually used here by Reformed writers, simply because they of course bring up a problem which cannot be dismissed offhand, that of the Roman Catholic doctrine of the change. Always and everywhere, in sacrament and in preaching and in the whole life of the Church, there is involved the fact that the existence of the earthly body acquires from its heavenly Head a new form, that it becomes the reality of revelation and of faith. Once more it would be out of place to regard it as a Nominalistic weakening of this becoming, when, e.g., Bullinger in the passage quoted so clearly rejects the doctrine of transubstantiation and so resolutely regards the new designation of the elements as just a designation. This designation is indeed not an interpretation arbitrarily imposed upon them, but the *nota a verbo Dei insculpta.* We would only show our failure to understand the meaning of earthly reality acquiring this new *nota* through the Word of God, were we to regard this way of looking at this new becoming as less " realistic " than that expressed in the Catholic doctrine of transubstantiation, or than that in the Lutheran doctrine of consubstantiation.

The presupposition of this actual event is the Word of God. Between this central concept of our prolegomena and of dogmatics generally on the one hand, and the concept of proclamation on the other, lie four decisive connections, whose mutual relation may be compared with that of four concentric circles: these we have now to analyse.

1. The Word of God is the commission upon the givenness of which proclamation must rest, if it is to be real proclamation. The need for proclamation cannot be based objectivistically on the fact that certain real relations and orders of value, immanent in the existence of man and things, craved to be known and disseminated. This craving is to be met not by proclamation but by fundamentally secular science, and there can be no question but that all such relations and orders, which we might think of as possible objects of Church proclamation, belong to the province of secular science and have absolutely no need of being proclaimed through preaching and sacrament. Neither can the need for proclamation be based subjectivistically on the fact that certain personal convictions of certain men pressed for this special articulation. For so far as these convictions are capable of rational presentation, the people in question should be referred once more to the way of scientific exposition—so far as the convictions may be wholly or predominantly of an irrational kind, they should be referred to the possibility of musical, poetical, or artistic expression generally.

Moreover, regarding all such objective or subjective motives—the more so, the more they claim seriousness and intrinsic worth— the question should suggest itself, whether apart from any scientific or artistic presentation whatever, they should not pre-eminently be expressed by a practical moral and political attitude to life appropriate to them. However that may be, we shall lose all insight into the need for proclamation if we recognise motives of such a kind. Of course motives purely of this nature are as necessary a concomitant in the Church as anywhere else, even when it is a question of proclamation. In fact, to put it still more clearly, they are the human motives of all so-called proclamation, and other than these human motives we cannot intrinsically have at all. It is not the case that we have power to reach out beyond them and to grasp and therefore make valid a higher motive, which is the necessary basis and so the realisation of the proclamation in question. What higher thing did we wish to make valid than real relations and orders of value on the one hand, and convictions on the other ? It is precisely the fact that it is impossible to point out and to validate any higher motive than this, and that means the need for Church proclamation and so proclamation which is real proclamation, it is precisely this that we acknowledge and confirm when we designate the commission from which we derive it as the Word of God. Certainly even so we speak implicitly, objectivistically of a real relation and an order of value, subjectivistically of a personal conviction. This human motivation is the medium above which we can as little raise ourselves as get rid of our shadows, above which we ought not to claim to raise ourselves either, because this medium is the point at which we have to expect the divine commission. God's Word signifies in this connection God's positive behest. God's positive behest ; and therefore a motive which, acting according to its own utterly superior principle, is present and active although in the midst of the entire inevitable world of human motivations. God's positive behest ; and so a motive which in its very godlikeness is not present and active in the way in which real relations and orders of value are present and active over us and convictions likewise in us, a motive which we cannot validate because we cannot grasp at it, but which is there and is active when and where it wills to be there and to be active. No proclamation but also depends upon such present human motives calling for validation. But no proclamation is real proclamation, so far as it does not also and beyond all that rest upon the commission, a commission we cannot take unto ourselves or take for granted in any way, which we can simply just receive and possess in the act of reception, which simply touches, elevates, and defines us and the entire world of our motivations from without, as a behest that comes to us in an unforeseen way, to which as we said earlier we can only take up an attitude by repeating it so far as we think we have heard it, and seeking to conform to it as well or ill as we can. Real proclamation thus means the Word of God preached, and the Word of God preached means, in this first and outmost circle, man's language about God on the basis of an indication by God Himself fundamentally transcending all human causation, and so devoid of all human basis, merely occurring as a fact and requiring to be acknowledged.

" So say ye now, ' whom God hath sent.' That is : God's Word is not named, for it is sent. That is : let none think that God's Word cometh to earth of man's device. If it is to be God's Word, it must be sent. Otherwise it is impossible that Holy Writ could be understood and expounded by any arbitrary device. It availeth not that one should speak and he not called, for God's Word cometh alone because God sendeth it. Where not, the whole world cannot utter that which could redeem from sins and comfort consciences. If He had not sent the Word and the office, we had had nought. Therefore we should neither utter nor hear aught, save the Word of God alone. Is it invented by man's choice and device, avoid it. It cometh not except it be sent from heaven. And let him that goeth about with the monks ask whether their thing be likewise God's Word. Then wilt thou hear that they give out, it is done of good intent to honour God. Hence 'tis thus a service to God and God's Word. But there is more to it than good intent, that one doeth God's service and payeth for sin. From thy heart floweth the device, the opinion. But say thou whether God hath sent it from heaven, also whether He hath commanded it. Yea, is it done for God's honour ? Therefore is it the wickeder and a twofold blasphemy that thou callest that God's Word and a service to God, which thou thyself hast invented. Therefore hath the Pope under the name and title of the Church led the world astray. But without God's sending cometh no Word into the world. Hath it grown out of my heart, cling I to Chrysostom, Augustine, and Ambrose, still 'tis not God's Word. For 'tis a vast difference 'twixt the Word that is sent from heaven and that which of my own choice and device I invent. As for Holy Writ, so it be grown on earth, thus saith John : He that is of the earth speaketh of earthly things. Therefore must we learn to base our blessedness soundly upon the power of God's Word and not upon our device or opinion " (Luther, *Ausl. des* 3 *und* 4 *Kap. Joh.* 1538 f. W. edn. 47, p. 193, l. 10).

2. The Word of God is the object which as such must be given to proclamation, in order that it may be real proclamation. Proclamation is asked how far it is proclamation about something, a relevant assertion or proclamation of a real object. Once more we assert that so far as this object is supposed to belong to the

province of objects of human apprehension and thought, to the province of objects of outer or inner perception, it is hard to see to what extent it would have to be proclaimed by preaching and sacrament particularly. Would not scientific, artistic statement, or even statement and publication in terms of political ethics, be incomparably more suited to objects of this class? Once more, of course, we must admit that we have no other objects save those of our outer or inner perception. Even of the object of proclamation it must be said, therefore, that if we have it at all as an object, then we shall also have it always as the object of outward or inward perception, as the object of experience and thought. If we did not have it in this way, we would not have it at all. But so far as we have it only in this way, we certainly do not have it as a possible object of proclamation. In that case metaphysics or psychology might, indeed would have to, take control of it. The same sciences which could not get control of a single object that was worth the trouble of proclaiming! By designating the object of proclamation the W o r d o f G o d, we mean that it is not only and not primarily the object of human perception. It must become the object of human perception if it is to be capable of being proclaimed. But so far as it is really proclaimed, it completely ceases to be the object of human perception. It is proclaimed so far as it presents and places itself for us and for the whole world as the object over against all our objects : certainly in the inevitable medium of perceptual objectivity, but in this medium as the object which we can in no wise get hold of, to which we can never point back as to something given, which is a presupposition as and only as it personally plants itself in a place where we are completely unable to plant it. In that way we have it, if we have it at all. We have it because it gives itself. Thus it is the object of proclamation in a different way from all possible objects of metaphysics or psychology. Between this object, and preaching and sacrament as the means of stating and imparting it, there should exist an inner connection. Preaching and sacrament are, as we saw, the promise of future revelation on the basis of revelation that has already taken place. How ought this object to be spoken of otherwise than in the form of such promise, a form that is distinct from science, art, and politics ? Real proclamation thus means God's Word preached, and God's Word preached means, in this second circle, man's language about God on the basis of God's self-objectifiation which is neither present nor predictable nor relatable to any design, but is real solely in the freedom of His grace, in virtue of which from time to time He wills to be the object of this language, and is so according to His own good pleasure.

Excellent delimitations on this point in H. M. Müller, *Glaube und Erfahrung bei Luther*, 1929 : " The concrete, contingent way in which faith becomes given, and to that extent the gift itself, is still only announceable in the proclamation of the Gospel, it is still an announcement " (p. 95). " As the mediation of the promise, preaching is distinctly not the handing down of revelation, but it is an indication that revelation is taking place " (p. 119 cf. also pp. 41, 149, 150, 162, 196, etc.).

3. The Word of God is the judgment in virtue of which proclamation can alone become real proclamation. True, proclamation is also asked whether it is true after all. What is to decide that ? What is the criterion here ? As a rule the truth of human language is to be judged partly by the nature of its object, partly also by the situation and desire of the speaker. Naturally this may and must also be the case with Church proclamation. It belongs to the sphere of human language : the proclaimer must submit to the questions, What do you know of the thing you speak of ? and, What interest do you represent in making this particular assertion ? He must and will submit his action to judgment by means of these questions. Only that, as proclamation, it is not touched by precisely all judgments thus brought to bear. But then it is its scientific or moral and political or æsthetic character that is here being judged. Proclamation as such, as it takes place in preaching and sacrament, presupposes that neither the nature of the object nor the situation or desire of the speaker are or can become so clear to any man as to put him in the position of making a judgment as to its truth. If there is judgment at all of Church proclamation as such, it must be formed from a different point of view. We mean and signify precisely this fundamentally different point of view of the judgment upon proclamation as such when we acknowledge it to be the Word of God. In so doing we do not deny that proclamation is also exposed to other criteria : that is really our confirmation of the fact that actually we only know these other criteria when we pass judgment upon them, i.e. at the actual moment ; that we therefore are not in a position to pronounce upon their truth in any other way. But even at this actual moment we cannot but (1) recollect that one criterion different from these others has given itself to our knowledge without it having been known to any one, and (2) expect that this criterion which at present we really do not know, or know only through that recollection, will

give itself again to our knowledge in the future. This recollected and expected criterion, which is not at the disposal of our or any actual moment, is the Word of God. This criterion we cannot handle. It is the criterion which handles itself, and apart from that is in no man's hands. The other criteria we can handle by recollecting and expecting this criterion. But only its own judgment holds as absolutely binding and inviolable. Proclamation becomes real proclamation when it is approved by this judgment. Real proclamation, therefore, means the Word of God proclaimed, and the Word of God proclaimed now means, in this third inner circle, man's language about God which, according to God's own judgment which cannot be anticipated and never passes into our control, and in view of the object proclaimed as well as of the subject proclaiming, is true language and therefore language to be listened to, language which rightly demands obedience.

4. Finally, the Word of God—and here at last we utter the decisive word—is the event itself, in which proclamation becomes real proclamation. Therefore, not only the commission which man must have received, not only the object which must take the centre over against human language, not only the judgment by which it must be established as true. Even from all these points of view the realisation of proclamation might be regarded as a merely external, accidental characteristic, a sort of vesture or illumination of an event, which as such still remained exclusively the event of the will and execution of the man proclaiming. That, of course, would involve an ill understanding of the significance of the "garment" and the "light" here in question, of the meaning of proclamation becoming real because God commands, God takes the centre, God gives judgment. But who would not continually misunderstand the subject here? Understanding of the subject in this proposition would, of course, necessarily render impossible all nominalist misunderstandings about the predicate. But it is deeply rooted in the nature of the case that here nominalist misunderstanding is not to be eradicated unambiguously or finally. It is the miracle of revelation and of faith when this misunderstanding does not recur every now and then, when, therefore, proclamation to us is not a human volition and execution qualified in some way, but also and primarily and decisively God's own act, when for us man's language about God is not only man's language, but also and primarily and decisively God's own language. It is this miracle that here, in the fourth and most circumscribed circle

of our deliberations, we have not so much to explain as rather to evaluate as this special miracle. " Not only—but also and primarily and decisively," so the formula must run. With the phrase " not only—but also " we primarily concede that even human language with its motives and objects and the judgments, among which as human language it stands, is there, because God's Word is there. The miracle of real proclamation does not consist in the volition and execution of the man proclaiming, with their completely conditioned state and in their utterly problematic nature, coming to be omitted, in a vanishing trick taking place somewhere in the reality of nature and a gap being thus created and somehow naked divine truth, scarcely hidden by a mere remnant of an appearance of human reality, entering into the gap.

The decisive sentence in the Roman Catholic doctrine of the change is to the effect that by the priest's act of consecration a *conversio totius substantiae panis in substantiam corporis Christi Domini nostri et totius substantiae vini in substantiam sanguinis eius* takes place (*Trid. sess. XIII, Decr. de ss. Euch.* cap. 4), and in such a way that only the *accidentia* of bread and wine *sine subjecto* are left over (*ib. can.* 2 and *Conc. Constantiense,* 1415 *Errores Joannis Wicleff* 2, *Denz. Nr.* 582).

The volition and execution of the man proclaiming is, however, by no means omitted in real proclamation. As Christ became true man and also remains true man to all eternity, so real proclamation becomes an event on the level of all other human events. It can be seen and heard on this level, and this being seen and heard, moreover, cannot be a mere appearance, but must happen in all essentiality. Without the ambiguity, the liability to misunderstanding and attack amid which it takes place, in which it is itself an event among a number of other events, it too could not be real proclamation. But as Christ is not only true man, it is not only the volition and execution of the man proclaiming. It is also and it is primarily and decisively the divine volition and execution. For that very reason the human element need not be omitted. The question here, apparently such a burning one, as to the mode of the operation of the two factors, side by side and together, is a highly irrelevant one. God and the human element are not two factors operating side by side and together. The human element is the thing created by God. Only in the state of disobedience is it a factor over against God. In the case of obedience it is the service of God. Between God and the true service of God there can be no rivalry. The service of God need not be omitted in order that God Himself may come to honour in it. Where God is really served, there—without omission of the human element, rather with the full, essential presence and activity of the human element in its entire humanity—the volition and execution of God are also in the centre, not only in co-operation as a first or second factor, but in the centre as the first and decisive element, as indeed befits God the Creator and Lord. Without depriving the human side of its freedom, its earthly substance, its humanity, without dissolving the human subject or turning its action into a mechanical event, God is the subject from whom the human action must acquire its new, true name. Its true name ! Therefore, not just a title pasted on : no, the name which accrues to it, in virtue of the complete superiority of the will of its Creator and Lord, as essentially, as primarily as possible. Where Church proclamation takes place according to this will of God, where it rests upon God's commission, where God Himself gives Himself to it as its object, where it is true according to His judgment, where, in short, it is the true service of God, there on the one hand its character as an event visible and audible on earth is not set aside.

Bread remains bread, wine remains wine, we should have to say, in the language of the doctrine of the Lord's Supper. The realism of sacramental consecration does not destroy the proper existence of the signs !

But, on the other hand, through the new robe of righteousness thrown over it, it becomes in this its earthly character a fresh event, the event of God speaking Himself in the sphere of human events, the event of Jesus Christ's vicariate plenipotentiary. Real proclamation as this new event, in which the event of human language about God is not set aside, but rather exalted, is the Word of God. Therefore, real preaching means once more the Word of God preached. Only now can it be clear that " preached " belongs to the predicate and how far it belongs there. The Word of God preached now means, in this fourth and innermost circle, man's language about God, in which and through which God Himself speaks about Himself.

Adolf v. Harnack in a fine essay (*Christus praesens—Vicarius Christi, Sitz.-Berichte der preuss. Akad. d. Wiss.* 1927 p. 415 f.) has shown how one might get and actually did get from the concept of the " Word of God " to the " admission of the Church into the high equations of theology " (God, Christ, Spirit, etc.) right down to the doctrine of the infallibility of the Roman Pope. In fact we are faced here, not only with the problem of the Roman Catholic doctrine of the change, but also with the problem of the Roman Catholic idea of all that is to be comprised in the concept of Church *potestas*.

In itself it might quite possibly be in line with our concept of the " Word of God preached," when Gregory of Nyssa (for the matter of that, likewise on the analogy of the new character taken on by the elements in the sacrament) says of the priest, that he who yesterday was one of the many, one from among the people, has now become, in virtue of his consecration as a priest a καθηγεμών, πρόεδρος, διδάσκαλος εὐσεβείας, μυστηρίων λανθανόντων μυσταγωγός (*Or. in diem luminum*). Or when Ambrose explains to the neophytes with regard to the Christian priest : *Vidisti illic levitam, vidisti summum sacerdotem. Noli considerare corporum figuras, sed mysteriorum gratiam . . . Quid tradiderit considera!* (*De myst.* 2, 6). *Non merita personarum consideres, sed officia sacerdotum* (*ib.* 5, 27). Or when Augustine, with special regard to the Church preacher, insists that : *Boni fideles non quemlibet hominum, sed ipsum Dominum obedienter audiunt*—the *locus superior sedis ecclesiasticae*, from which that utterance comes, forces of itself, he says, even the speaker, who perhaps is personally the very reverse of good, into good utterance (*De doctr. christ.* IV 27). Or when in these words he describes the earthly articulation of the voice of God : *quod creaturae motus expressit eam, serviens aeternae voluntati tuae ipse temporalis* (*Conf.* XI 6, 8). Or when he says of the *doctrina de superiore loco in conspectu omnium personante*, that it signifies from time to time the decision regarding the hearers, that *et qui faciunt audiant ad praemium et qui non faciunt audiant ad judicium* (*De civ. Dei*, II 28).

This perfectly plain designation of the function of Church proclamation is in itself also thoroughly familiar to the Reformers : " Now I and any man who speaketh Christ's Word may freely boast that his mouth is Christ's mouth. I am certain that my word is not mine but Christ's Word, therefore my mouth must also be His whose Word it speaketh " (Luther, *Eine treue Vermahnung*, 1522 W. edn. 8, p. 683, l. 13). " Hereby are all men upon earth subject to the preacher's office, as the apostles and their successors led on God's behalf, so that they must be submissive to the same and follow it, if they would otherwise have God's grace and be blest " (*Sermon on John* 16⁵ᶠ·, 1533 E. edn. 3, p. 434). " That is a power compared with which that of Emperor and King is naught, that an apostle, yea every disciple of Christ, may pronounce a judgment upon the whole world, that sin ought to go. And such judgment should be as potent and certain as though Christ Himself had uttered it " (*Sermon on John* 20¹⁹⁻³¹, 1533 W. edn. 52, p. 269, l. 18). " 'Tis a right excellent thing, that every honest pastor's and preacher's mouth is Christ's mouth, and his word and forgiveness is Christ's word and forgiveness. If thou hast sin and dost confess the same and believest in Christ, the pastor and preacher shall forgive thee that same sin in Christ's place, and the words which he saith to thee on God's behalf thou shalt receive, as if Christ Himself had said them unto thee. Therefore, we do well to call the pastor's and preacher's word which he preacheth, God's Word. For the office is not the pastor's or preacher's, but God's ; and the Word which he preacheth is likewise not the pastor's and preacher's, but God's " (Sermon on the same text, 1534 E. edn. 3, p. 376). " On the last day God will say to me, Hast thou also preached that ? I shall say, Yea, exactly. Then God will say to thee, Hast thou also heard that ? and thou shalt answer, Yea. And He saith further, Wherefore hast thou then not believed ? And then thou sayest, Oh, I held it for a word of man, since a poor chaplain or village parson uttered it. So shall the same word which sticketh in thine heart accuse thee and be thine accuser and judge at the last day. For it is God's Word, 'tis God

Himself thou hast heard, as Christ saith, ' He that heareth you heareth me ';
and I have sufficiently done mine office for the tribunal and presence of God,
in that I have shewn up thy sins and offences and chastised thee therefor,
and am pure of thy blood.   See thou then to it, how thou standest " (*Exposition of John* 3–4, W. edn. 47, p. 120, l. 28).   Hence might I be glad and say,
God who hath created heaven and earth, whose is the majesty divine, hath
spoken with me.   How ?   Through my brother man.   He doth it to us for
good, namely, for love and friendship.   But when one regardeth a preacher,
one reflects, This is a poor wretched man, and none considereth that beneath
lieth the majesty divine.   An angel might make the heavens full of fire which
hurleth lightning and thunder into it, and the heavens and earth turn black,
and everything collapseth.   Why then wilt thou not hear God, who putteth
Himself like a weak man, who hideth Himself and holdeth Himself equal to
the dear apostles ?   Therefore, it is not a preacher's word, but God's Word.
So long as it is God's Word thou shalt be beside thyself thereat, or glad "
(*ib.* p. 213, l. 26).   " If thou hear me who am a preacher, and hear me none
otherwise than thou hearest another man, and likewise believe my words
none otherwise than other men's word, thou art condemned along with me.
. . . Therefore thou shouldest not hear me as a man who preacheth man's
word.   If then thou hear me thus, 'twere much better thou heardest me not
at all.   Thus, too, thy pastor shouldest thou not hear as a man who speaketh
and preacheth man's word, but shouldest hear him as Him who speaketh the
word out of the mouth of babes and sucklings . . ." (Sermon delivered in
Merseburg, 1545 W. edn. 51, p. 15, ll. 30 and 36.)   *Repraesentant Christi
personam propter vocationem ecclesiae, non repraesentant proprias personas ut
testatur Christus : Qui vos audit, me audit.   Cum verbum Christi, cum sacramenta porrigunt, Christi vice et loco porrigunt* (Melanchthon, *Apol., De
ecclesia, C.R.* 27, 529).   But Calvin, too, explains most emphatically, that
certainly God is not bound to man's word about Him, and He is able to draw
His own to Him in any direct way.   But it has obviously pleased Him to let
us ripen into the manhood of Christ *educatione ecclesiae*, and therefore, without
ceasing to rule Himself and alone in His Church, without yielding His right
and His honour to a man, to avail Himself of man's word as a *vicaria opera*.
And now it holds, he says, of Christian preaching : *Deus ipse in medium prodit,
et quatenus huius ordinis autor est, vult se praesentem in sua institutione agnosci*.
There the point is to prove that man in practice can become a temple of God.
It is further a decisive test of our humility towards God that we learned to
render obedience to His Word not as one spoken directly from heaven, but
just as it meets us, in the mouth of a *homuncio quispiam ex pulvere emersus*,
who is in no relation better than ourselves.   And, finally, it is the strongest
bond of the love among us in which God wishes to bind us, that in preaching
He puts His Word in the mouth of a fellow-man and thereby forbids us to
seek to satisfy ourselves (*Sermon on Luke* 1[16 f.] *C.R.* 46, 39 ; *Instit.* IV 1, 5
and 3, 1 ; cf. E. Brunner, *Gott und Mensch*, 1930 p. 65).   The relation between
the ordinance that in proclamation *homines* are to be instructed *per homines*
and Christian *charitas*, was for that matter already a thought of Augustine's
(*De doctr. christ., Prol.* 6).

If we start with this concept of the Word of God preached, the well-known
distinction of the Bishop's office, as first represented especially by Ignatius
of Antioch, then by Irenaeus, Tertullian, and Cyprian, may likewise
not be designated impossible in itself.   We can neither estimate properly
the Catholic position nor relate the proper evangelical position, if with Harnack

(*op. cit.* p. 446) we begin by taking exception to the thought of the vicariate or succession in itself. To deny the *vicarius Christi* on principle would necessarily involve a denial of the *Christus praesens*. The dissent between Roman Catholic dogmatics and us, which, of course, we must always keep in view here, cannot touch the fact of this vicariate or succession, but only the manner of it. The following three questions should be decisive here : 1. How does a man become *vicarius Christi*, meaning *successor Petri* ? According to Roman Catholic doctrine he becomes so because of his place at the foot of a list of bishops which goes back without a break to an apostle, lastly to Peter, and last of all to Christ, the Founder of the Church. We ask how this profane, i.e. partly historical, partly juridical fact of such a list comes to ensure the regularity of the Church office ? What could documentary succession have to do with real, that is to say, spiritual succession ? 2. How does this vicariate (or succession) arise ? According to Roman Catholic doctrine it consists in a character which the Bishop or priest receives for life, in addition to his human existence, through his ordination. We ask : In what sense a character for life, if otherwise ordination can claim to affect only the official acts of the person consecrated, and even in connection with these acts cannot claim to mean more than the proclamation of a promise ? 3. In what does this vicariate (or succession) consist ? According to Roman Catholic doctrine, in an authority, permanently peculiar to the Church office, to draw up and to publish unalterable definitions in matters of faith and morals. We ask : To what extent can the exercise of such an authority to speak infallibly, permanently peculiar to such a human agency, still be regarded as service to God ? To what extent have we still to deal with a representation here, and not rather with a replacement of Christ ? All three questions summarised : Is not the vicariate in the Roman Catholic sense a thing in which only the accidents of the vicariate are retained, while in substance it is simply the rule of Christ become identical with the rule of the Church ? We realise that this whole doctrine is a truly significant attempt to come to terms with the problem of real proclamation. But does not this solution mean that proclamation (through the ideas of the historical succession, the *character indelibilis*, and the possibility of unalterable definitions) is dehumanised, i.e. drawn into a sphere in which it is only in appearance that it can signify a humanly assailable, responsible, surpassable, and therefore serviceable action ? It was certainly logical, but it is still a fact we face with discomposure, that on his consecration Innocent III preached simply—about himself (Harnack, *op. cit.* p. 441). Even Roman Catholic dogmatics is naturally aware that the Lordship of Christ is a lordship not only in His Church but over His Church. But where in this system can this lordship of Christ over His Church become concrete, where can it get proper play, when a complete transfer of all its power to the Church has already taken place, when its power in the Church is simply there ? And if it has no proper play, is it distinguished otherwise than merely by name from the power exercised in the Church by men without break, let, or limit ? Certainly a Catholic could approve of Luther's interpretation of the picture of the good shepherd in John 10 : " Thus he seeks the right shepherd's office, which is to help the control of consciences and souls, alone in His own person, when He who alone hath done and accomplished it, the work of our salvation, laid down His body and life for His sheep and founded the office, plies and maintains it, and thereby He brings them to Himself, rules and sustains them. And so in this office the whole preaching of the evangel includes, where and when and by whom it is preached, which after Christ are also called shepherds, not for their person's sake (for such can no one be, save Christ Himself) but because they are in the office which is proper to Christ alone, and He exercises it through them and works in the same " (*Crucigers Sommerpostille*, 1543 W. edn. 21, p. 323, l. 3). But on the question as to what " person " here means, the ways inexorably separate. In the evangelical view we can no longer speak of an action of the Person of Christ in and over His Church, where their humanity is taken from human authorities in the Church in the way mentioned, and where, on the other hand, Christ's own decision has vanished in the decision of these human authorities. That which can in the way described be part of the establishment, property, powers, and dignity of other persons, in the same proportion ceases to be an active person. A personal lordship must be a free lordship. A personal presence must be such that along with it there is the possibility of absence. A personal gift must be faced with the possibility of its refusal. And precisely this limitation of Church powers by the Person of Christ must prove the Church to be the true Church, serving Christ and for that reason also participating in the benefit of His lordship, of His presence and gift. But it is just this limitation that is excluded by the doctrine of the historical succession, of the *character indelibilis* and of the possibility of infallible definitions. Therefore, we must reject this doctrine. Luther continues in the sermon just quoted : " Therefore 'tis the same also in this spiritual control of conscience, where Christ doth not through His shepherd's office Himself guard, lead, and guide, there no other preaching helpeth or availeth aught, no matter if it be otherwise good and correct. For it cannot stand in straits against the devil when he gapes his gleaming vengeance through fear of sins and eternal death. For if it cometh to that, the poor sheep standeth alone and forsaken, all by itself ; and its act, directed by the doctrine of the law and our work, hath neither help nor stay more, with which to comfort itself and find rescue " (*ib.* p. 324, l. 17) ; and in a later sermon on the same text he is still more belligerent " But that such preaching, rightly used, may be useful and good, it must not itself enter the sheepfold like the other, nor imagine itself to be a shepherd. But only the doorkeepers and servants of the true Herd, Christ, who keep the sheep in watch and ward, that naught strange break in on them. And they make way for the Herd and give place to Him, who Himself leadeth them out and in to pasture. Therefore let such office be ordered, not to point to self, but to open to the Herd, that the sheep may hear Himself and be pastured by Him " (*ib.* p. 501, l. 8). In the Confession of the Synod of Strassburg of 1533 (contributed to the *Reformierten Kirchenzeitung*, 1931 No. 27, p. 211) we read in Article 6 : " Faith cometh of hearing. Yet neither is the planter aught nor the waterer, but God who giveth the increase is all. But in that way must there be detriment to divine grace and work if to the words and actions of evangelical preaching and sacraments they would attach somewhat of power to purify us of sin, which power they have in themselves, be they but preached and enacted by men, while those to whom they impart the Word and Sacrament may believe as they please. . . ." And once more Calvin has well said what must be said about the evangelical comprehension of the relation, which excludes any sort of *opus operatum*, between God and man in ecclesiastical office. *Et certe quum nobis constet Dei negotium hic nos et curare et agere, ipsum sibi operique suo minime defuturum confidimus. Caeterum qualiscunque exitus erit, nunquam nos coepisse, aut huc usque progressos esse poenitebit. Nobis spiritus sanctus doctrinae nostrae fidelis est ac certus testis.*

Scimus, inquam, esse aeternam Dei veritatem quam praedicamus. Ministerium nostrum ut mundo sit salutare, optamus quidem, sicuti par est : verum ut id consequamur, Dei est praestare, non nostrum (Suppl. Exhort. 1543 *C.R.* 6, 534). But we might also summarise our objection to the Roman Catholic doctrine in the indication given to the preacher by the greatest Catholic theologian, Augustine : *Oret, ut Dominus sermonem bonum det in os eius (De doctr. christ.* IV 15). What does it mean if this *oret* is taken not merely as an æsthetic and homiletic suggestion, but seriously in its material contents, more strictly than it needed to be taken even in Augustine's own opinion ? Must we really pray for the *sermo bonus* ? Can we only pray for it ? Does the act of Christ, real proclamation, the Word of God preached, belong to the Church office and therefore to man's act, or, on the contrary, as we should conclude from this *oret*, are office and act bound to the act of Christ, to the realisation of proclamation introduced by God's initiative, to the Word of God preached ? This question, from the standpoint of our thesis, is the puzzling cleft which has run right through the Church for four hundred years.

2. THE WRITTEN WORD OF GOD

We said that Church proclamation must be ventured upon in recollection of past, and in expectation of future revelation. The ground of the expectation is thus obviously identical with the object of recollection. We speak—hoping for what we cannot see, for what we cannot assume to be present—of a realised proclamation, of a Word of God proclaimed in the Church ; on the basis that God's word has already been spoken, that revelation has already taken place. We therefore speak in recollection.

What is the meaning of this recollection of revelation that has already taken place ? Recollection of God's past revelation might mean, first, the actualisation of a revealedness of God, originally immanent in the existence of every man, i.e. of an awareness of God originally proper to every human being. Recollection of God's past revelation would thus be identical with the discovery and fresh appropriation of a long hidden, forgotten, and unused part, and the most central and momentous part at that, of the timeless essential state of man himself, namely, his relationship to the eternal or absolute.

It was in this sense that Augustine understood *memoria*, naturally in definite connection with the Platonic doctrine of anamnesis. *Unde adest, nisi ex memoria ? Nam et cum ab alio commoniti recognoscimus, inde adest. Non enim quasi novum credimus, sed recordantes approbamus hoc esse quod dictum est. Si autem penitus aboleatur ex anima, nec admoniti reminiscimur. Neque enim omni modo adhuc obliti sumus, quod vel iam oblitos nos esse meminimus (Conf.* X 19, 28). God, according to Augustine, is that which we all seek, in that we all seek a *vita beata*. How do we come to wish to be happy, to love this *vita beata* ? Obviously we know it already. *Nimirum habemus*

eam nescio quomodo. . . . Neque enim amaremus eam nisi nossemus (ib. 28, 29).
All actual knowledge about God can, therefore, be but a confirmation of this
thing already known beforehand about God : *Neque enim aliquid de te inveni,
quod non meminissem ex quo didici te.   Nam ex quo didici te, non sum oblitus
tui.   Ubi enim inveni veritatem, ibi inveni Deum meum ipsam veritatem, quam,
ex quo didici, non sum oblitus (ib.* 24, 35).   Much later we have a completely
similar argument, when it is a question of introducing Cartesianism into
theology.   What help would any instruction or indoctrination be, thought
A. Heidan (*Corp. theol. christ.* 1686 Loc. I p. 9), *nisi ex nobis ideam Dei
formare possimus ?*   Not from without (*aliunde*) do we get the *idea Dei*, but
it is *potentia nobis semper inexistens.*   " Recollection " on these lines clearly
means (and Augustine has already expressed that clearly) man's turning
inward, his heartsearching and his homecoming from the dissipation of the
outer world to himself, to find God actually there.   *Sero te amavi, pulchritudo
tam antiqua et tam nova !   Sero te amavi !   Et ecce intus eras et ego foris et ibi
te quaerebam . . . mecum eras et tecum non eram (Conf.* X 27, 28).

Ought the recollection of God's revelation, on the basis of which
Church proclamation is ventured upon, to be t h i s recollection ?
That it cannot possibly be so, will clearly not admit of proof *a priori*.
Why could it not possibly have pleased God to be immanent in
His Church as her foundation, temporarily hidden but peacefully
abiding, because timelessly laid, really to stand upon which need
in that case have been for her only a matter of thorough-going
reflection upon self ?   Why should God not let the Church be founded
upon herself as the Church, in order, by an ever-new return to herself
as the Church—and that precisely would be the recollection of God's
past revelation—to let her ever and anon be founded upon herself
as the Church ?   Why not ?

The Neoplatonist and the Catholic Churchman might obviously exist very
well in personal union in Augustine.   Why should not both have been in the
right ?

If we start from the concept of the divine freedom or power,
no reason can exist why it could not possibly be so.   But such a
reason consists in the fact that God has not made this use of His
freedom or power.   It therefore consists in a fact which points
in a totally different direction.

Here, too, we must proceed in the first place, by a purely exegetical path (by which we are made conscious that it is the exegesis
of Church reality, as it is for evangelical Reform, that we are pursuing) to say that in regard to the Word of God the Church does
not find herself alone, pointed to herself or—which follows—to
self-reflection.   She has not the confidence to appeal, for her
venture of proclamation, to herself as the fountain of the divine
Word.   She seeks the commission, the object, the judgment, the

event, in recollection of which she is accredited in her proclamation and believes herself urged on to her proclamation, not in a hidden depth of her own existence. The homecoming to her own being, on the ground of which alone she actually ventures to proclaim, of course means for her the reversion to her proper being, but to her being which transcends herself, to Jesus Christ her heavenly Head, whom she confronts as His earthly body, bound to Him as such, and yet as such distinct from Him, who possesses the Church in Himself, but not the Church Him in herself, between whom and her there is no reversible, interchangeable relationship, as certainly as the relationship of master and servant is not reversible. He is immanent in her only because He transcends her. That is the fact which makes her recollection of God's past revelation different from one of reflection upon an essential ground timelessly her own : it hath pleased God to be her God, otherwise than in pure immanence.

But this fact needs more accurate description. The distinction between Head and body and His superiority to her is concretely expressed in the fact that over against proclamation in the Church there stands an entity extremely like it as a phenomenon, temporal like it, yet different from it, and in order superior to it. This entity is Holy Scripture. It is the concrete form of the reason why the recollection upon the basis of which we expect God's revelation cannot be recollection of a timeless essence of the Church herself It is the bolt here actually thrust home against the Platonic anamnesis. Simply, in the first place, by being there and telling us what God's past revelation, which we have to recollect, actually is. That is to say, simply, in the first place, because it is the canon.

Κανών means staff, then footrule, regulation, pattern, an appointed area. In the Church usage of the first three centuries the name was given to what was fixed in the Church as authoritative, i.e. as apostolic, the *regula fidei*, i.e. the norm of faith, in the sense of the Church doctrine of faith. From this (but only apparently) wider idea of the κανὼν τῆς ἀληθείας or τῆς πίστεως there has developed since the 4th century the more special one of the Canon of Holy Scripture, i.e. the list of the books in the Bible recognised in the Church as authoritative, because recognised as apostolic.

By recognising the existence of a canon, the Church declares that particularly in her proclamation she is aware of not being left alone, that the commission on the basis of which she proclaims, the object which she proclaims, the judgment to which her proclamation is liable, the nature of real proclamation as an event must

8

come from another source, from without, and concretely from without, in the complete externality of her concrete canon—as an imperative, categorical yet utterly historical, becoming articulate in time. And by acknowledging that this canon is actually identical with the Bible of the Old and New Testaments, with the Word of the prophets and apostles, she declares that this connection of her proclamation with something concrete and external is not a general principle or a mere determination of form, the content of which might be this or even a totally different one, but that this connection is completely determined in content, that it is an order received, an obligation imposed, that this bit of past happening composed of definite texts is her directions for work, her marching orders, with which not only her preaching but she herself stands or falls, which, therefore, cannot under any circumstances, even hypothetically, be thought away or under any circumstances, even hypothetically, be thought of as replaced by others, unless we mean to think away proclamation and the Church herself.

To make matters clearer, note what was just called the phenomenal similarity between Church proclamation and the second element contrasted with it in the Church, the canon of Holy Scripture. It consists in the fact that obviously even in Holy Scripture we are dealing with Scripture not in a primary but in a secondary sense : for it itself is the deposit of proclamation made in the past by the mouth of man. But even in its form as Scripture it claims to be not so much an historical monument as rather a Church document, proclamation in writing. Thus primarily both entities stand side by side within one genus ; there Scripture as the beginning, here the preaching to be carried out to-day, as the continuation of one and the same event ; Jeremiah and Paul at the beginning, the preacher of the Gospel to-day at the end of one and the same series.

Luther was well aware of this connection. On the one hand : " Gospel means nought else than a preaching and crying of the grace and compassion of God, gained and acquired through the Lord Christ by His death. And it is really not what stands in books and is composed of letters, but more an oral preaching and living word, and a voice that resounds there into the entire world and is publicly cried abroad, so that it may be generally heard " (*Ep. S. Petri gepredigt und ausgelegt*, 1523 W. edn. 12, p. 259, l. 8). On the other hand : " For we have John the Baptist's word and spirit, and we parsons and preachers are to our time what John the Baptist was to his time. We let John the Baptist's finger point and his voice ring forth : ' Behold the Lamb of God, that taketh away the sin of the world ' ; we carry on John the Baptist's preaching, point to Christ and say : That is the proper, only Saviour, whom ye should worship, on whom ye must depend. Such preaching must abide until the last day, even though it abide not in all places, all the time, alike, yet must it abide " (*Pred. über Matth.* 11²⁽· 1533 E. Edn. 1, p. 159).

In this same phenomenal likeness is next to be found also the unlikeness in order between Holy Scripture and proclamation to-day, the superiority, the purely constitutive significance of the former for the latter, the restrictedness of the reality of proclamation to-day by its foundation upon Holy Scripture and by its obligations to it—therefore, the fundamental distinction of the written word of the prophets and apostles above all other human words spoken later in the Church and needing to be spoken to-day. If what we said was correct, that the Church in regard to her preaching does not see herself alone, but finds herself in a concrete confrontation in which she recalls the past revelation of God ; and if the concrete form of her opposite is really the Biblical word of prophets and apostles, then compared with the former the latter must possess a fundamental distinction of its own. If the vicariate of Church proclamation is genuine, i.e. if the Church in her proclamation is not secretly founded upon herself, but upon the other who is her Lord, without her becoming His Lord, then the concrete form of the vicariate must be s u c c e s s i o n.

Even this concept from the Roman Catholic definition of the Church's office cannot therefore in itself be taken exception to. The series God, Christ, apostle, bishop, congregation, as seen in Church literature at the beginning of the 2nd century (e.g. *Clem. Rom. ad Cor.* 42, 44), the criterion almost formally applied, especially by I r e n æ u s, that the Church exists where the *traditio* or *successio apostolorum* exists (e.g. *C.o. haer.* III 2, 2 ; 3, 1 ; 4, 1 ; IV 26, 2, 5 ; 33, 8 ; V 20), but also the attack on the heretics from the point of view of an inquiry into their relation to the apostolic origin of the Church—*Edant ergo origines ecclesiarum suarum, evolvant ordinem episcoporum suorum ita per successionem ab initio decurrentem, ut primus ille episcopus aliquem ex apostolis . . . habuerit auctorem et antecessorem . . . exhibent quos ab apostolis in episcopatum constitutos apostolici seminis traduces habeant* (Tertullian, *De praescr. haer.* 32).—All this may in itself be fairly justified as expressing awareness of the concreteness of the form in which Christ and His Church are combined and yet contrasted : namely, that a p o s t o l i c i t y is in fact one of the decisive marks of the true Church (*credo unam sanctam catholicam et apostolicam ecclesiam*) and because of its direct connection with the superior character of what is Christian, the decisive mark of true Church proclamation. So too with her Scripture principle the evangelical Church too asserts and confesses : " Now when He says, Ye also shall bear witness, for ye have been with me from the beginning, He thereby specially placards the apostles for all preachers, and therefore so establishes their preaching that all the world should be bound to their word, and believe the same without any contradiction, and be certain that all they teach and preach is the proper doctrine and the Holy Ghost's preaching, which they have heard and received from Himself. As 1 John 1 adduces such witness, and says : " That which we have heard, that which we have seen with our eyes, that which we have beheld," etc. " of the Word of life, that declare we unto you." Such witness have no preachers on earth save the apostles alone, For the others are hereby commanded that they should all follow in the apostles' footsteps, abide by the same doctrine, and teach nothing more nor otherwise. And accordingly the proper sign is likewise indicated by which we should know and test such preaching of the Holy Spirit, for He says, " The Holy Spirit shall testify of me," etc. (Luther, *Crucigers Sommerpostille*, W. edn. 21, p. 426, l. 2). Thus the difference between the evangelical and the Catholic view consists here too not in the matter of the That but in the matter of the How. And even in the matter of the How no protest in principle can be raised on our part either against the summation of the apostolate in Peter, nor yet against the possibility of a primacy in the Church, which in that case might very well be that of the Roman community. The protest of Protestantism in the question of succession is directed singly and solely against the fact that *Tu es Petrus*, etc., is mechanically taken over the head of the first Peter to every succeeding Roman bishop as the second, third, and hundredth Peter, as if the succession and tradition of the Peter of Matt. 16, to whom flesh and blood did not reveal any such thing, could be other than pneumatic, or as if being pneumatic it could be tied down to the profane fact of such a list of bishops. " The visibility of the Church and the fixity bound up with it here demand a Church ordination, beginning with Christ the starting-point and continuing in un-broken succession, so that just as the apostles were sent by the Saviour, so they instituted bishops after them, these in their turn gave themselves suc-cessors, and so on until our own day. Principally by this episcopal succession, which started with the Saviour and continued without a break, as by an outward sign, it is recognised which is the true Church founded by Him " (J. A. Möhler, *Symbolik*, 3rd edn. 1834 p. 396). It is to that, that we can only say No. *Est enim ecclesia coetus non alligatus ad ordinariam successionem, sed ad verbum Dei. Ibi renascitur ecclesia, ubi Deus restituit doctrinam et dat Spiritum sanctum* (Melanchthon, *De ecclesia et de auctoritate verbi Dei*, 1539 *C.R.* 22, 598). And the ground of this protest is that under these circum-stances apostolicity, from being a divine gift and a human task, is bound to become an assured human possession, that, " principally " in a mechanically historical or juridical sense, it must cease to be the norm which confronts the Church as a pointer and a guide, and instead is completely fallen under the *judicium ecclesiae*, as to the disposal of the second, third, or hundredth Peter. Pneumatic Succession obviously implies that the *successor* is pneumatically identical with the *antecessor* but certainly not mechanically, and therefore in such a way that the *antecessor* is left with a field of operation of his own as contrasted with the *successor*. But such a field was assuredly not given to the first Peter in the Roman Catholic system, but here the *antecessor* is taken up and absorbed in the *successor* : in fact it is being the guard over Peter's grave that is here to constitute the apostolicity of proclamation. Because of this presupposition Peter, the apostolate, and Holy Scripture cease to be a free power in the Church and over against the Church, because on this pre-supposition the Church is once more left to herself, pointed to herself, and so to reflection upon herself, we cannot approve of the Roman Catholic concept of succession. Nor yet, in fact least of all in the form (to be characterised theologically, whether from the Catholic or from the evangelical point of view, as dilettante) in which it is set forth and represented by Friedrich

Heiler, *Im Ringen um die Kirche*, 1931 p. 479 (cf. esp. the " four grounds," p. 506 f.).

The apostolic succession of the Church must mean that she is guided by the canon, i.e. by the word of prophets and apostles as by the necessary rule of all expression valid in the Church—that she enters upon the succession of the prophets and apostles in their office of proclamation, and that in such a way that their proclamation comes first, freely and independently, while the proclamation of the Church is related to it, is ventured upon obediently in view of it, is measured by it, only therefore takes its place because and so far as it conforms to it—that she constantly acknowledges its free power over herself. Everything depends for the idea of a living succession upon the *antecessor* being thought of as still alive and possessed of free power as compared with the *successor*. But if, as is the case here, the *antecessor* is one who has long been dead, this can only happen when his proclamation is fixed in writing and when it is recognised that he still has life and free power to-day over the Church in this very written Word of his. It is upon the written nature of the canon, upon its character as *scriptura sacra*, that its autonomy and independence hang, and therefore its free power towards the Church, and therefore the living nature of the succession. Of course it might also have pleased God to give His Church the canon in the form of an unwritten prophetic and apostolic tradition, propagating itself from spirit to spirit and from mouth to mouth.

In that case it might be lawful and sensible that Peter's grave particularly should be the central sanctuary of the Church ! The canon might be the event of tradition, i.e. " the peculiar Christian sense present in the Church and propagated by means of Church education . . . the Word continuously alive in the hearts of believers " (J. A. Möhler, *Symbolik*, 3rd edn. 1834 p. 371).

It will not be disputed that there is somewhat of this kind in the Church apart from the real canon. But it would have to be said that, so far as it had pleased God to make this unwritten, spiritual-oral tradition the canon of His Church, the canon would be as faintly distinguishable from the life of the Church, as we can distinguish the blood of our fathers which flows in our veins from our own blood ; in other words, the Church is once more left to her solitary self and concentrated upon herself, upon her own aliveness. Whatever such spiritual-oral tradition there may be in the Church, obviously it cannot possess the character of an authority irremovably confronting the Church, because it lacks the written form. In the unwritten tradition the Church is not addressed, but is engaged in a dialogue with herself.

Papias's saying : Οὐ γὰρ τὸ ἐκ τῶν βιβλίων τοσοῦτον με ὠφελεῖν ὑπελάμβανον ὅσον τὰ παρὰ ζώσης φωνῆς καὶ μενούσης (Eusebius, *H.E.* III 39, 4) is significant for the turn, fateful in its operations, which had already set in here at the beginning of the second century ; the " alive-ness " is now no longer sought and found in the written word of the apostles themselves, but in the " voice " of such contemporaries as had themselves known the apostles, and this " living and lasting voice " is now already given the advantage over the " books," i.e. the apostolic writings. We find ourselves at the end of the same series—obviously the " alive-ness " has passed over completely from the *antecessor* to the *successor*—when K. Adam (*Das Wesen des Katholismus*, 4th edn. 1927 p. 162) can speak of the " dead Word " of the Bible in contrast to the " vitality " of Church tradition. But we find ourselves upon another tack rather than in the midst of the same one when we hear—Lessing refusing " to dream of suspending nothing less than all eternity by a spider's thread " (i.e. by the words of the witnesses of the first period ; *Eine Duplik*, *Lessing's theol. Schr., herausg. v. Chr. Gross*, II 2, p. 34), where yet (he holds) the *regula fidei* was once not identical with scripture (*Nötige Antwort, ib.* II 2, p. 215 f.) and where yet to this day it is solely " the undying miracle of religion " and, yet once more, not Scripture, that constitutes the effective proof of Christianity (*Eine Duplik, ib.* II 2, p. 33). " It must surely be possible for everything written by evangelists and apostles to be lost again and yet for the religion taught by them to persist " (*Fragm. eines Unbekannten, ib.* II 1, p. 262). Really ? His opponent M. Goeze had asked him about it, and Lessing stoutly replied, " God preserve me from ever thinking so meanly of Christ's teaching, as to dare to answer this question with an out-and-out negative ! Nay, this negative I do not utter, although an angel from heaven had dictated it to me ! Still less, when a mere Lutheran parson wants to put it into my mouth ! " (*Axiomata, ib.* II 2, p. 118). With greater right than the opening words of the Gospel of John, so Lessing thought, the Testament of John, " Little children, love one another," ought to be there to read in golden letters on the most visible part of every Church (*Das Test. Joh.* II 2, p. 19). " It is of course apocryphal, this Testament, but not therefore less divine " (*Ueber den Beweis . . . ib.* II 2, p. 14). At this last statement in particular who has not been sensibly reminded that with Holy Scripture even the Council of Trent *nec non traditiones ipsas, tum ad fidem, tum ad mores pertinentes, tanquam vel oretenus a Christo vel a Spiritu sancto dictatas et continua successione in Ecclesia catholica conservatas, pari pietatis affectu et reverentia suscipit et veneratur* (*Trid. sess. IV Recipiuntur libri . . .*) ? Was Lessing then guilty of Catholicising or the Council of Trent of modernising (in a manner already of course beginning in Papias) ? In what way are these two tendencies related to one another ? One thing is certain ; they agree in their result, in the relative independence which they give the present Church compared with the canon of Holy Scripture, i.e. in the relative devaluation of the said canon.

If then, apart from the undeniable and singular aliveness of the Church, there exists over against it a concrete authority with a singular aliveness of its own, an authority whose utterance means not a talking by the Church with herself, but a talking to the Church, which compared with the Church may hold the position of a free power and so of a criterion, obviously it must be distinguished precisely by its written Scriptural nature from the merely spiritual-oral life of church tradition and given a place before it. Certainly this real or Biblical canon is in a process of continual incorporation into the life, thought, and language of the Church, so far as the Bible is continually understood afresh, and therefore explained and interpreted. But exegesis is always a combination of taking and giving, of expounding and inserting. The very exegesis without which the norm cannot attain to validity as a norm is thus also a sign of the standing danger of a confiscation of the Bible by the the Church, of an absorption, a making up of its own life by the Church's life, of a transmutation of its free power into Church authority—in short, of an annulment of its character as the norm, which magisterially confronts the Church. All exegesis of the Bible means the presence of this danger. All exegesis may become predominantly an imposition instead of an exposition, and to that extent deteriorate into a dialogue of the Church with herself. And we shall not banish this danger, but only really begin to conjure it up and render it acute, by making right exposition depend on the verdict of an ultimately decisive Church teaching office, or on the verdict of an historical and critical science, comporting itself with an equal infallibility. If we assume that the one or the other of these authorities is worthy of the Church's highest confidence, in both cases the Church makes a mistake about the Bible, so far as she thinks that in one way or other she can control right exposition and thereby set up a norm over the norm, and ought to and can seize upon the proper norm for herself. Bible exegesis should rather be left open on all sides, not, as this demand was put by Liberalism, for the sake of free thinking, but for the sake of a free Bible. Self-defence against possible violence to the text must be left here as everywhere to the text itself, which in practice has so far always succeeded, as a merely spiritual-oral tradition simply cannot, in asserting its own life against encroachments by individuals or whole areas and schools in the Church, and in victoriously achieving it in ever-fresh applications, and so in creating recognition of itself as the norm.

" Inward truth," in spite of Lessing's protest (*Axiomata, op. cit.* II 2, p. 127), is " a wax nose that any knave can mould as he will to suit his own face " ; and if counter-Reformation polemics did apply the same tasteful metaphor to the Bible (*Scriptura est tanquam nasus cereus ; quia flecti potest hinc inde*—quoted by Calvin, *Articuli Fac. Paris. cum Antidoto*, 1544 C.R. 7, 31), that merely proves to us the rightness of demanding free exegesis for the sake of a free Bible.

The canonical text as a text already possesses the character of a free power, and the Church need do nothing except, after every exegesis promulgated within her, were it the very best, make clear to herself anew the difference between text and commentary, and let the text speak anew for itself without restriction, in order that she may experience the lordship of this free power and find in the Bible the partner or opponent which she must find in it (the text), if she is to take the living *successio apostolorum* seriously.

Of course there is the further question to be asked, how it comes about that the prophetic and apostolic Word in particular takes up this normative position over against the Church and her proclamation. We have just been trying to make clear to ourselves that there must be a written Word, a text, if there is to be a real canon distinct from the life of the Church herself. But the written form alone obviously does not make it the norm. There are also other texts about which corresponding assertions might be made regarding their exegesis, i.e. the free power inherent in them. Lastly, we also have as a text a large part of the uncanonical tradition, so far, e.g. as it has become fixed in dogma. What makes the Bible of the Old and New Testaments in particular into the canon ? Why must the Church's recollection of God's past revelation always have the Bible in particular as its concrete object ? It should imply no shirking of this question which it is always so right to raise afresh, if in the first instance we reply at once, The Bible constitutes itself the canon. It is the canon because it has imposed itself as such upon the Church and invariably does so. The Church's recollection of God's past revelation has computed that the Bible is her object, because, as a matter of fact, this and no other object is the promise of future divine revelation, which can make her proclamation a duty upon the Church and give her the courage and the joy for this duty. If we thought we could specify why this is so, we should once more be acting as if we had a measure in our hands with which we were in a position to measure the Bible, and on the basis of it to assign it its distinctive position. In that case our final and decisive wisdom would once more be the wisdom of a self-dialogue, although of a self-dialogue concerned with the Bible. No, the Bible is the canon just because it is so. But it is so because it imposes itself as such. And if we can only register this event as such, as the reality in which the Church is the Church, yet, after this has been done, it is still not impossible subsequently, by exegesis, to state wherein this self-imposition consists, and to what extent it sets a limit to the wisdom of our dialogue with ourselves. To anticipate we must already refer here to the content of Holy Scripture. The prophetic apostolic Word is the word, the witness, the proclamation and the preaching of Jesus Christ. The promise given to the Church in this word is the promise of God's mercy—expressed in the person of Him who is true God and true man—which takes to itself us who, because of our enmity towards God, could literally never have helped ourselves. The promise of this word is therefore in effect Immanuel ! God with us !—with us who have brought and always are bringing ourselves into the dire straits of not being able to be with God. Holy Scripture is the word of men who longed for, expected, hoped for this " Immanuel," and finally saw, heard, and handled it in Jesus Christ. It declares, attests, and proclaims it. And by its declaration, attestation, and proclamation it promises that it holds also and actually for us. He who hears its word in such a way that he grasps its promise and says Yea to it, believes. And this very grasp and affirmation of the promise, Immanuel with sinners ! in the word of prophets and apostles, is the Church's actual faith. In such faith she reminds herself of God's revelation already past, and in such faith she expects the future revelation still outstanding, she reminds herself of the incarnation of the eternal Word and of the reconciliation that took place in Him, and she awaits the coming of Jesus Christ and her own redemption from the power of evil. Thus it is in virtue of this its content that Scripture imposes itself. Scripture of this—really this !—content is in contradistinction to other scriptures Holy Scripture. Where the Church heard this word—she heard it in the prophets and apostles and nowhere else—she heard a magisterial, a final word which she could never again confuse or place on a level with any other word. Scripture of this content sets its natural bounds to recollection in the form of self-dialogue ; that is, if " Immanuel, with us, sinners ! " holds good, then our own deepest ground of being, whatever we may hold regarding it, at least cannot be God's past revelation, then our coming to ourselves—however significant, for that matter, such a coming to may be—has at least nothing to do with returning to God's revelation. Scripture of this content must remain confronting the life of the Church, which indeed can only be life in this relation, as an entity full of livingness of its own and full of free power, as the criterion that refuses to be dissolved into the historical life of the Church. And Scripture of this content, finally, must always turn again into the thing from which we started, the object of real, genuine recollection, in which the Church with her preaching reviews and meets the future. " I believe, therefore do I speak " (Ps. 116¹⁰). Hearing this word with faith in its promise controls proclamation and makes it possible.

The great historical example of this discovery of the canon, given to the Church in the Bible in virtue of its content, is the early period of the Reformation. What was enacted in Wittenberg and Zürich in those twenty, in Geneva in those thirty, years of the 16th century, is like a book of illustrations to what has just been set forth, of the Church seeing once more that she does not possess Christ with His gifts in herself, but must be found by His Word coming to her from without (" Salvation hath for us its source in grace and goodness pure . . ."). But she sees this because His Word, and He Himself actually in His Word, has already found her, because she has already ceased to be abandoned, because as her partner and opponent He has already come forward to comfort and raise us up in that very word of the Bible ; i.e. in concrete terms, because the Old and New Testaments have already spoken to her, already forced themselves upon her as the " canon of truth." Her proclamation is once more placed under the necessity of becoming a succession, an obedient following of the word of the prophets and apostles. Therefore now the Bible once more becomes important to her as a book, in its superiority and freedom over against herself, beyond all exegesis of the book, even her own, in its singularity which consists in and is actually ensured by the fact that it is the book about Christ, about the promise of grace, which cannot be heard anywhere else, and which makes an end of the need and pride of the man who stands upon himself and takes counsel with himself. And because this book is there as the canon, we must now preach in the measure and with the intensity that so astonishes us to-day, just as they did in those days ; therefore with the Bible, in the Bible, and through the Bible the Church is now completely rediscovering what Church proclamation is.

It now only remains for us to say the final word. Supposing we are right about the fact just described, that the Church is called, empowered, and guided to her proclamation by Holy Scripture, that involves the assertion that Holy Scripture too is the Word of God. And exactly in the same sense in which we made this assertion about the event of real proclamation. The recollection of God's past revelation, the discovery of the canon, faith in the promise of the word of the prophets and apostles, or, better, the Bible's imposition of itself on the strength of its special content, and therefore the existence of real apostolic succession—all that is an event and can only be understood as an event. In this event the Bible is the Word of God, i.e. in this word the human word of prophets and apostles represents the Word of God Himself, exactly in the way in which, in the event of real proclamation, the latter is to become the human word even of the preacher of to-day, namely, man's word with God's commission to us behind it, man's word to which God has given Himself as the object, man's word which is acknowledged and accepted by God as good, man's word in which God's own language to us is an event. This very fact of the language of God Himself becoming an event in the human word of the Bible is, however, God's business and not ours. That is what we mean when we call the Bible the Word of God. We confess and acknowledge thereby that the recollection of God's past revelation, without which it would be impossible to undertake Church proclamation, is as much God's grace and gift as is the realisation which our own proclamation needs. It is not in our power to achieve this recollection, certainly not in the form of our grip of the Bible ; but if and because the Bible grips us, therefore because we become reminded, this recollection is achieved. That this happens, that the Bible speaks to us of the promise, that prophets and apostles tell us what they have to say to us, that their word is imposed upon us, and that the Church from time to time becomes what she is because she is faced with the Bible, is God's decision and not ours—that is grace and not our work. The Bible is God's Word so far as God lets it be His Word, so far as God speaks through it. By this second equation as little as by our first (" Church proclamation is God's Word ") can we abstract from God's free act in which and through which here and now He lets it be true in us and for us, that man's word in the Bible is His own Word. The statement, " The Bible is God's Word," is a confession of faith, a statement made by the faith that hears God Himself speak in the human word of the Bible. Certainly a statement which by venturing it in faith we allow to be true quite apart from our faith and above all our faith, allow to be true even and actually against our unbelief, do not allow to be true as a description of our experience with the Bible, but allow to be true as a description of the act of God in the Bible, whatever the experiences may be which we have or do not have in that connection. But this is just precisely the faith which in this way sees and reaches beyond itself and all the experiences bound up or not bound up with it to the act of God, namely, to the fact that this act of God upon man has become an event, therefore not to the fact that man has reached out to the Bible, but to the fact that the Bible has reached out to

man. The Bible therefore becomes God's Word in this event, and
it is to its being in this becoming that the tiny word " is "
relates, in the statement that the Bible is God's Word. It does
not become God's Word because we accord it faith, but, of course,
because it becomes revelation for us. But its becoming revelation
for us beyond all our faith, its being the Word of God also against
our unbelief, we can, of course, allow to be true and confess as true
in us and for us only in faith, in faith against unbelief, in the faith
in which we look away from our faith and unbelief to the act of
God, but in faith and not in unbelief. And therefore precisely not
in abstraction from the act of God, in virtue of which the Bible must
from time to time become His Word to us.

Lutheran orthodoxy was familiar with a polemical doctrine, built up in
opposition to the Calvinists, Schwenckfeldians, Quakers, etc., of the *efficacia
Verbi divini etiam ante et extra usum*, to the effect that a divine power belonged
to the Word of God proclaimed and written, whatever its effect upon the
hearer or reader might be. In the Bible and preaching a divine *actus primus*
took place, whatever might be the case with the *actus secundus* in the heart
of men (Quenstedt, *Theol. did. pol.* 1685 I *cap.* 4, *sect.* 2, *qu.* 16 ; Hollaz,
Ex. theol. acroam. 1707 III 2, 1, *qu.* 4). So far as the aim of this doctrine
was to prove the truth of the credal statement that the Bible and preaching
are the Word of God, in their full compass, as independent of subjective
experience and superior to it, its claim must assuredly be admitted. But it
intended more than that, and in this more we cannot follow it. Quenstedt
denied specifically that the Bible is an *instrumentum* which requires *novo
motu et elevatione nova ad effectum novum ultra propriam suam naturalem
virtutem producendum*. The Bible and preaching were rather *media*, in which
summa vis et efficacia were inherent in themselves and permanently (*ib. ekth.* 7).
The Bible, so Hollaz thinks, is the wholesome Word of God, just as the sun
radiates heat even behind clouds, as a seed of corn retains its power even in
barren soil, as even the hand of a sleeping man is a living hand. And again
Hollaz explains in blunt language that the Word of God is not an *actio* but a
vis, a *potentia*, which as such has *efficacia* even *extra usum* ; in other words,
a *vis hyperphysica analoga efficaciae physicae*, i.e. *vera et realis*. As if apart
from the theological criterion of truth and reality the analogy with the physical
had to exist or needed to exist ! On this presupposition the theory is of course
logical and impressive. A power comparable with sunshine or the germina-
tive power of a seed of course does not require a *nova elevatio*. It is there
just as the powers in nature are there. But is God's Word there in that way ?
If it is really the Word ? And if it is the Word of God who is a Person ? We
shall surely have to choose between the concepts " Word of God " and " *vis
hyperphysica*," and in Evangelical theology no doubt should really be possible
as to how we must choose here.

3. THE REVEALED WORD OF GOD

The Bible is the concrete medium by which the Church recalls
God's revelation in the past, is called to expect revelation in the

future, and is thereby challenged, empowered, and guided to proclaim. The Bible is, therefore, not itself and in itself God's past revelation, just as Church proclamation also is not itself and in itself the expected future revelation. But the Bible speaking to us and heard by us as God's Word attests the past revelation. The proclamation that speaks to us and is heard by us as God's Word promises the future revelation. By really attesting revelation the Bible is the Word of God, and by really promising revelation proclamation is the Word of God. But the promise in proclamation rests upon the attestation in the Bible, the hope of future revelation upon faith in that which happened once for all. Therefore the decisive relation between the Church and revelation is the attestation of it by the Bible. The attestation of it ! The Bible, further, is not itself and in itself God's past revelation, but by becoming God's Word it attests God's past revelation and is God's past revelation in the form of attestation. Because in ruling, giving the order to march, and pointing the way the canon, or " staff," is moved by a living, outstretched hand, as the water was moved in the Pool of Bethesda, in order by that means and in that way to become healing, it attests and by this attestation establishes the relation between the Church and revelation, and thereby the Church herself as the true Church, and thereby her proclamation as the real proclamation. By its attestation ! To attest means to point in a definite direction beyond oneself to something else. Attestation is, therefore, the service of this something else, in which the witness answers for the truth of this something else. And this actual service is constitutive for the concept " prophet " as well as for the concept " apostle," concerning the difference between which this is not yet the time to speak.

When Paul, 1 Cor. 9[16], writes of himself : ἐὰν γὰρ εὐαγγελίζωμαι, οὐκ ἔστιν μοι καύχημα, ἀνάγκη γάρ μοι ἐπίκειται· οὐαὶ γὰρ μοί ἐστιν ἐὰν μὴ εὐαγγελίσωμαι, he is thereby describing (cf. say, Jer. 20[7f.]) the situation common to the prophet and to the apostle.

Engaged on this service, the Biblical witnesses point beyond themselves. If we regard them as witnesses—and only as witnesses do we regard them genuinely, i.e. in the way in which they themselves wished to be regarded—then their self, which in its inward and outward restrictedness and emotion constitutes, so to speak, the matter of their service, must decidedly be regarded by us from the point of view of its form, as pointing away from themselves. They speak and write not for their own sakes, nor for the sake of their deepest inner possession or even need, but under the orders of that something else. Not to assert themselves, nor yet as the heroes or advocates of the cause they plead, but away beyond any immanent teleology, for the reason that they must speak and write about that something else. It is not themselves, and not, emphatically not, their own special experience of and relationship to God, that they wish to present to and urge upon the Church, but that something else by their own agency. But " by their own agency " not in the sense in which the man himself must be a more or less perfect organ for the manifestation of objective facts and values or subjective excitations (as is the case with the productions of science, politics, and art), but by their own agency in such a way that it is solely and exclusively the something else which compels and limits the perfect or imperfect human organ from without, the thing attested itself, which is what makes man a witness.

We cannot at this point reflect too persistently " upon the difference between an apostle and a genius " (Kierkegaard, 1847).—The example of a Biblical witness in the unity of its form is John the Baptist, who stands so wonderfully midway between the Old Testament and the New, between prophet and apostle : Ἐγένετο ἄνθρωπος, ἀπεσταλμένος παρὰ Θεοῦ, ὄνομα αὐτῷ Ἰωάννης, οὗτος ἦλθεν εἰς μαρτυρίαν, ἵνα μαρτυρήσῃ περὶ τοῦ φωτός, ἵνα πάντες πιστεύσωσιν δι᾽ αὐτοῦ. οὐκ ἦν ἐκεῖνος τὸ φῶς, ἀλλ᾽ ἵνα μαρτυρήσῃ περὶ τοῦ φωτός (John 1⁶ᶠ·, cf. 3²⁷ᶠ·). In this connection one might recall John the Baptist in Grünewald's Crucifixion, especially his prodigious index finger : can any one point away from himself more impressively and completely (*illum oportet crescere me autem minui*) ? And can any one point to the thing indicated more impressively and realistically, than is done there ? This is what the Fourth Evangelist wished to say of this, and therefore, of a n o t h e r, and so, unmistakably, of e v e r y " John."

Why and in what respect does the Biblical witness possess authority ? In that it claims no authority whatsoever for itself, that its witness amounts to letting the Something else be the authority, itself and by its own agency. Therefore we do the Bible a poor honour, and one unwelcome to itself, when we directly identify it with this something else, with revelation itself.

This we may do by seeking revelation, and thinking we can find it in the heroic religious personality of the Biblical witness. We may also do so in the form of the doctrine of the general, equal and permanent inspiration oᵢ the Bible, which we shall come to speak about later. Kierkegaard says quite correctly in the work just named (*Der Begriff des Auserwählten*, edited by Th. Haecker, 1917 p. 314) that the mistake in asking whether an apostle is a genius is to be looked for not merely on the part of heterodoxy, but also on that of hyperorthodoxy, on that of thoughtlessness in general. We should not in practice forget that the historistic conception of the Bible with its cult of heroes and the mechanical doctrine of verbal inspiration are products of the same age and the same spirit. They have this in common, that they stood for the means by which man at the Renaissance claimed to control the Bible and so set up barriers against its control over him, which is its perquisite.

Such direct identification of revelation and the Bible, which is the practical issue, is not one to be presupposed or anticipated by us. It takes place as an event, when and where the word of the Bible becomes God's Word, i.e. when and where the word of the Bible functions as the word of a witness, when and where John's finger points not in vain but really pointedly, when and where by means of its word we also succeed in seeing and hearing what he saw and heard. Therefore, where the Word of God is an event, revelation and the Bible are one in fact, and word for word one at that.

" For this preaching means : ' Fear not, To you is born this day the Saviour, which is Christ the Lord.' Man's words which have grown in men's hearts are not like that. For the wisest folk on earth wot naught thereof. But this preaching rang down from heaven, of which same we, God be praised for ever, are become partakers. For 'tis all the same, if thou hearest or readest this preaching, as if thou hadst heard it from the angel himself. For the shepherds too saw not the angels, they saw but the light and the glory. But the word of the angels they heard, which we still hear in preaching, still read in the Book, if we will but open our eyes and ears and learn and rightly use such preaching " (Luther, *Predigt, Von der Engel Lobgesang*, 1544 W. edn. 52, p. 50, l. 13).

But for that very reason we should realise that and how far they are also always n o t one, how far their unity is really an e v e n t. The revelation upon which the Biblical witnesses gaze, looking and witnessing away from themselves, is, purely formally, different from the word of the witnesses just in the way in which an event itself is different from the best and most faithful narrative about it. But this difference is inconsiderable compared with the one which beggars all analogy, that in revelation we are concerned with Jesus Christ to come, who ultimately in the fulness of time did come. Literally we are, therefore, concerned with the singular Word spoken, and this time really directly, by God Himself. But in the Bible we are invariably concerned with human attempts to repeat and reproduce, in human thoughts and expressions, this Word of God in definite human situations, e.g. in respect of the complications of Israel's political position midway between Egypt and Babylon, or of the errors and confusions in the Christian Church at Corinth between A.D. 50–60. In the one case *Deus dixit*, in the other *Paulus dixit*. These are two different things. And precisely because, where the Word of God is an event, it is n o t two different things, but becomes one, we must maintain that it is not self-evident or intrinsically the same thing, that revelation is to be regarded primarily as the superior, the Bible primarily as the subordinate principle.

As early as the epistles of Ignatius of Antioch (e.g. *Ad Magn.* 13, 2) apropos of the relation of dependence of community on bishop, there arises likewise as its archetype the other relation of the dependence of apostle on Christ.   Augustine in his first homily on the Gospel according to John compares the Biblical witnesses with those hills from which, according to Ps. 121, cometh our help : But not from the hills as such, but from the Lord who made heaven and earth and who is above these hills ! For : *Audeo dicere, fratres mei, forsitan nec ipse Joannes dixit ut est, sed et ipse ut potuit ; quia de Deo homo dixit : Et quidem inspiratus a Deo sed tamen homo. Quia inspiratus, dixit aliquid ; si non inspiratus esset, dixisset nihil : Quia vero homo inspiratus, non totum quod est dixit, sed quod potuit homo dixit.* We have to distinguish, so says Augustine in another passage, between what *veritas incommutabilis per se ipsam ineffabiliter loquitur rationalis creaturae mentibus*, and its language *per mutabilem creaturam*, by means of spiritual images and a physical voice (*De civ. Dei*, XVI 6, 1).   In the same way Anselm of Canterbury distinguishes between the direct (*sine humana doctrina*) completed divine sowing in the hearts of the prophets and apostles, and the increase that accrues from the harvest there sprung up, the increase with which we now work (*De concordia, qu.* III 6).   Holy Scripture is *super solidam veritatem . . . velut super firmum fundamentum fundata* (*Cur deus homo ?* II 19), therefore not simply identical with it.   Luther speaks of the same direct revelation, when he distinguishes between prophets on the one hand, wise men and scribes on the other.   " They are prophets which preach out of pure prompting of the Holy Ghost, which have not fashioned it of Scripture or through men, as Moses and Amos were.   And these are the highest and best which are wise and know how to make others wise, who set out and expound Scripture ; such were almost all the patriarchs for and with Moses, and after him many also, especially the apostles, who were laymen and sorely unlettered folk, as Luke Ac. 5 says, 'ignorant of Scripture'" (*Kirchenpostille*, 1522 W. edn. 10[I], p. 271, l. 21).   On the contrary, wise men and scribes already presuppose the existence of prophetic Scripture.   But even Calvin, who approximated revelation and Scripture much more closely than did Augustine, says precisely in the most quoted passage, with a clear proviso, that Holy Scripture has with believers the authority pertaining to it, *ubi statuunt e coelo fluxisse, ac si vivae ipsae Dei voces illic exaudirentur* (*Instit.* I 7, 1), and formulates the concept of inspiration in the decisive passage to the effect that *summa Scripturae probatio passim a Dei loquentis persona sumitur* (*ib.* 7, 4).   And even in the subsequent period of orthodoxy which was the counterpart of the fatal doctrine of inspiration, there remains alive in the most manifold ways the memory of the difference in question.   According to Bullinger (*Comp. rel. christ.* 1598 p. 5, quoted acc. to Alex. Schweizer, *Glaubensl. d. ev. ref. Kirche*, vol. I 1844 p. 200) we must say : *Literae, verba caro sunt, sententiae vero Dei.*   According to W. Musculus (*Loci Comm.* 1564 p. 73, Schweizer, *loc. cit.* 199) the holy Scriptures are called holy, *quoniam de sacris rebus loquuntur.*   According to Peter Martyr (*Loci comm.* 1580 p. 13, Schweizer, *op. cit.* p. 200) Holy Scripture is an *expressio quaedam sapientiae*

Dei. According to J. Gerhard (*Loci theol.* 1610 *Prooem.* 18) the *verbum externum Dei* gets abroad, in one way *per inspirationem*, in another *per sermonem externum*, i.e. through angels, men, or human writing. In the *Syn. pur. Theol.* Leiden, 1624 Disp. 1, 8, it says : *Sacrae Theologiae revelatio a Deo prophetis et apostolis facta, est immediata, quae autem per hos Ecclesiae Dei manifestata est, mediata est.* And in the sense and frequently in the vocabulary of this very distinction there are set up at that time (cf. e.g. Bucan, *Instit. theol.* 1605 *Loc.* 4, 16) but also as early as the extreme ortho-doxy alike of Reformers (e.g. Fr. Turretini, *Instit. theol. elenct.* 1679 *Loc.* 2 *qu.* 2, 5 f.) and of Lutherans (Quenstedt, *Theol. did. pol.* 1686 I, *cap.* 4, *sect.* 2, *qu.* 3, *ekth.* 3, and I 7, 1, *thes.* 1, *n.* 2 ; Baier, *Comp. theol. pos.* 1686 *Prol.* 2, 1 ; Hollaz, *Ex. theol. acroam.* 1707 *Prol.* 3, *qu.* 2), side by side with full concentration upon Scripture as such, reflections also on revelation itself, to be distinguished from Scripture because constituting the first basis of it as inspired Scripture.

Revelation engenders the Scripture which attests it, as the commission, the " burden " laid upon the prophets and apostles, as the object which introduces itself personally into the scheme over against them, as the judge at once and the guarantor of the truth of their language, as the event of inspiration in which they become speakers and writers of the Word of God. Because revela-tion engenders the Bible that attests it, because Jesus Christ has called the Old and New Testaments into existence, because Holy Scripture is the document of a peculiar listening to a peculiar call, the document of a peculiar obedience to a peculiar behest, therefore it could become the canon, and therefore it can become from time to time the movable canon, the publisher of revelation, God's call and behest, God's Word to us. If in the prophets and apostles the Church possesses the concrete counterpart by which she is reminded of God's past revelation, transplanted into expectation of His future revelation and thereby commanded and authorised to proclaim it, the reason is that in them she really has the journeymen of this past revelation. But the prophets did not appoint them-selves to be such journeymen of revelation, nor are they at any moment such in themselves and obviously. What makes them so is that the revelation of God Himself happened apart from their existence. Did happen, and so we must designate this thing that happened to them as *Deus dixit.* What has generated Scripture and what Scripture now on its part attests, did really and finally, once and once for all, happen. Of what did happen we have already spoken in outline, when we said that God was with us, with us His enemies, with us who were struck and shattered by His wrath. God was with us, with the reality and completeness with which God does what He does ; He was with us as one of us. His Word

9

became flesh of our flesh, blood of our blood. His glory was seen here in the depth of our plight, and what was the deepest depth of our plight was first revealed when it was there and then illumined by the glory of the Lord ; when, that is, in His Word He descended into the lowest parts of the earth (Eph. 4⁹), so that there and thus He might take the power from death and bring life and imperishable being to light (2 Tim. 1¹⁰). That did happen, and that it is which the Old Testament proclaims as the word of prophecy, the New Testament as the word of fulfilment, but both as having happened, as having conclusively, completely, and adequately happened. That turns the Biblical witnesses into marvellous figures like John, incomprehensible by any morphology of genius ; therefore, it holds good of them, although in the most various ways, that " the zeal of Thy house hath eaten me up " (Ps. 69¹⁰) ; therefore, they who claim no kind of authority for themselves, from time to time claim and obtain the most unheard-of authority with their frail human speech ; that came upon them, and claims through them always to come anew upon the Church, and be cried abroad as the most utterly urgent thing that any time or any man at any time or any man in any respect can or must hear, that this " God with us " has happened. In the midst of human history and as a fragment of this history, but, of course, not as fragments of this history usually happen, i.e. without need of continuation or completion, without pointing beyond itself, without primarily striving for a distant goal, insusceptible of exegesis or of any, even the slightest addition or subtraction, incapable of changing its form, but in mid-stream of becoming, being moved only by itself, in mid-ocean of the unsettled, changeable, and self-changing, the fixed event, the fulness of time.

A bit of apocryphal Christian legend of the 2nd century may here be given currency, because for all its unhistorical foolishness it makes very clear, if clearness be possible here, what we are to think of as the fulness of time. In the so-called *Protevangelium of James*, chap. 18, we hear Joseph, the foster-parent of Jesus, narrate as follows, what he claims to have experienced on the night of the birth of the Lord in the neighbourhood of Bethlehem. " But I, Joseph, went about and went not about. And I looked up at the vault of heaven and saw it stand still, and I looked up into the air and saw it stiffened, and I saw the birds of heaven immovable, and I looked on the ground and saw a dish standing there and labourers lying down and their hands in the dish and the chewers chewed not, and those that were engaged in lifting up brought nothing to the top, and those who meant to bring to their mouths brought nothing to their mouths, but all faces were directed upwards, and behold sheep were being driven and remained standing, and the herd raised his hand to smite them, and his hand stayed up, and I looked at the

water-course of the river and saw the muzzles of the goats held down to it
and they did not drink : and in a moment everything resumed its course "
(*NT Apocrypha*, ed. Edgar Hennecke, 2nd edn. 1924 p. 91). The fulness
of time means practically, if in its perfect divine actuality it is to be the one,
unique, really moved and moving time, suspension of movement, complete
relativisation of all other time and of its content apparently thus moved and
moving.

This fulness of time, which is identical with Jesus Christ, this
pure event in relation to which everything else is not yet an event
or has ceased to be one, this " it is finished ! " this *Deuſ dixit*, to
which there are no analogies, is the revelation attested in the Bible.
To understand the Bible would mean, from beginning to end and
from verse to verse, to understand how everything in it is related
to that as to its invisible-visible centre. But because that is the
point, we shall have to say that we are not in a position to understand the Bible from our own standpoint. It can only be a case
of the Bible giving itself to be understood, of us being brought
to listen to the Bible as God's Word. But in that case listening to
the Bible as God's Word means to listen to it there and then, in
what is certainly always the very modest, changing, perhaps increasing, perhaps even decreasing compass in which it is true from
time to time for each individual, according as the human words of
the Bible are carriers of the eternal word, i.e. according as they are
intended from this centre in turn to intend this centre in all they
say. By itself being revelation at that time and in that way, the
Bible founds the Church, it makes proclamation necessary and
possible. The unity of the revelation guarantees the unity of
the Biblical witness, in spite of and within its utter multiplicity,
in fact contradictoriness. The unity of the Bible guarantees the
unity of the Church, in spite of and within the variety in the measure
of faith, in which the Bible becomes revelation to this man or that,
and to this man or that to-day or to-morrow. But the unity of the
Church thus founded guarantees the unity of the proclamation.

According to all that has been said, revelation is originally and
immediately, what the Bible and Church proclamation are derivatively and mediately, God's Word. We said of Church proclamation, that from time to time it must become God's Word. And
we said the same of the Bible, that it must from time to time become
God's Word. Now " from time to time " had to do, not with
human experience (as if our being affected by this event and our
attitude to it could be constitutive of its reality and its content !),
but, of course, with the freedom of God's grace. *Ubi et quando visum*

est Deo, not in themselves but in virtue of divine decision as expressed from time to time in the Bible and proclamation, because God who is free avails Himself of them, the Bible and proclamation are the Word of God. A statement in such form cannot be made about revelation. When we speak of revelation we are faced with the divine act itself and as such, which, as we had to remember in the past, is the ground and the limit, the presupposition and the proviso of what may be said of the Bible and proclamation as the Word of God. Because (1) it is only as repeating the Biblical testimony to past revelation that proclamation is real proclamation, i.e. the promise of future revelation, and because (2) it is only in its relation to the past revelation attested in it that the Bible is real attestation, i.e. the actual recollection of this past revelation —therefore the freedom of God's grace is the ground and the limit, the presupposition and the proviso of the statements, in virtue of which proclamation and the Bible are the Word of God. The decisive content of these statements, the positive fact which they express, and the manifest negations in which the positive fact is set, the relation in which they hold good, is precisely their relation to revelation. But revelation itself is nothing else than the freedom of God's grace ; not the principle of this freedom of course—this principle is in the first instance the certainly necessary product of human reflection upon this freedom—but the event in which God, being free, allows this free grace scope to operate. In this event of God's grace, proclamation and the Bible are elevated in the threefold sense of that word : (1) elevated in the sense of lifted upwards, marked out, made visible and knowable, so far as the Bible claims to attest this event and proclamation to repeat this attestation, so far as in the Bible and in proclamation it is this event that is properly intended by the human language ; (2) elevated in the sense of made relative, circumscribed, so far as this event also signifies the limits of what proclamation and the Bible can be in themselves or accomplish by themselves, the limits which obviously cannot be thought of as elevated solely by what men claimed or claim to say in them ; and (3) raised in the sense of well elevated, safe, secured, so far as this event is the confirmation and preservation, the fulfilment of what proclamation and the Bible are in themselves and accomplish by themselves, is the presence of what is intended in the human language of the Bible and proclamation. Thus when it is revelation we are looking at or starting from, we must say of proclamation and the Bible, that they are God's Word, by from time to time becoming God's Word. But for that very reason we must not say this about revelation itself, but the exact opposite, that it becomes God's Word, i.e. in the Bible and in proclamation, by being so in itself. It is itself the very thing that " elevates " the Bible and proclamation, in the threefold sense just discussed. Revelation is itself the divine decision, which takes effect in the Bible and in proclamation by availing itself of them, which therefore confirms, preserves, and fulfils them. It is itself the Word of God which the Bible and proclamation are, by becoming it.

ὃν γὰρ ἀπέστειλεν ὁ Θεὸς τὰ ῥήματα τοῦ Θεοῦ λαλεῖ· οὐ γὰρ ἐκ μέτρου δίδωσιν τὸ Πνεῦμα. ὁ πατὴρ ἀγαπᾷ τὸν υἱόν, καὶ πάντα δέδωκεν ἐν τῇ χειρὶ αὐτοῦ. ὁ πιστεύων εἰς τὸν υἱὸν ἔχει ζωὴν αἰώνιον· ὁ δὲ ἀπειθῶν τῷ υἱῷ οὐκ ὄψεται ζωήν, ἀλλ᾽ ἡ ὀργὴ τοῦ Θεοῦ μένει ἐπ᾽ αὐτόν (John 3³⁴⁻³⁶).

It is, therefore, unconditioned (we can say this only of our knowledge of revelation), is in fact itself the condition. We have to say of it, not *ubi et quando* but *illic et tunc visum est Deo*. Here we have to speak not of a possibility to be realised, but of the reality of the Word of God as the ground of all possible self-realisations. *Ubi et quando* may and must be said, because finally or primarily *illic et tunc* must be said. Because there is a moving hand, there is a moved and self-moving canon, a commissioned, objective, true and real proclamation in obedience to this canon. If we say " revealed Word of God," then " revealed " (as distinct from the " written " and the " proclaimed " in the first two forms of the Word) does not belong to the predicate ; it is nothing but a transcription, a second designation of the subject itself. If " written " and " proclaimed " signify the twofold concrete relation in which the Word of God is spoken to us, revelation signifies the Word of God itself, the act of its utterance. To designate it revelation is the same as saying that there is nothing other, nothing higher above this act from which it might be based or derived, that it is the condition which conditions everything without itself being conditioned. Revelation, *revelatio*, ἀποκάλυψις means the unveiling of the veiled. If it is really and strictly a question of that, then anything different from revelation is the veiling, the hidden state of the veiled.

The revealed Word is the mystery not made known to the ages but concealed, Rom. 16²⁵ ; Col. 1²⁶ ; Eph. 3⁹. In other words, no other reason for its being unveiled can be found or adduced except its actual state of unveiling itself. It is the νῦν characterised by ἀποκάλυψις or φανέρωσις, in which the witness to revelation as such speaks, in which alone the possibility resides of regarding it as unveiled ; and about this characterisation we really say the last word by pointing to the will of God : κατ᾽ ἐπιταγὴν τοῦ αἰωνίου Θεοῦ (Rom. 16²⁵), οἷς ἠθέλησεν ὁ Θεὸς γνωρίσαι . . . (Col. 1²⁷). " Christian faith and Christian life stand in the single literal revelation of God, for where that is not so, no heart can ever rightly be aware of this mystery, which hath been hidden there from the world, Now God revealeth it only to His eternally elected saints, to whom He will have it made known, otherwise it is, of course, hidden from every one and will remain a proper mystery. What good can the free or the enslaved and captive will here say or do about that ? How will it of its own might come to this light and mystery ? If the almighty strong God hide it from it, by no preparation or good work will it ever reach thereto. No creature can come to this knowledge, Christ Himself alone revealeth it to it in the heart itself. There all merit falls to the ground, all powers and abilities of reason, and count nothing with God, Christ alone must give it " (Luther, *Sermon on Matt.* 11²⁵⁻³⁹, 1527 W. edn. 23, p. 689, l. 4).

Thus we must think of every state of revelation as a process of revelation, that is, as conditioned by the very act of revelation ; of every happening in which revelation takes place as connected with what in this act happens once for all ; of all fulfilled time as fulfilled by the fulness of this time. But revelation itself is connected with nothing different or higher or earlier than itself. Revelation as such is not relative. Revelation in fact does not differ from the Person of Jesus Christ, and again does not differ from the reconciliation that took place in Him. To say revelation is to say, " The Word became flesh." Of course we may also claim to say by the word " revelation " something different, something purely formal, and in that case relative as such. But then we are not asserting what the Bible means by this word, and therefore not the thing with which Church proclamation is concerned, if it is connected with the Bible, nor yet what in Christian dogmatics must be called revelation, if it claims to take itself seriously as dogmatics. But if we mean by the word " revelation " " the Word became flesh and dwelt among us," then we are asserting something that is to be grounded only within the Trinity ; namely, by the Will of the Father, by the mission of the Son and of the Holy Spirit, by the eternal decree of the Triune God, i.e. not otherwise than as the knowledge of God from God, as knowledge of the Light in the Light. The result is the same when instead of " Jesus Christ " we say concretely " God with us." Certainly in place of this absolute we may mean something relative by the word " revelation," but the Bible means this absolute solely, and in the knowledge of this absolute the Church by means of the Bible reminds herself of past revelation, and for that very reason has to maintain a dogmatics which operates not in empty space but in the area of the Church. But if we say " God with us," we mean that which has no ground or possibility outside itself, which can in no sense be explained in terms of man and his situation, but only as knowledge of God proceeding from God, as free undeserved grace. The Bible by attesting God's revelation, and Church proclamation by obediently adopting this testimony, both renounce any other foundation, save that which God Himself has given once for all by having spoken. The Bible and proclamation appeal as it were to this once-for-all given thing to be present as such here and now as well. Just because it is the once-for-all given thing, they cannot reproduce it, or themselves bring it to the fore, but can only attest and proclaim it. It is not in the power of the Bible and proclamation to make it true that the *Deus dixit* of the Church is present in any given one of her times or situations. It is true—the *ubi et quando* now returns in force—where it is true, i.e. where and when, by having spoken, once for all, God willed to have it true according to His eternal counsel, where and when He lets it come true through His manifestation, preservation, and fulfilment of the Word in the Bible and in preaching. This being true and coming true of revelation thus consists in the Church really recalling past revelation, receiving, grasping and then genuinely proclaiming in faith the Biblical witness to it, as the real promise of future revelation. And by future revelation no other is to be understood than the one which took place once for all, but this as also now directed to us. As Christ of the Second Coming is none other than He that came, but now is also He that is to come to us. "God with us" becomes actual for us *hic et nunc*, as the promise received and grasped in faith, because it is the divine act *illic et tunc*. It is, therefore, that which is true in and for itself, that which comes true for us as a recollection and likewise as a promise, i.e. as the recollection of the Christ who came in the flesh and for that very reason as hope in the Christ who shall come again in glory. It is Jesus Christ Himself who speaks for Himself in it, and needs no witness save His Holy Spirit and is glad of the faith of His own in the promise received and grasped. It is this independent and unsurpassable origin for the Word of God which comes to us that we mean, when we speak of its third—materially we should say its first—form, its form as the revealed Word of God.

4. THE UNITY OF THE WORD OF GOD

We have been speaking of three forms of the Word of God, not of three several Words of God. In this threefold form and not otherwise—and also as the one invariably in this threefold form alone—it is given us, and in this form we must endeavour to understand it conceptually. It is one and the same, whether we regard it as revelation, as the Bible, or as proclamation. There is no distinction of degree or value between these three forms. For so far as proclamation really rests upon recollection of the revelation attested in the Bible and is therefore the obedient repetition of the Biblical witness, it is no less the Word of God than the Bible. And so far as the Bible really attests revelation, it is no less the Word of God than revelation itself. By becoming the Word of God in virtue of the actuality of revelation, the Bible and proclamation are also the Word, the one Word of God within which there can be neither a more nor a less. Still we should never regard any of the three forms of the Word of God in isolation. Of course the first one, revelation, is the form which establishes the other two. But it itself never meets us anywhere in abstract form, of it precisely our knowledge is only indirect, arising out of Scripture or in proclamation. It is just the immediate Word of God which meets us only in this twofold mediacy. But even Scripture, to become the Word of God for us, must needs be proclaimed in the Church. So to give a survey of the whole, the following brief schedule of mutual relationships might be drawn up.

The revealed Word of God we know only from the Scripture adopted by Church proclamation, or from Church proclamation based on Scripture.

The written Word of God we know only through the revelation which makes proclamation possible, or through the proclamation made possible by revelation.

The proclaimed Word of God we know only by knowing the revelation attested through Scripture, or by knowing the Scripture which attests revelation.

There is only one analogy to this doctrine of the Word of God. More exactly stated : the doctrine of the Word of God in its threefold form is itself the sole analogy to the doctrine which will fundamentally occupy us in unfolding the concept of revelation ; the doctrine of the three-in-oneness of God. In the facts that for revelation, Scripture, and proclamation we can substitute the divine " Person "-names of Father, Son, and Holy Spirit, and *vice versa,* that in the one case as in the other we shall encounter the same fundamental determinations and mutual relationships, that moreover the decisive difficulty, like the decisive clarity, is the same in both cases, in these facts we may see a certain support for the inner necessity and rightness of the present exposition of the Word of God.

The doctrine of the three forms of the Word of God in the sketch here attempted is not new. We have seen in detail how revelation, Scripture, and proclamation have from the beginning stamped themselves upon Christian thought as the special forms of the Word of God. Let us recall some further testimonies to the unity and coherence of these three forms. There are, above all, some passages in L u t h e r which are relevant here. Already in the *Dictata super Psalterium* (1513–1516) Luther says (on Ps. 45²) : *Quod verbum Dei triplici modo dicitur* : 1. There is a speaking by God *per verbum externum et linguam ad aures hominum*, the type of which Luther sees in the Word of the prophets and patriarchs of the OT, covered by the veil of mere literalness. 2. There is a Word of God, which He speaks through the Spirit to His saints now upon the earth, namely, in His Son, compared with the prophetic Word already a *verbum consummans et abbreviatum*, but also still enveloped in manifold veils. 3. There is a Word which God the Father speaks in Himself and to the saints in eternal glory. So we shall hear it some day, *cum nobis verbum suum ipse sine ullo medio revelabit. Unico et simplicissimo verbo suo* will He satisfy us then, and the Spirit Himself will take the place of all signs as the one sacrament (W. edn. 3, p. 262, l. 5). That the first form, the *verbum externum* of preaching, here gets short shrift, is not yet understood in its significance, is already shown by the fact that Luther saw no way of carrying out the Trinitarian articulation which was clearly before his mind in the second and third forms, because he could not of course connect with the Holy Spirit what he at the time still regarded as a *verbum externum*. How he thought out the advance from the first to the second form is likewise not clear in detail. And even the division between the Word which the Father speaks, in the third form *in se ipso* and in the second *in filio*, should not be carried out the way it is. But on the whole the three forms, up to and including the eschatologically qualified third, are very adequately viewed and described. An interesting variation on our theme is to be found in the already quoted sermon on Matt. 23³⁴ (*Kirchenpostille*, 1522 W. edn. 10¹, p. 272, l. 17), in which they are called " the three ways in which the truth may be revealed," " Scripture, word, thought ; the scripture through the books, the word through the mouth, the thought through the heart. There is naught with which to conceive the doctrine, save with heart, mouth, and scripture." The last one, which Luther here calls " thought," is of course nothing else than what we as the first have named revelation, by virtue of which Scripture and preaching reach man, touch his heart. More important is a passage from a sermon (likewise contained in the *Kirchenpostille*, 1522) on the wise men from the East. It surprises us above all by the completely new, one might almost say the over-emphasised, valuation which that same *verbum externum*, proclamation, has now acquired for Luther. The " oral and public sermon . . . the voice and the word cried forth by the mouth," is now for him the light spoken of in 2 Cor. 4⁴; 2 Pet. 1¹⁹. " Now Scripture is not understood until the light arises." By " scripture " is meant primarily the prophetic word to be found in the OT. At first Luther simply contrasts the NT with it as proclamation become living, i.e. oral, the task of which consists in opening up the prophetic word enclosed primarily in its written form. " For through the Gospel the prophets are opened up, therefore the star must first rise and be seen. For in the New Testament preaching should be made orally public with a living voice and bring forth to speech and hearing what hitherto is hidden in the letters and secret aspect. Since the New Testament is naught other than an opening and revealing of the Old Testament, as is attested in Rev. 5, where the Lamb of God opens the book with the seven seals. Also we see in the Apostles how all their preaching was naught else than to bring forth Scripture and to build thereon." And now Luther continues, astonishingly enough : " Therefore even Christ Himself wrote not down His teaching, as Moses did his, but did it orally and likewise commanded it to be done orally and gave no command to write it. Moreover, the Apostles also wrote little, and not all of them did that. . . . Even those who did write do no more than point us to the ancient scripture, as the angels pointed the shepherds to the manger and the swaddling clothes. And the star pointed these Magi to Bethlehem ! Therefore 'tis not like the New Testament to write books about Christian doctrine, but there should be, without books, in all places good, instructed, spiritual, diligent preachers who draw the living word out of the ancient writ and unceasingly din it into the people, as the Apostles did. For ere they wrote they first had preached to and converted the folk by the living voice, which was also their proper apostolic and New Testament work : that is likewise the right star which sheweth Christ's birth and the angelic messages telling of swaddling bands and cribs. But man's need to write books is a great injury, and it is a violation of the Spirit that the need hath compelled it and is not the way of the New Testament. . . ." NT Scripture as an adjunct or an interpretation of the Old is regarded as a defensive measure against the corruption in the Church. " It must be the last resort to do that, and need was, in order that some sheep should be saved from the wolves : so men began to write, and yet, through Scripture as far as possible, to bring the measure of Christ into Scripture, and thereby prepared for the sheep being able to pasture themselves and guard themselves against the wolves, where their shepherds refused to feed them or turned wolves." But further books had far better have ceased to be written in the Church. And the Star of Bethlehem, the Star of the Wise Men, should in every case be " the lively preaching and the simple revelation of Christ as the same is hid and promised in Scripture ; therefore he that seeth the star knoweth certainly the King of the Jews, the newborn Christ ; for the Gospel teacheth not otherwise than Christ, and Scripture likewise hath naught else than Christ. But whoso knoweth not Christ may hear the Gospel or hold the book right in his hands, but understanding of it he hath not yet, for to have the Gospel without understanding is to have no Gospel. And to have Scripture without knowledge of Christ is to have no Scripture, and is none other than to let this star shine and yet not perceive it " (W. edn. 10^1, pp. 625–28). The thought is to be found in Luther with this poignancy, particularly at that period in anything but isolation, that the OT and NT are related to each other as the written and the proclaimed Word of God. " Thus the books of Moses and the prophets are also the Gospel, since they have proclaimed and described beforehand concerning Christ, precisely what the apostles have preached or written subsequently. Yet is there a distinction between them. For as both according to the letter are written on paper, natheless the Gospel or New Testament should really not be written, but be put into the living voice, which then resounds and is heard everywhere in the world. But that it is also written has happened superfluously. But the Old Testament is composed only in writing, and therefore it is called ' a letter,' and so the apostles call it the ' writ,' for it alone hath pointed to the coming Christ. But the Gospel is a living sermon by Christ, who is come therein " (*Ep. S. Petri*, 1523 W. edn. 12, p. 275, l. 5 ; cf. also 259, 8, and 556, 9). That in other contexts also Luther attached the highest importance to the written nature of the New Testament and did not regard it as a necessary evil, and that it is inept systematically to hold him to this distinction, need not be proved. But it shows how he really devoted thought to the relation between Scripture and Preaching in general : both have the same content and object, in such a way that preaching receives it first of all from Scripture, and therefore can be nothing else than Scripture exegesis, but also in such a way that it must be derived absolutely from Scripture in the actual form of living proclamation and in that way become the Word of God to us. Allegorising on Luke 2[12], Luther about the same date summarised his idea in these terms : " Christ is involved in Scripture through and through, like the body in its clothes. Preaching is the crib in which he lies and is composed, and therefrom we get food and nourishment " (*Sermon on Luke* 2, 1523 W. edn. 12, p. 418, l. 24).— Protestant orthodoxy, which at the peak of its development was not fond of hearing talk of the variety of the forms of the Word of God and of the mobility of their mutual relations, the more energetically stressed their unity : which in itself is also true and instructive. Regarding the unity of the Word of God to the Biblical witnesses, and of the Word of God through them, *hae distinctiones non faciunt essentialem aliquam differentiam inter verbum Dei hominibus communicatum, sed tantum distinctos communicationis et revelationis modos exprimunt* (J. Gerhard, *Loci theol.* 1610 *Prooem.* 18). *Distinctio Verbi in* ἄγραφον *et* ἔγγραφον *non est divisio generis in species . . . quasi aliud esset Verbum non scriptum a scripto ; sed est distinctio subjecti in sua accidentia, quia eidem Verbo accidit, ut fuerit non scriptum olim et nunc sit scriptum* (Fr. Turretini, *Instit. theol. el.* 1679 *Loc.* 2, qu. 2, 4). *Nec vero aliud est verbum Dei quod a Deo vel quod inspiratum viris Dei, quam quod in scriptura traditur, aut praedicatur, vel mente humana reconditur* (Hollaz, *Ex. theol. acroam.* 1707 III 2, 1). Correct as all this is, we are still painfully aware of the absence, in all the utterances of this transition period, of the Reformers' insight into the dynamics of the mutual relationships between the three forms. This is shown in the doctrine of inspiration, which so to speak signifies a freezing up of the connection between Scripture and revelation. But it is shown above all in the fact that with the theologians of this period real and essential knowledge of proclamation, the third form of the Word of God, has apparently ceased. True, even with them " Word of God " means preaching, but the real point of connection between revelation and Scripture in the present is increasingly for them something quite different from the act of Church proclamation : it is the knowledge, faith, sanctification, holiness of the individual. But in that case their unity of revelation and Scripture, however stiff an objectivity it may be arrayed in, had to degenerate into the appearance of being, not so much a dealing by God with His Church, but rather a divine private institution for such-and-such a number of private individuals, for achieving which preaching and the sacraments were in that case still quite good enough as so-called " *media salutis.*" By forgetting that primarily the correlate to revelation and Scripture is simply but the beatitude or amelioration of the human individual, but (on the same level as revelation and Scripture) proclamation in service to God, the Church forgot no less than herself ; she made herself, instead of a place for the service of God, by which as such men are also helped, a place of very splendid service to man, in which God must figure exclusively as the most highly objective, most highly miraculous means, but still only as the means. The glory of objectivity in which the Word of God was enveloped, above all in its Biblical form, was even so something like the utterance of a bad conscience, by which the fact was concealed that men had ceased properly to be aware what they were saying, when they said " Word of God," ceased to be aware that they are thus expressing action taking place to-day—not of man in his relation to God, but of God in His relation to man—and thus expressing no less than the Church.   When that awareness ceased, was it surprising that Modernism in its recent inroads discovered that the goal of a very splendid service to man could also be reached by a simpler and less miraculous way than that which orthodoxy still continued to assert with great outward, but not quite so great inward, fidelity ? Was it surprising, if the objectivity which orthodoxy continued to claim for revelation and Scripture and theoretically also for preaching and the sacraments, struck one bright spirit and thousands of bright spirits, yes, even thousands of pious hearts, more and more as a superfluous idol, the smashing of which was bound to appear to them a good work, well-pleasing to God ? The catastrophic breakdown of orthodoxy in the 18th century, the consequences of which we have to shoulder to this day, is no greater a puzzle than the collapse of a house whose foundations are giving way.   It is not philosophy of the world become critical, but the Church's own theology become uncritical, ceasing to understand itself at the centre, which is responsible for that evil. The task set us of to-day, with all profound respect for the work achieved by orthodoxy, and with all understanding of the ultimate intentions of this service, must consist, in contrast thereto and by fresh adoption of Luther's thoughts, in taking proclamation in particular with seriousness as the Church's act, in and through which service should be rendered not to man but to God, in and through which God comes to express Himself ; and then, starting from that point, we must understand once more, that and in what sense first the Bible, and first of all revelation, is really God's Word.   It was at this point, before the inrush of the catastrophe of the 18th century, that forgetfulness set in.   It is obviously at this point that fresh reflection must begin.   Which implies that the direct object of a present-day dogmatics must be just Church proclamation.

§ 5

THE NATURE OF THE WORD OF GOD

The Word of God is in all its three forms the language of God to man. For that very reason it happens, holds good, and operates in the act of God on man. But precisely as such it happens in God's way, which is different from all other happening, i.e. in God's mystery.

1. THE QUESTION AS TO THE NATURE OF THE WORD OF GOD

At this point we have to depart from the first edition of this book in two points pre-eminently.—The first point refers to the arguments used there in § 5, 1 ; substantially to the effect that after establishing the concept of the Word of God in its threefold form, which we succeeded in doing by means of an analysis of Church proclamation, we had to pass over from the phenomenological to the existential mode of dealing with it, i.e. from the thought of one who deals with things from without, to the thought of one who by his existence participates in things. This passage was rightly resisted in many quarters (cf. Fr. Gogarten, *Karl Barth's Dogmatik, Theol. Rundschau*, 1929 p. 70 f. ; Th. Siegfried, *Das Wort und die Existenz*, I 1930 p. 35 f., 250 f.). The question is, whether the concepts of phenomenological and of existential thinking are properly specified and distinguished by the method under discussion. The question further is, whether existential is more than just a definite form of phenomenological thinking, or whether there is not some point at which the two concepts coincide. The question therefore is, whether the idea of a " passage " from the one to the other is not generally unrealisable. But these are philosophical and not theological questions. And the objection which I have since made to myself is this, that whatever their content and their mutual relationship may be, these concepts cannot in any way make or signify decisive salients on the path of dogmatic thinking, as seemed there to be taken for granted. However philosophers may or may not come to an understanding on these matters, they will do so as philosophers and not as theologians, i.e. they will not do so out of any responsible regard for the theme of theology, and so in such a way that theology can learn nothing from them, and indeed should learn nothing from them, unless she allows them to foist in a philosophical theme in place of her own, as has always happened, when she accepted material instruction from some kind of philosophy. Such adoption of a philosophical theme was not my purpose at this stage, even in the first edition. The statement of the " passage over " was intended to be more harmless and incidental than it has been taken to be. Clearly enough, in

141

dogmatics as in every science we need not, but we may avail ourselves of the specifically philosophical terminology as well as of any other, where it is suitable for incidentally illustrating and emphasising what has to be said with a theological intention, where the sense in which such a linguistic loan is made, is fixed with relative certainty by the context, and where the chance of being misunderstood is relatively remote, as though it were a question of proving theological statements by reference to similar ones with a philosophical content, i.e. of putting a philosophical theme in place of the theological one. In the passage under discussion such misunderstanding was relatively imminent and in any case promptly arose. Th. Siegfried (*op. cit.* p. 36), to my horror, interpreted this passage as follows : " Upon this foundation (meaning the existential thinking introduced) he proposes to build up his dogmatics." That really was not my intention. But apart from better intention altogether, I ought to have realised that to drag in those concepts at that very point, in relation to what I already wished to say on that occasion, was a superfluous and a dangerous game. Superfluous, because no proof of the doctrine of the Word of God by the fact that it was proved to be posited by existential thinking and that, therefore, an existential philosophy was asserted as its background and its justification, did as a matter of fact follow. Dangerous, because all that follows on the basis of that passage might be understood as indicating, although in obscure conjunction with the purposes of Catholic and Old Protestant theology, something of that nature, namely, an existential philosophical proof of theology. Moreover, there can and could be no serious question as to what I then practically understood by the " passing over." It would be fatal if hitherto we had not thought and spoken as participators in the things in our existence. But if this should not have been the case hitherto, it cannot be in our power to " pass over " to it now, and thus propose from now on to think and speak as participators. But further, whether before or after, we could never desist, when thinking and speaking of things, from always regarding them also from without, however much we might participate in them. And once more, of this consideration from without, we should have to say that it is nowise in our power really to get within sight of the things we speak of here, even merely from without. The two methods of consideration which I wished to keep separate there are, however philosophically they may be analysed and related, more or less proper to all human thinking and speaking, and a theological train of thought as such cannot become more correct or the reverse, more important or the reverse, because of this more or less. Even in subsequent transitions from more to less and *vice versa*, however naturally they may arise in theological trains of thought, practically there is no serious theological decision involved.—That leads us to the second point. In the first edition, at the point we have now reached, the doctrine of the Word of God is so continued that first in §§ 5 and 6 two analyses are given of the situation of man, first as preacher and second as hearer of the Word of God, and then in § 7 an analysis of the peculiar knowledge of the Word of God in general. Then in due course in the last section of the three paragraphs there is annexed to these three analyses, and presumably as the result of them, three times three " closer determinations of the Word of God," which in their totality explain what should now be unfolded as the doctrine of the nature of the Word of God. That arrangement in the first edition had three faults. (1) The " closer determinations " of the concept of the Word of God, scattered over three paragraphs and appearing almost in the form of appendices, were already withdrawn from readers' attention by this external placing, in a manner fatal to the under-standing of the whole. It might all too easily happen, and it actually did so happen, that these concluding parts of §§ 5–7 have been regarded as a mere echo, which perhaps might even be misleading, of the analyses which con-stituted the real and, apparently in part, stimulating content of the three paragraphs. (2) I did not succeed, perhaps luckily for me, in making these closing parts on the concept of the Word of God illuminating and credible, in terms of the advertisement, as " results " of the three analyses. Between the analyses and these closer determinations stood certain thought associa-tions, but, take them all in all, the latter were proved elsewhere ; at this point they were not even necessary, and therefore they neither impressed nor aroused attention alongside the former. (3) The unsuccessful attempt, necessarily incapable of succeeding, to derive the doctrine of the nature of the Word of God at all from the analysis of the concrete situation of the preacher and hearer, i.e. of the man who recognises the Word of God, meant in the same sense and in the same direction the following of a " false tendency," like the previously criticised introduction and application of the concepts of phenomenological and existential thinking. As a matter of fact these closer determinations were by no means gained from these analyses. But I acted as if they might and were bound to be so gained. An anthropology, even though a Church anthropology, was thus being put forward as the ground of knowledge for decisive propositions about the Word of God. In that way—combined with the general explanation that henceforth and particularly in §§ 5–7 we were dealing with existential thinking—I showed reverence on that occasion to the false gods, although only after the manner of the *libellatici* of the Decian persecution. If there is something the Word of God certainly is not, it is not a predicate of man, even of the man who receives it, therefore, neither of man who speaks, hears, and recognises it in the sphere of the Church. Such it would have to be, if the closer determinations of its nature were to be really derivable from an analysis of the concrete situation of this man ; and this, though it did not take place, was yet in my argument so intended and asserted.

In his already quoted review of the first edition of this book, Fr. Gogarten has in the main raised two objections to its contents : (1) It lacks a " proper anthropology " (p. 66), and (2) it speaks at least in places " one time of a God isolated in and for Himself, over against man, and the next, of man isolated in and for himself over against God " (p. 72), instead of altogether about God and man in their connection (cf. also *The Problem of a Theological Anthropology*, *Z.d.Z.* 1929 p. 493 f.). Towards the second objection a position will be taken up, particularly in the course of this section. In the case of the first, that has already been done in the previously expounded self-criticism, and it only remains for me to make this attitude explicit with regard to Gogarten. I might summarise all that has been said against myself by expressing my regret to-day that five years ago I was at least on the way to a ' 'proper anthropology.'' Gogarten ought really to have acknowledged this from his own standpoint. That he actually could not do so, but in spite of my obviously present tendency in this direction speaks of a " want " of real anthropology, is very comforting to me to-day, as proving that the harm has not been so great as it might well have been. For I should have been bound to regard it as a great disgrace really to do what Gogarten luckily has discovered I have not done, but which he would gladly have seen done, namely, erect a " proper anthropology " as the " centre," " the main task," " the real problem of theology " (*Z.d.Z.* 1929 p. 505), " the hardest bit of work," which theology could have to do to-day (*Th. Rundschau*, 1929 p. 67), and that of course just means that it is the fountain and criterion of all further theological propositions.—Gogarten has proved the c o n c e r n which moved him in his demand for a " proper anthropology " in two· ways. In the first place, h i s t o r i c a l l y (*Z.d.Z.* 1929 p. 502 f.). As a consequence of modern knowledge of nature and the world, man, he says, has been pushed from without from his central position which was so perfectly obvious in the Middle Ages, and in that way called to the discovery and inner consciousness of himself and his historicity. It was the " humanisation of life " that had already bound L u t h e r to the humanists of his time, and above all to the Renascence, and S c h l e i e r m a c h e r ' s theology, with all needful reservations, was to be estimated as the first great attempt to make this characteristic of Lutheran doctrine also the characteristic of a greatly conceived and executed theology. Because the thought of the more recent period was most strongly moved by the problem of man himself, anthropology must therefore be regarded as the proper problem of any present-day theology. If we assume that the historical backgrounds of this analysis of our time are in order—not all Lutherans, perhaps, would be pleased with this sketch—and if we further assume that this analysis is itself correct in substance—yet it was perhaps more correct before the War than in the present which so long ago became much more realistic again, in which it can scarcely be said any longer of a large and especially of the younger section of one's contemporaries, that the " humanisation of life " in particular is such a very significant concept in their living consciousness. Yet the question invariably remains whether in face of the alleged anthropologising of the modern (or once upon a time modern) living consciousness it is wise to follow in Schleiermacher's tracks, though under a different banner, and to take one's bearings by this living consciousness. Theology has far too frequently tried to seek out and to conquer the consciousness of a period on its own ground. We have already earlier addressed ourselves to the question of theology allowing her action to be prescribed by any sort of adversaries, because that simply means her already conceding them half or more than half of what she should never concede, namely, the Church's lack of independence in life and thought over against the world, the primacy of the questions which the world has to put to the Church over the questions which the Church has to put to herself. And might not a theology, which simply refused to co-operate even in method with such " humanisation of life," also be more timely to-day—if that is the real point—than one which by its pronouncement admits from the start that she can only contribute a second word, a so-called " word upon the situation," the situation prevailing outside the Church ? Gogarten's second concern seems to emanate from C h r i s t o l o g y. " Must not thought begin," he asks (*Theol. Rundsch.* 1929 p. 73), " with the Man God became ? Can we do other than start from the God who is in fact not isolated manwards, and does that not mean that thought must begin with the Man ? " I could understand that if for " starting from the Man " we had " working tȯ the Man." As a matter of fact theological propositions, are distinguished from those of all meta-physics or morals, according as they render the reality and truth of which they claim to speak, comprehensible, in a sense corresponding to the Immanuel who constitutes the content of revelation, as reality and truth proceeding from God to man. Ought it really to be a consequence of Christology, of the incarnation of the Word, that now, *post Christum*, thought ought to " start from man "—and for Gogarten that means, not from Jesus, the one and only

God-man, but from that other man, who over against God has ceased to be isolated, and yet is not identical with the God-man—in fact, must so start, and start as at the very centre of theology ? Is this man who has ceased to be isolated from God, apart altogether from the one God-man, in a position to form the possible or necessary starting-point of thought ? This con- clusion was at least not yet drawn even by the old Lutheran dogmatists, to whose Christology it might possibly have approximated. But the man who did draw it was first Schleiermacher, and then, from a bad motive, L. Feuerbach. Thus this second properly theological concern of Gogarten's seems to me not only to carry little conviction, but to be, in substance, thor- oughly dubious.—But I must regard the anthropology which Gogarten fails to find in me as harmful, because with it I do not see how we are to avoid the danger of handing over theology afresh to some sort of philosophy and so losing the real theological theme. I am quite aware that Gogarten (expressly in the essay in *Z.d.Z.* and inferentially also in the previous review in the *Theol. Rundsch.*, e.g. pp. 68, 73) has clearly explained that the theme of his " anthropology proper " is " man who cannot be thought of apart from the God who has united Himself with man in revelation " ; its content could therefore only be gained from the Gospel itself or from the context of the whole of theology (*Z.d.Z.* 1929 p. 494 f.). Gogarten's purpose in this seems to tend in the same direction which I previously designated by the concept " Church anthropology," in connection with my own procedure in 1927. What at that time I expounded as such, namely, an analysis of the self- interpretation of the man who preaches and listens to the Word of God and recognises it in this particular concrete situation, has failed to satisfy Gogarten as being " proper anthropology," so much so that he could never once acknowledge or give me credit for my (from his point of view, good) intentions in this direction. Why did it fail to satisfy him ? At the time, Gogarten wrote that with my undervaluation of anthropology was " very closely " connected my failure " to investigate thoroughly the question of the scientific nature of theology, i.e. the question of the relationship between theology and philosophy and of all that is otherwise involved in it " (*Theol. Rundsch.* 1929 p. 66 f.). Now it must not be assumed (and this assumption, moreover, is not established by the declaration, emitted in this connection, of his solidarity with Bultmann) that Gogarten's own estimate of anthropology is " very closely " connected with precisely this investigation. Yet if the service of anthropology is to make clear the relationship between theology and philo- sophy (and in harmony with Bultmann that certainly means to derive the possibility of theology from the discoverable relationship between philosopny and theology), how can we take seriously the theological independence of anthropology as desired by Gogarten, and its derivation from the Gospel and solely from the Gospel ? The decisive propositions in Gogarten's anthro- pological programme are to the effect that between the doctrine of man on the one side and the doctrine of God on the other there is a circle : " there is no understanding of man without understanding of God, but . . . this God again I cannot understand, unless I already understand man " (*Z.d.Z.* 1929 p. 496). Had Gogarten in the last sentence written " also " instead of " already," no objection could be taken. The thought would then be : understanding man presupposes understanding God ; but understanding God always includes understanding man also. But that does not appear to be Gogarten's thought. In fact no one could tell how far, from that standpoint, one could arrive at the primacy of anthropology, at clearing up the relation-

10

ship between theology and philosophy, and so at establishing the scientific
nature of theology. And Gogarten actually writes "already" of man.
By this "already" there appears to be ascribed to understanding man a
priority over understanding God, a priority which on its side seems unthinkable without presupposing some sort of "pre-understanding" with regard to
man, as is actually allowed for in Bultmann. But such a pre-understanding
with regard to man, by means of which we would as it were leap into the
aforementioned circle of understanding about God and man in their homogeneity, does not seem, again, to harmonise with Gogarten's unambiguous
declaration that man should be regarded primarily as a unit, "existing outside revelation, who may therefore be thought of without at the same time
thinking of the revelation of God " (*op. cit.* p. 497). The revelation of God !
What does that mean for Gogarten in this connection ? He interprets this
expression in the same passage by adding (the revelation) "in which God
has bound Himself to man from creation onwards as his God and Lord,"
and somewhat later with still greater clearness, "the revelation which is the
creation and preservation of man since the beginning of the world " (*op. cit.*
p. 498). And thereby we are set a final puzzle. What are we to understand
by revelation that takes place "from creation onwards," or by revelation
which is precisely the creation and preservation of man ? It might mean,
somewhat in the sense of *Qu.* 19 of the *Heidelberg Catechism*, the Gospel
which ever since creation has reached man. But why should Gogarten
adduce this in explanation in precisely this context ? And how, because the
one Gospel is the Gospel for all times since the beginning of the world, should
the conclusion be to the primacy of anthropology, which Gogarten seeks to
prove by his arguments ? What is now left over save the assumption which
is instantly applicable through Gogarten's second formula, namely, that
"since the creation " means God's revelation which is given itself in and with
creation and preservation, and which as such, even apart from the Gospel,
i.e. apart from God's second revelation which is distinct from creation, is
present and made known to us in the ordinances for the reality of our created
state, our creaturely existence ? The connection and homogeneity betwixt
God and man, on which Gogarten wishes to base his anthropology, would
thus be that which is posited in the relationship between God as Creator and
man as creature. Then at a stroke all would be clear. Gogarten could then
say, on the one hand, quite rightly, that for him too the point is absolutely
man and man only, who is only to be found within revelation, and on the other
hand and simultaneously he could, once more quite rightly, concede to the
understanding of man with his "already," a priority over the understanding
of God, i.e. God as He is to be understood from His revelation in the Gospel.
A slight terminological difficulty would remain, in that frequently Gogarten
speaks expressly of man as he is to be understood in the "Gospel," not merely
from the standpoint of "revelation." But in this passage by "Gospel"
might be understood this revelation which is given with creation itself, and
precedes the revelation proclaimed, or else the confirmation of this creation-
revelation implicitly given in the Gospel. The primacy of anthropology,
Bultmann's pre-understanding, the wonderful "already," and the still more
wonderful "starting from man," not to mention, in conclusion, the possibility of clearing up the relationship between philosophy and theology and of
establishing the scientific nature of theology, all this would be assured. If
by revelation in this context is meant a revealed state of God, preceding
revelation in the narrower and proper sense and given with our creaturely

existence as such, then an analysis of this creaturely existence of ours, i.e. of the revealed state of God inhering in it, must really be, as the " pre-understanding " of the proper, special revelation, the first step of theological common sense, the step by which we should jump into the circle including understanding of God and understanding of man, from, as it were, an outer, enclosing circle. In that case we could not in fact understand God, i.e. the God of proclaimed revelation, " without already (i.e. first) understanding man," man, i.e. to whom God is originally manifest as his creator. We should in fact primarily, i.e. in jumping into the inner circle, have in our thought to " start from man," i.e. from this man who by his created state is bound up with God. And this man who in the outer sphere of his created state is also in his own way already bound up with God, might really now be regarded as the common object of, or as it were the turn-table between, philosophy and theology, and be applied as an anthropology to clear up the relationship between these two sciences—in other words, to establish theology as a science. Were we thus to regard the " revelation starting with creation," of which Gogarten speaks, then I could think out for myself something at least sensible in itself about the " proper anthropology " which he fails to find in me and which he so obviously represents himself. Of course in that case I should not know what difference there was left between this sensible thing in itself and an everyday natural theology. The nature and purpose of all natural theology has always been to analyse man in the light of a revelation of God starting with creation, as the *introitus* to the inner circle of real theology, based upon *revelatio specialis*. And this is the compelling double question with which I am faced : how far is the nature and purpose of Gogarten's " proper anthropology," not, according to all he has said about it to be identified with the nature and purpose of all natural theology ? and how could it possibly be that Friedrich Gogarten really and deliberately wants to be understood in this sense ? How is this to be reconciled with the acute deliverances of Gogarten, set forth in this very context to combat natural theology (p. 495 f.) ? Which have we to take seriously in Gogarten, his anthropological programme or his emphatic renunciation of natural theology ? Or how far are we to take either seriously ? What is the relation of the one to the other, the other to the one ?—Be that as it may, I can only say for myself that I cannot supply what he finds lacking in me, because I cannot see that anything other than a new, or rather an old, natural theology could be the result. But natural theology in the sense just described is an undertaking possible only within the realm of Catholicism, because the presupposition involved is that the revealed state of God in our created state, the creation of man which is at the same time the revelation of God, is somewhere and somehow directly discernible by us, presumably because confirmed by the Gospel. This direct discernment of the original connection between God and man, discernment of the creation of man which as such is also the revelation of God, is, according to Reformed principles as to the seriousness of sin, taken from us by the Fall and only restored in the Gospel, in *revelatio specialis*. I.e. so restored to us that we must certainly regard the Word of God in revelation, Scripture, and proclamation as God's Word to man, as also related to man because he is God's creature—but not in such a way that statements can be derived from it which, apart from the availability of the Word of God in revelation, Scripture, and proclamation, can be made known by man, i.e. from the standpoint of man who now understands himself in his created state on the basis of the Word of God heard, and can—this is the crucial thing—on its side be made the presupposition of understanding the Word of God, in other words, the foundation of theology. There is of course a theological anthropology, but that will consist neither, as perhaps was Gogarten's original notion, in an explication and application of Christological propositions, nor yet in a supralapsarian analysis, now once more rendered possible, of the created state of man which is at the same time the revelation of God, but simply in showing forth man's original *status integritatis*, indicated in the Word of God itself and opened up in Jesus Christ, and his presently prevailing *status corruptionis* ; a process which simply cannot serve to make it comprehensible that by " starting with man " there are any possibilities of reaching God, but the content of which is very much rather the isolation of man before God, regarding which an understanding with any philosopher is as little possible as it is regarding any other *locus* in dogmatics ; to use it in the way for the sake of which Gogarten seeks to present his " proper anthropology," will be quite impossible. The circle connecting the understanding of God and man, of which Gogarten speaks so impressively, the circle in which the fact that man belongs to God is recognised, is really only one circle, and a tightly closed one at that. Even Gogarten only speaks of one and speaks of its being tightly closed. But I am not quite clear how far in either case that is permanent. For if it is only one and tightly closed, it is also impossible to begin with creation and jump into it from without—in other words, to display a common platform upon which to come to terms with the philosopher, be his name Grisebach or Heidegger, as to how far movement within this circle is possible at all, even from an external point of view. For we know nothing of our created state from our created state, but only through the Word of God, from which we can derive no independent, generally true items of knowledge, different from the Word of God and therefore leading up to it. And knowledge in this circle is irreversible. Movement in it does not go on automatically, down-up and up-down. It is by no means to be confused with Wobbermin's religious-psychological circle. We cannot at will claim now to understand man because we have understood God, now to understand God because we have understood man. But to understand God, because we have understood man by starting with God, is always an understanding new in itself, or rather in God's Word, and not one based upon a precedent understanding of man. To " start from man " can only mean to start with man of the lost *status integritatis*, that is, of the presently existing *status corruptionis*. Thus to understand God, " starting from man " signifies either a thing impossible in itself, or one such as can only be described in the form of Christology but not in the form of anthropology ; and so not in the form of a Christology translated into anthropology. There is a way from Christology to anthropology. There is no way from an anthropology to Christology.—On the basis of all these considerations I must not only decline Gogarten's invitation to improve my dogmatics by introducing a proper anthropology, but also eliminate everything in my own sketch of five years ago which might look like a concession in this direction.

In the first place, it must cease to look as if the doctrine of the Word of God ought to be based upon or even only subsequently supported by the fact that it is regarded as a bit of existential thinking. Secondly, no sort of anthropology, even only in appearance, must be allowed to come forward as the basis for understanding the Word of God. §§ 5–6 in the first edition, which deal with man as the preacher and as the hearer of the Word of God, may be dropped out completely, because their essential content is partly anticipated in §§ 3–4 of the new edition, partly it belongs to the problem of the knowledge of the Word of God, in part it has a more fitting place in homiletics than in dogmatics. That, and how far, the Word of God is the Word to man, is to be shown in the discussion of the epistemological problem, i.e. the question as to the truth of the Word of God. But the answer to the question, what is the Word of God ?, the doctrine of its nature, must no longer appear as conditioned by this investigation, must cease to show itself anywhere near a " proper anthropology "; it must be evolved prior to and independently of the latter.

We have spoken of the forms of the Word of God. Form is obviously always the form of a content. But may we actually speak of a content of the Word of God ? Can we answer the searching, popular question, yet frequently found in the mouths of theologians : What then is the Word of God ? In the question of the content of the Word of God we find ourselves faced with the same difficulty which will meet us much later in dogmatics, in the question of the nature of God in general. God and His Word are not presented to us in the way in which natural and historical entities are presented to us. We can never by retrospect, and so by anticipation, fix what God is or what His Word is : He must always repeat that to us and always repeat it afresh. But there is no human awareness corresponding to this divine utterance. In God's utterance there comes to be a meeting and a communion between His nature and man, but not an absorption of this nature into man's awareness. There can only be a constant repetition of fresh divine utterance. In this divine utterance there is realised, as such, together with the " God with us," the knowledge of God and His Word. Therefore we can only—i.e. by faith in the Word of God—say who God is ; He is the one God, Father, Son, and Holy Spirit. And so we can only—i.e. in view of the reality of the Church, within whose bounds we do our thinking—say what the Word of God is, here recalled and here expected : as the one Word of God, it is proclamation, Scripture, and revelation. But, of course, just as, knowing by faith who God is, we may and must therefore also say in what way God is, just as on the basis of the doctrine of the Trinity there is a doctrine of the attributes in which is manifested to us the hidden nature of God, unpredictable and irreproducible in human language, and therefore insusceptible of adequate expression in human language—so, knowing what the Word of God is, i.e. knowing about its three forms, we may say in what way it is ; we may say, when it is spoken to us in these three forms, in what series of determinations it is this Word, i.e. the Word of God. Thus we can, indeed, say what the Word of God is ; but we must say it indirectly. We must recall the forms in which it is real for us and from these three forms which it takes infer how it is. That "how" is the reflected image, attainable by man, of the unattainable nature of God. It is with this reflected image that we are here to be occupied.

2. THE WORD OF GOD AS GOD'S LANGUAGE

Church proclamation is language. Holy Scripture is also language. But revelation itself and as such is language too. If we hold to the Word of God in the three forms in which in fact it is heard in the Church, if we do not think beyond the Church to things which God could have willed and done, but once for all has not done, at all events in the Church, and therefore has not willed either, we have no reason for not taking the concept "Word of God" in its primary and literal sense. "God's Word" means, God speaks. "Speaks" is not a symbol (as P. Tillich, *Rel. Verwirkl.* 1930 p. 48, thinks), a designation and description (chosen by man on the score of his own judgment as to its greater or less symbolic force) of a totally other content totally foreign to the meaning of this proposition. But this proposition corresponds—certainly with human inadequacy, with the brokenness with which alone human propositions can correspond with the nature of the Word of God— with the possibility which God has chosen and realised at all events in His Church. We are not absolutising the human possibilities of the intellect. We might very well be of the private opinion that it would be better and nicer if God had not spoken and did not speak with such deliberate "intellectualism" and that it would be more appropriate to God if "God's Word" meant all sorts of different things, apart from the meaning "God speaks." But is this private opinion of ours so important, resting as it does upon some sort of philosophy? If perhaps it is not, let us simply stick to the fact, and not think beyond it, that in the form in which the Church knows God's Word—the one and only form which affects us at all necessarily because it affects us magisterially—in this form "God's Word" means "God speaks," and all further statements about it must be regarded as exegesis, not as limitation or negation of this proposition. We shall have to regard God's speech also as God's act, and God's act also as God's mystery. But as only God's act is really God's mystery (and not any other sort of mystery), so only God's speech is really God's act (and not any other sort of act). The concepts act and mystery cannot, therefore, because they are necessarily explanatory, point us away from the concept of speech or language, but because they are explanations can only point us back repeatedly to it as the original text. If they are trust-worthy commentaries, then of course in their own way they assert no less than everything, no less than the one and entire thing that needs saying here, just like the original text itself. We may there-fore very well and without danger also say with the concepts act and mystery what the Word God is, if thereby (otherwise than as in the case of Faust, who was looking for the right symbol) our purpose is not to translate the Logos in a way different from the concept of language, but to explain the only possible translation by the concept of language. Let us try, first of all without commentary, to understand the text itself in this its sole possible translation. What does it signify for the concept of the Word of God, if Word of God means originally and irrevocably, God speaks ?

1. It signifies first and foremost the s p i r i t u a l i t y of the Word of God, spirituality as distinguished from naturalness, corporeality, from any physical event. We hasten to add that also there is no Word of God without a physical event. We are reminded of that by the homogeneity of preaching and sacrament. We are reminded of that by the verbal nature of Holy Scripture. We are reminded of that finally and most highly of all by the corporeality of the man Jesus Christ. But nothing of that justifies us in saying that the Word of God is just as much and in the same sense spiritual as it is natural or corporeal. There is here in all forms of the Word of God an upper and under, an at first and a subsequently, which in its complete relativity can yet never be effaced or reversed. The Word of God is a l s o natural and corporeal, because without that it would not be the Word of God directed to us men as spiritual-natural beings, really coming to us in the way in which we are real. That is why sacrament must stand alongside preaching : that is why preaching itself is also a physical event. That is why the letter of Scripture is anything but a *pudendum* or a *negligendum*. That is why the Church (though in this is also emphatically and clearly shown the relationship of subordination) is called the body of Christ. The Word of God is a l s o natural or corporeal, because in the creaturely sphere which it enters as the Word to us men there is nothing spiritual which is not also natural or corporeal. But the fact that the Word of God ties itself not only to the spirituality but also to the corporeality of the creature need not hinder us from

realising that it is by no means neutral above both or in both, nor yet is it primarily and especially nature.

On this point we need not let ourselves be put out by the quite recently current realism and anti-spiritualism of modern times. That corporeality is the end of the ways of God—this utterance of Fr. Chr. Oetinger's which they are so fond of quoting was a good, although at the same time over-emphasised, expression of a very necessary opposition to the Enlightenment spirit of flight from Nature ; but it is not really suitable for conversion into a dogma. And if Erich Przywara once (*Stimmen der Zeit*, 1929 p. 231) reproached me with fixing on the two words, Word and Spirit, in so remark-able a way, thus betraying a " concealed spiritualism," and thereby an ultimate sublunariness in what I claimed as such a transcendent concept of God, whereas God is not confined to any one sphere of creation more than to another, but is free regarding both, the questions arise, whether God without prejudice to His freedom has not already in creation bound Himself in a different way and to a greater degree and in closer fashion to spirit than to nature ; whether also according to the uniform anthropology of the Bible, which verily must not be disturbed, man is not first and foremost to be con-sidered in the light of the invisible livingness breathed into him by God ; whether it is an accident that speaking about God is commanded hundreds of times in the Bible, whereas the setting up of likenesses of God is forbidden and barred *expressis verbis* ; whether it is just an accident that the words " Word " and " Spirit " play this special part also with regard to God Himself in the OT and NT, and whether in the doctrine of the Trinity words from the other sphere of creation could be applied equally well in place of *Logos* and *Pneuma*. It is an excellent thing for us to let the NT phrase about the bodily resurrection of Christ and the other one about the resur-rection of our body too be stated in a different form from the most of those immediately before us. It is an excellent thing for us, by means of the favourite doctrine of Eastern orthodoxy, that eschatological redemption includes in it in the most comprehensive sense, the cosmos, the creature as well, to let ourselves be reminded of a likewise long-neglected truth of the NT. But it would not be a good thing for us to overlook the fact that in the OT and NT man is addressed as a natural being also, but still as this distinct natural being, a natural being distinguished by spirit—we might even say simply that he was just addressed, that it is this and not any natural event, that even in the natural event it is always God's language, which is the way in which God visits him. A certain relative " canonisa-tion of the spirit as compared with nature " (Przywara)—more ought not to be asserted—we cannot avoid asserting even with all due recognition of the realistic interest.

The Word of God is primarily spiritual, and after that and in that form, in this its spirituality, for the sake of it and without prejudice to it, also a corporeal or natural event. That above all is what is meant when, in accordance with the forms in which we hear it, we call it God's language. The form in which reason com-municates with reason, person with person, is language, so too when it is God's language. Of course it is divine reason that communicates with human reason, the divine person with the human person. The complete inconceivability of this event confronts us. But reason with reason, person with person, primarily in analogy with what happens in the spiritual sphere of creation, not primarily in analogy with what happens in the corporeal or natural sphere. The Word of God—we should not evade the concept so much tabued to-day—is a rational and not an irrational event.

The reminder about supposedly " deeper " anthropological strata of being beyond the rational rests upon a philosophical construction and a philosophical value-judgment, about which philosophers must come to an agreement among themselves. We have nothing to say to it save that the meeting of God and man, according to what we know of it in the Church, takes place primarily, pre-eminently, and characteristically in this sphere, the sphere of *ratio*, however " deep " or the reverse of " deep " this may lie according to philosophical judgment.—" . . . the king of whom the psalm here speaketh, although of course IIe hath his kingdom upon earth, yet so ruleth spiritually and pointeth therefore to the heavenly kingdom, that although we really behold not His kingdom, nevertheless we hear it. But how ? ' Out of the mouths of babes and sucklings hast thou ordained strength.' And Christ's kingdom is a hearing kingdom, not a seeing kingdom. For the eyes lead and guide us not thither where we find Christ and get to know Him, but the ears must do that . . ." (Luther, *Sermon delivered in Merseburg*, 1545 W. edn. 51, p. 11, l. 25). " As when thou seest and hearest a preacher preach the Word of God, through which by Christ's behest he proclaimeth repentance and forgiveness of sins, thou seest there no plough or harrow, but thou seest and hearest that the preacher alone taketh up the tongues and the word. . . . Therefore likewise, when we see the holy sacrament achieve . . . rescue and freedom from sins and death, that thou shouldst no longer be holden fast in the devil's kingdom, thou seest not, but only hearest that which is announced and granted to thee with the preacher's tongue through the Word " (*ib.* p. 12, l. 9).

Language or speaking stands in correlation to hearing, understanding, and obeying. However sorely problematic these concepts may become through our being here concerned with God's speaking and with the hearing, understanding, and obeying correlated with God's speaking—it is faith that hears, understands, and obeys God's speaking—we shall not have to abandon the levels of these very concepts of speaking, hearing, understanding, obeying, unless we wish to take up a stand elsewhere than where the Word of God is heard.

Rudolf Otto's " Idea of the Holy," whatever it may be, is at all events not to be regarded as the Word of God, for the simple and patent reason that it is the numinous, and that the numinous is the irrational, and the irrational something no longer distinguishable from an absolutised power of Nature. Upon this very distinction everything depends, if we are to understand the concept of the Word of God.

The Word of God has also natural power, but primarily and pre-eminently and decisively the simple spiritual power of truth. —What we here assert of the Word of God does not hold equally of every word. It cannot be asserted of any other word that it decisively possesses the power of truth. For any other word physis signifies its limit, at which the lack of power in its spirituality is simultaneously exposed. Every other word lacks now rather truth, now rather reality, which of course implies lack of both. In every other word the significant thing is the uncertain swing between a spasmodic idealism and an equally spasmodic realism. The naturalness and the spirituality of every other word are those of fallen man. Only in God's word do we find the normal arrangement of spiritual and natural. But in God's Word we do find them, and we should not let ourselves be led astray by the aberrations of a human spirituality that flies from Nature, to level up that arrangement or to reverse it. We must therefore in the matter of language in theology and worship be perfectly clear as to what is involved in applying naturalistic concepts. In view of the language of the Bible itself we cannot possibly lay an absolute embargo upon speaking of life, light, fire, spring, stream, and storm, of outbreaks, shocks, overpowering events, and experiences. But in that case we must remember that, properly regarded, this occurs in the Bible invariably in a perfectly definite subordination ; and so reflect that in speaking naturalistically we are specifying the Word of God in its non-primary meaning, that in this way we are speaking of what it certainly also is, but of what it certainly is not primarily. We shall then have to reflect how easily at this point, with hearer and even with speaker, there begins a slip-back into the sphere of the natural, where there is no longer speech and answer, knowledge and decision, but only movement, pressure, and impact, where we are no longer concerned with truth but only with reality. This side of things has also to be kept in view, and that is why naturalism cannot be banished from theological language. But in the Word of God that is neither the primary nor the proper concern. And as soon as that became the sole concern in our statements, it would be all over with the service of God in theology and proclamation, according to human judgment, according to what we know about the Word of God through the Word of God itself. Awareness of the primary spirituality of the Word of God will exhort us to concentrate upon the spiritual sphere and to beware of trespassing on the natural.

2. " God's Word " means, God speaks. That signifies, in the second place, its personal character. God's Word is not a thing to be described, nor is it a concept to be defined. It is neither a content nor an idea. It is not " a truth," not even the very highest truth. It is the truth because it is God's person speaking, *Dei loquentis persona*. It is not something objective. It is the objective, because it is the subjective, namely, God's subjective. God's Word means, God speaking. Certainly God's Word is not the formal possibility of divine speech, but its fulfilled reality. It always has a perfectly definite, objective content. God always utters a *concretissimum*. But this divine *concretissimum* can as such neither be anticipated nor repeated. What God utters is never in any way known and true in abstraction from God Himself. It is known and true for no other reason than that He Himself says it, that He in person is in and accompanies what is said by Him.

Non satis est habere donum, nisi sit et donator praesens, sicut petivit et Moses, Ex. 33 : " *Si non tu ipse precedas nos, ne educas nos de loco ipso*," etc. (Luther, *Romans*, 1515–1516 *Fi. Schol.* 140, 15). *A Deoenim vivo disceditur dum a verbo eius disceditur, quod est vivum et omnia vivificans, imo Deus ipse* (Hebrews, 1513 *Fi. Schol.* 42, 1. 2). The Word of Christ is according to another utterance of Luther's the mouth of Christ : " That it therefore ever proceedeth out of Christ's mouth from one mouth to another and yet remaineth Christ's mouth " (*Pred. üb.* John 14²³ᶠ· *Cruc. Sommerpost.* 1543 W. edn. 21, p. 469, l. 3).

It was the third form of the Word of God, which bears and establishes everything that we attempted to fix in the concept of revelation, which forced us, when analysing the concepts of proclamation and of Scripture, to remain unfailingly mindful of this proviso. Just because we regard the Word of God not merely as proclamation and Scripture but as God's revelation in proclamation and Scripture, we must regard it in its identity with God Himself. God's revelation is Jesus Christ, God's Son.

" God's Son " in the language of the doctrine of the Trinity does not differ from " God's Word." When it reads in John 1¹ᶠ· : Ἐν ἀρχῇ ἦν ὁ λόγος, καὶ ὁ λόγος ἦν πρὸς τὸν Θεὸν καὶ Θεὸς ἦν ὁ λόγος. οὗτος ἦν ἐν ἀρχῇ πρὸς τὸν Θεόν, the fourth sentence would be a meaningless repetition of the second, did not the οὗτος, primarily indeed requiring likewise to be completed by λόγος, at the same time point, by an emphatic usage, beyond all that follows to the proper name Ἰησοῦς Χριστός, first mentioned in verse 17, with the bearer of which the Logos in the prologue of this Gospel is meant to be regarded as identical. And in Rev. 19¹²⁻¹³ the returning Christ, the rider on the white horse, is described as wearing a crown, ἔχων ὄνομα γεγραμμένον ὃ οὐδεὶς οἶδεν εἰ μὴ αὐτός, i.e. the wording of it is known to every one who sees it, but its literal meaning, the essence to which this name points, is known only to

Himself. Καὶ κέκληται τὸ ὄνομα αὐτοῦ (the wording of this name) ὁ λόγος τοῦ Θεοῦ. Thus here also, what the Word of God means does not admit of direct statement. It is the name of the revelation, i.e. of the revealer. He is the Word of God. From Him alone can, i.e. shall, we experience what the Word of God is. Of ourselves we can only say of what sort it is, i.e. He is.

The equation, God's Word is God's Son, makes anything doctrinaire in regarding the Word of God radically impossible. In it and only in it is a real and effective barrier raised against what can be made of proclamation according to the Roman Catholic conception or of Holy Scripture according to the theory of later Old-Protestantism, a fixed total of revealed propositions to be systematised like the sections of a *corpus* of law. The only possible system in Holy Scripture and in proclamation is revelation, i.e. Jesus Christ. Of course the converse also holds, God's Son is God's Word. Thus God reveals Himself in propositions by means of language, and human language at that, to the effect that from time to time such and such a word, spoken by the prophets and apostles and proclaimed in the Church, becomes His Word. Thus the personality of the Word of God is not to be played off against its verbal character and its spirituality. It is not the case that this second determination under which we must regard it would signify its irrationality and therefore do away with the first determination under which we had to regard it.

Such clearly is the opinion of P. Tillich, in whom is to be found the following, somewhat naïve polemic. " But it is quite wrong to equate the Word as a symbol for the self-impartation of the Being Beyond, with the word as the physical means of self-comprehension and self-impartation on the part of the human spirit, and in this way to mix up the Word of God and the word of Scripture or preaching. On the contrary, we must simply (!) point to the fact that for Christian theology Jesus Christ is the Word, not His words but His essence, which finds expression as much in His words as also in His action and passion " (*Rel. Verwirkl.* 1930 p. 49). Upon which the comment is, that on the one hand the words, the action and passion, and the essence of Jesus Christ cannot be separated from each other in such wise that words, action, and passion are but the " expression " of His essence, as if His essence stood equally behind words, action, and passion. The essence of this person is identical with His language, action, and passion. Now this essence of Christ is moreover not directly present to us, but it must become present to us, and it can only become indirectly present to us, namely, through the Word-proclamation first of Holy Scripture and next of the Church as well. If Christ's essence is present to us, that takes place absolutely in such a way that it is equated with the " word as the physical means of self-comprehension and self-impartation on the part of the human spirit," that therefore the word of Scripture and the word of preaching become the Word of God. " For where My word is, there also am I " (Luther, *Sermon on Matt.* 22, 1544 W. edn. 52, p. 509, l. 26). " . . . God could not otherwise send forth Christ into the world, He had to fashion Him into the Word and so spread Him abroad and bear Him to every man.   Otherwise Christ would have remained for Himself alone and unknown to us, and thus He would have died for Himself alone. But because the Word bears Christ to us, so it bears to us Him who hath overcome death, sin, and devil " (*Sermon on John* 8⁴⁶⁻⁵⁹, 1525 W. edn. 17ᴵᴵ, p. 234, l. 11).

The personification of the concept of the Word of God, which we cannot avoid when we remember that Jesus Christ is the Word of God, does not signify any lessening of its verbal character. But it signifies (and signifies of course) the knowledge of His personalness as distinguished from all thingness or materiality, even though and so far as it is the Word, the Word of Scripture and the Word in preaching.   Personalness means being the subject not only in the logical sense, but also in the ethical sense, being a free subject, free, even in respect of the periodical limitations which are given with its individuality as such, able to dispose of its own existence and nature, as much in so far as it is an express form, as in so far as it is a living development ; but free also to choose new possibilities of existence and nature.   If we represent to ourselves what that means, it will not occur to us to see in this personalising of the concept of the Word of God a case of anthropomorphism.   The problem is not whether God is a person, the problem is whether we are.   Or shall we find among us men one whom in the full and real sense of this concept we can call a person ? But God is really a person, really a free subject.   And as surely as we are faced with His inconceivability because we cannot think out this thought to a finish, so surely we should not, on hearing His Word, refuse to think this starting-point of all thought, to recognise Him as a Person precisely in His Word.   By which we mean that it is not something or other, not a θεῖον, but He Himself, that comes to us in His Word.   Precisely in His Word God is a Person. The concrete significance of that is, that He is the Lord of the verbal character of His Word.   He is not bound to it, but it is bound to Him.   He thus has free disposal of the verbal character of Holy Scripture, He can use it or not use it, use it in one way or in another.   And He can select a new verbal form beyond the verbal form of Holy Scripture ; for what Holy Scripture proclaims as His Word, can be proclaimed again as His Word in a new verbal form, always in such a way that it is He Himself who speaks in this form.   Again the personality of the Word of God signifies, not any diminution of its verbal character, but the sheerly active obstacle to reducing its verbal form to a human system, i.e. to using its verbal form to lay the foundation and raise the structure of a human system. It would be not the faithfulness but the unfaithfulness of God to us if He allowed us to make such use of His Word. That would mean that He allowed us to gain power over His Word, to take it under our own charge, and thereby to shut ourselves up against Himself, to our own hurt. God's faithfulness to His Church consists in Him making use of His freedom to come to us in His Word, and in reserving to Himself the freedom to do this again and again.

3. "God's Word" means, God speaks. That must signify, in the third place, what I might term the purposiveness of the Word of God. It might also be called its relatedness or pointedness, its character as an address. We do not know the Word of God, either in its form of proclamation or of Holy Scripture or of revelation, as an essence that exists for itself or could exist only for itself. The sole way we know it is as the Word directed to us, coming home to us. The fact that this is so is of course by no means self-evident. We cannot infer the fact from the general concept of language. It is so, but it might be different. Even in the life of God within the Trinity, of course, the eternal generation of the Son or Logos is the expression of God's Love, of His wish not to be alone. But the conclusion from that is not that God could not be God, apart from addressing us. Doubtless we only understand the love of God for man, or primarily, in the general sense, for a reality distinct from Himself, when we regard it as free, unbeholden love which does not rest on a need. God would be none the less God if He had not created a world and man. The world's existence and our existence is in no wise essentially necessary to God, even as the object of His love. The eternal generation of the Son by the Father itself asserts first and foremost that even apart form the world and us altogether God is not lonely ; His love has its object in Himself. And so it cannot be said that our existence as the existence of the " addressees " of the Word of God is in any way constitutive for the concept of the Word. It could not be less what it is, even without us. God might satisfy His love all by Himself ; for He is already an object to Himself, and an object truly worthy of love. God had no need to speak to us ; what God utters from eternity to eternity by Himself and to Himself, might really be uttered as well and better without our being there, as an utterance which for us would be eternal silence. Only if we are clear on that point can we estimate what it means that God has

created a world and ourselves—under no necessity on His side, but actually He has ; that His love is valid for us—under no necessity on His side, but actually it is ; that His Word is spoken to us —under no necessity on His side, but actually it is.   It is thus purposiveness, free, actual, essentially unessential to God, which meets us in proclamation, in the Bible, in revelation.   We estimate its reality correctly only when we regard it as the reality of the love of the God who does not require us yet would not be without us, yet has directed His regard precisely upon us.

In this context it is really and once for all appropriate and necessary to keep clearly before us what God really has not done but might have done, because only in this contrast is it evident what He really has done.—But from this point of view another result is, how ambiguous it is to set the doctrine of the Word of God in the framework of an anthropology.   In that case the freedom of the divine purpose for man can only be asserted as a corollary, while it is virtually denied by the statement of it.

Thus man who hears, as the object of the purpose of God who speaks, is included in the concept of the Word of God as a factual, but not as an essential necessity.   He is not—as I had stated in most amazing fashion on p. iii of the first edition—" co-posited " in it, like Schleiermacher's God in the feeling of utter dependence. It is God's free grace that he is co-posited in it as a factual necessity. —If our intention is to recognise in this sense " purposiveness " or relation to us as the third attribute of the Word of God, and if we now further inquire into the content of this purpose, into what this relatedness or pointedness signifies for understanding it, we recall that its content is a *concretissimum*, wherever and whenever God speaks to man ; that to every man from time to time it has something quite special to say, something that comes straight home to him, and only to him in that way.   The real content of God's speech, or the real will of the speaking person of God, is thus never to be conceived and reproduced by us as a general truth.   We may and must of course, as readers of Scripture and hearers and bearers of proclamation, work with definite general conceptual material, apparently repeating or anticipating what God has said to this or that man or is about to say to this or that man.   In no other way, obviously, can we remind either ourselves or others of the Word of God that once came and some day will come again.   We may do this in words of our own coining or in Scripture quotations. But in that case we must continually be reflecting that this conceptual material is our own work, and not to be confused with the fullness of the Word of God itself, which we are thinking of and waiting for : it only points to that. What God said was always quite different, and what He is going to say will always be quite different—quite different from what we may say and must say to ourselves and to others about its content. Not only the word of preaching heard as the Word of God, even the word of Scripture by which God speaks to us, really becomes quite different in the transition from the mouth of God Himself to our ear and to our own mouth. It now becomes the Word of God recalled and expected by us in faith, which the Word as such, spoken and again to be spoken by God, confronts anew in stark majesty. But even in this stark majesty, in which its real content remains inconceivable to us on our side, its purposiveness remains proper to it, it is the Word that comes home to us, aims at us, and is to that extent determined, determined not by us but by God Himself, as Him who aims at us. We anticipate nothing of its real content, we but make a note of the points of view from which we have to attend to its real content, when, in view of this purposiveness in it, in view of its being an address to us, we establish the following points :

(*a*) The Word of God as directed to us is first of all such a word as we do not speak to ourselves, as under no circumstances we could ever speak to ourselves. Every human word, even man's word in proclamation, even the word of the Bible, we perhaps could and can speak as such even by ourselves. The encounter with man's word as such is never a genuine, ineffaceable encounter, and cannot be one. The encounter with the Word of God is a genuine ineffaceable encounter, i.e. not one to be dissolved into fellowship. The Word of God always tells us something new, which otherwise we could never have heard from any one. It is the boulder of a Thou which does not become an I, that is here cast on our path. It is this otherness, then, which is yet related to us, which yet makes itself known to us, but yet does so in this way, which stamps it fundamentally and comprehensively as God's Word, as the Lord's Word, compared with which all other words, however profound and fresh and arresting they may be, are not the words of the Lord. Whatever God may say to us, it will at all events be uttered in this way, it will be uttered as the Word of the Lord.

(*b*) As such a word of the Lord directed to us the Word of God is, secondly, the Word which aims at and touches us in our existence. No word of man is competent to aim at us in our existence, no word of man has the power to touch us in our existence. There could aim at us in our existence and touch us in our existence only such a word as would interrogate and answer us, exactly as death, being the end of our existence, might interrogate and answer us. But death is dumb.   It interrogates not, and it answers not. It is in fact only the end, nothing really external and superior to our existence, a height from which it might be aimed at and touched. The Word of God is the Word of the Lord because it comes from this external and supernal, from which even death would not speak to us, even if it could speak.   The Word of God comes home to us, as no word of man as such can come home to us, and as even death does not come home to us, because it is the Word of our Creator, the Word of Him who bounds our existence and the end of our existence, from whose side it is affirmed and denied, because through this Word everything has its being and is preserved, and without it would not exist.   To Him we belong who here makes Himself heard.   Whatever He may say, it will at least also be said within this relation of the Creator to His creature.

(c) As the Word of our Creator directed to us, the Word of God is in the third place the Word which has become and does become necessary for the renewal of the original relationship between us and Him.   That God speaks to us, that He reveals Himself to us, which means that He turns wholly and anew towards us, that as the Unknown He makes Himself known—after He has created us, and although we still belong to Him—must signify on the one hand a criticism of the reality of the relationship existing between us and Him, but on the other hand a declaration also of His purpose to maintain it in standing and to establish it anew from His side in spite of and along with this criticism which He makes.   Neither of these can be the content of a word of man ; only He who has made this relationship can also confirm and renew it, if it has been disturbed or destroyed.   Only God can pronounce the verdict and give the promise and raise the claim, all of which are equally implied in the concept of revelation.   The Word of God under this third aspect of its purposiveness is the Word of reconciliation, i.e. of the Reconciler, of God who by a second creation sets up His covenant anew with us in judgment and grace.   Whatever God may say to us will at all events likewise be uttered in this relationship of renewal.

(d) But precisely as the Word of reconciliation directed to us, the Word of God is fourthly and finally the Word by which God announces Himself to man, i.e. by which He promises Himself as the content of man's future, as He who meets him on his way through time as the End of all time, as the hidden Lord of all times. His presence through the Word is exactly His presence as He that cometh, cometh to fulfil and complete the relationship founded between us and Him at Creation, renewed and confirmed at the reconciliation. Once more this final Word cannot be a word of man. Words of men are never final words, never the promise of a certain, conclusive coming of the Other. It is proper to God's and only to God's Word to be actually, as Word, the full, genuine presence of the Speaker, although of Him as Him that should come. God's Word is the Word of our Redeemer, i.e. of the Lord who is to be Lord, as He was and is, who in His relationship to us keeps eternally faithful to Himself and thereby also to us. And in that very way is the real righteous Lord, the Lord of all lords. And whatever God may say to us, it will at all events always be said too in this final, consummating, eschatological relationship.

Once more, what God says from time to time remains His mystery which is manifested in the event of His real speaking. The concrete fulness of what from time to time He has said and will say to men is and remains really His affair. We can only hold by the fact— we also must hold by it—that when He spoke it was, and that when He does speak it will be the Word of the Lord, the Word of our Creator, our Reconciler, our Redeemer. Because we regard it as pointed at us, as coming home to us, we are commanded to keep our human thinking and speaking about it open at least in these four directions, to be ready and watchful from these four points of view.

3. GOD'S LANGUAGE AS GOD'S ACT

Where God speaks, it is meaningless to cast about for the corresponding act. Distrust as to whether speech may have been " merely " speech is, of course, only too apposite in dealing with all speech of man. When man speaks—and the more so, the better, the more finely and the more truly he speaks—his wretchedness, the discord between truth and reality in which he lives, become at once visible. When man speaks, he seeks involuntarily to protect himself against this nakedness, perhaps by making it known in his tone and demeanour that he is really not merely speaking, but is himself engaged in action perhaps substantially by the fact that to the best of his ability he is speaking practically, i.e. as far as possible about acts, his own or others', past or future. The aforesaid suspicion that he might be " merely " speaking, the question of the corresponding act, will play round him in spite of all and from some side and in some sense assuredly touch him. Where God speaks this suspicion is vain. The man who hears God speak and can still inquire about the act corresponding, would simply show thereby that he actually has not heard God speak. We might, for example, hear Christian sermons preached and ask ourselves : What happens in virtue of the fact that this thing happens ? To all these words what corresponds in reality ? A question that most certainly needs raising ! We might listen to Holy Scripture and hear only words, a man's words, which we do or do not understand, but along with which invariably the corresponding event is still wanting. It is then sure that in the proclamation as in the Bible what we heard was not the Word of God. Had it been the Word of God, we could never have been looking round for God's acts. The Word of God itself would have been the act. The Word of God needs no supplementing by the act. The Word of God is itself the act of God. It is an act in proportion as everything that we are wont to call act, event, praxis, life, etc., and everything we usually miss and long for to supplement man's word, must as a real act appear extremely questionable alongside that other. The Word of God in the highest sense makes history.

" For He spake and it was done, He commanded and it stood fast " (Ps. 33[9]). When the Word of God comes to the OT prophets, that (e.g. Jer. 1) is described by the verb *hayah* (happen). Think of all the direct conjunctions of Word and creation, Word and calling, Word and forgiveness, Word and miracle, Word and blessing, Word and punishment, etc., in OT and NT. But even where the connection seems more indirect ; when the prophets speak of future events, or the evangelists speak in retrospect of the acts of Jesus, it is not a case of spoken reports about a far-off event, but of an immediate bringing to the front, through the agency of the Word, of things already or still regarded as happening. " Look at the creation of all creatures. ' In the beginning God created heaven and earth.' By what means ? By His Word, as Moses writeth : ' God said, Let there be light, and there was light.' ' God said, Let there be a firmament between the waters,' etc., ' and it happened so ' ; ' God said, Let the waters under the heaven be gathered into special places, that dry land may appear, and it happened so.' The speaking doeth it. If this Speaker saith something that He will have, it must happen so. So then of naught, solely by His speaking, God hath created heaven and earth and all creatures. How should He then not be able by His Word and Sacrament to effect what he wills, especially because His Word standeth fast, bearing us witness of such ? " (Luther, *Predigt am Sonntag Cantate über* 1 *Cor.* 15, 1544 W. edn. 49, p. 405, l. 33). " And so . . . we ought to hold His Word glorious and high, as an almighty power. For whoso hath that hath all and power for all. Again, whoso hath it not, him naught else can and should guard against sin, death, and Devil. For what our dear Lord Christ doth here with the nobleman's son, saving him from death by His almighty word and preserving him in life, that will He do for us all by His Word, if we will but accept it . . ." (*Sermon on John* 4⁴⁷⁻⁵⁴, 1544 W. edn. 52, p. 515, l. 4). " 'Tis for Christ but a matter of a little word to do it, so it is presently yea. And so God ruleth His Christian Church, yea He so ruleth the whole world, that for Him 'tis no tremendous work, but He effecteth all by a Word. Therefore ought we to learn to hold God's Word in honour and to believe in the same. The same Word we have in the preaching of the Gospel, in baptism, in the Sacrament, in Absolution. . . . If we believe in the Word, it will happen to us as it happened to this nobleman, namely, that we obtain what is promised us in the Word " (*Sermon on John* 4⁴⁷⁻⁵⁴, 1534 E. edn. 5, p. 215).

The difference between Word and act is that a mere word is the mere self-utterance of a person. An act is, over and above that, a relative alteration in the environment which proceeds from it. A mere word is passive. An act is, over and above that, an active participation in history. But for the Word of God these distinctions do not hold. For it is precisely as a mere word that it is an act. Nay, as a mere word it is the divine Person, the Person of the Lord of history, whose self-utterance as such is an alteration and an absolute alteration of the world, whose *passio* in history is as such an *actio*. What God does in speaking, pretty much, of course, like what He says, is insusceptible of general determination, either by reproduction or by anticipation. We can only point to the *concretissima* among the acts attested in the Bible, which are also to be expected of God in the future.

What is specially involved always was and always will be ὅσα ἡτοίμασεν ὁ Θεὸς τοῖς ἀγαπῶσιν αὐτόν (1 Cor. 2⁹).

We may and must take account of the significance of the fact that God's speaking, and therefore God's Word in all its three forms, is God's act.

1. That God's word is God's act means first its contingent contemporaneousness. The meaning of this is as follows: One time is the time of the direct, original utterance of God Himself in His revelation, the time of Jesus Christ—(which according to John 8⁵⁶ was also and already the time of Abraham)—the time of that which prophets and apostles heard, in order to attest it—another time is the time of this testimony, the time of prophecy and the apostolate, the time of Peter upon whom Christ builds His Church, the time when the Canon arose as the concrete counterpart in which the Church receives her norm for all times—and again another time is this or that time of the Church herself, the time of derivative proclamation, related to the words of the prophets and apostles and regulated by them. These are different times, dis-

tinguished not only by the difference in periods and in contents, not only by the remoteness of centuries and the gap in humanity between centuries and millennia, but distinguished by the varied attitude of God to men. Jesus Christ was not less a true man than the prophets and apostles, but in virtue of His unity with God He stood absolutely over against them as a master over against his slaves. The Biblical witnesses as men, even as religious men, held no fundamentally marked precedence over the later teachers of the Church or even over us or even over the teachers and leaders of other religions. Yet they stood and stand, in their office as witnesses, in an utterly unique and peculiar position in the Church compared with all the rest of us. Again, however fundamental the essential equality between our existence and that of Christ and that of the apostles, yet in virtue of our relationship to Scripture and through Scripture to revelation and again through the intervening experience of the Church, in which we have the advantage of the prophets and apostles and which at least distinguishes us from them, our situation in the Church is a third and quite special situation. It is that, the variety in order of before and after, above and below, which makes the times of the Word of God so varied. Three times it is a matter of an utterance of the Word of God by the mouth of man. But only twice, in the case of the Biblical witnesses and of ourselves, is it also primarily a matter of submitting to an utterance, and only once, in our own case, of an indirect submission to it mediated through the Bible. This varying position in God's order distinguishes these three times in a way not otherwise characteristic of man's times, a way in which they differ only here, in which only the times of the Word of God differ. This lack of contemporaneousness may naturally be dissolved by disregarding the variety of these three times in God's order, through consideration and exposition of them, not as times of the Word of God, but immanently, i.e. merely by assessing the variety of the periods and their human contents as such. In that case the assessment of this variety need not only form no hindrance to a direct insight into the continuity and unity of the times, to an insight into our contemporaneousness with Christ and all His saints—rather it is the first thing to make this grasp possible and provable, by teaching us to see and regard man in the past, were his name Jeremiah or Jesus or Paul or Luther, as a fellow-man and at the same time, of course, to criticise him, yet to esteem and love him as well, in short to keep company with him as a comrade of one and the same time.

That is the way which more recent Protestant theology, after overcoming the great crisis of the Enlightenment's split with history, has taken and still takes in all its typical representatives. People believed then and still believe that in this way, delivered from the stiff antitheses of the Old Church and her theology, they have discovered, in a perfectly new and now for the first time correct way, "revelation by God in history." The epoch-making name in this connection is, so far as I see and understand the matter, the name of Lessing. "The foul, wide ditch" (between the Bible and us) about which he has said in a well-known passage ("The Proof of the Spirit and of Power," *Theol. Schr.* ed. Gross, II 2, p. 13) that with all his goodwill he could not jump over it, was not and, for the author of *Laocoön*, could not be the general problem of historical understanding, leaping over the gap of centuries and the variety of their humanity. This leap Lessing, and after him Herder and Schleiermacher and the rest, down to A. Ritschl and Harnack, Lagarde and Troeltsch, could very well take, and take it with increasing excellence and skill. And likewise Lessing's other famous saying, that "accidental truths of history can never prove the necessary truths of reason," need not be turned into banality as though by truth of history we were to understand the special concrete empirical truth of an historical datum as such, and by truth of reason the timeless truth of mathematical and philosophical axioms. In this antithesis of the unique and the universal, the empirical and the rational Kant's philosophy of religion still moves, but certainly not Lessing's any longer, in this respect much the more modern of the two. Lessing recognises perfectly well a proof of Christianity by history. But it must be "the proof of the Spirit and of power"; i.e. history proves us no truth, so long as it is "accidental truth of history," truth merely told us by others but not as such "felt" and "experienced" by ourselves. It becomes "necessary truth of reason," i.e. it becomes for us necessary and real truth, when and so far as it is "felt" and "experienced" as such by us, experienced in the way the "paralytic feels the beneficent shock of the electric spark." "Religion is not true because the evangelists and apostles taught it, but they taught it because it is true. By its inner truth must Scriptural traditions be explained, and all the Scriptural traditions in the world cannot give it inner truth if it does not possess it" (*Frag. eines Ungen. op. cit.* II 1, p. 261 : *Axiomata, op. cit.* II 2, p. 122. The apologetic use of the concept of "experience" is already found, according to K. Aner, *Die Theologie der Lessingzeit*, 1929 p. 148 f. in the sermons of Abbot J. Fr. W. Jerusalem, 1745). And this inner truth Lessing clearly holds to be an entity thoroughly accessible to and apprehensible by us; as to its presence we can be judges in virtue of our feeling and experience. Therefore, he appeals from Luther's writings to Luther's spirit (*Anti-Göze, op. cit.* II 2, p. 140), from the letter of the Bible to the spirit of the Bible (*Axiomata, op. cit.* II 2, p. 112), from the recounted miracles to the still "constantly continuing miracle of religion itself" (*Eine Duplik, op. cit.* II 2, p. 33), finally from the Christian religion to the religion of Christ (*Die Religion Christi, op. cit.* II 3, p. 448 f.). "No one in Hamburg will ever again wish to dispute with me the utter difference between gross and net" (*Axiomata, op. cit.* II 2, p. 108). "Historical words are the vehicle of the prophetic word" (*op. cit.* p. 112). Such was Lessing's obstacle and such his conquest of the obstacle. It was the regular and, as he rightly saw, insuperable lack of contemporaneousness between Christ, the apostles, and ourselves that disturbed him, and that therefore he let drop in favour of an immanent and therefore also of an immanently superable lack of contemporaneousness. Henseforth all the more living spirits, in contrast to the Enlightenment and to Kant, found it no longer difficult or objectionable to explain revelation as history and history as revelation.

But if we drop the orderly variety of the three times, then however loudly and cordially we may continue to talk about revelation, its concreteness and historicity, and however illuminatingly and practically everything may take shape, we must drop the concept of the Word of God itself. Where we are in the position to do away with our lack of contemporaneousness with Christ and the apostles by placing ourselves on the same level as them, or them on the same level as us, in order by participating in the same prophetic spirit as them and by possessing in our own feeling the measure of inner truth to discuss with them the gross and net value of their words ; where therefore contemporaneousness rests upon the hypothesis of a merely quantitative difference between those there and us here, there the concept of the Word of God is bound to be humanised in such a way that it is no wonder people prefer to use it comparatively seldom and as (so to speak) a guide-post ; indeed the wonder rather is they don't prefer to eliminate it altogether in so many words. However seriously they may be taken as such, the differences inherent in history are not sufficient to justify a serious use of the concept " Word of God." For, fundamentally, the assessment of these differences does not amount to our letting ourselves be told something. Therefore in the region of these differences there cannot be any utterance of the Word of God. Within these differences there is only our togetherness with Christ and the apostles, a togetherness the norm and conditions of which, with all respect for the greatness and vitality of history, we, the living, who therefore are in the right, finally and ultimately set up and handle. The Church of the present, however historically she may feel and think, in that case speaks the last word as heiress and interpretress of history, and, without the Word of God in the serious sense of the term, stands solitary by herself and pointed in on herself. If we insist that the concept of the Word of God means precisely that the Church does not stand solitary by herself and pointed in on herself, then we must abide by the orderly distinction between the times, and the contemporaneousness of present-day proclamation with Scripture and with revelation can certainly not be regarded as a thing to be introduced by us by levelling up this distinction, by incorporating Scripture and revelation in the life of humanity. It can only be regarded as an expression of the fact that the Word of God is itself God's act. Thus, directly, it has nothing to do with the general problem of historical understanding. Of course the question of some sort of historical understanding always arises when the Word of God is manifest to us in its contemporaneousness. But it is not that sort of historical understanding as such which signifies the hearing, and is the basis of the proclamation, of the Word of God. Where the Word of God is heard and proclaimed, something happens which in spite of all interpretative skill cannot be brought about by interpretative skill.

The Biblical witnesses too had a definite relationship of historical understanding with Jesus Christ (ἐγνώκαμεν κατὰ σάρκα Χριστόν, 2 Cor. 5¹⁶). But in this relationship it was not through the power immanent in this relationship, that they came to recognise Jesus Christ as the Son of God.

And so certainly not through the power of Lessing's " feeling " and " experience," σάρξ καὶ αἷμα οὐκ ἀπεκάλυψέν σοι (Matt. 16¹⁷). Those who apprehend the light come into the world, who behold the Kingdom of God, do not do so in virtue of their earthly birth (John 1¹³, 3³ᶠ·). The Father hath hidden the mystery of the Son from the " wise and prudent " (Matt. 11²⁵)— i.e. surely, from the judgment based upon an inner truth already known to man.

Rather this knowledge is referred in OT and NT to election, revelation, calling, setting apart, new birth—clear concepts which, so to speak, shatter the immanence of the historical connection from within, so far as God Himself is the subject of the action indicated in them, so far as God's " good pleasure " (εὐδοκία, Matt. 11²⁶ ; Gal. 1¹⁵ ; Eph. 1⁹) as the altogether external truth first creates and posits the altogether inner truth as such in and by the free action described in these concepts : apart from all historical connections, though these undeniably exist ; in these connections but not through them. We should not regard these concepts as subsequent explanations of an event really and essentially immanent. They do not explain, they say, how it is primary. It is rather all the immanent interpretations of these concepts that here constitute subsequent explanations. We can only regard them as signifying free acts of God in the sense of the Biblical authors, or we do not understand them at all. They assert that without the removal of the difference the time of Christ is made contemporary with the time of the prophets and apostles by the free act of God.

The prophets prophesy of Christ and the apostles proclaim Him, neither of them as reporters, but both as witnesses, who speak not only "about Christ" but "in Christ," not because they have experienced Christ as one might also experience Plato, but because it pleased God ἀποκαλύψαι τὸν υἱὸν αὐτοῦ ἐν ἐμοί (Gal. 1¹⁶).

The Word of Scripture in its quite different time area, with its quite different time content compared with the Word of revelation, now reverts to its orderly position ; it is now described as the Word of the prophets and apostles, and as such, as the witness to Christ and in its subordination to the Word of Christ, it simultaneously utters the Word of Christ Himself.

It is the same step from one time to another understandable only as the act of God, when Church proclamation becomes real proclamation, i.e. God's Word, because in it Holy Scripture, and in Holy Scripture Christ Himself comes to expression. Once more we have here and must have here a definite relation of historical understanding, with all its relevant components, from philological analysis to skill in what is called "getting the feel" of the author. Proclamation is only possible in this relation of understanding, just as prophecy and the apostolate only existed in a definite relation of understanding. But in this relation proclamation of the Word of God is achieved not through the individual components of this relation or the sum of them, and therefore, e.g., neither through philological acuteness nor through the most talented and refined feel of the author, but purely and simply through the power of the Biblical Word itself, which now makes a place for itself in a quite different period and becomes the content of this period, because in proclamation the stage is held not by Paul the religious personality, but by Paul the apostle of Jesus Christ, and in him by Jesus Christ Himself. Because the Word of God is this act in this step from revelation to Scripture and to Church proclamation, i.e. in the full, strict distinction of times, it is one, it is contemporaneous—Ἰησοῦς Χριστὸς ἐχθὲς καὶ σήμερον ὁ αὐτός (Heb. 13⁸).

We said "contingently contemporaneous," just to emphasise the character of this contemporaneousness as an act, an event. We would have to speak of a twofold contingency, in so far as our concern, as much in the relation between revelation and Holy Scripture as in that between Holy Scripture and proclamation, is invariably both with a contingent *illic et tunc* from the standpoint of God who speaks, and also with a contingent *hic et nunc* from the standpoint of man who hears. Of a step from the one to the other we have indeed spoken in both relations. This "step" should not

be volatilised into the general truth of a fixed or continuous relation between the three forms. We are really concerned with a step,
which has reality only as this and that and the other step, i.e.
as a contingent act. The problem of the Word of God consists in
the fact that to this particular man to-day through the proclamation of this other particular man by means of this particular Bible
text this particular manifestation of God is imparted, that a particular *illic et tunc* becomes a particular *hic et nunc*. The problem
of the Word of God is thus from time to time a perfectly definite,
once-for-all, peculiar problem, and of this problem we must say
that it is solved by the Word of God itself, spoken by the mouth
of God, being contemporaneous *illic et tunc* and (i.e. exactly as
spoken *illic et tunc*) *hic et nunc*.

2. That the Word of God is God's act means, in the second place,
its power to rule. The speech of God is the action of God upon
those to whom He speaks. But as a divine action, as the action of
the Lord, His action is His ruling action. Where and when Jesus
Christ becomes contemporaneous with us through Scripture and
proclamation, where i.e. the " God with us " is uttered to us by
God Himself, we come under a Lordship. The concepts election,
revelation, setting apart, calling, new birth, which we previously
touched upon, all signify a promise, a judgment, a claim regarding
man, by which God binds him to Himself. Gospel and Law, as
the concrete content of the Word of God, always signify an arrest
of man. The Word of God says to man in each case—what it might
also say to him in a *concretissimum*—that he is not his own but is
God's property. If we regard the Word of God from its origin in
revelation, in Jesus Christ, as the summary of the grace of God,
grace means simply that man is no longer left to himself, but is
given into the hand of God.

The Gospel or the Word of the Cross is the δύναμις θεοῦ to them that
believe or to them that are saved, we read in Rom. 1¹⁶ and 1 Cor. 1¹⁸. The
Word of God is characterised as " living " and as " living and powerful,"
in 1 Pet. 1²³ and Heb. 4¹². And in Matt. 4⁴ it says of man, that he lives
πάντι ῥήματι ἐκπορευομένῳ διὰ στόματος Θεοῦ.

If a man knew nothing of this alike supporting and stimulating,
protecting and punishing, pacifying and disturbing power, if he
merely heard tell of it without knowing it as a power, he would
only prove that he knew nothing about the Word of God. We are
acquainted with the Word of God according as we are acquainted
with this power ; we are speaking of this Word of God when we

speak in remembrance and in expectation of this power, and in such a way that we understand that this power of the Word of God is not one power among others, nor one among other divine powers, but a peculiar divine power, which comes home to us, to which we are pointed, in face of which we stand at a crisis betwixt the obedience which is its due and the abysmal inconceivability of disobedience, and so at a crisis between blessedness and damnation. Moreover, the Holy Spirit (at least according to the Western notion of the Trinity of God) is inseparable from the Word, and His power, therefore, not a power separate from that of the Word, but the power that lives in the Word and through the Word. Moreover, of the power of God in His creation and government of the world we know nothing save through the Word revealed, written and proclaimed, and when we know of it through this Word, we cannot possibly separate it from the power of the Word itself.

Ἐδόθη μοι πᾶσα ἐξουσία ἐν οὐρανῷ καὶ ἐπὶ γῆς (Matt. 28, 18). τὰ πάντα δι' αὐτοῦ καὶ εἰς αὐτὸν ἔκτισται· καὶ αὐτός ἐστιν πρὸ πάντων καὶ τὰ πάντα ἐν αὐτῷ συνέστηκεν (Col. 1¹⁷).

Where once God has spoken and is heard, i.e. in the Church, there is no escape from this power, no getting past it, no acknowledgement of divine powers not summarised in this power, connected with its form, operative in its way.

Καὶ αὐτός ἐστιν ἡ κεφαλὴ τοῦ σώματος, τῆς ἐκκλησίας (Col. 1¹⁸; cf. Eph. 1²²ᶠ·). That is said of Christ. But Christ is actually the Word of God, contemporary in prophecy and in the apostolate and contemporary in the proclamation of His Church. If He is contemporary here, if He makes that step, we are necessarily here faced with the knowledge of the sole rule of the Word of God in the Church, with the significance it has for the Reformers' concept of God and of the Church. " The holy Christian Church, whose sole Head is Christ, is born of the Word of God, is incorporated in the same, and heareth not the voice of a stranger " (Zwingli, *Berner Thesen*, 1528 *art.* 1). " God's Word is a flowret, i.e. the longer the dearer. . . . That is, whoso once graspeth God's Word properly, loveth it so fondly that he always desireth it more and more " (Luther, *Sermon on Luke* 5¹⁻¹¹, 1534 E. edn. 4, p. 342) " . . . our preaching is this, that whoso heareth this preaching about Christ and believeth in Him, hath everlasting life. The Word of God is sent from heaven to be obeyed, to the end that if thou wert burnt to ashes, thou wouldst yet know the way out " (*Expos. of John* 3–4, 1538 f., W. edn. 47, p. 188, l. 28). " For 'tis certain we all have our blessedness through the Word of God alone. What should we know otherwise of God, of the Lord Christ and His sacrifice and of the Holy Ghost ? " (*Sermon on Mark* 7³¹⁻³⁷, 1544 W. edn. 52, p. 451, l. 39). " For God hath given us no other staircase and shewn us no other way up which we can go to heaven, save His dear Word, the holy Gospel. Whoso heareth the same gladly, marketh it diligently and sheweth desire and love thereto, is helped " (*ib.* p. 452, l. 16).

" For God will not reveal Himself in thy heart without the Word. Wouldst thou see and know Him, it must befall solely through the Word and the outward sacraments " (*ib.* p. 453, l. 31). " How doth the Father train us ? Through Christ. How through Christ ? By the Word. Thus He attracteth and charmeth thee ; so an thy need drive thee, go blithely to it, and boldly bring forth thine ill hap : but even bring the Word withal " (Sermon on John 8⁴⁶⁻⁴⁹, E. edn. 11, p. 130). " For the soul of man can be preserved by naught else than by the Word of God, that is its food and pasture, and so much as it availeth itself thereof, dependeth and believeth thereon, so far as it counselled and helped " (*Sermon on Luke* 11, 1527 W. edn. 17¹¹, p. 280, l. 30) According to Luther the correspondence of the Ascension and the Session of Christ on the right hand of God means the *regnum Christi* in the world, to be regarded as a *doctrinale regnum*, equivalent to the *ministerium Verbi* (*Enarr. ub. cap.* 53 *Esaiae*, 1544 E. edn. *Exeg. op: lat.* 23, p. 448 f.). " For through the Word He shall rule and not otherwise " (*Passion*, 5th Sermon, 1544 E. A. 3, p. 268). " That is the New Testament and kingdom of Christ which cometh home to us with so little might ; and yet with almighty power and might, which none can withstand. It appeareth to be foolish that Christ should initiate the New Testament in this wise " (*Sermon on Acts* 2¹⁻¹³, 1534 E. edn. 4, p. 86). " Yet there all is petty and naught to look at, both things, material and instruments. The material and preaching are petty ; the instruments, i.e. the apostles and disciples, whom Christ useth as tools for this preaching, are much pettier. Yet through this petty preaching and indifferent tools goeth the New Testament and Kingdom of Christ " (*ib.* p. 87). " This preaching is not come from men, but Christ hath Himself brought it and put it thereafter into the hearts of the apostles and their successors so that they grasped it, and into their mouths so that they spake and preached it. That is His kingdom, therefore He ruleth so that all His power standeth and lieth on the Word of God ; whoso then hear and believe it, belong to the Kingdom, and the Word then becometh so mighty that it createth all that is needed by man, and bringeth all good things that man may have. For it is God's power that it can and may make blessed all who believe therein, as saint Paul saith in Rom. 1 " (*Sermon on John* 10¹²ᶠᶠ· 1523 W. edn. 12, p. 530, l. 24). " But He keepeth specially before Him the two members, ears and tongue ; for the kingdom of Christ is founded upon the Word, which one cannot otherwise grasp or conceive, without these two members, ears and tongue, and ruleth alone through the Word and faith in the heart of men. The ears grasp the Word and the heart believeth it ; but the tongue uttereth it or confesseth it, as the heart believeth. So if we do away with the tongue and ears, there remaineth no marked difference 'twixt the Kingdom of Christ and the world " (*Sermon on Mark* 7³¹⁻³⁷, E. edn. 13, p. 308). " . . . *la parole de Dieu seule doit estre suffisante pour nostre foy. Si on demande sur quoy nostre foy est fondee et comment elle vient à sa perfection c'est par la parole de Dieu* (Calvin, *Sermon on Gal.* 1¹¹ᶠ·, *C.R.* 51, 361). *Iterum hic memoria repetere convenit, qualis sit regni Christi natura. Ut enim ipse aureo diademate ornatus non est, vel instructus terrenis armis ; ita non dominatur in mundo armorum potentia, nec sibi auctoritatem conciliat pomparum splendore, vel terrore et metu populum suum cogit ; sed evangelii doctrina regium eius insigne est, quo sub obsequium suum colligit fideles. Proinde ubicunque annunciatur pure evangelii doctrina, illic Christum regnare certum est : ubi vero reiicitur, simul etiam aboleri ejus imperium* (*Comm. Isa.* 11⁴, *C.R.* 36, 240). *Car Dieu regne, quand il conduit tout par sa providence ; mais cependant nous n'apercevons rien de son*

empire, quand nous luy sommes rebelles, que tout va pesle mesle et que sa parole
n'est point escoutee, laquelle est le sceptre royal par lequel il domine sur nous :
que Son Esprit ne domine point pour nous conduire en son obéissance, et pour
nous ranger tellement à luy, qu'il vive plustost en nous, que nous ne vivions à nos
appetits, et selon nostre naturel.   Dieu donc ne regne point en ceste facon sinon
quand l'Evangile nous est presché et que nostre Seigneur Jesus Christ, qui a este
constitué son lieutenant, nous gouverne tant par sa parole que par son S. Esprit.
. . . Or il est bien certain que . . . Dieu estant Createur de tout le monde, n'a
jamais quitté son authorite.   Il faut donc que sa puissance ait son estendue par
tout ; mais c'est d'une facon qui nous est cachée et incompréhensible, quand Dieu
gouverne, et que sa parole cependant n'est point preschee . . . puis de là nous
pouvons recueillir combien la doctrine de l'Evangile nous doit estre precieuse et
amiable, veu que par icelle Dieu nous prend sous sa charge et nous recognoist et
advoue pour son peuple . . . qu'il veut habiter au milieu de nous (Sermon on
Matt. 3[2]*, C.R. 46, 490 f.).*

It must follow from our knowledge of the power to rule residing
in God's Word that we are speaking of the Word of God.   Therefore we must speak of its power, of its might, of its operations, of
the changes it produces.   Because the Word of God makes history,
it is, as Word, also an act.

" Is not my word like as a fire ? saith the Lord ; and like a hammer that
breaketh the rock in pieces ? " (Jer. 23[29]).   " For as the rain cometh down
[and the snow] from heaven, and returneth not thither, but watereth the
earth, and maketh it bring forth, that it may give seed to the sower, and bread
to the eater : So shall my word be that goeth forth out of my mouth ; it
shall not return unto me void, but it shall accomplish that which I please,
and it shall prosper in the thing whereto I send it " (Isa. 55[10f.] E. tr.).   Cf.
the basic connection between καλεῖν, κλῆσις, ἐκκλησία, κλητός in NT, with the
totality of what ἐν χριστῷ becomes radically different for man and in man. ～ *This*
sentence is not clear.

The promise of the Word of God is not as such an empty
pledge which, so to speak, stands always confronting man, but the
transposition of man into the wholly new position of one who
has apprehended this promise, appropriated it to himself, who lives
no longer without, but, whatever his attitude to it, with this
promise.   The claim of the Word of God is as such not a wish or a
behest which, so to speak, remained external to the hearer, which
did not touch his existence, but it is the claiming, the commandeer-
ing of the man ; whatever his attitude personally to the claim of
God, as a hearer of His Word the man finds that he is now one
within the sphere of the divine claim, that he has become one
claimed by God.   Again, the judgment of the Word of God is not
as such a mere aspect beneath which man stood untouched in himself, as the same man from the ant's point of view may appear and
be judged a giant or a dwarf from the elephant's point of
view, without him in fact being a different person in either case.

But the judgment of God creates as such not only a new light and therewith a new situation, but with the new situation a new man, who previously did not exist at all but now does, identical with the one who heard the Word of God. Again, that would not be the blessing of the Word of God, which by being a *benedictio* was not immediately and as such known and regarded as a *beneficium*, a real enlistment under the good pleasure and protection of God.

We find that expressed in the strongest imaginable way in Jas. 1[18], where (cf. also 1 Pet. 1[23]) he is speaking of the Christian's being begotten by the λόγος ἀληθείας. And then (ver. 21) logically of a λόγος ἔμφυτος, and so of a λόγος which, so to speak, belongs to man himself, without which man would cease to be himself.

And because the word of which we are here speaking is God's Word, we shall have to add expressly that its effect, its power to alter is not, like other powers, a merely relative one, uncertain in itself, conditioned and confined by the relations of other factors, e.g. man. That may be true of all that it effects in man, all that is visible in man's existence as its effect. It is not true of its effect itself and as such. The power of the Word of God in itself and as such is absolute power.

" All flesh is as grass and all the goodliness of man is as the flower of grass. The grass withereth and the flower fadeth. τὸ δὲ ῥῆμα Κυρίου μένει εἰς τὸν αἰῶνα " (1 Pet. 1[24f.]). The Word of God is not only the λόγος ζῶν, but also the λόγος μένων. It is an " incorruptible seed " (*ib.* ver. 23) ; ὁ λόγος τοῦ Θεοῦ ἐν ὑμῖν μένει is said in 1 John 2[14] to the " little children," i.e. those not yet approved (cf. *ib.* ver. 27 : the anointing that " abideth ").

All this must be asserted of the Word of God, because the Word of God is not distinct from Jesus Christ, and because consequently its effect is not different from the lordship of Jesus Christ. To hear the Word of God is to be drawn into the sphere of the real power of this lordship. Of Him and for Him everything already holds which the Word of God asserts, whether as promise, claim, judgment, or blessing. It is not validated for the first time by preaching, but preaching explains and confirms the fact of its validity. It is proclamation of the Word of God in as much as preaching proclaims it as something already valid.

This also and specifically holds of preaching among coloured and among white heathen. If it did not proceed upon the more than axiomatic presupposition that its hearers are already dealt with as heathen, already drawn into Christ's sphere of power by the Word of God being proclaimed to them, in what way would it be any better than propaganda, in what sense would it b e the " mission," i.e. the sending, how would it be the proclamation of the Word of God taking place in faith ?   Though we utter all possible thoughts, and they ever so correct, about the convictions and circumstances of the hearers—by preaching the Gospel to them, because we believe in the promise of the presence and effect of the Word of God, only the one thing concerns us with regard to them : " T h o u hast borne all sin."

Nor is it faith which for the first time validates all that the Word of God asserts for us. Even faith, faith in particular, is just faith in Jesus Christ, and therefore the recognition and confirmation of the fact that the Word of God has been validated, before we believed and apart from our having believed. It is just faith that lives—we have already allowed this as the element of truth in the old-Lutheran doctrine of the *efficacia verbi extra usum*—by the power which is power before faith and apart from faith, by the power which gives it itself, faith, its object and thereby for the first time, from the standpoint of this object, gives it its existence. Therefore, as the sign of this real supreme power of the Word of God, baptism is instituted. It declares, as being on its part real action upon man and power of disposal over him, that he stands, prior to all his experiences and decisions, within the sphere of Christ's lordship. Long before he can adopt an attitude to God, God has adopted an attitude to him. Whatever attitude he may take it will take place within and on the ground of the attitude taken towards him by God. If he comes to faith, that will be but the confirmation of the fact that he does possess God's promise, that he is claimed, judged, and blessed by God. If he does not come to faith, neither will that be a possibility he was free to choose. He will sin against God's Word. He will display himself, certainly not as free man, but as an unfree. He will not choose, he will be rejected. It is not a possibility but the impossibility that he will grasp. In a word, he will, even in his very unbelief, be measured by the Word of God, touched by its power. It is just God's previous attitude towards him that will constitute his unbelief unbelief, his sin sin. Only in the realm of grace, and there for the first time, is there faith and unbelief, righteousness, and sin. Only through the power of the Word of God and through it for the first time are found the two categories, those that are saved and those that are lost.

Ἰδού οὗτος κεῖται εἰς πτῶσιν καὶ ἀνάστασιν πολλῶν ἐν τῷ Ἰσραήλ (Luke 2[34]). " The same stone laid in Zion becomes to some a stumbling-block and an offence, and whosoever believeth on him shall not be ashamed " (Rom. 9[33]). And Paul terms his preaching a Χριστοῦ εὐωδία τῷ Θεῷ ἐν τοῖς σωζομένοις καὶ ἐν τοῖς ἀπολλυμένοις· οἷς μὲν ὀσμὴ ἐκ θανάτου εἰς θάνατον, οἷς δὲ ὀσμὴ ἐκ ζωῆς εἰς ζωήν (2 Cor. 2¹⁵ᶠ·).

This whole consideration need not be limited to the relation of the Word of God to the single individual as such. All that has been said holds *mutatis mutandis* of the relation of the Word of God to the human cosmos in general ; concretely, of the relation of Church and history or of Church and Society. It is not the case that God revealed Himself somewhere and somehow, that somewhere there is a Bible and somewhere a Church of preaching and sacrament— and over against that would stand history or society untouched, sovereign, following their own laws, and so the Church would require to start from without, so to speak, from a God who remained alien to the cosmos, and represent and assert in attack and defence her interests, i.e. the interests of her God, against the cosmos. Thus the Church is not outside beside God, and the world is not inside apart from God. Things can only be seen thus if Bible and Church are considered apart from the revelation which constitutes them or if by revelation, with Schleiermacher, is meant merely the peculiar beginning of the religion which happens to be our own. But that does not mean remembering the Word that came and expecting the Word to come. If by revelation the Word of God is to be understood, and if moreover the Bible and the Church are to be understood in the light of such remembrance and such expectation, then the world of man which confronts the Word of God must also be considered as a whole, as a world subjected to a decisive change. In that case the world from the Church's standpoint cannot be the victim of its godlessness, cannot be taken seriously in its godlessness ; so far and so long as the Church takes this attitude she only proves that she herself does not seriously believe in the Word of God. If she did, she would also have to reckon concretely with its power. It cannot be a question of man being claimed for God, because by a survival in him from creation he still belongs, is bound to God—as if the Fall had no such radical consequences. It is a case not of natural, but very much indeed of supernatural theology. But such a theology, considering the power of the Word of God, will be bound to claim the world, history, society, as the things in the midst of which Christ was born, died, and rose again. Not in the light of nature but in the light of grace there is, not a profane realm self-enclosed and guarded, but only one called in question by the Word of God, by the Gospel, by God's claim, judgment, and blessing, one abandoned to its own legalism and to its own gods only in a preliminary and limited way. What the Word of God says stands, whatever the world's attitude to it, and whether it redound to it unto salvation or the reverse.

'Εγένετο ἡ βασιλεία τοῦ κόσμου τοῦ Κυρίου ἡμῶν καὶ τοῦ Χριστοῦ αὐτοῦ καὶ βασιλεύσει εἰς τοὺς αἰῶνας τῶν αἰώνων (Rev. 11¹⁵). Just because it is eschatological this ἐγένετο must be taken quite literally and really seriously. Christ does not for the first time become, but He already is βασιλεὺς βασιλέων καὶ Κύριος τῶν κυρίων (Rev. 19¹⁶ ; cf. Phil. 2⁹ᶠ· ; Col. 2¹⁵ ; Eph. 1²¹).

Thus neither is the world going to evolve on its own initiative into agreement with the Word of God, nor has the Church to achieve that by her work in and on the world. But the Church is the Church because she believes and proclaims that before all world developments and before all her own work the actually decisive word has already been spoken concerning the world exactly as it has been spoken concerning herself. Thus the world literally ceases to exist apart in a neutral attitude, over against revelation, the Bible, and proclamation. Whether it believes or not, whether it develops in this way or in that, whether the Church exercises a greater or a less influence, whether she consists of millions of confessors and pro-claimers, or whether only two or three are gathered together in the name of Christ—in whatever becomes of Church and world, the invariable centre of gravity is an event following upon that already spoken and decisive Word.

Sermo enim Dei venit mutaturus orbem, quoties venit (Luther, *De servo arbit.* 1525 W. edn. 18, p. 626, l. 26).

If the Church believes what she declares she believes, she is the place where the victory of Jesus Christ is not the last word heard and passed on, but the first. For that reason and in that way she is the place of revelation, of mercy and peace, Mount Zion which the heathen are on the way to, whether they know and desire it or not. The Church which is this place will have somewhat to say to the world and will be taken seriously by the world. In view of what is here said it will be fitting to recall that in the case of the power here being discussed the point is the power of the Word, power to rule, the power of God. All this distinguishes it from other powers, its effect from any other effect, what is effected by it from what is effected otherwise. It should not be forgotten here in particular that the Word of God is the speech of God and remains so, and is therefore His power, the power of truth which is not to be confused with any other power. But that the truth—which according to John 1¹⁴ is to be mentioned in the same breath

12

with grace—is power, we establish in our context without reservation.

3. That the Word of God is God's act means in the third place that it is a decision. It is in that way that an act is distinguished from a mere event. A mere event is in itself an occurrence subordinated to some sort of higher necessity. Above it, it has some sort of cause which occasions it. And it has every other event, in connection with which it takes place, to determine it in addition to itself. It causes because it is caused, and because something else beside it causes and is caused. This holds of the event in nature as well as of that in the individual and general life of man. It is a mere hypothesis when we call an event at the same time an act, a decision, a deed of free choice. At all events this predicate is not inherent in the concept of an event. That should be taken account of when the concept of the Word of God is connected with the concept of history. No doubt that must be done. According to all we have said about the contingent contemporaneousness and the power to rule of the Word of God, the Word of God is also an historical, temporal event. But if it were exhausted in being an event, its character as an act or decision would be as hypothetical as everything else that we usually claim as such. The Word of God is not to be regarded primarily as history, and then, and as such, as a decision also, but first and fundamentally as a decision and then, and as such, as history also. To think of an act which can be explained just as well, or better, as a mere event, an act which proceeds from a higher necessity and is conditioned right and left by other acts, is to think of the ambiguous thing usually called an act in the sphere of the human, but not of the Word of God. To let oneself be blinded by the circumstance that the Word of God in Jesus Christ, in the Bible, in proclamation, is of course also a human act, and then to take it as if it were only that and in consequence involved in that inevitable dialectic of human act and mere event, to look at it in the twilight of this dialectic, is *eo ipso* not to think of the Word of God. The Word of God is understood primarily as a decision or it is not understood at all. We might also say simply, understood as a divine act. As a divine act it is distinguished—although it is itself also a human act—from all human acts by the fact that it is not affected by the *Sic et Non* of the dialectic mentioned. It is also a human act, it is therefore also an event, but as an act and an event it is free, as free as God Himself, since indeed God Himself is in the act. God is the Lord,

above whom there is no other person or thing, beside whom, right or left, there is also no other person or thing conditioning Him, standing in relation to Him. God is *a se*. That holds without reserve of His Word also. But the aseity of God is not empty freedom. In God all potentiality is included in His actuality, and so all freedom in His decision. Decision means choice, freedom used. We should ill understand the Word of God without the unconditioned freedom in which it is spoken ; but we should further understand it ill, were we to understand it as a mere possibility instead of as freedom used, as a decision made, as a choice taking place. As a choice taking place, the Word of God in the humanity of Christ, in the Bible and in proclamation is also a human act and therefore a temporal event. But it is on the basis of choice that the Word of God is one with the humanity of Christ, with Holy Scripture, with proclamation, and therefore a temporal event. Both together, the choice and the event make the Word of God God's act in distinction from all other acts.—That the Word of God is God's act and so a choice which takes place, a decision that is made, freedom which is used, has the following concrete significance :

(*a*) The Word of God is not reality in the way in which reality can be predicted of an experienceable state of affairs, provided it is suited to our sense-perceptions and our understanding. Nor yet in the way in which reality belongs to the so-called laws of Nature, which are also the laws of the spiritual world in a special modification. Nor in the way in which, so far as there are such, the axioms of mathematics and physics have reality. Nor in the way in which it is real that I am I and not thou, and thou art thou and not I, or that yesterday is not to-day and will never be to-morrow. Not in the way in which the structure of the so-called character and the so-called destiny of each of us is real to the tiniest detail, being probably cosmically (note—cosmically !) legible, predetermined, perhaps in the lines of one's hands, perhaps in one's facial features, perhaps in one's handwriting, perhaps from the position of the constellations at the hour of one's birth. In a word, not reality in the way in which the totality of what we otherwise call reality is real. Although, and while yet, it also has part in this reality and encounters us in precisely this reality. Not reality in this way, because in distinction from all other reality it is not universal, i.e. not always and not everywhere present and therefore not universal, i.e. is not always and not everywhere fixable, or at least might be present and fixable *mutatis mutandis*.

It is the dropping out here of this " might," this potentiality on the basis of which perhaps comparable entities could be shown to exist, it is this that is significant. The Word of God "might" also not be universally present and fixable. This " might " would in fact be ever so characteristic of a created reality distinct from God in His aseity and actuality. The Word of God is uncreated reality, identical with God Himself, therefore not universally present and fixable, nor possibly so. Never under any circumstances is the Word of God reality in our reality in a general sense, but invariably and in all circumstances *suo modo, sua libertate, sua misericordia*, and being conditioned in that way and with that object and by those means—once more *suo modo*—it alone is also present and fixable.

Therefore there are, according to 1 Sam. 3¹, times when a revelation of Jahwe is something rare. Hence the remarkable prophecies of Amos 8¹¹ : " Behold the days come, saith the Lord God, that I will send a famine and thirst in the land, so that all its inhabitants mourn, not a famine of bread, nor a thirst for water, but of hearing the words of the Lord, so that they shall wander from one sea to another and run to and fro from north to east, to seek the word of the Lord, and shall not find it!" And of Mic. 3⁶ : " Therefore night shall be unto you, that ye shall not have a vision : and it shall be dark unto you, that ye shall not divine ; and the sun shall go down over the prophets, and the day shall be dark over them. Then shall the seers be ashamed, and the diviners confounded : yea, they shall cover their lips ; for there is no answer from God." Hence the concept of the Word, the Law, the commandment, the statute, the behest, the claim of Jahwe signifies for the prophets as for the others singled out by Jahwe, as for all Israel, as for the individual Israelite in the whole OT (I would not except even Ps. 119 and the later canonical literature generally) an event to be expected, to be revealed, to be besought from Jahwe and not a chance one according to immanent necessity, nor yet a higher inner condition, generally present and fixable. Hence also in the NT the existence of the true light in the world is described as an ἔρχεσθαι εἰς τόν κόσμον (John 1⁹), as an ἀποκαλύπτεσθαι or φανεροῦσθαι. Here, too, we recall the connection between revelation and the divine εὐδοκία. ὅπου θέλει πνεῖ (John 3⁸) holds as really of the Word of God as of the Spirit All of which obviously signifies that the Word of God is a decision.

It is only real and to be regarded as real, if and when it gives itself and gives itself to be understood. The question, what is the Word of God, is utterly hopeless if it means the question of the category under which the Word of God might fall, the question of the syllogism by means of which it might somehow be proved. The questions as to category and syllogism obviously imply that even the Word of God is one of the universally present and fixable, and therefore of the created realities. All concepts tending in this direction, including the concept of a highest essence, of an *ens*

perfectissimum or an unconditioned, the concept of the breaking
through and of the knowledge of such a highest essence, the concept
of its revelation, are as such—even as universal concepts—not the
concept of the Word of God. All universal concepts suppress the
essential feature, that the Word of God is a reality only by its own
decision. That the Word of God is a decision means that there is
no concept of the Word of God except the n a m e of God which we
love, fear, and adore, because it is identical with the Bearer of the
name.

(*b*) Because the Word of God is not, like created realities, universally present and fixable nor could possibly be universally present
and fixable, it therefore, as a decision in its relation to man, always
signifies a c h o i c e. The Word of God is an act of God which
happens *specialissime*, in this way and in no other, to this and
that particular man.

" Before I saw thee in the belly I knew thee, and before thou camest
forth out of the womb I sanctified thee, I ordained thee a prophet to the
nations ! " (Jer. 1⁵; cf. Isa. 49¹). This, of course, is the concept of prophetic
election to which nothing in the OT in general corresponds except the election
of Israel among the nations ; which strangely enough is seen in Deutero-
Isaiah in conjunction with the election of the individual prophet and servant
of God. But in the NT the concepts ἐκλέγεσθαι, ἐκλογή, ἐκλεκτός, no doubt
to correspond to the concepts καλεῖν etc., are also used of individual believers
as such, and in such a way that ἐκλέγεσθαι, or προορίζειν, seems to imply the
καλεῖν (Rom. 8³⁰), whereas not every καλεῖν has a corresponding ἐκλέγεσθαι.

This choice is made when the Word is spoken and apprehended,
a choice of grace unto faith and its righteousness or a choice of gracelessness to faithlessness and its sin. The *vocatio* may take place
efficaciter or *efficacissime*, yet the *electio* therein consummated may
be a *rejectio* ; i.e. the effect of the Word being spoken and apprehended may be complete, and yet the choice therein consummated
may be the choice of gracelessness.

Πολλοὶ γὰρ εἰσιν κλητοί, ὀλίγοι δὲ ἐκλεκτοί (Matt. 22¹⁴). The critical
relationship between κλῆσις and ἐκλογή is of course also intended when in
Matt. 24⁴⁰ᶠ·; Luke 17³⁴ᶠ· it speaks of two being together in the field, sleeping
in one bed, grinding at one mill, of whom it must yet be said that ὁ εἷς
παραλημφθήσεται καὶ ὁ ἕτερος ἀφεθήσεται. We think also of the parable of
the four different kinds of field, where the seed is expressly called the Word of
God, and especially of the general explanation given in Mark 4¹¹ : "Unto you
it is given to know the mystery of the kingdom of God ; but unto them that
are without, all these things are done in parables, ἵνα βλέποντες βλέπωσιν καὶ μὴ
ἴδωσιν, καὶ ἀκούοντες ἀκούωσιν καὶ μὴ συνιῶσιν, μήποτε ἐπιστρέψωσιν καὶ ἀφεθῇ αὐτοῖς.

We have already spoken, under the heading of the power to
rule in the Word of God, of this twofold possibility in its operation

The inner ground of this twofold possibility is that it is a decision and therefore a choice. Must we know an inner reason for this choice, a justification for God on account of the freedom which He takes to Himself and possesses, when He speaks to man, now of adopting him, now of rejecting him, of illumining one with His light and blinding another with the same light, of dealing with one as Peter and with another as Judas ? A sufficient justification for this view, as for the dogma of predestination generally which at this point comes within range, is that the decision made in the Word is God's and therefore it is a righteous and a good decision. It is a decision to which the hidden reality of the relation as subsisting between Jesus Christ and Peter, Jesus Christ and Judas assuredly and adequately corresponds, but which above all is justified in itself as the divine decision. The fact is that we may hear the Word of God and hear it again, and may thereby hear it correctly, adopt its promise as a promise, become obedient unto its claim, submit to its judgment, receive its blessing, find in it—in it, of course, outside ourselves !—the substance on which we feed and live ; or else we may not hear it rightly, adopt it, become obedient, subject, receptive only in appearance, in which case our life must continue without it as our nourishment. We may know the one or the other or both. But we must be aware that here the Word of truth itself decides as to " rightly " or " not rightly," i.e. that we receive grace or judgment in the way in which it comes to us from God and therefore for a right reason.

(c) As the divine decision the Word of God becomes operative on and in a decision of the man to whom it is spoken. What does the revelation, attested in Holy Scripture and proclaimed through preaching and sacrament, say to me ? What is revealed to me in it ? " God with us," in this form we summed up generally the content of the Word of God. But now, because this " God with us " is spoken to me, because *I* hear it, it must, without ceasing to be the divine content of the Word, or undergoing alteration as such, but rather as the actual, living, unalterable content of the Word, reach its goal in my situation over against it, created and defined in one way or another, in that modification of me accomplished by the Word of God spoken to me. This new modification of me is the decision as to my faith or unbelief, my obedience or disobedience, i.e. the divine decision as to whether my act is faith or unbelief, obedience or disobedience, correct or incorrect hearing.

This decision exists only over against the Word of God addressed
to me, only as the answer to it.

It is not one special case among the possibilities of human decision in
general. Therefore the understanding of it cannot be framed beforehand
in a universal anthropology. The most radical crisis, in which man may
discover himself—regarding himself in the light of universal anthropology—
has nothing to do with this crisis. For even in the most radical crisis of a
universally human kind, man at the same time discovers himself as the
individual selector of his own possibility. The decision does not come to him ;
he makes it. And this individual behaviour of his is the proper and primary
revelation of God. (Cf. on this H. E. Eisenhuth, *Das Irrationale als
philosophisches Problem*, 1931, especially the closing section, pp. 260–267 :
this book perhaps brings to a close, i.e. reduces *ad absurdum*, the theological
valuation of the philosophy of M. Heidegger.) From this standpoint
neither faith nor unbelief, obedience nor disobedience, nor decision between
the two, can come in sight at all. It must follow that the possibility of faith
and unbelief, obedience and disobedience regarding the Word of God, can
only be dealt with from within a theological anthropology.

Just as the Word of God is itself revelation, i.e. a word new
to me, so the situation into which it transposes me by being
addressed to me, is an utterly new situation, which could not be
foreseen or anticipated, one not comparable with any other situation, one based upon the Word of God and upon it alone. In fact a
situation for decision. But not the decision (which of course also
occurs !) of my varying resolution and choice, but the decision upon
a varying process of being judged and adopted, and so—because
the judging and adoption are the judging and adoption of God—
upon a varying state of truth, upon a varying meaning in my
resolution and choice. Because the Word of God means " God
with us," because it is the Word of the Lord, the Word of our
Creator, Reconciler, and Redeemer, it clearly pronounces our judgment upon ourselves. In it, it is decided who we are. We are
what we are on the basis of this judgment, we are what we are
as hearers of it, i.e. we are believers or unbelievers, obedient or
disobedient. We are neither the one nor the other, previously and
per se. Previously and *per se* we have not the slightest chance of
being the one or the other. Faith and unbelief, obedience and disobedience are only possible in that as our action in the judgment
of God they are the answer, one way or the other, to His Word
addressed to us. In faith and in obedience my own resolution and
choice are genuinely good before God, I exist, whatever else may
be said of me, according to the Word of God, I have adopted and
received His grace. In unbelief and disobedience my own resolution and choice, whatever else may be said of them, are genuinely

bad before God, I exist in contradiction to the Word of God, I have not adopted His grace. In one way or the other it is *I*—so that it is my, my extremely responsible decision. But it does not depend upon my decision for this character which it has, for my choosing now the good, now the bad. But what this decision of mine means, which I achieve with free will, is that in one case its meaning is a step to the right, in another a step to the left, that my choice one way is faith and obedience, while my choice another way is a denial of both—this characteristic of my decision is the truth, inherent in it, of the divine decision about me. By addressing me, God has regarded me as the man I am to myself as I am. The new quality which I acquire through the Word of God is my peculiar and essential quality. It is this peculiar and essential quality of mine that I cannot give myself. Only God can judge me. Thus I am altogether the man I am in virtue of God's decision. In virtue of God's decision I am by my own decision a believer or an unbeliever. And in this decision by which it is decided who I am by my own decision, and by which thereby it is decided what my decision in truth means—in this rendering of my reality, true (in this bringing of our works to light, John 3[20f.]; Eph. 5[12f.]), the Word of God is consummated as the act of God. It is always the act of the unsearchable judgment of God.

4. GOD'S LANGUAGE AS GOD'S MYSTERY

In a third series of the attributes of the Word of God, in order to point right beyond everything that was said from the standpoint of " Speech—act," we must speak of what is really the decisive thing, the fact, namely, that in everything we are concerned with God's speech, God's act. In fact we have already and repeatedly tried, in what has gone before, to anticipate limitations in this direction. But when we cast a glance over the whole of the concepts hitherto mentioned, spirituality, personality, purposiveness, and contemporaneousness, power to rule, decision, might not the question always arise whether the language was not about some other Logos, whether it was really about the Logos of God ? Or might not the temptation constantly persist, to think and speak of the Logos of God as we have described it, in such a way as one thinks and speaks of another spiritual entity perhaps difficult to grasp, but still graspable, in such a way, I mean, that one dreams of getting to know about it—and if perhaps after hard work, the better and surer the knowledge—dreams of examining into its structure, of understanding it in its operation, so that, at least in thought and speech one is master of it, as well or ill as mere man can come to master an object in thought and speech ?

At this point we may announce one cautionary consideration, which, of course, can only be proved emotionally, or even only understood emotionally, and therefore is easily sidetracked. Because and in that I continually hold it against myself, I hold it up a little to the whole of my senior and junior theological contemporaries, especially so far as they are engaged in so-called " systematic " theology. " Serious theological work " is an ideal which is in all our mouths. It appears that not only the Bible but also the Fathers of Protestantism and of the early Church are speaking to us once again with greater emphasis. The great concepts, God, Word, Spirit, Revelation, Church, Sacrament, etc., have once more entered our field of vision. Once more we are seeing that here theology has tasks to face. Once more many of us have the skill to talk cleverly, clearly, and definitely about these things. " Theological discussion " is taken up in many places in an extraordinarily intensive way. One can only be glad of the opportunity of being a theologian in these days of ours. But it is constantly to be feared that all of us are on the point of becoming far too positive. I am not thinking of the questionable and partisan meaning of this word, which to-day has become obsolete, although somewhat of the peculiar pathos of the old " positive " theology certainly continues to live, i.e. is being resuscitated, in what I here call " positive." I am thinking of a certain assurance of voice, speech, and attitude with which, it appears, we think we can work in the new (old !) field ; of a certain confidence with which we think we can take these mighty concepts upon our lips, analyse them, and unite them constructively one to the other, this way or that ; of a certain sprightliness with which we speak of the things signified by these concepts, as though we spoke about them, because we know how to speak above them with such comparative freedom from restriction. An assurance, certainty, and sprightliness which perhaps becomes but the greater, as we are clever enough also to work in the element of uncertainty or of " confident despair," or else a " line of death " or the like, into our more or less spiritual calculations. Is it also clear to our generation, in terms of life and not only of thought, that the " seriousness " of serious theological work is founded upon the fact that its object is never in any sense at our disposal, not even at the disposal of our profoundest " Biblical " or " Reformed " vision and knowledge, nor yet at the disposal of our most delicate and circumspect construction ? Practically any theological possibility may as such be pure threshing of straw and waste of energy, pure comedy and tragedy, pure deception and self-deception. Even the most zealous theological treasure-hunting is certainly mere folly apart from that " being rich toward God " (Luke 12^{21}) which no one can manufacture for himself or maintain for himself. In fact there can as little be a theology sure in faith, i.e. sure in its object, without awareness of this danger, as a clock with works and no pendulum. And this awareness must make itself noticeable, it must make theological thought and language in a real sense fruitful and substantial. To what extent does it make itself noticeable in the theological output of our day ? How far can such assurance, confidence, and sprightliness, such a leaven of the " positive " and of " positive people " be compatible with this awareness ? How far is our theological discussion not real talk at all ? *C'est le ton qui fait la musique.* No one can discuss tone in general, nor yet the tone which can make discussion into real talk, and never at all with those to whom at this point one thinks oneself nearest.   I fancy I can already hear the lamentations and the jeers and the " certainly—buts " with which these lines will be received.   Still, must it not repeatedly be said, Beware of this leaven ! ?

Obviously it would have confirmed our former question, we should really have been speaking of another Logos than the Logos of God, had we thought that regarding this question we should and could prove that we had not been self-deceived, that we had really been speaking of the Logos of God.   By the very idea that we could prove this in any sense we should be betraying the essential fact, or rather betraying the confusion we had made between this fact and some other fact.   For if anything serious was intended in what was said previously we must let ourselves be captured by the conviction that only the Logos of God itself can lead the proof, that where it is supposedly spoken of it is really spoken of. And in that way we would at least have already succumbed to the aforesaid temptation at times when we were looking for some means of keeping it at bay, securing ourselves against it and rendering ourselves immune.   For it would just mean claiming, in the most subtle way, to be masters of the Word of God, if we thought we could put ourselves into a position in which we should find ourselves securely in the right attitude towards it, the attitude not of a master but of a servant.   Would not that be the loftiest triumph of human certainty ?   But would it not also be the settlement of our query and a lapse into this temptation ?   For what would it signify if we had really consummated or were yet to consummate the delimitation of the divine over against the human ? If we could, we should then have said or should still be saying what the Word of God is.   The goal of all desire in theology is to achieve that, but the goal of an illegitimate desire !   The object of all pride in theology, to think one can really achieve that, but assuredly the object of an unhealthy pride !   For according to all that we can know of the nature of the Word of God, one thing is barred ; it cannot be an entity which we could delimit from all other entities and thereby make into an object, though it was done with the utmost humility and discretion.   Certainly it is delimited from all other entities, it is objective and it is *sui generis*. God's speech is different from all other kinds of speech, and His action is different from all other kinds of action.   But would it not imply a denial of this otherness of His, if we imagined we possessed a measure of this otherness and could apply it ?   Is it not a property of those other entities which are not identical with the Word of God, that we are able to delimit them more or less clearly from one another and to objectify them ? Is not this shown in the very fact that we review, understand, and ultimately master them, ultimately succeed in manipulating them, because ultimately we find that we are on the same level as them ? Would the Word of God be *sui generis*, if we could circumscribe *suum genus* and assign its fixed place to it, though it was still so very much the " wholly other " ? Is the Word of God not rather *sui generis*, God's Word, because we cannot do that, because it rather does that by itself alone ? So it will never do, by those already prescribed delimitations, to indicate to the Word of God, so to speak, its sphere within the world which is known to us and calls for conceptual classification. All our delimitations could only stand for signals or alarms to call attention to the fact that God's Word is and always remains God's Word, unbound, unattachable to this thesis or that antithesis. A sketch of the concept as the philosopher would like it has not arisen and ought not to arise. God alone conceives of Himself, even in His Word. Our concept of Him and His Word can only be a pointer of the limits of our conceiving, a pointer which should not claim to condense into a negative proof. Therefore, that cannot be our concern even at this point where certainly this decisive truth, that the Word of God is God's Word, has to be inculcated once again. Even now we can only inculcate it by once again and explicitly being mindful of our own limits, by inculcating it upon ourselves that even we could not utter one wretched syllable about the nature of the Word of God, if the Word of God had not been spoken to us as God's Word : which means, spoken to us in such a way that all our thought and speech about its How has its substance not in them but outside them, in the Word of God itself, in such a way, therefore, that from our thoughts and words about this How there can never, never issue the private system of a What. Therefore, and in this sense, we speak in conclusion of the language of God as the mystery of God. The question is, not of an ultimate assurance but, for the rest, of an always penultimate " de-assurance " of the theology of the Word of God : we might also say, of a theological warning against theology. The warning, namely, not to think that its peak propositions or principles are like the so-called axioms of the mathematicians and physicists, certain in themselves, and not rather related to their alone certain content and object, which they cannot dominate, but by which they must be dominated, if they do not wish to be soap-bubbles.

When we sum up what is here to be carried out precisely in the concept of my stery, we are thinking of the sense which the word *mysterium* has in the NT. *Mysterium* signifies not simply the hiddenness of God, but rather His becoming manifest in a hidden, i.e. in a non-apparent way, which gives information not directly but indirectly. *Mysterium* is the veiling of God in which He meets us by actually unveiling Himself to us : because He will not and cannot unveil Himself to us in any other way than by veiling Himself. *Mysterium* thus indicates sufficiently the divine givenness of the Word of God (divine in the sense of signifying our limits), by which it is of itself distinguished from anything given otherwise. Of itself distinguished ? That does not mean that we can fix the distinctness. In that case it simply would not be a mystery. But, of itself distinguished, in that it is given to us in that way and only in that way. Not in such a way that we come to a triumphant distinction, but in such a way that it remains reserved to itself to make the distinction.

1. The language of God is and remains God's mystery above all in its worldliness [in the sense of belonging to the world : and so here *passim*].[1] When God speaks to man, this happening is never so marked off from the rest of what happens that it might not promptly be also interpreted as a part of this other happening. The Church in fact is also a sociological entity with definite historical and structural features. Preaching in fact is also an address. Sacrament in fact is also a symbol in compromising proximity to all other possible symbols. The Bible in fact is also the document for the history of the religion of a tribe in Nearer Asia and of its Hellenistic offshoot. Jesus Christ in fact is also the Rabbi of Nazareth, historically so difficult to get information about, and when it is got, one whose activity is so easily a little commonplace alongside more than one other founder of a religion and even alongside many later representatives of His own " religion." And let us not forget that theology in fact, so surely as it avails itself of human speech, is also a philosophy or a conglomerate of all sorts of philosophy. Even the Biblical miracles do not burst these walls of worldliness. From the moment they took place they were interpreted otherwise than as proofs of the Word of God, and admittedly they may ever and anon be interpreted in a very different sense. The veil is thick. We do not possess the Word of God otherwise than in the mystery of its worldliness.

In other words, we always have it in a form which as such is not the Word of God and as such, moreover, does not betray that it is the form precisely of the Word of God. Otherwise expressed,

[1 Translator's note in these brackets.]

the self-presentation of God in His Word is not a direct one, yet not an indirect one either, in the way in which a man's face which we perceive in mirror may be called an indirect self-presentation of this man.

When St. Paul speaks in 1 Cor. 13^{12} of a βλέπειν δι᾽ εἰσόπτρου we must carefully consider the addition ἐν αἰνίγματι. He is calling attention to the fact that there is in question a twofold indirectness of vision. For the first thing to be pondered is that the Word of God meets us in a form to be distinguished from its content : the second is that this form as such signifies a " riddle," a veiling of the Word of God.—It is to the concept of the p a r a d o x that we must here point. A paradox is such a communication, as is not only made by means of a δόξα, a " phenomenon," but is to be regarded, if it is to be understood at all, παρὰ τὴν δόξαν, i.e. contrary to what the phenomenon as such appears to express. Just because the Word of God alone fulfils the concept of paradox with complete strictness, whereas in all other thinkable " paradoxes " the opposition between communication and form is such that it can be dissolved from some superior point of vantage, it is to be recommended that in theology more sparing use should henceforth be made of this concept now that it has done its part, not without causing all manner of confusions.

The self-presentation of God in His Word is not comparable with any other self-presentation, inasmuch as all that meets us elsewhere as self-presentation is either direct communication or if indirect characterised by a certain similarity and correspondence between matter and form, a feature which makes it possible (with the same significance as in perceiving an object in a mirror) to dissolve the indirect into direct communication, i.e. knowledge. This is the very thing which is excluded in the case of the Word of God. Its form is not a suitable but an unsuitable means for the self-presentation of God. It does not correspond to the matter, but it contradicts it. It does not unveil it, but it veils it. By the " worldliness " of the Word of God we must not only understand the fact that it meets us .in the garments of creaturely reality. But also, because this creaturely reality is that of fallen man, and because the Word of God meets us in this very reality, we must say that its form is not that of a pure nature which as such would straightway contrast with the unnaturalness of its environment. Moreover, our knowledge of the Word of God does not take place by means of an understanding that has somehow remained pure, and therefore pierces through to the mystery of God in the creaturely reality, but wholly by means of our fallen understanding. The place where God's Word is manifest is, objectively and subjectively, the cosmos in which sin rules. The form of the Word of God is therefore really that of the cosmos which stands in contradiction to God. It as little has in it the capacity of revealing God to us as we on our part have the capacity for knowing God in it. If God's Word is manifest in it, it happens, of course, " through it," but in such a way that this " through it " means " in spite of it." Worldliness as it is proper to the Word of God is not transparent in itself and as such, capable of being the translucent garment or the mirror of the Word of God. And in face of it there can never be any question of getting, by means of effort and skill, behind the fact that it is the worldliness precisely of the Word of God. What can be brought to light by interpretation or exegesis of this bit of world will always be itself (because it is our thought and exegesis with which we seek to help ourselves here) a hidden bit of world, requiring fresh interpretation and exegesis, but ultimately resisting all solution ; by it also being, once more, a contradiction of the Word of God and not a correspondence with the Word of God, and therefore a simple mirror of it. The real interpretation of its form can only be that which the Word of God gives itself.

The passage 1 Cor. 1¹⁸⁻²¹⁰ in this context cannot be seriously enough considered. What St. Paul preaches is ὁ λόγος ὁ τοῦ σταυροῦ, the Χριστὸς ἐσταυρωμένος who is indeed the power of God and the wisdom of God, through whom God turns the wisdom of the world into foolishness, who however, precisely as such, can from the world's point of view only be μωρία, who also stamps His preachers and hearers as fools, weaklings, underlings, nothings (μὴ ὄντα), who as σοφία ἐν μυστηρίῳ ἡ ἀποκεκρυμμένη can only illumine by divine election through the ἀπόδειξις πνεύματος καὶ δυνάμεως, through ἀποκάλυψις, " that no flesh may be able to boast itself before God," " that your faith should not stand in the wisdom of men but in the power of God." What God through him hath prepared for them that love Him, eye hath not seen, nor ear heard, neither hath it entered into the heart of man. It is the God-given Spirit that knows it, no one and nothing else.—*Quia mirandum est idcirco non creditur. Qualia enim decet esse opera divina, nisi super omnem admirationem ? Nos quoque ipsi miramur, sed quia credimus. . . . Nam si Deus et sapiens et potens . . . merito in adversariis sapientiae potentiaeque id est in stultitia et impossibilitate materias operationis suae instituit ; quoniam virtus omnis ex his causam accipit a quibus provocatur* (Tertullian, *De bapt.* 2). —This is a case of the insight which Luther in the *Heidelberg Disputation*, 1518 (W. edn. 1, p. 362 f.) opposed as the *theologia crucis* to a *theologia gloriae*, i.e. to a direct or only relatively indirect desire to know God. W. von Loewenich (Luther's *Theologia crucis*, 1929 pp. 7 and 12) is rightly of the opinion that there it is a question not of a special chapter in theology but of a special kind of theology, and in Luther's case a question not merely of a principle of Luther's in his young days but of a principle of his whole theology. *Iam adhuc agimus cum Deo velato, in hac enim vita non possumus cum Deo agere facie ad faciem. Universa autem creatura est facies et larva Dei. Sed hic requiritur sapientia quae discernat Deum a larva. Hanc sapientiam mundus non habet, ideo non potest discernere Deum a larva* (Komm. Zu, Gal. 2⁶, 1535 W. edn. 40¹, p. 174, l. 12). In an application of the doctrine of the *analogia entis* that might have been said at a pinch by a Catholic theologian brought up on Plato or Aristotle. (It is therefore not worth while out of such statements as that on the *larva Dei* character of the whole creature mysteriously to evolve, with K. Holl and his pupils, a specially deep new idea of the world according to Luther). The nerve of Luther's thought is that the *larva Dei*, the indirectness of His self-communication, is a twofold one, not only one caused by the creature's creatureliness, but also one caused by its sinfulness : *ut ergo fidei locus sit, opus est, ut omnia quae creduntur, abscond-antur. Non autem remotius absconduntur, quam sub contrario objectu, sensu, experientia. Sic Deus dum vivificat, facit illud occidendo : dum justificat, facit illud reos faciendo ; dum in coelum vehit, facit id ad infernum ducendo* (*De Serv. arbit.* 1525 W. edn. 18, p. 633, l. 7). " The Word I hear and Paul I see, who is a poor man. But this salvation, grace, life, and peace, these I see not ; but rather their counterparts I must see daily, sin, terror, ill-luck, suffering, and death ; that it seemeth there are no men so abandoned by God as the Christians, so must I hear this Word " (*Sermon on Acts* 13[26f.], E. edn. 8, p. 191). And still more sharply : *Nam fides ita dicit ; Ego credo tibi Deo loquenti. Quid loquitur Deus ? Impossibilia, mendatia, stulta, infirma, absurda, abominanda, haeretica et diabolica, si rationem consulas* (on *Gal.* 3[6], 1525 W. edn. 40[I], p. 361, l. 14). And in conclusion with almost unheard-of sharpness : " Therefore must God's faithfulness and truth ever first become a great lie, ere it become the truth. Though to the world 'tis an heresy. So seemeth it ever to ourselves as if God would leave us and not keep His Word, and in our heart looketh to become a liar. And in fine, God cannot be God, He must first become a devil, and we cannot come up to heaven, we must first go into hell, cannot become God's children, for we must first become the devil's children. For all that God saith and doth, the devil must have said and done " (*Ps.* 117 *expounded*, 1530 W. edn. 31[I], p. 249, l. 21).

Thus in all applications of the proposition that proclamation, Scripture or revelation is the Word of God, we shall need to have regard to the fact that it is true only in this twofold indirect-ness, that when the Word of God is spoken and becomes apprehended, what is involved is not merely an act of God generally, and not merely an act of God in creaturely reality as such, but an act of God in the reality which contradicts God, veils God, in which His revelation is not only His act, but His miraculous act, the rending of an unrendably thick veil ; in other words, His mystery.

Thus, for example, we cannot wish so to frame Church proclamation as to make it necessarily illuminating within the Cosmos as an element in the education, upbringing and care of the nation, of social progress, etc. We cannot wish, as was usual in the period of orthodoxy and the Enlightenment (as unfortunately even Calvin incidentally tried to do, *Instit.* I 8), and as was attempted from the time of Herder with all the apparatus of the new historical thought, to set up the Bible as a credible and commendable book from all sorts of human points of view. And above all we should on principle spare the revelation itself, Jesus Christ, for all our desire to prove directly or only relatively indirectly its superiority to all other religions (as, say, K. Holl has represented him, *Urchristentum und Religionsgeschichte*, 1925,

Ges. Aufsätze zur Kirchengesch, II p. 1 f.).   A purely historical treatment of Christianity shows itself here in the long-run to be repeatedly more fruitful theologically than such attempts at a breakaway which purport to be historical, but which ultimately rest upon a confusion of categories.

We ought not to conceive of the worldliness of the Word of God as, so to speak, a disagreeable accident, as an inconvenience some day perhaps to be removed in whole or at least in part. In this worldliness, and therefore in this twofold indirectness, we have really to do with a genuine and inseparable attribute of the Word of God itself.   Revelation means the Incarnation of the Word of God.   But incarnation means entry into this worldliness. We are in this world, we are ourselves thoroughly worldly.   Were God to speak to us in a non-worldly way, He would not speak to us at all.   To get round the worldliness of His Word would be to get round Christ.   No matter how completely we may first realise the meaning of saying that we are flesh and therefore not God, and without organ or capacity to receive God, but at enmity with Him and powerless to become obedient to Him—still, what at first looks like an absurd barrier which God puts in His own way, is nevertheless His real and therefore, of course, necessary and good way for us.   Not as if we could ever see why it must be or may be so.   We are not placed above God and ourselves and so can express no other opinion on the necessity and goodness of the relation into which God puts Himself towards us, but such as seeks to reproduce the reality of this relation.   But we have nothing else to reproduce but this, and reproduce this we must, that as surely as God comes into relation with us through His Word, so surely His Word must be as it is, a Word spoken in a worldly way, with a twofold indirectness.   The facts are not that God was veiled from us by some unfortunate disturbance and then unveiled Himself by removing this veiling—on this hypothesis man's attempts on his part to come as it were to the help of God by forcing his own way into the mystery, would be only too understandable and excusable, even where not actually necessary.   The facts are that God Himself veils Himself and in the very process—which is why we should not dream of intruding into the mystery—unveils Himself.   It is good for us that God acts exactly as He does, and it could only be fatal for us if He acted otherwise, if He were manifest to us in the way we should hold correct, directly and without any veil, without worldliness or only in that harmless transparent form of it *analogiâ entis*.   It would not be greater love and mercy, it would be the end of us and the end of all things if the Word were addressed to us thus. That it is addressed to us in the way it is in reality, unveiling itself in its veiledness, is the decisive way of saying that it has really come to us instead of us having to come to it, an attempt on which we could only suffer shipwreck. In its very worldliness it is, therefore, in every respect the Word of grace.

Among other places in a powerful exposition at the beginning of his commentary on *Galatians* (W. edn. '40[I], p. 75 ff.) Luther lays it down that this must differentiate us from the Pope, the Turks, Jews, and all *justitiarii, ut abstineamus a speculatione Majestatis*, which could only be fatal to us body and soul ; *scrutator enim Majestatis opprimitur a gloria.* To wish to know God directly means righteousness by works, and righteousness by works signifies the fall and despair of Lucifer. We, on the contrary, have to hold to the true and real Christ as he lies in the manger at Bethlehem and in the Virgin's lap. Calvin has expressed himself in the same sense : *Quand donc nous n'aurions sinon la majesté de Dieu qui se présentera devant nos yeux, elle sera pour nous effrayer et n'y pourrons pas avoir aucun acces à cause que nous sommes creatures fragiles, et mesmes qu'il n'y en nous que peché : nous campons ici sur la terre : mais nous sommes dignes d'estre engloutis jusques au profond d'enfer (Sermon on Gal.* 1[3f.], *C.R.* 50, 289). *Magnifions la bonte de nostre Dieu, veu qu'il luy plaist d'avoir regard à nous et à nostre rudesse et qu'il est content que sa gloire nous soit cachée, afin que nous n'en soyons point abysmez. Car . . . nous ne la pouvons porter estans ainsi fragiles que nous sommes (Sermon on Deut.* 5[1f.], *C.R.* 26, 248).—" Yea, if one really therefore feel it as actually 'tis in truth, the man must straightway from that hour die. For man being flesh and blood cannot understand it, in life man's heart is much too strait to conceive of such . . ." (Luther, *Sermon on Mark* 16[1-8], *Sommerpost.* 1526 W. edn. 10[I], 2, p. 216, l. 19). " It is forbidden, I must not see, hear, feel, know or acknowledge, but only hear it, and with faith cling to it and stand upon the mere Word of God.—And it goeth with us like as with one that hath a vertigo in his head, should he mount up to a high tower or come on to a bridge under which deep water floweth, so he must simply be blinded and led blindly and hang a cloak about his head, and he be led and borne, else he falleth from the tower and breaketh his neck or falleth into the water and drowneth. So, if we would be blest, we must also follow our guide, then are we thus safe. We, too, must shut our eyes tight and follow the companion, the divine Word, and say : I will let myself be wound in swaddling clothes and a cloak be wrapped about mine head and myself be led to that wherein I believe and see not, and will live therein and die. Otherwise we shall not feel it even although we are practically being torn to pieces therefor. Many have troubled themselves sorely thereanent and would gladly know where our dwelling or lodging is when we die, whither we are going, and many great people have become mad because they were not aware where one goes on leaving this life, and have coined this saying anent it :

I live and know not how long :
I die and know not when :
I go and know not whither :
Wonder 'tis there's joy in my song !

And 'tis true a non-Christian cannot know it at all, but a Christian must judge otherwise thereof, he hath a trusty conveyor, so he followeth his leader and guide, Christ, who saith what a man should do, saying : Hear what we speak, for we know what we speak, our words are truth, trust me, give thyself prisoner sublimely, and put thyself in my cloak I have wound about thy head, I will surely bear thee across.   If thou doest thus thou wilt not be led astray by Him.   But thou sayest : I know not whither I go, I feel naught, grope for and grasp naught.   That is quite true, but thou must rely on God's Word and trust God, who will sustain thee where, if thou fall from the tower, thou breakest not thy neck in twain or from fear fallest from the ship and must drown.   But there is naught there to see, we know not where the ladder or the steps are or the cord by which the ladder hangs, we can behold no way that leadeth to heaven.   But in Christ alone is the way to heaven prepared for us, which is reserved for us through the divine Word, otherwise thou treadest upon the air and so fallest. . . . This then is the difference between the Christian and the pagan that a godless man and a pagan departeth like a cow, seeing, opining, and judging all things according to the old birth as what he feels and grasps.   But a Christian followeth not as he seeth, but followeth as he seeth not nor feeleth and abideth by the witness of Christ, heareth what Christ saith, whom he followeth right into the darkness.   So we stay fast in the bag and are wound into His cloak and He leadeth us where Himself is and in Christ we walk up to heaven, who maketh him blessed " (*Exposition of John* 3–4, W. edn. 47, p. 33, l. 38).   " Lo 'tis this whereon St. John insisteth strongly in every passage in his gospel, that we should suffer only lofty fair thoughts to go their own gait, whereby the intellect and clever folk do circumvent and seek God in majesty apart from Christ.   He is ready in Christ to lie in the cradle and the mother's lap or to hang on the Cross : they would mount to heaven and find out how He sits and rules the world.   These are foolishly dreadful thoughts, unless rightly guided.   For they are all bound to this one spot where we should not grope and peer further.   Wouldst thou touch and grasp all that God is and doth and hath in mind, then seek it nowhere save where He hath put and laid it.   That thou hearest in the word, ' All that is thine is mine,' etc.   Therefore, a Christian ought to know not to seek or find God otherwise, save in the virgin's lap and on the Cross, or as and where Christ sheweth Himself in the Word " (*Sermon on John* 16[20], 1528–29 W. edn. 28, p. 135, l. 38).

In direct connection with these thoughts in Luther and in Calvin, we must now once more come back to Fr. Gogarten.   In the first edition of this book, apart from the " absence of a proper anthropology," he has objected principally to the fact that at least in part it speaks " at one time of a God isolated in and for Himself over against man, at another of man isolated in and for himself over against God " (*Theol. Rundsch.* 1930 p. 72). This is supposed to be shown in the application of the concepts " objective " and " subjective " to God and man, in the distinction between an " eternal history of God " and God's revelation as history, i.e. man addressed by God, between a " God in Himself " and a " God for us."   But that, he holds, is a mistake if we are to presuppose that in theology we should start our thinking " with the past incarnation of the Word."   I can scarcely be wrong in assuming that in this attack Gogarten had in mind Luther's attack, just instanced in one or two examples, against *speculatio Majestatis*.   True, he does not reproach me with actual failure to hear this warning of the Reformers.   He rather quotes a series of passages from my book itself, in which I contradict myself by abolishing that distinction. He even thinks me capable of holding this, the abolition of that distinction, as my own real opinion, which I myself contradict by that distinction. He professes " to see that Barth himself has come hard up against these things. But in coming up against them, he already abandons them again " (p. 73). Gogarten has two explanations of this mistake of mine. He supposes in the first place that it is the result of a man like me working " with ideas adopted without examination and unpurified," instead of first reducing them to order in this respect in a proper anthropology. It is these unpurified ideas which progressively introduced " alien hypotheses " into my thinking and so spoiled me my first draft (p. 78 f.). But at the close of his essay Gogarten also says something else, namely, that it is clear to him that actually in the very thing to which he has to take exception is to be noted " the true theological concern " of the book, the effort, namely, in all questions of dogmatics, to lay the emphasis on " God Himself," an intention in which he is quite at one with me (p. 79 f.).—In reply let me say, that the circumstance that I make the alleged distinction in order to abandon it again ; or *vice versa* that I come hard up against things (Gogarten obviously means against the clear and definitive abolition of the distinction) only to abandon them once more—this circumstance is correctly perceived. As regards " unpurified ideas " I likewise concede the fact, but can only repeat that I heartily reject any anticipatory cleansing of ideas in an anthropology of a theologically doubtful character, and for my part expect results only from a purification of ideas, achieved in the process of dogmatic research and exposition themselves. As for the theological concern which Gogarten sees at work even in my alleged error and in which he associates himself with me in spite of my error, it would certainly have been instructive if he had declared to what extent he also regards the aforesaid error as founded not merely upon certain unfortunate accidents with unpurified ideas, regrets for which are perhaps merely a form, but upon certain material necessities. In that case had he not perhaps come to realise that what he stigmatised was simply inevitable if thought is to start theologically and not philosophically " with the past Incarnation of the Word " ? Theological thought which starts there differs from a philosophical, in regarding " incarnation of the Word " not as the truth of a condition of things, e.g. the truth of the unity of subject and object, of the man-relatedness of God or the God-relatedness of man, to be laid at the foundation of dogmatics as the principle to be interpreted—that sort of thing Luther and the old-Lutheran dogmatists, in spite of their rejection of all *speculatio Majestatis*, never did—but as the truth of a divine act. But if they are to be regarded as an act, the *terminus a quo* (" God in Himself ") and the *terminus ad quem* (" God for us ") must first of all be differentiated, in order to be related to one another as such in the very description of the act. What would " God for us " declare, did it not emanate directly from the background of " God in Himself " ? For the sake of the abrogation, i.e. simply in order to speak of this matter, there must also be differentiation in this matter. To refuse to say No. 2 at all, would obviously be to be unable to say anything in saying No. 1. At this point we recall what was said in division 2 of this section on the " purposiveness," i.e. on the relatedness of the Word of God. There we sought to maintain that we understand the love of God for us correctly when we regard it as unbeholden and free, and thus also the Word of God as the sort of thing which possesses reality and glory not primarily because it is spoken to us, but in itself. It would be none the less the eternal Word of God were it not spoken to us, and what really constitutes the mercy of its revelation, of its being spoken to us is that it is spoken to us in virtue of the freedom in which God could be " God in Himself," but does not will so to be and as a matter of fact is not, but wills to be " God for us " and as a matter of fact is so. This freedom of God, without which we could not regard His Word as grace, would appear to me obscured, if in an excess of triumphant victory over so-called Greek thought we were simply to drop the opposition of " objective " and " subjective " in the concept of the Word of God, as Gogarten obviously wishes to do.

At this stage I must recall another critical discussion of my book, in which I am reproached from the very opposite side. In *Stimmen der Zeit* (Nov. 1928 p. 105) Erich Przywara, S.J., wrote that an " uncanny " reduction runs right through my book. For I affirm the entire world of Christian revelation only so far as it is the event of revelation become uniquely visible, in the way in which Kierkegaard conceived it, namely, as the utterance of God to man. With me the Trinity is said to dissolve into the threeness of revealer, revealing, and revealed state, while the Incarnation is but the concrete state of this event of revelation, grace but the subjective possibility of revelation. Thus the entire fulness of eternal life is reduced to the one " utterance," and in that way the ultimately pantheistic correlation-theology of Protestant liberalism is simply reversed with me, " from below upwards " is transformed into a " from above downwards " ; with me it is not God who is reduced to the nature of man, but (and so much the worse, Przywara obviously thinks) man who is exalted to the nature of God so far as the nature of God Himself is designated the " utterance of revelation." . . . Now that is certainly not just a correct estimate of my intentions or of what I actually said. But when such a clever and slightly malicious eye as that of Przywara finished by seeing and understanding me in this sense, I took it as a warning not to travel further in the direction desired by Gogarten. If one does not wish to be understood as Przywara, however wrongly, has understood me here, he must be quite clear in his own mind that his business is not a correlation-theology, i.e. a theology in which God in His relation to us swings up and down, either from below upwards so that God becomes a predicate of man, or from above downwards so that man would become a requisite in the nature of God. As regards the thought necessary in correlating God and man, we should not, as is done only too patently in Wobbermin and his pupil R. Winckler, or as I fail to see it clearly avoided in Bultmann, go the length of thinking away the free ground which this correlation has in God. If we reject this, the only sound, nay necessary, procedure left is to distinguish deliberately and sharply, as does the entire older theology, between the Trinity of God as knowable by us in the revealed, written, and proclaimed Word of God and His immanent Trinity, i.e. between " God in Himself " and " God for us," between the " eternal history of God " and His action in time, to remember continually how " God for us " does not self-evidently stand out from the background of " God in Himself," how it is true not as a condition of God which we could fix and assert by starting from the concept of man as participating in His revelation, but as an act, a step which God makes to meet man, by which the latter first becomes a man participating in His revelation. This becoming on man's part is one that is conditioned from without, from God's side, whereas God by making the step by which the whole correlation is first created at all, is not conditioned from without, from man's side. Therefore of course—here we agree with Gogarten—we cannot in theology speak of man in himself, in his isolation over against God. But naturally in theology, as actually in the proper doctrine of the Trinity as the presupposition of Christology, we must speak of God in Himself, in His isolation over against man. The only way we know ourselves is as those addressed by God's Word, but, of course, just because we are those addressed by God's Word, we should naturally have to know God as Him who addresses us in freedom as the Lord, who does not exist merely in addressing us, but as Him who is the cause and truth of this relation and correlation, who is also God previously, also God in Himself, also God in His eternal history. If this finding, if therefore this recollection of the immanent objective God-ness of God as distinguished from His God-ness for us, is already to be *speculatio majestatis*, then Luther himself would already have been guilty of *speculatio majestatis*, since he compares the Word, which was in the beginning, was with God and was God Himself (John 1¹), with the way in which love or anger, even without being expressed or made known, could absolutely fill a man, constitute the entire nature of this man ; and then he continues, " According to this picture God, even in His majesty, in His nature, is pregnant with a Word or utterance, which God in His divine nature holdeth with Himself and which is His heart's thought, which same is as complete and great and perfect as God Himself, but none seeth, heareth, nor conceiveth this same utterance save He alone. He hath an invisible and inconceivable utterance which hath been the word for all angels and for all creatures, for afterwards hath He through this utterance and word given their nature to all creatures ; in this utterance, word, and thought God is in heat so that He thinketh not otherwise therefor " (*Exposition of John* 1–2, 1537–1538 W. edn. 46, p. 545, l. 6). But what should that have to do with the *speculatio majestatis* against which Luther wages war in the commentary on *Galatians* and elsewhere ? Yet this war is not directed against acknowledging and regarding the Incarnate Word in all seriousness as the Word of God, and therefore in its invisible majesty, not against the distinction between what we succeed in hearing, seeing, or grasping intellectually, and what we have to believe as the presupposition of this entire visible aspect—but against the attempt to get round the necessity of faith by embarking upon an attempt at a direct, i.e. a merely relatively indirect knowledge of God, apart from the worldliness and the mystery, thereby given, of the incarnate Word. In pointing to the crib at Bethlehem and to the Cross of Christ, Luther is not implying thereby, that here in this phenomenon of the highest worldliness as such direct knowledge of God is possible and real, that here there is no need therefore to distinguish between what we see, hear, and conceive and what we have to believe, between true humanity and true Godhead, between the terminus *ad quem* and the *terminus a quo*, but he thereby points directly to the complete worldliness, i.e. to the hiddenness of the Word, and therefore to the sole reality of indirect knowledge, and so of course to the distinction in question, to its abolition (to be thought of, never as already completed but always as conceived in completion), and so to the immanent Trinity, to the eternal nature and eternal counsels of God. Here, in the *humanitas Christi*, we should seek and find all that—but seek and find here precisely that—seek and find but not see and possess directly. On the other hand, I am not quite clear how in the way indicated by Gogarten of a direct identification of " God in Himself " and " God for us " we can avoid trespassing upon what Luther has abjured as *speculatio majestatis*, upon a denial of the indirectness of our knowledge of the Word of God. If we really assert indirectness and mean by that not merely the harmless potentiality of the first degree, transformable into directness by virtue of the *analogia entis*, but the emphatic genuine indissoluble indirectness of the revelation and knowledge of God in the flesh, in the offence of the cradle and the cross, we must at this stage assert No. 2 if we are to assert No. 1; the No. 1 which alone is relevant here. Is it being serious with the worldliness and therefore with the hiddenness of the Word of God, to think one can express the One in one word instead of in two ? Naturally I do not assert that that is Gogarten's idea or that he dreams of denying the indirectness of our knowledge of the Word of God. But once again I am faced with the puzzle, since he obviously does not think the one and does not deny the other, as to what could he have in his eye or mind in his criticism. Has he broken with the conceptions of A. Ritschl, of which his criticism here has uncannily reminded me, as thoroughly as one should have broken with them (i.e. with the conceptions of Enlightenment theology) ? —Be that as it may, of actual materially important mistakes in my exposition Gogarten has made no mention, but, fairly considered, only of a source of possible material mishaps. On the contrary from Przywara's review, which comes from the opposite corner, I must infer how serious a danger to material comprehension any further advance in the direction desired by Gogarten would signify, in the very point which to me is all-important. So that in this respect, too, it is inevitable that I should rather speak with still greater emphasis along the lines disapproved of by Gogarten or should have to keep a still more expressive silence ; that at all events I cannot yield an inch.

2. God's language is and remains God's mystery in its one-sidedness. In that expression I am thinking of the relationship of veiling and unveiling actually conditioned by the " worldliness " of the Word of God. That God's Word is one-sided means that in being addressed to us and grasped by us it meets us, not partly veiled, partly unveiled, but either veiled or unveiled, without it therefore in itself being a different word, without its being one way or the other less really addressed to us or grasped by us. Its very veiling may absolutely change for us into its unveiling and its very unveiling change absolutely into its veiling. Absolutely ; i.e. it is for the time being, without alteration in itself, always for us the one or the other. Only for the time being can we conceive the other in the one, i.e. for the time being we can only grasp the other by grasping the one ; we can only grasp it in faith. With regard to the one we are transposed into the greatest clarity : such clarity, that we make ourselves very definite thoughts, clear in themselves, about what is told us, that we can react to it with our whole inner and outer attitude in life, with joy, thankfulness, confidence, zeal, seriousness, terror, confusion, anxiety, remorse. But this reaction is really reaction to the Word of God only when our clarity, our thought, our attitude in life, however determined, has its very determinate limit in the other : the limit set by the very Word

spoken to us, which does not admit of us arriving at a whole, a synthesis, a system, whether in our theory or in our praxis, the limit beyond which the Word remains a mystery to us in the entire clarity in which it is addressed to us and grasped by us, or rather for the first time becomes a real mystery. To grasp the Word of God does not from any standpoint mean being able to discern the connection between the two sides, being able to know or to express, why and how far at a given moment it is the veiled Word that signifies unveiling for us or the unveiled that signifies veiling. Could we know and state this, the Word of God would obviously cease to be a mystery, and would be a paradox like any other ; a paradox, behind the so-called mystery of which one could more or less comfortably penetrate. The language of God is and remains a mystery so far as its totality, as such, of course, i.e. with the entire weight and seriousness of the Word of God, is always manifest only on its one side, but on the other side it remains hidden. Hidden, therefore not simply withdrawn—in what is manifested to us there is always contained likewise what is hidden from us—but actually as hidden, only as such, i.e. only to be grasped and held in faith. In virtue of this one-sidedness in it, what God says to us remains what it is, His ways remain higher than our ways, and His thoughts remain higher than our thoughts (Isa. 55[8f.]), not only in their quantity but also in their mode and possibility. What remains hidden in the revelation made to us, remains always in God's own hand, remains to be sought and found there, with Himself, cannot be translated into an insight of our own or into an attitude of correspondence, because the meaning of the language of God is not to induce in us certain thoughts or a certain attitude, but by the clarity which He gives us and which, of course, induces both in us, to bind us to Himself. But that occurs, according as we are continually confronted with our limit, i.e. by His mystery.

We must approach this matter more closely. When by God's miracle His Word in its worldliness is addressed to us and grasped by us, that may mean first that we really hear the " God with us " there spoken to us, but hear it only in the worldly form in which it is spoken to us. But it may mean, on the other hand, that we indeed hear it in its worldly form, but really hear it in that way. From God's side that is the same thing, but for us it is altogether not the same thing but two things, or one thing only for faith. The one time God unveils Himself to us in His Word, but by the very fact that He veils Himself. The other time He veils Himself, but at the same time He actually unveils Himself also. Both times the question is to hear the whole, the real Word of God, i.e. the unveiling of God in His veiling equally with the veiling of God in His unveiling. The worldly form without the divine content is not the Word of God, and the divine content without the worldly form is also not the Word of God. We can neither remain rooted before the worldly form as such, nor fly beyond this and hope to enjoy ourselves still with the divine content only. The one would be realistic, the other would be idealistic theology, and both would be wrong theology. Both times, however, we in faith hear only the whole, the real Word of God. A removal of the distinction, nay opposition, between form and content we cannot achieve. The coincidence of both is God, but it is not discernible by us. What is discernible by us is always form without content or content without form. We may, of course, think realistically or idealistically, but we cannot think in a Christian sense. Obviously the thought of synthesis would least of all be Christian thought, because it would mean neither more nor less than that we wanted to achieve the miracle of God Himself. In faith and in the thought of faith it is not a case of thinking this synthesis. Faith means rather recognising that this synthesis cannot be achieved, committing it to God and seeking and finding it in God. By finding it in God we acknowledge that we cannot find it ourselves and so can neither achieve it in a definite attitude in life nor think it systematically. But by committing it to God and seeking it in Him, we do find it, we hear the whole, the real word of God, i.e. now the divine content in its worldly form, now in the worldly form the divine content. To hear in faith the whole, the real word of God does not mean discerning the unity of veiling and unveiling, of form and content, or accomplishing Christian thought by getting round faith. No, the thought of faith will always quite honestly be either a realistic or an idealistic thought, i.e. a thought in and of itself very unchristian. As such, and therefore without becoming different of and in itself, it is as the thought of faith a justified and sanctified thought. But justification and sanctification by faith means justification and sanctification by the object of faith, from God's side, without therefore the man of faith or his thought ceasing to be less defective. And because we cannot give ourselves faith, we cannot, therefore, by our thinking create for ourselves this justification and sanctification, cannot achieve any Christianity in our thought or even merely establish its presence in ourselves or in others, can only believe in it as God's grace : believe, because of the fact that our thought from either side is faced with a wall which we can neither throw down nor make transparent, i.e. because of the unchristianity which we cannot disown in our thought considered in and of itself. Thus believing now means hearing the divine content of the Word of God, although absolutely nothing but worldly form is discernible by us. And faith now means hearing the worldly form of the Word of God, although nothing but its divine content is discernible by us.

At this stage we may certainly recall the marvellous relation between the concepts "Father" and "Son" in their application to God as such, and to His incarnate Word as such, in the Gospel according to John. Both concepts are there used in such a way that one moment the content of the one is taken to be discernible, and next moment follows the declaration that from knowledge of the content of the one we must, may and shall arrive at knowledge of the content of the other. E.g. "that which the Father giveth me," 6^{37} ; or "whom the Father draweth," 6^{44} ; or "To whom it hath been given of the Father," 6^{65} ; or "Whoso is given to the Son by the Father," 10^{29}, he cometh unto me, the Son. On the other hand, "he that honoureth not the Son, honoureth not the Father," 5^{23}. "If any man serve me, him will the Father honour," 12^{26}. "No man cometh unto the Father but by me," 14^{6}. "He that hath seen me hath seen the Father," 14^{9}. "That the Father may be glorified in the Son," 14^{13}. Or in almost direct contrast, "I honour my Father," 8^{49} ; and, "My Father that honoureth me," 8^{54}. The declaration, "I and the Father are one," 10^{30} . . . "that they may be one, even as we are" (Father and Son : 17^{11}) obviously only underlines the fact that in John believing is as much going from the known Father to the unknown Son as from the known Son to the unknown Father. There would be nothing contrary to the sense of the Fourth Gospel if in this context for Father and Son we inserted our concepts of content and form in their variety and unity.

Faith is therefore invariably the recognition of our limits and the recognition of the mystery of the Word of God, the recognition that our hearing is bound to God Himself who wills to lead us now through form to content, and now through content back to form, and in both cases to Himself, who one way or the other does not give Himself into our hands, but keeps us in His hand.

It might appear as striking that the movement of faith or rather the movement of the Word of God itself, which of course faith can only follow, is thus expressly and thoroughly described as a twofold one. This is so not for the sake of a scheme, but because the fact here to be expressed allows of no other way. Indeed, above all, the fact is that in faith it is a case of as it were breaking through, or of recognising as broken through, the veiling in which, in proclamation, in the Bible and in Christ Himself, God speaks to us, i.e. of seeing and hearing that the very veiling of God is His true and real unveiling.

We think here of the well-known marvellous sermon of Luther's on the story of the Canaanitish woman, Matt. 15²¹ᶠ⁺. Believing steadfastly in the proclamation about Christ which she has heard (in " such a good crying "), the woman comes to Him, but lo, He takes " quite another cue, as though He would give her faith and good confidence a miss and make His own report false, so that she might well think, Is this the kindly, friendly man ? or are these the good words I have heard tell of him, whereon I have relied ? It must be untrue. He is thine enemy and favoureth thee not. Surely he might speak a word and say to me, I will not. Now He is silent as a stock. Lo, this is verily a hard blow if God show Himself serious and angry, and hide His grace so high and deep. . . . Now, what doth the wife thereupon ? She putteth from her eyes such unkind and hard bearing in Christ, is not led astray by all that, taketh it not to heart, but abideth downrightly and firmly in her confidence, holding on to the good report which she had heard and conceived of Him, and leaveth not off. So must we also do, and learn to cling fast to the Word alone, although God range Himself towards all creatures otherwise than as the word saith of Him. But oh, how sad that is for nature and reason that they should strip themselves thus bare and let go all they feel and lean alone on the mere word although they feel the opposite. God help us in straits and in dying to such courage and faith. Even the intercession of Jesus' disciples leadeth but to the answer, ' I am not sent but to the lost sheep of the house of Israel.' Here must all saints and all intercessions stand still. Yea, here must the heart let even the word go, where it would guide its gait by its feelings. But what doth the wife ? She leaveth not off, cleaveth to the Word, though it be dragged from His heart by force, replieth not to such a serious answer, still trusteth firmly that His kindness still lurketh beneath, and will not yet judge that Christ is ungracious or might be. That is the meaning of holding firmly. And once more her own ' Help me, Lord,' leadeth but to the reply, ' It is not meet to take the children's bread and cast it to the dogs.' What will she say here ? Then He answereth her ill that she is one of the damned and lost which should not be reckoned with the elect. That is a right unanswerable reply which none can deal with. Yet she leaveth not off, but even agreeth with His judgment and granteth she is a dog, but desireth not more than a dog, namely, to eat the crumbs that fall from the master's table. Is not that a masterpiece ? She taketh Christ at His own words. He likeneth her to a dog ; that she granteth and asketh no more than He would have, to let her be a dog as Himself judgeth ; what then ? He was fairly taken. To a dog one indeed leaveth the crumbs beneath the table, that is its right. Therefore He openeth right up and yieldeth to her will, that she is not now a dog, but even a child of Israel . . . here thou seest, though Christ taketh a seeming hard stand, yet giveth He no final judgment that He should say nay, but all His answers sound like no, yet are not no, but swing in suspense. For He saith not, I will not hear her, but is quite silent, replieth not yet a nay. Likewise He saith not, She is not of the house of Israel, but that Himself was sent to the house of Israel only. Thus leaveth it to swing in suspense twixt yea and nay. So He saith not, Thou art a dog and shalt not be given the children's bread, but, it is not meet, etc. Leaveth it once more in suspense whether she be a dog or no. Yet all three ring a bit stronger to nay than to yea, and yet there is more in them than nay. In sooth simple yea is in them but very deeply and secretly, and what appeareth is simple nay. Thereby is indicated how our heart standeth in temptation. According as it feeleth, so taketh Christ here His stand. Its thought really is, that simple nay is there, yet is it not true. Therefore must it turn from such feeling and grasp and hold the deep and secret yea beneath and above the nay with firm faith in God's Word, as the wife doth, and concede God the rightness of His judgment upon us. So have we gained and captured Him in His own words, as if we feel in conscience God chideth us for sinners and judgeth us unworthy of the kingdom of heaven, then we feel hell and bethink us we are eternally lost. Whoso then take knowledge here of this wife and capture God in His own judgment and say, Yea, Lord, 'tis true, I am a sinner and not worthy of Thy grace, yet Thou hast promised pardon to sinners and art not come to call the righteous but, as St. Paul also saith, to make sinners blest, lo ! so must God by His own judgment have mercy upon us " (*Fastenpostille,* 1525 W. edn. 17ᴵᴵ, pp. 201–204).

But conversely it is also the case that also in God's very unveiling His veiling is to be known and recognised, the close bond between the content and the form, the glory and the humility, the goodness and the severity of the Word of God. Only in the consummation, in which faith ceases altogether, can we bethink us of man as no longer requiring but relieved of this reverse movement of faith, this recollection of the worldliness of the Word. Even faith which breaks through or is led through in the visible to the invisible, in the nay to the yea, is after all regarded as human experience, action, and thought, the faith of the man, who even and precisely in his triumph stands in need of emendation and completion, in fact more than that, of the wholly new bond with God. He must therefore retrace the way already trodden ; in being freed by the Word he must be taken prisoner again by the same Word ; he must once more be placed before God—which must now mean, before the God who is veiled in His veiling. What else than *superbia* could man's experience of God's unveiling mean, if the matter is to rest there ? And what else than *theologia gloriae, speculatio Majestatis* could thought in this experience become, if thought claimed to hold fast to it ? Continually both Catholic and Protestant *theologia gloriae* has appealed to this experience, to victorious faith and never noticed that by abandoning indirectness in knowledge of God it also straightway abandoned real faith and the real Word of God. In fact faith and the Word of God are needed no less for this reverse movement, this return from finding to seeking, from being within to being without, from possessing to begging, from the triumph of experience and of thought to honest and complete spiritual poverty. Verily for the victor it is no less hard and inconceivable, that he, too, and he precisely must know and confess that he is beaten, than for the beaten man to have to know that as such he himself is a winner.

An important difference between faith and mysticism must consist in the fact that the mystic as such denies this reversal, ceasing in ecstasy in the very face of Unveiled Deity to be aware of His veiling, regarding proclamation, the Bible, Christ in their worldliness as mere symbols of the Godhead unveiled to him, with which he is able now to dispense and which lie fundamentally behind him ; and henceforth sees his future only in further unveilings, increasing in fulness, always leading further into the depths or the heights. On the contrary, the triumphant believer as such returns straight to proclamation, the Bible and Christ, sits down again, so to speak, in the lowest room and seeks his future only (really only !) in the God who for him as for any other sinner is wholly hidden—not already unveiled but wholly hidden ! It is in this very going and returning again that the believer as such, because in each case it is a matter of going at the behest of a God who calls, possesses a certainty which the mystic as such can never have.

Human experience and human thought might as such, in accord with their own dead weight, proceed in a straight line from despair to deeper despair, from seriousness to still greater seriousness (there is also a negative *theologia gloriae* !), or from triumph to higher triumph, from joy to still greater joy : to faith this straight line movement is forbidden by the Word of God, which calls us from despair to triumph, from seriousness to joy, but also from triumph to despair and from joy to seriousness. That is the meaning of *theologia crucis*. So, in this discipline by His Word, which never leaves us to ourselves whether in our humility or in our pride, God is faithful to Himself and to us, therefore always in an unmistakable one-sided forward or backward movement, in which one of the two remains unuttered, while on the other hand everything depends upon our hearing it, one way or the other, as uttered by God. How necessary it is to make this twofold movement of the Word and of the faith that follows it clear to oneself, is seen most conclusively in the fact that we need only produce the lines on both sides in order, from our start with the concepts of veiling and unveiling or form and content, to come up against the other antithetic concepts, to wit, law and gospel, demand and promise ; or in another direction, letter and spirit ; or in another direction still, God's wrath and judgment and God's grace. The Word of God in its veiling—its form—is God's demand upon man. The Word of God in its unveiling—its content—is God's turning to man. The Word of God is one thing ; for in the demand is consummated the turning, and the turning does not take place without the demand. By being really and seriously put under law, man comes to the gospel, and by coming to the gospel through revelation and faith he is really and seriously put under the law. God's wrath and judgment is only the hard shell, the *opus alienum* of God's grace, but it is the man who knows about grace, about the *opus Dei proprium*, who, and who alone knows what God's wrath and judgment are. It is the letter of proclamation and the Bible that conveys the Spirit : but it is the Spirit that will also bring us back every time to the letter. If we think of such pregnant concepts which are constantly developing out of the veiledness or the unveiledness of the Word of God, we shall not think of saying—we could only do so by a wicked weakening of all these serious concepts—that we could simultaneously experience their content in its truth and that we could systematically connect them with one another. But if one moment the one becomes true for us in experience and thought, we must the next moment have faith in the other which does not become discernible by us.

In Ex. 19–20 we find the narrative of the covenant made between Jahwe and Israel at Sinai. Of the nature of this covenant we receive a hint if we recollect the help hitherto received by Israel from their God, and from the promise, " Ye shall be my peculiar treasure among all the peoples." But it is not this that is the decisive content of this chapter, but on the one hand (in ch. 19) the astonishingly explicit and emphatically expressed order to keep away without fail from the place of manifestation of this gracious and kind God so as to avoid instant death, and then the description of the frightful occurrence of His manifestation, experienced at close quarters only by the one man Moses ; and on the other hand (in ch. 20) the enumeration of the conditions imposed upon Israel by Jahwe on His side, i.e. the commandments of His covenant, with the strict fulfilment of which the promise is bound up. In the same OT canon, in Jer. 31[31f.], we hear again of a covenant by the same Jahwe with the same Israel. It rests upon the pre-supposition that Israel has broken that first covenant, the commandments of which it should have fulfilled. As if that did not signify the end of any possible covenant, as if God were unfaithful to Himself, another new covenant is now proclaimed ; in it, too, there is of course still to be a law, but now no longer revealed from afar amid lightning and thunder, but a law—yet what is the meaning of " law " in this case ?—to be written in the heart of the Israelites, so very much, so realistically in their heart, that any instruction at all in the knowledge of the Lord from man to man shall become superfluous. This new revelation of law, this utterly new position of Israel close to Jahwe, this new covenant, simply inconceivable from the standpoint of the first, is to rest upon the forgiveness of sins : " and thus I will be their God and they shall be my people " (ver. 33). If now we are to listen to Ex. 19–20 and Jer. 31, obviously we cannot listen to both at the same time. An historical analysis of the two texts from the religious standpoint would instantly teach us in its own way that a systematic conspectus of both is an impossibility. We can therefore only listen to the one or to the other. Nor can it be a mere matter of harmonising exegesis but solely a matter of faith, to see the one in the other, the new in the old, the old in the new covenant, fully valid.—There should be a similar relation in the OT between the prophets' predictions of salvation and their predictions of catastrophe. The prophets admittedly surprise us by the abrupt onesidedness, with which one moment they relentlessly speak only of judgment to come and the next, with equal unrestraint, only of redemption to come. There was a time in which OT science regarded it as impossible for one and the same prophet to have spoken one way in one passage and another way in another passage. Nowadays we have grown more cautious. We shall say that predictions of salvation and catastrophe, in the absolute way in which they both appear, were naturally not possible simultaneously, or by any sort of inward connection ; there can therefore be no system of prophetic utterance. It took place either as a threat or as a promise. Precisely in this onesidedness it claimed to be the Word of God. To the understanding of them belonged and belongs what in the NT we call faith, or grasping also what from time to time has not been said.—And in the NT we may recall the connection between the Synoptic and the Johannine tradition regarding the humanity and the divinity of Jesus Christ. Certainly both speak of both, but with such variety in the direction of interest and emphasis that we could only misunderstand both if, as the " historico-critical " school once did, we thought of measuring the one by the other or (in what was once taken to be the " positive " method) of trying to equate the one with the other. That the Johannine representation is the direct antithesis of the Synoptic is not at all a bad historical hypothesis theologically, favoured by many more recent investigators. It is impossible to listen to the two state-ments at the same time, Jesus of Nazareth is God's Son, and, God's Son is Jesus of Nazareth. Here we listen to either the one or the other, or we listen to nothing at all. And so the second in that case can only be heard indirectly, only in faith.—As a final example I instance the relation of the Cross or death and the resurrection of Christ in the proclamation of St. Paul. Often enough he uses both concepts in the closest juxtaposition, but in what different directions they point each time as regards Christ Himself and as regards the reality of salvation for Christians ! True, St. Paul always means both when he simply says Ἰησοῦς Χριστός or ἐν Χριστῷ, but it is signi-ficant that it is only by this name that he can really express both. This name is anything but a system representing a unified experience or a unified thought ; it is the Word of God itself. In it Cross and Resurrection are one, but not—either for Paul, or for his first readers, or for us either—in what is stated in explanation over and above this name. We can only listen to the one or to the other, realising what is stated by the one or the other, and after that, in spite of and amid the veiling, listen to the other also in faith through the one.—These are but some of the great onesidednesses in the Bible, written and grasped as the Word of God. It is characteristic of the whole Bible when the Word of God (Heb. 4[12]) is described as " sharper than a two-edged sword " (cf. also Rev. 1[16]) and when it is then said of it that it pierces through and separates between soul and spirit, joints and marrow, and becomes judge of the plans and purposes of the heart, and that no creature can hide itself before it, but all is laid bare and becomes fixed before its eyes.

It is, as must already be stated here, this external onesidedness in the Word of God, resting as it does upon the inner twosidedness not apparent to us, that constitutes faith faith, makes it that grasped grasp—moving from depth to height and from height to depth—of God the ever invisible, ever beyond experience, ever unthinkable. From the Word of God faith thus has not only its existence but also this, its nature.

'Ο λόγον 'Ιησοῦ κεκτημένος ἀληθῶς δύναται καὶ τῆς ἡσυχίας αὐτοῦ ἀκούειν, ἵνα τέλειος ᾖ, ἵνα δι' ὧν λαλεῖ πράσσῃ καὶ δι' ὧν σιγᾷ γινώσκηται (Ignat. of Ant., Eph. 15²). Luther calls *fides Christi* a *res arduissima, quia translatio et raptus est ab omnibus quae sentit intus et foris in ea quae nec intus nec foris sentit scilicet invisibilem, altissimum, incomprehensibilem Deum (Hebr. Br.,* 1513 *Fi. Schol.* p. 39, l. 3). *Non enim habent nomen neque speciem ea quae fides intelligit. Nam praesentium rerum prosperitas vel adversitas penitus subvertit omnem hominem, qui fide non intelligit invisibilia. Hic enim intellectus ex fide venit, juxta illud " Nisi credideritis, non intelligetis " et est ingressus ille caliginis, in qua absorbetur, quicquid sensus, ratio, mens intellectusque hominis comprehendere potest. Conjungit enim fides animam cum invisibili, ineffabili, innominabili, aeterno, incogitabili verbo Dei simulque separat ab omnibus visibilibus, et haec est Crux et phase Domini (Oper. in Ps.* 1519 f., W. edn. 5, p. 69, l. 24). More than once Luther has described the situation of the believing man as a *pendere* or *haerere* between heaven and earth, by both sides now drawn and kept at a distance, now held fast and driven away (e.g. *Hebr. Br. Fi. Schol.* p. 71, l. 118; *Lect. on Isa.* 1527 W. edn. 25, p. 328, l. 33). Classically in the words, " But to watch is to cling to the eternal good and to behold and long for the same. But therein He is alone and none with Him, for they are all asleep. And He saith, On the housetop, as though He said, The world is a house, inside they all lie asleep and locked up, but I am outside the house, on the roof, not yet in heaven nor yet in the world, the world I have under me and heaven above me, thus 'twixt the world's life and eternal life swing I lonely in faith " (*Seven Pen. Pss.* 1517 W. edn. 1, p. 199, l. 1). All of which would have to be termed madness, were it not, as founded upon the " onesidedness " of the Word of God, bound to be exactly so and not otherwise.

3. God's language is and remains God's mystery in its spirituality. With this statement which should constitute the close of our exposition of the nature of the Word of God, we touch for the first time expressly upon the concept of the Holy Spirit. To say Holy Spirit in preaching or in theology is always to say a final word. For we are always speaking, whether we are aware of it or unaware —but 'twere good to be aware of it—of the event in which the Word of God is not only revealed to man but also believed in by him ; we are speaking of the fact that, and the way in which, the Word of God is so uttered to this and that man that he must listen to it, or of the fact that, and the way in which, this and that man is in such wise open and ready for the Word of God that he can hear it. So far as it belongs to the nature of the Word of God to be apprehensible by man, we must say of it that it is spiritual, i.e. that where it is real and where therefore it is believed in by man, it is finally and ultimately itself the ground of this event. The Bible and Church dogma and the entire older theology, when they come

to say of this event whatever it is possible to say of it at all, speak of the Holy Spirit. Whatever there is to be said about man—and here inevitably we must speak about man—all theological anthropology, i.e. all doctrine about man to whom the Word of God is manifested and by whom it is apprehended, will have to come under this category. The category signifies that even from this new point of view, even though we try to grasp the concept of revelation (which in fact is also constitutive for the concept of Holy Scripture and Church proclamation) so to speak from underneath, starting with ourselves, we must also and emphatically see and say that God is the Lord in this event. The Lord of the language is also the Lord of our listening to it. The Lord who gives the Word is also the Lord who gives faith. The Lord of our listening, the Lord who gives faith, the Lord through whose act the openness and readiness of man for the Word is true and real—is not another God but the one God in this way—and that is the Holy Spirit. We shall return at a later stage of our prolegomena to the entire aspect here opened up and to this category under which the aspect is to be regarded, irrespective of the place which these things have in dogmatics itself. Here we are concerned merely with the result, namely, that the Word of God is also God's miracle in reaching its goal among men, in the event of man's faith in the Word of God. We must believe in our belief (faith) no less than in the Word we believe in ; i.e. for all our sense of duty and need to regard our relation to the Word of God as a positive relation to it, and therefore for all our confession of our faith, we cannot regard it as positive, save as it is possible and real from God's side, save as the miracle of the Holy Spirit and not as our own work.

Luther's familiar but insufficiently valued exposition of Article 3 comes in here. " I believe that of no reason or power of my own can I believe in Jesus Christ my Lord or come to Him ; but the Holy Ghost hath called me through the Gospel, illumined me by His gifts, hallowed and maintained me in the right faith, even as He calleth the whole Christendom on earth, gathereth, illumineth, sanctifieth, and in Jesus Christ maintaineth it in the one right faith . . ." (*Smaller Catech.* 1531 W. edn. 30[I], p. 367, l. 4).

The meaning of that concretely is as follows. The hearing of the Word of God by a man and its apprehension by him can never be known by himself or others except in faith. We are expressing the same thing when we say, in the Holy Spirit. Faith, of course, is also a human experience. To this experience also a definite human attitude will correspond, and this human attitude will also find its expression in definite human thoughts. But that this experience is the experience of the faith, this attitude the attitude of the faith, and these thoughts the thoughts of the faith which has heard the Word of God, is decided spiritually, i.e. is decided not by the faith but by the Word believed in. Thus we cannot produce conditions, on the fulfilment of which hearing of the Word is assured. There is no method of converting revelation into revelation really apprehended, no method of Scripture exegesis which is really pneumatic, i.e. makes articulate the testimony to revelation in the Bible, and to that extent really brings the Pneuma to the front, above all, no method of living, rousing proclamation, which really touches its audience in an ultimate sense. There is nothing of that sort, because the Word of God is a mystery in that it really touches us spiritually, i.e. invariably only through the Holy Spirit, in full mediacy only immediately from God's side. In its spirituality it is finally distinguished from any mere idea of hypostasis, to which, so that it may even only be discerned by us as such, there must correspond some sort of experience, an attitude, a concept on our part, with some sort of certainty, be it ever so minute and difficult to grasp. We shall look in vain for a correspondence with the Word of God on our side, however little of it we would be contented with, however ready we might be to go to the ultimate depths and the outmost limits of human existence to look for it. Of course the Word of God is always real in perfectly definite human experiences, attitudes, and thoughts, but in its own power and dignity and not in that of these human experiences, attitudes, and thoughts, therefore, not in such a way that their being there could in any way ensure the presence of the Word of God, not in such a way that they would necessarily and manifestly be the signs of its reality.

As one of the most recent examples of how easy it is to forget this spirituality of the Word of God, I adduce what P. Tillich sets forth as to the task of Church proclamation to-day. Above all, he feels bound to advise it to renounce any direct exposition of religious contents as they are given in the Bible and in tradition. To that end it should note the following rules. " First, it must insist upon a thoroughgoing experience of the limiting situation ; it must take from the man of to-day the secret reservations which prevent him from placing himself with unconditioned resolve at the limits of his human existence. . . . Secondly, it must speak of the Yea that comes over man in the limiting situation when taken with unfettered seriousness. . . . Thirdly and lastly, Protestantism must bear witness to the new state from which alone it is possible to utter that Word with authority, i.e. so to utter it that it does not again become a source of assurance " (*Relig. Verwirkl.* 1930 p. 38 f.). Moreover, according to Tillich, it is to be the task of Protestant religious instruction " to make visible from the limits of what is human the situation of man in its secular and religious utterances, so far as these are known to the pupil

14

and understood by him " (*Ztschr. f. d. ev. Religionsunterricht*, 1931 p. 290).
Query : What is a " thoroughgoing experience of the limiting situation " ?
What is " unconditioned resolve " ?   How does one take from a man the
reservations which prevent him from placing himself at that spot with this
resolution ?   Does it go without saying that " in the limiting situation when
taken with unfettered seriousness " a Yea comes over man, and what does
it mean to speak about this Yea ?   What is the meaning of speaking from
the limits of the human or from the standpoint of the new state, of speaking
in such a way that man's word does not become an assurance again for the
hearer ?   Obviously Tillich reckons he can produce a new and better method
with all that.   A method for what ?   We must credit even him with meaning
by his language the proclamation of the Word of God.   But if that is so,
are not all his proposals pure child's play, compared with which one perhaps
comes very much closer to reality by sticking for the future as in the
past to the direct proclamation of the " contents of Bible and tradition " ?
By means of negations or delimitations on man's part, which, according to
Tillich, obviously we can achieve completely for ourselves, we are still far
from producing the Word of God for him and for ourselves.   Precisely by
proclaiming the " contents of Bible and tradition " we bear witness that we
are in no position at all to do so.

Naturally, too, it is not a case of recommending us, as the true
method, to realise that there cannot be any method here at all !
That is certainly a good thing to realise, but we can have and
use that realisation as well as any other, without it in the very
slightest having anything to do with proving that hearing of the
Word of God has taken place.   Even such a realisation is far from
putting this handle into our hands.   The search for the possibility
of getting hold of this handle, the search for such a receptacle of
human experience, attitude, and doctrine as would be now, surely
and unmistakably, the receptacle of a divine content, this search
is not one to be pursued further and further, right into any and every
sort of new and hitherto unknown or unthought-of areas of human
reality, in sublime indifference as to whether we are thus arriving
at new positions or merely at possible limits of this or that or maybe
of all possible positions.   What we must realise here is that this
search is aimless.

So far I am not clear either how far the concept of " experience " or
" temptation," introduced with a wholly new meaning into theological discussion by H. M. Müller in his previously cited book in answer to E. Grisebach, is really distinguishable from a long-sought and finally found limiting
concept, which in that case at least *per se* would be absolutely unsuitable for
signifying clearly the real hearing of the Word of God.   The only thing here
is to abandon altogether the search for a method of hearing the Word of
God, for an unambiguously " correct " description of its entry into man,
into the realm of his experiences, attitudes, and thoughts.—" So long as the
Word of God is not in man's power, either to speak or to touch fruitfully, but
only in God's hand, therefore 'tis needful that we pray Him to give us Himself

the Holy Word through itself or through a man " (Luther, *Exposition in German of the Lord's Prayer*, 1519 W. edn. 2, p. 108, l. 28). " No man can illumine another, but this light can light all of him, it alone, and preachers should only be forerunners and witnesses of this light to men, in order that they all may believe in that light " (*Sermon on John* 1[1-14], *Kirchenpostille*, 1522 W. edn. 10[I], 1, p. 223, l. 3). " Therefore 'tis already a wondrous realm : the Word is there and none wotteth it is so active and achieveth such gr at things for those that believe in it ; it must itself be felt and tasted in the heart. Therefore, we preachers can do no more than be our Lord Christ's mouth and His tools, by which He preacheth the Word bodily. The Word He letteth go forth publicly, that every man may hear it, But that we may feel it inwardly in the heart is the work of faith and is a secret doing of Christ's where He seeth that 'tis to be done of His own divine knowledge and good pleasure " (*Sermon on John* 10[12f.], 1523 W. edn. 12, p. 531, l. 4). " Christian faith and Christian life stand in the same literal revelation by God, for where that is not to hand, no heart is ever properly aware of this mystery, which is hidden there from the world's side. Now God alone reveals it to His saints elect from eternity, to whom He will have it made known, otherwise it remaineth indeed hid for every man and a proper mystery. What good will the freewill or the slavish imprisoned will say or do here about that ? How of its own power will it attain to this light and mystery ? If the Almighty strong God hide it from it, 'twill ne'er arrive at it with any preparation or good work. No creature can come to this knowledge. For Christ alone reveals it to it in the heart itself. Thus falleth to ground all merit, all powers, and faculties of reason and ranketh naught for God. Christ alone must give it " (*Sermon on Matt.* 11[25-30], 1527 W. edn. 23, p. 689, l. 4).

Only if we take for granted this renunciation, which must be expressly declared, shall we be able to speak in the next section about the knowability of the Word of God. There we shall have to speak of the fact that, and the way in which, it can be the object of human knowledge. But we shall not be able to speak of it in such a way as to produce accounts of how this object and this knowledge admit of clear and certain delimitation from other objects and the knowledge of them. That would be exactly the method of listening to the Word of God, which as such is impossible, because hearing the Word of God is faith, while faith is the work of the Holy Spirit. Obviously the human experiences, attitudes, and thoughts, which are bound up with the confession of any faith, and so with that of the Christian faith, lie in the realm of humanity and can as such be defined and mutually delimited. But they do not lie in the realm of humanity, so far as Christian faith is hearing the Word of God. As hearing the Word of God they can only be attested in the realm of humanity by an appeal to proclamation through the Church, to Holy Scripture, to revelation, in the form of an interpretation of this threefold form of the Word of God. But as hearing the Word of God they cannot be the object of

so-called "explanations" within this realm, i.e. as hearing the
Word of God they cannot be justified, delimited, and so domesti-
cated in this realm alongside of and over against what otherwise
belongs to this realm.

The renunciation here required can be realised with perfect clarity in the
three "imperishable verities," which Eduard Spranger as the assuredly
chosen mouthpiece of present-day German spirituality in theology "ventures
to submit to a fresh consideration" : 1. Man's responsibility for the basis of
his readiness to believe. 2. Adjustment to the known and peculiar legalities
of the so-called course of the world. 3. Adjustment to the existent manifold of religious convictions ("The War on Idealism," *Sitzungsberichte d.
preuss. Akad. d. Wiss.* 1931 XVII p. 436). One may be astonished at the
unsuspecting way in which Spranger submits to us for "fresh" consideration
what for really two hundred years and more has been said profusely enough
to Protestant theology and respectfully enough adopted by it. Satisfied
though he be with the applause which even to this day his "imperishable
verities" are sure to find in wide circles in the Church and in theology, he
must allow us to estimate them as admirable formulations of what in all
circumstances and without reservation must be abjured on the part of a
theology worthy of its name. Here, to-day as in the past, we can only reply
in sharpest opposition : 1. That in matters of the basis of man's "readiness
to believe," theology has no responsibility to any outside authority. The
responsibility of theology rather consists in making it clear that "readiness
to believe," looked at from without, has its ground in itself and so owes
no responsibility on the score of its ground. 2. Theology cannot compound
with the "peculiar legalities" of the course of the world, because she herself
stands within and not outside this course and because, like the Church in
general, she has to attest but not to achieve, within the course of the world,
God's composition with these peculiar legalities. 3. Theology, therefore, cannot
compound with the "existent manifold of religious convictions," because she
in fact finds this manifold in the area of human experiences, attitudes, and
thoughts, and she has no interest in compounding with it on this terrain,
whereas she does not find it at all in the area of faith and cannot for that
reason also compound with it.—The question whether this reply to Spranger
enlightens and impresses Spranger himself and his many like-minded associates
in philosophy and theology is immeasurably less important than the question
whether there will always be a "remnant" in the Church which, in regard to
the work to be done in theology, can only answer in these or in similar terms.

If with regard to the event of hearing the Word of God we point
not to a datum lying within man's existence, nor to the delimitation
of all data of man's existence, nor, finally, to the possibility of a
contingent experience, but only to faith, and that means, to the
Holy Spirit, we thus establish what was said at the beginning of
this section, that the question, What is the Word of God ? can only
be answered by indicating its nature through an interpretation of
its threefold form. Thus : What is the nature of the Word of God ?
Answer : It is on our lips and in our hearts, in the mystery of the
Spirit who is the Lord.

THE KNOWABILITY OF THE WORD OF GOD

The reality of the Word of God in all its three forms is based only upon itself. So, too, knowledge of it by men can consist only in acknowledgment of it, and this acknowledgment can only become real through the Word itself, and can only become comprehensible if we start with itself.

1. THE QUESTION AS TO THE KNOWABILITY OF THE WORD OF GOD

Our way so far has been briefly this. In § 3 we discovered in the concept of the Word of God the mandated content of Church proclamation, and along with that the criterion of dogmatics as the scientific testing of Church proclamation. In § 4 we became aware of the three forms, Proclamation, Scripture, and Revelation, in which the entity signified by that concept is real. And finally, in § 5, in view of these three forms we have inquired into the nature of this entity and have become acquainted with God's language, God's act, and God's mystery, as its three distinct but not different determinations.—Before turning, on the basis of these findings, to a preliminary determination of the concept of dogmatics, we have to answer explicitly the question as to the knowability of the Word of God.

In the concept of Church proclamation and so, too, in the concept of dogmatics it is obviously taken for granted that it is possible for men to hear the Word of God, in fact to utter it and so to know it. True, this is assumed in these concepts, not for human existence in general, but for a quite definite area of human existence, namely, the area of the Church. But even within the limits of this area, known to us to-day or real in God's sight, it is at all events men who are called to hear and to utter the Word of God. If the Church, and—in her—Church proclamation, and—in the service of Church proclamation—dogmatics may appeal to the truth, that must mean that men—not all men but particular men, and these particular men not always or everywhere but in a particular situation—

men can know the Word of God. Were it not so, then the entire conception of the Word of God would have to be emphatically designated a product of imagination, and Church proclamation together with dogmatics an objectless and therefore meaningless business and the Church a place of self-deceptions. For even if, that being so, some existent unknown to us corresponded to the concept of the Word of God, if we had really no knowledge of it, the thing signified by that concept, despite the correspondence, would not be a true reality for us, but a product of imagination. In the concept of the Church as a place where the truth is spoken and heard, and in the concept of Church proclamation and dogmatics as a sensible form of activity itself, it is taken for granted that knowledge of the Word of God is attainable by men.

By the knowledge of an object by men we understand the proof of their acquaintance with its reality in respect of its being there (or its existence) and in respect of its being thus and thus (or its nature). But "proof of their acquaintance" implies that the reality of the object in question, its existence and its nature, now becomes, while true in itself, somehow and with some degree of clarity and definition also true for them. Their acquaintance with it from being an accidental becomes a necessary, from being an external becomes an inward determination of their own existence. As knowers they are got at by the known object. They exist no longer without it, but with it. So far as they think of it at all they must think of it, with the entire trust with which they venture to think of it at all, as true reality, as true in its existence and nature. Whatever else and however else they may think of it, they must begin by thinking of the actual trueness of its reality. When faced with this trueness they can no longer withdraw into themselves in order from there to affirm, question, or deny it. Its trueness has come home directly to them personally, has become their property. And at the same time they themselves have become the property of its trueness. This event, this verification or proof we call, to distinguish it from mere knowings, knowledge. A knowing becomes knowledge when the man becomes a responsible witness to its content.

Knowledge of the Word of God in this sense is the presupposition of the Church. We may and must also reverse the statement and say that the Church is the presupposition of knowledge of the Word of God. One way or the other we assert that the Word of God becomes knowable for men. In particular, Church proclamation signifies that God's Word can be heard by men and uttered by men themselves. Were it not knowable, were a self-conserving knowledge of the Word of God impossible, were it impossible for its reality so to come home to men that they can no longer exist without it, but only with it, that they can only think of its reality as true, that they can only start their thinking with the truth of its existence and nature, were the freedom of self-withdrawal when faced by the Word of God limitless and inviolable—that would mean that to hear and to utter the Word of God in all seriousness was excluded. Such serious hearing and uttering rests upon the possibility of knowledge. The presupposition of the Church is thus the possibility of this relation, the knowledge-relation between man and the Word of God. Or *vice versa*, the Church is the presupposition of the possibility of this knowledge-relation. So far we have tacitly taken account of the presupposition ; or we might equally well say that the question as to its special kind and its essential correctness has already been discussed and answered implicitly, especially in the preceding sections on the nature of the Word of God. But this question is important enough to be dealt with now independently and explicitly. How can men know the Word of God ? That should be the form of the question.

A few preliminary notes on this particular way of putting the question may first lead the way to the matter itself.

1. We do not say, How do men know the Word of God ? In that form we should be asking a question as to the reality of such knowledge. But after all we have heard about its forms and its nature, the reality of knowing the Word of God could only be the content of the answer to be given by a man to this question, so far as this answer was to consist in repeating the Biblical promise given to the Church and in pointing to its coming fulfilment, and so far as then the Word of God itself was joined to this human repetition and indication and undertook the real answer. In other words, to the question so put a man's only answer would be proclamation. But just in order to be clear that this is so, our question must be, How can men know the Word of God ? We must inquire into the possibility of this event. The whole importance of realising that to the question concerning real knowledge about the Word of God, the Word of God alone can give the answer, demands that we should look about us and see whether it can only be so or whether it may not also be otherwise.

2. We do not say, How can men in general or how can man

know the Word of God ? We have already reminded ourselves that we are not concerned with man generally or with man universally; we are concerned concretely and definitely with man in the Church. Where the Word of God is known and so may become known, there it must be spoken, there it must have reached such and such men as a divine call. God knows them, those men who periodically as true hearers and proclaimers know the Word of God and so are capable of knowing it, and who for that very reason, as living human members in the Body of Christ, constitute the Church. We are concerned with the possibility of knowledge in these men.

3. Just because God knows them we prefer not to say, How do Christians know the Word of God? We could, of course, put it in that way, but in that case we should have to add, called and chosen Christians, and should thus be the reverse of clear ; for the question just is, how it is possible that men can become called and chosen and therefore real Christians, hearers and proclaimers of the Word of God through their knowledge. God knows those who become so. We know even Christians merely as men, who as such face us with the question how it should be possible for them to know the Word of God.

4. When we inquire as to the possibility of knowing the Word of God, we shall have to frame the concept of knowledge thereby taken for granted, as we did deliberately on a previous occasion, so generally, with such philosophical and epistemological indefiniteness that the possibility is kept open of any revision, restriction, or reversal that might befall from the side of the object of knowledge actually under discussion at this point. When previously knowledge was defined as self-authenticating acquaintance in its subject with the reality of an object, by that must be meant a mere indication of the epistemological problem and not an interpretation of it in advance. Any interpretation at this stage would simply imply philosophical and epistemological determination. But in such a determination the problem of knowledge ought not to be anticipated here, even as a problem, unless we are to run a most serious risk of anticipating the answer by our presupposition in a quite definite and, perhaps, in the long run, improper manner. The meaning of knowledge as knowledge of the Word of God must on no account be introduced into an investigation of this question in the form of an ultimatum.

I note as a counter-instance a statement by Fr. Traub. In *Monatsschr. f. Past. Theol.* 1928 p. 82, he reproaches me because in my dogmatics one gets no answer to the question " how I can succeed in affirming the Word of God, i.e. in affirming it as the Word of God and as reality." The preliminary interpretation here of " being able to know the Word of God" as "success in affirming it," is simply the premature introduction into the investigation of philosophical and epistemological determination of the problem, which in certain circumstances is quite enough to compromise the treatment of this problem of knowledge from the very outset. Who tells us that it is in our " affirmation " of the Word of God that the constitutive act of knowledge of it consists ? And, above all, who tells us that we can "succeed" in making such an affirmation ? The answer to the question put thus would obviously have to be the production of a way or method, by means of which this " success " might be realised. Who tells us whether this question may be put at all, and so a sensible answer be found at all ?

It might be the result of the peculiarity of this object of knowledge that the concept of the knowledge of it might literally not be commensurable in an ultimate sense with the concept of the knowledge of other objects, or with a general concept of knowledge, but that it admitted of definition at all only from the side of this its object. .

2. THE WORD OF GOD AND MAN

How very essential is the proviso already made in the last passage, is at once shown if we first of all steadily keep in view the meaning of saying that it is man who is here to be made comprehensible to us as the knower of the Word of God. Indeed it is implied in the concept of the Church that this is so. The Word of God which she hears and proclaims and which makes her the Church is God's Word directed to men. To men are directed preaching and sacrament, to men the word of the prophets and apostles, to men the revelation of God Himself in Jesus Christ, to men, therefore, the Word of God also, whose three forms we have accordingly once again described. If it is directed to them, it will obviously be known by them and therefore heard, but obviously not only known and heard, but known in the sense previously and generally fixed. Being mediated through their acquaintance with it, it will commend itself to them as reality. It is directed to them in order that they may let it be spoken to themselves and so may be what they are, no longer apart from it, but with it.

Consider here the connection between " grace " (" mercy ") and " truth " in Pss. 89[15, 25], 98[3], 117[2], and the way in which this connection is taken up in John 1[14, 17]. Consider the designation of the Gospel as the λόγος τῆς ἀληθείας in 2 Cor. 6[7]; Eph. 1[13]; Col. 1[5]; 2 Tim. 2[15]; Jas. 1[18]. Consider finally the designation of what is decisive in the position of a Christian as ἐπίγνωσις τῆς ἀληθείας in 1 Tim. 2[3], 4[3]; 2 Tim. 2[25], 3[7]; Titus 1[1].

As certainly as the Word of God is primarily and originally the Word which God speaks by and to Himself in eternal hiddenness—in developing the concept of revelation in connection with the doctrine of the Trinity we shall return to this great and inalienable truth—as certainly as it is, in revelation, Scripture, and preaching, the Word addressed to men, we cannot speak of it, we cannot think of it without at once remembering also the man who hears and thereby knows it.   The Word of God, Jesus Christ, as the being of the Church, faces us irresistibly with the realisation that men they were and men they will be, who are there intended and addressed and so characterised as the addressees, but also as themselves bearers of this Word.   The Word of God thus faces us with the so-to-speak anthropological problem as to how men as men can be that.   With the " so-to-speak " anthropological problem, I say ; and by that I indicate that it is entitled to that designation only with a definite proviso.   Or could it be otherwise ?   Are we to assert without reservation that the question of the possibility of knowing the Word of God is a question of anthropology ?   Are we to inquire into what man in general and as such (in addition to everything else of which he is capable) is or is not capable of in this respect ?   Is there a general truth with regard to man which can be made generally realisable, which would also include in itself his capacity for knowing the Word of God ?   We must put this question because an almost overpowering development in the history of Protestant theology since the Reformation has led to an impressive affirmative to this question throughout the entire movement in the Church which we have described as modernist.

We have already narrated by the way the discussions within Protestant orthodoxy over the question whether theology was to be regarded with Thomas Aquinas as an essentially theoretical science, or with Duns Scotus as an essentially practical one.   With increasing consciousness and universality the decision took the side of the second answer and signified this, that the object of theology was no longer given, as still in Chemnitz (*Loci theol. ed.* 1592 *De usu et util. loc. theol.* p. 12), as the nature and the will of God or, as in Walaeus, as *res divinae, nempe Deus ipse . . . et res omnes quae a Deo sunt* (*Loci comm.* 1640 p. 5), but, as already in J. Gerhard (*Loci theol.* 1610 *Prooem.* 28) as *homo quatenus ad aeternam beatitudinem est perducendus*, or, as in Wendelin (*Theol. christ. lib.* II 1657 *Prol.* 1, 3) as the *vera religio, quae est ratio agnoscendi colendique Deum*, or as in Burmann (*Syn. Theol.* 1678 I 2, 52) as the *vita hominis sive cultus ipsius erga Deum*, or as in Mastricht (*Theol. theor. pract.* 1698 I 1, 26) as the *vita hominis formanda et dirigenda Deum versus*.   One may interpret this turn of expression *in meliorem partem*.   One of their most cautious representatives, Fr. Turretini (*Instit. Theol. el.* 1679 I 5, 4), could show very nicely that, of course, even so theology was concerned with God, but with *Deus quatenus revelatus est*, with *Deus noster id est foederatus in Christo*. The aim was, assuredly in the spirit of the Reformation, to avoid any approximation to a *nuda speculatio de Deo*. (Quenstedt, *Theol. did. pol.* 1685 I *cap. 1, sect. 2, qu. 2, font. sol. 7*). Even then they were perfectly aware that there is nothing in a " non-existential " theology—*theologia nisi ad praxin referatur ne theologia quidem est* (Burmann, *op. cit.* I 2, 51, cf. Coccejus, *S. theol.* 1669 I 8). The statement that the orthodox had conceived and practised theology with a rigid objectivism as " *scientia de Deo et rebus divinis* " may be read in H. Mulert (*Religion, Kirche, Theologie*, 1931 p. 28) and other more recent authors, but it completely contradicts the sense of the explicit declarations to be found in these theologians, even in the older ones who had not yet adopted the new fashion. From the very outset the efforts of Protestant orthodoxy suffered rather from an excess than from a defect in considering the religious subject. At all events its intention—and that was assuredly also the meaning of the turn towards *scientia practica*—was to regard the Word of God altogether as the Word directed to man. Only that this turn had also still another meaning. It is notorious that by this turn the goal reached and, of course, also striven for was, in accordance with the increasingly definite demands of the scientific consciousness since the Renaissance, to transfer the object of theology from a Beyond which genuinely confronted man's position to the sphere of man himself. This object need not, but it could be thought of as embraced and conditioned by the general truths of man. So an attempt could be made to regard it or the possibility of it as lying within the self-interpretation of man. The simultaneous fresh construction of a *theologia naturalis* to be the science of the *praeambula fidei* in the old Thomist sense, the slow but noticeable withdrawal of the misgivings which the Reformers had had regarding the value of this undertaking, show the interest felt in this very connection of ideas from other standpoints also. By the 18th century at all events it is undeniable that the inferences pointing in this direction have been drawn. Now the definition crops up which still engages us to-day, that theology is the " science of religion " ; by which is meant " instructed knowledge of these doctrines and truths which supply us with the instruction, needful for our happiness and contentment, on our relations to God and our duties to Him arising out of these relations, and on the hopes which we should build upon these relations " (G. J. Planck, *Einleitung in die theol. Wiss.* 1794 vol. I p. 29). Of course a Herder and a Schleiermacher knew better than this how to conceive of the nature of religion in its depth, power, and independence. But the " we " which so strikingly dominates the statement of Planck's still remains or indeed becomes the cornerstone even of their view. It is the same Schleiermacher who, for the first time, quite fundamentally connects this newly-discovered and independent reality of religion with a corresponding possibility generally demonstrable on anthropological grounds, and who for the first time quite fundamentally undertakes to interpret Christianity itself in the form of a concretely historical analysis of human existence along the lines of a general doctrine of man : 1. Man's meeting with God to be regarded as a human religious experience historically and psychologically fixable; and 2. This experience to be regarded as the realisation of a religious potentiality in man generally demonstrable. Beginning with Schleiermacher, and notwithstanding the variety of types in particular interpretations, these are the two cardinal propositions in philosophy of religion in the 19th and 20th centuries. The decisive one is naturally the second of these statements.

If we apply it to what in our terminology we call the doctrine of the Word of God, it would mean that real knowledge of the Word of God is the realisation of a special potentiality of knowledge proper to man as such. If we affirm this statement, then we must acquiesce in the answer to the question of ability, with which we are here occupied, being given from an anthropological point of view, where it is a matter of secondary importance, whether we close with the actual anthropology of Schleiermacher and his school, or with one more congenial to our modern consciousness, like that of M. Heidegger. As it is, we are spared the choice, since we are not in a position to affirm the statement, on the basis of which we should be faced with such a choice.

The consideration which forbids us from saying Yes, here is this. In the first place, it is quite true (and that was at least in part the point, at least at the beginnings of the development) that the Word of God is to be regarded as something that happens in and to the reality of man.

Fundamentally there could be nothing to object to in describing this event as " experience," even as " religious experience." The quarrel is not with this term and still less with the right and important thing which this term might conclusively denote, namely, the extremely real and determinative entry of the Word of God into the reality of man. But the term is burdened (and that is why we avoid it) with the view in the background that man generally is capable of religious experience and that this capacity has the critical significance of a norm.

And in the second place, it is quite true that with this happening there must correspond logically and materially a possibility, an ability on the part of man.

Even the concept of the religious " *a priori*," which played so large a part in philosophy of religion round about 1910, would not require to be rejected utterly and for itself, had we not unfortunately, in connection with a right or a wrong understanding of Kant, to understand generally by that a capacity, a qualification grounded in man as such, and the freedom to dispose of it which it implied.

But the question is whether this event ranks with the other events that can enter man's reality in such a way, that to be able to enter it requires on man's part such a potentiality as is brought to meet it, so to speak, by man as such, such as consists in a predisposition appertaining to him *qua* man from the start, in an organ, in a positive or even negative qualification to be reached and discovered by an anthropological analysis of his existence ; in short, in what philosophy of the Kantian type calls a "faculty." It might be that in this the event did not so much presuppose on man's side this potentiality which it implies, as rather import it and by being an event lend it to him, so that it becomes his, the

man's, potentiality, without (by being that) ceasing to be out and
out its, the Word of God's, own potentiality, proper to it alone.
It may also be that what we are dealing with is a possibility of
knowledge, the nature of which is to be made understandable,
certainly as a possibility in man, but in this case, which differs
from all others, only by starting from the object of knowledge, i.e.
the reality of knowledge, and so absolutely not from the subject
of knowledge and so absolutely not from man. We have to decide
against the first and for the second conception of the " power " in
question in view of the nature of the Word of God and in particular
in view of what was said in § 5, 2, 2 under the concept of its " purposiveness," i.e. its manward connection and direction, its character
as an address to man. We have had to regard the Word of God
from this very point of view (the same that is occupying us at this
point) as the act of the free love of God : not in such wise as if man
who is addressed and listens belonged by any essential necessity
to the concept of the Word of God. That man is the addressee of
the Word of God is a fact, so far as it is true, and not derivable
from something else of which we might previously be aware concerning the nature of God. Still less—obviously !—from something
of which we might previously be aware concerning the nature of
man ; God's Word ceases to be grace or grace itself ceases to be
grace when we ascribe to man a disposition towards this Word, a
possibility of knowledge independent of it and peculiar in itself,
over against this Word. The same thing also results from what was
said in the similar passage regarding the content of the Word of
God directed to man. There we established the position that
however it might be constituted from time to time *in concretissimo*
for this man or that, this content would invariably be a genuine
unequivocal encounter with the Lord of man, a revelation which
man cannot achieve himself, the revelation of something new which
can only be told him. Further, the limitation of his existence by
the utter apartness of his Creator, a limitation on the basis of
which he can only regard himself as created out of nothing and kept
from falling into nothing. Further, the radical renewal and thereby
obviously the radical criticism of his entire present reality, a
renewal and criticism on the basis of which he can only regard himself as a sinner living by grace and so lost, from his own standpoint
locked up so far as God is concerned. Finally, the presence of
God as Him that cometh, Him that in the strictest sense is future,
the eternal Lord and Redeemer of man, on the basis of which

presence he can only regard himself as one hastening to meet this coming of the Lord and expecting Him. Of course it is not with these formulæ for describing the real content of the Word of God, but with the content of the Word which God Himself utters and in which He invariably expresses Himself in the way indicated by these formulæ, it is with the real content of the real Word of God that man is likewise informed, that any power on his part to listen or understand or know, any capacity which he the creature, the sinner, the one who waits, might have to meet this Word with, and so any possibility in the first sense, does not enter into consideration, but that the possibility of knowing corresponding to the real Word of God has simply come to him, man, that it sets forth a quite inconceivable *novum* in direct contrast to all his ability and capacity, and is only to be regarded as a pure fact, like the Word of God itself.

In 1 Cor. 2⁶ᶠ· we are told of the wisdom of God in Christ that it is a σοφία ἐν μυστηρίῳ unknown to the rulers of this aeon, invisible to any eye, inaudible to any ear, which has never entered any man's heart, and is accessible only to the πνεῦμα of God Himself and so only through the πνεῦμα of God Himself. And so not accessible to the ψυχικὸς ἄνθρωπος, who as such does not possess the πνεῦμα, who, therefore, cannot know what is accessible only to the πνεῦμα and through the πνεῦμα ; οὐ δέχεται, οὐ δύναται γνῶναι. Man must receive (λαμβάνειν) not only the Word of Christ, but also the πνεῦμα by which it is known, or he will not know it at all. Ἐδίδαξεν ἡμᾶς ὁ κύριος, ὅτι θεὸν εἰδέναι οὐδεὶς δύναται, μὴ οὐχὶ θεοῦ διδάξαντος, τουτέστιν ἄνευ θεοῦ μὴ γιγνώσκεσθαι τὸν θεόν (Irenaeus, *C. o. h.* IV 6, 4). " For what sort of a work is knowing ? It meaneth neither fasting, watching, mortification, nor aught a man may do or suffer with the body, but it lieth right within in the deepest foundation of the heart. In a word, knowing is no work but precedeth all works. For knowledge is of that which we receive and take. Thus by the sole wordlet ' knowing ' as by a mighty thunderclap is all doctrine smitten down which is founded on man's work, spiritual ordering and worship of God, as though thereby to get rid of sin, reconcile God and to merit grace " (Luther, *Sermon on John* 17³, 1528 W. edn. 28, p. 100, l. 21).

The modernist view against which we have to fix our limits goes back to the Renaissance and particularly to the Renaissance philosopher Cartesius with his proof of God from man's certainty of himself.

Among modern philosophers of religion of this school a few, like G. Wobbermin (*Syst. Theol.* vol. II 1921 p. 455) and Heinrich Scholz (*Religionsphilosophie*, 2ⁿᵈ edn. 1922 p. 310), were open or incautious enough to appeal expressly to Cartesius and to fortify themselves anew on his line of thought.

" The I-experience is for man the foundation of the surest certainty of reality that is thinkable, that is possible for him at all.

It is the presupposition . . . of all validation of reality connected
with the external world " (Wobbermin, *op. cit.*). We may ask
whether this Cartesianism, even when confined to the philosophic
plane, is quite so impregnable as it usually purports to be. But that
does not concern us here, and we shall beware of opposing to it
another philosophy somewhat better in accord with the instinct
of theology, or, weary of Descartes, of throwing ourselves into the
arms of Aristotle, which means Thomas. At this stage, having our
suspicions of the other side too, we merely make the point that in
theology at least thought cannot proceed along Cartesian lines.

In his essay, " What has the doctrine of justification to say to the man
of to-day ? " (1907 ; in *Gesammelten Aufsätze zur Kirchengeschichte*, vol. III
1928 p. 559) Karl Holl once formulated the fundamental proposition " common to all alive to-day " and constituting " the plumb-line of their religiosity "
to this effect, that the proper way is to " acknowledge nothing as religiously
valid, save what can be touched in the reality presented to us and can be
produced again from our own immediate feeling." This " fundamental
proposition " is precisely the fundamental proposition of the Cartesian
thought which is impossible in theology. On the basis of this proposition
there is no knowledge of the Word of God. For neither do we touch the Word
of God in the reality presented to us, but—and this is something different—
in the reality presented to us it touches us ; nor can it be reproduced from
our own immediate feeling, but if ever we had to know it we should have to
know ourselves, according to James 1[18], as produced by it.

The fact of the Word of God in no respect nor yet in the very
slightest degree receives its worth and validity from a presupposition
which we apply to it ; its truth for us, like its truth in itself, is
based purely upon itself. The procedure in theology therefore is
to base self-certainty upon God-certainty and to measure it by
God-certainty and so to begin with God-certainty without waiting
for this beginning to be legitimised by self-certainty. By the
making of this beginning—and only by the making of it !—it is then
likewise—though only subsequently, incidentally, relatively—legitimised by the necessary self-certainty. In other words, in the real
knowledge of the Word of God in which that beginning alone will
be made, there is also the event that it is possible, that that
beginning can be made. Once again, we base this rejection of the
Cartesian method not upon another and better philosophy. Here
we are not in the least interested to know whether there is such a
thing. In view of this object, the object of theology, we content
ourselves with saying that the possibility of it being known by men
in this way and in no other is to be affirmed. Men can know the
Word of God because and so far as God wills that they should know

it, because and so far as over against the will of God there is only
the weakness of disobedience, and because and so far as there is a
revelation of the will of God in His Word, in which this weakness
of disobedience is removed. We shall return to the problem here
indicated in the third part of our section. Here the preliminary
point to make was simply this, that if we are to call the problem of
the knowability of the Word of God an anthropological problem,
we must mean by that a problem of theological or Church anthropology. The question cannot be how man in general and as such
can know the Word of God. This question is objectless, for over
against the Word of God there is no such thing as man in general
and as such, but it is what it is by being spoken concretely to this
or that man. The question is how these men to whom it is spoken
concretely can actually know it. And at least the trend of the
answer to this question must be, that they can do so, if and in as
much as this ability is given them by the Word itself.—Of this
first finding we must first give two further explanations.

1. We have made a positive finding, have expressed a definite
Yea regarding the knowability of the Word of God. Right at this
first stage of our deliberations we must refer to this, because those,
who in spite of all that has just been said favour the way of answering our question which rests upon a general anthropology, usually
object that in this way the Word of God and man would conclusively
be held asunder or indeed " rent asunder." The answer to that is
that the other man ought not to listen so stubbornly only for the
Nay in it all. By what has been said we, to be sure, deny any connection between God and man, i.e. any knowledge of the Word of
God by man and therefore any knowability of the Word of God by
man, in the sense that a capacity in man in abstraction from the
Word of God is to be the condition of this connection. Of course
this condition cannot be fulfilled. It is the man who really knows
the Word of God who also knows that he can bring no capacity to
this knowledge, but must first receive all capacity. But might we
not expect of theologians even in modern times that they should
not set their hearts upon this once for all unrealisable condition ?
While we are on the subject, should we call the reference to God-
certainty, which precedes all self-certainty, an inadequate, an
unsatisfactory reference ? Is the reference to this way, the way
from God-certainty to self-certainty, not just the only,
but withal the absolutely certain and effective affirmation to give
to our question ?

2. No doubt by this reference we have made a positive statement only so far as it was a r e f e r e n c e, the reference to the event
of real knowledge of the Word of God. The force of this reference
does not lie in itself, but in the thing to which it refers. The thing
referred to here, the event, the actual priority of God-certainty over
self-certainty, the fact of the knowledge of the Word of God, which
does not presuppose its possibility in man, but in coming to man
brings it with it—this we can only " presuppose " in the way in
which man can " presuppose " God. " Presupposition " must in
that case mean recollection of its promise and hope of its advent,
i.e. an appeal to the Bible Word and expectation of its fulfilment.
Our reference therefore has every bit as much force, as the promise
is true and as the coming of the Lord is certain. In concrete
language, every bit as much force as the text adduced (1 Cor. 2⁶ᶠ·)
has truth and its content reality. The force of our reference therefore by no means lies with us. That holds not only of the affirmation which we wish to express, but also and just as strictly of the
accompanying negation. In other words, even the position of the
theologians who incline to Descartes, opposed as it is to the view
here set forth, cannot directly and really be reduced by us *ad
absurdum* or put out of gear. The force required to stop their mouths
is not at our disposal, nor have they themselves disposal of the
power to let their mouths be stopped. Even knowledge of the
impossibility of knowing the Word of God, apart from its reality, is
only possible on the presupposition of this real knowledge. There is
no philosophy which can do faith, i.e. theology, even this merely
negative service. The positive reference to the possibility of
knowledge which the Word of God itself brings with it can be
declined, and therewith also the negative reference to its unknow-
ability, apart from the possibility of knowledge which it imports
itself. Even with regard to ourselves when we affirm this twofold
reference, we have no control over its power. Our affirmation as
such might be a powerless one, because lacking in the real knowledge of the Word of God, a merely verbal and mental one instead
also being a real one over and above that. If it is real, that does
not depend upon it nor upon the seriousness and the honesty, nor
upon the existential participation with which we achieve it, but on
the reality affirmed by it. In short, for the obligatoriness of what
we here assert and deny, everything depends upon the fact that we
are involved in the matter as speakers and listeners. But if that
is so, it has absolutely nothing to do with us but only with the

15

thing itself. And for the very reason that this thing, the Word of God, is not a thing, but the living, personal, and free God.—This is the explanation which must accompany us in anything further that may be said on our question.

3. THE WORD OF GOD AND EXPERIENCE

What we have in view in this heading is the application and explication of what has generally been established as far as we have gone. We have established that knowledge of the Word of God becomes possible for men in the event of the reality of the Word of God. It " becomes possible for men "—this part of the thought above all is now to be explained. We attempt this by means of the concept of experience.

H. M. Müller (*Glaube und Erfahrung bei Luther*, 1929) has in connection with certain passages in Luther understood by the concept of experience, and kept it in view, the unusual experience of the temptation of faith, or the conquest of this temptation. Here we follow a more general usage.

If knowledge of the Word of God becomes possible for men, that must mean that an experience of the Word of God becomes possible for them. We defined knowledge as that confirmation of human acquaintance with an object whereby its trueness becomes a determining factor in the existence of the man who knows. It is precisely this factor determining the existence of the man who knows that we call experience. Man exists not abstractly but concretely, i.e. in experiences, in determinations of his existence by objects, by something external distinct from himself. As the object of experience, i.e. determined by this external thing which so far has come in contact with him, and in the way in which it has made contact, and as the subject of experience, i.e. as one who now a second time comes in contact with a definite external thing in a definite manner, he is what he is, he exists as a man, and not otherwise. If knowledge of the Word of God can become possible for men, that must mean that they can have experience of the Word of God, they can be what they are, as determined by the Word of God.

It should be stated explicitly that in this formula we would also include what might be rightly intended in the formula so dear to the 19th century, " the religious consciousness." Of course we shall not say, with the men of the 19th century, that " there is " or that man " has " a religious consciousness. But we might say that men may have a religious consciousness, or, in our own terminology, that the Word of God may become the ground and object of a man's consciousness. When, e.g. Schleiermacher spoke of the Christian consciousness or self-consciousness, he meant by that a " being affected " (to K. H. Sack, *g.* IV 1825 *Letters*, vol. IV p. 335), i.e. clearly somewhat similar to our " being determined." In preferring the concept of experience we do so, because it expresses something more comprehensive.

By experience of the Word of God which is possible to men on this presupposition as to its reality, we understand the determination of their existence as men by the Word of God.

If there is such a determination of man's existence by the Word of God, it must above all be stated that it is not to be confused with any sort of determination which man himself can give to his own existence. Experience of the Word of God, of course, takes place always in an act of human self-determination. But it is not as this act that it is experience of the Word of God. No determination which man can give himself is as such determination by the Word of God. But neither can there be room here for the other view, as if in this experience it were a case of co-operation between divine determination and human self-determination. Nor does the undeniable fact that this experience takes place in an act of human self-determination mean that man in this self-determination supplies, so to speak, a greater or lesser share in the whole, so as to leave the remaining portion over for determination by God. And in conclusion we must also reject the view often recommended as a solution—(it is Augustine's, and to-day the central dogma of the school of Holl in particular)—that it is a case of a " simultaneity," an " interwovenness," a " unity in tension " between divine and human determination. What viewed from the one side is grace is from the other side supposed to be freedom, and *vice versa*. All these theories are to be rejected, because they are in contradiction to the self-knowledge of man found in real experience of the Word of God, as we know it from the promise in the Bible. If a man lets himself be told by the Word of God that he has a Lord, that he is His creature, a lost sinner in receipt of His grace, a candidate for eternal redemption and, therefore, a poor stranger in this sphere of time, then this particular content of the experienced Word will flatly forbid him to ascribe to himself, wholly or in part, the possibility of such experience or even to equate dialectically with a possibility proper to himself the divine possibility which is realised in such experience. All those theories—not least the third of them— emanate not from the sole competent witness in this matter, namely, the man standing actually within the event of really knowing God, as he is set before us in Holy Scripture, but they emanate from an onlooker, interested in this event but only from without, who regards the two determinations obviously presented here, the one by God and the other by man himself, as the same kind of determinations as elsewhere may well be rivals of each other, and who, as with every right one usually tries to do with ordinary rival determinations, tries to look at them in their togetherness, to effect some sort of synthesis between them—obviously with the main concern of " somehow " asserting man's self-determination over against the determination of man by God. But the external on-looker with this interest fails to see—and because he is such an external onlooker with such an interest he must fail to see—that the togetherness of God and man as it occurs in experience of the Word of God, is not a togetherness on the same level, that it is, therefore, quite impossible to review this togetherness as it were from a higher watchtower and to diagnose it as a togetherness in its possibility. He also fails to see that there can be no meaning in wishing to assert " somehow " man's self-determination, even in the dialectical way indicated, against the determination of man by God. For the very reason that it is self-determination, it is subordinate to determination by God. Our very self-determination needs this determination by God in order to be experience of His Word. In this relation of utter subordination and need over against determination by God it cannot possibly, as Pelagius wished, take the place of the other, or, as the Semi-pelagians wished, co-operate with it, or, as Augustine wished, be secretly identical with it. Even if such elucidations were everywhere possible, where it is in other respects a matter of rival determinations of man or even of an object, here, where we are concerned with the question of the determination of man by God and by himself, they are impossible.

But it would also be the completely analogous misunderstanding of an onlooker, were we to regard the situation of man in experiencing the Word of God as the removal of his self-determination, as a condition of partial or complete receptivity and passivity.

Because it has almost of necessity given rise to this idea we shall prefer not to adopt Schleiermacher's concept of "dependence" in this connection.

In spite of an apparently very great appreciation of the thought of the omnipotence of God and of His Word, even so there would still be a failure to realise the nature of the opposition between God and man. So surely as in the experience of the Word of God it is seriously God who is involved, so surely it is as seriously a matter of man too. For it is precisely the man who is placed in a real knowledge of the Word of God who recognises himself completely as existing in the action of his life, as existing in his self-determination. Here we do not have to decide whether we really may and must say this of man at all and in general, so far as we have to regard him as not only a natural, but as essentially and primarily an historical being.

More recent philosophy of various complexions alleges this and thereby lives, perhaps more than is beneficial to it as philosophy, upon a loan from theology.

Be that as it may, the man who really knows the Word of God, as He meets us in the Biblical promise, can only regard himself as one who exists in his action, in his self-determination. The Word of God comes as a summons to him, and the hearing which he gives it is the right hearing of obedience or the wrong hearing of disobedience. Whether it is ultimately the one or the other, does not, of course, lie within his province. To that, the obedience or disobedience of his action, he cannot resolve and determine himself. Rather by his decision, by his resolution and self-determination, he stands in the secret judgment of the grace or disfavour of God, to whom alone his obedience or disobedience is manifest. And that is the overlapping determination by God which befalls his self-determination. But that makes no difference to the fact that his hearing is self-determination, action, decision. On this side also we must seriously recognise that the togetherness of God and man in man's experience of the Word of God is not a togetherness on the same level, to be surveyed like the coincidence of any other pair of ordinary entities, and, therefore, to be contemplated as a possible togetherness. Even one interested in the omnipotence of God, who thinks to solve the problem from this side, might actually be an onlooker from without, who thinks to behold and judge from a high tower, and precisely in that way and for that reason understands nothing of it all. Here we may simply repeat two previously formulated propositions with a somehow different emphasis. Our very self-determination is here subordinate to determination by God, and, our self-determination requires this determination by God in order to be experience of His Word. Were it not precisely human self-determination that is here indicated as, so to speak, the raw material, the subordinate, the thing in need, when we speak of the determination of human existence by the Word of God, how then would we speak of the determination of human existence and how at all of a determination by the Word of God ? If the Word of God is not spoken to beasts, plants, or stones, but to men, and if determination by the Word of God is really a determination of human existence, of what else then should it consist save in this, that the self-determination by which man is man receives in determination by God an Above which is absolutely superior to it, that a s self-determination and without in the least being infringed upon or destroyed as such, it is given a direction, is put under a judgment, has a character stamped upon it, in short, is determined exactly as a self-determining being is determined by a word, and as man in this case is determined by the Word of God. The fact that this befalls it and the nature of what thereby befalls it are not the work of man's self-determination. But conversely it is the work of man's self-determination which this befalls, to determine what may therewith befall it.

If that is clear, then the way should be free for a closer explanation of our statement that men may have experience of the Word of God. This statement must in that case mean that in their self-determination men may be determined by the Word of God. That is, not merely determined by any sort of external that may otherwise encounter them—that, of course, may also happen—but also determined by the Word of God. At this stage three points should be comparatively easy to realise :

1. In determining the anthropological spot at which experience of the Word of God becomes possible, we are not obliged to single out one or another among the various ways in which man can be self-determined, as if it and it alone were the chosen vessel of this experience. We have the will, we have conscience, we have feeling specially fixed as such distinct spots, and entire theological systems reared upon this or that preference.

The reason which made some prefer one and others another anthropological region was always that each thought or hoped he could best justify a definite synthesis of the relation between divine and human determination, whether non-determinist or dialectic or determinist, from one or the other anthropological centre accordingly. This unreality, of course, necessitated by assuming the need and possibility of such a synthesis, regularly avenged itself in the form of a very one-sided conception of religious experience, and also, in consequence, of the Word of God which they claimed to experience in this way. We saw that the synthesis in question is neither necessary nor possible. We have, therefore, no need to justify such a synthesis on anthropological grounds. We need single out neither the will, in order to underline human freedom, nor conscience, as the place where man becomes one with the will of God, nor feeling, in order to make clear man's utter dependence upon the omnipotence of God.

We may quietly regard the will and conscience and feeling and all other anthropological centres that come under consideration as possibilities of human self-determination, and then regard them in their totality as determined by the Word of God affecting the entire man.

2. Nor are we bound to envelope certain anthropological centres with so fundamental a distrust and suspicion as has frequently been the case in the history of theology. Here I am thinking chiefly of the extraordinary polemic which it has been the fashion in recent years to wage against the so-called " intellect " of man, his powers of comprehension and thought, as a centre of possible religious experience of the Word of God.

Two directly opposite reasons were and are held to establish the special incompetence of the intellect in matters of religious experience. In the eyes of one group its activity in this matter is a fatal sign that, instead of himself determining his life by acting, man is minded to sink into the lazy passivity of mere reflexion and meditation upon life. In the eyes of the other group, activation of the intellect is rather the peak of an overbold self-determination, which according to them ought to be broken and where possible to be smashed in experience of the Word of God. According to the one group it must lack the proper power, according to the other the proper humility, according to both the proper depth which one is much more hopeful of touching in one of the other anthropological centres, say in conscience or in feeling, as distinct from intellect. What shall we say in answer ? This, surely, above all, that we too see no reason anthropologically for a special preference of intellect in particular. What man does in making use of this power, in thinking and trying to understand, may in fact, like all human self-determination, equally well be laziness or else hybris or even both. But does not this also hold of feeling, conscience, will, or whatever else we may name here ? Are not they also self-determination, are they so in a less degree ? Proportionately less, as the differences regarding the relation of spontaneity and receptivity, which might at this point come under review, seriously drop in importance compared with the comprehensive determination of the whole of a man's existence by the Word of God ? Is it not arbitrary prejudice to suppose that in the act of thought in particular man is man in a worse sense than in his other self-realisations ? Should such a pre-judgment, as is so frequently alleged, really be the judgment of Christian faith ? It is notorious that it was only on the retreat before modern agnosticism and not earlier that Christian faith hit upon this extraordinary judgment ! This prejudice could only indicate an unfortunate close time for the Word of God. We recall the fact earlier established that the Word of God is quite literally language, not ultimately but primarily and predominantly so, i.e. is a spiritual event. If that be so the communication of it to man must at least also involve a claim upon the intellect, and the experience of it must at least also actually involve the co-option of the intellect. Does not the anti-intellectualism of modern theology mean on the one hand an effort after holiness which rests upon self-deception regarding the other anthropological possibilities and must inevitably end in disillusionments, on the other hand a restriction of possible experience of the Word of God at its

most crucial point which might very soon mean complete denial of it ? We
cannot regard this as at all a respectable proceeding. We regard it as a form
of convulsions, recovery from which is essential to a sight of what is really
to be seen here.

The Word of God determining man's existence is strong enough
also to deal with man as self-determining in thought. Naturally
the same would have to be said (and correspondingly proved), if
on the other side feeling or conscience were to become discredited
or excluded as a centre of possible experience of the Word of God.
If we must reject, as a more than suspicious attempt at despotism,
any calculated and preferential treatment of Christian experience
as the experience of feeling or of conscience, indubitably we are
also barred from assenting to the exclusion of this particular anthropological centre.

Particularly in this sphere evangelical theology runs a continual risk
of being tempted to elevate the needs of ephemeral polemics into denials in
principle : which as such cannot, of course, be carried out. We should resist
this temptation in every direction.

3. Nor, in order to prove that man may experience the Word of
God, are we bound to claim, or to discover and assert, any sort of
unusual or recondite anthropological centres. The existence of
such unusual centres, which to-day are more considered and investigated than at earlier periods, and the possibility that still
more of them may exist than are objects of consideration and investigation to-day, can indeed scarcely be doubted. There are, for
example, unconscious and subconscious, and apparently also semi-
occult and occult, possibilities in the soul of man. Unquestionably,
apart from discursive thought and in every variety of combination
with it, there is also an intuitive grasp of objects. It may be that,
apart from the possibility of æsthetic feeling and attitude, there is
also the possibility of a specifically religious variety.

One result of philosophical enlightenment as to the nature and limits of
theoretical reason in particular was that from the time of Schleiermacher's
discovery of the special " province " proper to religion in the heart of man,
theologians turned with a certain intrigued preference to these subsidiary
departments of psychology. On our own presuppositions we shall have to
say to this, that we can really take no special interest in the indication of
such so-called special centres of possible religious experience. Even the
possibilities which come under review in these subsidiary branches, both
those generally acknowledged and the problematical, are invariably possibilities of human self-determination. So far as they are to be claimed at all
as human possibilities, they are, in the comprehensive sense of the concept,
rational possibilities. Their hiddenness and rarity certainly do not qualify

them as points of entry for the determination of man by the Word of God. Here, too, we have rather to do with acts of human self-determination—and we repeat : so far as it is a case of human acts at all—and here that will always be our concern, whatever discoveries are still to be made here and whatever interpretations they may subsequently disclose. We do not say this in order to exclude these special centres as centres of possible experience of the Word of God, but simply in order to include them, together with the other, better known, anthropological centres, in the sum-total of human existence, which claims our interest here as the object of determination by the divine Word.

Why among the possibilities of human existence in being determined by this Word, should not the subconscious, or intuition, or whatever may be cited here, also have their place ? Yet, why alongside of and among the other better-known possibilities should they have a quite special value ? What psychology of the depths may have to say to us here in its various schools may serve to remind us of the broad lines along which the concept of human existence must invariably be conceived. Information on the accessibility of this human existence to the Word of God we shall not dream of receiving or expecting, even from the deepest psychology of the depths.

To summarise : human existence means human self-determination. If in experience of the Word of God the point is the determination of human existence, and so of human self-determination by the Word of God, by self-determination is to be understood the activity of the combined powers, in the activity of which man is man, without fundamental emphasis upon and without fundamental rejection of this or that human possibility. All such emphases or rejections are in this context to be refused on the score of method, because they are the results or presuppositions of a general philosophical anthropology, by the constructions of which we dare not let ourselves be influenced here, whatever right or wrong they may possess on their own ground. Determination of a man's existence by the Word of God when viewed from various sides may equally well be regarded as a determination of feeling, as of will or of intellect ; psychologically considered in the concrete instance, it may even actually be more the one than the other. But in substance it is definitely a determination of the whole self-determining man.

This settled, we push on a step further to the question, in what experience of the Word of God, i.e. determination of the whole self-determining man by the Word of God, might consist. To this question, so decisive for the whole problem of our section, the answer is the concept of acknowledgment in the introductory statement prefixed to the section. I am aware of no word relatively so appropriate as this to the nature of the Word of God, with the determining operation of which we are here concerned. And in view of what we know or think we know about man, this word is also adequate enough to express the special point which needs to be made here about it ; but is also general enough to express this special point with the comprehensiveness required by the present circumstances.—We develop the concept of acknowledgment by borrowing the nine bearings on the nature of the Word of God which we fixed and explained in § 5.

1. In the first place, the word acknowledgment involves the concept of kno wledge. This must be so, because the Word of God is primarily and predominantly language, communication from person to person, from mind to mind, spirit, a rational event, the Word of truth, because it is directed to man's *ratio*, by which, of course, we are not to understand the intellect alone, but the intellect at least also and not last of all. If that be so, then the experience of it must also correspond with it, so far as experience is possible. That point the word acknowledgment at least also indicates.

2. But in this word expression is also given to the fact that in experience of the Word of God we are concerned with a relationship between man as a person and another Person, naturally the Person of God. Of course we also speak of acknowledging facts and with such a fact we are concerned here, but a fact which is acknowledged is at least not a fact of nature—we do not acknowledge a landslip or a rainbow or the like—but a fact created and presented by a person or persons. Of such a creation is the determination of a man's existence by the Word of God ; it is determination by God's person. For that reason also we designate it acknowledgment.

3. Acknowledgment relates to the presence of a definite power of disposal, positive or negative, respecting the person who acknowledges something. But acknowledgment means not only submission to a necessity, but self-adaptation to the stark objectivity of the necessity, acceptance of it as good, not merely finding oneself in it, but seeing one's way about in it. Acknowledgment of the Word of God relates to the purposiveness of the Word of God, with its content as the Word of the Lord, as the Word of the Creator, Reconciler and Redeemer of man. It must, therefore, consist in the fact that man approves of this Word (though in a perfectly definite way), and sees his way about in this content of it

(though in a perfectly definite way) as in a truth which is valid for him. Acknowledgment of the Word of God by a man consists in admitting that he bows before the purposes of God expressed in God's Word, in affirming (of course in quite a special way) the " God with us," of which the Word of God has to tell its hearers.

4. Acknowledgment of the Word of God must, of course, also mean respect for the character of the fact which takes place in the Word of God. But this fact consists, above all, in its coming to us, in its contingent contemporaneousness as revelation, Holy Scripture, and Church proclamation. *Illic et tunc* becomes *hic et nunc.* Jesus Christ Himself lives in the message of His witnesses, lives in His Church's proclamation founded upon this message, moves as Lord of grace and of judgment to meet the existence of the hearer of the Word. Experience, therefore, of the Word of God must at least also be experience of His presence, and, because this presence of His does not rest upon an historical act of recollection on the part of man, but upon God's presentation of Himself in the life of man, therefore acknowledgment of His presence.

5. As we have already said, the word " acknowledgment " involves relationship to a power of disposal, to a necessity. We have to remember that the Word of God has power—power, just as any word has power—therefore the power of God's truth, the power of His promise, of His claim, of His judgment, of His blessing, which are its content ; but power. Acknowledgment of the Word of God by man is thus, of course, approval of the Word of God by man, but not such approval as is based upon persuasion between equals, but such as is based upon obedience, upon submission as between the utterly unequal. To have experience of the Word of God is to give way before its superiority. Whether it comes to us as law or as gospel, as commandment or as promise, it comes at least in such a way that it bends man, and, of course, his conscience and his will just as much as his intellect and his feeling—does not shatter him but really bends him, brings him into a conformity with itself.

6. Further, acknowledgment certainly means decision. The coming of the Word of God to man is the act of divine freedom and choice. It does not have to come to him, but it comes according to God's good-pleasure ; and once more it is God's good-pleasure how it comes to him, whether for grace or for judgment. Experience of the Word of God is, therefore, invariably experience of this divine freedom and choice and therefore itself decision, decision about man which becomes manifest by characterising man's decision as

a decision for faith or unbelief, for obedience or disobedience. By conformity with the Word of God of which we were speaking previously, we must therefore primarily understand both things, obedience and disobedience. Even in disobedience an acknowledgment of the Word of God takes place, although counter to the will of man and to his detriment. Even in his disobedience a man marks himself out for the man he is in presence of the Word of God. Even disobedience in its way is a confirmation, an approval of the Word of God ; so far as it is actual disobedience to the Word of God, and so far as man's self-determination, even in disobedience, is a completion of his determination by the Word of God. The corresponding thing should naturally be said about the decision to obey. Just because experience of the Word of God is such a decision, man may and must be called in the Church to ever new experience and therefore decision.

7. The concept of acknowledgment further implies that the act thereby indicated signifies calling a halt before an enigma, getting satisfaction about a situation which is not open but, from the acknowledger's point of view, unexplained. In § 5 we spoke of the worldliness of the Word of God, i.e. of its coming to us in a form which at the same time signifies its veiling. Experience of the Word of God must, therefore, consist in our receiving it in this form and veiling, in this twofold indirectness. Even our reception of the Word, which will be especially important for us later, will participate in this twofold indirectness. It, too, will have a worldly form, the form of all sorts of human acts, and this form will be its veiling, the calling of it in question. Otherwise than in this problematic form so deeply grounded in the facts there is no experience of the Word of God. It will also consist always in respect for, acknowledgment of, its mystery.

8. Just because it is concerned with the acknowledgment of the mystery of God in His Word, we must also stress the fact that the word " acknowledgment " signifies an act of man, a movement, a movement which, merely by being completed, is the acknowledgment here required, which therefore cannot be resolved into an attitude. What prevents this latter in experience of the Word of God and thus converts this experience, wherever genuine, into a movement, is comprised in what in § 5 we called the onesidedness of the Word of God. By that we meant that we are met by a complete Word of God which is always at the same time veiled and unveiled or unveiled and veiled, and that this is something special

for us every time, that we are met by it onesidedly, now in its
veiling and now in its unveiling ; in the unity of both it does not
become evident to us, yet every time its aim is to be heard as a
complete Word of God. In view of this situation, acknowledgment
of the Word of God must mean letting oneself continually be led,
continually taking the step, continually being in movement from
the experience felt at one time, from the thought grasped at one time,
to the opposite experience and thought, because hearing the Word
of God always consists of a simultaneous hearing of the one in the
other and the other in the one. In this movement, which cannot be
brought to rest by any synthesis, a man acknowledges the mystery
of the Word of God and he has Christian experience.

9. Where acknowledgment takes place there takes place on the
part of the man who acknowledges a giving way before the thing
or the person he acknowledges. He yields to the authority of
another. This is not in contradiction to the concept of self-determination, but it means that as such the self-determination of this
man takes place at a definite point in a definite context. It has
found its beginning and ground in another higher determination.
In the act of acknowledgment the life of the man, without ceasing
to be the self-determining life of this man, has its centre, its direction, the meaning of this attitude it takes up, also the criterion as
to whether this attitude really has the corresponding meaning—all
this it has outside of itself, in the thing acknowledged. So far
as it has it at all, it has it from the thing acknowledged. And so
acknowledgment as an attitude is out and out the act of the particular man and yet, looked at from the side of the meaning of this
attitude, it is likewise not his act at all but a determination befalling
him due to the thing acknowledged, the thing which forces his
acknowledgment. First of all, there is the thing acknowledged,
then, and in consequence and in the long-run completely due to it,
there is acknowledgment. We are faced with what in § 5 we called
the spirituality of the Word of God, i.e. the basing of not only the
spokenness of the Word of God, but also its really being heard by
man in the Word itself, the appropriation of the Word of God as
the gift of the Holy Spirit and, therefore, as the Word's own action
upon the man. And thereby we at the same time face the limits
of what we can say of experience of the Word of God as such. The
last thing to be mentioned here is the statement that the attitude of
acknowledgment towards the Word of God, while a real attitude
of the man and an act of his own self-determination, is the act of such

human self-determination that its meaning and ground, its final importance and peculiar content, its truth and reality can be ascribed by him not to himself but only to his determination by the Word of God. It is an act of pure acknowledgment, we might also say, an act in which acknowledgment consists in the claim to be merely the answer to an added-knowledge—for at this limit the concept must change its meaning !—which befalls the man on the far side of all his action and capacity, the subject of which is not himself, in the free truth and reality of which he must be acknowledged in order to acknowledge its truth and reality.

We shall, of course, do well to realise and express the fact that this experience ceases to be an experience by the very fact of taking place as an experience. In order to close the problem-circle of the question as to the possibility of man knowing the Word of God, or rather, in order to indicate the point at which it must finally be left open, we shall have to introduce and dwell upon, in the last division of our section, the concept of faith, which corresponds to the Holy Spirit of the Word of God. But before we do that, it is worth while stopping to look back and expressly establishing this, that experience of the Word of God is possible, but that precisely in view of its meaning and ground, of its ultimate seriousness and peculiar content, precisely in view of its truth and reality it is not experience, it is more than experience.

We preface this negative and amplifying statement with a positive point. Hitherto we have not denied the possibility of human experience of the Word of God, but affirmed it. We described it as genuine experience, by actually underlining as heavily as possible its character as human self-determination. We objected to the introduction neither of feeling nor of conscience into experience of the Word of God, nor, of course, to the introduction of the intellect. Nor did we combat the concept of experience : indeed we allowed the " religious consciousness " to keep its place in peace. We described this experience—not, of course, in the form of a psychological study, but in the form of a conclusion from our earlier gained understanding of the nature of the Word of God—by citing a series of acts which with the partial exception of the limiting case of the last are all to be completely claimed as human acts possible to man We shall not object if our 9 or 8 points in which we have developed " acknowledgment " are conceived and designated simply and straightforwardly as an attempt to describe—in this case formally— Christian religious experience or consciousness.

I must emphasise this, because to my regret I am continually having it said that my occupation is to put revelation and faith from the believer's standpoint up in the clouds, to teach a *fides quae creditur* " without considering the *fides qua creditur*, the intimate personal conviction and experience of faith." " Intimate personal experience of faith is to be completely eliminated." The conveyance of revelation is not to be thought of in such a way " that the ordinary nature of man also becomes a factor "—so the review, e.g. of G. Wobbermin (*Richtlinien ev. Theol.* 1929 pp. 22, 104, 139, 141, etc.) ; while from E. Schaeder I must again and again (the last time in *Das Wort Gottes*, 1930 p. 37 f.) listen to the certainly somewhat vague objection that I am exposed to the danger " of exaggerating in an untenable manner the protest against the place and validity of the ego in faith and in the theology of faith." With me people are compelled as " men of faith and theologians " to accomplish the impossible, namely, to jump over our own shadow." With me the necessary struggle with idealism tumbles head over heels, " and yet even so we are not " done with the sheer distance between God's spirit and the human spirit or finite ego (*op. cit. sup.* p. 41).—I do not doubt for a moment (and we shall have to return to it directly) that the contrast between the idea of Wobbermin and Schaeder (to cite them both as spokesmen for many others) and the idea here presented is as deep as it can be within the Protestant Church, and I really do not dream of commending myself to them by concessions. But it would serve to clear up the situation in dispute if they and others could forbear ascribing to me negations which I have never sponsored, even as long as ten years ago. The dispute really cannot be as to whether " intimate personal experience of faith " is to be " considered," and whether the ordinary nature of man is thereby to be " dealt with " also, or whether an " exaggerated," i.e. of course, an absolute " protest " is to be raised against the place and validity of the Ego in faith. What sense would there be in making here even a merely relative negation and protest, not to speak of an " exaggerated " one ! But, of course, I think that the quiet affirmative which may and must be made at this point, must be followed by statements other than those which a Wobbermin or a Schaeder would like to have follow, and upon which for them so much vitally depends in the whole dispute as it does for me upon my statements which follow.

We may concede everything that practically is to be conceded here ; we may, therefore, make the point, as we have done in every form, that in experience of the Word of God we are concerned with a genuine, humanly possible experience. But then we must, of course, go further and ask if experience of the Word of God is possible in such a way that by it the state of human possibilities is enriched by a further one, this, to wit, that man now possesses one possibility, one organ, one capacity more than he had before. Or looking at it from the opposite end : because the possibility of experiencing the Word of God is given to man in the power of its reality, is it given to him in such a way that it becomes an extraordinary possibility, perhaps one to be described as miraculous but yet independently proper to him, a special possibility of the religious man (pardoned man, as we may and must also say), but

all the same of man ?   Have we in the reality of this experience,
so to speak, a divine emanation in the direction of man or, from
man's standpoint, a divine influxus, the deposit of which would be
the possibility in question ?   From the actualised possibility of the
experience of the Word of God are we to conclude that, therefore,
there are men who possess this possibility—perhaps in the way
in which others as distinguished from many of their fellows possess
artistic possibilities ?   Do these men so exist that they can discover
and study themselves as possessors of this possibility, or can be
discovered and studied as such by others ?   Is experience of the
Word of God, therefore, real in such a way that its possibility can
be fixed and therefore presupposed as a predicate, as a definite
characteristic in definite men, as the property of a human I or We,
which can be asserted of this I or this We directly, unambiguously
and without reserve ?

This manifestly is, e.g. Schaeder's conclusion from his general presupposition, if he can talk of a " conjunction between the Word of God
and the finite Ego " (*op. cit.* p. 41) which takes place and is exhibited in faith,
of a " Word-bound Ego " (p. 45), if in the question as to the Word of God he
is ready to begin with the believing Ego "—" how should one do otherwise ? "
(p. 43), if he claims knowledge of a " Word-mediated active synthesis between
the spirit of God and the finite spirit " (p. 46), of an " inmost synthesis of
Word, history, the human ego, the spirit of God and faith " (p. 50), of an
" appurtenance of the Word of God to the strict presence of him who apprehends it " (p. 49), if on one occasion he can describe the Word of God itself
as " having arisen (!) out of the synthesis of divine self-offering or revelation
and the human relationship of faith effected by this revelation " (p. 105), if
he feels no obstacles to remarking incidentally : " we shall not make headway(!)
in promoting (!) the Word of God " until we have fulfilled such and such
conditions (p. 103) ; if, in conclusion, his doctrine of the Word of God reaches
its height by indicating certain " men of sensibility " who represented the
decisive effect of the Word of God, i.e. of the Church of the Word (p. 170).
It is a very serviceable fact which may be mentioned here, as it saves us
further remark, that Robert Winckler has not only specifically designated
this very theory as " substantially parallel " to that of his teacher Wobbermin, but also terms it " a platform " upon which to-day " all non-dialectical
theology may find itself united " (*Th. Lit. Z.*, 1931 Sp. 550 : cf. also Torsten
Bohlin, *Th. Lit. Z.*, 1931 Sp. 570).

Let us try, above all, to make clear to ourselves what it would
mean if this theory were correct.   It would obviously mean that
we might now assert an appropriateness in man to the Word of God,
the possibility of achieving man's determination by the Word of
God by means of human self-determination.   I say might, because
it is not in the first place asserted by the representatives of this
theory, i.e. not asserted as a general possibility, one proper to man

as such. As a possibility in this sense it can even be emphatically denied by them. It can be said on the ground of this theory with great zeal that the possibility of such experience is given to man from God's side and only from God's side.

There should be repeated here what was already expressly stated in the first edition of this book (p. 92 f.), that it would be an injustice to Schleiermacher (and to his followers up to the present day) to foist upon them the intention, which was of course Feuerbach's, of making the human subject the creator of his determination by God, to claim their theology therefore as direct Cartesianism. I do not think I missed the significance of the catchword used by Schaeder, " theocentric theology," in the campaign which I at that time conducted against him. Schaeder now sets store upon taking the Ego—which according to him is in theology to be catechised concerning the Word of God—in the sense of the " Word-bound Ego." Now, at the time I quoted sentences like the following, from his earlier book of course. " The entities which we deal with in knowledge are all of them entities of consciousness or they are not there for us to deal with. The God with whom theology has to do is the God of our consciousness and no other. Or He is the divine spirit-content of our consciousness. . . . The present finite spirit or the personal consciousness is investigated by theology in regard to its possession of God or the divine spirit and the conditions thereof. It is not easy to see how it could be otherwise. This I term the theocentric in theology. Naturally, for the very reason that it selects this name it starts with man or with the spiritual consciousness of man. What sensible man would fail to proceed thus ? But in consciousness or starting with consciousness it aims at grasping, by the means of knowledge available, the divine reality of the spirit, the pneumatic element, the reality of God " (*Das Geistproblem der Theologie*, 1924 pp. 2, 4). But already at the time I cited and considered Schaeder's further statement : " We reach God only in the way that He reaches us, i.e. only on the ground of His self-revelation to us, which is achieved in our consciousness, at least ultimately and conclusively, if it is to count as revelation " (*op. cit.* p. 63), and I believe that at the time I took up Schaeder pretty much in the way in which he has explained himself now (*Das Wort Gottes*, 1930 p. 43 f.), i.e. my impression of his meaning formed offhand on the first occasion was in accord with his present additional explanation. And it should emphatically be insisted upon that statements like the following may be read even in Wobbermin : " The way here in question leads from God to man and not *vice versa* from man to God. Man who is always finding himself entangled in sin and guilt does not of his own initiative come upon the way to God. For sin and guilt lead him right away from God. Only God can build up a connection between God and man, bridge over the chasm torn open by man's sin and always torn open afresh " (*Richtlinien ev. Theol.*, 1929 p. 102). Thus on the points that *a priori* and in general man is not suited for the Word of God, that in experience of the Word of God his relationship primarily is absolutely not creative, that the possibility of such experience is to be regarded not as one originally pertaining to him but as one accruing to him, there can be no quarrel with the representatives of this theory.

But what also seems to hold at first and is asserted on the basis of this theory, the action, creation, or gift of God in the experience

16

of His Word, all at once ceases to hold at a definite point. And what on the basis of this theory seems at first not to hold and is denied, man's suitability to the experience in question, nevertheless turns up all at once in full force at a definite point. The start apparently is not Cartesian, but the subsequent course is obviously Cartesian. For the reality of this experience, i.e. the determination of man by the Word of God, is thought of in such a way that in it God hands something over to man, with the result that practically it passes from the hands of God to the hands of man, or, viewed from man's angle, he receives something from God, in such a way that it is practically put into his hands. A " conjunction " or " synthesis " has taken place. Man's consciousness now has a " content of divine spirit," a consideration and investigation of which can be carried through. The statement *homo capax verbi Dei* suddenly comes to life. There arises in the reality of this experience as an entity capable of being met, indicated, and taken for granted a new man, new not only in being man addressed by the Word of God, new, that is, not just in Christ merely—who could or should say anything against that ?—but new in himself, transformed in the immanent state of his humanity. This man now gains, certainly in virtue of his being claimed by the Word of God, independence and an interest of his own, as a participator in the reality of the Word, so much so that the introduction of the concept of m y s t i c i s m, while not indispensable, becomes imminent and desirable.

Schaeder, *Das Geistproblem*, p. 118 f. ; and with more restraint in *Das Wort Gottes*, p. 54. I do not know whether to regard it as an uncertainty in terminology or as material wavering, when in his latest utterances Schaeder describes " faith-mysticism " primarily as the " active proximity of God," as the co-option, assumption, and justification of man (*Das Wort Gottes*, p. 33 f., cf. also p. 47), but then surpasses himself ; it is, he says, not only that but also " a characteristic inner transformation of the Ego and an enrichment of its content " (*op. cit.* p. 41). Not by his introduction of the concept of mysticism, but by his definition of it in this way, by his assertion of the " conjunction " or " synthesis," is the decisive step taken.

This man thus distinguished, is therefore certainly not man in general, and no possibility presupposed as such in man corresponds to the " content of divine spirit " in his consciousness. This man is rather the special man who is usually called the r e l i g i o u s man, the man who has f a i t h in the Christian sense. And the possibility proper to him of being the bearer of a " content of divine spirit," is the possibility which he has r e c e i v e d in the reality of experiencing the Word of God. But—and this is the whole point

—it is a possibility proper to him as this man, the religious man ; i.e. one which has become his own. In a hidden yet not quite hidden but realisable depth of his being, his existence, his self-determination is identical with the completion of his determination by the Word of God. He no longer stands merely upon the Word of God, but (of course with a constant appeal to the Word of God) also upon himself, upon the conjunction or synthesis realised in him and therefore possible to him, upon the *esse capax verbi dei* imparted to him.

His " own personal experience of faith " now becomes (to speak with Wobbermin) the " opposite pole " to the Word, and thereby an " aid in method " to knowledge of the Word, although regarded as a subordinate entity (*Richtlinien*, p. 140 f.).

And now the reality of experience of the Word of God itself no longer rests upon itself ; it has become an ellipse instead of a circle, one pole of which, and that the one nearest us, opposite to God, is the man who experiences.

Can we avoid the snag that man thus characterised as a subjective opposite pole is going to discover that he is nearer himself than the Word of God is, that therefore the order in knowledge, Man-God, will come into force anew—with the twofold reservation that we are dealing with man pardoned, and that the material order is the very reverse (cf. Wobbermin, *Wort Gottes und ev. Glaube*, 1931 p. 9, and Robert Winckler, *Theol. Lit. Z.*, 1931 *Sp*. 550–51)—but still will come back again, properly in force at last ? Can a theology which as a result is ready " in intervening in the question as to the Word of God to start with the believing Ego " (Schaeder, *Das Wort Gottes*, p. 43) do other than make this very believing Ego, the confessed Christian believer, the criterion and measurement of its pronouncements upon the Word of God ? And after that can it be denied that thereby the Cartesianism apparently rejected is drawn back again into theology—as, so we say, indirect Cartesianism, the Cartesianism of the believing Christian ? Has the concept " theocentric theology " not in that event become a *lucus a non lucendo* ?

Thus in real experience of the Word of God man becomes an independent and therefore also an independently interesting realisation of this experience and thereby also the thing that makes it possible. There are religious men whose existence and nature the Word of God has entered and in which it is therefore to be found, whose existence and nature are therefore bound to become the storehouse of knowledge of the Word of God and the first and decisive criterion and measure of it. Towards this thesis we must take up a position.

Only let us not believe that this thesis and our opposition to it are concerned with a subtlety of the theological schools, which might equally well be left unsettled. Behind the thesis of Professors Wobbermin and Schaeder of the independent being and possession of the religious man with its growing independent interest, stands the " *Ecclesiam habemus* " of General Superintendents Dibelius and Schian, stands the *common sense* of practically the whole of our positive and liberal ministry, stands (in this point intimately bound up with the prevailing tendency in the Church) the prevailing tendency in the pietistic community-movement.   Tell them what even Wobbermin and Schaeder mean to tell them, that the material order regarding experience of the Word of God must run " God-man " and not *vice versa*, and they will all be with you to-day and be agreed.   Tell them further that for man generally, man without or before faith, the order of knowledge must also run God-man, that without precedent revelation there can be no faith, and they will concede your point, themselves still quite unaffected.   But tell them this order of knowledge holds also and particularly of the religious man, that he also, he precisely, does not possess any possibility—not even as received—but can only receive the possibility of experience of the Word of God, only use it as lent in the reality of the receipt of it, tell them that this possibility is and remains God's possibility and does not pass from His hand to any other hand—tell them this and at once you stir up angry irreconcilable strife. When we say this, when we oppose this thesis by the counter-thesis which in fact is separated from it only by the breadth of a blade yet by the depth of the pit, we have the crushing majority of leaders and led in the Protestant Church to-day passionately against us.   Now the usual feeling on the other side, apparently, that just here faith, love and hope, thought and life, world and Church are wholly at stake—this feeling is utterly ours too, and whoever sees what is at stake must make this feeling his own, whatever his attitude to the question at issue.   But let every man choose and let no one continue to look around for tiresome new attempts at mediation !

We have now to develop the ground for our rejection even of this Christian or indirect Cartesianism, and at the same time evolve our own thesis regarding the possibility of experiencing the Word of God.

For that we must first briefly summarise again the positive content of our line of thought up till now. We have decided that if there is a Church and Church proclamation in any serious sense, that implies that knowledge of the Word of God is possible for certain men. That this knowledge is possible for them must mean that experience of the Word of God is possible for them, i.e. that it is possible for certain men, through the Word of God in their existence, i.e. in the totality of their self-determination, to be determined by the Word of God. It is possible, such was our closer definition starting from the nature of the Word of God, for the relation of certain men to the Word of God to be the relation of acknowledgment. Thus in the possibility of acknowledging the Word of God consists the possibility of the experiencing and therefore the possibility of knowing the Word of God. At this point we then encounter Cartesianism a second time, now as specifically Christian, or indirect Cartesianism, with its interpretation of this possibility as of such a kind that in the act of real acknowledgment (or experience or knowledge) of the Word of God in the form of an emanation from the Word of God addressed to the man or in the form of an influxus into the man addressed by the Word of God, it becomes the man's own, a predicate of his existence, a content of his consciousness, his possession. Against this interpretation of the possibility in question we have now to fix our boundaries.

To that end we return once more to the beginning : we are dealing with the possibility of knowing the Word of God. We are therefore dealing with possibility of verifying the knowledge that men have of the Word of God. We are dealing with the fact that the Word of God may become true for men who became acquainted with it through revelation, Scripture, and proclamation, in such wise that they themselves must also hold it as true, that its trueness becomes their possession, that they become responsible witnesses of its truth. We are dealing with the fact that in truth the Church and Church proclamation, among men and through men, may take place in truth. As we already established it all at the beginning of the section, they are no small things that depend upon this possibility. According to our understanding of this possibility is the nature of our understanding of the Church and Church preaching, and, for dogmatics, of our understanding of its special service in the Church, in testing, criticising, and revising Church proclamation. For the Word of God is the criterion of Church, of Church proclamation, and of dogmatics. In asking where the possibility of knowing the Word of God is to be sought, we are asking where we are to look for the criterion with which dogmatics has to work. It is not the same thing whether we answer this question with Christian or indirect Cartesianism, that it is given to the religious man, the man who believes in the Christian sense, in such wise that it is given over to him, that we must then seek it in him, in his intimate personal experience of faith as such, in his Word-bound Ego, among the contents of his consciousness—it is not the same thing whether we have to say this or whether perhaps we should not say it at all. Dogmatics will appear different and Church proclamation also, and in short the whole Church will look radically different according as we are committed or not to this statement. The whole question as to the relationship of the Church to truth will be put very differently according as we say yes or no at this point, and the relationship also of truth to the Church might be a different one accordingly. Its presence or non-presence in the Church might depend upon whether at this point the Church means to go to the right or to the left. Jesus Christ can and means to and will acknowledge in some sort of way, and that a wholesome and victorious way, even a Church with a bad dogmatics and proclamation, i.e. resting at this point upon a wrong decision. We may and should give ourselves this word of comfort. But we may not and should not rest there. We must open our eyes as widely as possible at the cross-roads, and only with the best conscience conceivable should we strike the way to right or left. We must be as certain of our facts as it is possible for men to be certain of their facts, when the one way or the other we are seeking the possibility of knowing the Word of God. And for that reason the question should be put thus : can we be sure of our facts if we look for this possibility in the religious man, the man who believes in the Christian sense ? Are we sure that in what we can get at, fix, consider, and analyse in him as the possibility of such a man—that therein we actually get at, touch, and therefore can affirm, the possibility of knowing the Word of God ? Or, putting it from the other side, are we sure that among the possibilities of such a man we can really get at, can affirm in one of the possibilities of such a man, the possibility of such knowledge, corresponding to real knowledge of the Word of God, this possibility upon the understanding of which so much subsequently depends ? Can we say with final human certainty that this is so ? Can we put our hand into the fire for it ? (We can only put the question in this form where such decision is involved, but in this form we must, of course, put it ; we must ask whether with ultimate human seriousness we can take the responsibility of ascribing the possibility of knowing the Word of God to the religious man as such.) And even when so put our answer to it must be No. We could affirm it only with penultimate seriousness, only with a wavering conscience, only with semi-certainty.

We could quite well take the responsibility of saying Yes at this point, were we concerned not with the possibility of knowing the actual word of God, but, say, the possibility of understanding Plato's wisdom and view of education. Where should we seek, find, and study them if not in the representatives of such wisdom and form, in men who are gripped by their pathos and ethos ? We might very well take the responsibility of saying Yes at this point, if we were dealing not with the criterion of dogmatics, but with the principle of a philosophy or view of the world, not with the proclamation of the Church, but with the message of a union of *illuminati* and peerers into the deeps, not with the Church at all, but with a community of emotional sensationalists whose game was emotion. If we were dealing with the possibility of human knowledge of things lying within the sphere of man, it would always be literally appropriate and obligatory to exhaust this possibility, without detriment to its objective content, among the appropriate experts, i.e. in ourselves if we belong to them, or in others, at all events in men who are participators in it. We might with ultimate human certainty entertain the expectation of really getting at it there, of being able to submit to getting our bearings and instructions there.

But with the possibility of knowing the Word of God the case is quite different. It too, of course, has its special exponents, its experts, its representatives. Of course there are men who have this possibility. We ourselves are perhaps among the men who have it, as the reflex, that is, an echo of its reality, in the act of the Word spoken to us, in the event of experiencing it. But if we mean to stick to ourselves or to other men like us in order to fix there, in ourselves or in them, this possibility infused into us as it were from God's side, do we not at once come up against an insuperable difficulty which straightway proves itself to be the end of all, yes, of all certainty in such a fixation ? If our aim is to investigate the content of divine spirit in the (pardoned) consciousness of man, is it not with us as with the man who wanted to scoop the reflection of the fair silver moon out of the pond in a sieve ? What can or shall we find there to fix and to investigate ? As the substance of man's experience of the Word of God, obviously what we have designated and described as the act of acknowledging the Word of God, an event in human life of a very characteristic, differentiated, and at the same time comprehensive kind. It is because this event in life is actually to be found, is capable of being experienced, fixed, and described, that we speak of a possibility of man experiencing the Word of God. By the very act of establishing this event in ourselves or in others, we are taking that possibility into account. But does this mean that we actually come across that possibility in this event in life, take that possibility into account because we have come across it in this event ? Or is it not the case that precisely in this event as such we completely fail to see and to grasp that possibility, that rather what we succeed in seeing and grasping is always merely the event as such, which as such might also be something quite different from that particular possibility ? Is it the case that the acknowledgment which takes place in ourselves or in others must really be the acknowledgment of the Word of God, that it literally can only be connected with this, the counterpart of the divine Word, that it is a true mirror of this counterpart, that in view of this human acknowledgment we may therefore conclude to this counterpart, and may regard man as faced with this counterpart ? Who tells us that ? Who is our guarantee for that ? When we envisage the fixable human possibility as such, who is our guarantee that it is precisely the possibility which corresponds to the reality of the Word of God and not quite a different possibility ? For all the nine elements which we summarised under the concept of acknowledgment (with the possible exception of the last, to which indeed we ventured only upon a partial application of the concept of experience) cannot striking parallels be adduced among possibilities of a totally different kind ? Ought this acknowledgment of the Word of God in its clear quality and individuality to be contrasted only with what happens in the so-called " other religions " ? So far as Christianity has its reality in such human acknowledgment, does it not undeniably belong to the field of general history of religion, in which, no doubt, there are hills and valleys, but no heavens ? And again, does not the entire field of history of religion lie in the comprehensive field of general history of civilisation ? Is there, moreover, even one so-called religious phenomenon which may not more or less happily and completely be interpreted as the prototype or residuum of a thoroughly sublunary attempt at shaping life, as a phenomenon of " work " in the broadest sense of the term ? And is civilisation anything other than man's vital activity as such, regarded from the point of view of work ? If we hold to what we may fix and investigate as man's acknowledgment of the Word of God, to the experienceable in Christian experience—where do we get the criterion for separating this experience from others, what is genuine in it from what is not ? Where are the limits to the possibility of re-interpreting everything in terms of religion in general or civilisation or humanity itself, or ultimately, of course, even of biology. With what certainty can we claim to know and assert that in what we see taking place in the act of acknowledgment in the religious man we really have before us the acknowledgment of the Word of God spoken to us and, therefore, the possibility of us experiencing, i.e. knowing it ? Nay, it is the certainty which dogmatics, Church proclamation, and the Church herself require regarding the possibility of knowing the Word of God, that cannot be attained to here. What can be attained to here are vague assertions, to support which we can scarcely avoid recourse to direct, philosophical Cartesianism.

Indeed, what Schaeder lays down is simply not true, that " every subjective explanation of these subjective phenomena of consciousness fails " (*Das Geistproblem d. Theol.*, 1924 p. 65). And when Wobbermin insists that the sentence about " the ultimate supreme reality," which must constitute the opposite pole of the " basic act of religion," is insured as against the suspicion of subjective illusion, because this basic act of religion *qua* I-related has for itself the " prime-reality of all certainty and validity in the real," namely the I-consciousness (*Syst. Theol.* vol. II 1921 p. 456), that only proves that as adherents of indirect Cartesianism we are forced, at the point upon which everything depends, to take refuge in its original and direct form and swear by the certainty of the self-certainty of man in general. Actually our experience, when we point to what the Word of God achieves on, in, and through us, is pretty much that of Aaron when, in presence of Pharaoh and his Court, he caused his rod to turn into a serpent: " then Pharaoh also called the wise men and the sorcerers : now the magicians of Egypt, they also did in like manner, with their enchantments : for they cast down every man his rod, and they became serpents " (Ex. 7[10f.]) ; only that we unfortunately cannot command the sequel, " but Aaron's rod swallowed up their rods."

It might, of course, be objected that all through we had grasped first, so to speak, the outward aspect of the experienceable act in question, that we had, so to speak, first envisaged it as a phenomenon. It would, of course, have to be conceded (it might be said) that in that way it could not come to be recognised as this particular act, that in that way we could not reach certainty as to its genuineness ; but surely it would be quite a different thing to ask what the man thought of as acting thus knew about himself ; whether for this man—and, so far as this man is appealed to as naturally the authoritative witness to the content in question, generally also—the act is not characteristically, unambiguously, visibly, and comprehensibly contrasted with all other acts and possibilities as this act and no other, and, therefore, visibly and comprehensibly as the possibility we are looking for, of experiencing (or knowing) the Word of God. Our answer is that, as a matter of fact, the relativity of the act, apparently so inevitable, might have its own limit in the limit of its external aspect, in the limit of its purely theoretical standpoint ; whereas beyond that (on the basis of its inward aspect, and so on the analysis of its existential character) it might open up new territory for itself, and there might result in addition a certain interpretation of the act in respect of its relation to the Word of God. How could we refuse to entertain the proposal thus to broaden or deepen the putting of the question ? One thing, however, we must stipulate : the man conceived of in this act, who must be the witness here, whose self-evidence must here be decisive, will have to be man as we know him from the promise. Only this man can tell us how it stands with the possibility which corresponds to real experience of the Word of God. My self-evidence here can only be important, so far as I regard myself as confronted by the promise, i.e. by the Word of God meeting me in revelation, Scripture, and Church proclamation, so far as I behold myself in the perfectly definite light which falls upon my existence from that quarter. Analysis of my self-evidence can only have the meaning here of an appeal to what the promise tells each individual about himself, to what only the promise itself can tell him about himself with decision and effectiveness. Asseverations about an individual set of conditions, if that is what " existential " language means, can be of no importance here. If on this proviso we were to adopt as our own the demand to allow the inward aspect also of the appreci-able act of acknowledgment and so of Christian experience to become articulate, what else could we say but this, that regarded from this particular point of view it is literally not the human act as such, the experienceable and the experienced as such, the thing really put into our hands, the thing man can achieve and fix as such, which absolutely distinguishes, characterises, and qualifies this act among and from man's other possibilities as the act in which determination of man by the Word of God takes place. Undoubtedly the man who is really determined by the Word of God will fulfil this act. There is no real knowledge of the Word of God without fulfil-ment of this act. When a man recognises the Word of God, all that we have said about this act becomes experienceable and experienced, psychologically real and definable : there takes place an understanding, a personal sense of being touched, an affirmation, assent, and approval, a concentration of remote times in the present, an obedience, a decision, a standing still before the mystery and a stimulation by its inner life, a founding of the whole man upon this mystery that lies upon his thither side. All that happens and must happen.

That man's encounter with God according to OT and NT is the opposite of a transcendental drama which man confronts almost as a bored onlooker, that the Biblical concepts of renewal and sanctification, of faith, knowledge, and obedience, of repentance, love, humility, thankfulness, etc., invariably point also to a perfectly concrete, experienceable, and psychologically fixable event and act, that admittedly no less a person than Luther repeatedly insisted upon. In this connection we recall only some of the most general passages in which in particular the nature of this event as experienceable is singled out. " The same peace hovers over all thought, reason, and understanding. Whereby thou must not understand that no one may feel or sense it ; for if we are to have peace with God, then must we first feel it in heart and conscience, how else could our heart and mind become assured thereof ? " . . . (*Adventspostille, Phil.* 4[4f.], 1522 W. edn. 10[1,2], p. 186, l. 15). " For if a man then surely entereth illusion as though possessing faith, and yet never experiencing it, he must rot and dry up, and naught is found, when it comes to the fight, where it should be found " (*Sermon on John* 4[10f.], 1532 W. edn. 36, p. 468, l. 29). " If then ye have grasped the resurrection of Christ with faith and have received power and comfort of the same, and are therefore risen together with Him, that must prove itself such in you that it is felt and in you traced according as it hath begun to work in you, that it is not alone word, but truth and life. For to those who have not thus felt it, hath Christ not yet arisen." . . . (*Cruc. Sommerpostille, Sermon on Col.* 3[1-7], W. edn. 21, p. 266, l. 20) . . . " take to thyself the Word of God, go and listen to man's preaching, or read or write or even sing it, so that thy sole concern and act is with it, then wilt thou feel somewhat that will not fail " (*Sermon on Luke* 24[13ff.], 1523 W. edn. 12, p. 500, l. 10) . . . " the call of the spirit in the heart must thou feel, for it is first also thy heart's call, how shouldst thou then not feel it ? . . . If thou feelest not the call, take thought and cease not to pray till God hear thee : for thou art Cain and it standeth not well with thee . . ." (*Kirchenpostille*, 1522 *Sermon on Gal.* 4[1f.], W. edn. 10[1,1], p. 372, l. 10 and p. 373, l. 2). Cf. also Calvin : *consequitur fidem a pio affectu nullo modo esse distrahendam* (*Instit.* III 2, 9). *Id autem* (the certification of faith) *fieri nequit, quin eius* (God's goodness) *suavitatem vere sentiamus et experiamur in nobis ipsis* (*ib.* III 2, 15).

But that all this happens and must happen, simply does not mean that in this event is to be seen and found the possibility of experiencing the Word of God, that in it man's self-determination becomes the opposite pole of the divine determination, that from man there results a " Word-bound ego," by the consideration of which we have to take our bearings when we raise the question of the Word of God. The very man who is really conceived of in this act will never in this world, even partially, even in the very tiniest part, see in this act as such something that makes possible the meaning, basis, and end, the truth and reality of this act. However genuinely or well or powerfully he may " feel," at least he will not feel himself an " opposite pole," he will not think of quitting his sphere to become a " Word-bound ego," he will not, even partially, expect fresh experience in the form of a self-experience. He will indeed be called by the Word of God in his whole existence, " with all his heart, with all his soul, with all his mind, and with

all his powers," he himself will be in it. But not for one moment
or in any respect will he adjudge his thus being in it as being even
approximately an adequate counterpart of the award and claim
which faces him. Not for one moment or in any respect, merely
because he is thus in it, will he put his confidence in the fact, take
his bearings by it, derive from it the measure for understanding the
reality in which he stands ; he will not reflect upon it at all, but
will simply be in it. Not for one moment or in any respect will he
dream of coming back on it, holding to it, or building upon it,
because he, he, has been in it. Upon his being in it, is passed the
judgment which the divine Word passes by its taking place. What
experienceable acknowledgment of the Word of God, what comprehension, impact, assent, obedience, etc., would even remotely
correspond to what would be worth calling real acknowledgment
of the Word of God ? What experienceable acknowledgment of
the Word of God would not in the act of taking place be discovered
and convicted by the Word of God itself—not of its undoubted
imperfection and insufficiency, but of its utter perversion, and
nullity ; for as surely as all else we do, it is the work of the human
heart, whose inventive efforts are bad from youth up and can only
be helped by forgiveness ? In what experienceable acknowledgment of the Word of God as such therefore could there be present
anything like a necessary and certain correspondence with the
Word of God ? If there really is, then it is certainly because of an
acknowledgment which man does not achieve and therefore cannot
fix, but which by grace counters his work, corrupted and dead by
sin, because of Christ and not of his own inner economy. How else
could it be with a religious man, one who has faith in Christ ?
Of course it is he who knows, who is the only person who does
know, that thus it is and not otherwise. The statement *finitum non
capax infiniti* at this point really could not prove what is to be
proved. If the real experience of a man addressed by the
Word of God were to speak against this statement, this statement would have to go, as every philosophical statement in
theology must go which contradicts this experience. As a
philosophical statement it does not interest us in the very
slightest. We shall not say *finitum*, but we shall say *homo
peccator non capax* — and we shall not continue *infiniti*, but
verbi Domini. It is this real experience of the man claimed
by the Word of God, which decides and proves that what makes
it possible lies beyond it.

3. The Word of God and Experience

We think of Peter's ἐξελθε ἀπ' ἐμοῦ ὅτι ἀνήρ ἁμαρτωλός εἰμι (Luke 5⁸), and the words of the father of the epileptic boy, Πιστεύω· βοήθει μου τῇ ἀπιστίᾳ (Mark 9²⁴). Therefore, the same Luther who puts experience so high can and must also say on the same lines : " faith is such that it feeleth not but droppeth the intellect, shutteth the eyes and simply surrendereth to the Word, followeth the same through death and life. But feeling goeth not beyond what can be grasped by intellect and mind, as what is heard, seen, and felt or known by the outward senses. Therefore, feeling is counter to faith, faith to feeling. Whoso then pursueth feeling is destroyed, but whoso counter to feeling dependeth heartily upon the Word will be carried through " (Sommerpostille, 1526 Sermon on Mark 16¹ᶠ·, W. edn. 10¹·², p. 222, l. 34). " But an I believe God and be born anew, I close my eyes and grope not and let the soul's being wholly perish and exclaim, Ah, God, in thy hand standeth my soul, Thou hast preserved it in my life and I have never yet known where thou hast set it down, therefore will I likewise not know what Thou wilt do with it now and henceforth, of this alone am I sure, it standeth in Thy hand, Thou wilt surely help it " (Sommerpostille, 1526 Sermon on John 3¹⁻¹⁵, W. edn. 10¹·², p. 301, l. 20). " The Word which I speak thou hearest of course : but thou knowest neither its beginning nor its end. Just as thou knowest not where the wind starteth or where it ceaseth, so also thou knowest not whence the Word cometh and whither it tendeth. The bodily voice and the outward sound thou hearest of course, but the power of the Word thou seest not, what it effects, how the Spirit worketh with and by the Word. Therefore, the Word must be believed against all sight and feeling of the understanding. If we would discuss much how it befalleth, 'tis all up " (Sermon on John 3¹⁻¹⁵, 1532 E. edn. 4, p. 177). " And so not a Christian do I see. Nor can I myself say, This hour or in that state shall I become a Christian. In short 'tis not within sight or time or state, 'tis beyond grasp and feeling, it dependeth not on apparel, or on this or that which we see and feel, 'tis literally naught.—Well, what concern of mine, if 'tis naught ? Yea 'tis naught if thou quiz thy five senses thereon or take counsel with thy mind and thy wisdom. But thou must set aside sense and mind and consider 'twere somewhat other that makes a Christian, whereof thou hearest no more than the breath and rustle. An thou hearest the voice, follow it and have faith in it, so shalt thou be born anew " (Expos. John 3, 1538–40 W. edn. 47, p. 29, l. 22). This, too, is the place to recall a thought which Calvin was often fond of expressing. This, he says, is the weakness and folly of all philosophical talk about the " highest good " that by it man is held fast to himself, quum necesse sit extra nos exire. Surely the highest good is coniunctio cum Deo. But this would demand conformatio on man's part with God. This again could only take place in a negation of man, in a complete quiescere ab operibus nostris. And therefore hinc semper faciendum est exordium, quum de regula pie sancteque vivendi agitur, ut homo sibi quodam modo mortuus Deum patitur vivere ; ferietur ab operibus propriis, ut locum Deo agenti concedat. Fateri enim necesse est, tunc recte demum constitutam esse vitam quum Deo subjecta est. Atqui propter ingenitam pravitatem hoc numquam fit, donec a propriis operibus supersedemus. Talis inquam repugnantia est inter Dei gubernationem et nostros affectus, ut in nobis agere, nisi otiosis, nequeat (Comm. Heb. 4¹⁰, C.R. 55, 48).

With this " collapse of the nature of the soul," with " 'tis literally naught " in Luther and with locum concedere Deo agenti, the passivity, in fact death, of man before the divine act in Calvin, a mystic train of ideas has already indubitably taken the stage. We ought not to object to it, because this train of ideas is scarcely to be avoided at this point. If experience of the Word of God is such that it can only have its basis and its certainty outside itself, then in regarding it as real, genuine experience we are bound in fact to take account of its proper, radical end, of the circumstances that here it really involves collapse and death on man's part. That is the new country which opens up, the very moment Christian experience is not only considered as a phenomenon, but is allowed to speak for itself. If we care to give the name of mystical thought to the thought of what is Beyond all experience and which becomes visible at that moment, it is not worth while objecting to the expression. So long as it remains clear—what in so-called mystical thinking often does not remain clear—that this Beyond cannot be, so to speak, a hinterland—still to be trodden and occupied—to the realm of man's acts, experiences, and possessions, a human act, or act-content, now to be determined by new methods. Rather it is the Beyond in which real experience itself actually seeks and finds its basis, in connection with which it is aware of itself as real genuine experience, in the acknowledgment of which alone it claims to consist, to consist apart from any claim to a content or importance of its own, so to consist that its claim to consist rests upon acknowledgment of its source and its end—this Beyond claims consideration as the genuine irremovable Beyond that cannot be brought to this side, claims consideration as the Beyond of God the Lord, the Creator, the Reconciler, the Redeemer. Human self-determination, even though it actually takes place in acknowledgment of the Word of God, i.e. human experience of the Word of God, will, if it is really that, never dream of seeing, contemplating, or regarding itself as determined by the Word of God. It will be so, without seeing or regarding itself in this being which it has acquired. It will quite simply be true from God's side, that human existence is here engaged in the acknowledgment of the Word of God. For it will be true that God hath spoken and man hath heard. In the act of such acknowledgment a new reborn man will arise as one addressed by God and listening to God—of course unknown as such to himself and others, in a newness that cannot be fixed ; what can be fixed will in his case always be what is old—not possessing himself : so far as he possesses himself, he will certainly not possess this newborn man—but it will be true that he is kept in the peace of God which passes all understanding. It will be true in utter independence of all standards of truth which the secular or even the religious man might first of all have to furbish up and review, or ever with the best intentions he comes to a conclusion as to what is true or admissible as true. All that will be true in itself, as the Word of God is true in itself ; nay, its trueness will be nothing else (neither an opposite pole ! nor a subjective correspondence !) than the trueness of the Word of God itself. The possibility of knowing the Word of God lies in the Word of God and nowhere else. Its reality can literally only ta ke pla ce, and as a visible miracle at that, visible to every man, secular or religious, Greek or Jew.

" It is but an appearance that the rainbow stands on the earth, in reality it is vaulted over the earth ; true it lets itself down to earth, but it stands not upon our earth, but is perceived only from there. So it is with the divine truth ; the same needs no human support, as little as the rainbow needs the earth. True it illumines man and he notices it. Still it is never dependent on man. It withdraws and man remains in darkness : it returns and man walks in the light. But man is not its assistant ; he cannot produce the light; likewise he cannot hoard it up!" (E d u a r d B ö h l, *Dogmatik*, 1886 p. xxv). " Therefore if I die—but I die no more—and some one finds my skull, let this skull still preach to him, saying, I have no eyes, yet I behold Him ; I have neither brain nor understanding, yet I comprehend Him ; I have no lips; yet I kiss Him ; I have no tongue, yet I praise Him with you all, who call upon His name. I am a hard skull, yet am I quite softened and melted in His love ; I lie outside here in the churchyard, yet am I within in Paradise ! All suffering is forgotten. That hath His great love done for us, since for us He bore His Cross and went forth unto Golgotha " (H. Fr. K o h l b r ü g g e, *Passionspredigten*, 1913³ p. 173 ff.). Thus speaks true Christian experience.

This miracle is fa ith, about which we shall have to say what is needful in this context in paragraph 4 of this section.

Let us here draw the last line in our course of thought so far. Faced with Christian Cartesianism we put the question, whether the thesis that the possibility of experiencing the Word of God resides in consciousness is to be defended with that ultimate human seriousness appropriate to its importance for dogmatics, Church proclamation, and the Church generally, whether we are to put our hand in the fire for it—whether, we might also ask, we are to pledge ourselves to present and uphold it as the *articulus stantis et cadentis ecclesiae*. We have seen that the act of acknowledging the Word of God, so far as its immanence in consciousness is fixable from without, whether historico-psychologically, through observation of self or through observation of others, cannot for a moment be clearly described as t h i s act, far less does it become knowable in its connection with a Word of God. What can be fixed are human possibilities in immovable proximity and indelible similarity to other human possibilities. And we have seen that here, too, a transition to " existential " thinking not only does not help us any further, but finally confirms us in the conclusion that there is nothing to be gained by it. For if this kind of thought is the self-interpretation of the man who has submitted to receiving a message about himself through the Word of God, then this inner aspect of Christian experience will actually testify that real acknowledgment of the Word of God by no means rests upon a possibility imparted to man and now inherent in him, immanent in him, but upon the Word of God itself which man can in no sense anticipate with his possibilities but can only follow.—And so for our part we must now assert the following positive conclusion, that this possibility as distinguished from those others which slip through our fingers, the possibility of human experience of the Word of God, regarded as the possibility of this Word itself—we may and must affirm it with certainty, with ultimate human seriousness ; it may and must in fact be presented and upheld as an *articulus stantis et cadentis ecclesiae,* for its character as a distinctive possibility we may actually put our hand in the fire. By connecting ourselves with this possibility in dogmatics, in Church proclamation, and in the Church generally, we shall invariably be building not upon sand but upon rock.

H. M. Müller (*Credo ut intelligam, Theol. Bl.* 1928 Sp. 167 f.) reproached me with countering, in my dogmatics, the " unheard-of assurance " of Neo-protestantism merely with another. Of course ! is my only possible reply. The " assurance " of the Neo-protestant thesis is not " unheard-of " because it is assurance, but because it simply is not, cannot be, but only purports to be. The certainty with which dogmatics, Church proclamation, and the Church have to deal in the possibility of human knowledge of the Word of God cannot be great enough, and it is, of course, my opinion—and naturally not mine alone—that in the case of the single distinctive possibility under consideration here, in the case of personal assurance about the divine Word it must be emphatically an " unheard-of " assurance.

The question, of course, will arise repeatedly whether we have knowledge of this possibility. Yet it stands or falls with the reality of the Word of God being uttered to us, which as such we cannot anticipate, which we can have before us and expect only as the event of the grace of God. In this event the possibility of knowing the word of God comes into sight for us, not otherwise and not previously. Which means that it comes into sight for us by being realised, by our having knowledge of the Word of God, by our self-determination being determined by the Word of God. We are acquainted with it from the moment we can still only affirm it, because we ourselves are its realisation in our entire existence. The question is whether we are acquainted with it, because by coming into view for us this event consists with the freedom of God. Grace would not be grace if God could not give or also refuse us this reality and with it, too, this possibility. The knowability of the Word of God therefore stands or falls with the act of really knowing it, which is withdrawn from our disposal. Upon this realisation therefore it also depends whether we can be acquainted with it and affirm it ; upon it depends also the assurance of this affirmation. It can only be the assurance of faith, the assurance of the man whom God in His free grace has not passed by, but whom by His Word He has called to faith, and who being called by His Word stands in the faith. In faith the man possesses and knows and affirms only this possibility of knowing the Word of God, that which lies in the Word of God itself, which came to him in the Word and is present to him in the Word. The assurance of his affirmation of this possibility can therefore only be that of the Word of God itself. Now that means that his assurance is not a self-assurance. He is sure not of himself but of the Word of God ; and, moreover, of the Word of God he is sure, not of and in himself but of and in the Word. His assurance is, of course, his assurance, but it has its seat outside him, in the Word of God, and so it is his assurance by the Word of God being present to him.

Quare facile senties, si advertas, hunc affectum ex tuis viribus in te non esse ; impetrandus ergo per humilem et in seipso desperatum spiritum. Fabulae ergo sunt opinatorum Scholasticorum, hominem esse incertum, in statu salutis esse necne. Cave tu, ne aliquando sis incertus, sed certus, quod in te ipso perditus : laborandum autem, ut certus et solidus sis in fide Christi pro peccatis tuis traditi (Luther, *Comm. Gal.* 1⁴, 1519 W. edn. 2, p. 458, l. 26).

If the Word of God is present to us that means that we are turned from ourselves and turned towards the Word of God, conformed to the Word of God. To stand in the faith means to be called to new faith. The presence of the Word of God and standing in the faith, therefore, mean keeping before one and expecting the Word and faith, fresh direction to the free realisation of the grace just experienced, fresh clinging to the promise, fresh vision after the event in which the possibility of knowing the Word of God comes into view for us.

ἐλάβομεν καὶ χάριν ἀντὶ χάριτος (John 1¹⁶). The righteousness of God is revealed ἐκ πίστεως εἰς πίστιν (Rom. 1¹⁷). But that may and must also mean παρ᾽ ἐλπίδα ἐπ᾽ ἐλπίδι ἐπίστευσεν (Rom. 4¹⁸).

17

The man, the Church, the Church proclamation, the dogmatics which claimed to be able to work with the Word and with faith as with a capital sum standing at their disposal, would simply prove thereby that they possessed neither the Word nor faith. Where there is possession of them, we simply do not take it for granted as such, we strain after it hungering and thirsting, the only way of blessedness. And so, too, after the possibility of knowing the Word of God. Exactly where we k n o w it, we e x p e c t to know it. Assurance in affirming it is thus assurance in expecting it, an expectation which rests upon its previous presence, upon the promise grasped, we might even at this stage say, which rests upon baptism received and believed in—but e x p e c t a t i o n. When we assert the possibility of knowing the Word of God, that means that we p u t o u r s e l v e s in r e l a t i o n with the event of its realisation. And that, of course, means, not that we assert it but that we confess it, as one must confess the faith one believes in, as alone one can confess to the event of the grace of God. This event, grace, and in and along with grace, faith, must come first. In confession, in connecting ourselves with the grace already proclaimed to us, already received by us, there results an affirmation of the possibility given to man of knowing the Word of God. Thus by affirming this possibility we are very seriously asked how we get to that point, whether we have not thereby presumed upon something which we must not presume upon, whether perhaps we were not of a mind to build a tower without having estimated the cost, whether thereby we are not claiming and purporting to be something, the right to be which we must have received, in order really to be it. The Church, Church proclamation, dogmatics must be aware that in affirming explicitly or implicitly the possibility of knowing the Word of God they stand at the crisis of this question, the question, From which side of the road ? Really from that of the Word, really from that of faith, really from that of baptism believed in ? And precisely also, if that is for them the real origin of it, their affirmation of this possibility can only be a relating of themselves to the fresh future event of the realisation of this possibility. This possibility is always being included and abrogated in this realisation. From that side it is always wanting to make itself known and to present itself to us, on that side, as made known and presented to us, it is always wanting to be sought and found afresh. The assurance of affirming it is thus really the certainty of expecting it. Assurance about grace, faith, baptism believed in, is the assurance of the faith that looks ahead in hope renewed. It cannot be otherwise : the assurance of this expectation is an assurance in profoundest jeopardy. Yet in this expectation a man must let go and abandon all his own imported assurance. But if he is thereby thrown completely upon free grace, the place of which might be taken by the condemnation he deserves, then without realisation in God's Word, even the possibility of knowing it would be done for, and what would then become of all our cocksure affirmation of this possibility ? Thus the assurance of this expectation is a trembling assurance. Its power lies in submission to grace or non-grace. Regarded by itself it is baseless, without hold upon God, and, moreover worthless, alongside the other forms of human assurance which have their seat not so strictly outside of man. It is more human, i.e. more unsure than all other human assurances, just because it is the assurance of expectation, this expectation. And yet "unheard-of assurance"? Yet an assurance which with calm and confidence may be set over against that assurance, anchored in human self-consciousness, of the directly or indirectly Cartesian thesis as to the knowability of the Word of God, set over against it as in every respect superior ? Yes, indeed ; for here even that cannot be otherwise ; just because it is in such profound jeopardy, just because it is connected with a sanction which we cannot create but can only hope for, just because it is included in the divine realisation and so withdrawn from our reach and so only to be sought there, only to be expected thence, for these reasons and in these ways it is an assurance which bears in itself a metal which makes it superior to any other assurance : because and so far as it is the confession of God's free grace, and therefore just because and so far as it is submission to grace and non-grace, i.e. an appeal to God Himself. Which, of course, once more, it only is so far as it is the assurance of grace already received, the grace of faith, the grace of baptism. If it is this assurance— the question is and it depends upon God, whether our assurance is this assurance—but if it is this assurance, then our affirmation of the knowability of the Word of God is the knocking to which it is opened. So it takes place in the region of the promise and of faith, in which there is no Yea and Nay, but only Yea. By praying that it may have power to be this boundless affirmation, it is in its utter humanness an affirmation of " unheard-of " assurance.

" (A man) must not doubt or waver as to whether he is one of those to whom such grace and mercy are given, who have surely received them by baptism or sacrament. Where then he believeth this, he must freely say of himself that he is holy, pious, good, and God's child, certain of blessedness, and must not doubt therein at all, not because of himself òr of his merit and work, but of the pure mercy of God, poured out upon him in Christ. The same he regardeth, however great it be, so that he doubteth not that it maketh him holy and God's child. And where he doubteth it, he doeth his baptism and sacrament the highest dishonour and accuseth of a lie God's Word and grace in the sacrament. For here should be no fear or wavering that he is pious and God's child by grace ; but only fear and carefulness as to how then he may remain steadfast till the end, in which alone all fear and carefulness stand ; for there all bliss is assured. But it is uncertain and matter of anxiety whether he stand fast and maintain it, since we must walk in fear ; for such faith boasteth not of work or self, but solely of God ; and the same grace of His can and may not leave him, so long as the boasting lasteth. But how long it will last he wots not : whether some temptation may drive him so that such boasting ceaseth, and so the grace ceaseth also. So Solomon means in Eccles. 9, ' The righteous and their works are in the hand of God ' ; yet is it all set in future uncertainty, so that man knoweth not whether he is worthy of grace or the opposite. He sayeth not that it is uncertain in the present but in the future. Wherefore it is that a man knoweth not whether he will withstand the assaults of temptation " (Luther, *Kirchenpostille*, 1522 *Sermon on Gal.* 1[4f.], W. edn. 10[I,1], p. 331, l. 17.)

Because surrounded by this ultimate lack of assurance, by the freedom of God, the assurance of our affirmation of the knowability of the Word of God cannot be great enough. Our care should be that when it takes place it should be limited enough, and really we need not fear the danger of " absolutising," so fearfully painted upon the wall at this stage by those who do not understand.

4. THE WORD OF GOD AND FAITH

At the beginning of this section we said that we could only inquire into the knowability, not into the knowledge of the Word of God, because knowledge of the Word of God is nothing else than the grace of God meeting the reality of men, the mode of which as a reality is as hidden from us as God Himself, and therefore we can only connect with it by our continual questions and answers. God has revealed it and will reveal it and man may proclaim it. Our question cannot be, " How does that come about ? " but only, supposing it does come about, how it can come about, how we should regard the fact, that men become the subject or object of this happening. But now this very question has led us back again, quite rightly for the first time, to that happening itself. We found that the possibility of knowing God was literally founded, raised, and bound up in the very event of its realisation, and our Yea to this possibility became a particular indication of this event. We cannot bring this event upon the stage and so we cannot prove our indication ; we could only prove it by bringing the event it indicates on to the stage and letting it speak for itself. We can therefore only ask further—and we must, of course, put the question—what is the meaning of this indication in our context, how far, in what sense, by what special compulsion we indicate that event as the centre at which the question of the knowability of the Word of God is decided. To the question so put the answer is that we indicate this event as the event of faith. Faith—in the discussions in paragraph 3 on experience towards the close we could, thus early, no longer avoid this concept—is what takes place in real knowledge of the Word of God and makes this knowledge possible. The event in question may and must still be regarded as one among many other concepts. In accordance with general Church and theological tradition we select this name at this point, because in practice it signifies, at once with precision and with comprehensiveness, the element in this event which constitutes it the thing that makes knowledge of the Word of God possible. To the question, what is that reality of the knowledge of God, so far as its knowability is included in it, which is so inconceivable in its mode, which is to be revealed only by God, and proclaimed by men only in His service and in virtue of His presence, the only possible answer which is adequate and exhaustive is, This reality is faith.

We best make this clear to ourselves if we think of the use of the concept πίστις in the NT. Πίστις may signify, as in Rom. 3³ and as in particular the use of the adjective πιστός shows, the faithfulness of God, His and His Word's reliability and trustworthiness, and so that attribute of God and His Word, in virtue of which a knowledge of God by man is attained to, which starts with God, because God is actually πιστός. But further, and as early as Paul (Rom. 12⁶ ; Gal. 1²³, 3²²ᶠ· ; 1 Tim. 4¹·⁶) and then Jude (³ and ⁶) πίστις is the teaching of faith, the Gospel revealed to man, and so the path on which, starting from God, knowledge of God is made possible to him by His making Himself known. Further and principally—think here of the so-called *genitivus mysticus* πίστις Ἰησοῦ Χριστοῦ, and of the many Pauline and Johannine passages to the same effect—πίστις signifies the position created by God's revelation in Christ, the existence of Christians, their existence ἐν Χριστῷ, by which they are put in the position of achieving knowledge of God, or knowledge of Christ as the Kyrios, on their own part also, the reality of men in which this achievement is an event. In πίστις Ἰησοῦ Χριστοῦ we see the divine decision taken about man. Next, from that point the concept begins, so to speak, to slip downwards into the sphere of human modes of acting ; πίστις now appears (here should belong the great bulk of Synoptic passages, though also many from the Epistles) described more or less often and clearly as trust, as that relationship of men in which they honour and reverence God's worthiness, His readiness to help, His power, His truth as it meets them in Christ, by their acknowledgment of them as such, by their submission to them : the possibility of knowing His Word, commanded by God in Christ, is now realised in this relationship. Πιστεύειν is now the decision achieved by the peculiar relationship of man. Admittedly in that case πίστις can be used in a further and more concrete sense to denote a Christian spiritual gift or virtue, besides which there are others, and beside which others it is not particularly prominent, beside which indeed it (1 Cor. 13¹³) may drop into the background. And in conclusion πίστις, πιστεύειν, πιστός come also simply to denote what we might term the Christian religion, meaning adherence to it, and so to denote the extremely and directly visible historical phenomenon (in the form of a particular communion, or particular cultus, or particular confession, or particular way of life) the relativity and questionable nature of which may then be accentuated with the familiar sharpness with which it is done in the Epistle of James. How far removed we apparently are here from the so objectively valid πίστις Θεοῦ of Rom. 3¹³, as also from the so cryptically significant and effective πίστις Ἰησοῦ Χριστοῦ. And yet in reality all these meanings of the concept have a single denominator : invariably, however objective or subjective, central or circumferential, single or multiple in meaning the use of the concept may be, from the mystery of God right down to what any one could see directly in the streets of Corinth or Rome, πίστις is the real thing that happens, which rests upon the will and Word of God, which is connected with the will and Word of God, in which at all events the fact also is included, that the proclamation of Christ to men is proved true, in which men, touched by its truth, themselves become bearers of it ; in a word, the event in which knowledge of God becomes real.—Πίστις expresses more than γνῶσις, but invariably it expresses γνῶσις too. A u g u s t i n e is therefore right in saying : *Si tollatur assensio, fides tollitur ;. quia sine assensione nihil creditur* (*Enchir.* 20). And likewise T h o m a s A q u i n a s is right in his definition : *fides cognitio quaedam est, in quantum intellectus determinatur per fidem ad aliquod cognoscibile* (*S. theol.* 1 q. 12, art. 13). And with corresponding decisiveness B o n a v e n t u r a : *Fides non est aliud nisi habitus, quo intellectus noster voluntarie captivatur in obsequium Christi* (*Sent.* III *d.* 23 *a.* 1 *q.* 1, quoted acc. to R. S e e b e r g, *Dogmengeschichte* vol. III 2–3 edn. 1913 p. 336). L u t h e r is likewise on the same lines : *fides nihil aliud esse quam veritatem cordis hoc est rectam cogitationem cordis de Deo* (*Comm. Gal.* 3⁷, 1535 W. edn. 40ᴵ, p. 376, l. 23). *Apprehenditur Christus . . . ratione seu intellectu informato fide et illa apprehensio Christi per fidem proprie est speculativa vita* (*ib.* Gal. 3¹³, W. edn. 40ᴵ, p. 447, l. 15). *Fides est in intellectu . . . Fides dictat et dirigit intellectum. . . . Est igitur fides doctrina seu notitia. . . . Fides habet objectum veritatem. . . . Primum omnium pius habere debet rectam opinionem et intellectum fide informatum. . . . Fides igitur est Dialectica, quae concipit ideam omnium credendorum* (*ib.* Gal. 5⁶, W. edn. 40ᴵᴵ, p. 26, l. 11 f., p. 28, l. 9 f.). And C a l v i n : *non in ignoratione sed in cognitione sita est fides* (*Inst.* III 2, 2). *Fateor . . . generale fidei obiectum . . . esse Dei veritatem* (*ib.* III 2, 30). But the content of the concept γνῶσις is so included in the concept πίστις that it is patent how God Himself or Christ is at once the object, the meaning, the warrant and the measure of true knowledge of God, without the latter ceasing to be a perfectly concrete act, achieved through men and experienced by men.

Thus it is in faith, as the possibility given in faith, that we must regard the knowability of the Word of God. In the event of faith it is as it were born, it comes into view, it is to be sought and found.

Of the event of faith as the NT understands it, according to the particular reading of it by the Evangelical Church, there are now three things to be said, at least because they are important in our context, the outcome of which must also be three different determinations of the concept of the knowability of the Word of God.

1. In faith as real experience through the known Word of God the control passes as it were to acknowledgment of the Word of God, which we regarded as the concrete form in which it is experienced by men. No matter in what perfection or imperfection of form human action, regarded as acknowledgment, may take place, in faith it is the right, the accepted, the acknowledged acknowledgment, not because man in himself has the power of, not because he has of himself succeeded in, achieving this right acknowledgment, but because what he actually can and does compass is acknowledged by the acknowledged Word of God, not as self-determination, but as self-determination determined by the Word of God. Let us hold on to the fact that faith is experience, a concretely fixable temporal act of this man's or that, the act, in short, of acknowledgment. But it does not go without saying that experience is real experience, experience of the Word of God. Of no experience as such, however perfect a form it may have, could this be said. Therefore, it is not as experience that faith is faith, i.e. real experience, although it is certainly experience. Or, the act of acknowledgment is not as such acknowledgment of the Word of God. Nor is it so in virtue of any degree of perfection with which it may be achieved. But it is the Word, it is Christ, to whom faith is related, because He gives Himself as object to it, who makes faith into faith, into real experience. Of course, because He gives Himself to it as object! For faith is not already faith because it has or is a relation—it might in fact be an objectless relation with an imagined object—but because the Word of God is given to it as the object of this connection, as the object of acknowledgment and therewith as the ground of real faith.

A particularly instructive document, especially in view of the epistemological problem, for the constitutive meaning of the object of faith for faith is the first chapter of Anselm of Canterbury's *Proslogion*. In closest material connection with the famous proof of the existence of God which immediately follows on it, there is brought up in the form of a prayer the problem, whether God is present at all to the thinker who sets about to understand and explain precisely the existence and the nature of God. He requires Him in order to be the man who can see and therefore understand Him properly, but particularly in order to have Him generally as the discoverable object of his search. *Quando illuminabis oculos nostros et ostendes nobis faciem tuam?* . . . *Nec quaerere te possum, nisi tu doceas, nec invenire, nisi te ostendas.* And Anselm anything but finds himself in this presence of God so necessary to him in a twofold sense. God's face is as much hidden from him as he finds himself blind. The twofold encounter which he needs from God's side does not take place. By that he means not the metaphysical inconceivability of God, but specifically the mystery of God which can only be regarded as a punishment upon sinful man, that as a son of Adam he knows his exact situation in this respect. At the same time he does not somewhat rhetorically transport himself into the condition of a heathen by so speaking. No: *Tu me fecisti et refecisti et omnia mea bona tu mihi contulisti et nondum novi te.* It is therefore altogether as a Christian that he feels he must say what he does say. Again, it can not be a case of this Christian experiencing an accidental and passing relapse from faith into unbelief, for in the same breath he describes his condition thus : *Desidero aliquatenus intelligere veritatem tuam, quam credit et amat cor meum.* In all this there is really no special need to remember that the whole thing takes place within the sphere of the Catholic Church, against the background of its unshakably acknowledged creed. " The Archbishop (? not till thirty years later !) is not a bad Catholic " (H. M. Müller, *Theol. Bl.* 1928 *Sp.* 169 f.). Of course by that and by all that is said before, it is conceded that the unrest, with which Anselm is on the look out for God's presence, is not an absolute unrest, not a negative counterpart to the peace of God, but a man's relative unrest, which as such has its definite place and free play, and which in the Church is countered by a rest somewhere and somehow, perhaps as his rest, but also perhaps not his rest at all! still at all events as a rest superior to his unrest. Would not a desire to be unrestful which excluded all outlook upon this superior rest, would not the assertion of an absolute unrest be the most foolish of all foolish human self-apotheoses ? For can and may a destruction of man's possibility of recognising God, as, of course, is the intention of this chapter from Anselm, be carried to its full consequences? May we, in the Catholic or in the Evangelical Church persist in standing at the cross-roads, as H. M. Müller appears to demand of Anselm and of theologians generally ? As if men this side the end of all things were in a position to stand at an absolute cross-roads! If there takes place in the sphere of the Church a real honest human search, must it not at once betray itself as one on which, for all its perhaps helpless despair, there still lies the reflection of search rewarded and already lies the reflection of fresh finds to come ? But be that as it may, humanly speaking, it is not pleasant, it has no basis in the text or in other texts of Anselm, and above all there is something extraordinarily foolish and unspiritual in it, when H. M. Müller abruptly finishes off with our chapter from Anselm because he assigns no serious importance to the question raised in it, his reason being that it is only raised within the " system," and so at once there is something mysterious about the answer to it. In so doing he suppresses the fact firstly, that as a question the question in the chapter in any case remains open absolutely, and is not settled either by appealing to the creed of the Church or to the *credere* of the Christian thinker, or even dialectically, or even by pointing to an already received answer to the prayer : why in the world should it not have been as deadly serious for Anselm as only an open question can be serious for a man—and for the very reason of his awareness that with this question of his he is within the sphere of the Church and therefore in the region of an answer which for him is wholly outstanding, and yet has already been given and certainly lies in the future ? And above all H. M. Müller fails to see that, if this question in Anselm practically stands in the reflection of its already achieved yet freshly future solution and nevertheless is a radically open question, to point to Anselm's " Catholicism " is really not to be taken as the only possible interpretation. We might add that it is still far from being proved that the suggestion of Anselm's " Catholicism " is bound to signify an interpretation *in malam partem*. Why should not the remarkable coincidence of ultimate disquiet and its ultimate solution, which, of course, is significant for this chapter of Anselm's, be viewed from the standpoint that Anselm prays by asking and asks by praying ? Is it not more pertinent and respectful to stick to this fact? May we ignore it, or discredit it as bad " Catholicism," because of an absolutely unprovable suspicion that there might be a " system " here ? Only by presuming this— and the inhumanity and at the same time the unspirituality of H. M. Müller's exposition of this matter is that he does presume this—only then can we treat Anselm's unrest as lightly as he does, against a background of the doctrine of absolute unrest, Anselm's unrest being, of course, not absolute but limited unrest. If we take the fact seriously that Anselm prayed in such unrest and in actual prayer was in such unrest, then we shall value the chapter as in its own way a distinctive illustration of how real, utterly certain, and hidden faith is always in transition from expectation to fresh expectation. All unrest in faith is in fact removed in prayer, but its actual prayer is its profound unrest. And alike as prayer and as unrest it is expectation, expecta- tion of its object. By its object it lives, at rest or in unrest, having found seeking, finding once more and seeking afresh. But this object is a free God, who is hidden from man because man is a sinner, who, of course, has transplanted him into the new state of faith in which He can be known by him, but who in this actual new state—it is the state of faith—will be sought and found anew and once more anew. He is and remains, of course, for faith, included in objectivity, in the externality of the Word of God, in Jesus Christ. He must teach man to seek Him, and He must show Himself to him, that he may find Him. But by this object, this external, Christian faith lives.

Non ex visione credentis, sed a visione eius cui creditur results that *deter- minatio intellectus ad aliquod cognoscibile* (Thomas Aquinas, *S. Theol.* 1 *qu.* 12 *art.* 13 *ad.* 3). *Non enim fides assentit alicui nisi quia est a Deo revelatum* (*ib.* 11² *qu.* 1 *art.* 1).—*Tolle verbum et nulla jam restabit fides* (Calvin, *Instit.* III 2, 6).—*Quoties nos de fide loquimur, intelligi volumus objectum scilicet misericordiam promissam. Fides non ideo iustificat, quia ipsa sit opus per sese dignum* (not . . . because in itself 'tis our work or ours) *sed tantum quia accipit misericordiam promissam* (Melanchthon, *Apology, art.* 4 *de justif.* 55 f. *cf.* 86). —*Non enim in sensum sed in promissionem recumbit fides* (C. Olevian, *De subst. foed.* 1585 p. 304, *cit. ap.* Heppe, *Dogmatik d. ev. ref. Kirche,* 1861 p. 388).—*Non propter fidem quatenus est virtus vel opus nostrum justificamur* (M. Chemnitz, *Loci theol.* 1591 vol. II p. 255) . . . *sed propter objectum quod fides apprehendit Christum* (*ib.* p. 252). *De fide non est statuendum ex sensu consolationis et gaudii spiritualis ; quia quintus ille gradus sequitur fidem, non est de essentia fidei et Deus sensum illum pacis credentibus saepe subtrahit* (*ib.* p. 252). *Ancoram fidei nostrae iactam esse in ipsum coelum et quidem ubi Christus pro nobis sacerdos* (*ib.* p. 257). Then with most delightful precision High Orthodoxy explains that *fides* is *justificans* not as a *qualitas inhaerens* or as an *actio* of man, but *ut est in praedicamento relationis*, as a relation (σχέσις) to its *objectum*. But once more not *per relationem* (through relating itself !) but *in relatione : quatenus sibi applicat et appropriat meritum Christi, cui unico dignitas illa competit*. In conclusion, it is to be said that the act of justifying faith (*fides quae justificat*) is, of course, correctly described by the concepts *notitia, assensus, fiducia*, but that this act as justifying (as *fides qua justificat*) is only to be regarded, so far as it is beyond what makes it into an act, as a *nuda apprehensio seu fiducialis acceptatio bonorum foeder- alium et beneficiorum Messiae passiva, admissiva motuum Spiritus, requietoria in sanguine et meritis Christi* (Quenstedt, *Theol. did.-pol.* 1685 III *c.* 8, *sect.* 2, *qu.* 6, *ekth*, 8–10).

In this context we must speak specially of L u t h e r. There are two sayings of Luther's, one of which especially is adduced over and over again by W o b b e r m i n in the theological discussion of to-day, with a persistency which obviously does not weary himself (finally, e.g. in *Richtlin. ev. Theol.* 1929 p. 124 f. ; *Wort Gottes und ev. Glaube*, 1931 p. 5) after having, together with its environment in Luther's text, already played an analogous part the previous century in A. Ritschl (*Rechtf. u. Vers.* 4th edn. vol. I p. 218 f. ; vol. 3, p. 201 f.). It runs, " faith and God belong together," and stands at the beginning of the exposition of the first commandment in the *Larger Catechism*. The other stands in the lecture on Romans and runs, so every reader of Wobbermin's likewise confidently believes : *fides et promissio sunt relativa* (instead of *relativa* Wobbermin persistently writes *correlativa*, cf. *Richtl.* pp. 109, 125, and *Wort Gottes*, p. 5). The first saying stands in the following context : " What does it mean to have a God, or what is God ? Answer : a God is that, by which one should be supplied with all good and with which one should take refuge in all necessities. Thus, to have a God is nothing else than to trust and believe in Him from the heart, as I have often said, which thing alone, the trust and faith of heart, maketh both, God and false god. If the faith and trust is right, so also is thy God right, and again where the trust is false and wrong, there also the right God is not. For the two belong together, faith and God. Whereon then (say I) thou hangest and confidest thy heart, that is really thy God " (*Deutsch Catechismus*, 1529 W. edn. 30[I], p. 132, l. 34). And the other : *fides et promissio sunt relativa : item cessante promissione cessat et fides et abolita promissione aufertur et fides et econtra* (*Gloss on Rom.* 4[14], Fi. p. 40, l. 24). We add for completeness sake two further sayings of Luther which tend in the same direction. The one as a parallel to the passage from the *Larger Catechism* : " As thou turnest and wheelest, so God, too, turneth and wheeleth. Thinkst thou, that He is wroth with thee, so He is wroth. Thinkst thou, that He is unmerciful to thee and wishful to thrust thee into hell, then so He is. As thou believest of God, so thou hast Him " (*Sermon on John* 4[47i.], 1534 E. edn. 5, 224). " There- fore as we believe so it befalleth us. If we hold Him for our God, He will certainly not be our devil. But if we hold Him not for our God, He is certainly likewise not our God, but must be a consuming fire " (*ib.* 5, p. 229). The other as a parallel to the *Gloss on Romans* : " So ought Word and faith to stand splendidly together. For the one cannot exist without the other. Whoso hath faith and hath not the Word, believeth like Turks and Jews. They have the faith that God is gracious and merciful. But the promise is lacking, for God will not be gracious apart from Christ. Thus, whoso hath the Word but not faith, there the Word accomplisheth naught. Thus Word and faith are given together in wedlock and naught can suffer them to part from one another (*Hauspost.* 1544 Sermon on Matt. 9¹ᶠ·, W. edn. 52, p. 498, l. 22). Wobbermin would prove by both these sentences that the relation between the Word of God and faith according to Luther is to be regarded as a relation of " connection," of " correlation," as a " circular " relation, a " relation of interchangeable connection," a " twin-pole " relation (*Richtl.* p. 125, 140 f. ; *Wort Gottes*, pp. 5 f., 14, 27 and frequently). I do not wish to make a fuss about these designations, although to me they are too ambiguous for me to adopt them, but here regarding Luther I would only make it clear that Luther says that in faith in man, whether wrong faith or unbelief, the decision depends upon the God a man has, and that therefore man always has the God he believes in. But that by no means implies that in a sense faith is the human counterpart of the Word of God, that the relation between the Word of God and faith is the symmetrical one of two partners—one superior and one subordinate, still, two partners—that this relation is as fundamentally founded on faith as on the Word of God. True, only faith has the right God, and this right God is, as the God believed in, that on which man sets the trust of his heart. But it is not the case that because He is believed in by man, the trust of his heart (not his " interest " in Him, as A. Ritschl said) makes Him the right God—as an object of faith or trust in itself He might even be an idol—but what makes Him the right God is that He is believed in with the right faith. The fact that the faith in which the right God is believed in is the right faith, is in no wise or sense due to itself, but to the fact that the right God has revealed Himself to it, due, i.e. to the Word of God. In this concept the circular movement of reflection must reach its end, and it reaches it in Luther too : for he indicates the point at which the real irreversible circular movement starts, a starts which is not in turn itself conditioned by an " opposite pole." In Wobbermin's view the sentence " faith and God belong together " may also be translated by the different one, " faith and the Word of God belong together " (*Wort Gottes*, p. 5). That might be thinkable, were this the only sentence we had to deal with. But in view of the rest of the content of the passage from the Catechism this translation does not hold : obviously Luther neither meant to say nor could say that the trust and faith of the heart constitutes the Word of God, that if man's faith and trust be right the Word of God is likewise right. In the Catechism passage his sole object is to say that " God " for man, in every case and in every sense of the Word, is that on which man puts his highest trust. There is then really no point in constructing one's understanding of Luther or one's whole theology upon this popular preamble. Neither in the Larger Catechism nor anywhere else has Luther himself taught the " God " thus defined, but just the right God of right faith ; nor in the question as to this God has he ever at any time pointed to faith as such and raised it to the dignity of an " opposite pole " or partner of the Word of God. But it runs thus : " To believe aught without God's Word is not faith but a false delusion that will nevermore come to aught, just as if thou wouldst believe thou shouldst yet become the Emperor of Rome . . ." (*Hauspost.* 1544 *Sermon on John* 4⁴⁷ᶠ·, W. edn. 52, p. 518, l. 22). " Whoso then hath not nor knoweth God's Word can have no such confidence and must get this delightful comfort for himself (*ib. Sermon on Luke* 5¹ᶠ·, W. edn. 52, p. 396, l. 7). " It is this, then, that I have said, that God will not suffer it that we should rely on aught else or with the heart depend on what is not Christ in

His word, be it as holy and spiritual as it may. Faith hath no other ground on which it can stand " (E. edn. 11, 26). " In faith everything must be lost to sight without the Word of God. Whoso alloweth aught else to come into view than the Word itself is already lost. Faith dependeth alone on the Word merely and purely, turneth not its eyes therefrom, regardeth naught else, neither its work nor merit. When the heart therefore standeth not simply, it is already lost " (*Sermon on John* 4⁴ᶠ·, 1522 W. edn. 10ᴵᴵᴵ, p. 423, l. 17). " This is the property and nature of faith that it may suffer naught beside it to which man contributes or turns, save the simple Word of God or divine promise . . . faith letteth go all creatures, all visible things in the world, even itself, and dependeth on God's Word : yea then, if it must go, dear friend, faith relieth on naught, gropeth not after ought, what it is sure of it will also hold to " (*Festpost.* 1527 *Sermon on Luke* 1²⁶ᶠ·, W. edn. 17ᵁ, p. 400, ll. 14, 32). In faith there takes place a *speculatio qua Christus apprehenditur,* a *speculatio theologica fidelis et divina inspectio serpentis suspensi in palo hoc est Christi pendentis in cruce pro meis tuis et totius mundi peccatis* (*Comm. Gal.* 3¹³, W. edn. 40ᴵ, p. 447, l. 18). And note that even in the gloss on Romans and in the sermon in which he speaks of the " marriage " between the Word and faith, the emphasis of Luther's expositions lies throughout on the thought that without the Word there can be no faith, while the dialectical fulfilment, that without faith we cannot have the Word, is only just achieved in the two passages but not carried further or in any way emphasised. In brief : when Luther speaks of the Word and faith, he of course says, that where there is no faith the Word cannot be or achieve anything ; but he says above all, and that is the point, that where faith is it has its ground and its truth and its measure, not in itself as an action and experience of man, but, although it is a human action and experience, beyond itself in its object, in Christ or in the Word of God. The designations circular relation, relation of interchange, relation of correlation are at least not very precise description for what Luther meant to say and did say in this matter. We obtain in Luther practically no other instruction, beyond what has been Reformed knowledge in this matter, than in Melanchthon.

From this standpoint it should now be further comprehensible that the interpretation of faith as *Fiducia,* trust, confidence, as we find it among the Reformers and then in the whole of Old Protestant theology (*Est itaque fides non aliud, nisi fiducia misericordiae promissae* . . . Melanchthon, *Loci* 1521 *De justif. et fide* IV ; cf. *Conf. Helv. post.* 16 at the beginning ; *Heidelb. Kat. qu.* 21) has nothing to do with pushing the reality of faith out of the object of faith into the believing subject. This emphasis on *fiducia* is meant to mark off real faith from a mere *opinio historica,* from a neutral recollective knowledge and affirmation of Biblical or Church statements, such as is possible even apart from the reality of faith. To exclude from faith the element of *notitia* or *assensus,* i.e. the element of knowledge, to conceive of faith as pure trust, which is intellectually without form or, in view of its intellectual form, indifferent, as any kind of trust in any kind of thing, to make the object of faith problematic and to transfer the reality of faith to the believing subject, was a possibility of which we can say with certainty (contrary to what K. A n e r seems to assume, *RGG*² *art.* " Faith — IV, from the standpoint of History of Dogma ") that even in the early period of the Reformation none of its responsible leaders took it seriously for one single minute. For Old Protestantism faith is *fiducia,* and more than *notitia* and *assensus* in view of the content of the Word of God, so far as man in faith adopts the merciful Immanuel! which the Word of God pronounces, i.e. lets the mercy of which the Word speaks rest on him, comforts himself with it on the strength of the Word, relies on it on the strength of the Word, so far as the believer is one who is comforted by the Word of God. True, faith is first faith when it is *fiducia*, and *notitia* and *assensus* by themselves would not be faith at all but just that *opinio historica*, which even the godless may have. But how should it be *fiducia* without at the same time and because it is *fiducia*, being *notitia* and *assensus* too, *fiducia promissionis*, trust in the mercy of God which meets us as the *misericordia promissa*, i.e. in the objectivity of the Word, which has form and the form of the Word at that, and therefore in the faith that adopts it the form of k n o w l e d g e also, the form of conviction ? Some lines before the famous definition of *fides* as *fiducia*, the same Melanchthon gives a definition : *Quid igitur fides ? Constanter assentiri omni verbo Dei.* Moreover, he certainly would not have said with W o b b e r m i n (*Wort Gottes*, p. 10 f. ; in *Richtlinien*, p. 131, he speaks of a " radical rejection of the *fides historica* " !) that this *assentiri* is " subordinate " to the *fiducia*, and that not because for him a real and serious, a theologically important subordination might arise, not between *assensus* and *fiducia* in real faith, but only between them and their object. It was, therefore, of faith regarded as *fiducia* that, as we heard, Melanchthon said that it was to be regarded as real justifying faith, not as an *opus per sese dignum*, but only in view of its *objectum*. But actually in connection with its object as such faith is necessarily and not in any way " subordinately " also *notitia* and *assensus* (apparently even in the *Loci* of 1559 *C.R.* 21, p. 242 f., Melanchthon does not distinguish these two elements), knowing, holding true the Word of the divine Person, on whom it bestows its trust. That so it was and had to be, we can also very well make clear to ourselves by the word *fiducia*. In addition to the psychological it has also a juristic meaning and philologically it should be quite legitimate, for understanding the one meaning, at least also to pay attention to the other. For juristically taken *fiducia* means abandonment of a possession out of loyalty and faith, or even the agreement drawn up about such an abandonment (e.g. in the case of a fictitious sale), or even the mortgage security one has given one in such a case. *Fiducia* therefore means what in a legal transaction, in which a personal claim is as a preliminary and for the moment put into another person's hand, a man retains in his own hand, as a surety, so to speak, to prove the legal claim, which exists before as well as after the transfer : whether it be the mere certainty that the other person's loyalty can be trusted, or an agreement for which this trustworthiness is security, or a deposit which is also security for this agreement. *Fiducia* is thus c o n n e c t e d with the reliability, the *bona fides* of the other, in whose hands my claim is now set aside without it ceasing to be mine. " I have confidence," therefore means, that I have grounds for relying for my part on this reliability of the other. Without the connection with this object, the *bona fides* of the other, there would be no *fiducia*. I have it by standing in this connection with the object and for the purpose of being able to stand in this relation to it, not otherwise. That is the *tertium comparationis* between the juristic and the psychological and then, of course, the theological concept also of *fiducia*. Note that already in the NT it can be said incidentally of God : πίστιν παρασχὼν πᾶσιν ἀναστήσας αὐτὸν ἐκ νεκρῶν, i.e. in the resurrection of Jesus He gave to all a surety, and this surety is nothing else than that which they can have in the form of faith (Acts 17³¹). *Fiducia* signifies, no less than *notitia* and *assensus*, the connection of faith with its object. But *fiducia* it is, it is the reliance upon God's reliability which is to be found in faith, that signifies this connection with the object pregnantly, and precisely because of the material content of faith expressed in the concept of *fiducia* the concepts *notitia* and *assensus*, with their indication of the divine opposite as such, should not be lacking to mark off its formal content. *Ultimus actus fidei nempe fiducia anima fidei justificantis est, sive perfectio eius formalis qua stante impossibile est hominem perire. Interim tamen praesupponit objecti justifici cognitionem explicitam et assensum generalem . . . et specialem* (Quenstedt, *Theol. did.- pol.* 1685 III *ch.* 8, *sect* 2, *qu.* 6, *ekth.* 7).

A word in closing upon a pair of concepts which recently have had a considerable new vogue (again in particular with Wobbermin), *fides quae creditur* and *fides qua creditur*. This distinction originates with Augustine: *Aliud sunt ea, quae creduntur, aliud, fides qua creduntur. Illa quippe in rebus sunt . . . haec autem in anima credentis est (De trin.* XIII 2, 5). Anselm of Canterbury next has split the element of *fides qua*, in his distinction between *credere id* and *credere in id, quod credi debet (Monol.* 76–78). Even this *in id* originates with Augustine (e.g. his *Tract in Johann.* 29, 6). Peter Lombard first adduces the first Augustine passage and then (is this original?) in view of the second one applies a threefold formula for the *fides qua creditur : aliud est enim credere in Deum, aliud credere Deo, aliud credere Deum (Sent.* III 23 C & D; cf. on the passage Luther's marginal note, W. edn. 9, p. 90, l. 15). Next, in Peter Lombard, J. Gerhard discovered first the first Augustine passage and in conjunction with it was probably the first expressly to use the concepts so familiar to us to-day, *fides quae creditur* and *fides qua creditur*, the first of which signifies the object of the second, the *materia circa quam*, the second the πεποίθησις et πληροφορία *in animo credentis (Loci theol.* 1610 ; *Loci*, 16, 66). But besides that, J. Gerhard discovered in the Lombard also the three-membered formula for the *fides qua creditur*, and seems to have regarded it, since he likewise takes it to be Augustinian, as confirming his own formula of *fiducia, assensus, notitia* (*ib.* 67). Since his day, at all events, *fides quae* and *qua* and, to explain *fides qua*, those three concepts have more or less become the common property of Protestant Scholasticism. We find both already in J. Wolleb (*Chr. Theol. Compend.* 1626 I 26, 1 and 7) taken up into Reformed dogmatics also, while M. Chemnitz, e.g. on the Lutheran and W. Bucan on the Reformed side, do not yet seem to have taken them for granted as familiar formulæ. The distinction of *fides quae* and *qua* can obviously only have the meaning of signifying the dialectic of the object-subject content of the concept of faith, as it has already met us in the use of the NT πίστις, the problem of faith and of the object of faith, as such. To the discussion of this problem itself this distinction makes no contribution, for, as the labours of Anselm and the Lombard show, all it would amount to would be to determine what is to be meant by *fides qua*. At the start we followed out the concept of *fiducia* and established the point necessary in our context, that it is *fiducia* —and with it *fides qua* in general, which for that very reason is not mere *fiducia* —which points beyond itself to the object, in connection with which it is *fiducia*. Even Augustine, the realist, who seems to have been the first to have spoken of this *quae* and *qua*, certainly did not regard his *fides qua* in any other way.

If, then, this is how it stands with faith, we shall have to say of the knowability of the Word of God given in the event of faith, that it is not a possibility contributed by man on his part to real knowledge ; nor yet is it a possibility accruing to man in real knowledge from some source or other as an enrichment of his existence. But as faith takes its absolute and unconditioned rise in the Word of God, independently of inborn or inherited characteristics and possibilities in man, and as it as faith has no other goal or source of life at any time or in any respect save in the Word of God, so is it also in all its parts with the knowability of the Word of God, into which we are here inquiring. We cannot fix it by, so to speak, turning our back upon the Word of God, in order to consider ourselves and to discover in ourselves an openness, a positive or at least a negative point of contact, for the Word of God. We can only fix it by staying fixed ourselves in faith and in the knowledge of faith, i.e. by turning away from ourselves and turning our face, or rather our ear, to the Word of God. In hearing it we have the possibility of hearing it. The fixing, therefore, is not the fixing of our possibility but the fixing of its reality, a fixing which cannot be made otherwise than by our staying fixed. In its reality we have also our possibility, though not for contemplation of it but only for use. By contemplating it we should cease to hear it, we should therefore lose its reality, and with it our possibility which we wished to contemplate. It is our possibility as coming to us in its, the Word's reality, just as faith also is our possibility as coming to us. Really our possibility, the possibility of the entire, creaturely, sinful man. But not in such a way that by considering this man we can discover it or read it off in or on him. But in such a way and only in such a way that this creaturely, sinful man waits for the Word coming to him, and so for his faith, and by that very fact already believes, he who in contemplating himself must invariably declare that he cannot believe.

P. Althaus' words on this point are very fine and striking : " I know not whether I believe ; but I know in whom I believe " (*Grundiss d. Dogm.* 1929 p. 19 ; cf. *Communio sanctorum*, 1929 p. 92 f.).

In faith that is pretty much how it stands with the knowability of the Word of God. It is not an extraordinary art. Or should one rather say the opposite, that it is a highly extraordinary art ? The exercise of it does not presuppose any special equipment, natural or supernatural. The believer is absolutely the same ungifted and idle or else gifted and excitable fellow he was as an unbeliever and may be again. As the man he is, with the inventory that corresponds to his condition, he believes. There is no question of a heightening or lowering of his existence, it is a question of the grace and judgment of God upon his existence. So not an extraordinary art, so far as it is entirely a matter of the man and his knowledge as he is. Highly extraordinary, of course, so far as for this man and his knowing the Word of God here becomes the truth. But whether extraordinary or not, at least a possibility given to us, but given only for use, not for inventorying or cataloguing, not for putting on ice or into the museum.

The story of the " manna," Ex. 16, down even to details, is an illustration of what has to be said in this context about faith.

So not a possibility we can exhibit but a possibility we can only hint at, as we might at faith, or the Word of God itself, or the child born of the Virgin Mary in the stall at Bethlehem. Wherefore, once more, the seriousness and the power of this hint must be the seriousness and the power of God, in order that we may really give the hint. So, the first thing we have to say of the knowability of the Word of God as the possibility given us in faith is, that it arises and consists purely in the object of real knowledge.

2. If what happens in faith is that acknowledgment of the Word of God, according as it can become man's act and experience, is, so to speak, put into force not by itself but by the Word of God acknowledged, so that it is real acknowledgment, we must now also lay it down positively that in faith men have real experience of the Word of God, and no *finitum non capax infiniti*, and no *peccator non capax verbi divini* either, should now hinder us from taking this statement seriously with all its consequences. This statement has indeed to do not with a human capacity, but with men on the assumption of their complete incapacity. The statement as to the incapacity of the *finitum* or *homo peccator* is conceded. And the statement about the man, who in faith has real experience of the Word of God, does not shelve that statement. But it overtakes it, brackets it. Faith is not one of man's various capacities, either as innate or as acquired. Among these there is certainly no capacity for the Word of God. The possibility of faith as it is given to man in the reality of faith can only be regarded as one lent to man by God and lent exclusively for use. The moment we wanted to regard it as in any sense one belonging to man, the second statement about man's incapacity would have to come back into force. We do not regard it as in any sense a possibility

belonging to man. But for that reason also no protest is to be raised from the side of men's possibilities, when we say that in faith there takes place a conformity of man with God. We do not say a deification, but a conformity with God, i.e. an adaptation of man to the Word of God. By really apprehending the Word of God in faith he is actually made fit to apprehend it. Were this to be denied we could no longer characterise and regard faith as the act and experience of man, or man as the subject of faith. But if we ascribe to man a qualification—not belonging to him, but one lent him in faith, and not one to be contemplated but only one to be used in faith, still a qualification—for apprehending the Word of God, then, we could not resile from speaking of a conformity with God proper to him in faith. Apprehension of the Word of God could not take place, were there not in and along with this event something in common between God who speaks and man who hears, an analogy, a similarity, for all the dissimilarity involved in the difference between God and man, a " point of contact "—now we may use this concept too—between God and man.

This point of contact is what theological anthropology, in correspondence with Gen. 1^{27}, calls the " image of God " in man. But in this respect and in this context we cannot possibly, with E. Brunner (*Gott und Mensch*, 1930 p. 55 f.), mean by that the humanity and personality remaining over to sinful man from the creation : for the humanity and personality of sinful man simply cannot signify conformity with God, a point of contact with the Word of God. In this sense, as a possibility for God proper to man *qua* creature the " image of God " is not only, as we say, with the exception of some remnants ruined, but annihilated. What is preserved of the image of God even in sinful man is *recta natura*, to which as such a *rectitudo* cannot be ascribed, even *potentialiter*. Man's capacity for God, however it may be with his humanity and personality, has really been lost. We cannot, therefore, see that at this point there comes into view a common basis of discussion for philosophical and theological anthropology, the opportunity for a common exhibition at least of the possibility of raising the question about God. The image of God in man of which we have to speak here and which constitutes the real point of contact for the Word of God, is the one awakened through Christ from real death to life and so " restored," the n e w l y-created *rectitudo* now real as man's possibility for the Word of God. The reconciliation of man with God in Christ includes in itself or else begins with the f r e s h establishment of the l o s t " point of contact." This point of contact is, therefore, not real outside faith but only in faith. In faith a man is created b y the Word of God f o r the Word of God, existing i n the Word of God, not in himself, not in virtue of his humanity and personality, nor from the standpoint of creation, for what is possible from the standpoint of creation from man to God has actually been lost through the Fall. Thus this point of contact also, like everything become real in faith, i.e. through the grace of recon-

18

ciliation, can only be spoken of theologically, and not theologically and philosophically. " Conformity with God " was the name we gave to the possibility of apprehending the Word of God. That is also expressed by the concept of the *imago Dei*. We must be quite clear that that puts us into hairbreadth proximity to the Catholic doctrine of the *analogia entis*. But even in and because of this proximity our doctrine will have to be quite a different one from that. We certainly regard the analogy, similarity or equiformity between God and man which in fact requires asserting here, not as an *analogia entis*, i.e. not as an analogy to be surveyed and seen through, one to be regarded as an analogy in a synthesis from the standpoint of an onlooker. Not a being which the creature should have in common with the Creator in spite of all the dissimilarity, but the action inaccessible to any mere theory, the human decision, is in faith, amid all its dissimilarity, similar to the decision of the grace of God. Of more than an analogy or similarity we should not speak. And it must be emphasised, as for that matter is also done by the Catholic doctrine of the *analogia entis*, that what we are dealing with is a similarity in spite of greater dissimilarity. Why the earlier mentioned theory of Augustine (and to-day of the school of Holl) of the secret identity between divine and human decision is inadmissible, can be understood from this point of view. If secret identity existed here, then we should have to speak not of similarity in the dissimilarity, but of equality in the inequality, but then we would be dealing not with mere conformity with God, but with a deification of man. But, in fact, we cannot be dealing with less than conformity with God. In rejecting the Thomist *analogia entis* we affirm the other Thomist thought, in which for that matter we might discern the content of truth in even the so-called *analogia entis : quum igitur christiana fides hominem de Deo . . . instruit . . . fit in homine quaedam divinae sapientiae similitudo* (Thomas Aquinas, *S.c. gent.* II 2). Thus, too, speaks Luther of the act of justification in faith ; he says it happens in such a way that God *nos tales facit, quale est verbum suum, hoc est justum, verum, sapiens, etc. Et ita nos in verbum suum, non autem verbum suum in nos mutat. Facit autem tales tunc, quando nos verbum suum tale credimus esse scilicet justum verum. Tunc enim iam similis forma est in verbo et in credente, id est veritas et justitia* (*Schol.* Rom. 3⁴, *Fi.* II p. 65, l. 16). And elsewhere : *Necesse est sapientiam carnis mutari et suam formam relinquere ac formam verbi suscipere. Quod fit, dum per fidem se ipsam captivat et destruat, conformat se verbo, credens verbum esse verum, se vero falsam* (*ib.* Rom. 6¹⁴, *Fi.* II p. 160, l. 3). And again elsewhere : *per fidem fit homo similis verbo Dei* (*Schol.* Heb. 3¹³, *Fi.* II p. 44, l. 4). And again in another passage : " As is the Word, so becometh also the soul by it, like as the iron becometh glowing red like the fire from the union with the fire " (*Freedom of a Christian Man*, 1520 W. edn. 7, p. 24, l. 33). In view of the righteousness which man receives in faith, Luther could, of course, say that *fides ita exaltat cor hominis et transfert de se ipso in Deum, ut unus spiritus fiat ex corde et Deo* (*Schol.* Heb. 7¹, *Fi.* II p. 74, l. 9). In view of the immovability and certainty of faith he can say outright : *fide homo fit Deus* (*Comm. on Gal.* 2⁷, 1535 W. edn. 40¹, p. 182, l. 15). In view of the power of real faith : " God help us, what a boundless, rich and mighty thing it is concerning faith ! for it maketh man, of course, in everything into a god to whom naught is impossible " . . . (*Kirchenpost.* 1522 *Sermon on Luke* 2²¹, W. edn. 10¹, p. 518, l. 5). And in view of the fact that in faith and in faith alone a man can give God His honour as God, still more boldly : *Ea (sc.*

fides) consummat divinitatem et, ut ita dicam, creatrix est divinitatis, non in substantia Dei, sed in nobis. Nam sine fide . . . nihil maiestatis et divinitatis habet Deus (Comm. on Gal. 3⁶, W. edn. 40ᴵ, p. 360, l. 21). In the same sense Augustine had already been able to assert, that in the *justificatio* of man so far as it makes us children of God, a *deificatio* takes place, whereupon in him also the comment is not lacking : *sed hoc gratiae est adoptantis non naturae generantis (Enarr. in Ps.* 49²). Neither in Augustine nor in Luther is anything said about the idea of a deification taking place in faith, in the sense of a change of man's essence into the divine essence. It is the *apprehensio Christi* or *habitatio Christi in nobis* or *unio hominis cum Christo* (as taught according to Gal. 2²⁰) as they are found in faith, which makes these expressions possible. In emphasising this more than mystical and more than speculative statement, that faith means unity with the thing believed in, i.e. with Jesus Christ, Calvin did not in the least lag behind Luther, or either of them behind an Augustine, an Anselm, a Bernard of Clairvaux. Without this statement the Reformed doctrine of justification and faith is impossible to understand. How in the Reformation period in particular it was distinguished from the idea of an essential deification of man can be realised from Calvin's discussion with A. Osiander (*Instit.* III 11, 5 f.) : in that there can be no question of a *mixtura Christi cum fidelibus (ib.* 11, 10). In *medio tenebrarum* (Luther *on Gal.* 2¹⁶, W. edn. 40ᴵ, p. 299, l. 18), in complete veiling this *unio* takes place, this self-presentation of Christ or therefore of the Word of God or therefore of God Himself in the believing man, this *inhabitatio totius sanctae trinitatis*, as was later said. Actually in this relation man remains man with his possibilities and his limits, and Christ Himself and alone or the Word, the object of faith and not a poured-in love or the like is the *forma fidei* (Luther, *ib.* 229, 28) i.e. the thing which distinguishes the believer from the non-believer, which makes his experience and his action real faith and at the same time a possibility given to him to use. But, of course, such a distinction takes place. Its complete hiddenness corresponds only with its complete reality as divine grace, a reality about which as such, without any exaggeration, too much can be said.

In faith man is conform with God, i.e. capable of apprehending the Word of God, capable in his own decision of so corresponding with God's decision made about him in the Word, that the Word of God is now the Word heard by him, he himself is now the man addressed by this Word. This capacity is not to be sought among the remainder of the possibilities belonging to him, the statement about the indwelling of Christ which takes place in faith may not be converted into an anthropological statement. From the lost condition of natural, sinful man, as whom the believer will for the first time properly recognise himself, no deductions will have to be made. But this natural, sinful man that he is and must recognise himself as being, precisely when in the state of faith, is when in faith, is when in Christ, dead according to Rom. 6³ᶠ·, and yet am I alive in faith, a miracle to myself, the other man, and as such capable of things, of which, as a natural, sinful man, I can only know myself utterly incapable.

To this capacity it also belongs, that for man in faith the Word of God is knowable, that it is spoken to him, and that he can hear it and apprehend it as a Word, and the Word of God at that.

It may happen in faith that a man has an ὑπόστασις ἐλπιζομένων, i.e. an open confidence corresponding to the nature of the thing hoped for, an ἔλεγχος οὐ βλεπομένων, a proof of the, to him, invisible and unattainable (Heb. 11¹). The man who in faith is righteous before God may say of himself, Ἐγγύς σου τὸ ῥῆμα ἐστιν, ἐν τῷ στόματί σου καὶ ἐν τῇ καρδίᾳ σου (Rom. 10⁸). What Irenaeus once urges now becomes possible, ἵνα ἀεὶ μὲν ὁ θεὸς διδάσκῃ, ἄνθρωπος δὲ διὰ παντὸς μανθάνῃ παρὰ θεοῦ (C. o. h. II 28, 3). This ability regarding the Word of God is the conformity of the believer with God and particularly the knowability of the Word of God, which is the object of our present inquiry.

To the image of God in man, lost in Adam but restored in Christ, it also belongs, that he can hear the Word of God. Only by the Word of God being really spoken into his sin in spite of his sin, only by the grace with which God replies to sin can even this possibility revive. But in grace it does r e v i v e. Not, therefore, as a natural capacity in man—it is grace, after all, which meets sinners, incapable men—as a capacity therefore in the incapable, as a miracle quite insusceptible of an anthropological interpretation, but as a real capacity already actualised in faith, regarding the existence of which there has ceased to be any room left for discussion, the existence of which can only be fixed, because by becoming an event it has already been exhibited as a possibility, or ever a question about it can be raised.

What eye hath not seen nor ear heard, what hath not entered any man's heart, that hath God prepared for them that love him (1 Cor. 2⁹). There are men—God has vouchsafed that there should be such men—who are aware of God's gracious acts (ib. 2, 12), who search out the " deep things of God " (ib. 2, 10) who can judge what is spiritual spiritually (ib. 2, 13), men who may be spoken about their acquaintance with the Word of God : δέξασθε τὸν ἔμφυτον λόγον (Jas. 1²¹), who can " stand " in the faith (1 Cor. 16¹³).

By being spoken to him, the Word is in man and man in the Word. There is no proof of this mutual involution of the Word and a man, as indicating that, by being spoken to some other man, the Word of God may reach such a mutual involution in his case. The proof of faith consists in the proclamation of faith. The proof of the knowability of the Word of God consists in confessing it. In faith and confession the Word of God becomes a human thought and a human word, certainly in infinite dissimilarity and inadequacy, yet not in utter alienation from its archetype ; but in its entire humanly sinful perversion of its real copy, as the veiling of the divine, its unveiling at the same time. By that is not meant an immanent transformation of human thought or human speech, nor a removal, however modest, of the offence, wherein here also the Word is flesh. Nor is there meant by that any weakening of the miracle of this mutual involution, any supernatural physics, claiming now to render the inconceivable conceivable. And once again and over and over again, what has to be said here cannot be intended as the analysis of a present reality, for as such it is withdrawn from our grasp and our knowledge, but strictly only as a reminder of the promise and as a hope of fulfilment to come. But in that case and in that way, this involution, nay, oneness of the divine *Logos* and the human in faith cannot and may not be either hushed up or denied. This involution or oneness is the knowability of the Word of God, the possibility of Church proclamation, regarded from the preacher's as well as from the hearer's standpoint, and thereby the possibility of dogmatics also. By the Church furnishing the ministry of proclamation, by our pursuit of dogmatics, we confess our belief in this possibility. We have every reason to be pretty clear at this very point, in spite of the threatening proximity of the *analogia entis*, mysticism and the philosophy of identity, and all other existing " dangers " so-called.

Uniatur tecum cogitatio mea, una et singularis sit tecum intentio mea ubi tecum a te misericorditer suscepta beata jam regnat substantia nostra (Anselm of Canterbury, *Medit.* I 6). So, too, Luther: *In ipsa fide Christus adest. Fides ergo est cognitio quaedam vel tenebra, quae nihil videt et tamen in istis tenebris Christus fide apprehensus sedet sicut Deus in Sinai et in templo sedebat in medio tenebrarum (Comm. on Gal.* 2¹⁶, W. edn. 40ᴵ, p. 229, l. 15). " The statement of revelation that God speaks, is identical with the statement that man hears ! " (Ed. Thurneysen, *Das Wort Gottes und die Kirche,* 1927 p. 222 : Wobbermin's indignation at this sentence, *Wort Gottes u. ev. Gl.,* p. 27, is neither actively nor passively very penetrating).

Along with our statement about man's conformity with God in faith, and therefore also in his possibility of recognising the Word of God, we now—as the second determination of the knowability of the Word of God—put this one ; that where and when the Word of God is really recognised by men, the nature of this recognition corresponds with the nature of the Word of God itself. If as the first determination of the knowability of the Word of God we understand that it is a human possibility, which in view of this object confronting man and over against the Word of God itself becomes a possibility as the reflex of its own, self-grounded possibility—we must now add that it becomes a possibility in the way in which the Word of God, itself and in itself, is possible. Therefore we have described what is acknowledgment of the Word of God by a man, not in the form of an analysis of human consciousness in faith, but in the form of a postulate directed by the nature of the Word of God to man's consciousness in faith. We have to think of man in the event of real faith as, so to speak, opened up from above. From above, not from beneath! Anything that can be seen, grasped, and analysed from beneath as human experience and action, as consciousness of faith, is not a fulfilment of this postulate, is in itself an " empty space " which also might be filled in quite another way than actually by the Word of God. Precisely the real believer will be fain to acknowledge that even his consciousness of faith as such is human darkness. We cannot, therefore, omit to investigate the consciousness of our admitted ego with regard to its content of Word of God. The opening up from above, achieved in the event of real faith, remains as hidden for us as this event itself and as God Himself. But we must also state that it is also as manifest to us as this event and as God is manifest to us, to wit, in remembrance of the promise, in hope of its fulfilment. Just as we should and must believe in the Word itself, are called upon to believe in it, so is it also with our faith in the Word, so too with our possibility of knowing it, or its knowability for us, so with the presence of the *forma verbi* amid man's darkness, the presence of Christ in the *tenebrae* of our heart. If the event of faith is the event of the presence of the Word believed in, in the case of man, man's becoming one with it, that must imply that man's darkness—we can never see or regard it as anything else—can turn into light. Thus man's possibility, insufficient in itself, can become the sufficient divine possibility. In its fulfilment it is the sufficient divine possibility. By affirming the knowability of the Word of God occurring in the event of faith, as it is promised to us, we are affirming the divine possibility. So far as we can affirm it only in its hiddenness, in the husk of the human possibility which meets us as darkness, we shall on that account not deny the dissimilarity between the divine possibility in itself and the thing it becomes in our hands: we can see the stick dipped in the water only as a broken stick. But unapparently for us, invisibly and yet really, it is the completely unbroken stick. For all its dissimilarity the human possibility of grasping the promise in faith is not without resemblance to the divine possibility of its realisation. Not in itself, not as a human possibility but naturally, in accordance with our first determination, from the standpoint of its object, as a possibility of grasping the promise. In virtue of this resemblance our possibility of knowing the Word of God is the possibility of a certain, clear knowledge not equal but similar to the certainty and clarity with which God knows Himself in His Word. In virtue of this similarity confession of faith, as it corresponds to the knowledge of the Word of God, acquires that definiteness which fundamentally differentiates it from the expression of human convictions however deep and serious, that ultimate human seriousness which alone can be the material of confession, especially confession of faith. In virtue of this similarity it is possible for there to be a Church, Church proclamation, dogmatics. Certainty and clarity of knowledge, confession of faith, the Church, rest on the fact that the Word of God, wherever and whenever it is really known, becomes known in the manner of the Word of God itself, in this resemblance to the thing believed in and known.

We thus do not oppose the Catholic doctrine of the *analogia entis* by a denial of the concept of analogy. But we say that the analogy in question is not an *analogia entis*, but according to Rom. 12[6] the ἀναλογία τῆς πίστεως, the correspondence of the thing known with the knowing, of the object with the thought, of the Word of God with the word of man in thought and in speech, even as it distinguishes true Christian prophecy taking place in faith from all that is untrue. This *analogia fidei* is, of course, also the meaning of the wonderful Pauline passages in which human knowledge of God is converted into man's being known by God. Paul calls the Christians γνόντες θεόν, only to emend it into μᾶλλον δὲ γνωσθέντες ὑπὸ θεοῦ. Obviously it is this γνωσθῆναι that distinguishes their γιγνώσκειν as Christians from their earlier heathen non-knowledge about God (Gal. 4[8f.]). If here in the Christian community any one thinks to have known somewhat, he does not yet know what must be known. One can never look back upon the human, even upon the Christian act of knowledge as such, as upon an already successful work which corresponds with its object. Whoso loveth God, οὗτος ἔγνωσται ὑπ' αὐτοῦ. Once more it is the divine act of knowledge, performed not through man but upon man, which distinguishes him whose knowing is grounded in the love of God and so in real fellowship with Him, in the presence of God (1 Cor. 8[2f.]). But this being known, the divine possibility, even in the Christian remains distinct from the human possibility of knowing: the latter cannot exhaust the former, the resemblance, the analogy remains. Seeing God " face to face " without dissimilarity remains reserved for the eternal consummation, even for the Christian : τότε δὲ ἐπιγνώσομαι καθὼς καὶ (i.e. not only correspondingly, similarly, analogously as, but exactly as) ἐπεγνώσθην (1 Cor. 13[12]). We have the same reversal before us in the words of Augustine : *Qui autem per Spiritum tuum vident ea (sc. opera Dei) tu vides in eis. Ergo cum vident quia bona sunt, tu vides quia bona sunt : et quaecunque propter te placent, tu in eis places et quae per Spiritum tuum placent nobis, tibi placent in nobis* (Conf. XIII 31, 46). At the same time one must be sufficiently impartial not to overlook what amid much that is doubtful can be explained *in bonam partem* in the words of the Hegelian Ph. Marheineke: " In the human spirit God is manifest to Himself not through it but through Himself, and in that way is manifest to the human spirit also. The latter, as reason, is annulled in Him. The hardest thing science requires in all its devotees is that pure Substance itself should show itself as subject, man with his spirit to be subject to the divine spirit and be patient under it. His true knowledge of the absolute is itself an absolute knowledge " (*Grundlehren d. chr. Dogm. als Wissenschaft*, 1827 § 115).—It is precisely when we regard man's conformity with God which takes place in faith, and the " point of contact " with the Word of God posited in this conformity, not as an inborn or accessory attribute of man, but as the sole work of the actual grace of God, that the only final word left us at this point is that God acts in His Word on man. It is because man's work in faith is the thing to which God's work happens, that man can know the Word of God. He knows by being known of God.

3. With this last turn in the discussion of the concept of the *analogia fidei*, we have already reached the third and last point to be made in this context about faith and the knowability of the Word of God for man. If it is the case that a man really believes (1) that the object of faith is present to him ; (2) that he himself is assimilated to the object, the conclusive result is, thirdly, that his being a believer is wholly dependent upon this object. By believing he can regard himself as based not on himself but only on his object, in fact as existing only through his object. He has not personally created his faith himself ; His Word has created it. He has not reached faith, faith has reached him through the Word. Moreover, he has not taken faith unto himself ; faith has been gifted to him by the Word. As a believer he cannot regard himself as the active subject of the work which there takes place. Without prejudice to the fact that it is a matter of his experience and action, that in faith he is by no means a block of wood or a stone, but actually a self-determining man, without prejudice to the fact that in faith he by no means sinks into a passive apathetic con-templation—even in such sinking he would for that matter still always be a self-determining man—but in whatever special state of soul, at least in thinking, willing, feeling, he is utterly by himself, he lives his own life. But the point is that in faith he must regard this by no means diminished self-determination of his, must regard his very self in its activity, in its living of its own life, as determined by the Word of God, that in his very freedom, in the full use of his freedom as a man, he must regard himself as some one else whom he had no capacity to become, whom he has also no power to be, whom, therefore, he is not free to become or to be (although he is free by becoming and being him !)—in short, whom he can only be

by being him. Man acts by believing, but the fact that he believes by acting is God's act. Man is the subject of faith. It is not God but man who believes. But the very fact of a man thus being subject in faith is bracketed as the predicate of the subject, God, bracketed exactly as the Creator embraces His creature, the merciful God sinful man, i.e. so that there is no departure from man's being a subject, and this very thing, the Ego of man as such, is still only derivable from the Thou of the Subject, God.

The old theology described this state of affairs, when it designated faith a gift of God, of the Holy Spirit. That, of course, might be meant and stated with a great variety of emphasis. We must regard it in a more thoroughgoing sense, than for example it is stated and regarded in Augustine. Augustine, of course, taught against the Pelagians very expressively and very impressively that faith is grace. Yet his *Ut credamus Deus dedit* remained ambiguous, for the other statement remained, *fides in potestate est*, in which *potestas* signified the *facultas faciendi* (*De spir. et lit.* 31, 55) and the relation between the two propositions was described thus : *Quid habeat et quid accipiat, Dei est ; accipere et habere utique accipientis est* (*ib.* 34, 60). In one of his latest writings against the Semi-Pelagians he certainly tried to put this right also : *Habere fidem gratiae est fidelium* it now runs ; but now also there still stands against that the other sentence : *Posse habere fidem naturae est hominum* (*De praedest.* 5, 10). Here, since we cannot fail to see how this mere *posse habere fidem*, not to mention *habere*, must be founded upon man, we must rather say with Luther : *fidem esse . . . simpliciter donum Dei, qui ut creat ita conservat fidem in nobis* (*Comm. on Gal.* 1¹², 1535 W. edn. 40ᴵ, p. 130, l. 13). " Here we must not regard reason or its work, when we speak of faith and God's work. Here God worketh alone and reason is dead, blind, and compared with this work an unreasoning block, to which Scripture refers when it says : " God is marvellous in his saints." Also Isa. 55 : " As the heaven is high above the earth, so are my ways high above your ways " (*Fastenpost.* 1525 *Sermon ou Matt.* 8¹ᶠ·, W. edn. 17ᴵᴵ, p. 85, l. 10). " But those who gladly hear God's Word, and to whom Christ hath said, as here to the deaf : ' Ephatha, O ear, thou shalt stay open,' 'tis these are rightly holpen against the devil, For God hath given us no other staircase nor shown another way whereon we may mount to heaven save His dear Word, the holy gospel. Whoso gladly heareth the same, marketh it with diligence, and hath desire and love thereto, he receiveth help. That is the one miraculous work, which still runneth daily in Christendom, that our ears which the devil by sin hath stopped are opened again by the Word, that we hear God's Word " (*Hauspost.* 1544 *Sermon on Luke* 18⁹ᶠ·, W. edn. 52, p. 452, l. 14). " Like then as God giveth the Word, 'tis His and not our Word, so too giveth He faith in the Word. For both are God's work, Word and faith " (*Hauspost.* 1544 *Sermon on Matt.* 9¹ᶠ·, W. edn. 52, p. 501, l. 19). " But that thou hearest and apprehendest such, is likewise not of thine own power, but of God's grace, who maketh the Gospel fruitful in thee, so that thou believest it " . . . (*Adventspost.* 1522 *Sermon on Matt.* 21¹ᶠ·, W. edn. 10ᴵ·², p. 30, l. 5). " Where Christ sat not on the right hand of God, nor daily poured forth of His spirit, the Christian faith could not exist. For 'tis counter to all human reason and the devil is hostile to it. Therefore, where the outpouring of the Holy Ghost kept not continual guard, the devil would not let a single man abide by the Easter preaching and by faith in Christ ! " (*Sermon on Acts* 2¹⁴ᶠ·, 1534 E. edn. 4, 105). Note there that Luther has traced back and nailed the actual, existing, living, direct relation to Christ, as distinguished from merely regarding it as true, the faith that lives by works, to the fact that it is not a work of man (regarding it as true might also be that !), but the gift of God. " There be some that hear or read the Gospel and what is said anent faith, and swiftly fall thereon, and give the name of faith to what they think. But they think no further than that faith is a thing that standeth in their power to have or not to have, like any other natural human work ; therefore, when in their heart they achieve a thought, which saith, Verily the doctrine is right, and I believe it is so ; at once they think faith is there. When then they see and feel in themselves and in others that there is no change. . . . Behold they fall from their height and cry and say : Ah, faith doeth it not alone. Why ? Ah, for this reason that there are so many of them who believe and do nothing more than before, they find in themselves likewise no change of mind from before. These are they whom Jude in his Epistle, v. 8, calleth dreamers, who deceive themselves with their own dream. For what is such thought of theirs, which they call faith, other than just a dream, and a mere ghost of faith, which they themselves of their own power, without God's grace, have made in their hearts ? who become thereafter more idle than they were before . . . But proper faith, whereof we speak, letteth not itself be made of our thoughts, but 'tis a pure Work of God in us, without any aid of ours. . . . Therefore, 'tis likewise a mighty, active, restless, busy thing, which alike reneweth a man, beareth him elsewhere, and leadeth him altogether into a new way and nature, such wise that 'tis impossible that the same should not do good without intermission (*Sermon on Luke* 16¹ᶠ·, E. edn. 13, 235 ; cf. *Hauspost.* 1544 *Sermon on John* 16⁵ᶠ·, W. edn. 52, p. 292, l. 31).

The application to the epistemological problem follows automatically.

We may now rejoin A u g u s t i n e : *Non parva ex parte intelligit et scit Dominum, qui intelligit et scit etiam hoc a Domino sibi dari, ut intelligat et sciat Dominum* (Conf. XVII 4, 8). And A n s e l m o f C a n t e r b u r y : *Intellectus ex auditu gratia est* (*De concordia qu.* III 6).

The Word of God becomes knowable by making itself knowable. The application of what has just been said to the epistemological problem consists in the fact that we hold fast to this statement and not one step beyond do we take. The possibility of knowing the Word of God is God's miracle on and in us, just as much as are the Word itself and the utterance of it. We are not here concerned to assert a passivity in man, which would set aside or even only limit his freedom. But we are concerned here to realise that the mutual involution, in fact oneness of human and divine possibility, of man's knowing and his becoming known by God, is an event in man's freedom, and cannot in any sense be regarded as the product of it, and therefore as the result of an intuition, of a thinkable or achievable deepening or heightening of the life of the soul of man. Should such ever take place—and why should it not ? but it absolutely need not !—it is at least not the one which introduces the unification, and therefore the knowability of the Word of God. Even the idea of the *sacrificium intellectus* is but a last desperate attempt to make of the knowledge of God a work of man, to have a human possibility correspond to what is the sole work of God. If we have understood that the knowability of the Word of God is really an inalienable affirmation of faith, but that precisely as such it denotes the miracle of faith and indeed a miracle for us only to be recalled and anticipated, then as a final necessity it must now also be understood, that, as the original subject, as the primary power, as the creator of the possibility of knowing the Word of God, man must be set aside and God Himself introduced.—Christ does not remain outside. And it is quite true that a man must open the door to Him (Rev. 3[20]), but even the fact of that event is, *quoad actum* and *quoad potentiam*, the work of the Christ who stands outside. So that the other thing also remains unreservedly true, that the risen Christ passes through closed doors (John 20[19f.]).

§ 7

THE WORD OF GOD, DOGMA, AND DOGMATICS

Dogmatics is the critical question as to Dogma, i.e. as to the Word of God in Church proclamation : or, concretely, as to the agreement of the Church proclamation achieved and to be achieved by men with the revelation attested in Scripture. Prolegomena to Dogmatics, in the sense of coming to an understanding about its path to knowledge, must therefore consist in expounding the doctrine of the three forms of the Word of God, as revealed, as written, and as proclaimed.

1. THE PROBLEM OF DOGMATICS

In the three preceding sections we characterised the criterion of dogmatics : its three forms, its nature, and its knowability. Our meaning, when in § 3 we called the Word of God the measure by which Church proclamation is to be measured by dogmatics, should now have become conceivable in a preliminary way and in its entire inconceivability. Become conceivable in a preliminary way, we shall have to say : yet all that has been said only meant, so to speak, an attempt at turning ourselves round and putting ourselves in the direction we must look, in order to see the point from which the Church is aware that her proclamation is understood and judged, from which, therefore, she too must be at pains to think it out herself, so as, in full consciousness of her responsibility, to submit herself to the necessary self-test in regard to her proclamation. In all that has been said up till now we have sought to sketch first, so to speak, the region of this criterion, to visualise its peculiarity as distinct from other objects of human and also, of course, Christian reflection and therefore its difference from other criteria, possible in themselves. We have, although with a steady view to the concrete content of this criterion, primarily put the formal question and received the corresponding formal answers. There may and must be—always in recollection of the promise that came to the Church and always in expectation of its

284

fulfilment —more said of the Word of God than has been said so far. The recollection to which the Church is aware of being called, is connected with a perfectly concrete content of the Word of God, and so also is the expectation inseparable from this recollection. This concrete content of the criterion of dogmatics has not yet been placed in the centre of our attention or put independently into words. But that must be done. Only when we have regarded it in its unity of form and concrete content, only when it is clear that the form with which we have been busied up till now is the form of a perfectly concrete content, have we regarded the Word of God in such a way that the validation of it as the criterion of Church proclamation has meaning and justification. Our doctrine, therefore, of the Word of God may still be far from perfect. Its perfectly characteristic propositions are still outstanding. In one sense, of course, we cannot go any further or expect to hear any more. We have just said that the meaning of the Word of God must now become conceivable in its entire inconceivability. For we do and shall rest content, first, with the inconceivability of the fact that the Word of God is spoken to men. No consideration yet to be adduced, not even that necessarily to be directed to its concrete content, will ever help us to realise how this reality comes to be. We have investigated, and shall further investigate what its nature is. We shall be able *a posteriori* to inquire into its possibilities, i.e. the possibilities based on itself. How it has and does come to be of this nature, what the possibility is of its possibilities, must and will remain for us inconceivable. And we do and shall rest content, secondly, with the inconceivability of the nature of the Word of God in itself. First then, because being what it is, it is but the content of what happens from time to time when it is uttered to this and that man. Second, because even that which this man and that apprehends and adopts as the Word of God in the event of faith and of which he can give an account, has already ceased to be what the Word of God addressed to him is in itself, and is his recollection of the Word addressed to him and his expectation of the Word to be addressed to him afresh. This double limit dogmatics likewise cannot pass, for the reason that it applies its interest to the concrete content of the Word of God. Even its concrete content it, with the whole Church, can only know in recollection and in expectation and so neither in its That nor in its (in the narrower sense) concrete What, neither with a proof that lies outside itself, nor as the *verbum concretissimum*, as it from time to time affects this man and that, and yet also remains hidden to him in being made manifest to him. Of dogmatics nothing superhuman is to be expected : it cannot be part of its office to tear down the bounds of faith prescribed for the Church. It belongs rather to its task to make known these bounds as such, to say what may be said and at the same time to warn against encroachments, or illusions, regarding things which may not be said. In this sense it should, therefore, be conceivable by this time what meaning attaches to the two expressions about the Word of God, conceivable in a preliminary way, and conceivable in its entire inconceivability. By the first we indicate the possibility of further realisations. And by the second we assert that even with such further realisations our course must lie within certain bounds.

But before we can enter upon this further path, we must once more, now in some measure instructed as to the one thing there essential, return to the task of dogmatics as such. In § 1 we defined it generally as the Christian Church's task of self-testing in respect of the language proper to her in speaking about God. In § 3 we then stated more fully that it was a question of investigating the " responsibility " of this language, i.e. of Church proclamation measured by the Word of God which she claims to proclaim. Thus our first result was the need for asking and stating what was to be understood by this measure by which Church proclamation is to be measured, by means of which, therefore, this self-testing is to be carried out. After this has been done we proceed to a third determination of the dogmatic task. Let it likewise be noted that it cannot yet be the last one. That can only be the case when we have also investigated our criterion as to its concrete content, or rather in the last stage of this investigation itself. But in order actually to fix the direction of our further advance, we must for a moment turn anew to the task as such, for the sake of which the question as to the criterion has been put and is still to be put.

The task then of dogmatics is to be that of investigating Church proclamation as to its agreement with the Word of God, as to its suitability to what it would proclaim. In the human form of the proclamation put forward by the Church the Word of God itself should, of course, be in the forefront. Such is the sense of the claim with which the Church validates her proclamation, such, too, the sense of the expectation in which it is enveloped. Dogmatic work begins with this claim and this expectation being taken perfectly seriously, with the Church being, so to speak, taken at her word about this claim and this expectation. In dogmatics the Church is herself bound by what she undertakes in her proclamation. She puts her undertaking to the touch by confronting it critically, by therefore suspending that claim and that expectation for a moment, in so far as she separates in thought her proclamation and the Word of God, not so as to be able to measure the Word of God by her proclamation, but so as to be able to measure her proclamation by the Word of God. She does not cease to believe that God will confess her and her doings, that He will put His Word into her proclamation and thus turn her proclamation into real proclamation. But this belief of hers means that she lays hold on the promise of God. Her believing does not mean that she thinks to possess it, but she hopes it may be given her. Thus faith's reflection will actually consist in the Church first of all holding apart God's Word and her own and seeing the latter questioned by the former. Faith is actually aware of being called in question as to whether as a human work it is also obedience. Actually for faith the judgment of God, to which all human work as such is exposed, will be no idle thought, but the call to add her own judgment upon this work. The corresponding critical labour regarding Church proclamation is the task of dogmatics. But who is to do justice to this task ? How and where is it to catch sight of the Word of God as an entity distinct from Church proclamation, so as to compare the latter with it and measure it by it ? Is there a possibility of that at all ?

Were there no such possibility we should now be faced with a remarkable dilemma.

Even in that case we could work away at Christian proclamation in a variety of ways. Even so we could ask whether it is really suitable to the Word of God which it purports to proclaim, in fact to be. Even so, disturbed by its human imperfection, we might try to look into this suitability and to improve it in respect of this suitability. We might test it philosophically for its epistemological, logical, cosmical, psychological content, or historically or ethically and educatively or politically for its form. We might fit it into the most modern view of the world for the moment, or the most pressing practical needs and tasks of the moment, or the most eloquent forms of expression of the moment. There is, in fact, no lack of such other criteria which might be given entry, as substitutes, so to speak, for the missing criterion of the Word of God,

It might even be that Church proclamation was felt to correspond to the Word of God in proportion as it stood the 'test of this or that one of these other criteria or of all of them together. Theology would in that case consist in handling these other criteria and their relevancy with the utmost possible stringency of application, always taking it for granted that in this way sufficient treatment was dealt out to the inconceivable, proper criterion of theology, the Word of God.

In this way and from this standpoint we may try to understand the theology of Modernist Protestantism. Gripped and urged in its own way by anxiety for the Church, even it wished to do justice to the task transmitted by the Reformation and the older Church, wished in its own way to continue the effort after correct Church proclamation that corresponded to the Word of God. Even it desired and therefore had its dogmatics. But it had lost the proper criterion for and over against Church proclamation, as it had been put into its hand by the Reformation in particular. It was still acquainted with it, but it had ceased to regard it as a criterion, as distinct from the present state of Church activity and superior to it. It still continued to take account of it, but it had ceased to understand its dignity, its character as an authority from which there can be no appeal. It forgot its duty of looking to it and to it alone in the question as to the Word of God, by which Church proclamation is to be measured. On this question it invariably looked another way. The place of the criterion of Reformed theology, which had as it were become empty, had to be otherwise occupied and was in fact otherwise occupied. Even if we regard as heretical this newer theology which took the lead with Pietism and the Enlightenment, we must admit that it wished to continue the critical function of theology ; it wished first and last to be the conscience of a preaching Church ; it was also aware that a conscience must have criteria. And if it had ceased to understand as such the criterion of Reformed theology, and therefore seized upon other criteria, it did so with the idea of possessing in these other criteria a full and equal substitute, in a measure representing what had been lost. Not of ill-will, but with a right goodwill it is as philosophical, cosmical, moral, secular, in a word as Protestantly civilised as it has become and was always becoming with ever new variations, right through the 18th and 19th centuries and up to our own. Even the golden calf (Ex. 32) was not to set forth a strange God, but the God who led Israel out of Egypt. Even Israel acted piously in that, and even Aaron met it in that with the best intentions. In this way we may regard the theology of Modernist Protestantism. It had ceased to envisage any possibility of getting within sight of the Word of God as an entity distinct from Church proclamation. But it was very much in sight of other entities, likewise distinct from Church proclamation and likewise very authoritative, comprised in the modern consciousness of being civilised. This consciousness, therefore, it thrust as a substitute into the place of the Word of God, become unreal to it, volatilised into an idea. And now it delivered judgment from that standpoint.

If we cannot achieve that distinction, if for us the Word of God, as distinct from Church proclamation, is not a concrete entity, then the treading of this road—which is not the only one that opens up at this point—may likewise be imminent for us. But in that case we must be very conscious of the difficult problems of this road, and the question is whether it is tolerable.

1. How do we know, as obviously we claim to know on that roadway, that the event of losing the Word of God as a concrete theological criterion, i.e. of losing a specifically theological relevancy, is a necessary and good event, the result of which must and may simply be accepted ?

2. How do we know whether the criteria newly chosen in place of that which was lost are really suitable for this undertaking, Church proclamation ? whether by applying them we are not creating confusion where the aim is order, and destruction where the aim is to build up ?

3. How do we know whether here, where perhaps only an absolutely given criterion ought to be considered, we are not decidedly in the wrong, when, however good our intentions, we look about generally for criteria, choose criteria and introduce them as such ?

4. How do we know, finally, whether any other criterion can act at all as a substitute for the Word of God, no longer in our grasp, whether, if we ought to be content with the impossibility of coming face to face with the Word of God, we had not better renounce all critical efforts about Church proclamation, i.e. all theology ?

These questions will, of course, really weigh with and possibly force from the road mentioned only those for whom the Word of God as a concrete, independent criterion has not completely disappeared from the field of vision, for whom, therefore, the possibility of comparing this criterion with those others has at least not been completely excluded.

This has not been the case even in the age of theological Modernism. The uneasiness caused by the quite different way of putting the question in the first century of the Church of the Reformation did not cease to have its effect. Many a time, of course, it was reduced to a minimum. If anything served to suppress it and so to harden the modernist attitude, it was the opposition which the official Church body offered to theological liberalism from the days of Wöllner's edict on religion, through the vexatious period of Frederick William IV up to the time before the World War ; because this opposition rested, not upon a better theology, upon a real vision of what Modernism had ceased to see, but in the main upon somewhat gloomy, conservative instincts, and because it worked out not in the way, alone possible in the Church, of spiritual conquest, but in the form of strong, political

19

repression of this, at that time, new theology. The human glory which has enveloped theological Liberalism right up to its last phase, distinguished by the names of Harnack and Troeltsch, the religious passion with which it could come forward at that very time in the theology of W. Herrmann, were the glory and the passion of a martyrdom by which the Church leaders, powerless to confront it with a superior utterance, ever and again put it in the right in its own eyes and in the eyes of the world. What an ecclesiastical " orthodoxy," so little sure of its business as that of the 18th, 19th, and 20th centuries, could bring or has brought about in view of the great Modernist *Quidproquo*, was certainly anything but a healthy unrest in this new Protestantism, due to the standpoint of the Reformation. And if over against the Liberal there has always, right into the last phase, been in addition a " positive " theology, so-called, borne along by considerable forces, one which formally sustained the Reformed thesis as to the criterion of dogmatics, it should, on the one hand, have kept aloof from an alliance with the unspiritually conservative Church authorities and declined their strongly political support, and on the other hand shown itself more unambiguously as the thing it claimed to be, the " theology of revelation." Had the " modern positive " group, in which the ruins of a whilom Erlangen and Leipzig school were once more found assembled in the first decade of our century, so much to reproach their Liberal opponents with, as they thought they had ? Where, in the last resort, was the " theological orthodoxy " of which Liberal periodicals had so much to say ? How it had co-operated in the hunt for other criteria ! What a line it had taken apologetically ! How many a one in their ranks could without special transformation waken up one morning a tolerably genuine religious philosopher, religious historian, or religious psychologist ! How it further increased the confusion of points of view, especially in the sphere of exegesis, by a historism which was none the better because it was a supernatural historism on friendly terms with tradition, without making the slightest impression on the enemy and without being able to prevent the frontiers between " Positive " and " Liberal " OT men, " Positive " and " Liberal " NT men, from being increasingly and finally altogether obliterated, and that entirely to the advantage of the so-called " Positives " ! And how utterly in the end, when the great moment came in which at least to some extent a " theology of revelation " should have distinguished itself from the theology of civilisation as based upon the relativity of everything human, did it go hand-in-hand with it, in ethos and in ethics ! I make these points, in which in themselves I have really no interest, only because continually (especially in the writings of E. Schaeder, but cf. also P. Althaus, *Die Theologie*, in C. Schweitzer, *Das relig. Deutschland der Gegenwart*, vol. II 1930 p. 140) the lament rings out, how much these days it is forgotten, that the theological protest against a *Kulturprotestantismus* has for ever so long and indeed always been to the fore. Certainly it was to the fore, and we add that it was also to the fore in Liberal theology itself ; how else should it have been, if as theology it was not going to sell up completely and retire ! Even Liberal theology was not actually as bad as it frequently claimed to be. Under pressure of the problem there were not wanting even in their own ranks certain counter-currents worth noting. No less zealously than E. Schaeder, Wobbermin to-day is continually announcing, e.g. *Richtlinien* 1930 in the Preface, *Wort Gottes* 1931 p. 4, note 2, that he has long been " in sharpest conflict not only against all psychologism, but also against all historism " (*op. cit.* p. 6). But what value, what meaning can there be in contesting or asserting priorities here ? If and so far as " it " was really said ages ago, by Positives and Liberals themselves, it had at the time just the effect and significance it was capable of having, in the form in which it was uttered. This is certain, that the real force of unrest emanated neither from the ecclesiastical authorities nor from the theology of that time, but quite simply from the fact that the Church continued to live and her proclamation also continued—led or misled, aided or only brought to ruin by Modernist theology, yet still continued even in the 18th, 19th, and 20th centuries. The Church continued to live, for the Bible still remained for the Church, a Bible frequently relativised on historico-psychological principles and misinterpreted in the interests of philosophy of religion, a Bible whose claim and need to constitute the textual basis of Church proclamation was questioned, more as a matter of fact than of insight extensively affirmed as against theological theory, a Bible to which one felt only more or less bound—but nevertheless the Bible, and with the Bible the problem and with the problem the unrest over the neo-Protestant solution. By the continuance of a proclamation somehow—very much " somehow " !—bound up with the Bible, by the continuing life of the Church in this her decisive function, the querying of the Modernist answer in this matter was always kept alive.

When, faced with the whole possibility of the other criteria being introduced in place of the Word of God in dogmatics, we put up those four questions, when we assert that what we are supposed to know in all the four points we cannot possibly know, when therefore we declare for the unsoundness of the whole suggested possibility of a solution—we thereby appeal to the simple fact that Church proclamation whether understood or not understood, whether inwardly grounded or merely in accordance with usage, is actually confronted with the Bible. So long as this confrontation is not set aside, no one can properly say that the whole problem does not exist for him, that the possibility of the Word of God being the true and concretely independent criterion of Church proclamation is entirely withdrawn from his field of vision.

From the book by Wilhelm Pauck, *Karl Barth, Prophet of a New Christianity ?* 1931 p. 99, I take the following information : " It is important to remember . . . that the difference between modern preaching in America and Protestant Europe is fundamental. The American sermon is seldom Biblical and expository. Its reference to the Scripture is in the majority of cases casual or superficial. It deals generally with ' religious ' topics. The European Protestant, however, follows the old tradition of preaching the ' Word,' whether he is affiliated with liberal or orthodox theology." If what concerns America is pretty generally correct, even the actual confrontation of the Church with the Bible here presupposed is there no longer or scarcely any longer an event. In that case naturally the problem based on this confrontation likewise does not arise. In that case I may expect among the successors of the Pilgrim Fathers neither interest nor understanding for what follows and at the same time for the whole of this dogmatics. But perhaps even there there is at least a dim recollection that the preaching of the Church might stand in some sort of distinct connection with the Bible. And even there it will surely happen some day that " religious topics " get for some so stupid and stale that from that dim recollection a clear one may arise once again.

From the situation of the parson in the pulpit,who has not merely to say something somehow, but to say it in face of the open Bible and presumably in accordance with the Bible and in exposition of the Bible, from this situation the man outside the Church, the abjurer of faith, can gather at least this, that here a protest against the introduction of other criteria of Church proclamation or, which comes to the same thing, that the validity of the Bible as the criterion, as the concrete form of the Word of God, might at the very lowest be possible. And yet it may also be that the Bible as the Word of God has already spoken or is yet to speak to us, that we should, therefore, have to think and judge in this matter not as outsiders but upon the terrain of the Church. The Church, re-garded as the human centre of human volition and action, rests indeed not upon the presupposition, of course, but upon the recollec-tion and expectation, that God has actually spoken the Word in the Bible and is speaking it to us. Can we stand by this recollection and expectation and to that extent by the Church, without having to propound the four questions ? And are the questions in that case to be answered otherwise than as follows ?

1. If it is really the case that we no longer know concretely whether and to what extent the Word of God is the measure by which Church proclamation is to be measured, if for us the Word of God has really been volatilised from a concrete " over-against " into a bare idea, then we have not to accept that as a historic fate in the history of mind ; it is the sign of the wrath of God, the tempta-tion of faith, a relapse into the consequences of disobedience, in which one cannot be a spectator of oneself, with which one cannot come to terms in the Church ; it is the event to which, in the knowledge that it is a matter of divine discipline, the only possible answer is a cry to the hidden God, that He would be pleased to restore one His gift of the lost measure. Thus it agrees with the recollection and expectation of faith. Faith may at any moment fall headlong into unbelief, and then the relevance of theology is actually lost and the temptation arises to make oneself a golden calf to represent the God of Israel, the temptation as it were to settle down comfortably in unbelief and fend for oneself. Faith overcomes this temptation. Faith does not make a virtue of

necessity. Even and actually in the depths of unbelief faith hears the new summons to faith. Thus even in the struggle about the Word of God, which undoubtedly befel it more than once before the 18th century, faith may quite well lose theological relevance, but lose it only to find it again.

2. In fact Church proclamation is not an undertaking which in view of its content could come under any other criteria than the very Word of God. What is undertaken in it is removed, not, of course, in respect of human motives and forms, but in respect of its intention in faith, from any claim to be judged from the standpoint of any philosophy or ethics or politics whatsoever. The introduction of another criterion can only mean here that the undertaking itself is also becoming different, that it is ceasing to be the Church's mandated undertaking, accompanied by the divine promise. For the introduction of another criterion means renouncing the believed intention of the undertaking. So far as a measure is really being applied here other than the measure of the Word of God itself, however right and weighty this measure may be, considered by itself, the practical result can only be confusion and ruin. The Church cannot listen to any other voice than the voice of her Lord, as the decisive word about her proclamation. If she fails to hear this, the darkness of complete want of counsel and leadership would be ever so much better than the light of strange lights however bright.

3. As a matter of fact a decided error is involved in the assumption that in matters of Church proclamation in general we can look round for criteria, select and apply them. The criterion to which she is aware of being subject the Church has not chosen and taken herself, it is given her. It is in force prior to and in the act of undertaking proclamation : it is undertaken on the basis of its being already in force. It may indeed be noticed or not noticed, acknowledged or not acknowledged, but when noticed and acknowledged it can be noticed and acknowledged only in an act of obedience, only in a finding unpreceded by any human seeking. The choice of other criteria in place of the Word of God is at once, by being a choice or act of human embarrassment and acuteness instead of an act of acknowledgment of prevenient divine goodness, betrays itself as an act signifying the abandonment of the Church's terrain, of her recollection and expectation, and, to that extent, of her faith.

4. But, finally, if it is objected that there is no question of really surrendering the one criterion of the Word of God, that the other

criteria are to be introduced merely to represent this sole one (in consideration of the inconceivability of this sole one !), that theology is not abandoning her task but merely, so to speak, assuming an incognito, by setting the other measures alongside the one, which is not thereby denied and deposed, but merely (always in view of its own inconceivability !) bound as it were to maintain substitutes or a substitute—our reply is, that the other criteria are to be rejected as irrelevant and injurious, because they cannot here act substitute, because a vicariate here is fundamentally impossible. Philosophy, ethics, politics or whatever might be offered us here, may have their importance and their rights in their own sphere, but they are the philosophy, ethics, politics of sinful, lost man, whose word, however deep and true it may be, cannot be acknowledged as judge over the Word which is to be directed in God's name to this sinful lost man, nor yet as judge over Church proclamation. In desiring here to judge himself man would not be judged. In desiring to serve proclamation from this standpoint, dogmatics would simply not serve it with a real, serious criticism and revision. Even theology would then be nothing else than one among the many forms of dialogue which man holds with himself about himself, whereas it is supposed to be a service to the language addressed by God to man. The real need of Church proclamation, the need to ask how sinful man can be the messenger of the divine Word, would be left unheeded, for in this need there is no help in the best-founded most highly-considered human judgment. Thus, if theology had no answer to give to this peculiar need of the Church, it might as a matter of fact just as well be discontinued.

The second possibility in the dilemma in which we should be placed if we were not aware of a concrete form of the Word of God as the supreme criterion of Church proclamation, would consist in our having to start from the fact that with her proclamation the Church is practically left to herself and dependent on herself. But, it might now be asked, does that mean that she is without the Word of God and therefore not in a position to control, criticise, and correct herself by the Word of God ? May not, must not the contraposition of the Word of God and Church proclamation be regarded as a relative one ? Did we not say ourselves that the reflection in which the Church makes this distinction, is the reflection of faith, which by making the distinction simultaneously grasps the divine promise, Lo, I am with you alway ! and precisely thereby already abrogates the distinction again ? Ought not the distinction therefore to end up in a distinction within the reality of the Church herself, in the distinction between the human and the divine element in her reality, both of which elements are yet to be regarded as elements in her reality? Is not the Word of God handed over to her as the Church of Jesus Christ, and is not therefore the missing concrete authority set up and alive in herself? Is not this very thing the Church's glory, her Lord's presence in her, namely, that she may and ought on the one hand to proclaim the Word of God and on the other hand herself to regulate, criticise, and revise this act of hers by means of the same Word of God?

In this possibility, in the first place, we are once more faced with a conception already discussed at an earlier stage, the Roman Catholic conception of the relation of the Bible to the Church's teaching office. According to this conception the Church has, of course, one Lord and Judge of her action, she, of course, has the Word of God over her. But she has it over her because she has it in herself, indistinguishable from herself. The Roman Catholic Church too possesses, reads, in fact reverences the Bible, without prejudice to her setting tradition by its side. But, of course, not the Bible by itself, not an emancipated Bible, not a Bible which confronts the Church as the authority. Here it is not acknowledged that the Bible as it stands is the Word of God and, as such, the supreme criterion of Church doctrine. Here, on the contrary, we are dealing with the Bible authentically interpreted by the Church herself, namely, by her teaching office through which Christ yet liveth and speaketh, with the Bible as belonging to the Church, properly understood, properly expounded, properly applied by her teaching office. It is the Word of God by which all proclamation is to be measured. Thus the *regula proxima fidei*, the nearest immediate plumb-line of Catholic belief is not the verdict of the Bible, but the verdict of the Church's teaching office on the Bible. (Cf. Diekamp, *Kath. Dogm.* vol. I 1930 p. 63 f.). By her actual view of the Bible the Church retains both proclamation and the norm for its needful criticism, in her own hands, i.e. the Bible rightly understood and rightly applied, which actually is the norm which is applied in such criticism. Actually there is only a relative distinction between the two, and the synthesis of them can cause no surprises to the Church who in her head is at once the *norma normata* and the *norma normans*, the *ecclesia audiens* and the *ecclesia docens*; for, at least in her head, i.e. in her teaching office, she has oversight of both and has full authority and power of disposal to complete the synthesis and, therefore, also the dogmatic criticism at her own free judgment. But in this possibility we are confronted not only by the Roman Catholic conception of the Church's teaching office. According to the doctrine of Protestant Modernism, too, we find the Church ultimately dependent on herself and left to herself. Here, too, that need not mean that the Church must be without the Word of God and therefore without any criterion of her proclamation. Here, too, the Bible was not simply thrown aside in favour of philosophical, historical, political, and other criteria. Here, too, there was still adherence to the connection between proclamation and the Bible, and also to a certain critical right of the Bible to speak in dogmatics. As a rule there was also still adherence, which largely served to obscure the issue, to the strong traditional theoretical propositions on the normativity, in the sense of the sole norma-

tivity of the Bible. " I am thoroughly serious in bringing to full and un-
modified validity Luther's basic proposition, that the Word of God alone is
to set up articles of faith . . . that quite exclusively and unconditionally
Holy Scripture alone is competent to be the source of dogmatic work, with the
severest rejection of so-called sub-sources." So—Wobbermin! (Chrt. u.
Wiss. 1932 p. 179.) But even here the Church does not hold the Bible as a
concrete and supreme criterion of herself. True, there is no infallible teaching
office here, to expound authoritatively the Bible's being in the Church, to
erect by its interpretation of the Bible the concrete regula proxima fidei.
But the fact that in Catholicism the Church in her unity as the norma normata
and the norma normans has precisely these two coefficients is not, even there,
the essential thing in this position. It is rather the presupposed relativity
of the opposition between Church and Bible that is essential, the insight into
this relativity ascribed to the Church, the capacity ascribed to her of herself
determining how far she will let herself be judged by the Bible, and therefore
ultimately be herself the judge in her own cause. That is what even Protestant
Modernism does, without any infallible teaching office. This state of things
is perhaps most clearly seen in that one of its various schools in which, apart
from Schleiermacher, its nature has in general been most clearly and
logically worked out, namely, in the theologians who philosophically take
their bearings on Hegel. When Ph. K. Marheineke ascribes quite unreservedly to the Christian community the " holy spirit of Jesus Christ,"
who " not only has knowledge in himself but himself is it " (Grundlehren der.
christl. Dogmatik, 1827 § 25), when therefore he can say of the Christian religion
that " in it God is known humanly as He knows Himself. It is truth in and
for itself " (§ 69), when in this Christian " spirit " he lets not only reason but
also Church tradition and Scripture be " abrogated in their aseity " (§ 113)
and then expressly makes this " spirit " the normative expositor not only of
tradition but also of the Bible (§ 112, 588), the expositor who by being himself
the spirit of the Bible takes in this his own standpoint, and therefore in
dogmatics as in Church tradition merely repeats what he already has, in
fact is himself (§ 116)—can this mean anything else than that the Bible continues to be preserved as a stage which the self-movement of the Christian
spirit must also pass beyond, yet which precisely as such is utterly lacking
in the character of a power independent of this self-movement and really
directing it ? Does it mean anything else than that, as it opens up to the
Christian thinker, the opposition between the divine and the human word is
also already perceived in its relativity and overcome ? Is there any fundamental significance in this Christian thinker not being exactly a Pope, and
also not having a Pope over him, if he can decide authoritatively as to the
extent of this perception and conquest ? Does not the nature of the same basic
view come but the more clearly to light if every one is called to be his own
Pope in virtue of the spirit which is alive in him as a member of the Christian
community ? And when A. E. Biedermann sets dogmatics the task of
gaining " autonomously," by logical working up of our experiential knowledge
of the Christian act of faith, knowledge of its nature, of the Christian principle
(Christl. Dogm. 1869 § 92), when he thinks to see this Christian principle in
the " religious personality of Jesus," i.e. in " that mutual relation between
God and man which in Jesus was the fact of his religious self-consciousness "
(§ 99), when accordingly he makes the Bible the place where the Christian
principle is " primarily " (next to it comes, as in Marheineke, on the same
level Church tradition, i.e. the historical development in question), as " the

prime form of Christian faith," to be transmitted by history and science
(§ 140)—what else does that mean than that the relation of dogmatics to the
Bible is regarded as a dialectical circle, the course of which is determined by
the dogmatist himself ? He works up his experiential knowledge of the
act of faith, exactly as he (now as an historian) claims to judge of the Christian
principle, so far as it meets him in the prime form of Christian faith in the Bible,
and in the development of the Church. In spite of the validation of this historical connecting point in terms of this theory, confrontation with a ἕτερος
νόμος is not achieved. All we get to is the grandiose loneliness of the
Church of the present, which always has the Word of God already in herself.
And it should be a sub-question of no very great moment as to whether
this loneliness is to be found more expressively symbolised in the Roman
Catholic institution of an official teaching office, or in the manifest lack
of such a thing in Protestant Modernism. The Roman Pope infallibly interpreting the Bible, or the Neo-protestant Professor of theology, as assuredly
the vehicle of the Christian principle or Christian spirit as the rediscoverer
of it in the Bible, are figures which perhaps really stand out from the same
background with the same effectiveness.

Regarding this second possibility also there is no direct proof
of its impossibility. Were we to pretend to lead such a proof, we
should, so to speak, abolish ourselves ; we should *ipso facto* prove,
not its impossibility, but, in profoundest accord with the adversary
here to be contradicted, its possibility on our part. To prove
that the contraposition of the Word of God and Church proclamation is not only, as is asserted here, a purely relative one, itself a
distinction within the Church of the present, that the Word of
God in the Bible rather confronts Church proclamation as the
judicial authority and remains in that position, that the Bible as
this supreme authority addressing the Church from without cannot
possibly be the Bible, as already interpreted dogmatically or
historically by the Pope or the Professor, but the Bible not yet
interpreted, the free Bible which remains free in face of all interpretation—to prove that we should obviously have to put ourselves
in a position above proclamation and the Bible, we should have to
share the opinion that to render this relation clear was a matter
of our ordering, in one sense or another, that we had the power
to establish the supremacy of the Word of God in this relation.
Obviously, too, the Bible whose supremacy we had the power to
prove would not be the free Bible which by being free constitutes
a real authority, but obviously it would likewise be a Bible already
interpreted in a definite way, our Bible made our own and thus
become an instrument in our own hands and to that extent, for
all its perhaps demonstrable supremacy, still also merely an element
within the Church of the day, which we ourselves constitute.

We shall, therefore, guard against venturing forth upon such a proof. It could only prove the opposite of what ought to be proved. Here, too, we can but indicate a fact, and in view of this fact, with the same absence of demonstration as before, introduce a contradiction. The fact is, once more, the meaning which the Bible practically has in the life of the Church (apart from all theories as to its meaning !).

It has it even in the Roman Church in spite of the mischievous doctrine of the Church's teaching office, and it has it even in Protestant Modernism in spite of the equally mischievous doctrine of the spirit of the community or of the Christian principle.

The Bible has never in any way completely lost the significance of a relative authority over against the consciousness and the proclamation of the Church of the day, the significance, so to speak, of a second voice, which she always wished to hear alongside her own and in harmony with her own. A certain apprehension and trouble over this harmony, over its establishment and maintenance, has never completely ceased. But that also means that counter to the theory or in a fulfilment of the theory, which was better than the theory itself, the possibility always remained, not that the Church ruled the Bible, but that the Bible ruled the Church, that the relationship of disposal, in theory ordered so entirely in favour of the Church, i.e. of man in the Church, the relationship of " above " and " in " the Church could actually be susceptible of reversal. At least, resistance by a free Bible, perhaps never completely the captive of any interpretation, remained a possibility. Even the Bible apparently assimilated by the Church was yet never so completely assimilated that men failed altogether to recall to consciousness from time to time at least the relative distance between it and herself, or that they fathered an attempt at complete denial of even the formal—perhaps really grown purely formal— difference as such. The Bible found and the Bible finds utterance in the Church. Thereby the possibility is not ruled out, that it may also find utterance over against the Church. True, this fact and the possibility that goes with it is only a sign. It may be overlooked. The history of the Bible in the Church may be so regarded and interpreted as that the Pope and the Professor have always done as they wished with the Bible. But it need not be so regarded and interpreted. Even in the case of such an outlook and interpretation it will have to be conceded that it might also be regarded and interpreted differently—perhaps as a matter of fact can not, but still might! Whether regarded or not regarded as such, regarded in this way or in that, the sign refuses to be denied away altogether. Of course the sign as such does not mean the answering of the question whether the Bible is the Word of God over the Church and to the Church. This question is a question for faith. How could it be answered by the existence of the sign? Neither may we assert generally that the question for faith is at least put by the presence of the sign. We may only say that by the sign the question for faith might be put. In answer to the sign it might happen that man in the Church is called to faith. It might be that in the Bible which ever and anon finds utterance in the Church man hears the Word of God, and really the Word which will not be imprisoned or bracketed by the Church, which refuses all inclusion in her own reality and cannot by any interpretation be translated into a word of man, the Word which confronts the Church, with which she cannot sing a duet, but which she simply has to listen to in its complete and unique solo voice. The happening of this event, the event of faith, we cannot take .for granted. We can only relate ourselves to this event, so far as it is the content of the promise given to the Church—we might also say, of the command given to the Church. We cannot speak about this event when it is there, being fulfilled, but only in recollection and in expectation. Because this event will take place in accordance with the promise, because the Church is to be the Church of Jesus Christ, the Bible will be heard as the Word of God. It is to this fulfilment to come of the promise received that we relate ourselves. The Word of God is the speech, the act, the mystery of God, and so not a substance immanent in the Church apart from the event of its being spoken and believed, or discoverable and demonstrable in her. Therefore, even the Church is not constantly, continuously the Church of Jesus Christ, but such she is in the event of the Word of God being spoken to her and believed by her. Therefore the sign, too, set up in the Church, of the Bible somehow speaking and being heard, is a genuine sign, but none the less, also, no more than that. If in regard to the event we could talk about a fulfilment that had already happened and as such wa s illuminating now, instead of about God's promise and command, about the present instead of about the future, if we could argue from faith and with faith, as with an available and handy assumption, then the sign would cease to be a sign. The presumption of the presence of faith would dissolve the sign as such into a directly visible and palpable datum. This datum being presumed, the Bible might then be regarded directly as the Word of God. This datum, together with faith or faith together with this datum, would then constitute the proof that the Bible is the Word of God. But by being led this very proof would contradict what it meant to prove.

It would lead us back pretty much to the point we started from, namely, the twofold formation of Roman Catholicism and Protestant Modernism. Nothing is more significant of both than the presumption that the event of faith in the Word of God has already taken place and therefore that faith is already present, a faith from which and with which one can argue. It is by means of this presumption that the sign as a sign is dissolved and thereby, of course, a proof made possible ; the proof that the Word of God as an authority is not o v e r the Church but i n the Church, that it is an authority properly and finally incorporated in and subordinated to the Church.

The Word of God o v e r and t o the Church is not susceptible of any proof, not even and least of all of this proof by the faith present in the Church. With the conclusion, Because I believe and because for me as a believer the Bible is the Word of God, therefore and to that extent it is God's Word—with this conclusion it is all over with the divinity of the Word of God, it is no longer regarded as the Word standing o v e r the Church, directed t o the Church. With this conclusion we are pursuing a *theologia gloriae* which—however loudly it may asseverate the opposite—is not in fact subdued to the Word of God. There is, therefore, no question of this conclusion, if the Bible is to be regarded here as the free, supreme criterion of Church proclamation. The relationship in which we do this, relationship with the event of faith, of the Word of God becoming uttered and heard, does not raise any claim to be a proof. By appeal to relationship to this event it is not meant that an argument should be brought forward—an argument seeking to prove the final percussion effect of the immediately religious—one which would transpose us into the position of proving against Catholicism and Modernism the perfect correctness of our own position and of defending it by attack. We must realise that the relationship to this event may quite well be turned against ourselves, because we do not hold this event in our hands, because in its nature it is a divine decision, the result of which we may not anticipate. Whether the Bible will speak to us as God's Word, whether we shall hear it, whether we shall believe in it as the Word of God—we and those with whom we are speaking—that we can neither take to ourselves nor give to them, the happening of that we cannot presume, from that point and with it we cannot argue. What we might presume to be our faith might even be God-forsaken unbelief, and to argue from that and with that might be extremely impotent. We can only point out that in the event, in faith in the Word of God in the Bible, the decision would, of course, be given smoothly and without contradiction against any conception of the Bible as an authority set up and superintended by the Church, as a merely relative counter-authority to Church proclamation of the day. Otherwise, if it did not achieve this decision by happening, it would not be this event.

But, very true, it is not for a moment a direct pointer to this event which achieves the relationship here in question. If we presumed to point directly to it, to dream of coming forward ourselves, somewhat in the attitude of Grünewald's John, as witnesses to this event, we should be alleging what one should never think of alleging, that we had, so to speak, its reality at our back, that we based on it, that by appealing to it we could contradict others. The word " pointer " would then be merely another word for " presupposition." But we cannot say, either as prophets or as apostles, and, therefore, certainly not with the full assurance of Biblical witness, " We beheld His glory " (John 1¹⁴). What we beheld and what—not warrants but, to put it simply, induces us to give the pointer in question, the *ratio* of our pointer, is once more very simple : it is the Bible, not yet removed out of the Church, not yet actually and entirely alienated from her proclamation, not yet stripped of all authority as compared with her, this actual fact, this sign, as we said before. We relate ourselves to the event of faith, by relating ourselves to this sign. The thing we indicate is thus itself an index or pointer.

Catholics and Modernists will be able and bound to grant that neither they nor we personally have created this sign and set it up. We all found it there. Amid many other signs which perhaps point in quite another direction, there is in the Church which claims to believe in herself as the Church of Jesus Christ at least this sign also, the voice of Moses and the prophets, of the evangelists and the apostles, not quite unnoted, not quite suppressed. What they say is, of course, a direct indication of the event of the Word of God and of faith : " we beheld His glory " and " we have believed and known " (John 6⁶⁹). We cannot say that of ourselves in that way. Once again, we are not witnesses in the same sense as the prophets and apostles. But it is before our eyes and ears that they said so about themselves and that they thereby claimed to have spoken not any sort of word of man, but the Word of God in human words, the Word which God Himself speaks to men, the Word in which God acts upon man, the Word in which God's mystery is manifest. That is the sign of the Bible which is set up among us. And to this sign, i.e. to this utterance of the prophets and apostles, to the claim they raise, we can pay as much or as little attention as we can pay to other facts. By living in the sphere of the Christian Church we are in a position and indeed called upon to attend to it. What comes·by our perhaps doing so is an act of recollection. Nothing has changed in itself by this attention, except that the world of our spiritual pictures has been increased by one more picture. *Notitia* has taken place, we have formed for ourselves an *opinio historica*. It does not turn us into prophets and apostles, it therefore does not place us within the reality of the Word and of faith, to which they bear witness. No unfolding or enrichment of this picture, no deepening of this recollection of ours, no systematic clearing up of its content, can bring us nearer the reality it indicates by the breadth of a line. Therefore, we are not referring to a method of realisation, placed in our own or any one else's hands together with the Bible, when for our part we now indicate this sign, this index that has been given to us. Naturally, we can only achieve this indication by already interpreting the Bible, be it in the briefest words, in some definite sense which then becomes our own sense. But this interpretation itself can make no other claim than that of drawing attention to the set-up sign as such. Interpretation itself can only be an indication, certainly not the discovery of the Holy Spirit or of the Christian principle in the Bible, certainly not mediation of the Word spoken in it. What happens or does not happen beyond this indication and its being indicated, beyond this recollection and *notitia*—the speech or silence of the Bible, the utterance of prophets and apostles *hic et nunc* and the impulse to utterance on the part of the men of to-day, the confirmation of the claim that it is God's Word, the decision being made, the occurrence of faith or else its non-occurrence—all this is withdrawn from our or any man's sight or grasp. It is true by being true. It lies not behind but before us. So and only so do we refer to it as to the decision against the relative and for the absolute validity of the Bible as the Word of God, as the genuine, supreme criterion of Church proclamation and thereby also of dogmatics. In making such a reference we, so to speak, take no responsibility for our action. Meaning that there is no sense or manner in which we have to answer for the Bible really being God's Word. Any wish to answer for it would here be a denial of what we wished to answer for. We can say no more than this, that in this matter the Bible can answer for itself.

As little as we can say clearly, directly, and generally that it answers for itself, so little may we or any one else say that it cannot answer for itself. We say it can, and in that way and thereby we associate ourselves with the event of faith in which the decision is made that it is for the Bible to speak and for the Church to hear. If we are asked what right we have to say that, we answer, No right that we have and claim for ourselves : but we have the right which is proved a right in the event of faith, if it occurs. If we are asked why we do this, why in view of the possible self-responsibility of the Bible we say No to the Catholic and Modernist doctrine of the Word of God, we reply : We as little know why we do this as we know why we got out of bed to-day not with the left but with the right foot first ; and, finally, neither question comes home to others in the same way. Once for all the fact is that once for all we oppose the doctrine. Were we further pressed and asked whether therefore it is an accident that we entered this opposition, we shall bite off our tongue rather than put the responsibility on the Holy Spirit or our faith or our conscience, so as in that way to give ourselves the necessary authority with the people, and we shall reply that accident springs from accidents. Therefore, it may have befallen us to raise and present this opposition. Not because so it is for me, but because once for all the fact is that here there is opposition, will ye have to come to terms with it as with a further modest little fact and sign.

And if it should further be said : Just so, a secret appeal to a special receipt of grace, to a Luther-like "I can no other," to a prophetic illumination, of course, once again we should cheerfully answer : Nothing of all that, nothing special, no whit of prophecy and apostolate, a perfectly earthly, harmless, ambiguous business, devoid of all mystic splendour or mystery, merely a little—Protestantism is what this opposition means, a sign to which we really cannot give any demonstrative power, a sign which may be opposed on all sides, which may be completely unremarked and completely misunderstood, a sign regarding the unimportance of which, amid the many other signs in which the world and the Church are so rich, we are under no illusions ! Is it a sign at all ? That we can neither desire nor know. With perfect ingenuousness and modesty we can simply act accordingly, i.e. enter our dissent. But, of course, by doing this we, being faced with the task of dogmatics, have therein decided to let the Bible stand as the absolute authority set up over against Church proclamation. That dogmatics cannot be " dogmatics " in the sense of the Roman Catholic Church, i.e. not an unfolding of the revealed truths immanent in the Church, and not *Glaubenslehre* in the sense of Protestant Modernism (the exposition of the faith of the men united in the Church)— that we have decided by our opposition, which, in view of the Biblical sign, must be made good only factually and not by proof. By this opposition we declare that the possibility of visualising the Word of God as an entity different from Church proclamation is given to us—as we saw, actually as a possibility—in the fact that in the Church the Bible is read, and we relate ourselves to this fact, when, not in a Catholic and not in a Modernist, but just in a Protestant way, i.e. in opposition, we take practical account of this possibility. By this opposition, which, of course, we take for granted in every form, we assert that dogmatics, as the inquiry about the Word of God in Church proclamation, must be the critical inquiry as to the agreement of Church proclamation, not with any norm of human truth or human value (that was the first possibility of our dilemma), nor with a standard of divine truth already known and proclaimed by the Church herself (that was the second possibility) but with the revelation attested in Holy Scripture. That is the concrete meaning of the inquiry to be set up in dogmatics concerning the Word of God. In view of § 4 we may also say that the task of Dogmatics is to deal with the problem of the equation of the Word of God and man's word in its form as Church proclamation with a view to its verification, and it does this by measuring Church proclamation as man's word by the second form of the Word of God, namely, by Holy Scripture, so far as, once more, the latter itself is the witness to its third and original form, revelation.

Because, and so far as this is the task of dogmatics, dogmatics or *theologia dogmatica* is its name. Therefore, we translate this concept, not by " The science of dogmas," but by " The science of dogma." Dogma is the agreement of Church proclamation with the revelation attested in Holy Scripture. Into this agreement, and therefore into dogma, dogmatics inquires. We thus oppose the Roman Catholic definition of the concepts dogma and dogmatics. According to it a dogma would be a truth of revelation defined by the Church ; and dogmatics the combination of and commentary upon these dogmas.

(For the following, cf. A. Deneffe, S. J., *Dogma, Wort und Begriff, Scholastik* 1931 p. 381 f. and 505 f.) In the colloquial usage of heathen antiquity, but also of the Greek OT and NT, the word " dogma " meant primarily a behest, a statute, a decree. E.g. the " law of the Medes and Persians " mentioned in Dan 6[16], because of which Daniel is put into the lion's den, is a dogma ; the command which according to Luke 2[1] went forth from Cæsar Augustus, is a dogma ; according to Eph. 2[15], Col. 2[14] the decrees of the OT Law are dogmas. But there is also a second meaning of the word in antiquity to be considered, that of a doctrinal proposition in philosophy or in science generally, emanating from an individual teacher, a school or movement ; and it is apparently with more of the latter than of the former significance that the word, almost always used in the plural to signify Christian truths, has by the 2nd century (first in Ignatius of Antioch *Ad Magn.* 13[1]) passed over into the usage primarily of the Greek Church. But Cyprian, Tertullian, Ambrose, Augustine, Leo the Great, and Gregory the Great were still unacquainted with it in this significance or did not wish to use it, in fact as late as Thomas Aquinas it is seldom used with this meaning. The rival of this meaning right up to the present day is the directly opposite one (found as early as Irenaeus, *C. o. h.* I 31, 3). Perhaps this is the only one Augustine knew ! : dogmas, distinguished as such by all manner of adjectives of evil connotation, are the false doctrines of heathen or heretics. (In the Encyclical " *Quod Apostolici,*" 28th Dec. 1878 Leo XIII still speaks of the *prava dogmata Socialistarum*). But ever since the 16th century the word apparently has come into currency with special emphasis in the second meaning mentioned (in the sense of *dogma fidei, dogma catholicum, dogma Ecclesiae*). At all events it is from this point of view that theological efforts begin in the Roman Catholic Church to define the concept. The result of them is summarised by Deneffe (*op. cit.* p. 531), in agreement with Diekamp and Bartmann, in the proposition, *Dogma est veritas a Deo formaliter revelata et ab Ecclesia sive solemniter* (by an *ex cathedra* decision or *conciliar* decree) *sive ordinarie* (by the fact that it is generally taught in the Church without opposition) *definita.* (As against R. Seeberg, *Lehrbuch der Dogmengeschichte*, vol. I 3rd edn. 1920 p. 1, we should therefore have to say that the formal acknowledgment of the propositions in question by the Church is far from exhausting the concept of Church dogma.) In the Catholic view dogmatics is consequently the systematic exposition of these revealed truths. (Cf. Bartmann, *Lehrbuch d. Dogm.* 7th edn. vol. I 1928 p. 2 ; Diekamp, *Kath. Dogm.* 6th edn. vol. I 1930 p. 11.) But, on the Evangelical side also, R. Rothe (*Zur Dogm.* 1863 p. 14) regarded the task of dogmatics in this sense.

In the first place we make the point, that even we, though, of course, in a way to be explained in greater detail, acknowledge that there are dogmas in the sense of this definition. We shall have to deal at a later part of our Prolegomena with dogmas, i.e. the doctrinal propositions acknowledged and confessed by the Church which are deposited in the Church symbols, with their relative authority and with their importance even for dogmatics. But—

20

and this is our first objection to the Roman Catholic concept of dogmas and dogmatics—we must deny that dogmas constitute the goal of dogmatic work, that dogmatics is called dogmatics because of them. For dogmas are not *veritates a Deo formaliter revelatae*. In dogmas there speaks the Church of the past—venerable, worthy of respect, authoritative, *non sine Deo*, as befits her—but the Church; she defines (i.e. circumscribes in dogmas) revealed truth, the Word of God. And thereby out of the Word of God comes the word of man, not unworthy of notice but extremely worthy of it, yet the word of man. The Word of God is above dogma as the heavens are above the earth.

The closeness of *dogmata ecclesiastica* to *dogmata haereticorum* must surely recall at once the fundamental assailability of dogma as defined by the Church, and keep at a distance any idea of an infallible dogma of this description. But we may also point to the fact that according to Roman Catholic doctrine itself dogmas are not yet known or defined by the Church, in their full number, that without prejudice to the substantially closed character of revealed truth there is rather a dogmatic progress (cf. Diekamp, *op. cit.* p. 15) and that as the unalterable and infallible truth in the formulæ of the dogmas there is finally offered, not the formulæ, but their "material content" (*sensus*) (Bartmann, *op. cit.* p. 38). In this explanation there might lurk an admission of the humanness of the dogmas. But, of course, it is always the Church herself who is to be the subject likewise of the dogmatic progress kept in view, and, moreover, the *sensus* to be distinguished from the dogmatic formula will always be none other than the *sensus, quem tenuit ac tenet sancta mater Ecclesia (Conc. Vatic., Constit. dogm. De fide cath., cap. 2)*. Here it can never come to a real attack on dogmas, i.e. on the Church which proclaims the dogmas and explains them more fully in particular cases, to a clear and serious distinction between dogmas and the Word of God.

In the identification of the Word of God and Church proclamation as it meets us in this definition of the concept, we can only have in view the coefficient of that grandiose isolation in which a Church must find itself which has sequestered the Word of God beforehand for herself by an embargo and taken it under her own management, and has lost the capacity of listening to the voice of a Confronter. If it is this voice from opposite that should be heard as the criterion of what the Church says and does, then dogmatics cannot hold to the inquiry into Church dogmas, then Church dogmas cannot be the form in which it hears the voice from opposite. Otherwise, looked at from this side as well, dogmatics would be a dialogue by the Church with herself, by the Church of to-day with the Church of yesterday and the day before. In the context of the dialogue which God conducts with His Church, even this dialogue by the Church with herself may acquire its meaning. Precisely a dialogue by the Church of to-day with the Church of yesterday and the day before will likewise have to be conducted in dogmatics, as we shall still need to show in principle. But if dogmatics chose to exhaust itself in that, it would certainly not do justice to its task as the Church's responsibility to the Word of God. It simply would not have taken up this task at all. Thus the dogma after which dogmatics inquires certainly cannot be the *veritas ab Ecclesia definita*. The *veritas ab Ecclesia definita* is itself an inquiry after dogma. It may and should guide dogmatics. It cannot claim to be the dogma which is the goal of dogmatics.

But secondly we shall have to say that the dogma after which dogmatics inquires is not the truth of revelation, but it is on the way to the truth of revelation. That will also be to be said about the dogmas of the Church to which at this point we make no closer approach as yet. They are propositions which grasp and reproduce the truth of revelation only so far as they strive towards it.

Even Thomas Aquinas associates himself with a definition of the concept of the *articulus fidei* and so of the single concrete Church dogma by Isidore of Seville: *articulus est perceptio divinae veritatis tendens in ipsam* (*S. th.* II², qu. 1 art. 6).

The inner meaning of all possible propositions of the kind, the thing all dogmas mean to express when they strive towards the truth of revelation, is the dogma after which dogmatics inquires. In calling it the inner meaning of all propositions of the kind, we as good as say that it is not itself a proposition, that it is not proclaimed at any time by any Church. It is what is intended in all possible propositions of the kind, it is the dogma for the sake of which the Church proclaims dogmas. Dogma signifies the essence, of which dogmas, as well as dogmatic propositions, i.e. the propositions of dogmatic science, claim to be manifestations, the essence from which real dogmas and real dogmatic propositions may arise, namely, when they reproduce it. For the sake of dogma, dogmatics must also associate itself with dogmas. Dogmas call upon it to give attention to dogma, they give it directions— just as the Church can give directions—to inquire after dogma. Upon a third and lowest grade it then builds its propositions, the scientifically dogmatic propositions. Dogmatic propositions, dogmas, and dogma have this in common ; taken together they are not the truth of revelation, but dogma is, and the dogmas

and dogmatic propositions aim at being (they are so under the
proviso that by the grace of God, by dint of watching and prayer
they become so) on the way to the truth of revelation. Dogma
in the original and proper sense, as the inner meaning of all dogmas
and all dogmatic propositions, is a concept of relation, and arising
from it so too are all dogmas and dogmatic propositions. Only that
in their case it is set up under the conscious proviso in question
as to whether they are complete relating concepts, i.e. concepts
of a relation that really exists. Of the relation in point we are
already aware : it is a matter of the relation with the agreement
between Church proclamation and the Bible as the Word of God.
Dogma may thus be defined as Church proclamation, so far
as it really agrees with the Bible as the Word of God.
If we knew about dogma, if we had dogma, then we would know
and have the Word of God itself in a definite and definitely indicated form and manifestation of Church proclamation, because
dogma is Church proclamation in real agreement with the Word of
God. But a theology which would assert its knowledge and possession of dogma would be *theologia gloriae*, which ought not to
claim to be the dogmatics of the Church. What it is faced with is
always actual Church proclamation in the entire humanity of its
form and manifestation on the one hand, and on the other hand
the sign set up in the Church, namely, the promise and commandment of the Bible. And the task set it is the inquiry after the
Word of God in Church proclamation and so the inquiry after
dogma, after that attitude towards the Bible as the Word of God
which is essential to Church preaching. Each answer, each realisation of such an attitude and agreement could only be one of two
things, either the event of the Word of God itself which dogmatics
can neither presuppose nor postulate nor create, or one of the great
illusions and prolepses in a dogmatics which is not aware that for
all its presupposing, postulating or attempts at creation it is nothing
in respect of this event. Thus the real results of dogmatics, even
when they take the form of the most positive declarations, can
themselves only be new questions, questions as between what
the Church seems to want to proclaim and what the Bible seems
to want to have proclaimed, questions which can only be put
with the greatest modesty and with a consciousness of being
under the greatest stress, especially if perhaps they are serious,
important questions. If inquiry ceased, if instead of dogmas and
dogmatic propositions dogma itself took the boards, if one could

exhibit the agreement of definite Church proclamation with the Word of God and therefore show the Word of God itself in this particular Church proclamation, then along with the *ecclesia militans* dogmatics would be at an end and the Kingdom of God would have dawned. The second possibility of such a manifestation of dogma, or of the Word of God itself, can only be that of the great illusions and prolepses.

To that extent, as I myself did in the first edition of this book (pp. 112–113), one may term dogma an " eschatological concept."
The old Lutheran theology (e.g. Quenstedt, *Theol. did. pol.* 1685 I. *cap.* 1, *sect.* 1, *thes.* 3–14) made a very sensible distinction between the *theologia archetypos* which God has and in fact is Himself, and *theologia ektypos*, as with the exception of Christ according to His humanity and the angels it may belong to men as well, where too the *theologia hominum* possible to us has once more one of two meanings, as *theologia patriae* in the eternal redemption and as *theologia viatorum* in this world, and here in this world a different one *ante* and *post lapsum*, again a different one *post lapsum* as *theologia naturalis* and *supranaturalis* and as *supranaturalis* once more a different one as *theologia immediatae* and *mediatae revelationis* ; the former only for prophets, apostles, and evangelists, the latter for us, as persons directed to their writings. This *theologia ektypos mediatae revelationis hominum viatorum post lapsum* which reaches us may obviously once more be treated under a double aspect ; first in its relation to its original type, *theologia immediatae revelationis*, which accords with its meaning but is hidden from us, purely future for us, not to be realised by us and so constituting the object of our inquiry ; then and to that extent it is dogma. Secondly, in its completion as the Church's concrete work of thought completed in time and always completed at a particular time, the work of the Church and in the Church, the inquiry after the relation laid upon us for the sake of Church proclamation. Then and to that extent we shall have to understand by *theologia ektypos mediatae revelationis hominum viatorum post lapsum* on the one hand Church dogma, and on the other hand the thing with which we are busied here, the scientific work of dogmatics.

We shall next, in the third place, have to ask concerning the Roman Catholic concept of dogma and dogmatics, whether it is not the symptom of a wrong development which set in every early, that the concept of " dogma " was taken up into Church language in the sense of " doctrinal proposition " instead of in the sense of " behest " or " decree " which is so much more readily suggested by Biblical usage. Assuming that Church dogma is to be equated with *veritas revelata*—that it aims at the truth of revelation even we admit—is *veritas revelata* the truth of a doctrinal proposition ? Is the truth of revelation—so we must ask by further cross-examination—like other truths in that it may be fixed as ἀλήθεια, i.e. as the unveiled state of a hidden characteristic in human thoughts, concepts, and judgments and in the form thus limited and minted, held in preserve, so to speak, quite apart from the event of its becoming revealed as truth? Such obviously is the case with the truth of a doctrinal proposition. But will the truth of revelation submit to such materialisation and depersonalisation? Can it be possessed in abstraction from the person of Him who reveals it, and from the revealing act of this person, in which it is given to another person to perceive? Can the possession of this truth take place otherwise than, once more, in an act of the person perceiving it, in a decision, i.e. in the taking up of an attitude? If the truth of revelation is the truth of a doctrinal proposition, then, obviously, yes.

The truth of a doctrinal proposition may be viewed neutrally as a neutral truth. Of course one may go so far as to agree or not to agree with it. But it is not of the essence of it to demand this decision. Nor is it of the essence of encountering it that we should take up an attitude to it. That is what the Catholic definition of dogma as a doctrinal proposition in fact excludes. That dogma as such means only doctrine and not also commandment is, in the usage of the 2nd and 3rd century Fathers and as late as the 4th in Eusebius and Athanasius, the reverse of clear. But it becomes clear in Cyril of Jerusalem, Gregory of Nyssa and Cyril of Alexandria, in whom dogma as the doctrine of faith and dogma as moral commandment are kept separate as two distinct entities, (cf. Deneffe, op. cit. pp. 508–13). The result of Roman Catholic dogmatics equating not only dogma with veritas revelata, but also veritas revelata with the truth of a doctrinal proposition is one of its most prominent characteristics. We have already touched upon it at an earlier point. It is that Catholic doctrine is theory qua theory and for theory's sake, certainly affirmed theory, but essentially, according to the prevailing Thomist conception, pure theory. Theory qua theory means that the affirmation of veritas revelata as such is the judgment of a thinker who as such is not forced to this verdict or to its opposite. In itself it is primarily not so much the challenge of this verdict, the compulsion to take up an attitude, as rather for its own part pure, neutral truth. It is true in itself in the fixed, minted form of the doctrinal proposition, and then for us, whatever our attitude to it may be, in the form of perception and understanding of the proposition in question. Theory for theory's sake means that theory, the treatment of the veritas revelata, has its aim and purpose in itself. It has no necessary correspondence with an action, to say nothing of it being itself regarded as an action. The whole joining up of the task of dogmatics with Church proclamation, as we here take it for granted, is quite uncatholic, for the simple reason that for Catholic dogmatics the question as to a task of dogmatics lying outside itself is as impossible as the question as to a special task of the mystic, of the angels, or of the blessed in heaven in their vision of God. The task which awaits the Catholic dogmatist can only be to grasp and expound in its articulated wealth the world become visible once for all in the veritates revelatae, the God-ordered world of definite spiritual ingredients (cf. on this E. Peterson, Über die Forderung einer Theologie des Glaubens, Z.d.Z., 1925 p. 282).

It is this reserve with which the truth of a doctrinal proposition

may be confronted, this possibility of a purely theoretical attitude
to it and the idea objectively answering to this possibility of a
purely material, impersonal presence of truth in the proposition,
it is this that for us makes the equation between *veritas revelata*
and doctrinal proposition doubtful and more than doubtful.

We might also ask for a moment—and it is instructive to do so
—whether we cannot establish the validity of our doubt by manag-
ing to follow out the other Catholic equation in virtue of which we
had to equate Church dogma with *veritas revelata*. Even on this
Catholic ground itself should it not be asked whether *veritas
revelata* or Church dogma can be a truth separable from the Person
of God who speaks and acts by speaking, a truth which does not
as such compel to decision, to action, and in the acceptance of
which there is neither decision as such, nor service as such to a task
lying outside itself? Whether, by having to do with such a neutral
truth that allows himself to be neutral, man has to do with God?
Whether a doctrinal proposition as such can be regarded as the
Word of God? Must not dogma, also and especially on Catholic
ground where it is identified with the Word of God, be regarded,
in conjunction with Biblical usage as it was at least still possible
in the first century Fathers, primarily as a command? And so
as a truth which we may possess as a truth only by it being told us
by God, and by the acceptance of it being impossible otherwise
than by the decision of a definite attitude to what is said to us?
And so as a dogma, which, of course, is also a " doctrinal proposition " (it is not a question of excluding this meaning ; why should
we ? Why should not also and particularly a behest be able to
instruct us ?), but a doctrinal proposition which can teach us and
be a dogma, only so far as it " goes forth " from God, as the decree
" went forth " from Cæsar Augustus, and so just as a behest goes
forth—and comes to us in the act of obedience (or does not come to
us in the act of disobedience, teaches us nothing, does not as
dogma exist for us) and so just as an order comes or does not come
to us; goes forth in a divine, comes to us in a human decision?
But, of course, we must realise that we can only tread Catholic ground
with this question and with this offer in order to leave it again at
once, or if we should with this question find a hearing on Catholic
ground, it would have to cease being Catholic ground. For how
could it be otherwise ? This question or this offer would at once
have to call in question even the assumed Catholic equation
between Church dogma and *veritas revelata*.

According to the Catholic conception Church dogma must primarily
have the character of a doctrinal proposition, precisely in order that intrinsically it may be an object of contemplation, in order that anything
problematic may be removed from the truth of it, as well by man's attitude
to it as by God Himself. The character of dogma as a doctrinal proposition
is meant to guarantee—to guarantee in a way that its character as a command
could not, in a way that would literally be endangered by its character as a
command—its objectivity, its truth in itself and therewith its credibility
as *veritas revelata*. Catholic theology prefers to take the materialisation and
depersonalisation of revealed truth into the bargain as that, of course, is given
in the fact that dogma is interpreted as a doctrinal proposition. It prefers
to make a virtue of the necessity thus arising and to explain that the materiality and lack of personality in the doctrinal proposition, its abstraction
from all human and divine decision, its unparadoxical state of being unveiled to which as a doctrinal proposition it gives expression, are the marks
and credentials of dogma as revealed truth. Catholic theology prefers to
say that, rather than depart in any sense from the equation. By that equation, by the assumption that revealed truth is given over to the Church
in the form of dogmas (not only in this form, but also in this form), that she
possesses and has to guard them as such, has to see theologically to their
validation as such, to the credibility of their truth *per se*, particularly by
the idea of revealed truth as contemplative material put into the Church's
hands, Catholic theology stands or falls. It must make a virtue of the
necessity. Or rather, for her the necessity is not a necessity at all. She not
only takes into the bargain, as Catholic theology she means to affirm from the
very start, pretty well everything that is given with the character of dogma
as a doctrinal proposition. Only in our eyes not in hers was what happened
then in the matter of the word " dogma " a wrong development. In her
eyes everything had to come out as it did. She would have had to abandon
herself, had she meant to return to the question whether in the concept of
dogma there was not proposed the meaning of command or behest and
whether then it might not also be determinative of its meaning as doctrinal
proposition. If our demand or proposal in this connection is to be taken
seriously—as seriously as we naturally mean it—if the doctrine of dogma
should really be regarded as a behest (and not, of course, its behest, once more,
as a doctrine to be contemplated : which naturally is not denied by Catholic
theology), it must then be immediately clear that the dogma set up by the
Church herself cannot itself be this behest, but only a serious reminder of this
behest.

We cannot give ourselves an order which is what it is only by
the act of Him who orders and of him who obeys or disobeys, in
the way in which the Church gives herself Church dogmas. Moreover, the truth of doctrine which we can receive by a behest we
cannot possess in the way in which the Church possesses the truth
of her dogmas. If *veritas revelata* is a behest, then it cannot be
identical with Church dogma. Church dogma and *veritas revelata*
necessarily part company. We must therefore withdraw, realising
that there is no room for our views on Catholic terrain.

Or rather we must say polemically, that the impossibility of the Catholic equation between revealed truth and Church dogma is for us betrayed by the fact that out of revealed truth must issue what has issued from it in Catholicism. The material, impersonal truth-in-itself ascribed to dogma, its objectivity for contemplation (which is the whole point for Catholic theology when it stresses in the concept of dogma the meaning of a doctrinal proposition), is what for us is the mark of a truth conditioned and confined not only by man's creatureliness but also by his sin, in contrast with which the truth of God in His revelation is quite a different truth. In virtue of the very fact that as a doctrinal proposition it can also be treated simply, that as a doctrinal proposition it is neutral and permits of neutrality, that precisely as a theory—and who would deny that Church dogma is also that ?— it itself bears witness to its place of origin, namely, to the Church, her language, her testimonies, her proclamation, her dialogue with herself— all this certainly in a marked manner, but we are not thinking of urging that Church dogma should be brought down to this level of hers—but to the Church, and not to the Word in which God addresses the Church. We do not think and never can think that that truth should be the truth of the Word of God, which is put in the hands of the Church as is the case with Church dogma. We claim to know the truth of the Word of God from the witness of Holy Scripture as a truth that is sovereign in quite another way.

Our recalling of the older use of " dogma " is not to be taken as meaning that we wished to identify Church dogma as a behest with the Word of God. So far as Church dogma is a behest—and, of course, we think it our duty to indicate that it would have been much more suitable from the OT and NT point of view to introduce it into the Church's vocabulary with this signification—it is a human behest, a behest imposed by sinners, although sinners assembled in the Church, and as such surrounded and permeated by the utter ambiguity, frailty, and perversion of human behests. Heaven is as high above Church dogma regarded as a behest as it is above it regarded as a doctrinal proposition, and we are not thinking of putting the Church in possession of the Word of God by an indirect move regarding this second or rather first signification of the concept. But assuredly the recollection of this first signification of the concept may lend us important light for understanding the concept of the dogma which dogmatics inquires after, for understanding the concept of the agreement of Church proclamation with the Word of God in Holy Scripture. Recalling the first signification of the word we shall have to regard the relation implicit in this concept of dogma as the relation between behest and obedience, and also but only then as the relation between doctrine and instruction. Agreement of Church proclamation with the Word of God naturally also signifies the truth of Church proclamation. But truth cannot be the last word on this agreement. For what truth is, is measured by the thing that in this case is higher, by what God's will is. His Word comes home to sinful men assembled in the Church as the Word of the Lord, the knowledge of which must be achieved in the form of acknowledgment. It must first (not in a temporal but in a logical " first " !) be believed and only then and in that way can it be known as truth. *Credo ut intelligam.*

The Catholic Church has herself expressed this very finely in the formula, *Credimus non propter intrinsecam rerum veritatem naturali rationis lumine perspectam, sed propter auctoritatem ipsius Dei revelantis, qui nec falli nec fallere potest (Conc. Vatic. Constit. dogm. de fide cath., cap.* 3). Of course the *auctoritas* is also *veritas*, but it is not its being *veritas* but its being *auctoritas* that makes it credible.

It would be knowledge of real dogma if we knew of such a form of Church proclamation as was conform to the will of God, in which God's behest to the Church was executed, in which the faith of the Church coincided with the orders of the Lord. Then and to that extent it would also be the perfect truth, while on the contrary any truth which might belong to it otherwise than in fulfilment of the divine behest would not make it real dogma at all, but would rather be shown to need the inquiry after dogma, because measured by it, it would still always be untruth. Therefore, since knowledge of real dogma will never come to pass before the end of all things, the meaning of our search for dogma must be, not primarily the search of a pupil who is anxious for his thoughts to agree with the superior thoughts of his teacher, but primarily the question of a servant who has to inquire into the agreement of his action with the purposes of his master, in order then, by this occasion, to discover for certain how to learn something he did not know before. When we call dogma, about which we inquire in dogmatics, a concept of connecting relation, we mean by that that it is the concept of a relation which exists between a demand and a decision corresponding to the demand. Dogma is the relation between the commanding God and the man who hearkens to His command, the relation which takes place in the event of this commanding and hearkening. Therefore, it is not an *opus supererogationis*, or a luxury or an academic game to work at dogmatics in the Church. It is certainly not the case that the Church carries on her proclamation orderly in good faith and according to the will of God, and then incidentally also raises the question—it may perhaps only be the question of certain people specially interested for intellectual reasons—whether and how far this proclamation is also true, while dogmatics would then exist to satisfy this special need. It is not the case that in respect of the Church's obedience in her proclamation all is arranged for the best, only the so-called " permeation by thought," the explication of faith is lacking, that only the cry for a world view, for the relation between this faith, so attractive in itself, and knowledge would still be unsatisfied, and that then to this demand of curiosity or would-be truthfulness dogmatics would also have to be offered somewhere by some one, alongside something else which the Church offered her members. No, the fact is, the subject of debate in dogmatics is the Church's relation of obedience to her Lord with regard to her proclamation which is at the root of everything. It is not a question of a little bit of truth for such as feel specially disturbed on that score, although generally they are as undisturbed as all the rest ; it is a question of the will of God, the acknowledgment or non-acknowledgment of which in the Church's proclamation is a matter which must verily disturb the whole Church, the Church as such and in all her members. The Church stands or falls with what is sought for in dogmatics. Therefore, she must inquire after it. She cannot work or not work at dogmatics. A dogmatics which she might just as well not work at, in whose inquiry she did not altogether participate, as inquiry as to her own existence, a dogmatics which let itself be crowded into the corner of the religiously intellectual or the intellectually religious, could only be a bad, useless and boring dogmatics which in that case would be much better not worked at all. We work at dogmatics, because urged by the fact of the Bible we are not free of the question as to the obedience of Church proclamation. In the question as to obedience is included that as to its truth. But the question as to its truth may be put merely as the question as to its obedience. As the question about obedience it is the question about dogma.

2. DOGMATICS AS A SCIENCE

Already in an earlier context we made the point (§ 1, 1) that if theology generally and with it dogmatics regards and designates itself a " science," it does not do so on principle ; i.e. it does not raise this claim as one by the acknowledgment of which it would stand or fall, and it raises the claim without being able or even willing to prove and justify it before a tribunal outside itself. Nor does it recognise the need of regarding or legitimating itself generally as a science. Nor does it acknowledge the universal concept of science in authority to-day as also authoritative for itself. Nor does it acknowledge the obligation to oppose to this another concept of science, including and so justifying itself. It regards and designates itself a " science " because it has no interest in anything but a *de facto* separation from the other so-called efforts of man after knowledge, because it must protest against a concept of science which would exclude precisely this effort it is making after knowledge, because it affirms a unity in all man's efforts after knowledge which though hidden are on the way to it and as such are real ; we might also say, because it affirms the Church as the hidden yet ever so real area of all human efforts after knowledge. What it understands by " science " in designating itself as such, it itself defines in responsibility to the Church which it serves—which the other sciences too might and must and finally and ultimately will serve — in responsibility to its object and to the task set by that object. It is aware first of all that in its inquiry into dogma, i.e. into the agreement between Church proclamation and the Word of God, it has to tread a defined path to knowledge, the path defined by this special problem. And it is aware secondly that it itself, i.e. every one participating in its problem, has to submit an account of this its path to knowledge. In this twofold obligation inwardly towards itself consists the concrete meaning of its outward claim (not provable before the tribunal of a general concept of science) to be a science : its scientific quality consists in its being effected (in fact in its being effected with a consciousness that constantly calls for renewal) in the inquiry as to dogma as that is set by the existence of the Church. Where the investigation is conducted with this effectiveness, we might even say, with this objectivity, there dogmatics as a science takes place.

At this point we shall have to maintain a relative distinction. There is a regular and there is an irregular dogmatics.

By regular dogmatics we are to understand an inquiry into dogma such that in it we concentrate upon the completeness appropriate to the special task of the School, of theological instruction. If it is to be a good school the theological school must give training in independent inquiry as to dogma. For that reason it must be as complete as possible ; it must impress on the pupil how the one question breaks up into many questions and how these many questions are open practically all along the line and from every possible point of view, and stand in connection with one another. A regular or school dogmatics must, therefore,

cover the whole ground regarding the range of concepts and themes
'of significance for Church proclamation, regarding the Biblical
testimony in which this proclamation has its concrete criterion,
regarding its bearings on the history of dogmas and of dogmatics,
i.e. on the concrete forms of Church proclamation available to date,
regarding the real and imaginable difficulties and oppositions which
must be dealt with for every separate question, lastly regarding
the implicit and explicit clarity of the path to knowledge. These
are demands which arise of themselves if dogmatics is to be taught
and if this instruction is to be deliberate guidance, in fact guidance
to independent dogmatic work and not merely the imparting of
the results of a particular teacher's work.

Regular systems of dogmatics in this sense are, in the ancient Church,
Origen's work Περὶ ἀρχῶν, Gregory of Nyssa's great "Discourse,"
Cyril of Jerusalem's *Katecheses*, Augustine's *Enchiridion*, John of
Damascus' Ἔκδοσις ἀκριβῆς τῆς ὀρθ. πίστ., in the Middle Ages the writings
of Anselm of Canterbury (regarded as a whole and according to his
purpose!), the *Sentences* of Peter Lombard, and naturally the *Summas*
of the Great Dominicans and Franciscans. The unmistakable increase
in "school" tone which takes place between the Church Fathers and the
Scholastics, is repeated again upon Evangelical ground between the regular
dogmatics of the Reformation time itself (Melanchthon's *Loci*, at least
in their later drafts, Zwingli's *Commentarius de vera et falsa religione*, and
above all Calvin's *Institutio*) and Protestant Orthodoxy, particularly of the
17th century, which was quite peculiarly industrious and fruitful as well
in comprehensive books on doctrine as in compendious outlines, and which
was faced by a Catholic theology no less learnedly equipped. With the
18th century there set in once more a slow but distinct depression. Since
the middle of the 19th century Catholic dogmatics has recovered from it,
chiefly by its universal and deliberate return to Thomas Aquinas. Thanks
to the services of Schleiermacher and under his influence (for example
in the works of A. Schweizer, A. E. Biedermann, J. A. Dorner) Evangelical dogmatics likewise experienced a new golden age, even before the
recrudescence on the Catholic side. But this undeniable formal rise in Evangelical dogmatics in the first half of the 19th century had too little inner necessity, was too little due to a fresh understanding of the matter of evangelical
theology, too much conditioned by taking over the acquisitions of contemporary philosophy and, in that connection, too much conditioned
by an all-round abandonment of the theme of evangelical theology, to prove
itself true. It was a tired age, which thought it saw a gleam of hope in the
theology of A. Ritschl, which ultimately merely reached back over Idealism
and Romanticism to the quintessence of Enlightenment dogmatics. The
spasmodic concentration which made the dogmatics of this school impressive
for a time, ended in an individualistic simplification and abbreviation of all
questions, which has given (this holds true as compared with its own past,
even before Ritschl) a markedly journalistic stamp to modern Evangelical
dogmatics. To see what is meant here one should compare say the *Glaubenslehre* of Troeltsch, the leading figure of the period linked up with Ritschl,

with the dogmatics of A. E. Biedermann or with the work done by a follower
of that period so worthy of honour in his way as H. Lüdemann. Let us be
under no illusions ; this declension has not been overcome to-day ; as for
scholastic exactitude, nothing we are producing to-day is comparable either
with the productions of mediæval and post-Reformation dogmatics, or with
those of idealist or with those of Thomist or, I need hardly say, with those of the
dogmatics of the Reformation. Would that we had only got the length at
last of regular dogmatics being once more, at least for us, a persistent ideal
worth striving after !

It is part of the human reality of the Church that in her there
must be not only theology but also a theological school or school
theology (*theologia scholastica*), i.e. theology introduced not only
for free spiritual exchange but also for instruction. It was a fatal
theological error, there was Baptist spiritualism involved in it, to
think that it could be dispensed with. Whoever looks the fact
of the humanity of the Church straight in the face will be unable to
absolve the Church from the task of working at even school theology,
but in that case he will also have in principle to assent to the task
of a regular dogmatics.

By irregular dogmatics on the other hand is meant an inquiry
into dogma such that in it the task of a school is not visualised
primarily and, therefore, there is no primary concentration on the
completeness we spoke of. As a free statement about the problems
arising in Church proclamation from the point of view of the inquiry
as to dogma, dogmatics may and must also be worked at in the
Church outside the theological school and apart from its special
task. Such free dogmatics existed before there was regular school
dogmatics, and alongside the latter it will ever anew be necessary
and possible. It will be distinguished from the latter by not cover-
ing the ground with the same consistency, either in respect of Church
proclamation itself, or in respect of the decisive Biblical testimony,
nor in respect of the history of dogma, nor in respect of Systematic
Theology in detail, nor in respect of strictness and clarity of method.
It will perhaps for definite historical reasons only pick out a definite
theme and put it in the forefront. It will perhaps take a rather
untrammelled line as regards the Biblical basis and the selection of
partners in the discussion. It will perhaps be mainly an exposition
of results, and take shape in theses or aphorisms, and only partially
or not at all preserve the distinction between dogmatics and proclamation. It will perhaps leave much to be desired regarding the
implicit and explicit clarity of its path to knowledge. In this or
that respect or in several respects or in all at once it will be

a fragment and mean to be one, and it will have to be estimated as such.

What remains preserved for us of the dogmatic work of the ancient Church even from the pens of its most significant and most learned representatives, is mainly not regular but irregular dogmatics in the sense described. Athanasius as distinguished from Origen and John of Damascus wrote no dogmatics proper. As distinguished from Melanchthon and Calvin, Luther is a most characteristically irregular dogmatician. But even from a more recent and less classical past one may recall names like those of J. G. Hamann, G. Menken, H. Fr. Kohlbrügge, J. Chr. Blumhardt, H. Kutter, whose work in a formal respect unquestionably belongs to this category. From ancient times till the present day irregular dogmatics has been deposited in dogmatic treatises, Bible commentaries, historical expositions, sermons, pamphlets, and other so-called devotional literature. Irregular dogmatics to some extent is worked at quietly, or perhaps even in public, by every one who has an interest in the problem of dogmatics, yet has neither the call nor the wish nor the time nor the tools to co-operate in regular dogmatics. On the whole it must be said that in spite of its name irregular dogmatics has in fact at all periods of the Church constituted the rule, regular dogmatics on the contrary the exception. And it must be noted that regular dogmatics has always proceeded from irregular, and without its impulse and co-operation could never have existed.

If in point of matter and of history we keep the entire difference between the two clearly in view, we shall be on our guard against overhasty valuations or the reverse on the one side or on the other. Above all, we shall not without more ado attribute a scientific quality to regular, and an unscientific quality to irregular dogmatics. If the nature of dogmatics as a science consists in its special objectivity, namely, in its effectiveness for the inquiry as to dogma, then one cannot see why both regular and irregular dogmatics should not be both scientific and unscientific.

Of course it did happen, and this was the case precisely in the age of orthodoxy, that the quality of dogmatics as a science had to be vindicated by school dogmatics against the free-lances. But the other thing also happened, that it had to be vindicated by the free-lances against School dogmatics. Of course it is undeniable that the aversion slightly traceable in every century against school dogmatics often rested upon a kind of enthusiasm and not at all on solid Christian insight, and had little or nothing to do with the seriousness of the inquiry into dogma, and so was assuredly no sign of scientific quality. But the other side is also undeniable, that the passage from irregular to regular dogmatics—when perhaps the school had ceased to be aware that t had to serve life, i.e. the Church—was often enough accompanied by a declension in the seriousness, liveliness, and joyfulness of Christian insight, by a lameness in the inquiry into dogma, and therefore by a loss of the scientific quality of real dogmatics.

A word must be said here about the two aspects of openness and readiness. No general statement can be made, but the question arises from case to case whether at times the aphorisms of the irregular or the systematics of the regular are more or less proper to the task of dogmatics. The call for the one as for the other may become a necessity, and it may become necessary to restrict the one or the other to its proper limits.

What is to be attempted here is regular dogmatics. The Church will not be able to dispense with it completely at any time, even and especially in the most disturbed times, and on every hand signs indicate that especially for Protestantism to-day an ordinary school dogmatics might be healthier than a further excess of irregularities, with which in somewhat parlous wise it has always been well provided, and particularly in the modern period. The results of irregular dogmatics, more than those of regular, are exposed to the danger of being purely accidental, because nearly always at least in form they tend to be conditioned by the person and biography of their author. The seriousness of their significance for the Church must at least be proved by the fact that they can be presented not only as the results of irregular dogmatics, and so, e.g., not only in sermon form or in the pamphleteering key, not only as the expression of religious, perhaps even of prophetic experiences and impressions, but also in the stricter form of critical reflection, as in the schools. Almost all the parts of knowledge in our sphere have first seen light in aphoristic form and in the key of proclamation. Dogmatics, i.e. the criticism and revision of proclamation to date, usually takes its rise in proclamation itself. But a knowledge bound to the aphoristic form or the key of proclamation, a knowledge not also susceptible of being taught, would not be genuine knowledge ; and therefore dogmatics must—not begin but continue as regular dogmatics. Nothing that claims to be truly of the Church will need to shrink from the sober light of " scholastic," but in whatever freedom and individuality it may first come to expression, as surely as it aims at being universally valid, it will itself make a push to set up a school and therefore to become school doctrine. The fear of scholasticism is the mark of the false prophet. The true prophet will manage to submit his message even to this test.

The phenomenon of Luther's theology, which might be given a quite different name, is instructive enough for the dangers by which an irregular dogmatics is threatened. But it is also significant of its importance for the Church that it bore entry into the school theology of Melanchthon and Calvin and their successors, and all that it may possibly have lost in this process should not prevent us acknowledging that this process was a necessary process for the sake of the Churchly character of the Reformation.

Any one who aims at working at regular dogmatics has then, of course, special cause to recall that this way of pursuing the task ought not to take to itself any right of monopoly, or make the slightest claim to scientific quality. It is surely useful to reflect that any moment it is possible for the inquiry as to dogma to be put and answered much more seriously and fruitfully at some unknown country parson's modest Bible Class than in the most exact academic discussion imaginable. School dogmatics may not claim to be regarded as the better but only as the necessary other form of dogmatics. And it should not disdain to listen ever and again to the voice of free dogmatics.

The results of Protestant school dogmatics in the 19th century, therein much prouder than that of the age of orthodoxy, in largely disdaining to do this and thereby simply sleeping through the existence of phenomena like Kohlbrügge and Blumhardt, have been ruinous.

The decision as to the scientific or unscientific nature of regular and irregular dogmatics depends on the answer to the question how far both are busied with their task and not, through absentmindedness, with quite other things. But this task of theirs consists in the criticism and revision of Church proclamation regarding its agreement with the revelation attested in Holy Scripture. Of a scientific dogmatics (no matter whether regular or irregular) three things are therefore to be required.

1. It has to busy itself with the problem of Church proclamation as such, not with any sort of problems of thought which might crop up in proximity to certain concepts in Church proclamation, but have absolutely nothing to do with the latter itself. The system of Christian truth can be the task of dogmatics only so far as it is a matter of the Christian truth proclaimed and to be proclaimed, the exposition of which will then be much less a system than the narrative of an event. Dogmatics as gnosis without concentration on the task of Church proclamation, dogmatics as metaphysics in movement and at rest within itself, would, however profound, spiritual, and logical in its aspect, be *qua* dogmatics unscientific. As to when and where the transition to such metaphysics takes place, no general account can, of course, be given. It should be realised that concepts of a pure metaphysics may become concepts of proclamation and *vice versa* concepts of proclamation may become concepts of a pure metaphysic ; that, therefore, the range of the lawful object of dogmatics is *in concreto* movable

21

It is a nuisance not to be respected, when uneasy limited spirits or those whose reading is fundamentally cursory think they should reject a theological exposition at once, because it operates with such concepts as they also meet elsewhere in metaphysical use. The legitimacy of their occurrence is decided by the context in which they occur. But by the context is decided the legitimacy of the occurrence of all concepts, even those that appear clearly to belong to proclamation. Even they might turn into concepts of a metaphysic which has nothing to do with proclamation. And the question is whether this is not pre-eminently the case with A. Ritschl from whom those anxious souls received their cue.

But that does not alter the fact that here from time to time a question is put to dogmatics and a boundary is drawn for it. Not all propositions in dogmatics are suited to become directly propositions of Church proclamation. To be adequate we shall have to say that no proposition in dogmatics is suitable for that as such. Dogmatics is the equipment for Church proclamation, it formulates the propositions to be pondered before Church proclamation formulates its propositions. But it is by this very relation that the propositions of dogmatics must bear being tested. They should never hang in the air (perhaps as propositions constructed merely for the sake of logical or cosmological or moral completeness), in such a way as to be incomprehensible as the equipment for Church proclamation, as to be comprehensible only as pure gnosis. There are boundary cases (we shall meet them in the doctrine of God, in the doctrine of creation, in eschatology —least in the doctrine of reconciliation, but even there precisely in Christology), which cannot be evaded, but which as such must be treated with twofold caution. But by saying, There are boundary cases, we say, " There is also a boundary." It is now easier, now harder to find, but it is always to be remembered and never to be crossed with impunity.

The question of being unscientific in this respect arises with regard to the parties in mediæval and Old Protestant dogmatics, where it appears to have been more a matter of satisfying the formal need for completeness felt by teacher and taught in general, than of logicality and exactitude in teacher and taught as belonging to the Church. But it arises still more regarding certain undertakings in modern dogmatics in which the concern seems to be not so much the Church's task as such, as rather all sorts of understandings about its possibility in relation to this or that general idea of the world. The apparently loftiest peaks of science in our domain in ancient and modern times must have been the very ones to be threatened by the unscientific quality which was always making to break in in the form of a transition to pure gnosis.

2. Scientific dogmatics has to busy itself with the criticism and revision of Church proclamation, not merely with a repetitive

exposition of it. Dogmatics cannot merely be an historical report on the classical expression of the faith proclaimed at this or that past period of the Church. Nor yet just the clearing up and exposition of the faith as the dogmatician in question thinks it right to proclaim it personally. Nor merely the phenomenology of a cross section of the common faith as proclaimed in the varying present.

The first according to R. R o t h e, the second according to S c h l e i e r m a c h e r and H o f m a n n, the third according to A. S c h w e i z e r, was the task of dogmatics. Against all these forms of putting the question the objection is that in them the Church is, so to speak, looked at from without, is her own onlooker. But the real Church exists in the act of hearing and proclaiming the Word of God by means of men. To the inquiry of this real church such a dogmatics alone answers which examines the problematic nature of its own existence, which intends not merely to say something but by saying something to serve, to be of use.

Repeated exposition, in harmony with the intentions of the theologians named, will, of course, be indispensable for dogmatics at every step. But dogmatics is not meant to be exhausted in exposition. Its scientific quality consists not so much in confirming as rather in disturbing Church proclamation as it meets it in its concrete forms to date, and above all in the present concrete form of the day ; in putting it at variance with itself as it truly belongs to itself, in driving it outside of itself and beyond. The historical report on the facts and the personal confession of faith or that expressed in the name of contemporaries can be but means to that. Dogmatics becomes unscientific when it becomes easy-going. But it becomes easy-going, indolent—even when urged by feeling ever so lively and by sagacity ever so great—when it limits itself to the unfolding and display of some possession or other already to hand. There is absolutely no need for it to be merely the so-called " stiff " dogmatics of the old style (frequently Catholic style) which in this sense must be termed unscientific. Just the same may and must be said of the most fluid, active, and pious modern dogmatics so far as its critical nerve is perhaps dead, so far as for its Church environment it signifies nothing but a pleasant certification that everything is in order and may continue as before. So long as the Church on earth is the Church of sinners and her proclamation therefore involved in the hardest problems, we shall be able to say with all definiteness that a dogmatics which assumes this attitude and has this result is in the wrong. The real Church is waiting for something else than certification. Once more it will have to be said that the boundaries between a merely reporting and an, appropriately, critical dogmatics cannot be defined generally. Even and precisely a critical dogmatics will simply have to report very seriously over wide stretches and, in reporting, to criticise and correct.

It is clear that for the task of dogmatics in certain circumstances more can be achieved by simply adducing a single passage from the Bible or even from the Fathers, than by the most thoroughgoing dialectical discussion.

And on the other hand a dogmatics which criticised and corrected at every step might veritably end up in a mere report.

The *Glaubenslehren* of Schleiermacher and A. Schweizer assuredly contain enough criticism and correction, but the question is whether all the criticism and correction does not and is not meant to end up, in marvellous accord with the Catholic conception of dogmatics, in a certainly grandiose certification.

Appearances may be deceptive both ways and, of course, there is no outward assurance here against slipping back into the forbidden opposite. But here too the question is put, and every dogmatics will also have to answer this question : is dogmatics to be a bit of Church history, of present-day Church knowledge, or itself a bit of Church activity ? Only in the latter case is it science in the sense of the task set it.

At the beginning of his book *The Theology of Facts versus the Theology of Rhetoric* (4th edn. 1876 p. 1), A. F. C. Vilmar tells of a teacher of dogmatics he heard in his young days, who used to accompany and conclude certain sections of this discipline with the words " *In futuram oblivionem*, gentlemen." To these sections, extraordinarily enough, belonged those on faith, justification, the Person of Christ, the sacraments, and the gifts of grace of the Holy Spirit. But whatever it be, anything in dogmatics a man can teach and learn *in futuram oblivionem*, and therefore as mere material of knowledge, can possess in black and white and confidently carry home, has certainly nothing to do with science. Dogmatics is scientific not as the exposition of all sorts of material, although it must be that too, but as the movement of this material or as this material in motion. So long and so far as this act and this state of movement has not set in, dogmatic work has not yet begun.

3. Scientific dogmatics inquires—and now we come to the decisive point—into the agreement of Church proclamation with the revelation attested in Holy Scripture. That is what we showed in part one of our section to be the meaning of dogma. If the scientific nature of dogmatics consists in its special relevance, i.e. in its being effected in the inquiry into dogma, we have here to do with the decisive test by which its scientific quality must ever and anon be proved. We heard already at an earlier stage that

Church proclamation could and can also be criticised and corrected from quite different standpoints. What might happen in that way might be science from these other standpoints. Only dogmatic science it certainly would not be. Neither of the previously mentioned mistakes need be fatal to dogmatics ; gnostic as well as uncritical dogmatics might at least incidentally do justice to the task of dogmatics. That is excluded if it is a case of the third error, of the confusion of the criterion of dogmatics with other criteria. The result of that, humanly speaking—and our speech here need only be human—can only be absurdity. Dogmatic work stands or falls according as the measure by which Church proclamation is measured is the revelation attested in Holy Scripture : not a philosophy or an ethic or a psychology or a political theory. Manifestly, every one who works at dogmatics also works more or less with perfectly definite presuppositions of mental science. The only question is whether apart from that he is further aware of the sign of the divine promise set up in the Church, and whether he is in the position and willing, in a way which admits of no further proof, to take this sign so seriously that in this connection its direction takes complete precedence of all directions for which he may have to thank the mental sciences. If and so far as this is the case his work is scientific ; if and so far as this is not the case it is unscientific, however scientific it may be considered from other standpoints. It is perfectly right—and not only is doubt not being thrown on this right here, but it is being emphatically underlined—that of no theologian or dogmatician should there finally be demanded education in mental science, familiarity with the thought of the philosopher, the psychologist, the historian, the æsthetician, etc. Of course even the dogmatician must think and speak in a definite period and for that must be a man of his period, but that means also a man of the past which constitutes his period, in other words an educated man. But no element in education makes him a dogmatician save the one which is not provided for in all these disciplines, which consists in undemonstrable modest attention to the sign of Holy Scripture, gathered about which the Church from time to time becomes the Church. By this attention the theologian becomes a theologian, by nothing else. So it is not a case of undervaluing the other disciplines. It is nonsense in this connection to speak of " educated criticism " for the elementary reason that after all attention to Holy Scripture also may be designated an element in culture or education. Nor is it a question of the barbarous demand that to the theologian as such the problem of culture as such must be indifferent. The problem of culture is the problem of being a man, which verily exists even for the theologian as such, as surely as theology too is a definite activity of man's nature. We may even view the problem of theology and dogmatics as being altogether within the framework of the problem of education ! It is rather a question of realising simply that this special problem, like all other problems of education, for that matter, has its own legality, not to be confused or mixed up with any other.

It is a question of what L u t h e r once, when he wished to prove why theology just like law and medicine has and must have its own language, to wit the *phrasis Spiritus sancti*, formulated in the sentence, *Non debet ars artem* [1] *impedire, sed unaquaeque debet retinere suum quasi cursum et uti suis terminis* (*Comm. Gen.* I [14], W. edn. 42, p. 35, l. 35). Why should we wish to have it otherwise ? Dogmatics is practically one *ars* among *artes*, capable of being learned and taught like them, but the " art " whose law points us to Holy Scripture as to the criterion decisive for it becomes sheer bungling unless its criterion is held valid and respected.

Assuredly this problem is a very special, an extremely remarkable problem. We shall have to take good care not to level it down or to dream of deducing, or proving, that and how far it can be seen set in the frame of the culture-problem at all. To assert that this is the case and to be aware what that means is nothing else than to be of the opinion that here we have to do with t h e culture-problem, with the framework of all culture-problems. He who does so will therefore be bound to know that not only must he leave this problem its own laws ; he must renounce any derivation of its lawfulness from a universal lawfulness superior to it, and, of course, also renounce any wish to prove as a general necessity the supremacy of this problem over all other problems in the form maybe of a theological philosophy of culture. He will be sufficiently well aware of the nature of the problem to know that all that is forbidden him. It cannot be expected of any one that for him too this problem should be set in the context of the problem of his being a man, in fact as the problem that actually controls this whole context—just as certainly we cannot expect any one to be aware that he is in the Church, when he does not know that he is. But we may expect of the man who professes to be stirred by this problem, who wishes to participate in dogmatic work, that he stick to the proper laws of this problem however remarkable they may be, just as in any other department he would stick to its special

[1] *Sic* !—TR.

laws although perhaps less remarkable. We may expect of him that he should behave himself in this department as a man of knowledge and not as a bungler. Without any arrogant " educated criticism " he may be expected to realise that in this department the criteria of philosophy cannot play a part which might perhaps belong to them in all other departments.

If any one absolutely refuses to accept this and insists on deriving his final standard here, too, from this or that logic or ontology or psychology or sociology, his attention must be called kindly to the fact that, of course, all the country is open to him, only he should refrain from his activities here, where with such other final standards he can only create confusion.

Against the corruption of theology which has now been so long in vogue, introduced by the desire to regard and work at it as a branch of general mental science we may for once enter a protest in the name of neatness and decorum ! Of course to prove this protest inwardly more will be needed than phenomenological interest in paying respect to ordinances and categories which after all exist, or the jealousy of a spiritual Trade Unionism greedy of its own special consequence. We can and may even here indicate the formal necessity for independence in theology, but we should not then forget that the seriousness of this indication stands or falls with the fact that attention to the witness of Scripture is not merely spoken of, but is actually given. The really effectual call to theological objectivity will only proceed from a theology that is itself utterly objective, in fact ultimately it will only be able to exist in the work of such an utterly objective theology. It is not the description but the existence of such a theology that says what has really to be said here, that can get a hearing as the thing that has really to be heard here, namely, that at no time and in no circumstances and on no pretext can theology know a more stringent concern than this, of remaining true to itself and always growing truer as Scripture theology. Without the existence of such a theology there is no object in debating the question of the right theology, and it certainly brings no result even if the answer which we here propound as the right one had been ever so powerfully and impressively actualised. Only the actual worker at such theology is aware what is the meaning here of neatness and decorum, only he, moreover, can make representations on its behalf with real emphasis, not the fellow who somewhere and in general claims to know that in theology as in everything else things should be done neatly and with decorum and that therefore

Scripture should be, become and remain master in theology's house. A single attempt to think and speak about a concrete question on this presupposition is more convincing than the most exact statement as to the fact, reason, and extent of its being spoken and thought in that way. Precisely at this stage the question should become pressing, whether it has not more often been irregular than regular dogmatics that simply exists in this sense as proper theology and has thereby done decisive service in exhibiting the scientific character of dogmatics. But be that as it may, i.e. however this third sign of the scientific nature of dogmatics comes to be substantiated, it is certain that we have here to do with the sign at which the roads to right and left most mercilessly and momentously separate. So much so is everything involved at this point that if the boundary between a dogmatics finally determined by Scripture and one finally determined by other authorities could be stated generally, all further discussion between the one side and the other would be cut off. We could only agree mutually that under the same name we were engaged on a matter that differed *toto coelo* and had nothing to learn mutually from one another except a warning against the utterly forbidden, which in that case would have to mean giving a share to the other side. We must not be deceived as to the sword of this complete separation hanging as much over our opposition to Roman Catholicism as over our opposition to Protestant Modernism, and somewhat of its menace will always make itself felt in the necessary discussions with both. Only that in strict reality the course of even this boundary cannot be stated generally but must be discovered from one case to another, and in the last resort remains hidden completely from our sight.

Dogmatic work which really submits itself to the criterion of Holy Scripture is finally and properly matter of a call, the givenness and continuation of which are withdrawn from human influence in the same way as the call to real proclamation of the Word of God. In view of the possibility of such a calling as it is brought home to us by the Bible promise, it may become the matter of a resolution in constant need of being renewed. Only to that extent can it then be a programme as well. But no programmatic attention to this decisive sign of scientific dogmatics can imply a mechanical insurance against a reversion to unscientific procedure, i.e. one not in accord with Scripture. As a matter of fact there has never appeared even during the Reformation a clearly Scriptural dogmatics not determined by other authorities as well. On the other hand it will have to be admitted that determination by Scripture and therefore scientific character may be achieved in dogmatics at least partially, and fortunately has often enough been achieved, even where there was more or less a serious lack of fundamental insight and therefore of detailed consideration of this sign. That this is true both ways, explains the fact that a discussion with Catholicism and with Modernism is not quite cut off ; actually it is now and again possible and even necessary that even where, to a large extent mutually, people can only regard one another as heretics, they must now and again take account of the Church's area as comprising even the heretic, and for all the ominousness of the situation cannot utterly separate from each other.

But once more and even here the fact that the boundary is not exactly definable, that all concrete judgments on the matter are held in reserve, that the actual course of this boundary is a matter for decision on each occasion, in virtue of which first may become last and last first—once more and even here that need not mean that this boundary is not drawn from time to time. Even here the question is put to all dogmatic work and as we must once again insist is put here in such a way that the real answer to it, the actual meaning which a definite dogmatics, considered from this point of view, has or has not (however much or little we know about it *in concreto*), means a verdict of life or death on its scientific quality. We have every reason to be cautious in our verdict as to whether a particular dogmatics has or has not for its standard the revelation of God attested in Holy Scripture. There can be no doubt about it that at all times in the heat of controversy men have been much too ready with their positive as with their negative judgments. It will be appropriate to be clear that even when in the particular case one feels one may and ought to pronounce such a judgment, one can always, so to speak, make only a temporary pronouncement, for the actual moment, and must give another hearing to-morrow, to see whether one may not perhaps have been deceived one way or the other and ought thus or thus to alter judgment. Such verdicts, even those that are ever so well founded, even those which the Church internally rent has most solemnly deposited in her mutually opposed and mutually accusing confessions, should be regarded fundamentally merely as questions very sharply put and not as pronounced judgments of God. But when all that is said and realised, it must also be said and realised that the sword of the real judgment of God nevertheless hangs over our heads—over our own as well as over those of our heretical partners in the dialogue—by the very fact of our taking up this work and carrying it on. Whether it is regular or irregular dogmatics that we are working at, cannot be the ultimate question. Nor can the ultimate question be to avoid the mistakes of a gnostic or uncritical dogmatics, of which we spoke before, however certainly these faults as such must be kept in view and avoided as well as we can. Ultimately everything depends upon whether a dogmatics is scriptural. Were it really not so, it would definitely be finished with ; for in that case it would have to be said of it with all definiteness that in it the Church is distracted, i.e. busy with other sorts of things, and is not doing justice to the scientific task set her by the problematic nature of her proclamation.

3. THE PROBLEM OF DOGMATIC PROLEGOMENA

We come to the real goal of our section. Dogmatics regards and designates itself a science, as we said. By that is meant that consciously and expressly it treads its own perfectly definite path to knowledge, defined by the matter. But in the position in which the Church has found herself for the last four hundred years, agreement as to which is the perfectly definite path to knowledge cannot be presumed automatically. The way of Roman Catholicism and the way of Protestant Modernism is a different one from that of the Evangelical Church. Evangelical dogmatics has to explain to itself why it thinks it must go its own way which is different from the others, and what this its own way is. According to the considerations we adduced in § 2 this is the task of prolegomena to dogmatics. What we have already done for this task was to define the criterion of dogmatics. But we have not yet spoken of the application of this criterion. We have therefore—and to that extent we cannot yet break off at this point, to that extent the greater part of our task still lies before us—not yet spoken of the path to knowledge as such which must be trodden in dogmatics. We arrived at the definition of the criterion of knowledge—and this was the purpose of our first chapter now drawing to a close— by reflecting upon and about the promise and task of proclamation given to the Church. As we saw, it is the promise and commission of this proclamation to be the Word of God to man. We have first put and answered the formal questions, where and how the Word of God is to be found, what it is and how it is knowable. All of this on the presupposition that its promised and commissioned identity with Church proclamation (in view of the fact that in the latter we have to do with man's work) in reality stands in question, that Church proclamation must become what because of its promise and task it is, and that from this " becoming what it is " there grows up for the Church, alongside the commission of proclamation itself, the commission of dogmatics, i.e.

the commission of testing, criticising and revising its actual proclamation from time to time. We next saw how the Word of God
concretely confronts Church proclamation in the form of Holy
Scripture as the witness given to the Church concerning God's
revelation. Church proclamation in agreement with Scripture is the fulfilment of the concept of dogma, after knowledge of which dogmatics strives. We have so far not
reached further than this definition of the criterion of dogmatics.
How are we now to proceed to determine its path to knowledge
as such, to determine the application of this criterion ? The
choice here to be proposed cannot be arbitrary, but it arises out of
the facts, as we have already learned. If it was relevant to reduce
the problem " proclamation and the Word of God " to the concrete
denominator " proclamation and Holy Scripture," we shall now
have to reach back to the point in our investigation so far where
we already meet with proclamation and Holy Scripture in
their context. This took place in § 4 which dealt with the three
forms of the Word of God. In the connection there revealed between
proclamation and Holy Scripture there obviously inheres the
thing we are now inquiring after, the path of knowledge to a
critical investigation of the agreement of proclamation with Holy
Scripture. There we had to do with proclamation and Scripture
as such, or rather as forms of the Word of God, and not so far
with this inquiry of ours as to how the first is to be measured by the
second and to be criticised and revised on the basis of it. Therefore, in order to answer this inquiry of ours we must return to
that connection. Should the path to knowledge into which we are
now only beginning to inquire become clear, the following points,
so far not yet cleared up, must obviously be made clear.

1. We must show how we are to take it when we regard the
Bible as the sign of the promise set up in the Church, namely, as
the witness of God's revelation, and to that extent as the Word
of God by which proclamation is to be measured. We must show
what is meant by possessing this sign as the Church and in the
Church, and by hearing it and giving effect to it as such. And we
must show how men can come to let this sign be given them. In
other words we must give an explicit doctrine of Holy Scripture.

2. We must show how we are to regard the other point, that
man's word in the proclamation of the Church may and should
become God's Word according to the promise. The norm must be
exhibited to which man's word is subordinate in view of this

promise. And we must describe the nature of the thinking which is ready to subscribe to this norm. In other words, strictly in accordance with the doctrine of Holy Scripture to be prefixed, there must be attempted an equally explicit doctrine of Church proclamation. If we are successful in exhibiting this correspondence then we are obviously saying about the application of the criterion of dogmatics, i.e. about the path to knowledge in dogmatics, all that can be said generally about it.

3. But now, thirdly, an investigation of this correspondence, even the doctrine of Holy Scripture and of Church proclamation itself, would be strangely in the air, were the question as to the Word of God itself and as such not also and indeed pre-eminently brought up once again and quite freshly. The whole meaning of the correspondence between Holy Scripture and proclamation and so too the whole meaning of the path to knowledge in dogmatics actually consists in our having to do with the Word of God both in Holy Scripture and in proclamation, with the difference that in the former (Holy Scripture) we have simply to discover it so far as it affects the task of dogmatics, whereas in the latter (proclamation), at least in connection with the task of dogmatics, we have not so much to discover it as to inquire into it, to investigate proclamation in relation to it—but in either case we have to do with the Word of God. If the correspondence is to be not only asserted but intelligibly understood in itself, we shall not be able to circumvent the question as to how the correspondence can come about at all, what we mean when we speak of discovering the Word of God in the Bible and of inquiring into the Word of God in proclamation. We cannot leave it as something to be taken for granted that this comes under consideration at all in either case, that dogmatics has to take account at all of this identity. That requires and is susceptible of no outward proof, though, of course, it admits of an inward one. And if correspondence really does take place between the Bible and proclamation and so a path to dogmatic knowledge becomes visible, even that may not be left looking like an accident or as a result of general didactic considerations ; it must arise out of the matter, out of the fact that the Bible and proclamation are or may become the Word of God. It must be shown that, and to what extent the questions previously raised about the Bible and proclamation are not without foundation, are not questions of casual curiosity, nor do they spring from a logical scheme which might as well be applied here as anywhere else, but

that these questions necessarily result from the fact that both things, the Bible and proclamation, are or may become the Word of God. For that very reason the question as to the Word of God itself and as such must also be raised once more and quite freshly. Quite freshly ! The facts that it exists in three forms, that it is God's language, God's act, God's mystery, that (and the extent to which) it is knowable by men, should no longer be repeated explicitly : to this determination of the criterion of dogmatics— it will remain increasingly of actual importance—we shall in the future relate ourselves as to opinions taken for granted for the nonce. But there is one point in our deliberations so far which requires renewed and most thoroughgoing clarification in the interests of an answer to our inquiry regarding the path to knowledge. In § 4 we spoke of three forms of the Word of God : of proclamation, of the Bible, and then in the third (but in fact the first and decisive) place of revelation, as of the source of the Word of God in the Bible and in proclamation, as of the primary form of the Word of God, by connection with which, by participation in which the Bible and proclamation may also become the Word of God ; of the Word of God so far as it simply is the Word of God without any becoming, of the event of the Word of God in virtue of which the Bible and proclamation become the Word of God. The Bible and proclamation are the Word of God in virtue of the Word of God revealing itself. It is thus the concept of revelation which must give us the key to understanding the relations between the two, from which we must already gather the questions with which we approach these two. It alone can make clear what is involved in the proclamation of to-day and yesterday being measured by the Bible. But we shall not be able to inquire into revelation in general, into what is commonly so called in all religions, and with which all that the religion of the Bible and of Christian proclamation calls revelation would then have to be incorporated in its special character. By putting such a general question we should at once prove that we were not inquiring into the revelation of the Word of God, and would then certainly fail to obtain any answer to that question. And what cause, moreover, could we have in our context to inquire generally into revelation or into a revelation in general ? We are inquiring into the revelation on the basis of which proclamation may and must be measured by the Bible, with which Bible and proclamation are in common related and so also mutually related to one another. We have to do with the concrete concept of revelation which the Bible attests as having taken place and which proclamation promises as about to come, with the very concrete bracket which encloses, in the Scripture adopted in the proclamation of the Church or in the proclamation of the Church moved by Scripture, a definite past, to wit the epiphany of Jesus Christ, and with equal regularity a definite future, to wit the recurring moment in which men shall hear the Word of God. We are inquiring into the presence of the Word of God between the times, a presence as certain as it is inconceivable, as unique as it is ever new, but at all events concrete. Naturally, beyond the c o n c e p t, even and especially the concept of revelation gathered from the Bible and proclamation, stands the r e a l i t y of it. We cannot wish to have to do with the reality of it. Neither in proclamation nor in dogmatics can we introduce the attested past or the promised future as present. Nor can we dream of introducing with the present which we can introduce t h i s past or t h i s future. We have to do with the c o n c e p t of revelation, i.e. with the pre sence of the Word of God b e t w e e n the times. But, of course, with a c o n c r e t e concept of revelation, with a c o n c r e t e presence of the Word of God. We have to do with the concept of the revelation of the God who, according to Scripture and proclamation, is the Father of Jesus Christ, is Jesus Christ Himself, is the Spirit of this Father and of this Son. Naturally, we may also inquire into the concept of quite different revelations and possibly into a general concept of revelation. But in that case we should be leaving the task of dogmatics where it was. For the concept of t h i s God and it alone interests dogmatics. From it and only from it can it expect light on understanding the connection between the Bible and Church proclamation and on guidance in criticising and revising this latter. If we do not wish to effect the transition to some other science, perhaps also good and useful enough, but which in that case would not be dogmatics, we must at this point, at which actually the relation between the Bible and proclamation is in question, confine the inquiry to this concrete revelation.

But how shall we make the inquiry ? Clearly in such a way that we envisage and analyse first of all the fact of this revelation —this one, be it noted, the one attested in Scripture as having taken place and the one promised in proclamation as on the way —analyse it exactly as this fact, " God reveals Himself," is itself actually put before our eyes in the Bible and proclamation, analyse it as it is enjoined upon us by the fact itself and by the way in which it makes itself known to us. Again, we must gather from the fact itself how far it can be regarded as possible *per se*, as self-realising. The analysis of this fact as such can be nothing else than the explication of what, in the dogmatics of all ages, has played its distinctive part under the name of the doctrine of the divine Trinity. The answer to the query as to the inner possibility of this fact is given on the one hand by the basic propositions of Christology, on the other hand by the basic propositions about the effectiveness of the Holy Spirit. But we set about the investigation of the concept of revelation in order to clear up the presuppositions of the doctrine of Holy Scripture and the doctrine of Church proclamation, with which we are practically concerned. From the concept of revelation we must arrive at the extent to which the Bible and proclamation are to be regarded as the Word of God, the nature of the correspondence that holds between the two, and the way in which the second is to be measured by the first. Thus the investigation of the concept of revelation belongs to the beginning of the whole. Hence in the further course of our prolegomena we shall have to speak in three chapters about revelation, about Holy Scripture and about Church proclamation : so that the whole may be regarded as an exposition of the doctrine, announced in § 4, of the three forms of the Word of God, only that we no longer concentrate upon the mere exhibition of these forms but upon their inner structure and their mutual relations ; so that, as we suggested at the time in the case of proclamation as the problematic entity in the whole context, the way must now be the reverse one, and revelation must constitute the starting-point and proclamation the goal.

CHAPTER II
THE REVELATION OF GOD

CHAPTER II

PART I

THE TRIUNE GOD

§ 8

GOD IN HIS REVELATION

God's Word is God Himself in His revelation. For God reveals Himself as the Lord and that according to Scripture signifies for the concept of revelation that God Himself in unimpaired unity yet also in unimpaired difference is Revealer, Revelation, and Revealedness.

1. THE PLACE OF THE DOCTRINE OF THE TRINITY IN DOGMATICS

When, to make it clear how Church proclamation is to be measured by Holy Scripture, we first of all inquire into the prior concept of revelation, in this very inquiry we are already bound to stand by Holy Scripture as the witness to revelation. Perhaps more important than anything that dogmatics can say about the distinctive place of the Bible in the Church and over against the Church is the example it itself has to give in laying its foundations. It must endeavour, what indubitably is commanded it along with the Church generally, to give heed to Scripture and therefore to allow itself to be set no problems from any source save Scripture. But the fundamental problem with which Scripture faces us regarding revelation consists in this, that the revelation attested in it refuses to be regarded as just any sort of revelation, alongside of which there is or might be other revelations. It absolutely insists upon being regarded in its uniqueness. That means, it absolutely insists upon being regarded from the side of its subject, God. It is the revelation of Him who is called *Yahweh* in the OT and θεός or concretely κύριος in the NT. But the inquiry about the self-revealing God, which therefore forces itself upon us as primary, cannot, if we will further follow the testimony of Scripture, be separated at all from the second question, how it happens,

339

how it is real, that this God reveals Himself. Or from the third, What is the result? what is the effect of this event upon the man whom it befalls? Just as also on the other hand these second and third questions cannot possibly be separated from the first. So impossible is any separation here that the answer to each of these three questions, for all the independence and individuality which must belong to it and continue to belong to it as the answer to each special question, is essentially identical with the answers to the other two questions. God reveals Himself. He reveals Himself **through Himself**. He reveals **Himself**. If we wish really to regard the revelation from the side of its subject, God, then above all we must understand that this subject, God, the Revealer, is identical with His act in revelation, identical also with its effect. This is the at first merely indicative fact from which we get the hint to begin the doctrine of revelation with the doctrine of the **Triune God**.

In the first edition of this book (p. 127) I indicated these three questions and then continued in these words : " Logically the questions are quite simply about the subject, predicate, and object of the short sentence, ' God speaks,' ' *Deus dixit.*' " On various sides these words have been taken amiss. I have been seriously and contemptuously reproached with it being a grammatical and therefore a rationalistic proof of the Trinity, so that here I am practising the very thing I otherwise oppose, namely, deriving the mysteries of revelation from the data of a generally comprehensible truth. According to this procedure a doctrine of the Trinity might be constructed likewise upon the utterance of the revelation of any other God, a merely supposed God, in fact upon the sentence, " I show myself " (so Th. Siegfried, *Das Wort und die Existenz*, 1928 p. 52).—The answer is that those words which to-day I can still repeat in all formality, were actually at the time used somewhat unguardedly and ambiguously. Attentive readers of goodwill had already at the time noted the sense in which they were used ; namely, that these words naturally did not themselves aim at being a proof but merely at reducing in a preliminary way a proof already achieved, to a formula suited to it and as perspicuous as possible. Naturally I never dreamt then, nor do I now, of deriving the truth of the dogma of the Trinity from the general truth of such a formula ; but from the truth of the dogma of the Trinity the truth of such a formula is perhaps derivable for this definite purpose, to wit, for the dogma of the Trinity. " Perhaps," we must say ; for the truth of the dogma of the Trinity does not stand or fall with any such formula. Even yet I cannot tell why it should not be correct as a formula for the questions demanded by the matter. All dogmatic formulæ are rational and so is every dogmatic procedure, so far as general concepts, i.e. human *ratio*, are employed in it. But it could only be called rationalistic if it were proved that the use of it was determined, not by interest in dogma, and therefore by subordination to Scripture, but otherwise, most probably by the principles of a definite philosophy. But if we are clear that in dogmatics rational formulation is generally and of necessity involved—a rational formulation, of course, related to an already completed proof and taking account of Scripture—then no objection can be taken even to logical or grammatical formulæ as such—it is as difficult to see in their case as in that of certain juristic formulæ, why they should be specially suspect—only we shall ask whether or not they are appropriate to the matter under review. So in this concrete case, we shall ask whether it is an arbitrary anticipation, simplification, or even complication to say that we are driven by what Holy Scripture tells us about the revelation which it attests, to inquire into the subject, object, and predicate of the short sentence in question. And whether we are compelled to say that by these three questions, i.e. by the answers to them which we find in Scripture, our attention is drawn to the problem of the doctrine of the Trinity. And, therefore, to say further that in these three questions there is opened up a way not to prove, but rather to understand the doctrine of the Trinity. Whether a doctrine of the Trinity is also derivable from the short sentence, " I show myself," we need not investigate here. The chief question, of course, will be whether it can be regarded as a command with the same meaning as is involved in the short sentence culled from the Bible, " God speaks."

The nature of the Bible's answer to the question, " Who is God in His revelation ? " is practically such as to involve an immediate answer to the other two questions as well, " What does He do ? " and " What does He effect ? " and not a merely preliminary answer, such that what we manage to hear in it can be neutralised on the next occasion on which these other questions are also being put, but such that, in receiving the answer to the first question, we are also bound to hear the answers to the other two—so that the first answer is rightly heard, only if it is heard as an element in the other answers. Are we to believe that this is also the case in other records of revelation ? Perhaps, perhaps not : it is no concern of ours here. In the Holy Scripture of the Christian Church at all events the situation is such that the first questions calling for answer are, who is revealing Himself in it, who God is in it ; and then also and subsequently, what this God does ; and thirdly, what He effects, accomplishes, creates, and gives in His revelation. But if question one is put intelligently, not only is it answered, but at once questions two and three also ; and only when the answers to two and three are received, is the answer to question one really received.

1. The Bible, of course, also tells us who the G o d is whom it attests as self-revealing.

It names and describes Him as *Elohim* (perhaps, Him that is to be feared), as *Yahweh* (we shall yet have to come back to this most important name), as *El Shaddai* (perhaps, the all-sufficient), as the Lord and Protector of Israel, the Creator of heaven and earth, the Ruler of the world and its history, the Holy and the Merciful ; in NT as the Lord of the Kingdom to come, as the Father in heaven, as the Father of Jesus Christ, as the Redeemer, as the Spirit, and as Love, etc.

2. But would any one here really hear and understand, without at the same time hearing and understanding what is further said of the That and the How of the revelation of this God ? That this revelation happens, and in a particular way, is not an accident, in view of the fact that it´is the revelation of this God that is involved. It is also and precisely in the That and How of this revelation that He shows Himself as this God. In fact, this God will and can show Himself in no other way than in the That and How of this revelation. Moreover, in this That and How He is completely Himself.

If this is already true in OT, in view of the fact that here it is the figures of Moses and the prophets round which the narrated event of revelation is concentrated (they are really not only instruments in God's hand, but as such they are at the same time his representatives, not only witnesses of revealed truths, but delegates of the self-revealing God), we must already in OT point to the remarkable figure of the angel of the Lord who at certain points comes into action in a way identical with *Yahwe*—still more so in NT where revelation actually coincides with the appearing of Jesus Christ. Thus in the event of revelation itself we have now to look for and to recognise the Revealer.

3. But as to who God is in His revelation, that is, thirdly, to be answered likewise according to the indication of the whole Bible in view of the men who receive revelation, in view of what the Revealer intends and does with them, what His revelation achieves in them, what therefore His revealedness signifies for them.

In the Bible revelation is always a happening between God and certain men. Here one is separated out and led into the far country like Abraham, there one is called and anointed to be a prophet, another a priest, another a king, here a whole nation is chosen, led, ruled, blessed, disciplined, rejected and taken up again, there faith and obedience are aroused, or else hearts are completely hardened. Here in the light of this whole occurrence a Church is gathered together, preaching and sacrament are introduced as signs of recollection and expectation, because now, " in Christ," man has acquired a future and along with that a present between the times [i.e. past and future— Tr.]

But all this, this revealedness of God attested in Scripture is not merely " the effect " of the Revealer and His revelation, only to be distinguished from these last—it is also to be distinguished from them—but at the same time the answer to the question, Who manifests Himself ? and to the second one, How does He manifest Himself ? Thus if we are inquiring about the God who reveals Himself according to the testimony of the Bible, we must pay attention to His self-manifestation as such, as well as to the men who are reached by this self-manifestation.

It is this fact that in putting the first question we are at once led on to a second and a third, which brings us in a preliminary way into proximity with the problem of the doctrine of the Trinity. Into proximity : because we could not say just yet that we were called upon by these considerations to evolve precisely the doctrine of the Trinity. In fact we are at this point first aware of the one thing, that the self-revealing God of the Bible must always be known also in the process of His revelation as such and in His revealedness as such, in order to be known at all. These observations gain significance and, in our context, decisiveness, only when we make the following two points :

4. The question " Who is the self-revealing God ? " always gets its unlimitedly complete answer, also in what it gives us to hear about His self-revelation as such and about His revealedness as such among men. This God Himself is not only Himself but also His self-revelation.

He comes as the angel to Abraham, He speaks through Moses and the prophets, He is in Christ. Revelation in the Bible does not mean a minus, a something other over against God. It means the equal of God, a repetition of God. Revelation is, of course, the predicate of God, but in such a way that this predicate coincides exactly with God Himself.

And again, He Himself is not only Himself but also what He creates and achieves in men.

For that reason the Word which the men in the Bible hear and hand on may be called the Word of God, although it is heard by their ears, is formed by their mouths, is indubitably their Word. All gifts and graces, as well as all punishments and judgments in the Bible are important, not for what they signify in themselves apart from the revelation and from Him who reveals Himself, but because they are His work upon man, because in them He is nigh unto men or far from them, friend or foe to them.

Thus, it is God Himself, it is the same God in unimpaired unity, who according to the Bible's understanding of revelation is the revealing God, and the event of revelation, and its effect upon man.

5. It does not appear possible, nor in the Bible is any attempt made, to dissolve the unity of the self-revealing God and His revelation and His revealedness into a uniformity, to remove therefore the boundaries which separate from each other the above three forms of His being God in revelation, to reduce them to a synthetic fourth reality.

Nowhere in the Bible are we left in any doubt about God as God, without detriment to His revelation, being and remaining " invisible," i.e. inaccessible to man as such, because, as distinguished from him, eternal and holy. If this God reveals Himself—and without detriment to His invisibility He does reveal Himself, He makes Himself accessible to the same man—He is in His revelation in a way with which that first state of His admits of being identified indirectly indeed, but not directly, not simply, not by removal of the differentiation. The " angel of the Lord " in OT is obviously identical with the Lord Himself a n d not identical. It is quite impossible that the non-identity too should not become and remain visible. So in NT with the inexchangeability of the names Father and Son. But the same also holds good regarding the revealedness of God attested in the Bible : if God gives Himself to man, He is yet Someone other than the Giver, Someone other than the gift, and yet the names Christ and Spirit or Word and Spirit also remain inexchangeable.

Thus, to the same God who in unimpaired unity is Revealer, Revelation, and Revealedness, is also ascribed in unimpaired v a r i e t y in Himself precisely this threefold mode of being.

Only now, by consideration of the unity and variety of God in His revelation attested in Scripture—and also really by that—we are confronted with the problem of the doctrine of the Trinity.

So once more, and perhaps comprehensibly, it may be affirmed by way of a supplementary formulation of a fact previously presented by the Bible, that we are faced with the problem that in the sentence " God speaks "— not in the general sentence " God speaks," but in the one taken from the Bible —subject, predicate, and object are to be both equated and differentiated. It is cheap to assert that this may also be said of the equivalent general sentence or equivalent sentences, presumably connected with some other god, or even capable of being asserted by the sentence " I show myself." We " may " say anything. But in this case it obviously cannot be a matter of no importance that there is much that we " may " do on theory but don't do in practice, because we have neither cause nor need to do it. If any one wishes to assert that even outside the Biblical witness to revelation—not as a possibility but as a fact—we are faced with the problem of the doctrine of the Trinity, he would have to show—he would actually have to take upon himself to develop the other doctrine of the Trinity in another dogmatics in another Church—that there was cause and need to do what in regard to those other sentences we perhaps merely " may " do, if at this point he is to produce a substantial objection.

Therefore if it is right, for the understanding of the concept of revelation, to ask first who God is, and if guided by the Bible we are bound to raise the question in the way in which we have just done in brief, we have cause, in accordance with the question now come into view, to pursue the reply which likewise has already come into view, i.e. to turn first—naturally, again, following this answer just become visible, namely, Holy Scripture—to developing the doctrine of the Triune God.

In putting the doctrine of the Trinity at the head of the whole of dogmatics we are adopting a position which, looked at in view of the history of dogmatics, is very isolated.

Still, not quite isolated : in the Middle Ages it was Peter Lombard in his *Sentences* and Bonaventura in his *Breviloquium,* who likewise took up this attitude.

Otherwise the custom was and is not to give this place to the doctrine of the Trinity. The reason for this really odd fact can only be that with overwhelming unanimity it was thought right and possible to pursue a certain scheme of inquiry, formally very natural and illuminating, and accordingly to speak first of Holy Scripture (or, in Catholic dogmatics, of the authority of the Church's teaching office, or, in modernist dogmatics, of the reality and truth of Religion) as the *principium cognoscendi* (irrespective of the concrete content of faith) and then once more in the doctrine of God, first to deal with God's existence, nature, and attributes (again irrespective of the concrete givenness of what " God " means for a Christian).

Even Melanchthon and Calvin, and Protestant Orthodoxy in both confessions after them, joined this company with a remarkable lack of hesitation, and similarly none of the later movements in Catholic and Protestant theology here led to the taking of a different path.

Our reason for deviating from this custom is this. It is difficult to see how in regard to Holy Scripture we can tell what is significant for the holiness of this very Scripture, unless previously it has been made clear—naturally from Holy Scripture itself—who that God is whose revelation makes Scripture Holy. And again, it is difficult to see how what is significant for this God should be made clear, if, as has been done repeatedly in old and new Catholic and Protestant dogmatics, we reserve the question to which the doctrine of the Trinity is the answer (namely, Who God is) and deal first with His existence and His nature, as if this That and What could be determined otherwise than on the presupposition of the Who.

Here an appeal may be made to Calvin himself against the procedure which he too adopts : *Quomodo enim immensam Dei essentiam ad suum modulum mens humana definiat . . . ? Imo vero, quomodo proprio ductu ad Dei usque substantiam excutiendam penetret . . . ? Quare Deo libenter permittamus sui cognitionem. Ipse enim demum unus, ut inquit Hilarius, idoneus sibi testis est, qui nisi per se cognitus non est. Permittemus autem, si et talem concipiemus ipsum qualem se nobis patefacit : nec de ipso aliunde sciscitabimur quam ex eius verbo (Instit.* I 13, 21).

As if there were not a very serious risk, in the case of the doctrine of Holy Scripture as well as in the doctrine of God, of getting lost in considerations and seeing oneself forced to conclusions totally irrelevant to the ostensibly concrete object of both doctrines, if one first discards His concreteness, as it is actually made plain in the Trinitarian form of the Christian concept of God. And as if the doctrine of the Trinity itself were not threatened with the like danger, the danger of irrelevant speculation, when it is first allowed to be articulate only at a later stage, instead of being given the first word, since it has to give us our information on the concrete and decisive question, Who God is.

By regarding it always as a duty to follow the formally far too apposite, far too illuminating scheme of, How do we know God ?, Does a God exist ?, What is God ?, and then only finally and ultimately, Who is our God ?, we directly contradict the highly important explanations, which we cannot get out of giving, as to the practical, comprehensive significance of the doctrine of the Trinity. What we seek to bring into practical recognition by putting it first has not been altogether concealed throughout the history of dogmatics and has often been expressed in very strong words. It is the point at which it is fundamentally decided whether the truly important expression " God," important in every aspect, is used in Church proclamation in the manner appropriate to its object which is its norm. It is the doctrine of the Trinity which fundamentally distinguishes the Christian doctrine of God as Christian—it is it, therefore, also, which marks off the Christian concept of revelation as Christian, in face of all other possible doctrines of God and concepts of revelation. Of course decision has to be repeated at every stage. But the state of things should be such that it is repeated from this standpoint, from this it gains its income, from this it becomes so serious, so simple at once and so complicated, as in fact and in the last resort it invariably is.

If we do not know God in the way in which He reveals Himself as the one, namely, *distincte in tribus personis*, the inevitable result is that *nudum et inane duntaxat Dei nomen sine vero Deo in cerebro nostro volitat* (Calvin, *Instit.* I 13, 2)—*Quia de Deo sentiendum est sicut se patefacit : Credimus, agnoscimus, confitemur et invocamus tres Personas, Patrem, Filium et Spiritum sanctum. . . . De re summa et excellentissima cum modestia et timore agendum est et attentissimis ac devotis auribus audiendum, ubi quaeritur unitas Trinitatis, Patris, Filii et Spiritus sancti. Quia nec periculosius alicubi erratur, nec laboriosius quaeritur, nec fructuosius invenitur* (M. Chemnitz, *Loci*, 1591 I p. 31).—*Ignorato vel negato Trinitatis mysterio tota salutis* οἰκονομία *ignoratur, vel negatur* (J. Gerhard, *Loci*, 1610 III 1, 7).—*Deus Deus esse non potest, nisi tres habeat distinctos existendi modos sive personas* (B. Keckermann,

Systema S. S. Theol. 1611 p. 20, cited according to H. Heppe, *Dogm. d. ev.-ref. Kirche*, 1861 p. 86).—*Qui non addunt mentionem trium personarum in descriptione Dei, eam nequaquam genuinam aut completam sistunt, quum sine iisdem nondum constet, quisnam sit verus Deus* (A. Calov, *Systema loc. theol.* 1655 f. II 182, cited according to H. Schmid, *Dogm. d. ev.-luth. kirche*, 4th edn. 1858 p. 78).—So long as theism " only distinguishes God and the world and never God from God, it always stays caught in the reversion or transition to the pantheistic or other denial of absolute being. A perfect protection against atheism, polytheism, pantheism, or dualism there can only be with the doctrine of the Trinity. . . . Faith in the eternal, holy love, which God is, can only be perfected, theoretically and practically, by knowledge of the perfect eternal object of the divine self-knowledge and love, i.e. by the thought of the Father's love for the only-begotten Son. Finally the full quickening nature and impartation of God, which is neither a diminution nor a limitation of His nature, will be kept in preservation only by the Trinitarian doctrine of the Spirit " (C. J. Nitzsch, *System der christl. Lehre*, 6th edn. 1851 p. 188). —" With the confession of God's tri-unity stands and falls the whole of Christianity, the whole special revelation. It is the kernel of the Christian faith, the root of all dogmas, the substance of the new covenant. From this religious, Christian interest the development of the Church doctrine of the Trinity has therefore taken its origin. It was in fact not a matter of a metaphysical theorem or a philosophical speculation, but of the heart and being of the Christian religion itself. To such an extent was this felt that all who still set store by the name of Christian acknowledge and honour a positive Trinity. In every Christian confession and dogmatics the deepest question is this, how God can be one and yet also threefold. And exactly in proportion as the question is answered does Christian truth come less or more to its own in all parts of the teaching. In the doctrine of the Trinity there beats the heart of the whole revelation of God for the redemption of mankind " (H. Bavinck *Gereformeede Dogmatiek*, vol. II 4th edn. 1918 p. 346 f.).—" The Trinitarian name of God expresses the specifically Christian consciousness of God, and since that consciousness is the ground and content of all faith, the Trinitarian name of God is the Christian Gospel. Which is why Christian baptism is in that name " (Ad. Schlatter, *Das chr. Dogma*, 2nd edn. 1925 p. 354).— And even Troeltsch found in the Trinitarian formula, naturally in the sense in which he understood it, " a short expression of Christianity as the revelation of God, given in Christ and operative in the Spirit . . . the abiding classical formula of Christianity into which the entire doctrine of faith can be concentrated " (*Glaubenslehre*, 1925 p. 124). Cf. also Joseph Braun, S.J., *Handlexikon der kathol. Dogmatik* 1926 p. 55 : " The doctrine of the most holy Triplicity is the basic dogma of Christianity."

If this can be said thus or in similar words, one really cannot see why it should not become articulate in the external and above all in the internal position of the doctrine of the Trinity in dogmatics.

There is a series of modern dogmaticians who have taken account of this need at least externally by building up their so-called special dogmatics according to the threefold division of God the Father, Son, and Holy Spirit : Ph. K. Marheineke, *Grundlehren der christl. Dogm. als Wiss.* 1827 ; A. Schweizer, *Glaubenslehre d. ev.-ref. Kirche*, 1844 f. and *Christl. Glaubenslehre nach prot. Grundsätzen*, 2nd edn. 1877 ; H. Martensen, *Die chr. Dogm.* 1856 ;

Th. Haering, *Der christl. Glaube*, 1906; M. Rade, *Glaubenslehre*, 1924 f. The need for such an emphasis, and so the constitutive significance of the doctrine of the Trinity, is indeed mostly not very plain from what these authors actually have to say about the doctrine itself and as such ; e.g. in A. Schweizer it is greatly obscured by the tremendous preliminary Part I, a natural theology on broad lines. Nor am I aware of any of those named, in whom in the working out of this doctrine, although it serves them as a framework for the whole, one comes in sight of a material decision which has significance for this whole. But in the choice, however founded, of this arrangement there is unmistakably a practical confirmation of the presence and the urgency at least of the problem of the doctrine of the Trinity. The same naturally holds good of Schleiermacher, who was able to employ the doctrine of the Trinity outside the series of the other dogmatic *Loci* as a solemn conclusion to the whole dogmatics. Of course, from the fact that Schleiermacher's doctrine of the Trinity can only constitute the conclusion of his dogmatics but cannot so well constitute the beginning, the inference to be drawn is that for him, too, no constitutive meaning attaches to it, so that here, too, the fact is more important than the purpose and manner in which it is used.

Our concern really must be not that externally it should receive a prominent place, but only that by our actually giving it such a place, its content may be made decisive and dominant for the whole of dogmatics. The problem of the doctrine of the Trinity meets us in the question put to the Bible about revelation. When we ask, Who is the self-revealing God ? the Bible answers us in such a way that we are impelled to consider the Three-in-oneness of God. Moreover, the other two questions, what this God does and what He effects, are, as we saw, primarily answered by new answers to the first question, Who is He ? The problem of these three, like and yet different, different and yet like, answers to these questions is the problem of the doctrine of the Trinity. The problem of revelation stands or falls primarily with this problem.

In this conviction that the discussion of the doctrine of the Trinity belongs directly to the context of a discussion of revelation we also feel ourselves strengthened (apart from the way indicated, by which we reached it) by two mutually connected historical facts. The Old-Protestant Orthodox, whether or not they knew what they were saying, could not sufficiently emphasise the character of the Trinity as a, in fact as the, mystery of faith. *Mysterium trinitatis neque lumine naturae inveniri, neque lumine gratiae, neque lumine gloriae potest comprehendi ab ulla creatura* (H. Alsted, *Theol. scholast.* 1618 cited after Heppe, *op. cit.* p. 86 f.). *Sublimitas tanta est, ut ὑπὲρ νοῦν, ὑπὲρ λόγον καὶ ὑπὲρ πᾶσαν κατάληψιν: Quare ex ratione nec oppugnari nec expugnari, nec demonstrari, sive a priori, sive a posteriori potest aut debet* (J. Fr. König, *Theol. pos acroam.* 1664 I § 78). For that very reason, and also in harmony with the Church Fathers and with the mediæval Scholastics, and nowhere so insistently as here, they have spoken of the necessity of revelation as the sole source of the knowledge of this mystery which dominates all mysteries. But also there fits most adequately into this the denial which modernist Protestantism, from the days of Servetus and the other anti-Trinitarians of the Reformation period, brought against this very doctrine. As Schleiermacher very rightly saw and declared, it is emphasised above other Christian doctrines because it can not be made comprehensible as the immediate utterance of the Christian self-consciousness. " Or who would assert that the impression made by the divine in Christ obliges us to conceive such an eternal distinction (in the highest Being) as the ground of it (namely, the impression) ? " (*Der christl. Glaube*, § 170, 2). We take the actual fact, that this theology declares that, from the standpoint of its under-standing of revelation, it has no access to this matter, as a sign that this matter should be noted and considered in the first place, at the point where real revelation is involved.

2. THE ROOT OF THE DOCTRINE OF THE TRINITY

So far the only position we have established in an initial way is that in inquiring into what Holy Scripture attests as revelation we come up against the problem of the doctrine of the Trinity, that therefore we have cause first of all to turn our attention to it. At this stage it is worth an adequate examination, in order to make clear to ourselves that in reality the Christian concept of revela-tion already includes in itself the problem of the doctrine of the Trinity, and that it cannot be analysed at all without its first step being to try to give expression to the doctrine of the Trinity.

According to Scripture God's revelation is God's own immediate speaking, not to be distinguished from the act of this speaking, therefore not to be distinguished from God Himself, from the divine I which confronts man in this act in which it addresses him as " thou." Revelation is *Dei loquentis persona*.

From the standpoint of the comprehensive concept of the Word of God we must say that here, in God's revelation, God's Word is identical with God Himself. Among the three forms of the Word of God that can be said unconditionally and with strictest propriety only of revelation, not with the same unreservedness and directness of Holy Scripture and of Church proclamation as well. For if the same may and must also be said of them, it must at all events be added that their identity with God is an indirect one Without wishing to deny or even merely to limit their char-acter as God's Word, we must think of the fact that here the Word of God is mediated, through the human persons of the prophets and apostles, who received and handed it on, and again through the human persons of their expositors and proclaimers ; that Holy Scripture and proclamation must always be becoming the Word of God in order to be it. Although in Holy Scripture and in Church proclamation the Word of God is God Himself, it is because that is the case in the revelation to which they bear witness. Of course, in regarding the Word of God as the thing that is proclaimed and written, we do not regard it as the Word of God in a less degree. But we do regard the same Word in its relation to revelation. On the other hand, if we regard it as revealed, we are regarding it apart from such relations, or rather as the ground of those relations in which it is also the Word of God. We regard it as indistinguishable from the event in virtue of which, in these relations, it is also the one Word of God, and therefore as indistinguishable from God's own direct speaking, and therefore as indistinguishable from God Himself. It is this that—we shall not say marks off, because a distinction in rank and value does not arise here—but simply marks revelation, as distinct from Holy Scripture and from Church proclamation (cf. § 4, 3 and 4).

According to Holy Scripture God's revelation is a ground which has no sort of higher or deeper ground above or behind it, but is simply a ground in itself, and therefore as regards man an authority from which no appeal to a higher authority is possible. Its reality and likewise its truth do not rest upon a superior reality and truth, are under no need of an initial actualisation or legitimation as a reality from any other such point, and so are also not measured by reality and truth such as might be found at such another point, are not to be compared with such, nor to be judged and regarded as reality and truth in the light of such. On the contrary, God's revelation has its reality and truth wholly and in every respect— i.e. ontically and noetically—within itself. Only by denying it can we wish to ascribe to it a higher or deeper ground different from itself, or regard, adopt, or reject it from the vantage of such a higher or deeper ground. Obviously the adoption of revelation from the point of view of such a ground, differing from it and presumably superior to it—e.g. an affirmation of revelation, in which a man previously set up his conscience to be the judge of it—can only be achieved by denying revelation. Revelation is not real and true from the standpoint of anything else, either in itself or for us. It is so in itself, and for us through itself. That also distinguishes it from the witness given about it by the prophet and the apostle, and by the expounder and proclaimer of Scripture, at least so far as this witness is considered *per se*. If we may also say the same of this witness, that it is grounded in itself, and for us through itself, that is so in virtue of the fact that this witness does not merely wish to be connected with revelation, but really is connected, because in it, too, revelation has become an event. That may be the case. And it must also be the case, in order that Scripture and proclamation may be the Word of God. They must become it. Revelation must not first become it. In it reposes and lives the fulness of the original being of the Word of God, existent in itself.

For this whole context cf. E d u a r d T h u r n e y s e n, *Revelation in the History of Religion and in the Bible, Z.d.Z.* 1928 p. 453 f.—OT and NT are thoroughly at one in the view that the utterances of God, as they have reached men according to their testimony, constitute a self-contained *novum* over against everything that men can say to themselves or to each other. One may obey or not obey, believe or not believe what is called revelation in the Bible— either is open—but one cannot from another standpoint perceive, or from another standpoint take one's bearings, as to whether it has really taken place and whether its content is true. We can not only not produce it ourselves (as the priests of Baal wished to do on Carmel, 1 Kings 18), nor can we control it as revelation (like the vain attempt on Jesus when they asked Him for a sign). We can only stand or rather move within its closed circle, or— the puzzling possibility, always lying so uncannily close at hand, of the *mysterium iniquitatis*, " concluded under unbelief " (Rom. 11^{32})—stay or go outside. J e s u s speaks ὡς ἐξουσίαν ἔχων (Matt. 7^{29}). What does that mean ? It goes on, Not as their scribes ; i.e. obviously, not like those who at best must refer to the other higher authority of a witness to revelation already before them. Therefore, for Paul it is so important to have seen and heard the Lord Jesus Himself and not just to be acquainted with Him through tradition. His apostolate stands or falls with this immediate touch of his with revelation, i.e. with this immediacy of revelation itself. Equally grounded in itself and of final authority is the entity which is introduced, especially in the NT, as the S p i r i t, with its decisions in things both great and small (down to the route of the apostles' journeys). According to the Bible a man who became participant in the revelation of God and obedient to it had no motives or grounds for it, he was not instructed or convinced, he followed neither his reason nor his conscience nor the reason and conscience of other men—all of that might a l s o happen, but the Bible speaks little of it and it is not t h a t that is important in this matter—he was confronted with this ἐξουσία, and he bowed to it and to no other person or thing. He h e a r k e n e d unto a c o m m a n d.

All that we sum up in the statement, G o d r e v e a l s H i m s e l f a s t h e L o r d. This statement is to be regarded as an analytical judgment. The distinction between form and content cannot be applied to the Biblical concept of revelation. Hence, where according to the Bible revelation is an event, there is no second inquiry as to what its content might be. And its content could not become manifest in some other event just as well as in this. But here revelation as such is, of course, in accordance with the riches of God, never one time like another but always new, yet, as revelation, invariably the announcement of the βασιλεία τοῦ θεοῦ, the lordship of God. And how otherwise could the announcement of this βασιλεία follow than just by means of what is here called revelation ? To be Lord means to be what God in His revelation is towards man. To act as Lord means to act as God in His revelation acts on man. And to acquire a Lord is what man acquires in God by receiving His revelation—revelation here always being regarded in the unconditional sense in which we meet it in the witness of Scripture. All else we know as " lordship " must be a copy, and is in reality a sad caricature of this Lordship. Without revelation man is unaware that there is a Lord, that he, man, has a Lord, and that God is this Lord. He is aware of it through revelation. Revelation is the revelation of lordship, and at the same time of the Lordship of God. For that is the godhead of God, it is that of which man is unaware and which God must reveal to him and does reveal according to the witness of Scripture —lordship. Lordship is present in revelation, just because its reality and truth are so utterly grounded in itself, because it need be actualised and legitimated in no other way than by the fact of its occurrence, because it is not in any relation to anything else, but is revelation by its own agency, because it is the self-contained *novum* we spoke of. Lordship means freedom.

The previously emphasised Biblical concept ἐξουσία admittedly expresses both things.

Godhead in the Bible means freedom, ontic and noetic independence. In the decisions taken in this freedom of God the divinely good becomes an event ; truth, righteousness, holiness, mercy, deserve to be called what their names declare, because they really are so in the freedom of God. In this way, as this Free, the alone Free, the God of the Bible has lordship. In this way, too, He reveals it. It is precisely that self-sufficiency or immediacy, so characteristic of Bible revelation, which characterises this revelation on the one hand as the revelation of God, on the other hand as the revelation of lordship. But that does not become completely characteristic until we notice that it is not an abstract matter of the revelation of lordship but a concrete one of the revelation of the Lord, not of godhead (even were it godhead regarded as freedom), but of God Himself, who in this freedom speaks as *I* and addresses by thou. The happening of this is called in the Bible revelation, and therefore revelation of His lordship. Because this I speaks and addresses by thou, God announces His kingdom and He distinguishes this announcement from all speculations upon freedom, lordship, godhead, as man might perhaps set them up without revelation. As freedom, lordship, godhead are real and true in God Himself and only in God Himself, and so inaccessible and unknown unless God Himself, unless this I speaks and addresses by Thou—so, in God Himself, they are the meaning of the event which the Bible calls revelation. " God reveals Himself as the Lord " means that He reveals what only He Himself can reveal, Himself. And so, precisely as Himself He possesses and exercises His freedom and lordship, He is God, He is the ground without grounds, with whose word and will man can but begin without asking Why, in order therein and thereby to receive everything worthy the name of true and good. It becomes and is true and good because we receive it from Him, because God as Himself is with us, with us as only a man who says I and addresses us as Thou is with another man, yet with us as Him whom He is, as the Lord who is the Free. God's being with us in this way is according to the Bible the event of revelation.

The statement, "God reveals Himself as the Lord," understood in this sense, i.e. the meaning intended by this statement, and therefore the revelation itself attested by Scripture we call " the root of the doctrine of the Trinity."

We mean by the doctrine of the Trinity, in a general and preliminary way, the proposition that He whom the Christian Church calls God and proclaims as God, therefore the God who has revealed Himself according to the witness of Scripture, is the same in unimpaired unity, yet also the same in unimpaired variety thrice in a different way. Or, in the phraseology of the dogma of the Trinity in the Church, the Father, the Son and the Holy Spirit in the Bible's witness to revelation are the one God in the unity of their essence, and the one God in the Bible's witness to revelation is in the variety of His Persons the Father, the Son, and the Holy Spirit.

When we designate the statement, God reveals Himself as the Lord, i.e. the actual revelation designated by this statement and attested by Scripture, as the root of the doctrine of the Trinity, two things are involved :

First (negatively) : the statement or statements about the Trinity of God can not claim to be directly identical with the statement about revelation, or with revelation itself. The doctrine

23

of the Trinity is an analysis of this statement, i.e. of what it designates. The doctrine of the Trinity is a work of the Church, a document of how she regards that statement, or its object, a document of how she knows God, i.e. how she struggles against error and for the relevancy of her proclamation, a document of her theology and to that extent a document of her faith and only to that extent, only indirectly, a document of revelation itself. The text of the doctrine of the Trinity, whether we are thinking of one of its ecclesiastically dogmatic formulations or of our own or another theological-dogmatic explication of the Church dogma, is therefore not identical with a bit of the text of the Bible witness to revelation. The text of the doctrine of the Trinity is throughout connected with texts in the Bible witness to revelation, it includes also certain concepts taken from that text, but it does so just as an interpretation does, i.e. it translates and expounds that text, and that e.g. involves its availing itself of other concepts than those contained in the text before it. That means that it not only repeats what is there, but it confronts what is there with something new, to explain what is there. We designate this difference between revelation and Scripture, of which the Church and theology at their tasks must be aware, by designating our statement about revelation—even it now is to be regarded as an interpretation—merely the root of the doctrine of the Trinity.

Already in the early Church the doctrine of the Trinity was attacked with the argument that it is not Biblical, i.e. it stands in the form in which it was formulated by Church theology it cannot be read anywhere in the Bible. In particular, it was argued, this held good of the decisive concepts " essence " and " Person " with which it worked, but, more than that, it held good of the concept " Trinity " itself. Now, this objection may be raised against any dogma, against theology in general and as such, but in that case it would also inevitably have to be raised against any proclamation which is also an explanation over and above the reading of Holy Scripture. Now explanation means repeating in other words what has been said already. Of the fact that the doctrine of the Trinity " is not in the Bible," the Fathers of the Church and of the Councils and, a good deal later, the Reformers in their struggle with the new anti-Trinitarians were naturally also aware. But they rightly denied that for the legitimacy, i.e. " Biblicity " of Church dogma and of a Church theology it was a matter of *ipsa etiam verba* (i.e. the word of Holy Scripture) *totidem syllabis et literis exprimere* (M. Chemnitz, *Loci ed.* 1591 I p. 34) That would mean an *iniqua lex* for the Church, a condemnation of all Scripture exposition, which really consisted of *explicare quod Scripturis testatum consignatumque est* (Calvin, *Instit.* I 13, 3). *Si oporteret de Deo dici solum illa secundum vocem quae sacra scriptura de Deo tradit, sequeretur quod nunquam in alia lingua posset aliquis loqui de Deo, nisi in illa in qua prima tradita est scriptura veteris vel novi testamenti. Ad inveniendum autem nova*

2. *The Root of the Doctrine of the Trinity* 355

nomina antiquam fidem de Deo significantia coegit necessitas disputandi cum haereticis (Thomas Aquinas, *S. th.* I *qu. 29 art.* 3). Inaccurate explanations of the Bible, even when given forth in the speech of a later time had to be countered in the speech of the same time. In that at all times consisted the task of dogma and dogmatics. In that dogma and dogmatics have their specific character as distinct from the Bible. But not for that reason necessarily as un-Biblical, i.e. contrary to the Bible. They find themselves, as must be granted without ado, in the same parlous realm as, from time to time, the false doctrines which have to be rejected. But what realm is that but that of the *ecclesia militans*, which seeks to listen to the prophets and apostles, to understand what they have to say, although in the language of a later time, to understand it rightly at the risk of being misunderstood? *Nec enim Deus frustra donum prophetiae dedit ecclesiae ad interpretandas scripturas, quod inutile sane foret, si rem scripturis traditam nefas esset aliis vocabulis exprimere* (Fr. Turretini, *Instit. theol. elenct.* 1679 I *l.* 3 *qu.* 23, 23). But if this objection is to be rebutted, we shall not only draw from it a reminder of the risk of all theology, but also gather with Calvin that in doctrine as such, with regard to its object, it is a question of an *impropria loquutio*, that the explanation as such, so far as it differs from the text, so far as it is forced to work with concepts foreign to the text, might well and with pleasure be " buried," if the right understanding of the text were otherwise assured. (*Utinam quidem sepulta essent, constaret modo haec inter omnes fides, Patrem et Filium et Spiritum esse unum Deum : nec tamen aut Filium esse Patrem, aut Spiritum Filium . . . ib.* 5). On the other hand it signified a confusion of categories as well as a forcing of the facts, if it was thought a duty to secure that : *Trinitatis dogma non est ecclesiae traditio tantum, sed doctrina in sacris literis expressa* (T. Wolleb, *Christ. Theol. Comp.* 1626 l. 1 *cap.* 2 *can.* 2, 1).

Second (positively) : By describing revelation as the root of the doctrine of the Trinity we also assert that the proposition or propositions about the Trinity of God, of course, claim to be, not directly but indirectly, identical with the proposition about revelation. The newness, the otherness, with which they stand alongside the first proposition (or its content) can not mean that a first period, say the Biblical, still had a faith without revelation or knowledge of the Triune God—what it meant by the contrast and the unity between *Yahweh* and the angel of *Yahweh*, between Father, Son, and Spirit, was in reality an imperfectly cleared-up monotheism, a greatly broken-up polytheism or the like—then came a second period, say that of the early Church, which thought it had, for all sorts of reasons, to formulate the same faith now in a really trinitarian way in the sense of the dogma—and now (such is the theory) we would be standing in a third, say the modern period, for which once more the Bible as well as dogma have become documents for the faith of past periods, regarding which we should have all liberty to express our faith either in the same way or otherwise. No, we regard dogma—with what right and in what sense we shall, of course, first have to show—as a necessary and relevant analysis of revelation, and therefore revelation itself throughout as properly interpreted by the dogma. The Bible can as little explicitly contain the dogma of the Trinity as it explicitly contains the other dogmas : for its witness, which was also given in a definite historical situation or in a plurality of such situations, does indeed stand as the witness of the revelation to erring humanity in general, but not as contrasted with these or those specified errors of Church history as such. But its witness is as witness to the revelation not only the record of the faith of a definite period, but, because it is that, at the same time the authority by which faith at any time must let itself be measured, and also can be measured irrespective of the difference of times.

There is no reasonable way in which we could or can contradict either Arius or Pelagius, Tridentine Catholicism or Servetus, Schleiermacher or Tillich directly out of the Bible, as though their false doctrines were already contradicted there to such and such an extent *totidem syllabis et literis*, chapter and verse, as though the Word of God had already been expressed there upon the temporary concerns of the various periods and only needed to be turned up, to yield the proper decision. On the contrary for dogmatic decision in the temporary concerns of the various periods we may and must argue on the basis of Scripture which must be discovered afresh from time to time, if we do not wish to argue as arbitrarily and as untheologically as our adversaries apparently do.

From this it follows that the proof of the truth of dogma, which as such " is not in the Bible," is not led by the fact that it is now a dogma once for all, but only by the fact that we may and must regard it as a just interpretation of the Bible. We shall have to speak later of the fact that and the reason why we have to approach dogma with a certain prejudice in favour of its truth, with a quite definite respect for its (not absolute but relative) authority. But that does not exclude, it includes the need for dogmatics to prove dogma, in the sense of indicating its basis, its root in revelation, i.e. in the Biblical witness to revelation. If dogma had no such root, if it could be shown that at its formation it was chiefly or entirely inserted in instead of excerpted from revelation, if in short it could not be regarded as the analysis of revelation, it could not be regarded as dogma.

In this sense there is a whole series of dogmas of the Roman Catholic Church which we could n o t acknowledge as dogmas, such as that of justification coinciding with sanctification, or that of Mary or that of purgatory or that of seven as the number of the Sacraments or that of the infallibility of the Pope. As little, naturally, the specific dogmas of Protestant Modernism, like that of the historical evolution of revelation or that of the continuity between God and man in religious experience. We fail to see the " root " which these doctrines would need to have in revelation, i.e. in the Biblical attestation of it, in order to be able to be dogmas.

In describing revelation as the root of the doctrine of the Trinity, we thus indicate that we simply do not confuse or equate the Biblical witness to God in His revelation with the doctrine of the Trinity, but, of course, claim to see between the two a genuine and truly found c o n n e c t i o n. By which obviously we are saying that also for ourselves, for the dogmatics of our time—which certainly is quite a different time from that of Athanasius and Augustine—the doctrine of the Trinity has a thoroughly actual and not only an historical relevance, i.e. that the criticism and revision of Church proclamation, to-day as then, must be completed in the form of developing the doctrine of the Trinity, that the text of the doctrine of the Trinity—it too, naturally, as expounded by o u r s e l v e s ! for to renounce exposition would mean renouncing the text altogether—becomes for us a commentary which we are bound to use for the exposition of the Bible and thus for the use of the dogmatic criterion.

But let us come to our point, namely, that the ground, the r o o t, of the doctrine of the Trinity, if it has one and so has the right to be a dogma—and it has one, it has the right to be a dogma —lies in r e v e l a t i o n.

Qu. 25 of the H e i d e l b e r g C a t e c h i s m runs as follows : " Since there is but one divine Being, why namest thou three, Father, Son, and Holy Ghost ? " The question is taken over almost word for word from the *Geneva Catechism* of 1545, where C a l v i n himself answers it as follows : *Quoniam in una Dei essentia Patrem nos intueri nos convenit . . . deinde Filium . . . postremo Spiritum sanctum* (K. Müller, *Bekenntnisschr. d. ref. Kirche* 1903 p. 118, 25). What is the meaning of *Quoniam nos convenit* ? Calvin has answered more clearly in the *Institutio* (I 13, 2) : *nam ita se praedicat unicum esse, ut distincte in tribus personis considerandum proponat.* And accordingly the *Heidelberg* formulates its answer : " B e c a u s e t h a t God hath thus revealed Himself in His Word, that these three distinguishable Persons are the one true eternal God." Therefore, then, and to that extent *convenit.* We might here object that by this appeal to revelation Calvin and his followers had certainly only meant that like much more the Trinity of God was attested in Scripture. But that the actual introduction of i t is established in this strange way, would at once of itself be very striking. And at this point we should recall the words of Calvin among others, which we cited earlier, the conclusion of which is that for the old Protestants the Trinity was simply not one article of faith among others, but the fundamental answer to the question, Who is God ?, to which all the other articles of faith are related. If we answer this question with the doctrine of revelation as such, we are, of course, thereby technically doing something, which was not done in that way four hundred years ago. But materially we certainly do not diverge from the purposes of that time when we indicate that revelation as such—Biblically attested revelation, that is—is the ground of the doctrine of the Trinity, i.e. that the doctrine of the Trinity is the proper interpretation of this very revelation as such.

By that we do not assert that the doctrine of the Trinity is merely the interpretation of revelation and not also an interpretation of the God who reveals Himself in revelation. That would be meaningless, because after all revelation is the self-interpretation of this God. If we have to do with His revelation we have to do with Himself and not, as modalists of all periods have thought, with an entity distinct from Himself. And it is as the answer to the question about the God who reveals Himself in revelation that the doctrine of the Trinity interests us. Which means that it is a part, in fact the decisive part of the doctrine of God, which at this point is not yet under discussion. We here anticipate the discussion of this part of the doctrine of God and shall later build up all that remains to be developed in this context upon this very presupposition, the Triunity of God. In a dogmatics of the Christian Church we cannot speak correctly of the nature and attributes of God without presupposing that it is God the Father, Son, and Holy Spirit of whom we are speaking. But this fact, that the doctrine of the Trinity is the basic presupposition of the doctrine of God as such also, does not in any way prevent it from being regarded also and at this early stage as the interpretation of revelation as such. Not as an exhaustive interpretation ; to give such a one we could not only speak of God who reveals himself, but we should also have to speak of the way in which and of man to whom He reveals Himself, and for that we should require further anticipations from the realm of the so-called special dogmas ; there are definite parts of Christology and Pneumatology of which we should have to take account. But from the doctrine of the Trinity we actually gather who the God is who reveals Himself and therefore we let it find expression here as the interpretation of revelation. By that then we do not mean that revelation is the ground of the Trinity, as if God were the Three-in-one only in His revelation and for the sake of His revelation. But, of course, we say that revelation is the ground of the doctrine of the Trinity ; the doctrine of the Trinity has no other ground than this. We come to the doctrine of the Trinity by no other way than by that of an analysis of the concept of revelation. And *vice versa*, revelation, to be rightly interpreted, must be interpreted as the ground of the doctrine of the Trinity. The question, decisive for the concept of revelation, about the self-revealing God cannot be answered by ignoring the answer given in the doctrine of the Trinity to this very question, but the doctrine of the Trinity itself is the answer to be given here. Our assertion then is that we designate the doctrine of the Trinity as the interpretation of revelation, or revelation as the ground of the doctrine of the Trinity : we find revelation itself so attested in Holy Scripture that our understanding of revelation (which is related to this testimony), i.e. of the self-revealing God, must be this very doctrine of the Trinity.

By that we do not mean only those passages which with strong probability might be or had to be regarded, in view of their language, as explicit indications of the doctrine of the Trinity which rightly lay in the future and was therefore already presented in revelation, or in the actual witness to it in the Bible ; hence we do not mean only the passages which speak quite clearly of a threeness in oneness or of a oneness in threeness of the self-revealing God.

In the OT perhaps the passage Isa. 61[1f.] may be mentioned as such an explicit indication, where the prophet is speaking in one breath of the Lord *Yahweh* and of a bearer of the message of salvation anointed by this Lord, upon whom in turn rests the Spirit of this Lord. In the NT we naturally have here before all to think of the command to baptise Matt. 28[19], in which, whatever layer of tradition it may belong to, Father, Son, and Holy Spirit are not only expressly and distinctly named and in the order which later became classic, but are also summarised in the concept of the divine " name " into which (i.e. into the divine reality indicated by this name) the " Gentiles " were to be baptised. Beside this passage may be set Rom 1[1-4], where the Gospel is described according to its Author as the εὐαγγέλιον θεοῦ, according to its content as dealing with the υἱὸς θεοῦ, while the πνεῦμα ἁγιωσύνης is described as the agent by whom this " Son of God " is " set apart " as such in His resurrection and to that extent (for those to whom He is manifest and who believe in Him) as such " installed " (ὁρισθείς). At the climax of the same letter there then (11[33]) appears the famous saying, ἐξ αὐτοῦ καὶ δι᾽ αὐτοῦ καὶ εἰς αὐτὸν τὰ πάντα, on which, of course, so many and such heavy stresses, exegetically and systematically, need not be laid, as Wobbermin has done (esp. *Syst. Theol.* III 1925 p. 392 f.), because most emphatically it signifies not so much a pronouncement upon God as rather a pronouncement upon the world and its relation to God. This saying is in this respect the more illuminating for the connections in which the divine αὐτός becomes knowable as thrice the same, but thrice the same in a different way. Nor can it be accidental, the way in which the concepts θεός, υἱός, πνεῦμα turn up and are used in 2 Thess. 2[13]. (On the other hand the passage 1 John 5[7], still greatly treasured in the age of Orthodoxy, while in its original reading—Spirit, water, and blood—an interesting testimony to the unity and variety as between Christ and the Spirit, is not to be used in the textual form, in which it later had a partial publicity and notoriety—Father, Son, and Spirit—for the ascertainment of the NT doctrine as such.) Beside these four passages should next be placed a series of those in which likewise and more or less clearly the same three appear in the same special functions, but now in a considerably more mobile order. We find, according to 1 Peter 1², the election of believers grounded in the πρόγνωσις θεοῦ πατρός, completed in the ἁγιασμὸς πνεύματος and directed εἰς ὑπακοὴν καὶ ῥαντισμόν αἵματος Ἰησοῦ Χριστοῦ. We hear in Rev. 1⁴ about the grace and peace wished for the seven Churches, that they are derivable ἀπὸ ὁ ὢν καὶ ὁ ἦν καὶ ὁ ἐρχόμενος (note here how the first fundamental concept is once again paradoxically broken up into a significant threeness), καὶ ἀπὸ τῶν ἑπτὰ πνευμάτων ἃ ἐνώπιον τοῦ θρόνου αὐτοῦ (here obviously the one Spirit is supposed to be described at the same time as the special spirit of each individual of the seven churches)—καὶ ἀπὸ Ἰησοῦ Χριστοῦ the faithful witness. If in these two passages Christ, although certainly important, stands in the third place, in two others He returns to the first. That occurs in 2 Cor. 13¹³, where the so-called apostolic benediction ascribes grace to Jesus Christ, love to God the Father, and κοινωνία to the Holy Spirit, and Mark 1⁹ᶠ·, where the Holy Spirit descends upon Jesus as the principal subject of the baptism story, after which a voice from heaven confirms His Divine Sonship. (Cf. Fr. Turretini, *Instit. Theol. elenct.* 1679 I *Loc.* 3, *qu.* 25, 7 : *Alius auditur, sed nec videtur, nec descendit. Alius non auditur, sed visibili specie descendit. Alius descendit et ascendit e flumine baptizatus in conspectu omnium.*) But once more, too, there are not wanting passages in which the Spirit is named as the first and in the context most notable member of the Threeness. The Holy Spirit is followed in Jude 20–21 by God and the κύριος Ἰησοῦς Χριστός, or apparently in 1 Cor. 12⁴ and Eph. 4⁴ the classical order of Father, Son, and Holy Spirit is actually reversed, whereby these last two passages are once more specially remarkable through the emphasis laid upon the unity by the αὐτός or εἷς, with which the three concepts are introduced.

We have agreed that we need not expect to find the doctrine of the Trinity actually expressed in the Old or New Testament. But already in view of the presence of these explicit indications we are unable to deny that the problems which developed later in the doctrine of the Trinity, are not foreign to the Bible but at least preformed in it. And this explicit indication first gathers weight from the fact that it is wrapped up in a perfect network of implicit indications, and above all from the fact that the entire theme of the revelation of God as it is handled in the Old and New Testaments, centrally in the New, cannot be touched, far less grasped, without encountering the pre-formation of these problems. That is what we have now to show.

God reveals Himself as the Lord : in this sentence we have summed up the way we regard the form and content of Biblical revelation. The question now is : must we, without approaching too closely to the unity of its content, regard this sentence in a threefold sense and, without too closely approaching its threefold sense, as unified in its content ? If this sentence, not in any general signification but in relation to what the Bible calls revelation, demands this way of looking at it, then we have realised what on the basis of the passages just adduced could only be conjectured as extremely probable, that this sentence is actually the " root " of the doctrine of the Trinity, that the problems of the doctrine of the Trinity are represented in the fact of revelation, as it is attested in the Bible.   Thereupon we shall no longer proceed with the scheme of Subject, Predicate, Object (Revealer, Revelation, Revealedness) which was only to make it clear to us that and to what extent we were led by revelation itself to the problem of the three-in-oneness.   Or rather we now dissolve this scheme— it has and retains its significance—in the manner suited to the concrete content of Biblical revelation on the one hand and to the doctrine of the Trinity on the other.   The inquiry about Revealer, Revelation, and Revealedness corresponds with the logical and material order both of Biblical revelation and also of the doctrine of the Trinity.   Subsequently, therefore, when it comes to be developed, we shall return to this order.   But we must put our question in a different order, if we now wish to see how Biblical revelation and the doctrine of the Trinity are interconnected, how the second could and did proceed from the first.   That is an historical question which as such has its own special form.   But it is determined by the fact that on the one hand Biblical revelation has a definite historical centre, while the doctrine of the Trinity has a definite historical occasion, in Biblical revelation.   Historically speaking, the three questions answered in the Bible as to Revealer, Revelation, and Revealedness have not the same weight ; it is rather the second of these concepts, God's action in His revelation—revelation in answer to the question, What God does, and thus the predicate of our sentence—which is the real theme of the Biblical witness.   Within the framework of this theme then both the other questions—actually just as important—will be answered. And so, too, the doctrine of the Trinity historically considered, in its origin and construction, has not been interested equally in Father, Son, and Holy Spirit ; here also the theme was primarily the second Person of the Trinity, God the Son, the divinity of Christ.

What we have to realise from the standpoint of history of dogma is what Harnack (*Lehrbuch d. Dogmengesch.* 4th edn, 1909 vol. I p. 90) formulated in the sentence, " Confession of Father, Son, and Spirit is . . . the unfolding of the belief that Jesus is the Christ." O. Scheel (*RGG*[2] art. *Dreieinigkeit*, III) is in material agreement : " The history of the doctrine of the Trinity is primarily a history of the Logos-concept in Christianity." The same insight is involved, which Irenaeus developed, linking it up with the name of Christ in an appeal to Isa. 61[1] : *In Christi enim nomine subauditur qui unxit et ipse qui unctus est et ipsa unctio in qua unctus est. Et unxit quidem Pater, unctus vero est Filius in Spiritu qui est unctio (C.o.h. III 18, 3).*

In the framework then of this theme, of the question of the divinity of Christ, although in logic and in substance they at once claim the same weight, the other two questions here, too, have achieved expression primarily as a necessary counterpart to the question about the Son, namely, that about the Father and that about the Spirit of the Father and the Son.

If this was so necessary and correct we should then have to say that in 2 Cor 13[13] in the order Christ, God, Spirit we have before us the most genuine form of the Biblical witness in this matter. At all events the historical development of the doctrine of the Trinity out of the witness to revelation was achieved by this route, and this route we must now follow.

1. Revelation in the Bible means the self-unveiling, imparted to men, of the God who according to His nature cannot be unveiled to man. The element of self-unveiling in this definition may be described not as the logically material, but as the historical centre of the Biblical concept of revelation. When the Bible speaks of revelation it does so in the form of narrating a story or a series of stories. But the content of this story and of each one of these stories is just the self-unveiling of God referred to. When it gives us this narrative, our experience, of course, also is that it is the God who according to His nature cannot be unveiled to man who unveils Himself there, and that this self-unveiling is imparted to particular men. Logically and substantially that is at once just as important as the self-unveiling in the narrative. Historically the latter constitutes the centre. But what is the meaning here of self-unveiling ? Since it is the God who according to His nature cannot be unveiled to man, who unveils Himself there, self-unveiling means that God does what man himself cannot do in any sense or in any way ; He makes Himself present, known, and significant to them as God. In the historical life of men He moves into a place and a very definite place at that, and makes Himself the object of human contemplation, human experience, human thought, human speech. He makes Himself an authority and an agent, and a concrete authority, an historical agent at that, an element in their human existence, significant and effective in time and in temporal relations. He exists Himself, He exists as God for them exactly

as quite other things or persons exist for them—as Esau existed for Jacob, as Mount Horeb or the ark of the covenant for the people of Israel, as John for Peter or Paul for his Church—naturally in His own special form, not to be confused with any other, but really and concretely exists in definite form, so much so that the men specially involved could say, without the slightest speculation or metaphor, Immanuel, God with us ! so that without the slightest fiction or self-deception they could say Thou to Him, could pray to Him. That is what self-unveiling is, that is the thing man cannot supply himself with, what only God can give him, but what He actually does give him in His revelation. It is the concept of form which we must single out from what has been said as the decisive one. Whoever and whatever the self-revealing God may be otherwise, this is certain that in His revelation, according to the witness of the Bible, He takes form, and that this taking form is His self-unveiling. For Him it is not impossible and for Him it is not too petty a thing, to be His own double in His revelation, double so far as His self-unveiling, His taking form is obviously not a thing that goes without saying but an event, and an event at that which can be explained by or derived from neither the will and act of man nor the rest of the world's course, so far as a move on His part is necessary to this event, and so far as this move obviously means something novel in God, God's distinguishing Himself from Himself, a being of God in a mode of existence, not subordinate as compared with His first, hidden mode of being as God, but just different, one in which He can also be existent for us. He who reveals Himself here as God is able to reveal Himself ; already the fact of His revelation declares that it is His property to distinguish Himself from Himself, i.e. in Himself and hiddenly to be God and yet at the same time in quite another way, namely, manifestly, i.e. in the form of something He Himself is not, to be God a second time.

In another way God a second time—in the OT that is shown primarily in the fact that practically the whole of the attributes significant of the *Yahweh* of Israel (His " righteousness " with which He watches over His covenant with Israel, His "lovingkindness" and "faithfulness" towards His own, His "glory," and also His "Word" and His "Spirit," the "wisdom" of the later OT and also the "countenance" anthropomorphically—or we had better say not at all anthropomorphically—ascribed to Him, His "arm," His "hand," His "right hand") are from time to time given expression to in such a way as though they were not only in or of *Yahweh* but simply *Yahweh* Himself in another way a second time. Revelation means, that all these human, only too human concepts are not only that, are not only descriptions and expositions of the reality of *Yahweh*, but are themselves the reality of *Yahweh*, that in these concepts and therefore in space, in the spiritual but also in the physical space of men genuinely different from Himself *Yahweh* possesses what we previously called " f o r m," that in them all *Yahweh* Himself is there, subsists, has objectivity for those to whom He is manifest. The Science of Religion usually terms the concept so used hypostases, i.e. simply distinguishably-indistinguishable realities of the one God, and why should we not agree with this description ? The Science of Religion has notoriously, on its part, borrowed them from Christian History of Dogma. As a matter of fact one of the series of hypostases stands out in a significant and, if we are not completely deceived, comprehensive way as the inner meaning of what God is in His self-unveiling " in another way a second time," the concept of the n a m e of God. Knowledge, fear, love, trust, hope, praise, preaching, appeal—all that is continually connected with this apparent sub-centre alongside of *Yahweh* and yet thus unmistakably connected with *Yahweh* Himself. In it, in this name, the pious man thinks, speaks and acts, when he stands before *Yahweh*, in His service, under His protection, under His blessing. To this n a m e of *Yahweh*, not to Him who dwells on Sinai, or according to the later idea in heaven, a house in Jerusalem, the temple, is built. On the other hand this name is the authority for the sake of which *Yahweh* forgives, is gracious, leads, does not abandon Israel ; His name in fact dwells—thus hath · *Yahweh* chosen it for Himself—in Jerusalem. But likewise the already mentioned angel of *Yahweh* stands in the closest connection with the name of *Yahweh* : what makes him, according to Ex. 23²¹, the angel of *Yahweh* and gives him authority as such is that " My name is in him." In His name is concentrated everything in H i s r e l a t i o n s h i p to His people, i.e. to the pious, and from the name of *Yahweh* somehow proceeds everything the people or the pious who stand in this relationship to Him, have to expect from Him. What does all that mean ? Any one's name, not only for the OT but to a large extent for ancient thought generally, perhaps also for so-called primitive (in reality, of course, not at all primitive) thought generally, is not at all something attaching externally to the person in question, something accidental or unessential, not a mere *nomen* in the sense of the mediæval debates ; but at this very point (perhaps, in distinction from the previously named " attributes " of God, only at this point) it must be said that the name is a being belonging, of course, to another Being, identical with Him in a way not to be explained, yet a separate being, so that pronouncements upon the name and the bearer of the name are distinct from each other and yet on the other hand may represent each other : " where the name is, there is the bearer of the name : what happens to the name, happens also to Him to whom it belongs : where the name works, the bearer of it works " (H a n s S c h m i d t, *RGG²*, *art. Namensglaube* I). If the OT applies this realistic thought about the name to *Yahweh*, that means on the one hand that there is a distinction between *Yahweh* who dwells on Sinai or in heaven, and *Yahweh* who dwells in C a n a a n, in S h i l o h and later in J e r u s a l e m, there is a distinction between *Yahweh* in His hiddenness and *Yahweh* in H i s h i s t o r i c a l f o r m, in which—and this is what is asserted in the givenness of His name—He is k n o w n i n I s r a e l a n d d e a l s w i t h I s r a e l. " God's name is the expression for His personal nature as it is present in His sanctuary, in His people " (O. P r o c k s c h in G. Kittel's *Theol. Wörterbuch zum NT*, 1932 *art.* ἅγιος, p. 90). But, on the other hand, it also means that the OT does not pretend to knowledge of two gods or of many gods, but it knows of the one God : the hidden *Yahweh* Himself is present in His name and all predicates of His name are those of the hidden *Yahweh* Himself—but it is acquainted with this one God once and then a second time in quite a different way. And just this fact that it knows of Him in this way, that is, " a second time in quite a different way " is the all-important one for Israel or for the pious. For this *Yahweh* who exists " a second time in quite a different way," the name of *Yahweh* is the form in which *Yahweh* gets at Israel, acts on him, is manifest to him. Therefore, the decisive act of the revelation by which Israel is chosen as Israel, becomes the people of this God, is just the revelation of the name of God. That this revelation of the name (Ex. 3$^{13f.}$) is in fact, in content, a refusal of any name—" I am that I am " can scarcely mean anything else than just, I am He whose name proper no one can repeat—is significant enough ; for the revealed name itself by its wording is to recall also and precisely the hiddenness of the revealed God. But still under this name, which itself and as such expresses His mystery, God *does* reveal Himself to His people, i.e. He begins, as Ex. 3 instructively shows, to deal with Israel through the announcement of His deliverance out of Egypt, communicated to Moses. From this point of view it will be necessary to add to the concept of the name of God the concept of the covenant which belongs to quite a different stratum, in order to get a full view of all that the form of God, and to that extent His existence in His self-unveiling, signifies in the OT. In the covenant with this people— " I will be their God and they shall be my people " Jer. 31^{33}—the name of God is realised : within the covenant with its divine promise and claim, with its record deposited in the law, everything takes place that takes place through the name of *Yahweh*. In the language of our historians, " the thought of the covenant is the form in which is clothed Israel's consciousness of the bond made in history with this God and at the same time of the element of the divine will in this bond " (J. Hempel, *RGG*^{2} *art.* Bund IIA). To have knowledge of the name of *Yahweh* and to that extent knowledge of *Yahweh* Himself and so to participate in His revelation, means simply to be partners in the Covenant founded by Him. In this respect and in this way *Yahweh* is God " in another way a second time," that He chooses a people, makes it His people and rules it as His people.

And now it is possible to get a relatively simple view of the fundamental matter with which the NT is concerned. God " in another way a second time " —that is obviously the point here too ; only in a way incomparably more direct, unambiguous, palpable. So much more direct that even the " hypostases " of the OT beside it appear pale, or, to speak in the famous figure of Hebrews, as mere " shadows," so much more direct that the former, particularly the remarkable place and meaning of the " name " of *Yahweh*, may be regarded quite unrestrictedly and at the same time quite meaningly, as the Church has always maintained as against Judaism, yet from this standpoint only, as " prophecy " of the " fulfilment " present here. Into the place—not of the *Yahweh* on Sinai or in heaven, but certainly of the name of *Yahweh* that in the end really dwells in Jerusalem in a house of stone—there now comes the existence of the man Jesus of Nazareth, " My Lord and my God " He is called at one of the peaks of the NT message (John 20^{28}). The remote yet also constantly near and actual background here, too, is the God who has no historical form, the " Father in heaven." But even this God the Jesus of the NT calls not only the Father who has sent Him, but emphatically His Father with whom He may range Himself, nay with whom He knows Himself ranged, because He exists as man among men, because He does His will, i.e. because He reveals Him, the Father, from whom, it is true, He is separated by this form of His as man, or His ability to be God in this form, but by nothing essential. Inalienably important as this background is, little as it can be thought away even for a moment, the actual picture which the NT witness sets before us is the picture of the self-unveiling of this Father, in which He is not the Father but just t h e S o n, the historical form of this man on his way from Bethelehem to Golgotha, the " name " J e s u s. Once more : the concreteness and reality of the self-unveiling of God for man and withal the puzzle of the self-differentiation which renders this self-unveiling possible and takes place in God Himself, has here, compared with the OT, not merely increased quantitatively. Is not perhaps here for the first time everything cut away, that is merely speculative, merely figurative, merely fictitious in the way of regarding God's real becoming-an-object in His revelation ? Is not the question of f a i t h in the revelation, the question of affirming the " God with us " so put here for the first time that it calls for decision, here— where in place of the invisible form of the name of the manifest God which is primarily real only in the region of human conception—the unique, contingent, somatic, human existence of Jesus has entered ? Has it not become shatter-ingly clear in the rejection of Jesus by the Jews that it was possible to affirm the God of the OT apparently with the deepest reverence and most zealous faith and yet in reality to deny Him, so far as His form, now become quite concrete, became an offence to these pious souls ? Or what else has Israel to object to in Jesus except the divine self-unveiling which now encountered it—not for the first time, but now for the first time quite unambiguously— the self-unveiling which now approached it (Israel) so to speak in the body ? Inasmuch as Israel thought it had to defend the name of God that dwelt in the house of stone in Jerusalem against Jesus as against a blasphemer, it is this name it denies, separates itself from, and therefore it separates itself from its own Holy Scripture, which is a peculiar witness of this very name as of God's real presence and action in the human sphere. This presence and action of God Israel begs to decline. Why does the Lord's Prayer in the NT begin in such an OT way, Hallowed be thy name ! ? How else should it begin ? one might almost reply. That is what happens precisely with the name of Jesus. Not something new but something primæval and initial, the God who wills to be God " in another way a second time " and to be known as God, as the God of Abraham, Isaac, and Jacob, the God who will be manifest in His name and hallowed in His name. And therefore in explanation of this first petition the Lord's Prayer must continue, Thy Kingdom come ! Thy will be done, as in heaven so (*N.B.* !) also on earth ! This καὶ ἐπὶ τῆς γῆς was the self-unveiling, the form of God, which Israel found attested in its Holy Writ on every page, and which now when it stood fulfilled before it, it denied once more, exactly as its fathers in the desert had murmured against Moses and later stoned the prophets, not from irreligion but in the protest of the most refined, most ponderable religion against revelation, which definitely does not leave the pious man to himself but confronts him l i t e r a l l y with God. Therefore, the Jesus-revelation ends with the crucifixion of Jesus by these most pious folk of their time, who, with Immanuel daily on their lips and in their heart, refused this particular Immanuel ! in its fulfilment which had now unconditionally taken place. But just because Immanuel was now, in Jesus, unconditionally fulfilled, the crucifixion of Jesus had to signify something different from the stoning of even the greatest prophet, namely, the end of the history of Israel as the special people of revelation, the pulling down of the house of stone as the dwelling of the name of the Lord, the free issue—not of a new but of the one old gospel now to Jews and heathen. Because the Word became flesh, λόγος συντελῶν, completely bringing to light what revelation in the OT had invariably first brought to light as a pointer, it had also to become λόγος συντέμνων, the dissolution of this revelation and of its written testimony—not contradiction or abolition or destruction, but dissolution of it into itself, just as morning twilight disappears in the brightness of the rising sun itself (Rom. 9²⁸) : Christ the τέλος of the law (Rom. 10⁴). We are face to face with the theme of the great struggle which Paul beyond all others waged, at the rise of the Church. It was not a struggle against, but like the struggle of Jesus Himself, of whom it only wished to testify, the great struggle for the OT, i.e. for the one eternal covenant of God with men, now sealed in time, for the acknowledgment of the perfect self-unveiling of God.

That God is capable of what the Bible ascribes to Him in its narratives of what happened from the patriarchs through Moses and the prophets, past Golgotha and up to Easter and Whitsunday, namely, that God can become manifest to men in the strictly real sense in which that becomes conclusively visible in the Jesus-revelation, i.e. that God can become so unlike Himself that He is God in such a way as not to be bound to His secret eternity and eternal secrecy, but also can and will and really does assume temporal form—this ability, desire, and real action of God we might now regard as a first confirmation of our sentence, God reveals Himself as the Lord. As against talk of other revelations outside that attested in the Bible the question above all would have to be put, whether in those cases it is really a matter of such genuine assumption of form by the godhead over against men and not perhaps merely of phenomena such that identity with the godhead is not seriously claimed for them but merely a certain participation in it. And secondly, it would have to be asked whether the lordship which perhaps even in these cases is ascribed to the godhead is also in these cases viewed as implying the same sort of freedom in God in Himself, i.e. the freedom to be unlike Himself. Where these two questions cannot be answered in the affirmative or in the degree that they cannot be answered with certainty, one should at least go very carefully to work in including the revelation of the Bible in the series of other revelations. But, be that as it may, the Lordship which becomes visible in the Biblical revelation consists in God's freedom to distinguish Himself from Himself, to become other than Himself, and yet to remain as He was : in fact more, to be the one God equal to Himself and to exist as the one sole God by the very fact that He thus, so inconceivably deeply, distinguishes Himself from Himself, that He is not only God the Father but also—in this direction this is the comprehensive meaning of the entire Biblical witness—God the Son. That He reveals Himself as the Son is what is primarily meant by saying that He reveals Himself as the Lord. Actually this Sonship is God's lordship in His revelation.

2. Revelation in the Bible means the self-unveiling, imparted to men, of the God who according to His nature cannot be unveiled to man. By emphasising this element we return to the Subject of the revelation. The revelation attested in the Bible is the revelation of the God who according to His nature cannot be unveiled to man. There are other things, there are also other gods, who also cannot be unveiled to man, i.e. of which in fact he has actually no experience and no conception but of which he might very well have experience and a conception, whose inscrutability [1] is only factual and might some day be removed by some other fact, because it is not based upon the nature of the thing or of the god in question. Inscrutability, however, hiddenness, belongs to the nature of Him who is called God in the Bible. As Creator, this God is distinct from the world, i.e. as the person He is, He does not belong to the realm of what man as a creature can know directly about God. Nor can He be unveilable to him even indirectly, in the created world, because He is the Holy One, whom to see, even to see indirectly, would require other eyes than ours which are corrupted by sin. And finally this God by His grace, i.e. by His self-unveiling, says to every one to whom it is imparted, that of himself he cannot do what is there done for him and to him. Thus it is of the nature of this God to be inscrutable to man. Of course, inscrutable in His revealed nature. It is the *Deus revelatus* who is the *Deus absconditus*, the God to whom there is no way and no bridge, of whom we could not say or have to say one single word, had He not of His own initiative met us as *Deus revelatus*. Only when we have grasped this as the meaning of the Bible do we take in the bearing of its pronouncement that God reveals Himself, i.e. that He has assumed a form for our benefit. We cannot withdraw one iota from our previously given interpretation of revelation, that it consists in God having assumed a form. If we deny that, we deny revelation itself. But that it is the God who according to His nature cannot be unveiled to men,

---

[1] For non-unveilability *unenthüllbarkeit* : and so always for *convenience* in this context—TR.

who there reveals Himself, is a fact with its own very definite significance for understanding His unveiling. It must signify that even in the form which He assumes by revealing Himself, God is free to reveal Himself or not to reveal Himself. In other words, we can regard His self-unveiling in each separate instance only as His act in which to a man who has no power to unveil Him He Himself unveils Himself, which means, shows himself in a definite form, but Himself reveals Himself. Revelation always means to reveal, even in the form, even in the means of revelation. The form as such, the means, does not take the place of God. It is not the form that reveals, speaks, comforts, works, helps, but God in the form. The result therefore of God assuming a form is not a medium or a third thing between God and man, nor a reality different from God, which as such would be the subject of revelation. That would mean that God could be unveiled to man after all, that there was no longer any need of God for His revelation, or rather that God was given into the hands of the man who, by God's form being given to him, could more or less dispose of God as of other realities. God's assumption of form means that He disposes of the form in which He meets man, just as He disposes of man. God's presence is always God's decision to be present. The divine Word is the divine speaking, the divine gift is the divine giving. God's self-unveiling remains the act of sovereign divine freedom. Here it may be for one man what the Word says, there for the next only then the veiling of God. For the same man it may be the first thing to-day, and the second to-morrow. In it God cannot be grasped by man or attached by sequestration, or caught at work. To count upon it means to count upon God's free loving-kindness, not upon a credit granted once for all, not upon an axiom to which one can revert once for all, not upon an experience which one has had once for all. Were that so, we should not be dealing with the God who according to His nature cannot be unveiled to man, we should rather be dealing with one of those mysteries which some fine day unveil themselves to us, and cease to be mysteries to us any longer. The world's mysteries are of such a kind that in a moment they can cease to be mysteries. God is ever and again a mystery. Revelation is ever and again revelation in the full sense of the word, or it is not revelation, at all events not what is so called in the Bible.

We have already noted the remarkable circumstance that the great revelation of the name in Ex. 3 according to the most probable interpreta-

24

370 § 8. *God in His Revelation*

tion of the text consists precisely in a refusal of the name. " Wherefore askest
thou after my name, seeing it is wonderful ? " answers the angel of the Lord
even to Manoah, Judg. 13^{18}. A delivering over of God to man, as awareness
of His peculiar name would imply, is not to take place even in revelation, but
revelation itself is to be regarded and to continue to be regarded as the
revelation of the free loving-kindness of God. This reserve of *Yahweh*, His
remaining hidden in His very revelation is also indicated, Ex. 3, by that
urgent " Draw not nigh hither : put off thy shoes from off thy feet, for the
place whereon thou standest is holy ground ! " Just as generally the concept
of holiness in the OT has nothing to do with a speculation about the transcendent God, but belongs, strictly to His immanence, i.e. to His revelation, to
His name. Holy in the OT is all that is connected with what we call the form
of God in His revelation and that in this connection and because of it demands
another attitude from man than the profane one, in whose sphere and environment it is visible and audible as the form of God, a distinguishing, reserved,
utterly reverent attitude, an attitude in which man has to get rid of all
arbitrariness, all clumsy intereference—think of the evil experiences a man
could have by meddling with the " ark of the covenant " ! Everything the
OT says of God's self-unveiling stands *eo ipso* under apparently the very opposite sign as well : " Am I a God at hand, saith the Lord, and not (also) a
God afar off ? " (Jer. 23^{23}). The " angel of the covenant " is, Mal. 3^1, expressly himself called " Lord," which does not prevent him from having at
the same time to be sent by the Lord. Holy according to Isa. 6 is the manifest
God, the mere skirt of whose garment fills the temple, while He Himself sits
on a high and lofty throne, incomprehensible to the prophet and to his whole
people, in the very moment of His turning to him with His revelation. Holy
is God and holy is what is connected with God, because and so far as God in
unlocking and imparting Himself also draws and makes fast the bounds which
separate man from Him, and which the latter (man) therefore may not pass.
Holiness is the separation in which God is God and as God goes His own
way, even though and just because he is " God with us," the reservation
of His gracious or ungracious decision with which one must reckon concerning Him and because of which He is ever to be sought afresh and ever with
the same humility. Holy has also unquestionably the meaning of " uncanny " : God comes indeed to men, but not to be at home with them. This
God is not exhausted in His action, as the institution of the Sabbath puts
it with special beauty : He can not only work, He can also rest from all His
works : in entering the sphere of our existence, He inhabits and also asserts
His own sphere, proper to Him and only to Him. With regard to this God, as
we may gather equally from the attitude of the prophet and from that of
the psalmists, it is always a case of the whole thing over and over again,
and the history of His acts is a history of ever renewed beginnings. Of
course there is and ought to be a tradition of revelation, an institutional
worship, but opposed to that in the keenest dialectic stands prophetism, ever
ready and armed properly to unsettle afresh everything that wanted to
settle down, to face afresh with the mystery of *Yahweh* everything that wanted
to explain itself humanly, far too humanly. From this standpoint we can
understand the sharpness of the prohibition of images as a ban not so
much on sense enjoyment as rather on the pious obtrusiveness and cocksure-
ness of the religion of Canaan. We cannot sufficiently notice that this hiddenness of God in the OT nowhere becomes a matter of esoteric metaphysics,
that rather it becomes and remains always extremely practical, just because

it is only the hiddenness of the revealed, the active God. But that this God can only be seen and heard as active ; not at all or anywhere (or merely *per nefas*) as exhausted in and bound up with a medium, this fact is guaranteed by His hiddenness, by His inconceivability.

In the NT also this relationship is not altered. On the contrary there, too, it is true now in a pointed way, that God hides Himself in revealing Himself, that even and precisely in assuming a form He remains free to be manifest in this form or else not to be. The form is here the *humanitas Christi*. And there we come up against one cf the hardest problems of Christology which will have to occupy us more than once : Can the Incarnation of the Word according to the conception of the Bible witnesses mean that the existence of the man Jesus of Nazareth might have been as it were in itself, in its own power and continuity, the revealing Word of God ? Is the *humanitas Christi* as such the revelation ? Does Jesus Christ's Sonship to God mean that God's revealing has now, so to speak, passed over to the existing of the man Jesus of Nazareth, and the latter has now become identical with the former ? At this point we can only make the following reply, that where things have really been conceived in this way, invariably to a greater or less degree there has shown up clearly the thing the OT, as we heard, specially wished to guard against with its holiness concept of the manifest God, the possibility of letting God be unveiled through man, of allowing man to place himself on the same platform as God, there to comprehend Him and so to become His master. The " fairest Lord Jesus " of mysticism, the " Saviour " of pietism, Jesus the teacher of wisdom and friend of man in the Enlightenment, Jesus the inner meaning of exalted humanity in Schleiermacher, Jesus as the embodiment of the idea of religion in Hegel and his school, Jesus as a religious personality according to Carlyle's picture in the theology of the outgoing 19th century—all that looks at least pretty doubtful in the light of what in the OT sense is a sacrilegious profane intrusion, whereby it was believed possible, so to speak, to come to an understanding about the presence of God in Christ, to take possession of it with the aid of a few conceptions emanating from the humanity. We may at once conclude from the fact that such attempts at secularisation are not undertaken in the NT, that in it, too, the *humanitas Christi* comes under the reservation of God's holiness, i.e. that the power and the continuity in which the man Jesus of Nazareth, according to the testimony of the evangelists and apostles, was in fact the revealed word, consisted here also in the power and continuity of the divine action in this form and not in the continuity of this form as such. As a matter of fact even Jesus certainly did not become revelation to all who met Him, but only to a few. But even these few could deny and abandon Him and one of them could be his betrayer. Manifestation is clearly not in itself or directly ascribed to His existence as such. This existence of His as such indeed is also given to death, and thus from the side of death, i.e. of its boundaries, because He rose, the Crucified becomes manifest as the Son of God ; but thereby the resurrection is described not as an effect belonging to the *humanitas Christi*, but as one befalling it, as a becoming awakened from the dead by God (frequently, e.g. Gal. 1¹ ; Rom. 6⁴ ; in Eph. 1²⁰ expressly by God the Father). To speak in the language of the later period, the divinity is not so immanent in the humanity of Christ as not also to remain transcendent over it, not so that its immanence could cease to be an event quite in the sense of the OT, a constantly recurring new thing, that becomes real from God's side in definite circumstances. In Paul's comprehensive formula 2 Cor. 5¹⁹ θεὸς ἦν ἐν Χριστῷ κόσμον καταλλάσσων ἑαυτῷ, we need not lay such emphasis on the ἦν that its connection with the verb καταλλάττειν is overlooked. This reconciling action of God is the being of God in Christ, but this reconciling action of God is the being of God in Christ. The Son " glorifies " the Father, yes, but not without the Father glorifying Him, the Son (John 17¹). It is not any son that is here the spokesman, but the Son of this Father, who also as the Father of this Son remains the Father in heaven, the Father who sends the Son, to put this Johannine description of the divine action here at the close.

And now we repeat that the God of the Biblical revelation is also able for what is ascribed to Him in this respect by the Biblical witnesses: that His revelation does not in the least betoken a loss of His mystery, that, true, He assumes a form, but without any form compassing Him, that in gifting Himself He remains free to give Himself afresh or to refuse to, so that it is always His new self-giving that remains man's sole hope, that His " second time in quite another way " really does not prevent him from remaining quite equal to Himself—in the fact that this is so we hear confirmation for the second time, obviously in a very different way compared with the first, that God reveals Himself as the Lord. Once again here we should have to ask an additional question, whether in other cases which purport to speak of revelation the abiding mystery of the self-revealing God really belongs to the concept of revelation, and whether the lordship there ascribed to " God " can really exist there together with such freedom in God with regard to His own utterances—or whether in those cases revelation does not always consist in God becoming the world and so in an empowering of man, in consequence of which " God " does not remain free at all, but at best must become a partner, at worst a tool of the pious man. We may indeed even speak of " revelation " there, but, let us repeat, it would be well not to be in too great a hurry to put Bible revelation on a par with the other variety. But that merely by the way. Certain it is that the lordship of God as visible in Bible revelation does consist in this freedom of His ; in His abiding freedom to unveil or to veil. God reveals Himself as the Father, that is to say the Father of the Son in whom He assumes form for our benefit. God the Father is God who even in assuming form in the Son always does not assume form, God as the free ground and the free power of His being God in the Son. It were no revelation within the bounds of the Biblical witness in which God would not also be manifest thus as the Father. His doing this is the other thing—it is really something else, the same and yet not to be brought to the same denominator as the first—that is meant when we say that He reveals Himself as Lord. God's Fatherhood, too, is God's lordship in His revelation.

3. Revelation in the Bible means the self-unveiling, imparted to men, of the God who according to His nature cannot be unveiled to man. We inquired previously about the source of the revelation. And now we ask where it goes to? The revelation attested in the Bible takes place not only in man's sphere, as might be said of the theogonies and cosmogonies which comprise the object of testimony in the records of the Babylonian religion. But it reaches man, and not any kind of mythical man, not man in general, but always man occupying a quite definite, a definite historical position. It belongs to the concept of Biblically attested revelation, to be an historical event. Historical does not mean fixable as historical or fixed as historical. Historical does not therefore have its usual meaning of "historical." We should have once more to discard all that was previously said about the mystery in revelation, did we wish now to describe just a single one of the events of revelation narrated in the Bible as "historical," i.e as apprehensible by a neutral observer or as apprehended by such an one. What the neutral observer of these events might apprehend or may have apprehended of these events was the form of the revelation, not regarded by him as such and, moreover, not to be regarded by him as such, some sort of happening unrolling itself in the human sphere, having all the possibilities of interpretation appropriate to this sphere, but in no case revelation as such.

Millions in the ancient East may once have heard the name *Yahweh* and sometime or other have seen His temple. But this historical element was not revelation. Thousands may have seen and heard the Rabbi of Nazareth. But this historical element was not revelation. Even the historical element at the resurrection of Christ, the empty grave regarded as an element in this event, that might possibly be fixed, was certainly not revelation. This historical element, like everything historical, is admittedly susceptible of an even highly trivial interpretation.

On the question of the "historical" certainty of the revelation attested in the Bible we can only say that in the Bible itself it remains out of account in a way explicable only on the ground that this question is simply foreign to it, i.e. obviously and utterly inappropriate to the object of its testimony. The neutral observer who understood the events narrated in it as revelation, ceased by that very fact to be a neutral observer. And for the non-neutral, who heard and saw, who believed, there was and there remained simultaneously in the mere form of the revelation the mystery of it, i.e. he above all could not but be aware that here historically there could be established not merely little but nothing, that is to say, a thing that invariably was merely different, quite without importance for the event of revelation. This cannot be what is meant when we describe Biblical revelation as being, according to its concept, an historical event. By that we rather mean the fact that the Bible always regards what it calls revelation as a concrete relation to concrete men. God in His inconceivability and God in the act of His revelation—that is not the formula of an abstract metaphysic of God, the World, or religion, claiming to hold good always and everywhere. It is rather the narrative about an event which took place uniquely, i.e. in a place and at a time always more or less exactly determined. That this place and time lies for us, historically, to a large extent in obscurity, that the separate data provided by the Bible about them are open to historical criticism, is obvious in the case of documents of a date and civilisation which had no knowledge at all of an historical question in our sense, quite apart from the fact that no serious part, even in the sense possible in that time and in that civilisation, could be played by historical interest in the composition of those documents which did in fact claim to be documents of revelation. But that makes no difference to the fact that by the thing it calls revelation the Bible always means a unique event, one occurring in that place and at that time. Thus, for all its " errors " in such and such a variety of cases— and in this respect it is simply quite unconcerned—in its statements about place and time, according to the canons of present-day historical science, the important thing is not the more or less " correct " content of these statements, but the fact of them. This fact, that the Bible of the OT and NT repeatedly and with extraordinary emphasis makes chronological and topographical statements, that therefore it means every time to ascribe to the revelation of God of which it tells a temporally and spatially circumscribed place, that it includes the events narrated by it, in which revelation is imparted to men, in the framework of other events which happened at that time and place, that ancient Egypt, Assyria, and Babylon come into view as the horizon of the experiences of the nation Israel, that Cyrenius, the governor in Syria, cannot be left out of the story of Christmas, and that Pontius

Pilate genuinely belongs to the Creed—all that asserts the Bible's claim, in its account of revelation, to relate history, i.e. however, a claim to recount not a relationship between God and man existing generally, always and everywhere, or discoverable in process, but an event that took place there and only there, then and only then, between God and certain perfectly definite men. The divine self-unveiling of which it tells, together with the holiness it ascribes to God in this act of His, is imparted not simply to man, but to such and such men in a perfectly definite situation. Each time it is a quite special event, and as such incomparable and irrepeatable. To listen to the Bible as the witness to God's revelation is in all cases to hear about such history through the Bible.

To listen to such history as that which is an event in the revelation attested in the Bible, clearly cannot mean to hold such a happening to be possible, probable, or even real, on the basis of a general concept of historical truth, Even stories of events which have taken place between God and men, of course, fall, on their human side and therefore particularly in view of the data industriously stressed in the Bible, as regards their temporal form under this general concept of history. But they do not fall under it on their divine side. Thus, the " historical judgment " presupposed by this general concept can relate fundamentally only to this temporal form. It can neither assert nor deny that there and there God has acted on man. To make this assertion or denial it would have to abandon its presupposition, the general concept, and come to a confession of belief or unbelief regarding the Biblical witness. About the special historicity of the story recounted in the Biblical witness it can really form no " historical " judgment. But the listening to such history as that which is an event in the revelation attested in the Bible may also—and this is not quite so obvious—be independent of the " historical " judgment upon its temporal form. The judgment in virtue of which a Biblical story may be regarded with probability as " history " in the sense of the general concept of historical truth, is not necessarily the judgment of faith about the Biblical witness. For the judgment may be passed without the Biblical story being regarded in its special sense, i.e. as history between God and man. Again, the judgment in virtue of which a Biblical story was not to be regarded with probability as " history " in the sense of the general concept, but perhaps with probability in the sense of the general concept to be regarded not as " history "—this judgment is not necessarily the judgment of unbelief upon the Biblical witness : for such a judgment may be passed and the story yet be regarded in its special nature, i.e. as history between God and man. The question that decides the hearing or not hearing of the Bible story cannot be the question as to its general historicity : it can only be the question as to its special historicity.

The view that a Bible story is to be regarded partly or wholly as saga or legend need not therefore necessarily attack the substance of the Biblical witness. It might merely declare that according to the canons by which otherwise and in general historical truth is usually judged, this story is one which more or less eludes certain demonstration that it ran the course corresponding to the narrative. " Saga " or " legend " can only describe the more or less pervasive share of the narrator or narrators in the story narrated. There is no narrated story in which according to the general concept of historical truth one must not at least count upon such a narrator's share, i.e. upon elements of saga or legend. That holds also of the stories narrated in the Bible. It would have to be without temporal form if it were to be otherwise. This fundamental uncertainty about its general historicity, but combined with the positive judgment that there and there saga or legend is actually present, need not necessarily attack the substance of the Bible witness, (1) because invariably this judgment can concern and contest only the general historicity of a Biblical narrative, (2) because by its nature, even in the apparently clearest instance, it may be merely a judgment of probability, (3) because even " saga " or " legend " at least means history, and without prejudice to the " historical " judgment can be heard as the communication of history. So long as this is the case, the question of the special historicity of the narrative in question is at least not answered negatively.

It is different with the introduction of the category of myth. The view that a Bible story is to be regarded as a myth necessarily attacks the substance of the Biblical witness. And for the reason that " myth " does not intend history but only pretends to be history. Myth in fact means the exposition—brought forward in narrative form, but claiming to be true in itself irrespective of time and place—of certain basic relationships of human existence, which always exist everywhere, in their connections with their own origins and conditions in the natural and historical cosmos, or in the Godhead, reduced to narrative form on the supposition that man has knowledge of all these things and can expound them one way or the other, that he controls them, that in the last resort they are his own things. The myth (cf. for what follows Eduard Thurneysen, *Christus und die Kirche, Z.d.Z.* 1930 esp. p. 189 f.) imputes to the event narrated by it no exclusive character —in other words, " What the myth narrates as a fact may happen any time anywhere, it is not a unique happening, but one that can be repeated. . . . But a thing that can be repeated and can happen over and over again, however surprisingly, is a general possibility akin to a natural event. A thing that happens in this way rests simply on the assumption that the man to whom is imparted this revelation narrated in myth, stands in the last resort in an original and natural connection and relationship (hidden, of course, but at least potentially present everywhere) to the ultimate ground of his existence, to his God. In the events of revelation then recounted by the myth, this latent possibility becomes, so to speak, active. In ever new theophanies man experiences the ground of the world as present and himself as bound up with it. But that means that there here exists an ultimate identity between God and man. There is no thought of a profound and final distinction. What therefore myth recounts as having happened uniquely is not unique at all ; it is the same unfailing final root-relationship, which, enticed forth by all sorts of wizardry and magic, is " just once more " experienced and undergone, to be continually experienced and undergone afresh."

> Joyous was it years ago—
> So eagerly the spirit strives !—
> To inquire, to come to know,
> How nature in creating lives.
> And 'tis the eternally One,
> In its manifold revealed :

Small is great and great the small,
Each peculiarly sealed.
Ever changing, standing fast,
Near and far and far and near,
Forming thus and then transforming—
As a wonder stand I here.

(Goethe, *Parabase*, Jub.-Edn. vol. II p. 246).

That is the birth of myth ! (The difference between myth and speculation proper consists in the mere fact that in speculation the narrative form is stripped off again, like a garment grown too tight ; in consequence of which, what in myth is adduced as a fact is now exalted to the sphere of the pure idea or concept, and the existing and acknowledged wealth of the origins and relationships of human existence now achieves expression in its " in and for itself." Myth is the preform of speculation, and speculation is the essence of myth coming to light.) True, we cannot prevent an historian applying the category of myth to certain events related in the Bible. It might, of course, be asked whether he really found his supposed myths in the text of the Bible and not rather somewhere behind the text of it, by dissolving the context in which the passage in question possesses its meaning, and by ignoring what it says in this context, by assuming so-called sources of special character and independent content, conjectured to lie at the basis of the Biblical text, by combining definite parts of the Biblical text with portions of extra-Biblical texts which perhaps may really be claimable as mythical. In a word, it must be questionable whether the verdict " myth " applied to the Biblical accounts is not, on purely historical and scientific grounds, intrinsically a wrong verdict, because it can perhaps only be made through failure to detect what the real Biblical texts claim to say and do say if read exactly as we have them before us in their narrower and broader context, as, after all, Biblical texts ! But even should this objection appear incomprehensible, the historian whose mind is made up for such a verdict must at least be quite clear that the possibility of such a verdict being reached by him at all implies the fact that he has read the Bible, so to speak, outside the Christian Church ; inquiring, not into the evidence for revelation, but into something different, perhaps actually myth or speculation—perhaps himself quite unaware or forgetful of the fact that such a thing as revelation may exist, perhaps himself aware only, or even for the moment aware only, of man's general capacity for controlling the origins and relations of his existence whether by fable, thought, or other means, because they are actually his own concerns. It is really perfectly obvious that an age, whose thought, feeling, and action are mythical to so high a degree as the so-called modern period which culminates in the Enlightenment (including Idealism and Romanticism), must hunt for myth even in the Bible—and find it. Historism is " the self-interpretation of the spirit so far as it is a matter of its own productions of itself in history" (E. Troeltsch, *Ges. Schriften*, vol. III 1922 p. 104). Good! The person who is not inquiring after revelation has, of course, nothing left him but to inquire after myth, and the person who is inquiring after myth because he must do so, because myth is his own last word, will not, because of our objection which, perhaps after all, is also before the mind of the historian as such, feel hindered from inquiring after myth in the Bible as well, in order certainly, or even really to find it, indeed in strictness to find it a little everywhere. We can only declare that the interpretation of the Bible as witness to revelation and the interpretation of the Bible as witness to myth are mutually exclusive. The category of saga, the throwing doubt upon the general historicity of Bible narratives is not an attack on the substance of Bible as witness. But the category of myth is, because "myth" not only throws doubt upon the history as such and thereby also upon the special historicity of the Biblical narratives, but fundamentally denies them, because revelation regarded as myth would not be an historical event but a so-called non-spatial, timeless truth, in other words, a human creation.

The Bible lays such extraordinary weight upon the historicity of the revelation it recounts, because by revelation it does not mean a creation by man. It declares so emphatically that revelation was imparted to such and such men in such and such a situation, because thereby it describes it as a thing that is being imparted to men. This is what is overlooked or denied in applying to the Bible not, so far, the concept of saga but the concept of myth. The revelations attested in the Bible do not claim to be the naturally special phenomena of a universal, an idea, which man might then be comfortably in the position of comparing with this idea and regarding and estimating in its speciality.

Because this is not the case, the Philosophy of Religion of the Enlightenment from Lessing by way of Kant and Herder to Fichte and Hegel, with its intolerable distinction between the eternal content and the historical " vehicle," must be described as the lowest depth of modern misunderstanding of the Bible.

The revelation attested in the Bible claims to be an historical event where naturally—if at this point we drag in the concept of history to explain it, the only *tertium comparationis* can be the fact that in revelation as in history we are dealing with a definite event, distinct from all others, and therefore incomparable and unrepeatable. If with the Enlightenment we sought to conceive of the historical event as once more being itself the mere exponent of a general occurrence, a special case under a rule, or the realisation of a general possibility, if " history " were to be regarded as a frame within which a thing like revelation could take place, then at this point we should have to reject the concept of historicity with the same emphasis as that of myth. " Historical " in relation to " revelation " must rather mean an event as a fact with no court of reference above it by which it could be inspected as a fact and as this fact. It is thus that, according to the Bible, revelation is imparted to man, and for that reason that the Bible lays stress upon chronology, topography, and contemporary world-history, i.e. upon the contingency and uniqueness of the revelations narrated by it. What it thereby declares is just this, that revelation takes place vertically from heaven, it befalls man in the same incidental way in which he is such and such a man living in such and such place at such and such a time and in such and such circumstances, i.e. at such and such a stage of his inner and outer life, with only this difference that this historical contingency of his can none the less be surveyed and explained from all possible dimensions. The statement, *individuum est ineffabile,* may indeed be asserted about it but, characteristically, not proved, whereas revelation simply is the *ineffabile* confronting man, getting at man; and as such it proves itself. Thus, and from this standpoint we at last reach final clarity regarding what we said in 1 and 2 about the unveiling and veiling of God in His revelation. By these two relationships in which the Bible regards God as existing there cannot be intended two elements in a present, known truth and reality, which have to be proved by the general necessity of thought. Otherwise, even though we never wanted it to have a hearing, we should still be regarding Biblical revelation as myth! That *Deus revelatus* is also *Deus absconditus* and *Deus absconditus* also *Deus revelatus,* that the Father glorifies the Son and the Son the Father, is not just obvious, i.e. not intelligible *per se,* as (say) the immanent dialectic of this or that sphere of human life, or perhaps as a dialectic such as Hegel's " In itself " and " For itself " is intelligible *per se,* i.e. resolvable into a third. If the goodness and the holiness of God are themselves neither experiences which we could manufacture, nor concepts which we could construct for ourselves, but divine modes of existence to which human experiences and concepts can at all events respond, so far as they are asked the appropriate question, then at last their togetherness, their dialectic in which alone both are what they are, is really not a cognisable dialectic, i.e. one achievable by ourselves, but merely one that can be ascertained and acknowledged as actually taking place. It is this factual circumstantiality, its becoming ascertainable and acknowledgeable, that constitutes the historicity of revelation. By such a concept we mean that in the Bible revelation is the matter of God's being imparted, of a revealedness in God, by which the existence of definite men in a definite situation was so signalised that their experiences as well as their concepts were able, not to grasp God in His unveiling and God in His veiling and God in the dialectic of unveiling and veiling, but to follow Him, to respond to Him.

It is the element of calling in the Biblical concept of revelation to which we have to attend at this third point. Once more we find OT and NT at one in the notion that in no wise can man produce revelation for himself. We already instanced the priests of Baal on Carmel, who in their efforts to call up the " god " exactly indicate how for men there is simply no access to *Yahweh*. And along the same lines the so-called "false" prophets of the OT are obviously also regarded as proclaimers of a self-grasped revelation, which for that very reason is not revelation at all. Similarly in the NT (e.g. Mark 10[17f.]; Luke 9[57f.]) those who wish of themselves to acquire eternal life, i.e. follow Jesus, are put down as the very people who are literally incapable of doing so. On the other hand the promise given to Abraham not only for Sarah, but according to Gen. 17[17] also for Abraham himself, is simply an object of mirth, Jacob-Israel (quite apart from his other traits of character which to-day are felt to be so objectionable) actually in Gen. 32[22f.] appears as a fighter against God, and a victorious fighter at that, whilst resistance to the call, as illustrated chiefly in a Moses, Isaiah, Jeremiah, or Jonah, actually seems to belong to the nature of the true prophet. To this class naturally belongs, as the great NT example, the calling of Saul to be Paul. And also with regard to Peter, the meaning of the tradition perhaps was that his real call came about only through the Risen One, and therefore after his denial. To him in particular it is said very emphatically, that flesh and blood had not revealed that (namely Christ's sonship to God) to him. Naturally it would be foolish to regard all this as a negative attitude towards revelation on the part of the man in question. In such and such a number of calls this resistance of the men is not specially stressed. Of course, nowhere either is it a preparation for the call ! What the Bible means in this respect is obviously that there is no disposition towards it in man. Calling is a non-derivative fact, or only derivative from divine election. Prophets and apostles stand there as such, not exalted to anything heroic, in their complete humanity, yet for all that as prophets and apostles fallen, so to speak, from heaven, as surprising to themselves as to their neighbours, in an office inexplicable by their existence, bearers of a " burden " which they have not taken upon themselves, but which was laid upon their shoulders. In the NT the puzzle or the solution of the puzzle of this inconceivably actual presence of real men at God's revelation is expressed by the concept of the πνεῦμα. As by unveiling we ultimately mean nothing but Easter and then, with an inevitable glance back at the source of revelation, by veiling nothing but Good Friday, so now, with a glance forward, with a glance at man in whom and for whom revelation becomes an event, with a glance at the threshold over which revelation enters history, we mean nothing but Pentecost, the outpouring of the Holy Spirit. The πνεῦμα is the miracle of real men being present at revelation. What is involved at Whitsuntide is nowise different from the event of Good Friday and Easter. But precisely the fact that here for real men, for men as human as are the apostles in the NT description, it may be and really is a matter of Good Friday and Easter happening in the sense of a happening that touches them, befalls them, calls them, the fact that not only does Jesus Christ exist, but Jesus Christ is in the Church of Jesus Christ, is in the faith in Jesus Christ—precisely that is the distinctive thing about Pentecost and the Spirit in the NT. It was of Pentecost we were thinking when we termed revelation an event that from man's standpoint drops down vertically from heaven. How else can it be expressed if we wish to keep close to this particular text and, indeed, perhaps to all the NT passages bearing upon the " Spirit of God " or " Spirit of Christ " ? The miracle which here cannot be too strongly stressed corresponds only, on the one hand to the mystery of God from which the revelation proceeds and in which it always remains involved, and on the other hand to the paradox that in revelation there takes place a real procession of God out of His mystery This is the character of God's revealedness.

Without this historical revealedness of God, revelation would not be revelation. God's revealedness makes it a relationship between God and man, the effective meeting between God and man. But it is God's own revealedness that makes it that. In this respect, too, and therefore with respect to its aim, our statement that God reveals Himself as the Lord is confirmed. God's power to do what the Biblical witnesses ascribe to Him, not only to assume form, not only to remain free in this form, but in this form and this freedom of His to become the God of such and such men, Eternity in a moment, this is the third sense in which He is Lord in His revelation. We speak of revelation outside the Bible as well, and there is no reason for describing that as absolutely impossible. But there is reason for asking now this third question as well, whether in the concept of revelation presupposed in such an assertion this element of God's revealedness is to be considered as an act of God Himself, whether this conception of the adoption of revelation is to be regarded as a sheer bestowal without any disposition ; or whether in those cases—the other places where it is felt the attestation of revelation should be assumed—it is not perhaps rather precisely the positive, or perhaps (as in Buddhism) the negative disposition of man that plays the part of decisive importance, whether what in those cases is called revelation is not perhaps better described as myth, because there we have decidedly a case of man debating with himself. But we lay no stress on these side-issues. Our only interest is the positive one that in the Biblical witness this thing, God's lordship in the third sense, is the jointly decisive mark of revelation. God reveals Himself as the Spirit, not as any spirit, not as the discoverable and arousable subsoil of man's spiritual life, but as the Spirit of the Father and of the Son, and so as the same one God, but this time as the same one God in this way as well, namely, in this unity, nay, in this self-disclosing unity, disclosing itself to men, unity with the Father and the Son. The fact of His doing this, this third thing also— which does not follow obviously from the first and second, as surely as there is nothing, absolutely nothing, obvious in their existence and co-existence either—that there is such a manifestation of the Father and the Son, is what we mean when we say that He reveals

Himself as the Lord.   The fact, too, that according to John 4²⁴
God is a Spirit is God's lordship in His revelation.

We look back and come to a close.   We have inquired into the
root of the doctrine of the Trinity, into its root in revelation ;   not
in any sort of revelation, not in a general concept of revelation,
but in the concept of revelation to be derived from the Bible.
We asked whether revelation had to be regarded as the ground of
the doctrine of the Trinity, or the doctrine of the Trinity to be
regarded as having grown up from this ground.   And now after a
side-glance at the passages in the Bible witness, which are in immediate harmony with the doctrine of the Trinity itself, we have
investigated the meaning of revelation in the Bible, asking, but
concretely, asking in view of the Biblical texts, whether the statement, " God reveals Himself as the Lord," really has in these
texts a threefold ¹ meaning, yet a simple ² content.   If it was right to
emphasise in the Biblical witness to revelation the three elements
of unveiling, veiling and impartation, or of form, freedom and historicity, or of Easter, Good Friday, and
Pentecost, or of the Son, the Father, and the Spirit, if
we have rightly described these three elements separately, and if
we have put them in the proper relation to each other—if our
threefold conclusion that " God reveals Himself as the Lord,"
was therefore not an interpolation but a real result, and if in this
statement we have really thrice said the same thing in three indissolubly different ways, our conclusion now must be that revelation must in fact be regarded as the root or ground of the doctrine
of the Trinity.   As the root or ground, we say.   The doctrine of the
Trinity is not yet directly encountered by us.   Even in the passages with a Trinitarian ring the elements are lacking which
characterise the doctrine of the Trinity itself.   Our concepts of
" unimpaired unity " and " unimpaired variety," the concept of
the one essence of God and of the three Persons or modes of existence to be distinguished in this essence, lastly, the polemical statement briefly touched upon by us at the outset, that the Trinity of
God is to be found not only in His revelation but, because in His
revelation, in God Himself and of itself ;   that therefore the Trinity
is to be regarded not only as " economic " but also as " immanent "
—none of that is directly Biblical, i.e. explicitly expressed in the
Bible ;   it is Church doctrine.   We have established no more than
this, that the Biblical doctrine of revelation is implicitly, and in

¹ *dreifach*   ² *einfach*

some places explicitly also, an indication of the doctrine of the Trinity. In its ground-plan it must be interpreted as the ground-plan also of the doctrine of the Trinity. If the doctrine of the Trinity itself and as such admits of proof and completion, we must say that from the side of revelation there exists a genuine and necessary connection with the doctrine of the Trinity. The doctrine of the Trinity, together with its corollaries, distinctions, and summaries, is occupied with a problem actually and most centrally put by the Biblical witness to revelation. Actually it is the exegesis of this text. It is not—even at this stage we may say this—an arbitrarily posed speculation with its object elsewhere than in the Bible. Any child knows that it operates with certain philosophical terms of the outgoing pagan antiquity. But according to our findings that cannot mean that it is a non-Church construct, i.e. one which did not become necessary in the Church as such, which did not arise in its time from the basis of Scripture, from the faith in God's revelation which arose from Scripture, a doctrine dealing with a theme of pagan antiquity. On the contrary, its statements admit of being regarded as, not directly but indirectly, identical with those of the Biblical witness to revelation. It is Church exegesis, i.e. it interprets this text, the witness to revelation which as such is valid in the Church. When we come to expound it in detail as the Church's exegesis of the Bible text, it will be our duty never to omit a continual reference back to this Biblical text, to ask whether and how far in so doing we are dealing with real things. By the proof which we have already led, there should be preliminary assurance that it is church exegesis, that the statements of the doctrine of the Trinity confront Biblical revelation as directly as any answer can confront a question.

3. *VESTIGIUM TRINITATIS*

Before we turn in the next section to develop the doctrine of the Trinity itself, one critical consideration is necessary regarding the result we have already arrived at. We have been inquiring as to the root of the doctrine of the Trinity. By attempting to analyse the Biblical concept of revelation we reached the conclusion that this very analysis, when reduced to its simplest expression, the triply one lordship of God as Father, Son, and Holy Spirit, is the root of the doctrine of the Trinity. In other words, the Biblical concept of revelation is itself the root of the doctrine of the

Trinity. The doctrine of the Trinity is nothing else than the unfolding of the knowledge that Jesus is the Christ or the Lord. By saying that from this root proceeds the doctrine of the Trinity, we are saying in a spirit of polemical criticism that it can proceed from nowhere else. It is this " nowhere else" that must now be specially visualised. Occasion for this is found in the problem set by the history of the doctrine of the Trinity, that of the *vestigium trinitatis*. The expression presumably originates with Augustine and means an analogue of the Trinity, i.e. of the Trinitarian God of the Christian revelation, in this or that reality which is distinct from Him and therefore creaturely, a creaturely reality such that, not as an assumed form of God in His revelation, but quite apart from God's revelation, in its own crea' :re-like structure, it shows a certain similarity to the structure of the Trinitarian concept of God, and is therefore to be regarded as a copy of the Trinitarian God Himself.

Augustine deals with this e.g. *Conf.* XIII 11, 12 ; *De civ. Dei* XI 24 f., but principally *De Trin.* IX–XI. For a general understanding of the problem as the Church Fathers and Scholastics saw it put, the passage *De Trin.* VI 10 is instructive. *Oportet igitur, ut creatorem per ea quae facta sunt intellectum conspicientes, trinitatem intelligamus, cuius in creatura, quomodo dignum est, apparet vestigium. In illa enim trinitate summa origo est rerum omnium et perfectissima pulchritudo et beatissima delectatio. . . . Qui videt hoc vel ex parte, vel per speculum et in aenigmate, gaudeat cognoscens Deum et sicut Deum honoret et gratias agat : Qui autem non videt, tendat per pietatem ad videndum.*

We must sharply insist that (unfortunately !) our concern here is not with the distinction imparted in revelation to a creaturely reality, whereby a man, an angel, a natural or historical event, human words or actions, or—at its best and highest and most simultaneous point, as an epitome of the whole created being thus signalised—the *humanitas Christi*, becomes the divine organ or tool or medium. We might, of course, call that, we may call the form assumed by God in His unveiling as the Son or the Word, the *vestigium trinitatis*. But that is not what was intended when the concept arose and was applied. There our concern is with a Trinitarian adaptation of essence, belonging immanently, as is alleged, to certain created realities and thus quite apart from their being invariably claimed by God's revelation, with a genuine *analogia entis*, with traces of the Trinitarian Creator-God in what exists as such, in its pure createdness. If it be admitted that there are *vestigia trinitatis* in this second 'sense, then the question obviously arises—and therefore in our context we are bound to take the matter up—whether we have not to assume a second root of the doctrine of the Trinity alongside of that indicated in the previous paragraph. Obviously the *vestigium trinitatis*, if such a thing exists in the second sense of the concept, would have to be taken into consideration as such a second root of the doctrine of the Trinity. In that case the question would have to be raised, whether the origin of the doctrine of the Trinity must not be attributed at least also to the insight into those traces of the Trinity present and apprehensible in the created world even apart from the Biblical revelation. And were this question once admitted, one could scarcely avoid proceeding to the further question, which of the two contiguous roots of the doctrine of the Trinity under review is the real and primary, which on the other hand the subsequent " runner." But then the question would also have to be allowed, whether the derivation of the doctrine of the Trinity from Biblical revelation might not be merely the subsequent confirming from His revelation in creation of a knowledge of God which could be gained quite apart from this revelation. And then the last question could hardly be omitted, whether the *vestigia* in question, upon which in that case the doctrine of the Trinity would really be grounded, were really to be regarded at all as the *vestigia* of a Creator-God transcending the world and not rather as determinations of the cosmos now to be regarded as strictly immanent ; and, because the cosmos is man's cosmos, as determinations of human existence ; whether therefore the concept of natural as well as that of Biblical revelation might not have to be struck out and the doctrine of the Trinity adjudged to be the bold attempt of man's understanding of the world and, in the last resort, of self, i.e. adjudged to be myth. The problem set us by the assertion of the presence and knowability of those *vestigia trinitatis*, is thus really of the greatest importance, not only for the question of the root of the doctrine of the Trinity, but for the question of revelation generally, for the question of basing theology solely upon revelation, and lastly and in particular for the question as to the meaning and possibility of theology as distinct from a mere cosmology or anthropology.

The question is whether these *vestigia trinitatis* do not, by the conclusions which result from recognising them—even were the list of questions mentioned the only one bound to arise from this recognition—compel us to pass over first to that cheery double track of " revelation " and " prime revelation " (P. Althaus), and then from this half measure, as quickly as possible, to the genuine Roman Catholic theology of the *analogia entis*. But in that case

25

would they not call our attention in the nick of time to the fact that theology would do well to cease regarding itself generally in an impossible fashion as theology and give itself out for what alone it can fundamentally be, a bit of man's way of looking at the world and self, in the unfolding of which the concept " God," like a superfluous X in numerator and denominator, needs merely to be cancelled out to simplify the counting on both sides, because whether with or without this concept the sole concern is man, in our case man's own three-in-oneness ? Of course, the question may also be put, whether in this concept of the *vestigium trinitatis* we have not before us a primeval Trojan horse, which once upon a time (to echo Augustine, for its *pulchritudo* and *delectatio*) was all too unsuspectingly allowed entry into the theological *Ilium*, in the belly of which, so much wiser have we grown through certain experiences not yet felt in Augustine's time, we can hear a fearful clank, so that we have cause to execute a vehement defensive movement (perhaps the actual situation admits of no other action than this !) by which we explain (e x p l a i n perhaps really only in a perfectly unsophisticated sense !) that we wish to have nothing to do with this affair.

To inform ourselves first of all about the *quaestio facti*, the question as to what has been and can be thought of concretely in speaking of *vestigia trinitatis*, let us subdivide into phenomena from nature, from culture, from history, from religion, and lastly from man's soul-life.

Since any sort of systematic completeness in detail is out of the question we give some characteristic examples from all five spheres. (For what follows cf. H. Bavinck, *Geref. Dogmatiek*, 1918 vol. II p. 332 f.)

1. Nature—Anselm of Canterbury compares Father, Son, and Spirit in the Trinity with the existence and mutual relationship of spring, stream, and lake, which as a single whole might be called the Nile. But not only the single whole : spring, stream, and lake are also, each for themselves, the Nile. Although the spring is not the stream, the stream not the lake, and the lake not the spring ; although on the other hand there are not three Niles, but only a single one. The one complete Nile is, of course, spring, stream, and lake. It is just as difficult, or impossible, as with the " Persons " of the Trinity, to say what is the common concept under which these three, fall. Yet it is as clear in the one case as in the other, that the spring is derived neither from the stream nor from the lake, while the stream is not from the lake but certainly from the spring, and the lake on the contrary from the spring and from the stream (*Ep. de. incarn. verbi c.* 13).—Luther apparently, at all events in table-talk, was fond of sponsoring the statement that *in omnibus creaturis licet invenire et cernere trinitatem istam esse expressam,* and to illustrate it by the example of sun, water, stars, plants, etc. A concise account of one of these expositions of his, actually with regard to natural phenomena, is to the effect that " in all creatures there is and is visible an indication of the Holy Triplicity. Firstly, their nature signifies the almightiness of God the Father ; in the second place their shape and form show the wisdom of the Son ; and in the third place their usefulness and power is the sign of the Holy Ghost ; showing therefore that God is present in all creatures, even in the tiniest little leaf and poppy seedlet " (W. edn. *Tischreden,* I pp. 395 ff.). Let it suffice us by way of example to mention that similarly weight, number, and measure, or the solid, fluid, and gaseous states, and the

three dimensions of solids, the primary colours, yellow, red, and blue, and the harmony of keynote, third and fifth, have been brought into connection with the Trinity.

2. Culture—The teaching, military, and food-supply professions in society, epic, lyric, and drama in poetry, not omitting the three main disciplines of mediæval science, were here held to be *vestigia trinitatis*. Once more we let Luther speak : " In divine things the Father is *Grammatica* ; for He giveth the Word and is the fountainhead from which, if one may so speak, floweth good, excellent, pure speech. The Son is *Dialectica* ; for He giveth the arrangement whereby a thing should be set in excellent order of succession, so that conclusion and consecution be certain. But the Holy Ghost is *Rhetorica*, the Speaker since He excellently upholdeth, breatheth, and acteth, maketh quick and powerful, so that impressions are made and hearts occupied " (W. edn. *Tischreden* I p. 564).

3. History—To this section belongs a doctrine which is continually cropping up in Church History, that of the three kingdoms which were supposed to be discovered in the ages of the OT, the NT, and the Christian Church, or, with an eschatological intention and in combination with the three great apostolic figures, in the three ages or kingdoms : (1) the Petrine, past, the kingdom of fear, i.e. of the Father, (2) the Pauline, present, the kingdom of truth, i.e. of the Son, and (3) the Johannine, future, the kingdom of love, i.e. of the Spirit. In this connection if the Holy Spirit became the special catchword of all so-called fanatical, or better, all chiliastic parties in the Church, we might almost say, became the God who was specifically non-Church or even anti-Church, it might happen that Luther, for example, in face of its one-sided appeal, felt that he really had to be equally one-sided in his appeal to the Word, and that " spiritualistic " came to be a concept by which was expressed a definite criticism, namely, that directed against anything fanatical. Moeller van den Bruck (*Das dritte Reich*, 2nd edn. 1926 p. 13) has called the thought of the third kingdom a " cosmological thought which carries us beyond reality." " It is no accident that the ideas already foisted into the concept in the name third kingdom . . . betray themselves from the outset as ideological, are unusually nebulous, are sentimental and in the air, and thoroughly eschatological." Moeller v. d. Bruck admittedly wished to " remove it from the illusionist sphere and connect it entirely with the political." Still, even by such secularisation, he has retained something of the feeling of the ancient and mediæval philosophy-of-history implied in the *vestigium trinitatis*, as it lived—to name but one name—in Giacchino de Fiore.

4. Religion.—As early as the Middle Ages attention had been drawn in this connection to the phenomena of the subjective religious consciousness ; *cogitatio, meditatio, contemplatio ;* or *fides, ratio, contemplatio ;* or the *via purgativa, illuminativa,* and *intuitiva* of the mysticism influenced by the Areopagite, the nature and order of which reflected the Trinity. Alongside of that should be set Wobbermin's assertion that Christian Trinitarian monotheism brings the fundamental conviction of all religious faith to a conclusion, in so far as it generally includes three motives which reach expression in the religious feeling of dependence, the religious feeling of security, and the religious feeling of longing (*Wesen und Wahrheit des Christentums*, 1925 p. 432). But it was certainly not our modern age with its interest in History of Religion, but the old theology, as is clear e.g. in J. Gerhard, *Loci*, 1610 l. 3, 30, that was the first to realise, that the number three, particularly in the Godhead,

played a notable part in the objective phenomena of religion as well, and non-Christian religion at that. We emphasise one point: the ancient Babylonians knew of two triads of gods, one cosmic, *Anu*, *Enlil*, and *Ea* (the gods of heaven, earth, and water), and one superior, sidereal, *Shamash*, *Sin*, and *Ishtar* (sun, moon, and the planet Venus). The ancient Egyptians knew of the family of gods, *Osiris* with his spouse *Isis* and their son *Horus*, and in a similar relationship the ancient Canaanites, Syrians, and Carthaginians knew a supreme god, the *Magna Mater*, later worshipped also under the name of *Cybele* and, e.g., the son of God known under the name of *Attis* or *Adonis*; and presumably once more in a similar relationship ancient Etruscan Rome with its so-called Capitoline Triad, *Jupiter optimus maximus*, *Juno regina*, and *Minerva*. Later Brahmanism knows the so-called *Trimurti*, the mystical unity of *Brahma* who brings forth the world, *Vishnu* who sustains it, and *Siva* (or *Rudra*) who destroys it. To this day the confession of a convert to Buddhism runs : " I take my refuge in the *Buddha*, I take my refuge in the *Dhamma*, I take my refuge in the *Sangha* " (the " three *Kleinodia* "), where Buddha signifies personality, Dhamma the teaching, Sangha the community of the Founder of the religion.

5. The Human Soul.—Here, according to Augustine, the point is first of all the three powers of the soul, *mens* the power of inward, *notitia* the power of outward apprehension, *amor* the power to connect the one with the other and so to complete the apprehension—next, the three corresponding elements in the real process of consciousness, *memoria*, i.e. the basic act of self-consciousness and objective consciousness generally and in itself, as the pure form ; *intellectus*, i.e. the consummation in thought of an idea of self or of an object in a definite image ; *voluntas*, i.e. at once the affirmation of this image and the reversion from the image to pure consciousness. Thus, it was not a different *vestigium* but a repetition of the same one in different words, when Augustine could also distinguish, *amans, id quod amatur, amor*. Let us hear Augustine himself in a specially pregnant formulation of his thought : *sine ulla phantasiarum vel phantasmatum imaginatione ludificatoria mihi esse me, idque nosse et amare certissimum est . . . Quid si falleris ? Si enim fallor, sum. Nam qui non est, utique nec falli potest. . . . Consequens est autem, ut etiam in eo quod me novi nosse, non fallor. Eaque duo cum amo . . . quiddam tertium . . . eis . . . adjungo* (*De civ. Dei* XI 26). It was more than a *vestigium* rather the *imago Dei*, or *trinitatis*, that Augustine thought to find in this structure of human consciousness. It is this theory of the *vestigium* which above all others has made an impression and a school throughout the centuries. We find it in all sorts of modifications, e.g. in Anselm of Canterbury (*Monol.* 67 and *passim*), Petrus Lombardus (*Sent.* I *dist.* 3), Thomas Aquinas (*S. theol.* 1 qu. 45, *art.* 7), Bonaventura (*Breviloq.* II *c.* 12), in the Reformation period in Melanchthon (*Enarr. Symb. Nic.* 1550 *C.R.* 23, 235 ; *Loci*, 1559 *C.R.* 21, 61 and often), in the Reformed Churchman, B. Keckermann (*Syst. S. S. Theol.* 1611 p. 20 f.), in the Enlightenment in Lessing's *Education of the Human Race*, § 73, in the 19th century in A. Twesten (*Dogm. d. ev.-luth. Kirche*, vol. II 1837 p. 194 f.), at the present day in none other than Ad. Schlatter : " Since we are in possession of our image, there continually arises in us a kind of three-in-oneness ; to the knower comes the person known, but not in the way of both standing side by side, but straightway the third appears, the knower who knows himself in the person known " (*Das chr. Dogma*, 2nd edn. 1923 p. 24). Equally Trinitarian according to him is the order of our volition :

" we have an immediate volition, an elective volition, and the union of the two, the volition elected by us, which now contains in itself the power of action " (*op. cit.* p. 148). The relation which from this standpoint must result, Schelling's triad of substance, object, subject-object, and Hegel's " In itself " of the subjective spirit as thesis, " for itself " of the objective spirit as antithesis, and " in and for itself " of absolute spirit as synthesis, need only be indicated. We may calmly assert that these very peaks of idealist philosophy would simply be unthinkable anywhere else than against the background of Christian dogmatics, even were they nothing else than fresh variants on the Augustinian proof of the Trinity itself. It is clear that to this context the logico-grammatical scheme of subject, object, and predicate would also belong, if we were to take it as our real key to the doctrine of the Trinity. And it is equally clear that here, too, the mediæval construct of the religious consciousness, no less than Wobbermin's, must be assessed also as a variation upon the general Augustinian argument from consciousness.

What are we to say to all this material, what are we to do with it ? The first task is to try and conceive it in the sense in which it was originally intended, as an interesting, edifying, instructive, and helpful hint towards understanding the Christian doctrine, not to be overvalued, not to be applied as a foundation or proof in the strict sense, because we must already know and believe in the Trinity, if we are really to apprehend its *vestigia* as such in macrocosm and microcosm—but still to be valued as supplementary, non-obligatory illustrations of the Creed, which yet are to be thankfully received.

Already Irenaeus sounded the warning that we have not to understand *Deum ex factis, sed ea quae facta sunt ex Deo* (*C. o. h.* II 25, 1). To his exhortation that man should learn to view the Trinity in himself, Augustine himself has expressly linked the further exhortation, *cum invenerit in his aliquid et dixerit, non iam se putet invenisse illud, quod supra ista est incommutabile* (*Conf.* XIII 11). Petrus Lombardus also visibly draws back : *Non enim per creaturarum contemplationem sufficiens notitia trinitatis potest haberi vel potuit sine doctrinae vel interioris inspirationis revelatione. . . . Adjuvamur tamen in fide invisibilium per ea quae facta sunt* (*Sent.* I *dist.* 3 f.), and expressly delivers himself upon the *dissimilitudines* actually to be found precisely in the Augustinian *similitudo. Trinitate posita, congruunt hujus modi rationes ; non tamen ita, quod per has rationes sufficienter probetur trinitas personarum* (Thomas Aquinas, *S. Th.* I *qu.* 32 *art.* 1). So certainly we may also regard Luther's utterances on this matter not as a theological foundation but only as theological table-talk.

We need not adjudge the services of the old theology at this point as a mere idle game, however trifling much of what is adduced may seem to us to be.

The other impression we have of the whole material is undeniably this that there must be " something in it," although in different degrees, in the connection between the Trinity and all the threenesses to which we are there pointed. Why should not there be something in it ? The only question is what. Theology and the Church, and before them the Bible itself, speak in fact no other language than that of this world, shaped in form and content by the creaturely nature of this world, but also conditioned by the limitations of humanity : the language in which man as he is at the moment, therefore sinful and perverted man, tries to come to terms with the world, as it meets him and as he sees it and is able to understand it. Bible, Church, and theology speak this language, undoubtedly on the supposition that there might be " something in it," namely, that in this language something might also be said of God's revelation, evidence be given, God's Word be proclaimed, dogma be formulated and explained. The only question is whether this ability should be regarded as an ability proper to the language and so to the world, i.e. to men, or as a risk expected of the language and so of the world or man, so to speak, from without, so as to be not really the ability of the language, the world, man but the ability of revelation, if we are really speaking in the form of concepts and ideas which also exist otherwise and in themselves, in conformity with the created world and with the power of man in his analysis of this world—in one word really speaking about revelation, the Trinity, forgiveness of sins, and eternal life, about things over which this language of men as such has absolutely no control. Now it is not to be asserted that the discoverers of the *vestigia trinitatis* had achieved this distinction. In achieving it ourselves we are brought back to a realisation that the real *vestigium trinitatis* is just the form assumed by God in revelation. So far as I can see, that was not the meaning of the Fathers and Scholastics when they spoke of the *vestigium trinitatis*. But by means of this distinction one can understand subsequently how they were brought, on the one hand to affirm the thought of the apprehensibility of the *vestigium trinitatis*, on the other hand immediately to bracket or qualify it again with the explanation, that real apprehension could only take place or the presupposition of revelation, *trinitate posita*. They might actually have meant something different from what they appeared to say, that they were in search of language for the mystery of God, made known to them by revelation and, as they were always repeating, only by revelation, and able to be made known to all men only by revelation. In this search for language they were admittedly faced, apart from the material offered by the Bible, in the first place with a number of applicable abstract categories from contemporary philosophy.

Strictly speaking the concept *trinitas* as such would have to be regarded as a *vestigium trinitatis* already found in the field of logic. And F. Diekamp, *Kathol. Dogm.* vol. I 6th edn. 1930 p. 260, correctly points out that the analogies adduced by the Church Fathers are in the long run only further expositions and multiplications of the Biblical concepts, Father, Son, and Spirit, which are likewise already analogical.

In this language of the Bible and philosophy the dogma was then formulated. But the mystery of revelation, still as alive as ever even in the formulated dogma, made a further demand, only now in accordance with the decision as to how it was to be regarded, for language. And only now was it discovered, not that the language could grasp the revelation, but that the revelation, particularly the revelation now properly and authoritatively appreciated in the formulated dogma, could grasp the language, i.c. that always starting from revelation, sufficient elements were to be discovered in the familiar language spoken by all, to make speech about revelation possible, not exhaustively or suitably or exactly, but still to a certain extent comprehensibly and clearly, elements which with more or less range of vision were usable to describe certain factors and relations in what could be said of revelation. Men wished to say Father, Son, and Spirit, or *unitas in trinitate, trinitas in unitate* ; they opened their eyes and ears and discovered that they both must and could say, with this end in view, spring, stream, and lake ; weight, number, and measure ; *mens, notitia,* and *amor* ; not because these things were suited for that in themselves or of themselves, but because as figures of the Trinity, as means of speaking about the Trinity, they were suitable for appropriation or, so to speak, capture, because, being aware of God's revelation in Scripture, men thought they might presume upon their ability to express what they in themselves and as such, of course, do not express and cannot express. There is nothing in saying that source, stream, and lake, *esse, nosse,* and *velle* are mutually related like Father, Son, and Spirit ; but there is something in saying that Father, Son, and Spirit are related like spring, stream, and lake. Men were quite certain about the Trinity, on the other hand they were uncertain about the language of the world in relation to the Trinity. But in this language they had to speak about the Trinity. Therefore, they had to claim it for the Trinity, namely, as witness on behalf of the Trinity. The case then was not that men wished to explain the Trinity by the world, but on

the contrary that they wished to explain the world by the Trinity
in order to be able to speak of the Trinity in this world.   It was a
matter not of apologetics but of polemics, not of proving the
possibility of revelation in the world of human reason, but of
fixing the actual possibilities of this world of human reason as the
scene of revelation.   *Vestigia trinitatis in creatura*, they said, and
perhaps really rather meant *vestigia creaturae in trinitate*—naturally
in the self-revealing Trinity, in the Trinity so far as it assumes
creaturely form. They did not think things capable of having
the Trinity immanent in them or of possessing the property of
being able to reflect the Trinity—on this side, admittedly, everything remained incomplete, questionable, and conditioned by the
preceding revelation—but they did regard the Trinity as being
capable of reflecting itself in things, and all those more or less
happy discoveries of *vestigia* were an expression of this confidence, not confidence in the capacity of reason for revelation,
but confidence in the power of revelation over reason.   In
this sense it may be said that the problem involved was that of
theological language, which can be none other than the language
of the world and which, whatever the cost, must always speak and
believes that it can speak, contrary to the natural capacity of
this language, in this language, as theological language, of God's
revelation.   Regarded in this fundamental fashion—so far as it is
susceptible of being so regarded—the doctrine of the *vestigia* was
anything but playing with words !

But why then does it largely and as one constantly feels inevitably and rightly make this impression upon us, the impression
that after all this is a matter of mere table-talk, not to be taken
so very seriously, and somehow, in the background, a matter of
parlous profanation of what is Holy ?   We can only reply that it
is because we are not so clear about the purpose which alone we
can legitimately pursue thereby, that any moment the whole
order thus evolved might not be even reversed, and polemics
produce apologetics, and the attempt to speak theologically become
the surrender of theological language in favour of some alien speech,
the asserted and assumed intelligibility of revelation become the
assertion of an original commensurability of reason with revelation,
the synthetic " God into the world " become an analytic " God in
the world," the claim of revelation upon the world become a
claim of the world upon revelation, and the discovered pointer
therefore become a self-begotten proof.   Were there no guarantee

against this reversal—and to a great extent there was not—the idea of a second root of the doctrine of the Trinity was bound to assert itself. It might then be supposed that fundamentally the Trinity could just as well be derived from and grounded upon human self-consciousness or other creaturely ordinances as from and upon Holy Scripture, and first of all the danger already indicated was bound to arise, because interest turned more and more to the trinities within the world which are so much nearer to man, because it was increasingly thought that the divine Trinity could be discovered in them as such. Was it really thus discovered? Was the triune God supposed to be rediscoverable first of all in the world and then also discoverable independently, really the One called God by Holy Scripture? Or was it not merely a comprehensive idea, a supreme principle of the world and ultimately of man himself? Is it not therefore the case that the proof led, not proved nothing, but did not prove what it really should have proved, and, if that were not realised, rather led away from what it should have proved? Was the proof of the Trinity thus led not logically bound to lead to the denial of the Trinitarian God of Holy Scripture, because it proved and put in His place a god constituted *totaliter aliter*?

Suppose some one wished seriously to prove the truth of the divine Trinity from its attestation in the history of religion. What would he, what could he prove? The two Babylonian triads and the Brahmanic Trimurti are demonstrably nothing else than just formulations of a triply membered world-principle. In the Egyptian, Canaanite, and Etruscan triads it is equally clear that the primary connection of the family is what is really meant and honoured as divine. In the " three regalia " of Buddhism, the person, the doctrine, and the community of Buddha, we have manifestly, so far as we have to do with a divine trinity at all, to do with the deified historical event of the founding of a religion. If all that crops up as triadic godhead merits the appellation " God," then the history of religion is a confirmation of the Christian Trinity ; but not otherwise. For what is left over after deducting the question of the nature there described as the nature of God, is really only the number three. And for science of religion to found divinity upon the actual number three (" it is presumably holy because primitive man was not yet acquainted with a larger number," *RGG* ² art. *Dreieinigkeit* I) can certainly not be described as particularly illuminating. J. Gerhard has really said (*op. cit.*) everything there is to be said as to the fruitfulness of the history of religion for our problem : *In verbis nobiscum consentiunt, in verborum istorum explicatione ac sensu dissentiunt.* We should only step into the void, were we really to think of planting foot here.

Let us further suppose that some one wished incidentally to base faith in the Triune God also upon philosophy of history. It would be easy to show that the three-beat rhythm of historical development, as it is constantly being asserted, is nothing else but the rhythm of the arrangement into past, present, and future in which man the actor who reflects upon his action always finds himself. We may certainly depend upon it that the third element, decisive in all philosophy of history, denotes pretty regularly the place where the philosopher of history in question is standing himself or which he is striving to reach ; alternatives which are not so very different. If the dream he dreams from that standpoint is the wisdom of God, then such a philosophy of history is a proof of the Trinity, certainly not otherwise : otherwise the philosopher of history has proved nothing, literally nothing, except just his own vision and his own will.

The menace of the Augustinian argument from the consciousness had already been indicated by Luther. We heard how delighted he was in his own way to take a hand in all other possible arguments of this kind. The more is his instinct to be admired which at this very point would not let him co-operate, as compared with Melanchthon. For he explained that from the Augustinian doctrine of the *imago Dei* in man, present in *memoria, intellectus,* and *voluntas,* must follow the annoying *disputatio de libero arbitrio. Ita enim dicunt : Deus est liber, ergo cum homo ad imaginem Dei sit conditus, habet etiam liberam memoriam, mentem et voluntatem. . . . Ita nata est hinc periculosa sententia, qua pronuntiant Deum ita gubernare homines, ut eos proprio motu sinat agere (Comm. Gen.* I²⁶, W. edn. 42, 45, 25). The advance of anthropological speculation *via* Descartes and Kant to Schelling and Hegel, and finally and logically to Feuerbach, has clearly justified him. Certainly Augustine thought he was remote from any possibility of such a reversal. But if B. Keckermann (*op. cit.*) could venture to say, *quam est necessarium, hominem esse rationalem . . . tam est necessarium in Dei essentia tres esse personas,* then the way to this reversal was laid. Could it be avoided once this *quam . . . tam* was attempted ? The image of God in consciousness is primarily and without question, in itself and as such, the image of free man. To see in this image as such the image of God is to declare that free man is recognised as God. If this free man really is God, then the proof has succeeded. But if God is simply not to be free man but to confront free man imperially, then obviously this very proof, at once the most manifest, most profound and historically most powerful, would have missed its mark in a specially distinct way in that respect.

And so it is with the whole of the remaining material, the moment we consider it in its own actual strength by asking whether and how far *vestigia trinitatis* could really be present *in creatura. Vestigia trinitatis* there, of course, are ; no one can deny it. The only question is, of which Trinity ? If it is to be the divine Trinity that meets us in the three dimensions of space or in the three notes of the simple harmony or in the three primary colours, or even in spring, stream, and lake, then God is—just, as seen first in ancient Babylonia and India, the mysteriously threefold law or nature of the world known to us, the mystery of the cosmos, traces of which meet us in this triplicity of all or many things, and which in that case would obviously be in most intimate touch with the mystery of man and the mystery of his religion. If that is God—it is just possible that it might be God—why should not the wealth of three-in-onenesses in nature and culture not really prove the three-in-oneness of this God ? But only the three-in-oneness of this God. The question remains whether this God is also really to be claimed solely as the Creator-God and whether therefore he perhaps has no right to bear his name of " God " ?

And now so far we have not touched at all upon the thoroughgoing incongruities of the *vestigia*, never denied even by the representatives of this doctrine, in their relation to the Biblical and ecclesiastical doctrine of the Trinity. We shall find that the decisive propositions of this doctrine, that of the indissoluble unity and that of the indestructible variety of the three elements, cannot be carried through in any of these *vestigia*, but that the proof which may be led from them can never be more than the proof either of three divine beings standing side by side, or of a single divine monad without hypostatic self-differentiation, that therefore, even if the divine being therein presupposed were worth calling God, the three-in-oneness of this God in the sense of the Christian doctrine of the Trinity could not be proved from these *vestigia*. Quenstedt is perfectly right : *nulla vera et plena similitudo trinitatis in creatura reperitur (Theol. did.-pol.* 1685 *P.* I *c.* 6 *sect.* 2, *qu.* 3, *font. sol.* 5). The Lombard expressed the same thing in his reference to the *dissimilitudines* in the *similitudo*, and finally, in spite of all, even Augustine might have said so. And so in half-conceding the possibility of the doctrine—it is seldom contested outright—the objection likewise has always been raised against it, that it is far too easy, that the jeers of unbelievers are called forth by it, while simple souls are led into error (cf. Thomas Aquinas, *S. theol.* I *qu.* 32 *art.* 1; Calvin, *Instit.* I 13, 18; Quenstedt, *op. cit. font. sol.* 6) and, in fact, in spite of Augustine's authority and in opposition to it, the problem is by most ancient dogmaticians simply touched upon and then dropped again as useless and dangerous. What meaning can this objection and this distrustful attitude have, in a matter which one cannot and does not wish to deny altogether, except this, that people felt the foreign-ness of that which should be proved to be " God " by means of the *vestigia*, its utter difference from the God of Abraham, Isaac, and Jacob, from Father, Son, and Holy Spirit in the NT, with which the doctrine of the Trinity should be concerned.

Hence obviously the impression of trifling, and even frivolity, of which one can scarcely divest oneself in pondering this *theologoumenon*, however pleasing and credible at first its touch on one in the words of Anselm or Luther. The moment it is taken seriously, it leads, clearly and inevitably, straight into an ambiguous terrain, in which in a trice with the best will in the world we speak no longer of the God of whom we wished to speak, whose footprints we wished to discover, but of some principle of the world or humanity, of some alien God. The original aim was to speak of God's revelation. But what really happened was talk about the world and man, and that, regarded as talk about God's revelation, must actually end by being talk against God's revelation. The conqueror was conquered ! Such a game cannot yield serious results. Taken seriously it can only signify a profanation of what is holy. Hence the feeling of frivolity without which we cannot have any dealings with it.

What follows is not that the game can be forbidden on principle, that the undoubtedly distinguished theologians who have been occupied with it more or less seriously must be regarded out of hand as heretical in this matter. Indeed, we have tried to indicate the good intentions with which it might be pursued and its basis in the problem of theological language. But even in respect both of this good intention and of this problem of language there is a lesson to be learned here. Clearly there are possibilities in language—and here apparently we have to do with one such—in using which the Church and theology undertake something which is not indeed to be forbidden on principle but is certainly quite unobligatory, outside their commission and undoubtedly dangerous, so far as in so doing the translation, refounding and resetting of the theme, which is their task, comes precariously near to taking up a totally different theme, so far as in so doing there can suddenly take place a μετάβασις εἰς ἄλλο γένος. The inventors of the *vestigia trinitatis* had no wish to produce a second and different root of the doctrine of the Trinity parallel to revelation, far less did they wish to represent this other as the only true one or to deny the revelation of the Trinitarian God. But their action is deeply overshadowed by the question whether nevertheless this is not precisely what they have done. That non-obligatory, uncommissioned and perilous possibility is clearly involved in every case in which theological language, as was undoubtedly the case here, claims to pass beyond the interpretation to the illustration of revelation. Interpretation means saying the same thing in other words. Illustration means saying the same thing in other words. Where the line between the two lies, cannot be stated generally. But here there is a line, in that revelation will not submit to illustration but only to interpretation. To illustrate revelation is to set something else at the centre of attention. It is a failure in proper trust in revelation with respect to its own power of self-evidence; it is calling for support, strength, and confirmation of one's language about it from a source other than itself. This other source at least shares the interest. Its power to illustrate (and who knows but we ought to say at once, its power to prove?) revelation now becomes a circumstance important in itself and at the same time, obviously, so does the proper being and nature of this other source, which as a so-called illustration of revelation has already acquired such weight that, because it lies much closer to man than revelation, because in the last resort it is his own being and nature, it must become a menace to his attention to revelation, and signify a limitation of the seriousness with which revelation is regarded. Is not the wish to illustrate revelation, not to speak of asserting the necessity for such illustration, not to speak of asserting that this or that does illustrate revelation, already to be regarded as tantamount to a desertion of revelation ? Has not unbelief already taken place there ? Does not the transition from interpretation to illustration as such already come under the interdict, Thou shalt not make unto thee any likeness ? Obviously this transition should not take place in the very language of theology. The point, therefore, is whether in the doctrine of the *vestigia* we have this transition perhaps typically before us and ought to reject it as such. Let us grant that there is no interpretation of revelation—the most careful dogmatics, even Church dogma itself not excepted—in which there are not elements of illustration to be found. Let us grant that, at a distance from the vocabulary of Scripture, by merely opening our mouths or taking up our pens we depart from revelation in the direction of that possibility which in every case is non-obligatory, uncommissioned, and perilous ; in the present instance, in the direction of the *vestigia trinitatis*. We must, e.g. be quite clear that, with our arrangement of the Biblical concept of revelation, which we attempted in the previous sub-section, according to the elements of veiling, unveiling, and impartation, we have brought ourselves into extraordinarily close proximity to Augustine's vexatious argument, that we are by no means insured against the suspicion that even we may have availed ourselves of an illustration, even we may have had a little game with a so-called *vestigium trinitatis* (perhaps to be traced back to the little sentence " I show myself "). Have we not thereby consented to let ourselves be actually supported, strengthened, and confirmed by an entity different from revelation, namely, by a logical possibility of construction ? In the last resort is it the Bible that has spoken to us or really just this possibility ? Have we discovered the root of the doctrine of the Trinity in revelation and not in the end this quite different root ? We wished to discover the root of the doctrine in revelation, not a different one. We have done everything to make it clear that this and nothing else was our object. But if any one chose to reproach us with being concerned with that quite different root, we could never accuse him of malice ; for with the best will in the world we can never completely or unambiguously escape the appearance of that being the case. It is good to make all that clear to ourselves. As theologians, here as elsewhere, we are not in a position ourselves to anticipate the justification of our action or to promise it to ourselves. But that again cannot in the least alter the validity of the command here laid upon the theologian about the line between interpretation and illustration, invariably drawn for theological language, if it means to be and remain theological language. Nor can it alter, therefore, in any way the necessity for attending to this line, the necessity for the constant query, where we find ourselves when we speak, on this side of it or on that. The decision of this is not in our hands—just as also we have not finally to decide whether the discoverers of the *vestigia trinitatis* have really crossed it or not—but anxiety certainly is laid upon us regarding this decision, which demands of us reflection and care. Theological language by no means holds a brief entitling it to venture anything and everything. Precisely in thinking upon the crisis in which we always stand and which we nowhere escape, we shall make distinctions in what we do. It is in fact not the same thing consciously and purposely to derive the Trinity from the scheme of human self-consciousness or from another creaturely ordinance instead of from Scripture, and while deriving it from Scripture to grasp at a scheme which has admittedly no small resemblance to the scheme of human self-consciousness and other creaturely ordinances. True, that is only a relative distinction. We are not thereby justified in doing the second and not the first ; ultimately, at the same risk as all the rest, including the inventors of the ancient *vestigia trinitatis*, we can only venture an indication that the root of the doctrine of the Trinity lies in revelation and can lie only in revelation, if it is not forthwith to be the doctrine of another, alien god, of one of the gods, the man-gods of this world, if it is not to be a myth. In the sense of such an indication we reject the doctrine of the *vestigia*. We cannot lay claim to drive them from the field in the name and power of revelation. Revelation would not be revelation if any man were in a position to set up a claim against others and prove it justified, that he forsooth spoke from and about revelation. If we know what revelation is, then in our deliberate talk concerning revelation we shall let the issue be that revelation speaks about itself. Just to prove that this is so we confront the doctrine of the *vestigia* conclusively with a perfectly simple, unassuming nay, a nay by which we would merely state that in this doctrine the line seems to be crossed, but a nay the strength of which stands or falls with the fact that we also and by no means lastly relate it to ourselves, and that in the last resort we delicately leave it unproved. Proof could only consist in it being said to us, No man can serve two masters! The Lord who is visible in the *vestigia* we can only regard as a different Lord from the one so called in the Bible.

There is, of course, and with this we conclude, a real *vestigium trinitatis in creatura*, an illustration of revelation, but it we have neither to discover nor to validate ourselves. According to our understanding of it as the real right meaning of the *vestigia* doctrine, it consists of the form which God Himself in His revelation has assumed in our language, world, and humanity. What we hear when with our human ears and concepts we listen to God's revelation, what we apprehend in Scripture (and can apprehend as men), what the proclamation of the Word of God actually is in our life, is the triply one voice of the Father, the Son, and the Spirit. In this way God is present for us in His revelation. In this way He manifestly creates Himself a *vestigium* of Himself and so of His three-in-oneness. We add nothing to that, but say the same thing when we say that God for us is there in the threefold form of His Word, in His revelation, in Holy Scripture, in proclamation.

In view of this real *vestigium trinitatis*, if we are to apply Luther's table-talk, quoted above, about *Grammatica*, *Dialectica*, and *Rhetorica*, we should say that the encyclopædic sketch must run as given in §1, 1: exegetical, dogmatic, and practical theology.

This *vestigium* is clear and reliable. It is the *vestigium* of the God who deserves to be called God. And it is really the *vestigium* of the Triune God in the sense of the Church doctrine of the Trinity. But this *vestigium* will be better described in the sense described above as *vestigium creaturae in trinitate*. And in adhering to this one we are not maintaining a second root alongside the first, we are maintaining the single root of the doctrine of the Trinity.

GOD'S THREE-IN-ONENESS

The God who reveals Himself according to Scripture is One in three of His own modes of existence, which consist in their mutual relationships, Father, Son, and Holy Spirit. In this way He is the Lord, i.e. the Thou who meets man's I and unites it to Himself as the indissoluble Subject, and who actually thus and thereby becomes manifest to him as his God.

1. ONENESS IN THREENESS

In order to achieve the proper conceptual clarification of the question as to the Subject of revelation, we now turn to the development of the Church doctrine of the Trinity.

The doctrine of the three-in-oneness of God, as it has been built up and rightly asserted in the Church, to interpret Biblical revelation regarding the question of the Subject of this revelation, means—this above all must be emphasised and established—not a removal or even a mere querying, but rather the final and decisive confirmation, of the insight that God is One.

The concept of the unity of God as such will have to occupy us later in the doctrine of God. It interests us here solely in respect of the further realisation that three-in-oneness in God, so far from conveying a threat to, rather asserts the establishment of the Christian thought of the unity of God.

In our proof that the doctrine of the Trinity is rooted in Biblical revelation, we started from and always returned again to the revealed name Yahweh-Kyrios, which binds together OT and NT. The doctrine of the Trinity itself neither is nor claims to be anything else than an explanatory confirmation of this name. This name is the name of an unique entity, of a single, unique Willer and Doer, whom Scripture designates as God.

It will at once be clear that no difference can or will be made to this by the distinction, in Holy Scripture itself, between the *Yahweh* who dwells on Sinai and Him who dwells at Jerusalem, or in the NT by the distinction between Father and Son, or by the distinction made manifest in the contrasts between Good Friday, Easter, and Whitsunday. The man who prays to the Father or believes in the Son or is moved by the Holy Spirit, is met and bound to Himself by the one Lord. We quoted the Pauline passages 1 Cor. 12^{4f.}, Eph. 4^{4f.} : but in them must be noted not only the distinction of θεός, κύριος, πνεῦμα, but also, in them, the unity emphasised by the repetition of αὐτός or εἷς. Even the Church doctrine of the Trinity aims, not only at obscuring the εἷς θεός, but rather at setting it as such in the light. From the very outset it is directed against the anti-Trinitarians as those who actually fail to confess the one God. The presumption and aim of the Church in this matter is the doctrine of the unity of God, the divine μοναρχία, in which she recognises τὸ σεμνότατον κήρυγμα τῆς ἐκκλησίας θεοῦ (Pope Dionysius, *Ep. c. Tritheistas et Sabellianos a.* 260 *Denz. Nr.* 48).

The Trinitarian baptismal formula could not be more wrongly interpreted, than by regarding it as the formula of a baptism into three divine names.

Tertullian, *Adv. Prax.* 26, still spoke of *singula nomina.* But the ὄνομα of Father, Son, and Holy Spirit, Matt. 28¹⁹, is one and the same. *Ita huic sanctae trinitati unum naturale convenit nomen, ut in tribus personis non possit esse plurale* (*Conc. Tolet.* XI *a.* 675 *Denz. Nr.* 287). Baptism is *in nomina,* not *in nominibus Patris, Filii et Spiritus sancti,* as the *Cat. Rom.* II 2, 10, so excellently insists.

The faith confessed in this formula, and likewise faith in the great tripartite confessions of the ancient Church is thus not a faith with three objects.

Non habes illic : credo in maiorem et minorem et ultimum ; sed eadem vocis tuae cautione constringeris, ut similiter credas in Filium, sicut in Patrem credis, similiter in Spiritum sanctum credas, sicut credis in Filium (Ambrosius, *De myst.* 5, 28). *Quid sibi vult Christus, quum in nomine Patris et Filii et Spiritus sancti baptizari praecepit, nisi una fide in Patrem et Filium et Spiritum credendum esse ? Id vero quid aliud est, quam clare testari Patrem, Filium et Spiritum unum esse Deum?* (Calvin, *Instit.* I 13, 16).

Three objects of faith would mean three gods. But the so-called three " Persons " in God are never three gods.

Deus Pater, Deus Filius, Deus Spiritus sanctus. Et tamen non tres dii sunt, sed Unus est Deus. Ita Dominus Pater, Dominus Filius, Dominus Spiritus sanctus, et tamen non tres domini sed unus est Dominus (*Symb. Quicunque*).

We may unhesitatingly equate the concept of the lordship of God, with which we found the whole Biblical concept of revelation to be related, with what in the language of the ancient Church is called the essence of God, the *deitas* or *divinitas,* the divine οὐσία, *essentia, natura,* or *substantia.* The essence of God is the being of God *quâ* divine being. The essence of God is the godhead of God.

The more explicit development of this concept must be reserved for the doctrine of God. At this point Quenstedt's definition suffices us (*Theol.*

26

did.-pol. 1685 *P.* I *c.* 9 *sect.* 1 *th.* 11) : the essence of God is the *quidditas per quam Deus est, id quod est.* From the Bible standpoint, it is that which makes *Yahweh-Kyrios,* or that wherein *Yahweh-Kyrios* is, the person whom he describes Himself to be by this name, the name of Lord.

Of this essence of God it must now be said that the unity of it is not only not removed by the threeness of the " Persons," but that it is rather in the threeness of the " Persons " that its unity consists. Whatever is to be said about this threeness, it can by no means signify the threeness of the essence. Three-in-oneness in God does not mean a threefold deity, either in the sense of a plurality of deities or in the sense of the existence of a plurality of individuals or parts within the one deity.

The Church doctrine of the Trinity may be summed up in the equation *Deus est Trinitas*—when at once the note on *Trinitas* is *non triplex sed trina* (*Conc. Tolet.* IX *Denz. Nr.* 278). *Quidquid est in Deo, est ipse Deus unus et solus ;* whatever may have to be said about the distinctions in God, it can never mean a distinction of the divine being and existence (*essentia et esse* ; Bonaventura, *Breviloq.* I 4).

The name of Father, Son, and Spirit means that God is the one God in a threefold repetition ; and that in such a way, that this repetition itself is grounded in His Godhead ; hence in such a way that it signifies no alteration in His Godhead ; but also in such a way that only in this repetition is He the one God ; in such a way that His Godhead stands or falls with the fact that in this repetition He is God ; but also precisely for the reason that in each repetition He is the one God.

As regards the name Father, Son, and Spirit we have to distinguish *alius—alius—alius,* but not *aliud—aliud—aliud,* as if it were a case of parts of a whole or individuals of a species (Fulgentius, *De fide ad Petrum, c.* 5). *Personas distinguimus, non deitatem separamus (Conc. Tolet.* IX *Denz. Nr.* 280). —*Quibus est unum esse in deitatis natura, his est in personarum distinctione specialis proprietas (Conc. Tolet.* XVI *a.* 693, *Denz. Nr.* 296). It is a case, with the so-called " Persons," of a *repetitio aeternitatis in aeternitate ;* therefore not of a threeness of eternity *extra se,* but of a threeness of eternity *in se ;* so that *quotiescunque repetatur aeternitas in aeternitate, non est nisi una et eadem aeternitas* (Anselm of Canterbury, *Ep. de incarn.* 15). *Simplicissimam Dei unitatem non impedit ista distinctio . . .* for *in unaquaque hypostasi tota intelligitur natura* (Calvin, *Instit.* I 13, 19). *Ipsa etenim Dei essentia est maxime unita individua et singularis, idemque de tribus personis tamquam species de individuo nullo modo dici potest (Syn. pur theol.* Leiden, 1624 *Disp* 7, 12).

It is the idea of a mere unity of kind or of a mere collective unity that we would exclude, the truth of the numerical unity of the essence of the three " Persons " that we would stress, in availing ourselves first of all of the concept of " repetition " to describe

the " Persons." It will be good to note at this early stage that it
is to the one single essence of God, which is not to be tripled by the
doctrine of the Trinity, but emphatically to be recognised in its
unity, that there also belongs what we call to-day the " personality " of God.

With this concept also we shall have to deal fully in the doctrine of God.
The concept—not the thing designated by it, but the designation, the explicit
assertion of God as not an It but a He—was as foreign to the Fathers as to
the mediæval and post-Reformation scholastics. They always spoke—
from our point of view, not theirs—too innocently and uncritically of the
deitas, of the *essentia divina*, etc., i.e. apparently of God as of a neuter. The
concept of the " personality " of God—we emphasise it in a preliminary way
by defining the essence of God as the lordship of God—is a product of the
struggle against modern naturalism and pantheism.

" Person " in the sense of the Church doctrine of the Trinity
has nothing directly to do with " personality." Thus the meaning
of the doctrine of the Trinity is not that there are three per-
sonalities in God. That would be the worst and most pointed
expression of tritheism, against which we must here guard. The
doctrine of the personality of God, of course, goes along with the
doctrine of the Trinity in so far as (as is yet to be shown) the utmost
care is taken, by the Trinitarian repetitions of the knowledge of
the lordship of God, to prevent the divine He or rather Thou from
becoming in any way an It. But in it we are speaking not of three
divine " I's," but thrice of the one divine I. The concept of the
equality of essence ($\delta\mu oo\upsilon\sigma\acute{\iota}a$, *consubstantialitas*) in Father, Son,
and Spirit is thus at every point and pre-eminently to be regarded
in the sense of identity of essence. From the identity follows the
equality of essence in the " Persons."

The assertion that by her doctrine of the Trinity it is the knowledge of the unity of God and thus monotheism that the Church
has maintained against the anti-Trinitarians, may at first seem paradoxical, because apparently the concern of anti-Trinitarians of all
times has been precisely the proper relationship between the
peculiar significance and power of the revelation in Christ and
the principle of monotheism. The question might be asked whether
perhaps all that can be said is not merely that in spite of the doctrine
of the Trinity, the Church desired to retain and has retained the
unity of God as well ; she has so shaped the doctrine of the Trinity
that at the same time she tried to do justice to Christian monotheism, and succeeded. But to this qualifying interpretation we
must stedfastly say, No ; that also and precisely in the Church

doctrine of the Trinity as such the whole point was and is also and precisely Christian monotheism. We simply have not understood the point here, if what we see here is the play of a rivalry between two different interests, in asserting the rights of which tensions, gaps, etc. may arise. From this point of view we can indeed understand the anti-Trinitarian heresies, which were all of them heresies because they were answers to wrongly-put questions, i.e. attempts to reconcile with one another falsely-opposed interests, i.e. to remove irrelevantly - manufactured tensions. On the other hand the Church's line is already formally marked off from the heretical line by the fact that what happens on it is just as much and just as radically intended to be responsibility towards the one interest as towards the other, and must be understood as such, because, as a matter of fact, they are not two interests opposed to one another and then brought artificially into agreement. Upon this thin but fixed line where the fundamental concern is very simply neither this principle nor that but the interpretation of Scripture, we are dealing radically and obviously as much with the oneness as with the threeness of God, because we are dealing with revelation, where the two are one. On the other hand all anti-Trinitarianism feels that it must confess the threeness because of Scripture, but the oneness because of reason, and combine the two ; and naturally cannot possibly do so, because of the difference of the sources from which, and of the sense in which it affirms them both. Inevitably—as we must realise, if we are to understand the strictness with which it must be combated by the Church—all anti-Trinitarianism falls into the dilemma of denying either the revelation of God or the unity of God. According as it really asserts the unity of God, it must call revelation in question as the act of the real presence of the real God : the unity of God in which there are no distinct persons will make it impossible for it to take revelation seriously as the genuine presence of God in its manifest otherness, as compared with the invisible God who is Spirit. According as, contrariwise—and this is our primary concern here—it is ready to assert revelation but without recognising the Son's and the Spirit's equality of nature with the Father in heaven, it will call the unity of God in question. It will not in fact, in its concept of revelation, be able to avoid foisting in a third thing which is not God, an hypostasis not divine —not that it wants that—but half-divine, between man and God, and making it the object of faith. So far as it is not a denial of revelation, anti-Trinitarianism in any form is a coarser or a subtler idolising of revelation.

When A r i u s and his followers wanted to see and to honour in Christ the one God's first, highest, and most glorious creature, of which it may be said that ἦν ποτε ὅτε οὐκ ἦν καὶ οὐκ ἦν πρὶν γένηται, that it is created out of nothing, that as compared with the Father it is ἀλλότριος καὶ ἀνόμοιος, that as the υἱὸς τοῦ θεοῦ κτιστός it comes to be named God without really being so— they encroach obviously just by the r e v e r e n c e which they still wish to offer to this creature (and the more so, the more seriously this reverence is intended !) too nearly upon the u n i t y of God. If Christ is not true God, what else can faith in Him be but superstitition ? So when the Arian and non-Arian P n e u m a t o m a c h i, a E u n o m i u s or a M a c e d o n i u s of Constantinople, regarded the Holy Spirit as a created, ancillary spiritual power— how could it be otherwise than that all serious religious pronouncements upon this creaturely *pneuma* should let it appear as a semi-divine authority alongside of God and thus cause a very severe breakaway from the very monotheism which this whole tendency was meant to serve ? Christ and the Holy Spirit are " the powers of life by which God created the will to good and its achievement in men " (K. H o l l, *Urchr. u. Rel. Gesch.* 1925 *Ges. Aufs. z. Gesch.* vol. II 1928 p. 27). It was against talk of such " powers of life " that the monotheistic spearhead of the Church dogma of the Trinity was directed. S u b o r d i n a t i o n i s t Christology—we are thinking chiefly of O r i g e n—will allow Son and Spirit to participate in the essence of the Father, but in graduated proportion. Here into the essence of God Himself thought projects a hierarchy, a more and less in the matter of divine essence. This solution also could not be described as compatible with the unity of God. Of the man Christ armed with special divine power and ultimately exalted to divine dignity, as taught by the a d o p t i a n i s t Mona r c h i a n s, an A r t e m o n followed by a P a u l of S a m o s a t a, the same would have to be said in this respect as of the Christ of Arius. And when, finally, the m o d a l i s t i c M o n a r c h i a n s, a N o e t u s of S m y r n a, a P r a x e a s, a S a b e l l i u s in particular, a P r i s c i l l i a n—in whose footsteps S c h l e i e rm a c h e r and his school have walked in modern times—asserted equality in essence of the Trinitarian " persons," but only as phenomenal forms under which God's real single essence was concealed as something different and higher—it must still be asked whether revelation can be believed in, with the thought in the background that in it we have to do not with God as He is, but only with a god as He appears to us. If the τρόπος ἀποκαλύψεως is really a different one from the τρόπος ὑπάρξεως, and if the ὑπάρξις is the proper being of God, then that means that God in His revelation is not properly God. To take this improper God seriously as God, is clean against m o n o t h e i s m, which one did and does mean to protect by this distinction. In that case, faith in revelation—and it is from here that the questions arise which must also and precisely be put to modern Sabellianism—must become i d o l a t r y.

If revelation is to be taken seriously as the presence of God, if there is to be a legitimate faith in revelation, then in no sense can Christ and the Spirit be subordinate hypostases. In predicate and object in the concept of revelation we must be dealing over again and in no less a degree with the Subject itself. Revelation and Revealedness must be equal to Revealer. Otherwise, if this last is the one God, there is no room for them beside Him. The unity of God would otherwise render revelation and revealedness impossible. As Arius said, in parlous proximity to denying all revelation, Christ and the Spirit would not only be " foreign to and quite unlike " the Father, but would cease to have anything to do with Him, being creatures of some other sort. The only thing compatible with monotheism is that Christ and the Spirit should be equal in essence with the Father.

In hac trinitate nihil prius aut posterius, nihil maius aut minus. Sed totae tres personae coaeternae sibi sunt et coaequales (Symb. Quicumque). Nullus alium praecedit aeternitate aut excedit magnitudine aut superat potestate (Conc. Florent. a. 1441 Decr. pro Jacobitis, Denz. Nr. 704).

2. THREENESS IN ONENESS

As the doctrine of the *repetitio aeternitatis in aeternitate*, the doctrine of the Trinity confirms the knowledge of the unity of God. But not any knowledge of any unity of any God.

A sort of monotheism is represented not only by Judaism and Islam, but, as we know to-day, whether in the background or as the culminating superstructure of its pantheon or pandemonium, in some form by pretty well every religion, right back to the animisms of the so-called nature-religions of Africa. A sort of monotheism — this cannot be sufficiently emphasised — had long permeated philosophy, syncretistic cult teachings and above all the feeling for life in the late antiquity of the West, when Christianity took the stage; say, when Paul's Romans reached the Rome of its day. We need not expect that the dogma and dogmatics of the Church will submit to confirming a sort of monotheism, to being measured by a sort of monotheism. From this false presupposition the anti-Trinitarian heresies arose and are bound continually to arise.

What is in question is the revealed knowledge of the revealed unity of the revealed God—revealed according to the testimony of the OT and NT. The unity of God established in the doctrine of the Trinity is not to be confused with singularity or isolation.

Sustulit singularitatis ac solitudinis intelligentiam professio consortii (Hilarius *De trin.* 4).

Singularity and isolation are the limitations necessarily associated with the concept of numerical unity in general. But the numerical unity of the revealed God does not have these limitations. No logical necessity need hinder us from simply admitting that this is established.

For the numerical concepts in the doctrine of the Trinity generally we must hold : *Haec sancta trinitas, quae unus et verus est Deus, nec recedit a numero, nec capitur numero (Conc. Tolet.* XI *Denz. Nr.* 229). *In divinis signifi-cant (termini numerales) illa de quibus dicuntur,* they are to be taken meta-phorically, they do not posit quantity in God, they assert ultimately only negations (Thomas Aquinas, *S. theol.* I *qu.* 30 *art.* 3). *Quid ista ibi significant, ipso de quo loquimur aperiente, insinuare curemus* (Petr. Lombardus, *Sent.* I *dist.* 24A). So the number 1 asserts the negation of all plurality of or in God. All further conclusions from the application of this concept of number are to be rejected as irrelevant. We must be quite clear that the use of the number concepts and of rational concepts generally in the doctrine of the Trinity (and not only in the doctrine of the Trinity !) in the ancient Church stands under the sign of Hilarius' statement (*De trin.* 4) : *Intelligentia dictorum ex causis est assumenda dicendi, quia non sermoni res, sed rei sermo subjectus est.* Without attending closely to this statement we cannot grasp this point even historically, and he who does not make this statement his own as an axiom of method is no theologian and will never be one !

God is One, but not in such wise that as such He requires first a Second and Third in order to be One, nor in such wise as though He were alone and had to do without an opposite, therefore not in such wise—this will become decidedly significant in the doctrine of creation and man, though also in the doctrine of reconciliation—as though He could not exist without the world and man, as though between Him and the world and man there existed a relation of reciprocity. But in Himself these limits to what otherwise we regard as unity have already been done away : in itself His unity is not a singularity and isolation. Herewith, i.e. with the doctrine of the Trinity, we have stepped on to the soil of Christian mono-theism.

Μὴ συμπαραφέρου τοῖς Ἰουδαίοις πανούργως λέγουσι τὸ Εἷς θεὸς μόνος, ἀλλὰ μετὰ τοῦ εἰδέναι ὅτι εἷς θεὸς γινώσκε ὅτι καὶ υἱός ἐστι τοῦ θεοῦ μονογενῆς (Cyril of Jerus. *Cat.* 10, 2). *Confitemur : Non sic unum Deum, quasi solitarium (Fides Damasi a.* 380 ? *Denz. Nr.* 15).

The concept of the revealed unity of the revealed God thus does not exclude but includes a distinction (*distinctio* or *discretio*), an arrangement (*dispositio* or *oeconomia*), in the essence of God. This distinction or arrangement is the distinction or arrangement of the three " Persons "—we prefer to say, the three " modes of being " in God.

Herewith, like all who before us have busied themselves with this matter, we enter upon the most difficult section of our investiga-tion. What is meant here by " Person," as commonly used ? Or to put the question generally, what is meant in God by what is distinguished or arranged as Father, Son, and Spirit ? What is the common concept under which these three are to be interpreted ? What are these three—apart from the fact that, as well together as each separately, they are the one true God ? What is the common principle of their being, now as Father, now as Son, now as Spirit ?

In the opening sentence of our section we avoided the concept " Person." Neither was it on its introduction into ecclesiastical language made sufficiently clear, nor has the subsequent interpretation, imparted to it and enforced as a whole in mediæval and post-Reformation scholasticism, really issued in such a clearing up, nor has the introduction of the modern concept of personality into this debate produced anything else but fresh confusion. The situation would be hopeless if our task here were to state the proper meaning of " Person " in the doctrine of the Trinity. Fortunately that is not our task. But, of course, the difficulties in which we see ourselves involved regarding a concept once for all become classical, are but a symptom of the difficulty of the question generally, which has to be answered here one way or the other.

The concept *persona*, πρόσωπον, originates (like the concept *trinitas*, supposed to have been used first by Tertullian) with the struggle against the Sabellian heresy, and was therefore meant to indicate the being in and for themselves of Father, Son, and Spirit respectively. But did not *persona*, πρόσωπον, also mean " mask " ? Did not the concept give fresh support to the Sabellian idea of the three mere phenomenal forms, behind which stood a hidden fourth ? In consideration of this the Greek Church largely preferred to translate *persona* by ὑπόστασις rather than by πρόσωπον. But on the other hand if by ὑπόστασις Westerners of necessity thought of *substantia* in the sense of *natura* or *essentia*, they could not but regard themselves as threatened by the proximity of tritheistic ideas. If the West, finally held to *persona* and the East to ὑπόστασις, neither party could be perfectly content with the other nor either, finally, with itself.

It is somewhat of a relief to find that a man of Augustine's standing declared openly (*De trin.* V 9, VII 4) that to call the thing " Person " was a matter of a *necessitas* or *consuetudo loquendi*. A really suitable concept for it simply does not exist. Certainly, by the three divine Persons something quite other was intended than a juxtaposition like that of three human persons, and for this reason, that a juxtaposition of human persons denotes a separation of being (*diversitas essentiae*), which in God is completely excluded—thereby the possibility of the Greek objection to πρόσωπον was formally acknowledged ! To the question, *quid tres* ? i.e. what is the *nomen generale*, the general concept for Father, Son, and Spirit, a proper answer could not be given, *quia excedit supereminentia divinitatis usitati eloquii facultatem. Verius enim cogitatur Deus quam dicitur et verius est quam cogitatur.* (The more the distinction of Persons is regarded as taking place and being grounded in the divine essence itself, the more conceivable in fact becomes the inconceivability of this distinction : this distinction participates in the inconceivability of the divine essence, which would not be the essence of the revealed God, if it were conceivable, i.e. apprehensible in the categories of *usitatum eloquium*. Neither *persona* therefore nor any other concept can do the service of rendering this concept really conceivable. What may be in place here can only be more or less fruitful and clarifying designations of the incomprehensible reality of God.) If, as is Augustine's opinion, we still use the expression *tres personae*, that is done *non ut illud diceretur, sed ne taceretur omnino. Non enim rei ineffabilis eminentia hoc vocabulo explicari valet :* not in order to say that the three in God are precisely *personae*, but in order to say by means of the concept of *persona* that there are three in God—in which connection also the numerical concept 3 can express no more than the negative point, that Father, Son, and Spirit are as such not one. Following Augustine, A n s e l m of C a n t e r b u r y spoke of the *ineffabilis pluralitias* (*Monol.* 38) of the *tres nescio quid : licet enim possim dicere trinitatem propter Patrem et Filium et utriusque Spiritum, qui sunt tres, non tamen possum proferre uno nomine propter quid tres.* Against the concept *persona* Anselm also has the soundly based reflection, that *omnes plures personae sic subsistunt separatim ab invicem, ut tot necesse sit esse substantias, quot sint personae.* That is true of human, but is untrue of the divine Persons. He, too, only speaks of *personae, indigentia nominis proprie convenientis* (*ib.* 79).

Under the influence of Aristotle the Middle Ages then tried to secure a special systematic content for the concept " Person." The point of departure for the considerations here set on foot was constituted by the definition of B o e t h i u s (early 6th century, *C. Entych. et Nest.* 3) ; *P e r s o n a e s t n a t u r a e r a t i o n a b i l i s i n d i v i d u a s u b s t a n t i a.* According to T h o m a s A q u i n a s (*S. Theol.* I *qu.* 29 *art.* 1–2), *substantia individua* (equivalent to *singulare in genere substantiae* or to *substantia prima*) means an essence existing in and for itself, one separate in its existence from others, unable to impart its existence to others, a single essence. *Natura* denotes the general essence, the *essentia speciei*, the *substantia secunda*, to which such a single essence belongs. *Natura rationabilis* or *rationalis* is thus rational nature (according to the mediæval view it includes God, angel, and man) as opposed to *natura irrationalis*, non-rational nature (including all other substances from animals downwards). *Persona* then is nothing but just *substantia individua* (which may also be called *res naturae, subsistentia*, or, with the Greeks, ὑπόστασις), so far as the single essence indicated belongs to rational nature. Boethius' definition is therefore to be translated in the sense of Thomas thus : Person is the single rational individual essence. The applicability of this concept to God Thomas proved by the assertion that *persona* involves the attribute of a dignity, in fact *persona* exactly denotes the *perfectissimum in tota natura.* This dignity, this *perfectissum* must be attributed to God in an eminent sense, *excellentiori modo.* Unfortunately, Thomas made no deliverance as to what it is this dignity contained in the concept of Person, this *perfectissimum* in the *persona*, in his opinion consists of. Is it a matter of the superiority of the single r a t i o n a l essence over the non-rational ? Or of the superiority of the s i n g l e rational e s s e n c e over rational nature as such ? Or of both ? Be that as it may, Thomas o n c e shows himself aware of the objection that the *principium individuationis*, which at least shares in being decisive for the concept of Person, is a material which exists in individuation, a somewhat with an individual existence, a potentiality. But, according to Thomas, God is also and emphatically *immaterialis, actus purus.* Thomas must therefore admit that of the element of *individua substantia* there remains, on application of the concept of Person to God, only the attribute of the *incommunicabilitas*, non-communicability, of the existence of the essence in question to others, while of the concept of the single essence there remains only what makes it a s i n g l e essence, when the fact that it is a single e s s e n c e is set aside (*ib. art.* 3 *ad.* 4). And naturally Thomas is e q u a l l y aware of that still more important objection, already raised by Augustine and Anselm, that a plurality of persons necessarily involves a plurality of essences as well—therefore, when asserted of God, a plurality of divine essences, or at least a division of the one divine essence. He must therefore establish it, with material correctness, but still in a way very serious for his concept of Person, that the *personae* of the Trinity are *r e s   s u b s i s t e n t e s   i n* (i.e. in the one) *d i v i n a   n a t u r a*. Thomas cannot escape acknowledging that the ὑπόστασις of the Greeks is in this respect nearer the facts than the Latin *persona*, and that he avoids ὑπόστασις only on account of the fatal translation *substantia*. But also the *res subsistentes* in *divina natura* are according to him nothing but *relationes*, relations within God (*ib. qu.* 29 *art.* 4 ; *qu.* 30 *art* 1). Glad as one is to follow him in this and glad as we are to agree with him in point of method, when he appeals here also to the incomparability of the concept in its relation to what is here intended, namely, the divinely revealed—*aliud est quaerere de significatione huius nominis " persona " in communi et aliud de significatione personae d i v i n a e* (*ib. qu.* 29 *art.* 4c)— as little one can feel convinced that even only relative conformity to meaning (no other in fact comes in question) in the application of the actual concept of person has been so explained by Thomas, that one is practically bound to abandon towards this concept the reserve, for which one may always make an appeal to A u g u s t i n e and A n s e l m. The proper explanation, within the limits of the possible, of what is involved in the three in three-in-oneness Thomas also has n o t given in the form of an interpretation of the concept of person, but by means of the concept of r e l a t i o n s !

Quite in line with Augustine and Anselm (and materially not in contradiction to Thomas) C a l v i n could carry on a controversy against the concept of person in these words : *Les anciens docteurs ont usé de ce mot de personne et ont dit, qu'en Dieu il y a trois personnes : Non point comme nous parlons en notre langage commun appelant trois hommes, trois personnes ou comme mesmes en la papauté ils prendront ceste audace de peindre trois marmousets* (mannikins) *et voilà la trinité. Mais*—thus Calvin continues his opinion—*ce mot de personnes en ceste matière est pour exprimer les propriétez lesquelles sont en l'essence de Dieu* (*Congrégation de la divinité de Christ, C.R.* 47, 473). J. G e r h a r d (*Loci* 1610 l. III 62) also spoke later of a *magnum imo infinitum discrimen* between the divine Persons and the human ones familiar to us.

What in the conceptual language of the 19th century is called " personality " is distinguished from the ancient and mediæval *persona* by the addition of the attribute of s e l f - c o n s c i o u s n e s s. In that way the whole question comes to be thoroughly complicated. One obviously had and has the choice, either of attempting to complete the doctrine of the Trinity by assuming the concept of Person with this new accentuation, or of holding to the old concept of Person which, since this accentuation of linguistic usage, has become completely obsolete and incomprehensible outside monastic and a few other studies. It was the teaching of the Catholic theologian A n t o n   G ü n t h e r, condemned by Pope Pius IX in 1859, in which the former possibility was chosen : according to him the single Persons in the Trinity were single substances, three subjects thinking and willing for themselves, proceeding from each other and connected with each other and thus joined together in the unity of an absolute personality. On the Protestant side along the same lines Richard Grützmacher (*Der dreieinige Gott—unser Gott*, 1910) has ascribed severally to Creator, Son, Spirit a special I-centre with a special consciousness, will, and content. But according to him each individual of the three was also an absolute personality, one with the others in the fact that the nature of all three is love and holiness, so that they are always experienced as operating side by side and together. It must, of course, be admitted that it is difficult here not to think of the *trois marmousets* rejected by Calvin and hence to call this doctrine tritheism. We can as little speak seriously of a tripersonality of God as of a triessentiality. The definition given in more than one passage by Melanchthon (e.g. *Exam. ordinand.* 1559 *C.R.* 23, 2) and often quoted later : *Persona est subsistens vivum, individuum, intelligens, incommunicabile, non sustentatum ab alio*, has a somewhat suspicious ring in this respect, especially if we put beside it the fact that he was able to say likewise in the plural, *tres vere subsistentes . . . distincti seu singulares intelligentes (Loci*, 1559 *C.R.* 21, 613). *Vita and intelligentia*, as attributes of the concept of Person, of necessity import at least a tritheistic appearance into the doctrine of the Trinity. But even the attribute of individuality, connected with Father, Son, and Spirit as such instead of with the essence of God, and so the idea of a threefold individuality, is scarcely possible without tritheism. " In God, just as there is o n e nature, so also there is o n e knowledge, one self-consciousness " (F. Diekamp, *Kath. Dogmatik*[6] vol. I 1930 p. 271).

Clearly in face of the danger here imminent, almost the entire Neo-Protestant theology thought it had to fly to Sabellianism. On the one hand was the desire also to apply to Father, Son, and Spirit the modern concept of personality, but a justifiable fear of doing so, with a Günther or Grützmacher, in an ontological sense. Thus they were limited to a doctrine of three persons, merely phenomenological in intention, to a Trinity dispensing revelation, and so to three Persons such that behind them God Himself might still be " absolute " personality. As regards this conception it was never quite clear, either in ancient or in modern times, how far really—and the more seriously revelation was taken the greater the risk of its happening—they were speaking of a Quaternity instead of a Trinity. It was at least understandable that Schleiermacher preferred simple silence about the concept of the personality of God, or that D. Fr. Strauss (*Die christl. Glaubenslehre*, vol. I 1840 § 33) and A. E. Biedermann (*Christl. Dogmatik* 1869 §§ 618 and 715 f.) went the length of eliminating it altogether, or of banishing it from the realm of truth in which God is nothing but Absolute Spirit, to the lower region of the inadequate religious idea. It of course remains to ask whether the assumption of a triple divine self-consciousness is not also to be described as polytheistic, if this triplicity is described " merely " as a matter of the dispensation of revelation or of the religious idea. What does " merely " really mean here, if man still certainly and actually lives with God just in virtue of the dispensation of revelation, or in the religious idea, if none the less precisely at this point the *trois marmousets* are to be the last word ?

The second possibility has been adopted by Roman Catholic theology, in the Trinity doctrine of which to this day " Persons " are so spoken of as if the modern concept of personality did not exist, as if Boethius' definition still continued to be actual and intelligible and above all as if at that period of the Middle Ages the meaning of this definition had been so clarified that by means of it one could speak profitably of the Trinitarian three.

In view of the history of the concept of Person in the doctrine of the Trinity one may well ask whether dogmatics is wise in further availing itself of it in this connection. It belongs to another part, namely, to the doctrine of God proper, and as a deduction from the doctrine of the Trinity. It follows directly from the Trinitarian understanding of the God revealed in Scripture that this one God is to be regarded not only as an impersonal lordship, i.e. as power, but as the Lord, and so not only as absolute Spirit but as a Person, i.e. as an I existing in and for Itself with a thought and will proper to It. It is thus that He meets us in His revelation. It is thus that He is God thrice as Father, Son, and Spirit. But is it really also the concept that explains this thriceness as such, that can therefore be made the foundation of the doctrine of the Trinity as its hermeneutical principle ? The man who wishes to keep to it throughout will scarcely find another valid argument to put alongside the undoubtedly honourable position it holds by hoary ecclesiastical and scientific usage, save that he has not another better one to put in its place. We shall constantly be having to ask ourselves the serious question whether the first reason of piety and the second technical one are sufficiently weighty to cause the dogmatician still further to overload the thought of the Trinity, difficult as it is in any case, with an auxiliary thought, itself in turn so serious and applicable only with so many precautions. We have, indeed, no cause to wish to outlaw the concept of Person outright or to withdraw it from circulation. But we could only apply it in the sense of a practical abbreviation and as a reminder of the historical continuity of the problem.

The really valuable determinations of the principle of God's threeness in oneness were derived neither by Augustine nor by Thomas nor by our Protestant Fathers from the analysis of the concept of Person, but, under the urge of their usually over-laborious analyses of the concept of Person acquired from quite a different source. We prefer to let this other source rank even externally as the primary one and therefore, at least preferably, to say not " Person " but " mode of being," with the intention of expressing by this concept the same thing as should be expressed by " Person," not absolutely but relatively better, more simply and more clearly. That God as Father, Son, and Spirit respectively is God in a special way, this element—not that of the participation of Father, Son, and Spirit in the divine essence which is identical in all and therefore simply not significant for Father, Son, and Spirit as such, nor yet that of the " reasonable nature " of the Father, Son, and Spirit, which once again cannot be described as a threefold one without Tritheism—is usually emphasised, even by those who think here that they must analyse the concept of Person, in these analyses as the first and decisive element. It is thus a case not of introducing a new concept, but of bringing to the centre a subsidiary concept used in the analysis of the concept of Person from time immemorial and with the greatest effect. The statement " God is one in three modes of being, Father, Son, and Holy Spirit " thus means that the one God, i.e. the one Lord, the one personal God is what He is not in one mode only, but —we appeal in support simply to the result of our analysis of the Biblical concept of revelation—in the mode of the Father, in the mode of the Son, in the mode of the Holy Spirit.

" Mode of being or existence " is the literal translation of the concept τρόπος ὑπάρξεως, already in use in the Early Church debates, *modus entitativus*, as B. Quenstedt e.g. (*Theol. did.-pol.* 1685 *P.* I *c.* 9 *sect.* 1 *th.* 8) has said in Latin. But also the concept ὑπόστασις understood in the sense in which it was finally received instead of πρόσωπον by the Eastern Church after initial doubts and against the lasting doubts of the West, means *subsistentia* (not *substantia*) i.e. mode of existence of one who exists. It was perhaps in this sense that Heb. 1³ already called the Son the χαρακτὴρ τῆς ὑποστάσεως θεοῦ, i.e. in His mode of existence an " impress," a countertype of God the " Father's " mode of existence. We heard above of the Thomist definition of the concept of the divine Persons : they are *res subsistentes in natura divina*. The concept *res* might not be quite happy, for *res in natura* has a dubious ring. But, of course, the concept *subsistere* is one of the two usable elements in the old concept of person. In Calvin's (*Instit.* I 13, 6) definition the main concept is to the same effect : *Subsistentia in Dei essentia* (for that matter Calvin has expressly explained in the previously adduced *Congrégation*, that with the Greeks he would regard the concepts *substance* or *hypostase* to denote the matter in question, also on account of the Biblical basis in Heb. 1³, as *plus convenable*). In the succeeding period I. Wolleb e.g. said (*Chr. Theol. comp.* 1626 I *c.* 2 *can.* 1, 4) that *persona* means *essentia Dei cum certo modo entis ;* or the *Syn. pur. Theol.*, Leiden, 1624 *Disp.* 7, 10, *substantia divina peculiari quodam subsistendi modo ;* or Fr. Burmann (*Syn. Theol.* 1678 I *c.* 30, 13), *essentia divina communis et modus subsistendi proprius.* But here we may also appeal to modern Catholic authors : M. J. Scheeben (*Handb. d. Kath. Dogmatik* vol. I 1874 new edn. 1925 p. 832) expressly explains that the individuality of the divine Persons is identical with the special form, belonging to each of them, of possessing the divine substance, it is a modality of this individuality essentially pertaining to the individuality of the divine substance itself. And B. Bartmann (*Lehrb. d. Dogmatik* 7th edn. vol. I 1928 p. 169) writes : " That whereby the three persons are distinguished from one another is not to be sought in the essentiality, nor yet primarily in the Person in itself, which is perfectly equal to the others and complete and eternal, but in the varying mode of possessing the essentiality."

It is what these theologians call *subsistentia, modus entis,* form or mode of possession, that we, by saying " mode of existence " at the critical point, would bring to the focus of attention, where as a matter of fact it has always stood, even in the various analyses of the concept of Person, although, as it seems to us, far too much obscured by the context.

It is a question of special, distinct, absolutely in d i v i d u a l modes of God's existence. In other words these modes of God's existence are not to be confused or mixed up with each other. Of course, in all three modes of existence God is, in Himself and compared with the world and man, the one God. But this one God is God three times in another way, so other that it is precisely only in this three-times otherness that He is God, so other that this otherness, His existence in these three modes of existence, is absolutely essential to Him, therefore, so other that this otherness is i r r e m o v a b l e. Neither can we contemplate the possibility of one of the divine modes of existence just as well being the other, say, the Father the Son, or the Son the Spirit, nor of two of them or of all three coalescing and dissolving into one. Were that so they would cease to be modes of existence essential to the divine existence. Just because the threeness is grounded in the one essence of the revealed God, because in denying the threeness in the oneness of God we at once mean another God than the one revealed in Scripture—for that very reason this threeness must be regarded as an irremovable one, the individuality of the three modes of existence as an ineffaceable one.

We saw how in T h o m a s A q u i n a s, apart from the element of *subsistere*, the element of *incommunibilitas* proved itself tenable in his concept of Person, i.e. proved itself usable for the concept of Person in the doctrine of the Trinity. And now it is no mere accident, that the *Conf. Aug. art.* 1 included precisely these two elements in its definition : Person in the context of the doctrine of the Trinity means *(quod) p r o p r i e s u b s i s t i t.* We shall, indeed, have to bracket the " *quod* " in this definition. W h a t *proprie subsistit* is not just the Person as such, but G o d in the three Persons : God as *proprie subsistens* in a threefold way. It is noteworthy that F r. D i e k a m p also *(Kath. Dogmatik,* vol. I 6th Edn. 1930 p. 352 f.), who works with the Thomistic *res subsistentes,* comes to the conclusion that absolute subsistence belongs only to the divine substance as such ; to the Persons as such, on the contrary, only a relative subsistence. But this relative *subsistere* of the Persons is a *proprie subsistere.* So C a l v i n declared that Person meant *subsistentia in Dei essentia quae . . . p r o p r i e t a t e i n c o m m u n i c a b i l i distinguitur (Instit.* I 13, 6). In *Conf. Aug. art.* 1 M e l a n c h t h o n added in explanation, *Non pars aut qualitas in alio* : and in the *Loci, Non sustentata ab alio.* And Q u e n - s t e d t *(op. cit. th.* 12) in extending Melanchthon's formula further strengthened the *incommunicabilis* by the description, *p e r s e u l t i m a t a e t i m m e d i a t a subsistens.* If we consider this and emphasise the fact, that the individuality in question can actually be sufficiently described only by adverbs *(proprie,* etc.) or ablatives (*proprietate*) describing the word *subsistere*, while the subject of this *subsistere* and therefore of the *proprie subsistere* as well cannot be a *res* or *subsistentia* different from the one essence, but only this one essence of God itself, then the concept of " mode of existence," now further strengthened and explained by the adjective " individual mode of existence," should ever more clearly reveal itself, as the kernel of what dogmatics has to hold fast to of the old concept of Person. Of course, there is more to be said about God the Father, Son, and Spirit than what is said in the formula " individual mode of existence." What we are concerned with is the modes of existence, the threefold otherness of God. Calvin's definition is perfectly correct that *persona* means *natura divina cum hoc quod subest sua unicuique proprietas* (*Instit.* I 13, 19). But the conclusion of these and really of all the definitions of the ancients adduced, is that the " more " in question—what Father, Son, and Spirit are " more " than " individual modes of being ! "—is the *natura divina*, the one undistinguishable divine essence, with which, of course, Father, Son, and Spirit are identical. But if we now ask about the non-identical, the distinguishing and distinct element, about what makes the Father the Father, the Son the Son, the Spirit the Spirit, about *quod subest sua unicuique proprietas*—and clearly we should have to ask about it, if we wish to ask about the threeness in the oneness—then we should have to stick to the less expressive formula " individual mode of existence." Thereby we also describe the one divine essence, but we thereby describe it (and with exactness only thereby) as the one divine essence, which is not only one, but one in three.

For that very reason then Father, Son, and Spirit are not to be regarded as three divine attributes, as three parts of the possessed being of God, as three departments of the divine essence and activity. The threeness of the one God as we met with it in our analysis of the Biblical concept of revelation, the threeness of Revelation, Revealer, and Revealedness, the threeness of God's holiness, mercy, and love, God's threeness on Good Friday, Easter, and Whitsunday, the threeness of God the Creator, God the Reconciler, and God the Redeemer—all that may and should, as will have to be shown directly, draw attention and point to the problem of the threeness in God. Inasmuch as we sometimes hold these three elements apart, we have in these three elements as such respectively not yet reached the concept of the three really individual modes of God's existence. For whether it be a case of the inner content or of the outer form of the essence of God, all that can be said may and must ultimately be said in like manner of Father, Son, and Spirit. There is no attribute, no act of God, which would not in like manner be the attribute, the act of the Father, the Son, and the Spirit. Of course, knowledge of the revelation of God means knowledge of various definite attributes which we cannot reduce to a common denominator, by which we can also thereafter make clear God's existence as Father, Son, and Spirit. But just because it is of the essence of the revealing God to possess such and such attributes, in His essence they are also indistinguishably one, and not to be apportioned ontologically to Father, Son, and Spirit. Certainly God meets us in the Biblically attested revelation, as we saw, in constantly different action, always in one of His modes of existence, or better put, distinguished or characterised from time to time by one or other of His modes of existence. But this relatively distinct manifestation of the three modes of existence does not imply a corresponding state of distinctness among themselves. On the contrary, we shall have to say that as surely as the relatively varying manifestation of the three modes of existence points to their corresponding variety among themselves, so surely does it also point directly to their unity in this variety.

We might, for example, visualise the essence of the Father to ourselves by the concept of eternity, but how would that be possible without at once construing also the Son and the Spirit similarly under the same concept ? We may with Paul and Luther recognise in Christ the revelation of the righteousness of God if we at once proceed to regard the Father and the Spirit in exactly the same way. In the Spirit we may see the inner concept of the divine life, but that must at once signify that we are conceiving the same life as the life of the Father and the Son. We shall—here I follow an exposition of Luther's (*Von den letzten Worten Davids*, 1543 W. edn. 54, 59, 12)—in the story of the baptism of Jesus, call the One that appears in the form of the dove, not the Father or the Son but the Holy Spirit, the voice ringing from heaven not the voice of the Son or the Spirit, but the voice of the Father, the man baptised in Jordan, not the incarnate Father or Spirit but the incarnate Son, without forgetting or denying that everything, the Voice from Heaven, the Incarnate and the Gift from above, is the work of the one God, Father, Son, and Spirit. *Opera trinitatis ad extra sunt indivisa.*

The variety of the modes of existence, the *alius—alius—alius*, into which we are now inquiring, can not be proved from this standpoint. But if not from this, from which standpoint then ? The only possible answer that can be given and as a matter of fact has been given from the beginning, once more confirms us in thinking that we do well to set in the centre of the whole investigation not the concept of Person but that of mode of existence. This answer is to the effect that the distinguishable form of the three divine modes of existence is to be understood in terms of their individual relations, indeed of their individual genetic relations to one another. Father, Son, and Spirit are distinguished from one another because without inequality in their essence or dignity, without increase or decrease in divinity the original relations in which they stand to one another are unequal. If we have rejected the possibility of reading off the distinction between the three modes of existence from the varieties of content in the thought of God contained in the concept of revelation, because in the last resort we cannot speak of such things, so now we should and must assert that the formal individual characteristics of the three modes of existence can quite well be read off from the concept of revelation—what actually constitutes them modes of existence —namely, the characteristics due to their relation to one another. Naturally the why of these characteristics cannot be stated, any more than a why of revelation can be stated. But, as we have tried to do, the that of revelation can be stated and described, and that cannot be done—in fact we could not do it—without encountering certain formal characteristics (in and together with the characteristics in content which are not under consideration here) which as characteristics of the one essence of God the Lord prove themselves also to be inalienable characteristics.

Here and rightly reference has been made first and foremost to the NT names Father, Son, and Spirit. If these three names are in their threeness really the one name of the one God, it follows that in this one God, there is at all events primarily—let us say it with circumspection—something like fatherhood and sonship, and therefore something like begetting and begottenness, and in addition a third thing common to both, which is not likewise a begottenness, nor yet likewise a procession merely from the Begetter, but, to put it generally, a bringing forth, a bringing forth which originates in common from Begetter and Begotten. But we should also, applying our ternary of Revealer, Revelation, and Revealedness, say that there is a source, an authorship, a ground of revelation, a Revealer of Himself, as certainly distinct from Revelation as such, as Revelation signifies something utterly new over against the mystery of the Revealer, which is laid aside in the Revelation as such. Thus, distinct from the First there is, as the Second, Revelation itself, as the event of the manifestation of what previously was hidden. And as the common result of these two elements, constituting the Third, a Revealedness, the reality which is the purpose of the Revealer and so at the same time the meaning, the trend of the Revelation. Put more briefly, only because there is a veiling of God can there be an unveiling, and only by there being a veiling and unveiling of God can there be a self-impartation of God.

We might say further that God being the Creator is the presupposition of the fact that He can be the Reconciler; that the Creator being the

27

Reconciler is based upon the fact that He can be the Redeemer. Or : the fact that God can be merciful to us in Christ, is founded upon His holiness, and hence the Love of God towards us is founded upon His holiness and mercy. Calvin was fond of making clear these original relationships in the God of revelation by the concepts *principium* (i.e. *principium agendi*), *sapientia* (i.e. *dispensatio in rebus agendis*), *virtus* (i.e. *efficacia actionis*) (*Instit.* I 13, 18; cf. *Cat. Genev.* 1545 in Karl Müller, p. 118, l. 25).

Of course, God's real modes of existence cannot be read off from the varieties in content of these and similar conceptual ternaries. For everything here distinct in content must be thought of as being in its variety sublimated once more in the unity of the divine essence. But they can certainly be read off from the regularly recurring mutual relations of the three concepts respectively, as they are most simply to be found between the concepts Father, Son, and Spirit themselves. On these relations is founded God's threeness in oneness. This threeness consists in the fact that in the essence or act in which God is God there is first a pure origin and then two different issues, the first of which is to be attributed solely to the origin, the second, different in kind, to the origin and likewise to the first issue. According to Scripture, God is manifest, He is God, in such a way that He is Himself in these relationships to Himself. He is His own producer and He is in a double and quite distinct respect His own product. He possesses Himself as Father, i.e. as pure Giver ; as Son, i.e. as Receiver and Giver ; as Spirit, i.e. as pure Receiver. He is the beginning, without which there is no Middle and no End ; the Middle, which can only exist by starting from the Beginning and without which there would be no End ; the End, which starts absolutely and utterly from the Beginning. He is the Speaker, without whom there is no Word and no Meaning ; the Word which is the Speaker's Word and the bearer of the Meaning ; the Meaning which is as much the Meaning of the Speaker as of His Word. But let us be on our guard against the zone of *vestigia trinitatis* on which already we have almost trespassed. The *alius—alius—alius* representable in such different ternaries does not signify an *aliud—aliud—aliud* ; One and the Same may be This and That in the truly corresponding determinations of these original relations, without ceasing to be the One and the Same ; and each of these original relations as such is at the same time the One in whom these relations occur—to these facts there are no analogies, this is the unique divine threeness in the unique divine oneness.

In what we have just been developing we are concerned with the thought familiar in the history of dogma under the name of the doctrine of relations. It must already have been known to Tertullian : *Ita connexus Patris in Filio et Filii in Paracleto tres efficit cohaerentes, alterum ex altero* (*Adv. Prax.* 25). The Cappadocians (e.g. Gregory Naz., *Orat.* 29, 16) were the first to speak expressly of σχέσις, relation or connection, as the Person-constituting element in God. In the West the doctrine next clearly appeared in Augustine : *His enim appellationibus* (Father, Son, and Spirit) *hoc significatur quo ad se invicem referuntur* (*Ep.* 238, 2 14) . . . *quae relative dicuntur ad invicem* (*De trin.* VIII *prooem.* 1) . . . *Non quisque eorum ad se ipsum, sed ad invicem atque ad alterutrum ita dicuntur*(ib. V 6). In the Middle Ages Anselm of Canterbury (*De proc. Spir.* 2) coined the formula : *In divinis omnia sunt unum, ubi non obviat relationis oppositio*, a formula which was actually raised to a dogma by the Council of Florence, 1441 (*Decr. pro Jacob., Denz Nr.* 703). In another passage he formulated the matter thus : *Proprium est unius esse ex altero et proprium est alterius alterum esse ex illo* (*Monol.* 38, cf. also 61 and *Ep. de incarn.* 3). Next Thomas Aquinas introduced the concept of relation into his concept of Person, and therefore defines the Trinitarian *persona* as *relatio ut res subsistens in natura divina* (*S. theol.* 1 *qu.* 30 *art.* 1 *c., cf. qu.* 40 *art.* 1–2). Correspondingly in Calvin the definition, now to be quoted in full, runs : *personam voco subsistentiam in Dei essentia, quae ad alios relata, proprietate incommunicabili distinguitur.* With complete accuracy with respect to the doctrine of relation the whole doctrine of the threeness in oneness was expounded by Luther as follows : " The Father is my and thy God and Creator, who hath made thee and me, The selfsame work that thou and I are, the Son also hath made, is as much thy and my God and Creator as the Father. Therefore the Holy Ghost hath made just the same work that thou and I are, and is thy and my God and Creator, just as much as the Father and Son. Yet there are not three Gods or Creators, but one single God and Creator of both the twain of us. Here by this faith I guard myself against the heresy of Arius and his like that I divide not . . . the single divine essence into three Gods or Creators, but retain with correct Christian faith not more than the single God and Creator of all creatures."—" Once more, if I now pass beyond and outside the creation or creature into the inward, inconceivable essence of divine nature, I find, as Scripture teacheth me (for reason is here nothing) that the Father is another distinguishable Person from the Son in the one undivided eternal Godhead. His distinction is that He is the Father, and hath not divinity from the Son nor from any one. The Son is a distinguishable Person from the Father in the same one Fatherly Godhead, His distinction is that He is the Son, and hath divinity not from Himself nor from any one, but solely from the Father, as eternally born of the Father. The Holy Ghost is a distinguishable Person from Father and Son in the same one Godhead, His distinction is that He is the Holy Ghost who proceedeth eternally from the Father and Son at once, and hath divinity not from Himself nor from any one, but both from Father and Son at once, and all that from eternity to eternity. Here by this faith I guard myself against the heresy of Sabellius and his like, against Jews, Mahomet, and all such others as are cleverer than God Himself ; and mix not the Person into a single Person, but retain in correct Christian faith three distinguishable Persons in the single Divine eternal essence, all three of which, to usward and the creatures, are a single God, Creator and Worker of all things " (*Von den letzten Worten Davids*, 1543 W. edn. 54, 58, 4). In contrast to which it is characteristic of the tritheistic weakness of the concept of Person in Melanchthon that, to the detriment also of the Lutheran orthodoxy which followed him, he at least did not take up the concept of relation into his definition, but usually, if at all, introduced it only subsequently, for purposes of explanation.

The relations in God, in virtue of which He is three-in-one essence, are thus His being Father (*paternitas*), in virtue of which God the Father is the Father of the Son, His being Son (*filiatio*) in virtue of which God the Son is the Son of the Father, and His being Spirit (*processio, spiratio passiva*), in virtue of which God is the Spirit of the Father and of the Son. The fourth relation, logically possible and also actually existing, the active relationship of Father and Son to the Spirit, therefore cannot constitute a fourth hypostasis, because between it and the first and second hypostases there is no relative opposition, because it is rather included already in the first and second hypostases, because *spirare* belongs to the full concept of Father and Son. *Spiratio convenit et personae Patris et personae Filii, utpote nullam habens oppositionem relativam nec ad paternitatem nec ad filiationem* (Thomas Aquinas, *S. Theol.* 1 qu. 30 art. 2 c.; cf. J. Pohle, *Lehrb. d. Dogmatik*, vol. I 1902 p. 329; B. Bartmann *op cit.* p. 211). These three relations as such are the divine Persons, explains Thomas (*paternitas est persona Patris, filiatio persona Filii, processio persona Spiritus sancti procedentis, ib. art.* 2 *ad* 1) and with him the entire newer Catholic dogmatics. The matter which is designated by the concept of Person, so explains M. Scheeben (*op. cit.* p. 834) although formally the concept of Person has no relative significance, is a subsisting relation, or substance in a definite relation. " The divine Persons in themselves are nothing else than subsistent relations " (J. Pohle, *op. cit.* p. 328). " The trinitarian Persons do not possess a proper subject to inhere in, but exist as *relationes subsistentes* " (B. Bartmann, *op. cit.* p. 211). A divine Person is " an intradivine relationship, in so far as it exists for itself and is completely incommunicable " (Fr. Diekamp, *op. cit.* p. 350). " The relationships . . . are . . . what makes the separate Persons into these Persons " (J. Braun, *Handlexikon d. kath. Dogm.* 1926 p. 228). Of all which, particularly of the explanation of Thomas himself, still more of those of his modern pupils we may well ask :

1. What really has become of the definition, that the Persons are *res subsistentes in natura divina* (*S. theol.* 1 qu. 30 art. 1 c.) ? Why are Catholic dogmatists silent about it ? Why do they speak only of the reality of the relations as such ? They are, of course, right; there is nothing else to be done. The duplication (or quadruplication) of the subject expressed in the *res* and *natura* must certainly be abandoned as misleading, to say the least of it.

2. If we may hold Scheeben to his declaration, that the name " Person " as little of itself expresses relativity for God as for the creatures, that formally it has no relative significance, but if on the other hand that relativity is precisely the thing that should be stated here, why hamper ourselves with the concept of Person which invariably obscures everything ? " The terminology has been fixed in such a way by ecclesiastical and theological usage, that it can no longer be discarded " (J. Pohle, *op. cit.* p. 25).

The relevance of this argument does not leap to the mind. Manifestly, in the first place, the ancient concept of Person, which is the only one in question here, has to-day become obsolete; in the second, the only possible definition of the entity in question is not for one moment a definition of this ancient concept of Person. Therefore, wherever ancient dogmatics, or Catholic dogmatics even to-day, speaks of " Persons," we prefer to call Father, Son, and Spirit in God the three individual modes of existence of the one God, consisting in their mutual relationships.

Such then is the repetition in God, the *repetitio aeternitatis in aeternitate*, by which the unity of the revealed God stands apart from everything that may otherwise be termed unity. We postpone the criticism of the separate concepts which here come in view, particularly the concepts, *paternitas, filiatio* and *processio*, for discussion in their several appropriate contexts. At this stage an answer had to be given to the general question as to the threeness in oneness, to Augustine's *quid tres* ?

It is a good thing to be quite clear that even after the answer has been given the question is still constantly being put. Attempts have always been made to give the answer at this stage. We, too, have just been making ours. We wished to give a relatively better answer than was conventionally given by means of the concept of Person. But already the fact, that ultimately we could only group the well-known elements of the concept of Person (though somewhat more sensibly, we hoped) round the concept of mode of existence, may remind us that our answer certainly cannot lodge a claim to be an absolutely better answer. The great central difficulties which in all ages have oppressed the doctrine of the Trinity at this same point, oppress us also. We, too, cannot say how an essence can be at once its own producer and in a twofold sense its own product. We, too, cannot say how an original relation of an essence should at the same time be this essence itself, in fact how three original relations should at the same time be this essence itself and yet not the same as each other, but irremovably different from each other. We, too, cannot say how the original relation of an essence should at the same time be a permanent mode of existence of this essence and how, further, the same essence, standing in two other opposed original relations should simultaneously and with equal truth and reality exist in the further two corresponding modes of existence. We, too, cannot say how far in this case three should really be one and one really be three. We, too, can only establish that in this case this must all be so, and only by expounding the Biblically attested revelation and in view of this object can we establish it. No single one of the concepts applied, call it essence or mode of existence or original relation, be it the numerical concept of one or the numerical concept of three, can here express adequately what it should express, what we want to express by it in applying it.

Were we here anxious to pay heed to what these concepts can express as such, in their immanent potentiality for significance, were we anxious and able not to enter upon the hint they are supposed to give, we should only cause ourselves endless trouble. Or who could fail to be constantly faced here with the question, whether these concepts really a r e pointers for him, or whether, by clinging to their immanent potentiality for significance, he is not just letting himself in for unlimited trouble ? The axiom, *non sermoni res, sed rei sermo subjectus est*, without assimilating which no man can be a theologian, really is not and never can be a self-evident axiom. The truth of this will be obvious also and precisely here. It remains true that each of all the concepts in which we here try to express ourselves is of considerable use for what should here be expressed, only to cease obviously to be of any use, or only to be useful to the extent of pointing by its very uselessness, along with other uselessnesses of the same type, beyond itself to the problem as it is set us by Scripture. When we have said what is meant by Father, Son, and Spirit in God, we must continue, and say that we have said nothing. *Tres nescio quid* was the final answer which even Anselm could return to Augustine's query, indeed had to return. The danger we here incur with regard to all concepts as such is, however, repeated with regard to the actual object. The inadequacy of all concepts not only signifies the threatening proximity of a p h i l o s o p h i c a l c r i t i c i s m, arising from the immanent potentialities for significance contained in these concepts—that might be borne with, because ultimately as such it is incompetent. It signifies besides the threatening proximity of t h e o l o g i c a l e r r o r. We, too, cannot avoid every step of ours being exposed to danger in this very region, whether the menace comes from the tritheistic or the modalistic error, from at least the suspicion felt on either side that there is a danger of the opposite error. We, too, cannot so take a middle course, that every misunderstanding is excluded, and our " orthodoxy " is clearly assured. We, too, even in this respect can give but a r e l a - t i v e l y satisfactory answer to Augustine's question. Thus, on all sides it is provided that the *mysterium trinitatis* shall r e m a i n a mystery. There can be no talk of " rationalising," because here neither theologically nor philosophically is rationalising p o s s i b l e. In other words, neither as philosophers with a previously elucidated apparatus of concepts can we here bring the interpretation of the object to a conclusion—rather we can never get away from the fact that the decisive act of interpretation from the side of the object takes the form of elucidating a conceptual equipment radically unsuited to this object. Nor as theologians can we really insure ourselves by means of such equipment against the two opposite errors which threaten us here ; we never get away from the fact that over against a theological language which avails itself of the apparatus and is therefore uninsured, the truth creates for itself the needful assurance. Theology means taking rational trouble over the mystery. But all rational trouble over this mystery, the more serious it is, can only lead to interpreting it anew and genuinely as a mystery and making it visible as such. For that reason it is worth while to give in to this rational trouble. If we are unwilling to take the trouble, neither shall we know what we mean when we say that here we are dealing with God's mystery.

3. THREE-IN-ONENESS

In the doctrine of the Trinity our concern is with God's oneness in threeness and threeness in oneness. Past these two obviously one-sided and unsatisfactory formulations we cannot get. They are both one-sided and unsatisfactory, because in the first a slight over-emphasis on the oneness and in the second a slight over-emphasis on the threeness is inevitable. The concept " three-in-oneness " must be regarded as the conflation of both these formulæ, or rather as the indication of that conflation of the two, which we cannot attain to, and for which therefore we have no formula, but of which we can be aware only as of the inconceivable truth of the Object itself.

Three-in-oneness we say. " Threefoldness," as Luther once declared, is " a right bad German." " Threefoldness hath an odd sound." His objection to this word was obviously its tritheistic ring, reminiscent of the disagreeable *triplicitas*. Instead of that Luther wished to speak of a " three-hood in God " (*Sermon on Luke* $9^{28f.}$, 1538 W. edn. 6, 230). Yet adherence to the expression " three-in-oneness " is to be recommended, first because better than *trinitas* or τρίας, certainly also better than "threefoldness," and, of course, also better than "threehood" it gives expression to both the decisive number concepts ; secondly, because with the einig (three-in-oneness=Dreieinigkeit) it indicates, as distinguished from the word " triunity " (=Dreieinheit) which might also call for consideration, that the point about the threeness in God is, of course, oneness, but the oneness of a single being (Einsseins), which is invariably also a single becoming (Einswerden).

Yet the advantage of this concept " three-in-oneness " can never be more than the dialectical union and distinction in the mutual relation between those two, in themselves, one-sided and unsatisfactory formulæ. We see on the one hand how for the Biblical hearers and seers of revelation Father, Son, and Spirit, or however the three constituents in the Biblical revelation may be named, coincide in the knowledge and concept of the one God. And we see on the other hand that for them the source and goal of this very knowledge and concept is never in any sense a bare one, but rather the Three, however they may be named. In the movement of these two thoughts consists the advantage of the concept of three-in-oneness.

Ex uno omnia, per substantiae scilicet unitatem, et nihilominus custodiatur oikonomiae sacramentum, quae unitatem in trinitatem disponit, tres dirigens Patrem et Filium et Spiritum—tres autem non statu sed gradu, nec substantia sed forma, nec potestate sed specie—unius autem substantiae et unius status et unius potestatis, quia unus Deus, ex quo et gradus isti et formae et species in nomine Patris et Filii et Spiritus Sancti deputantur (Tertullian, *Adv. Prax.* 2).   Calvin repeatedly (e.g. *Instit.* I 13, 17) referred to a saying of Gregory Nazianzene (*Orat.* 40, 41), which in fact gives very fine expression to this dialectic of the knowledge of the three-in-one God : οὐ φθάνω τὸ ἓν νοῆσαι καὶ τοῖς τρισὶ περιλάμπωμαι· οὐ φθάνω τὰ τρία διελεῖν καὶ εἰς τὸ ἓν ἀναφέρομαι.   (*Non possum unum cogitare quin trium fulgore mox circumfundar : nec tria possum discernere quin subito ad unum referar.*)   Similarly Gregory Naz. (*Orat.* 31, 14) showed that we could only represent God's doing and willing and His essence to ourselves as one ; and then, in view of the distinct origins, it was three—not that we had to worship side by side, but to know as the object of worship.   Very beautiful also is the form in which the Trinitarian dialectic meets us in the " Preface on the All-holiest Triplicity " in the *Missale Romanum : Domine sancte, Pater omnipotens, aeterne Deus* ! *Qui cum unigenito Filio tuo et Spiritu Sancto unus es Deus, unus es Dominus : non in unius singularitate personae, sed in unius trinitate substantiae.   Quod enim de tua gloria, revelante te, credimus, hoc de Filio tuo, hoc de Spiritu sancto, sine differentia discretionis sentimus.   Ut in confessione verae sempiternaeque Deitatis et in personis proprietas et in essentia unitas et in maiestate adoretur aequalitas.*   Note how in the three-membered conclusion of this passage the *personae* and the *essentia* in God are offset by the *maiestas*, the *proprietas* and the *unitas* by the *aequalitas* (obviously equivalent to ὁμοουσία), and so an attempt is made to give a space of its own to the third member, to which Trinitarian dialectic points.

Three-in-oneness in God, therefore, necessarily also means oneness in Father, Son, and Spirit among themselves. The essence of God is indeed one, but yet the various original relations assert no sort of separations, but—where there is distinction, there is also community, a definite participation by each mode of existence in the other modes of existence, and indeed, because the modes of existence are in fact identical with the original relations, a complete participation by each mode of existence in the other modes of existence. Just as, according to the Biblical witness, in revelation the one God is only knowable in the Three, the Three only as the one God, so too none of the Three is knowable without the other Two, but each of the Three only with the other Two.

It need not, of course, be shown specially, that where in the OT and NT the question is raised of the distinction within the Trinity the emphasis from time to time upon one of God's modes of existence never in any sense asserts its separation from the others, rather throughout—think of the express pronouncements upon Father and Son in John (e.g. John 10[30.38], 14[10.11], 17[11]) or of the relation between Christ and Spirit in Paul—it is not the identity of one mode of existence with the others, but, of course, the co-presence of the others in the one, that is implicitly or explicitly asserted.

Since John of Damascus (*Ekdosis*, I 8 and 14) this view has found expression in theology in the doctrine of the *perichoresis* (*circumincessio*, passing into one another) of the divine Persons. It asserts that the divine modes of existence condition and permeate one another mutually with such perfection, that one is as invariably in the other two as the other two are in the one. This has been proved now more from the side of the unity of the divine essence, now more from the side of the original relations as such. Both are right and in fact ultimately make the same assertion. *Nec enim Pater absque Filio cognoscitur, nec sine Patre Filius invenitur. Relatio quippe ipsa vocabuli personalis personas separari vetat, quas etiam, dum non simul nominat, simul insinuat. Nemo autem audire potest unumquodque istorum nominum, in quo non intelligere cogatur et alterum (Concil. Tolet.* XI *Denz. Nr.* 281). *Propter unitatem naturalem totus Pater in Filio et Spiritu Sancto est, totus quoque Spiritus sanctus in Patre et Filio est. Nullus horum extra quemlibet ipsorum est* (Fulgentius, *De fide ad Petr.* 1). *Est et enim totus Pater in Filio et communi Spiritu et Filius in Patre et eodem Spiritu et idem Spiritus in Patre et Filio . . . Tanta igitur . . . aequalitate sese complectuntur et sunt in se invicem, ut eorum nullus alium excedere aut sine eo esse probetur* (Anselm of Canterbury, *Monol.* 59; cf. also Petr. Lomb. *Sent.* I *dist.* 19 E ; Thomas Aquinas, *S. Theol.* I *qu.* 45 *art.* 5). On the basis of this doctrine the inner life of God would appear as a kind of circular course among the three modes of existence, so that we are glad to be reminded of the inappropriateness of this figure (the result of the literal meaning of περιχώρησις), by the fact that instead of a temporal sequence the Latin Church adopted a spatial togetherness of the three Persons and so preferred to speak of a *circuminsessio* (dwelling in one another, *immanentia, inexistentia*) rather than of a *circumincessio*. One way or the other this theologoumenon—which is less far removed from the necessary basis of genuine dogmatics in Scripture than may at first sight appear—signifies at once the confirmation of the distinction between the modes of existence (none of them would be what it is—not even the Father !—apart from its coexistence with the others) and the relativisation of it (none of them exists as a special individual, all three " inexist " in one another, they exist only in common as modes of the existence of the one God and Lord who posits Himself from eternity to eternity). With considerable justification therefore J. Pohle (*Lehrb. d. Dogm.* vol. I 1902 p. 355) terms the doctrine of Perichoresis " the final total of the two chief factors under discussion," that is, of the doctrine of the *unitas in trinitate* and of the doctrine of the *trinitas in unitate*. In fact it has to be regarded as the one important form of the dialectic required to complete the concept of " three-in-oneness."

To the oneness of Father, Son, and Spirit among themselves corresponds their oneness outwardly. God's essence and His operation are not twain but one. God's operation or effect is His essence in its relation to the reality distinct from Him, whether about to be or already created. The operation of God is the essence of God, *qua* essence of Him who (*N.B.* with a free decision, grounded in His essence but not constrained by His essence) is the Revealer, Revelation, Revealedness, or the Creator, Reconciler, Redeemer. In His operation God is revealed to us. All we can know of God according to Scripture testimony is His acts. All we can assert of God, all attributes we can assign to God relate to these acts of His. And so not to His essence as such. Although the operation of God is the essence of God, it is necessary and important to distinguish His essence as such from His operation : in order to remember that this operation is a grace, a free divine decision, also to remember that we can only know about God, because and so far as He gives Himself to our knowledge. God's operation is, of course, the operation of the whole essence of God. God gives Himself to man entirely in His revelation. But not in such a way as to give Himself a prisoner to man. He remains free, in operating, in giving Himself.

On this freedom of His rests the distinction between the essence of God as such and His essence as the Operator, the Self-manifesting. On this freedom rests the inconceivability of God, the inadequacy of all knowledge of the revealed God. Even the three-in-oneness of God is revealed to us only in God's operation. Therefore the three-in-oneness of God is also inconceivable to us. Hence, too, the inadequacy of all our knowledge of the three-in-oneness. The conceivability with which it has appeared to us, primarily in Scripture, secondarily in the Church doctrine of the Trinity, is a creaturely conceivability. To the conceivability in which God exists for Himself it is not only relative : it is absolutely separate from it. Only upon the free grace of revelation does it depend that the former conceivability, in its absolute separation from its object, is yet not without truth. In this sense the three-in-oneness of God, as we know it from the operation of God, is truth. In a bridging of the gulf (taking place from God's side) between divine and human conceivability, the event takes place that within the sphere and limits of human conceivability there is a true knowing of the essence of God at all, and so also of the three-in-oneness. Within this sphere and within these limits revelation takes place. Otherwise how could it be revelation if this sphere were merely our sphere ? How should we realise the three-in-oneness otherwise than within this sphere and within these limits ? Revelation, of course, goes bail for its truth solely as being God's step towards us. As surely can we not go bail for it, as on our side we are not able to take the step across the gulf. We can only let it be guaranteed to us. Nor should we be astonished at the inconceivability in which it persists for us after becoming conceivable to us. Nor should we confuse our conceiving with its truth as allotted and appropriate to us, with the truth of the three-in-oneness itself, from which for us by the grace of God it comes to our conceiving, itself actual in a truth appropriate and allotted to us. It is therefore legitimate for us, on the basis of a revelation which takes place within the sphere and within the limits of human conceivability, to distinguish the three modes of existence of the one God.

God's revelation attested in Scripture forces us to this distinction. Scripture itself speaks continually in terms of these distinctions, and in all seriousness, i.e. in such a way that we are not in a position to do away with these distinctions without exegetical violence. It shows us God in His operation as Revealer, Revelation, and Revealedness, or as Creator, Reconciler, and Redeemer, or as Holiness, Mercy, and Loving-Kindness. In these distinctions we can and should become aware of the distinctions in the divine modes of existence in terms of the truth allotted and appropriate to us. The limit of our conception lies in the fact that in conceiving these distinctions we do not conceive the distinctions in the divine modes of existence. These do not consist of such distinctions in the acts or attributes of God. If that were our assumption, we should be assuming three gods or a tripartite essence of God. God's operation would then be a strange combination of three divine truths or powers or even individuals. Thus we must believe that those distinctions in the operation of God really take place within the sphere and limits of our conceivability, but that even here they neither properly nor primarily signify the last word in the hidden essence of God, that in these distinctions cannot rest the distinctions in God Himself.

But why should they not call our attention to the, to us, inconceivable distinctions in God Himself, to those distinctions which rest upon the various ways in which God posits Himself in the secrecy of His Godhead, is His own origin ? Why should not the conceivable distinctions in God's revelation in their utter preliminariness face us with the problem of His inconceivable and eternal distinctions ? We must at least say that they may be regarded as fit and proper to give us this hint. There is an analogy—we here recall our exposition of the doctrine of relations in this respect—between the concepts Father, Son, and Spirit and the various other formulations of the triad in revelation, on the one hand, and on the other hand the three divine modes of being that consist in the various original relations, in which we have known the truly inconceivable, eternal distinctions in God. In these analogies (not, like the so-called *vestigia trinitatis*, present in the world but set up in the world by revelation) by which the mystery is not as it were delivered and solved but just signified, and signified precisely as a mystery, we have the truth of the three-in-oneness appointed and appropriate for us. We shall not overestimate this truth. If we did that, if we confused the analogy with the thing itself, equated the distinctions conceivable by us with those inconceivable by us ; in other words, if we thought we had conceived the essence of God in conceiving His operation, we should be standing forthwith right in the error of tritheism. But why should we therefore underestimate that truth ? Why should we not, recognising the unattainability of the thing itself, let it stand as a hint about the thing itself ? *Abusus non tollit usum* : why not use this hint as it is intended to be used, as the creation and gift of revelation ?

In the language of the old dogmatics, what has to be said about this positive relation between Father, Son, and Spirit in God's operation and Father, Son, and Spirit in God's essence is called the doctrine of appropriations (attributions, assignments). By special attribution of a word or deed to this or that Person of the Godhead there should be brought to our consciousness, according to the teaching of Leo the Great (*Sermo* 76, 2), the truth of the three-in-oneness, which in its operation is actually undistributed and yet exists in the three Persons. *Ob hoc enim quaedam sive sub Patris, sive sub Filii, sive sub Spiritus sancti appellatione promuntur, ut confessio fidelium in trinitate non erret : quae cum sit inseparabilis, nunquam intelligeretur esse trinitas, si semper inseparabiliter diceretur. Bene ergo ipsa difficultas loquendi cor nostrum ad intelligentiam trahit et per infirmitatem nostram coelestis doctrina nos adiuvat.* Augustine (*De doctr. chr.* I 5) appropriated *unitas* to the Father, *aequalitas* to the Son, *connexio* to the Spirit. Thomas Aquinas, *potentia* to the Father, *sapientia* to the Son, *bonitas* to the Spirit (*S. theol.* I *qu.* 45 *art.* 6 *ad.* 2). Bonaventura (*Breviloq.* I 6) has a host of appropriations, partly taken over from older sources, partly indicated by himself: unity to

the Father, truth to the Son, loving-kindness to the Holy Spirit ; or eternity
to the Father, appearance (*species*) to the Son, event (*usus, fruitio*) to the
Spirit ; or principle to the Father, exposition to the Son, consummation to
the Spirit ; or all-power to the Father, all-knowledge to the Son, goodwill
to the Spirit. A peculiarly characteristic Biblical appropriation has always
been found in the ἐξ αὐτοῦ, δι' αὐτοῦ, εἰς αὐτόν of Rom. 11[36]. Naturally also
we have an appropriation before us, when in Luther's Catechism the concepts Father and creation, Son and redemption, Holy Spirit and sanctification
are brought into the well-known close relation to one another; whereupon
it must, of course, be noted how Luther himself, when he comes to speak of
the Trinity, never fails to indicate the real unity of the apparently—and yet
not only apparently but in their own way genuinely—threefold pronouncements about the operation of God. Naturally, too, the ternary preferred by
Calvin, who is manifestly borrowing from the great Mediæval tradition, is
an appropriation, *principium, sapientia, virtus.*

The clearest and most complete definition of appropriation has been
given by Thomas Aquinas: *appropriare nihil est aliud quam commune
trahere ad proprium . . . non . . . ex hoc quod magis unae personae quam
alii conveniat . . . sed ex hoc quod id quod est commune, maiorem habet similitudinem ad id quod est proprium personae unius quam cum proprio alterius*
(*De verit qu. 7 art. 3 cf. S. Theol. I qu. 39 art. 7–8*). The two rules to be considered here in the sense of this definition, run as follows according to the
directions of Catholic dogmaticians (cf. e.g. B. Bartmann, *Lehrb. d. Dogm.*
7th edn. vol. I 1928 p. 215) :

1. The appropriation must not be arbitrary, but must take place
intelligently. Not each and every triad, however sensible in itself, is suitable
for signifying even truthfully the mystery of the three-in-oneness. There
must exist manifestly a connection, a similarity, an analogy between the
three things signifying and the three signified, as there manifestly exists
one between Father, Son, and Spirit on the one hand and the three original
relations on the other. Lacking this the appropriation lacks significance.

And 2, the appropriation must not be exclusive. By the appropriation
of this or that attribute or act of God to this or that mode of existence there
must not be created any property for this mode of existence, any distinction
that is constitutive for this mode of existence. What is appropriated belongs
in fact to all the modes of existence, and the real distinction between the
modes of existence cannot really be achieved by any appropriation, in the
last resort not even by the designations Father, Son, and Spirit.

Evangelical dogmatics will have to add as a third and decisive rule, that
appropriations must not be invented freely. They are genuine when taken
literally or substantially or both from Holy Scripture, when they are a rendering, or interpretation, of the appropriations already found there. If they are
this, they will certainly also be neither arbitrary nor exclusive.

The position reached as to the conceivability of the Father,
the Son, and the Spirit in God's operation clearly requires—we are
now inquiring into the oneness of the three modes of existence
externally as well—a dialectical counterpart. Already it has
always been visible on the periphery of what has hitherto been
said, but it must now be emphasised, that also and precisely in the

operation of God, also and precisely in God's entry into the sphere of the creature and so into the sphere and limits of our conceivability, God in His eternal truth and God also in the truth appointed and appropriate to us is one. It were heathen mythology to picture the operation of God in the form of a (so to speak) dramatic appearance and withdrawal of now this, now that one of the divine Persons, of an up-and-down surge of half or completely individualised powers or forms or ideas, of a varying coexistence and rivalry of the three hypostases. Once more the boundary does not admit of being unambiguously and universally indicated, as between permitted and enjoined " appropriation " and this forbidden mythology. The one may here often bear a confusing resemblance to the other. But the boundary is drawn : to the involution and convolution of the three modes of existence in the essence of God there corresponds most completely their involution and convolution (*Ineinander und Miteinander*) in His operation. That now in this act or attribute, indelibly and characteristically opposed to the others He becomes specially visible, now in this or that mode of existence, may not and should not mean that we had not also to believe in and worship God in His other modes of existence, which for the time are hidden. As surely as Scripture is meant to be read in its context as the witness to God's revelation, as surely as e.g. Good Friday, Easter, and Pentecost merely unite in asserting what they should assert, so surely we must declare that all God's operation, as we are bound to conceive it on the basis of His revelation, is a single act, occurring simultaneously and unitedly in all His three modes of existence. Of creation, past revelation and reconciliation, to the redemption to come it holds good, that He who here acts is the Father and the Son and the Spirit. And of all perfections to be asserted in view of this action by God it holds good, that they are as much the perfections of the Father as of the Son, or of the Spirit. *Per appropriationem* now this act, now that attribute in respect of this or that mode of existence must be brought to the forefront, to make it possible to designate it as such at all. But it is only *per appropriationem* that this may be done, and therefore never through forgetting or denying the presence of God in all His modes of existence, in His complete being and action even over against us.

The rule for theologising on the Trinity, *opera trinitatis ad extra sunt indivisa*, is first found, not literally, of course, but substantially, in Augustine : *Sicut inseparabiles sunt, ita inseparabiliter operantur* (*De trin.*

I 4). *Ad creaturam Pater et Filius et Spiritus sanctus unum principium, sicut unus creator et unus dominus (ib.* V 14). For : *non potest operatio esse divina ubi non solum aequalis est, verum etiam indiscreta natura (C. Adrian.* 15). In the dogma of the Catholic Church this view has found most pointed expression in the statement of the *Conc. Florent.* 1441 *(Denz. Nr.* 704) *Pater et Filius et Spiritus sanctus non tria principia creaturae, sed unum principium.* Let us recall here once more the emphasis with which L u t h e r supported this very truth. We shall have to say of it, no less than of the doctrine of perichoresis, that it is to a certain extent the proof or test of the sum, in view of the opposed series of propositions about the *unitas in trinitate* and the *trinitas in unitate.* Together with the doctrine of appropriations it constitutes the other form of the dialectical completion of the concept of three-in-oneness.

4. THE MEANING OF THE DOCTRINE OF THE TRINITY

By the doctrine of the Trinity we understand the Church doctrine concerning the oneness of God in the three modes of existence of Father, Son, and Holy Spirit, or concerning the three-fold otherness of the one God in the modes of existence of Father, Son, and Holy Spirit. All that had, and still needs, to be expounded here in detail, could and can only be an exposition of the oneness in threeness and the threeness in oneness of God. As such this doctrine is not to be found in the texts of the Old and New Testament witness to God's revelation. It did not arise out of the historical situations to which these texts belong. It is the exegesis of these texts in the language, which means also in the light, of the questions arising out of a later situation. It belongs to the Church. It is a theologoumenon. It is a dogma. We have inquired (§ 8, 2) into its root, i.e. into the possibility on the basis of which it could become dogma in a Church which wished to regulate its doctrine by the Biblical witness. And we saw that its possibility consists in the fact that in the Bible revelation signifies the self-unveiling, imparted to men, of a God who according to His essence cannot be unveiled to man. This content according to the Biblical witness is of such a nature, that in view of the three elements of the veiling, unveiling, and impartation of God, we have cause to speak of a threefold otherness of the one God, who according to the witness of the Bible has revealed Himself. The Biblical witness to God's revelation faces us with the possibility of interpreting the one proposition, " God reveals Himself as the Lord," three times in a different sense. This possibility is the Biblical root of the doctrine of the Trinity. But in the Bible it remains on the level of possibility. We now ask what it would mean to actualise it, what need and what right the Church had to formulate this doctrine. She could do so. But had she to ? What insight has she expressed in this dogma, and what reason have we therefore to be at pains to understand it ?

Obviously there can be no sense in discussing this question if the Church of earlier days, which framed this theologoumenon and exalted it to a dogma, has become alien to us, to such a degree that we can view her and her achievements in thought only historically, i.e. in this case, externally, as an alien so far as we are concerned, without really thinking her thoughts along with her, and can only estimate them one way or the other in the light of their intentions.

That e.g. would be the case, if we could not rise above the reflection that, in the discussions before and after Nicæa, very undogmatic antagonisms, namely, of ecclesiastical and civil politics, of courts, provinces, and certainly of economics as well, had also played a very considerable part. Or could not rise above the reflection that the framing of the doctrine of the Trinity had simply been also a bit of history of philosophy in late antiquity, an offshoot of Stoico-Neoplatonic Logos-speculation. Or, with the historians and systematic writers of the school of A. Ritschl, could not rise above the reflection that the belief in revelation held by the Christian world in which this dogma arose was for us shrouded beyond recognition in the vapour of an ancient mystery religion fed upon all possible Orientalisms, was imbedded in a predominatingly physical attitude towards the salvation revealed, in a predominantly cosmic interest in the knowledge of revelation, in a piety with a predominantly sacramental trend, with which we could not really identify ourselves, the validity of which we should have to call seriously in question, from the side of the Reformation rather than from that of the NT. If considerations of this sort—and in addition, perhaps, a mere feeling of reverence for a form consecrated by its age—were to claim the last word in matters of our participation in the origin of this dogma, what else would that mean but just this, that those events and with them their result, the dogma, and in addition all later work attempted along the lines of this dogma, would be fundamentally alien to us. We should be confronting the capital issue as to the intention of the dogma, namely, Christian knowledge of God, with the deep suspicion if not with the actual certainty, that there was nothing in it, or rather that it was merely Byzantine politics talking, merely the Stoa and Neoplatonism, merely the piety of an ancient mystery cult. In that case any discussion as to the meaning of the doctrine of the Trinity could only emanate from the aloof temper of an astonished and disapproving onlooker, and in the end might just as well be dropped.

We must be quite clear that, if we adopt such an attitude towards the Church of that early period, we credit her with having, so to speak, lost her theme, so that in what she really aimed to be, namely, the Church of Jesus Christ, she need no longer be taken seriously, that her work is therefore no concern of ours, save as an object of such observation from without. By estimating her as at worst we should try to estimate a heresy or an alien religion, we naturally cannot make any serious inquiry, i.e. in sympathy with her, into the meaning of her intention. But still further we must be quite clear that this is an exceedingly risky and dangerous verdict. Risky because we thereby declare the Church of that early period to be substantially a heresy or an alien religion, a judgment which, formally, is indeed not impossible, but at least involves a great responsibility, especially when, as here, there is in question the line of history of dogma, along which, ever since the great and decisive struggles of the 4th century, all Church theologians of any importance, including the Reformers and their successors in the 17th century, have unswervingly advanced. And such a verdict might be dangerous, because if in the Church a man is determined to look upon and regard others in this purely external fashion, he must submit to the interrogatory as to whether on the contrary he himself is not perhaps the outsider, as being the adherent of a heresy or of an alien religion. At all events it might be more normal and safer at least to start with the presupposition that the Church of the early period, more especially the Church of this early period, is one and the same with the Church we know and which we like to call the Church ; that there is therefore sense in asking seriously, i.e. asking along with her, what she intended by this dogma. The assumption that Jesus Christ did not quite abandon His Church at this time, and that therefore in spite of all that might perhaps rightly be said against her, it would be in place to listen to her, as we listen to the Church—this assumption might in any case have a very definite advantage over the opposite one. The reasons would in every instance have to be very weighty if one were to be forced to resolve really to let drop, as it were, the Church of any period, and to give place to such discussion and judgment from without, to a listening to her voice which was no longer serious. Are the reasons in favour of such a course so cogent in the case of the Church's early period during which the doctrine of the Trinity took its rise ?

Profane motives of every kind have, in the history of dogma and theology of all periods, those of Protestantism certainly not excluded, played a part that went to obscure everything else. In spite of the disgraceful delight with which it was done, it was a good thing that the writing of Church History by Pietism and the Enlightenment so incontrovertibly established the position, that the history of the Church, even in such mighty times of decision as that in which the doctrine of the Trinity arose, was anything but

28

a history of heroes and saints. But in that case we should be just and sensible and say to ourselves that not only the Church of Byzantium, but also that of Wittenberg and Geneva, and in a word even the purest Church of the Quietest in the Land, when examined at close range, have always and everywhere been abodes of frailties and scandals of every sort, and that at all events on the basis of the Reformers' doctrine of justification it is unseemly and not worth while to play off the worldliness of the Church against the serious import of what she knows, a knowledge gained perhaps in spite of and in the midst of this worldliness. The same must be said of the undoubtedly existent connections of dogma with the philosophy of that period. By proving philosophical limitations we can entrench ourselves against the confessions and the theology of any period and any school, the more effectually the less we see the beam in our own eye. As regards terminology, theologians have always lived by some sort of philosophy, and in that respect they always will. But instead of getting into a Pharisaic froth about it and consigning whole periods to the Hades of a philosophy accused of denying the Gospel—only because one's own philosophy is different!—it were better to canvass the question, and in strictness that question alone, as to what the theologians of the early period really meant to assert in the language of their philosophy. And the first thing really to be cautious about is when we insist on the differences in the so-called piety of the various periods, and hold it against the dogma of the Trinity, that the piety from which it arose is so utterly different—as people said, e.g. thirty years ago—from our own, so soberly focussed upon " world-view and morality." Who gives us the right to consider our own " piety "—even if its agreement with the Reformation and with the NT did appear ever so impeccable—the only one possible in the Church, and to exalt it into a standard by which to measure the attainments of past periods ? Let us be sure of our cause as far as we can. But antithetical hostilities of attitude, especially in forming an opinion on the subjective " religion " of others, should be a thing against which one can only issue a warning.

The possible grounds for an attitude towards the Church of the 4th century particularly, and so also towards her dogma, so mistrustful as to lead to dropping the question of its meaning, seem to us to be unconvincing.

But it is clear that if any one wishes to assert them we cannot meet them with counter-arguments. The formal possibility, that that Church might be an apostate Church which does not concern us and has nothing to say to us, cannot be contested. If we actually deny this possibility, that, as in all analogous cases, is a decision of faith or, we might say with greater caution, a decision which might regard itself as a decision of faith, which can only have meaning as a decision of faith, a decision for the rightness of which we can, ultimately, only appeal to the dogma itself and to Holy Scripture confronting the dogma, with the question whether, for all the undeniable and ineradicable limitations of its origin, it does not express a view to which a Church with an ear for Holy Scripture not only could come, but must come at a definite time. Whether by letting Scripture and dogma speak for themselves, we can escape being convinced, that here divine truth has received a human formulation in a way in which it had to be formulated some time, and in such a way that this formulation, once made, can never be lost or forgotten again ? Whether there did not then arise— what is certainly exegesis and therefore not infallible revelation, but still and for the time being exegesis that can always confidently be described as not merely correct but also as important ? And if we answer this question in the affirmative, if we thus admit the possibility of regarding ourselves as being in the same sphere as the Church of the past which knew and confessed this dogma as such, i.e. as being the same Church as herself, if then we inquire as to the meaning of the doctrine of the Trinity, that does not signify merely an accidental personal decision. We ought to take account of the fact that to this day this decision is not just that of the Roman and the Orthodox Churches, but is fundamentally also that of all great Evangelical Churches.

Not one of them has actually revoked what is implied in the fact that an express confirmation of the ancient Church symbols which give expression to the dogma of the Trinity was in the 16th century made an integral part of the Reformed Confessions. The reading at services of the so-called " Apostles' Creed," as is customary in the Prussian and other provincial Churches, repeats in its own fashion this significant event. And at least we are faced with the problem of the doctrine of the Trinity, every time baptism is validly administered in our Churches.

No one can say that he knows, and no one is entitled to declare, that it is merely a pious feeling for an old and honourable landmark of Christendom, which even in the Evangelical Church, ravaged as it is by modernism, still in fact contrives a modicum of space for the doctrine of the Trinity in more or less clear form. This fact also gives us the external right, in fact it faces us with the task, of asking here for a reason.

Our proper starting-point should be, that the origin of the doctrine of the Trinity, however varied the motives which may have contributed thereto, was at least conditioned by the need to clear up a question with which the Church saw herself confronted in the delivery of her message by Holy Scripture itself. On the supposition that the Church was not only unfaithful to her essence, as, of course, was actually the case at all times, but in a certain measure and sense also faithful to it, and therefore by her proclamation intended to take up the witness of the Old and

New Testaments, it can occasion no surprise that she came up against the question which found its answer in the doctrine of the Trinity. Neither should it occasion surprise that in such a relatively early period she came up against this question in particular ; nor need there be surprise at the strenuousness of the conflicts into which she was hurled by this question, or at the inexorability with which, the centuries through, she has adhered to the broad lines of the answer then achieved. The question which arose for her out of the fact that her proclamation was bound to Scripture and to which she replied in the doctrine of the Trinity, was actually a basic question, a life question of first rank for Church preaching and therefore likewise for Church theology. For that reason we consider it right to put the discussion of this doctrine in the forefront of all dogmatics : a practical exposition of what was held in theory from earliest days by many regarding its significance.

But the question answered by the doctrine of the Trinity is a definite question regarding the fundamental concept, or the fundamental fact attested in Scripture, of the revelation of God.

Even if it be regarded as a mere offshoot from the Logos-speculation of late antiquity, it would at all events have to be conceded that at least the occasion of it is the appearance of Jesus Christ, viewed as the revelation of the Logos. Its aim is to discuss the divinity of this revealed, incarnate Logos. Its second object—the concept of the Spirit—in that case points likewise in the same direction. And when it speaks of the Father, it is dealing with the point of origin and relation of these two, the Son and the Spirit.

But the definite question regarding revelation answered by the doctrine of the Trinity is the question who it is that reveals Himself, the question as to the Subject of revelation. The meaning of the doctrine of the Trinity may be summed up briefly and simply by saying that its answer, strict and logical, to this question is, that He who reveals Himself is God. But if this meaning of it is to be completely obvious, the same statement must be emphasised in the reversed order also, that He who reveals Himself is God. For the strictness and logic of the answer to the question about the Subject of revelation consists precisely in the fact, that in our inquiry into the interpretation of this answer we at once see ourselves referred back again to revelation itself. The Church doctrine of the Trinity is a self-enclosed circle. Its predominant and decisive interest consists in stating adequately and completely that the Revealer is God. But how could it state precisely that with adequacy and completeness without thereby announcing that none other than the Revealer is God ? It might be put more simply by saying that the doctrine of the Trinity states that our God—namely, He who makes Himself ours in His revelation—is really God. And to the question, But who is God? it would be equally simple to reply, Just this God of ours. Is it not the case that the former principal answer together with the latter subordinate one are the presuppositions, as simple as they are in the highest degree momentous, of all Christian thought and language about God? The first and last criterion of Christian proclamation is, whether it moves in the circle described by these two answers. Christian theology can signify nothing else than exercise in this movement. The question, not solved but put with its full force in the Bible itself, as to the Subject of revelation and hence of all action by God on man, had indeed to be answered. Is not the haste understandable, with which men felt called to answer it, and the certainly uncanny zeal with which they set to the task? And this just because it involved such a simple but also such a central problem? And could this question be answered otherwise than thus? Or is this problem somehow not set in the Bible? Or could it be answered any otherwise than it has been answered in the doctrine of the Trinity?

The problem pointing to the Church doctrine of the Trinity, which we imagine we see set us in the Bible, consists in the fact that there the being, language, and action, and therefore the self-revelation of God is described throughout by the moments of His self-veiling or His self-unveiling or His self-impartation to man, that His characteristic attributes are holiness, mercy, and love, that His characteristic proofs in the NT are indicated by Good Friday, Easter, and Pentecost, and accordingly His name indicated as that of the Father, the Son, and the Holy Spirit. The Bible lacks the express declaration that the Father, the Son, and the Holy Spirit are of equal essence and therefore in an equal sense God Himself. And the other express declaration is also lacking, that God is God thus and only thus, i.e. as the Father, the Son, and the Holy Spirit. These two express declarations, which go beyond the witness of the Bible, are the twofold content of the Church doctrine of the Trinity.

The doctrine of the Trinity means on the one hand, as the denial of subordinationism, the express statement that the three moments do not mean a more and a less in the Godness of God. The Father is not to be regarded as the proper God as distinguished from the Son and from the Spirit, and Son and Spirit are not, as distinguished from the Father, favoured and glorified creatures, powers of life aroused and set in motion by God, and as such and in this sense revealers. But it is God who reveals Himself in a like manner as the Father in His self-veiling and holiness, as He does as the Son in His self-unveiling and mercy, and as the Spirit in His self-impartation and love. Father, Son, and Spirit are the one, single, and equal God. The Subject of revelation attested by the Bible, of whatever nature His being, language, and action may be, is the one Lord, not a half-god, either descended or ascended. Communion with Him who reveals Himself there means for man, in every case and under all circumstances, that He confronts him as a Thou confronts an I, and unites with him as a Thou unites with an I. Not otherwise ! All communion with this God is barred, of the kind of communion we might have with creatures, such that the Thou can be changed by the I into an It or a He, over which or whom the I thereby acquires powers of disposal. Also and precisely as Son and as Spirit, He who reveals Himself according to the witness of Scripture is not an It nor a He ; He remains Thou. And by remaining Thou He remains the Lord. The Subject of revelation is the Subject that remains indissolubly Subject. We cannot get behind this Subject. It cannot become an object. All subordinationism rests upon the design of making out of Him who there reveals Himself such a subject as we ourselves are, a creature whose "thouness" has its limits which can be reviewed, conceived, and controlled, which can be objectified, over against which one's ego can be asserted. Note well ; even the Father, supposedly thought of as the Creator, is, according to subordinationist doctrine, actually drawn into the creaturely area. According to this doctrine He is related to Son and Spirit as idea to phenomenon. Though actually standing in this commanding position, even He betrays Himself as an entity to be concocted and controlled by the I. In the last resort subordinationism means the denial of revelation, the incorporation of the divine subjectivity into the human and—*via* polytheism —the loneliness of man with himself, in his own world, in which ultimately there is no Thou and therefore no Lord. It was this possibility that the Church was striking at when she rejected Arius and every form of subordinationism. Our question is : did she do well in this, or not ?

But on the other hand the doctrine of the Trinity means, as the denial of modalism, the expressed declaration that those three elements are not foreign to the Godness of God. The relationship is not that we should have to seek the proper God beyond these three elements, in a higher being in which He was not the Father, the Son, and the Spirit. The revelation of God, and therefore His being as Father, Son, and Spirit, is not an economy foreign to His essence, limited as it were from above or from within, so that we should have to inquire about the hidden Fourth, in order really to inquire about God. But if we inquire about God, we can only inquire about Him who reveals Himself. It is He who according to the witness of Scripture exists, speaks, and acts as Father, Son, and Spirit, in self-veiling and self-unveiling and self-impartation, in holiness, mercy, and love, it is this and no other, who is God. Communion with God means for man, strictly and exclusively, communion with Him who reveals Himself, who is Subject in His revelation, and indissolubly Subject at that. It is this indissolubility of subjectivity that is guaranteed by the knowledge of the final reality of the three modes of existence in the essence of God, above or behind which there is no higher. Here is barred all communion with God which might signify an escape from His revelation, an over-stepping of the reality in which He shows and gives Himself. God is completely the person He purports to be in His manifestation and gift of Himself to us. To hasten past Him who addresses us as Thou in a threefold confrontation according to the Biblical witness, can only be to hasten into the void. Modalism in the last resort means the denial of God. Our God and only our God, the God, that is, who makes Himself ours in His revelation, is God. To relativise this God, as is done in the doctrine of the real God beyond this manifest God, is to relativise, i.e. to deny, the one real God. Here also the Thou, the Lord, drops out. Here also man obviously wants to get behind God, behind God as He really shows and gives Himself, and therefore behind what He is ; for the two things are the same. Here also, therefore, it is a matter of making God an object. Here also the divine subjectivity is absorbed by the human, inquiring after a God who does not exist. Here also man finds himself, this time *via* mysticism, alone with himself in the end, in his own world. This possibility, coinciding with the first one at its root and at its top, the Church wished to guard against, when she rejected Sabellius and all forms of modalism. And again we ask : are we to think that she did not do well in this ?

The doctrine of the Trinity declares—and that is the positive point it stands up for on its fighting front—that and how far He who reveals Himself to man according to the witness of Scripture can be our G o d, that and how far He can be o u r God. He can be our G o d, because He is equal to Himself in all His modes of exist-ence, is one and the same Lord. Knowledge of revelation as it may arise on the witness of Scripture, means, in terms of the doctrine of the Trinity, in all elements of the event to which this witness points us, knowledge of the Lord as Him who meets us and unites us to Himself. And this Lord can be o u r God, He can meet us and unite us to Himself, because He is God in these three modes of existence as Father, Son, and Spirit, because creation, reconcilia-tion, redemption, the entire being, language, and action in which He wills to be our God, is grounded and typified in His own essence, in His Godness itself. As Father, Son, and Spirit God is, so to speak, ours in advance. Thus the doctrine of the Trinity tells us the two things, that He who reveals Himself according to Scripture is to be feared and loved; to be f e a r e d because He can be God, to be l o v e d because He can be our God. That He i s both, the doctrine of the Trinity as such cannot tell us. No dogma, no theology as such can do that. The doctrine of the Trinity as such is not the Word of God, which might tell us that. But if there is a service of the Word of God, a proclamation which may become the Word of God, and a service of this service, namely, dogmatics, as critical reflection on the proper content of proclamation, then naturally the question of the Subject of revelation, to which the doctrine of the Trinity is the answer, should be the first step in such reflection. Scripture, in which the problem of the doctrine of the Trinity is set, is and remains the measure and the judge of the solution of this problem. It stands above the dogma of the Church, and therefore above the critical reflection to which we let ourselves be led by the dogma of the Church. But, everything considered, we venture to maintain, pending better instruction, that this leading is a suitable one.

GOD THE FATHER

The one God reveals Himself according to Scripture as the Creator, that is, as the Lord of our existence. As such He is God our Father, because as the Father of God the Son He is so antecedently in Himself.

1. GOD AS THE CREATOR

In the event described by the Bible as revelation, God deals as the Lord with man. Not as a being of the kind and order to which man himself belongs, and so not as a being of which man on his own part might equally well be lord. Nor yet as a being who exists and remains for Himself in His own kind and order. These are the two errors, the two lies about God, which it is the function of revelation to remove. He acts as the Lord, i.e. as the authority utterly superior to man, in distinction from all other authorities ; an authority which none the less, with all this utter superiority, literally concerns him and claims him. To say that God reveals Himself, i.e. that He deals as the Lord with man, is not equivalent to saying that God has and uses power over man. Power is, of course, the presupposition and medium of lordship. We are speaking of lordship, where one person brings himself before the consciousness of another, an I before a Thou, as the bearer of power, where a superior will makes known its power. That is what takes place in the event described in the Bible as revelation. Hence the prevailing name for God, *Yahweh* in the OT and *Kyrios* in the NT.

But who is the Lord, and therefore the God, who is spoken of there ? As we already saw, it is characteristic of the Bible in both Testaments, that primarily its answer to this question points

¹ [Deliberately in the sections on the Trinity no capitals have been used for pronouns and some nouns denoting Jesus Christ and the Holy Spirit (save in a few noticeable instances), so that the reader may at once know which "Person" of the Trinity is intended, where two (or three) are being spoken of.—Tr.]

us first of all not to a region beyond human history, but to the midst of this history itself.

At the climax of the Biblical witness the answer is to the effect that Jesus of Nazareth is the Lord. He it is who approaches man in utter superiority. He is the self-revealing God. In the next section we return to this confession, so significant for the whole form and the whole content of the Biblical witness, and so decisive as the presupposition of the Christian Church.

Even in the NT the answer that Jesus of Nazareth is the Lord, is by no means to be taken for granted ; neither did it become so in the Church, nor will it ever do so. Why not ? If this Jesus of Nazareth was a true and real man, the answer obviously includes an inequation. At best it must become realisable as an equation. True and real divinity, as expressed in the predicate *Kyrios*, the NT already ascribes in the first instance to a completely Other than Jesus.

In the name Christ which it applies to Jesus, it recalls the prophets, priests, and kings of the OT as the authorised and sanctified men of *Yahweh*, behind whom and over whom stands He who has primarily and properly authority and sanctity. It calls Jesus the Word or the Son of God, the Sent of God into the world to be the life and light of men. It regards Jesus' dignity, Jesus' lordship, Jesus' superiority as fundamentally other and subordinate compared with that of the Other, who is properly called θεός. In the so-called Synoptics this mode of treatment seems quite particularly to hold the foreground. It strikes almost like a false note, at least as a puzzle, when, here above all, Jesus is also called *Kyrios*. For what else is Jesus here than a single indication of the Lord, Whose kingdom (not his own !) Jesus announces, proclaims by words and deeds, in form and matter hardly very differently from John the Baptist, over against Whom, the " One good " (Mark 10¹⁸), Jesus includes himself with his disciples in the address, Our Father !, Whose will he most definitely distinguishes even from his own will (Mark 14³⁶), to Whom, as is repeatedly emphasised, he prays, obedience to Whom ultimately appears to be the whole meaning of his calling and work. Therefore an apparently ancient but, in the literature of the 2nd century, very respectable layer of tradition (Matt. 12¹⁸ ; Acts 3¹³·²⁶, 4²⁷·³⁰) calls him the (ἅγιος) παῖς of God, like David and the Servant of God of Isa. 53. How could this Jesus be more emphatically put at a distance and distinguished from Him who is really called God, than by there being put into his mouth the doubly disconcerting *Eli, Eli, lama azabhtani* ! (Mark 15³⁴) ? He who here, in the Synoptics, is really called God, seems undoubtedly to be the " Father in heaven," who constitutes the background, and, in so doing, with incomparable significance, the meaning-ground, of the event narrated. But even in John there not only stands the much-noted " The Father is greater than I " (John 14²⁸), but usually Jesus explains himself as the emissary of the Father (the μόνος ἀληθινὸς θεός, John 17³ !), who lives to do the Father's will, to speak His words, to finish His work, whose triumph consists simply in his " going to the Father," and " through " whom men come to the Father (John 14⁶). With regard to all the Gospels, the Fourth included, A. von Harnack was right in saying of Jesus ; " Aim, power, insight, result, and stern inevitability—everything comes to him from the Father. Thus it stands in the Gospels : there nothing can be turned or twisted " (*Wesen d. Christentums*, 51st thousand, 1906 p. 80). And so, too, Paul is never weary of pointing, alongside of Jesus and in a certain sense past Jesus and above him, to the Father, the " Father of Jesus Christ." The form of greeting in nearly all his letters runs : Χάρις ὑμῖν καὶ εἰρήνη ἀπὸ θεοῦ πατρὸς ἡμῶν καὶ κυρίου Ἰησοῦ Χριστοῦ. Is it that " God our Father " is thereby expressly designated the Father of our Lord Jesus Christ as well ? According to Eph. 1¹⁷, where He is called ὁ θεὸς τοῦ Κυρίου ἡμῶν Ἰησοῦ Χριστοῦ, ὁ πατὴρ τῆς δόξης, this might undoubtedly be the case. Or do the two entities θεὸς πατήρ and κύριος Ἰησοῦς Χριστός, as is assumed in the translation of the Vulgate and of Luther, stand together as the common source of grace and peace ? Certain it is that the κύριος Ἰησοῦς Χριστός is distinguished from the Θεὸς πατήρ and placed after Him ; ἡμῖν εἷς Θεὸς ὁ πατήρ . . . καὶ εἷς κύριος Ἰησοῦς Χριστός (1 Cor. 8⁶). Ὑμεῖς δὲ Χριστοῦ, Χριστὸς δὲ Θεοῦ (1 Cor. 3²³). Ἀνδρὸς ἡ κεφαλὴ ὁ Χριστός ἐστιν . . . κεφαλὴ δὲ τοῦ Χριστοῦ ὁ Θεός (1 Cor. 11³). Jesus Christ is κύριος εἰς δόξαν θεοῦ πατρός (Phil. 2¹¹). He is the προσαγωγὴ πρὸς τὸν θεόν (Eph. 2¹⁸). He will ultimately hand over the kingdom τῷ θεῷ καὶ πατρί (1 Cor. 15²⁴). He is the εἰκὼν τοῦ θεοῦ (2 Cor. 4⁴ ; Col. 1¹⁵). And so Hebrews calls him the ἀπαύγασμα τῆς δόξης (Heb. 1³), the πιστὸν ὄντα τῷ ποιήσαντι αὐτόν (Heb. 3²), who offered himself without spot to God (Heb. 9¹⁴), and gives that picture of his passion so entirely reminiscent of the view of the Synoptists : ὃς ἐν ταῖς ἡμέραις τῆς σαρκὸς αὐτοῦ δεήσεις τε καὶ ἱκετηρίας πρὸς τὸν δυνάμενον σῴζειν αὐτὸν ἐκ θανάτου μετὰ κραυγῆς ἰσχυρᾶς καὶ δακρύων προσενέγκας καὶ εἰσακουσθεὶς ἀπὸ τῆς εὐλαβείας, καίπερ ὢν υἱός, ἔμαθεν ἀφ' ὧν ἔπαθεν τὴν ὑπακοήν (Heb. 5⁷⁻⁸).

Looked at on these lines the Lordship of Jesus as the Son is merely an appearance, exercise, or application of the Lordship of God the Father. The essence of the Divinity ascribed to Jesus is to make clear, impart, and carry out who God the Father, God in the proper sense is, and what He wills and does for man, to represent this God the Father.

Filius revelat agnitionem Patris per suam manifestationem (Irenaeus *C. o. h.* IV 6, 3) . . . *ut in suis verbis non tam se quam Patrem adspiciamus* . . . *ut sic defixis oculis in Christum recte trahamur et rapiamur ad Patrem* (Luther, *Comm. Gal.* 1⁴, 1535 W. edn. 40¹ p. 98, I 25). We should : " Know that Christ is the proper epistle, the golden book wherein we read, Learn to see before our eyes the will of the Father " (*Two German Fast Sermons*, 1518 W. edn. I p. 274 l. 41), " who is a mirror of the Fatherly heart " (*Gr. Kat.* 1529 W. edn. 30¹ p. 192 l. 5). Along these lines A. von Harnack (*op. cit.* p. 91) once formulated the then much disputed proposition : " Not the Son, but the Father alone belongs to the Gospel as Jesus proclaimed it " ; in which, more explicitly, Harnack's meaning was that Jesus' witness to his own Person belonged to the Gospel proclaimed by him, not as one part or proposition alongside another, but, of course, as the expression of the fact that he was aware of himself as the way to the Father.

Precisely, if, in answering the question as to Him who in Scripture is called the Lord, it is right to start with the confession, Jesus is the Lord !, it should again be right to let ourselves first of all be turned in this other direction, seemingly the very opposite, and to ask, What is the goal to which Jesus is the way ? Whom or what does he reveal, so far as he reveals God the Father ? What do we see in him, so far as he is God's " reflection " and " mirror " ? Who is the " Father of the Lord Jesus Christ " ? The answer given us here by the NT is a very different one from that which a too natural and edifying but utterly arbitrary exposition of the word " Father " might give here. What is knowable as the manward-turned will of the heavenly Father in what actually takes place in and through Jesus, lies not at all, in the first instance, in the direction of a genial affirmation, protection, and insurance of human existence, but rather in a radical questioning, nay abrogation of it.

Note that already in the OT the concept " Father " is as much interpretable by the concept " Lord " as *vice versa* (Deut. 32⁶ ; Mal. 1⁶). That men as such are the children of God, that God is a Father to them as such, neither OT nor NT states. But according to the OT Israel is chosen and called out of the mass of the nations to be the children of *Yahweh*. " Out of Egypt have I called my son " (Hosea 11¹). And by a " new birth," and so by a re-foundation of his natural existence, utterly inconceivable in any human sense, away beyond the dissolution of it, man, according to the NT, is transposed into this sonship (John 1¹²ᶠ·, 3³ᶠ·). " Every plant, which my heavenly Father hath not planted, shall be rooted up " ; so runs the inexorable law that holds here (Matt. 15¹³). It is in fact the suffering servant of God of Isa. 53, who is rediscovered in Jesus (Acts 8²⁶ᶠ·). The story of Jesus' life in all four Gospels is described as from the outset, on an adequate estimate, a story of his death, self-proclaiming and self-realising on an increasing downgrade. Ἡμεῖς δὲ κηρύσσομεν Χριστὸν ἐσταυρωμένον writes Paul (1 Cor. 1²³), fully conscious that that is the wisdom of God, which must be to the Jews an offence and to the Greeks foolishness. It is as the High Priest of the new covenant, who is himself the sacrifice which he offers, that the author of the Epistle to the Hebrews regards him. His obedience is an obedience of suffering (Heb. 5⁸). Obedience μέχρι θανάτου, θανάτου δὲ σταυροῦ (Phil. 2⁸). And therefore hath God exalted him and given him the name κύριος Ἰησοῦς Χριστός (Phil. 2⁹⁻¹¹). The Lamb that was slain is worthy to receive power and riches and wisdom and strength and honour and glory and blessing (Rev. 5¹²). Ἐν τῇ ταπεινώσει ἡ κρίσις αὐτοῦ ἤρθη. Therefore the continuation of his life is unthinkable, ὅτι αἴρεται ἀπὸ γῆς ἡ ζωὴ αὐτοῦ (Acts 8³³). He is the corn of wheat which must fall into the earth and die, in order to bring forth much fruit (John 12²⁴). Beyond the death of the man Jesus of Nazareth lies the place from which falls upon him the light, which makes him the revelation of God the Father : ἐξ ἀναστάσεως νεκρῶν is he " declared to be the Son of God " (Rom. 1⁴). God the Father acts in him and through him, by raising him from the dead (Gal. 1¹ ; 1 Cor. 6¹⁴ ; Rom. 4²⁴, 6⁴ ; Eph. 1²⁰). Him who thus reveals Himself in Jesus, the believer calls Ἀββὰ ὁ πατήρ (Gal. 4⁶ ; Rom. 8¹⁵). He who sees Jesus sees this Father (John 14⁷ᶠ·). The Jesus " who was delivered for our offences, and was raised again for our justification " (Rom. 4²⁵), he it is of whom this exclamation holds. And because faith is faith in Jesus, it is itself faith in the will and work of this Father. Being baptised into Christ means being baptised into his death, " being planted together in the likeness of his death " (Rom. 6³ᶠ·, cf. Phil. 3¹⁰), being crucified and dead with him in his crucifixion (Gal. 5²⁴ ; Rom. 6⁶ ; Col. 3³ ; Eph. 4²²). Hence already in the Synoptists, following Jesus is identical with self-denial and taking up one's cross (Mark. 8³⁴), and one can only save one's life by losing it for Jesus sake (Mark 8³⁵). Beyond this strait gate lies literally all that the NT can say about καινότης ζωῆς (Rom. 6⁴) in the baptised and believing. And Him who " in Christ " so deals with man, and leads them this way to the goal, Him believers call Father and " Father of the Lord Jesus Christ." He is the Father of the Son who was dead and is alive again, was lost and is found again (Luke 15²⁹ !). Μετανοεῖν, to reverse one's thinking, to think afresh, to think through to God and His kingdom, really also means, particularly in the NT, to think upon the fact that we must die (Ps. 90¹², cf. Ps. 39⁵). It does not only mean that ; but everything else it may mean, it can only mean, by first of all and decisively meaning this. Note that T h y name, T h y kingdom, T h y will are the objects of the first three petitions in the prayer to be directed to " Our Father, which art in heaven " (Matt. 6⁹ᶠ·), upon which the three which follow them come to rest. This " Thine " makes these petitions in the NT context absolutely equivalent to, Teach us to reflect that we must die !

He whom Jesus reveals as the Father is known absolutely in the death of man, at the end of his existence. His will enters the life of man, not identically with death, nor yet merely in the manner of death, but really along with death, executing death upon man, impressing the signs of death upon man. Not until the sharply drawn, repeatedly to be drawn boundary-line of the Cross, is His will manifest as the will to quicken, bless, and benefit. The life that His will creates will be a life that has passed through death, risen from death, eternal life, really a new birth.

What does all this mean for our question, who God the Father is ? As stated it cannot mean that God the Father is identical with death, with the negation of man's existence. Here rather in death death is vanquished, in negation negation. Resurrection in fact is the power of the Cross, life gained is the power of life lost. But it is strictly and exclusively as the power of the Cross, of life lost, that resurrection and life gained are here reached. That implies that in any case God the Father is by no means identical even with what we know as our life, or perhaps with its meaning and power, that His will confronts our will to live from above, without being bound, rather with complete power of disposal. Not only will it be impossible to establish, by way of self-interpretation of any analysis of our own existence, what God the Father wills with us. Rather it cannot be hidden from us, that this own existence of ours, to its deepest foundations and powers, is radically placed under judgment by the will of God, that it must become new by the action of the will of God the Father upon it. God the Father wills neither our life in itself nor our death in itself. He wills our life in order to lead it through death to eternal life. He wills death in order to lead our life through it to eternal life. He wills this passage of our life through death to eternal life. His kingdom is this new birth.

Hence the extraordinary relativisation of the concepts "life" and "death," which we find especially in Paul: 1 Cor. 3[22]; Rom. 8[38], 14[8]; Phil. 1[20]. Eternal life, resurrection life is undoubtedly for Paul the re-living of this life of ours, willed by God and to be expected from God (1 Cor. 15[53]; 2 Cor. 5[4]). But the very re-living of this life of ours on the other side of the passage through death means that on this side of this gate it must lie on the scale with death, jointly counterbalanced by the hope of faith.

We summarise this by saying that God the Father, whose will and work for men are such, is the Lord of our existence. This He is strictly, so far as He is the Lord over man's life and death. Any other lordship, not knowable upon this line of death, could not be lordship over our existence, but at best a lordship in our existence. The lordship of a God who was identical with our will to live would be limited by the lordship of death. And the lordship of a God who was identical with death would only be the limit of our ability to live. Neither would be lordship over our existence. For our existence is our will and ability to live in its limitation by death, not our life only nor yet merely its limitation by death. Nor would it in that case be real lordship. It would not be the bearer of a power really superior to us, who met us there. The real Lord of our existence must be the Lord over life and death. And this is just God the Father, as we find Him attested in Scripture as Him who is revealed in Jesus. But "the Lord of existence" means the Creator. For if God is the Lord of our existence in the full meaning of the concept that means that our existence is held by Him, and only by Him, over the abyss of non-existence. It has no independent reality either in its certainty as life or in its threatening by death. It is real, so far as He wills and posits it a real existence. It has an Originator from whom as such it is utterly distinct, with whom it is yet utterly connected—but not in such a way that it is at all essentially proper to this Originator to have such a real outside-of-itself, not in such a way as to constitute this relationship a necessity for Him. It has an Originator outside of whom nothing is necessary, who is necessarily related to nothing outside Himself. It has an Originator, who calls it into existence and maintains it in existence out of free loving-kindness and according to His own free will and plan, in free contrast, determined only by Him, to the nothing in which it might remain, without the Former losing anything. It has—what we have been describing in all we have said—a Creator. And it is as the Creator that Jesus shows us God the Father. He shows us Him likewise negatively as Him whose will is done on Golgotha, where, in and with Jesus Christ, the life of us all is nailed to the Cross and dead, in order that thus and thereby eternal life might be manifest, as Him who is that which the concept Creator signifies.

Note how in Rom. 4^{17} the God of Abraham is described in one breath as the ζωοποιῶν τοὺς νεκρούς and as the καλῶν τὰ μὴ ὄντα ὡς ὄντα.

By the name "Father" we signify, of course, the natural human originator of our existence. But our natural human father is not our Creator. He is not the lord of our existence, not for a moment the lord of our life, far less of our death. In calling God our Father, Scripture adopts an analogy, only to break through it at once.

So we must not estimate by natural human fatherhood, what is meant by God being our Father (Isa. 63^{16}). But from the Fatherhood of God natural human fatherhood acquires any meaning and value inherent in it : God is the Father ἐξ οὗ πᾶσα πατριὰ ἐν οὐρανοῖς καὶ ἐπὶ γῆς ὀνομάζεται (Eph. 3^{15}).

God our Father means God our Creator (cf. for this statement Deut. 32^{6} and Isa. 64^{7}). And it should now have become clear that it is precisely "in Christ," as "the Father of Jesus Christ," that God means our Creator. It is not a general truth, knowable antecedently or to be acquired by our own powers ; it is the truth of revelation that God is our Creator. Only by what we otherwise know as the relation of father and son being broken through by the Word of Christ the Crucified and Risen, only through its being interpreted by this Word, i.e., in this case, through its acquiring from this Word a meaning which on its own merits it could not have—only so do we come in sight of what Creation means. But in that way we can come in sight of it. The "Father of Jesus Christ," who according to the witness of Scripture is manifest in Jesus, His servant, possesses the attributes of a "Lord of our existence." The witness concerning Him leads us to the place where the miracle of creation can come into view. It attests the holy God, the God who alone is God, the free God. It is this witness that we now have to understand by means of the fundamental positions of the doctrine of the Trinity.

2. THE ETERNAL FATHER

The decisive proposition by which the answer just heard to the question, who is God the Father ?, is elevated into an element in the knowledge of the Triune God in the sense of the Church dogma must run thus : as "the Father of Jesus Christ " God can be our Father, because already beforehand, quite apart from the fact that He reveals Himself to us as such, He is what He reveals Himself as being, namely, the Father of Jesus Christ His Son, who as such is Himself God. He can be so, because He is Himself the Father in Himself, because Fatherhood is an eternal mode of existence of the divine essence. In Him whose name, kingdom, and will Jesus reveals, in His actual individual distinction from this His revealer, though also in His individual communion with him, we have to do with God Himself.

How is it that with the Church dogma we come to look in this way at the Biblical witness about God the Father ? The answer must simply be that we do so by adopting the Biblical witness and taking it with literal seriousness, in so far as formally it shows the content of the revelation of the Father to be completely limited and tied down by its impartation in the Person of the revealer, Jesus of Nazareth. Its content cannot be abstracted from this form. There is here no question of any possibility of distinguishing content and form, and regarding the content as divine and necessary, the form as human and accidental ; the former as the essence, the latter as the historical appearance of the revelation. The form here is essential to the content, i.e., God as our Father, as the Creator is unknown, in so far as He is not made known through Jesus.

It is especially the Johannine tradition which expresses this exclusiveness with ever-renewed emphasis : John 1[18], 5[23,37], 6[46], 8[19], 14[6], 17[25] ; 1 John 2[23] ; 2 John 9. Καθὼς γινώσκει με ὁ πατήρ, κἀγὼ γινώσκω τὸν πατέρα (John 10[15]) ; and therefore ὁ ἑωρακὼς ἐμὲ ἑώρακεν τὸν πατέρα (John 14[9]). But it is to be found as conclusively, with the same unmistakable clarity, in the Synoptists : Πάντα μοι παρεδόθη ἀπὸ τοῦ πατρός μου, καὶ οὐδεὶς ἐπιγινώσκει τὸν υἱὸν εἰ μὴ ὁ πατήρ, οὐδὲ τὸν πατέρα τις ἐπιγινώσκει εἰ μὴ ὁ υἱὸς καὶ ᾧ ἐὰν βούληται ὁ υἱὸς ἀποκαλύψαι (Matt. 11[27]).

If this exclusiveness is adopted and taken seriously, if therefore the abstraction between form and content is seen not to be permissible, then any possibility is barred of conceiving the first article in the creed as an article of natural theology. Jesus' message about God the Father must not be regarded as if Jesus had expressed the familiar truth, that the world must have and really has a Creator, and then had ventured to designate this Creator by the familiar human name of " Father "—not as if on his part he intended what all serious philosophy has named as the highest cause, or as the highest good, as *esse a se* or as the *ens perfectissimum*, as the universal, as the ground of meaning and the abyss of meaning, as the unconditioned, as the limit, the critical negation or the origin ; intended it and dedicated it by the name of Father, not altogether unknown to religious language, gave it a Christian interpretation and, as it were, baptism. To that we can but say that this entity, the supposed philosophical equivalent of the Creator God, has nothing to do with Jesus' message of God the Father, with or without the name of Father attached. Nor would it have anything to do with it even were it brought into relation and perhaps identified with the principle of " Die and become ! ", with the superior origin and aim of the dialectic of life lost and life gained. An idea, constructed with the claim to be the idea of God, is as such, not as an idea but simply because of this claim, an idol from the standpoint of the exclusiveness expressed in the Biblical testimonies. Even the genuinely pure, and for that reason treacherously pure, idea of God in a Plato cannot count as an exception. If the exclusiveness holds, then Jesus did not so much reproclaim the familiar world creator and interpret it by the likewise not unfamiliar name of Father, but he revealed the un-familiar Father, his Father, and thereby, and first thereby, and only thereby explained that and what the Creator is, and that He as such is our Father.

It is important, then, as an interpretation of the address " Our Father," that according to John 20[17] Jesus does not say, I go to our Father, but ἀναβαίνω πρὸς τὸν πατέρα μου καὶ πατέρα ὑμῶν καὶ θεόν μου καὶ θεὸν ὑμῶν. It is not κατὰ φύσιν but κατὰ θεοῦ χάριν καὶ θέσει, ἀφάτῳ φιλανθρωπίᾳ, through the Son and the Holy Spirit, that we have God to our Father (Cyril of Jerusalem *Cat.* 7, 7–8).

But for the knowledge of God the Father this means, that God is not God the Father, only because He is the Creator and therefore our Father. He is so for that reason also, and that is the *opus ad extra* which becomes manifest in Jesus. But from the fact that in Jesus and only in Jesus He becomes manifest as the Creator and so as our Father, it follows that He is already what corresponds thereto, antecedently and in Himself, namely, in His relation to him by whom He becomes manifest, hence in His relation to Jesus. If it is true that we have to recognise fatherhood in God's will executed in and through Jesus, and if it is further

29

true that any abstraction of this will from the fact that it is fulfilled precisely in and through Jesus, is barred by the exclusiveness mentioned, then apart from what His fatherhood means for us, we must regard it as that fatherhood which holds previously for Jesus, and therefore as that which corresponds to a sonship of Jesus. There is therefore a fatherhood of God in Himself, the truth of which does not first consist in Him being the Creator and in us by His grace being His children, but already and primarily in the fact, that a revelation of our new birth, and therefore a revelation of creation, i.e. of His lordship over our existence, c a n be an event. The possibilit y in God for this event is the Son of God, who is identical with Jesus of Nazareth. In relation to him, therefore, as the Father of this Son, God is antecedently Father in Himself.

Faith in God the Father must be so proclaimed, that at once unexpressed and unconfused by recollection of other fatherhoods, faith in the only-begotten Son may be impressed upon the hearers. Τὸ γὰρ τοῦ πατρὸς ὄνομα ἅμα τῷ τῆς ὀνομασίας προσρήματι νοεῖν παρέχει καὶ τὸν υἱόν· . . . Εἰ γὰρ πατήρ, πάντως ὅτι πατὴρ υἱοῦ (Cyril of Jerus. Cat. 7, 3–4). Per prius paternitas dicitur in divinis secundum quod importatur respectus personae ad personam quam secundum quod importatur respectus Dei ad creaturam (Thomas Aquinas, S. Theol. 1 qu. 33 art. 3c). God is the Father secundum relationem quam habet ad personam filii (Polanus, Syntagma theol. chr. 1625 III 5 ; from Heppe, Dogm. d. ev.-ref. Kirche, 1861 p. 92).

In view of this original fatherhood of God the dogma of the Trinity speaks of the " Person," or as we say, of the mode of existence of God the Father. Not only in this mode of existence is God God. He is likewise so, in the possibility—or, we must also say, in the possibilities—in which He becomes manifest as Him who acts upon us in the new birth. He is so, if there really is not to be an abstraction between revelation and its content, also in the modes of existence of the Son and of the Holy Spirit. But precisely if this is so, the content of the revelation, so far as it is simultaneously the revelation of the Creation, of the divine lordship over our existence, points us back to a corresponding inner possibility in God Himself, which, as far as order goes, must be regarded as the first, original one, presupposed in the other possibilities. In this first, original possibility He is God the Father in the sense of the dogma of the Trinity, namely, the e t e r n a l Father.

Πρὸ πάσης ὑποστάσεως καὶ πρὸ πάσης αἰσθήσεως, πρὸ χρόνων τε καὶ πρὸ πάντων τῶν αἰώνων τὸ πατρικὸν ἀξίωμα ἔχει ὁ θεός (Cyril of Jerus. Cat. 7, 5).

We must n o t say that the use of the name " Father " here is a transferred, im p r o p e r, inadequate one. That could only be said, if the measure of propriety, here and generally, were our language, meaning the created reality to which our language is related. If the Creator is the measure of the propriety of the created, and therefore of our language also, then we should on the contrary have to say, that it is not only the application of the name of father that is improper for the originating relation in which one creature stands to the others, but also ultimately its application to the relation between God as Creator and the creature, as we have read it off from the revelation of the new birth. God alone, as He whom He is by Himself, i.e. as the eternal Father of the eternal Son, is properly and adequately to be called Father. From the power and dignity of this alone proper name of Father, there flows by grace and for faith the improper—not, of course, therefore untrue, but really improper—name of Father for God as the Creator, and from this again the naming of the original intra-creaturely relation, the thing which is called fatherhood in heaven and on earth (Eph. 3^{15}); this too to be regarded as a true but improper appellation, dependent upon the power and dignity of the intra-trinitarian name of Father for God.

Οὐ γὰρ ὁ θεὸς ἄνθρωπον μιμεῖται, ἀλλὰ μᾶλλον οἱ ἄνθρωποι διὰ τὸν θεόν, κυρίως καὶ μόνον ἀληθῶς ὄντα πατέρα τοῦ ἑαυτοῦ υἱοῦ, καὶ αὐτοὶ πατέρες ὀνομάσθησαν τῶν ἰδίων τέκνων (Athanasius, *Or. c. Ar.* I 23).

The Trinitarian name of Father for God, God's eternal fatherhood, signifies God's mode of existence, in which He is the Originator of His other modes of existence.

Fons ergo ipse et origo est totius divinatatis (*Conc. Tolet.* XI 675, *Denz. Nr.* 275). In this mode of existence the Fathers describe Him as αὐτόθεος, ἄναρχος, ἀγέννητος, θεὸς ἐπὶ πάντων, as *a nullo originem habens, a se ipso existens, ingenitus, innascibilis, principium sine principio.*

It must be strictly noted that this origination (the incomparable type of the relation between Creator and creature, which again is the incomparable type of all intra-creaturely originating relations) is connected with the mutual relations among the divine modes of existence, and therefore may not be interpreted as if, between the Father on the one hand and the Son and the Holy Spirit on the other, there existed a relation of superiority or inferiority regarding their divinity. The divine essence would not be the divine essence, if there were in it superiority and inferiority and also, of course, various *quanta* of divinity. The Son and the Spirit are of one essence with the Father. In this unity of the divine essence the Son is from the Father and the Spirit is from the Father and the Son, while the Father is from none but Himself. In other words, the intra-divine possibility, in virtue of which God can become manifest to us as the Creator and as our Father, is not a possibility grounded and resting upon itself. Rather it presupposes such a possibility and it presupposes something that occurs in God, in virtue of which it is posited as a possibility. It arises in God out of a possibility, grounded and resting upon itself. It is—everything to be regarded as an intra-divine relation or movement, as the *repetitio aeternitatis in aeternitate !*—the copy of a type, the outcome of an origin, the word of a knowledge, the decision of a will. This thing, the type, origin, knowledge, will in God, in which He distinguishes Himself from Himself, from which proceeds the other thing, to wit the copy, outcome, word, decision ; in short, this fact that He can relate Himself as Creator and as our Father to one distinct from Himself outside Him—this First in God Himself is the eternal Father, in the sense of the dogma of the Trinity. God is the eternal Father so far as from eternity and in eternity He is the Father of the Son, who participates with Him, from eternity and in eternity, in the same essence. In this relation and not otherwise God is God—the God who reveals Himself in the Son as the Creator and as our Father. From this perception arise two conclusions with regard to this revelation of His through the Son.

1. From the eternity of the relation between Father and Son in which also that of the relation of the two to the Holy Spirit is already contained, it follows in the first place of necessity, that not only God the Father is to be claimed as the Creator and as our Father, and that God the Father is to be claimed not only as the Creator and as our Father. We said above that the use of the name Father for this relation and act of God outwardly is a derivative and improper one. Revelation, so far as it is the revelation of God the Creator and our Father, and so far as this content of it is inseparable from its form as revelation in Jesus, leads us to the knowledge of God the eternal Father. But in this very knowledge we cannot in fact separate the Father from the Son and from the Holy Spirit. In this very knowledge, therefore, must become clear to us the merely relative significance of the way of isolation, by which we reach this knowledge. It signifies an " appropriation" (cf. § 9, 3), when by isolation we regard precisely God the Father as the Creator and as our Father, and God the Father as precisely the Creator and as our Father. The three-in-oneness does not mean the side-by-sideness of three parts of God acting in three different

functions. *Opera trinitatis ad extra sunt indivisa*, just as likewise the essence of God is a single and undivided essence, and as the *trinitas* itself is an *individua trinitas*. Thus, not only is the subject described in the first article of the creed the Father, Almighty, Creator of heaven and earth, but with Him, in the order and sense pertaining to each, also the subjects of the second and third articles. And again, the subject of the first article is not only the Father, Almighty, Creator of heaven and earth, but again in the order and sense pertaining to it therein, also the subject of reconciliation like the subject of the second, and of redemption like the subject of the third article. Thus, not only the Father is the Creator God, but the Son and the Spirit are that with Him. And the Father is not only the Creator God, He is with the Son and the Spirit also the Reconciler God and the Redeemer God. The very knowledge of the intra-trinitarian s p e c i a l i t y of the name Father thus guarantees the knowledge of the u n i t y of God, which would be endangered by the view of the speciality of the revelation of God as the Creator and as our Father, if this view were not forestalled by the apparently but only apparently—so speculative intra-trinitarian realisation just noted. Because God is the eternal Father as the Father of the Son and, together with him, the origin of the Spirit, therefore, the God who acts in reconciliation and in redemption, who reveals Himself as the Reconciler and Redeemer, cannot be a second and third God, or a second and third part of God; therefore, He is and remains God *unus et individuus*, in His operation as in His essence.

Hence all theological favouritisms are forbidden; that of a one-sided faith in God the Father, as was customary in the Enlightenment, as much as that of so-called Christocentrism, of which Pietism was so fond and still is, in short, like all excess which has been and can be indulged in in an isolated veneration of the Spirit. We cannot call God the Father, without the S o n and the S p i r i t, and we cannot call the Son Saviour or the Spirit Comforter, without implying the F a t h e r in both cases.

This knowledge ensures the Trinitarian dogma of the eternal Father, the Father of His only-begotten Son.

2. But from the same eternity of relationship between Father and Son, in which is also expressed the eternity of the relation of both to the Holy Spirit, there now also follows the second point, that the necessary relativisation of the knowledge of revelation, which leads us to the realisation of this eternal relationship, cannot mean any devaluation or discrediting of this way of knowledge. That to regard precisely God the Father as the Creator and God the Father precisely as the Creator, is an improper procedure, because

God is one in His essence and operation, does not mean that it is an untrue, or a forbidden procedure that must be abandoned. " Improper " here can only mean that it is not in itself an exhaustive but a one-sided way of looking at it, which needs to be completed, a way to which we cannot and may not surrender exclusively, which we cannot and may not make exclusively valid, a way of looking at it which must also include meanings which are not contained in it itself as such. The " appropriation " which we achieve by regarding God the Father or Creation in this special way, is not only permitted but even enjoined, and the knowledge based upon it, in its entire relativity, is true knowledge. Without making this appropriation, we could not realise that it is " only " an appropriation. It is upon the way of knowledge based upon it and upon it only that the goal is attainable, from which the relativity of the way as a way can be recognised. The appropriation in fact simply corresponds with the reality of the revelation attested for us in Scripture, and the impropriety of the knowledge based upon the appropriation corresponds with the reality of the faith apprehending the revelation, which is certainly not sight. The dogma of the Trinity, which earlier reminded us of the unity of the essence and operation of God, will not lead us to a right understanding of itself by passing over revelation and faith, but by penetrating to revelation and faith. It cannot, therefore, be a question of the appropriation of precisely God the Father for creation, or of creation precisely for God the Father, being a preliminary and surmountable view, which would subsequently dissolve and disappear in a higher gnosis of the one God. In fact the oneness of God in no sense signifies the dissolution of His three-in-oneness. God reveals Himself as the God He is. Which is just what the dogma of the Trinity also asserts. It is the eternity of the relation of Father, Son, and Spirit which, because this relation includes unity and variety in the three modes of existence, also declares that God's operation outwards is just as really varied in its unity in itself as it is unified in its variety. Earlier, with regard to the unity of operation of Father, Son, and Spirit outwards, we introduced the stipulation about them operating in the order and sense pertaining to each. That means that the unity of their operation is to be regarded as the communion of the three modes of existence, in the sense of the doctrine of " Perichoresis " (cf. § 9, 3), according to which all three, without loss or mutual dissolution of their independence, interpenetrate one another interchangeably,

inexist interchangeably in one another. This unity cannot therefore be understood, as though the truth regarding God's operation
outward were just a vanishing of the independence of the three
modes of existence in a neutral, undifferentiated fourth, so that with
modalism no statement relating to this *opus ad extra* could be
made seriously about a definite mode of existence, while all statements relating to this *opus ad extra*, might be made indifferently
about each separate mode of existence. At this point we merely
emphasise what is relevant to our theme, that the Father is not the
Son and not the Spirit. That remains true also in the *opus ad
extra*, as surely as it is true from eternity and in eternity. To this
distinction is related the appropriation, in which we equate the
Creator with God the Father and God the Father with the Creator.
It is a mere appropriation, so far as it does not include the expression of the truth of perichoresis, the intercommunity of Father,
Son, and Spirit in their essence and operation. But it expresses
the truth and also communicates true knowledge, so far as, along
with the equation, it touches upon and signifies the distinction
also found in the *opus ad extra*, the order and sense in which God,
as the Three-in-One, is the Subject of the *opus ad extra indivisum*.
It expresses the truth, so far as by its emphasis precisely upon the
Father, or Creator, it points to the affinity between the order of
God's three modes of existence on the one hand, and that of the
three sides of His operation as Creator, Reconciler, and Redeemer
on the other. Between the relation of the Father to the Son and
the relation of the Creator to the creature there e x i s t s once for
all an a f f i n i t y : in the one case as in the other, although in a
sense differing *toto coelo*, we are concerned with origination. In
view of this affinity it is not only allowed but enjoined upon us, to
ascribe creation as a *proprium* to God the Father in particular, and
to regard God the Father *peculiariter*, precisely as the Creator. And
on the contrary, the result of the eternal truth of the distinction,
valid also in consequence for the *opus ad extra*, is the realisation that
certain statements about the operation of the Son and the Spirit
can n o t be appropriated to the Father, although God the Father is
no less the Subject of reconciliation and redemption than are the
Son and the Spirit.

We cannot say of God the Father that He was conceived and born, that
He suffered, died, and rose again. Nor can we say of Him that we must
pray for His coming, and that He is to be poured out upon all flesh. For
on the one hand all these statements stand in affinity with the relation of the

Son or the Spirit to the Father, but not *vice versa* : their content, therefore, pertains *peculiariter* to the Son and to the Spirit, and not to the Father. On the other hand the statements in the second article especially relate to God the Son, so far as, in acting as Reconciler, he has assumed humanity, and therefore creatureliness. They would, therefore, applied to God the Father, collide with His affinity to the essence and action of God as the Creator. Of course, in the Incarnation of the Word the Creator became a creature, and, of course, the Holy Spirit for whom we pray, is the *creator spiritus;* and a presence of the Father also in the Son who was born, suffered, and died, and in the Spirit outpoured at Pentecost, no one could or should for that reason deny. But we ought just as little to say, God the Father died, as we ought to say that Jesus of Nazareth or the Spirit of Whitsunday created heaven and earth.

An absolutely unambiguous boundary between bidden and forbidden cannot, of course, be drawn. We can only say that the doctrine of perichoresis, which admits of misuse in a one-sided emphasis on the involution or interpenetration (Ineinander) of the three modes of existence, also includes the other element, by which we should be warned against misuse, namely, regarding the involution as a convolution (Miteinander), presupposing the eternal independence of the three modes of existence in their eternal community. And in any case it may be stated quite definitely, that to systematise the one-sidedness, as we partly find it in the ancient modalism (e.g. in the form of " Patripassianism "), is absolutely forbidden, because it would mean the dissolution of the three-in-oneness into the neutral fourth. The eternity of the fatherhood of God means not only the eternity of the communion of the Father with the Son and the Spirit, but it also protects Him from being made to coincide with the Son and the Spirit. This forced coincidence is also inadmissible on the ground of the statement that *opera trinitatis ad extra sunt indivisa.* It would not only collide with the dogma of the Trinity. It would also be irreconcilable with the adoption and serious use of the Biblical witness, which makes the Father and the Son one in their variety. It is, therefore, right and necessary that the knowledge of the Father as the Creator and as our Father, for all our awareness of the unity of the Father with the Son and the Spirit, should always be a special piece of knowledge. Only in this speciality taken seriously does it lead to the awareness mentioned, and this very awareness will lead us constantly to take it seriously in its speciality too.

GOD THE SON

The one God reveals Himself according to Scripture as the Reconciler, i.e. as the Lord, amidst our enmity towards Him. As such He is the Son come to us, or the Word spoken to us, because He is so antecedently in Himself, as the Son or the Word of God the Father.

1. GOD AS THE RECONCILER

We return to the starting-point of our previous section, where we opened with the question, who is He whom Holy Scripture calls the Lord, who deals with man in revelation?, and where we replied, that at the peak of the Biblical witness it is stated (generally with the intention of stating what is true and valid for the whole Biblical witness, and so for the OT witness also) that Jesus of Nazareth is this Lord. Then we first of all followed the lines of the NT message, according to which, in apparent contrast to this statement, Jesus of Nazareth is regarded rather as the servant of God who proclaims and executes the will of his Father in heaven. But then we saw how also and precisely the revelation of the Father, of whom Jesus might appear at first as the mere mediator, does not according to the Biblical witness admit of being abstracted from this Mediator. What God reveals in Jesus, and the manner of His revelation of it, namely, in Jesus, are according to the NT not to be separated; and, assuming that this prohibition is to be respected, we are bound to regard the concept of God as the Father in His actual relation to this Mediator of His revelation, as a mode of existence finally and really pertaining to Him, and we must regard His Fatherhood as an eternal one.

We now once more turn our attention to the other line of Biblical witness, first touched upon at that earliest point and at once abandoned, in which the emphasis is precisely not upon the distinction of Jesus from the Father, but, without denying this distinction, directly upon his communion, in fact unity, with Him.

To the statements about the relation of the Father to the Son, with which we got into touch in the previous section, corresponds most completely a series of statements on the relation of the Son to the Father. With these statements indeed the construction of the dogma of the Trinity started, and *a priori* we must expect to have to attend to it at this particular point also, if the dogma means to take the unity of the Son with the Father attested in these statements, i.e. the divinity of Jesus Christ, as a final, proper, and essential unity.

Here we must first indicate the application to Jesus of the name K y r i o s, an application surrounded, of course, with all manner of obscurity. Does the Apostle's language here grasp at the title of divine ruler of the world, familiar in Hellenistic Egypt ? Or at the title belonging in Syria to the cult god, as opposed to his slaves, the adherents of the cult ? Or at the title of Cæsar in the Roman Cæsar-religion ? Be that as it may, the name, in view of its significance outside of contemporary Judaism, at once carries the person indicated by it far away from the rest of men to the side of " divinity " (in the more or less serious acceptation of the concept, which might come under consideration in this religious world), to the point where in any case that bending of the knee pertains to him, of which Paul has spoken in Phil. 2¹⁰. But—and thereby the matter really at once becomes almost plain—in view of the close connection between the early Church and the synagogue of Palestine and Hellenism, it cannot possibly have happened unawares or unintentionally, that with this word people at least also translated the OT n a m e f o r God, Yahweh-Adonai, and applied it to Jesus. We are pointed in the same direction by the practical m e a n i n g of the name Jesus, as the name in which they prophesied, taught, preached, prayed, baptised, in which sins were forgiven, devils driven out, and other miracles performed, in which his followers must assemble, in which they must admit each other, in which they must believe, upon which they must call, by which they must remain stedfast, for the sake of which they must indeed be even hated and scorned, and lose every earthly possession, in fact perhaps even die ; in which, once more, they are also " washed, sanctified, justified " (1 Cor. 6¹¹), which, so to speak, is the place, the region in which their entire language and action should take place (Col. 3¹⁷). It is pretty much the same, comprehensive, pervasive meaning which (cf. § 8, 2) the name of Yahweh has in the OT : the n a m e of Yahweh is just Y a h w e h m a n i f e s t to m e n. Who then is Jesus, if his name has the same meaning ? Does it still need the express declaration of Paul (Phil. 2⁹) that God hath given him the name which is above every name ?

As the second general phenomenon pointing emphatically in the same direction—we owe the express indication of the fact to K. L. S c h m i d t (*RGG*² *art.* Jesus Christ)—must be cited the fact that NT tradition has set forth the revealing activity of Jesus as an intertexture, impossible to dissolve, of w o r d a n d d e e d, and indeed of word and miracle. Τὰ περὶ Ἰησοῦ Ναζαρηνοῦ, apart from the final events of his life which are decisive for the meaning and trend of the whole, admit of being summarised in the words, ἐγένετο ἀνὴρ προφήτης δυνατὸς ἐν ἔργῳ καὶ λόγῳ (Luke 24¹⁹) or ἃ ἤρξατο ποιεῖν τε καὶ διδάσκειν (Acts 1¹). But such and similar " summary descriptions," which for that matter often enough (e.g. Acts 2²², 10³⁸) seem to be acquainted only with

Jesus the miracle-worker, do but formulate the impression which an impartial reading, say, of the Gospel of Mark must in any case leave, that the teaching, which, of course, is also set forth here, is meant to be understood not apart from, but through the action which is its invariable accompaniment. It is a lack in R. Bultmann's book *Jesus* (1926), that it passes over this insistent demand of the texts in order to construct " Jesus " one-sidedly out of his sayings. The deeds, which join in the dialogue without a break and which should also be listened to, are miracles. How they hang together with the central content of Jesus' sayings, is shown by the story of the paralytic (Mark 2¹⁻¹²), where to the horror of the scribes—they at once speak of blasphemy, and rightly from their standpoint—Jesus not only speaks of forgiveness of sins but forgives sins, and to show his authority for this act-word makes the paralytic whole. God's act taking place visibly, the whole fact of a gracious happening to man, underlines the spoken word as God's word. That is the meaning of the miracles ascribed to Jesus, and—in the light of the authority transferred to them by Jesus, expressly to his apostles also—a meaning which marks off these miracle stories, whatever the practical verdict upon them, as at least something very special amid the wealth of miracle stories of that whole age. But their speciality lies in their thorough-going and indissoluble conjunction with the word of Jesus, a conjunction which as much distinguishes this word from a mere prophetic utterance, as it distinguishes the miracles from mere thaumaturgy, a conjunction in which word and deed equally render visible a Higher, something beyond ethos (" history "!) and physis, a loftier authority confronting the whole estate of human, nay of cosmic reality. Who is this, who, obviously acting for this higher authority, can speak thus because he can act thus, act thus because he can speak thus ?

It might be said of the further titles assigned to Jesus in the NT, the title Messiah-Christ, the title Son of Man and the title Son of God, that they are in themselves ambiguous or obscure. " Son of God," e.g. was a widespread designation in the ancient East simply for the king. But the context of NT Christology makes this title also eloquent in quite a definite way. He whom the Gospel will depict, so the Fourth Evangelist begins, the Word which, become flesh, tabernacled among us and was seen by us in His glory (John 1¹⁴)—this Word was not, like all other words, a created human word, merely relating to God, merely speaking from God and about God. As the Word it is spoken in the place where God is, namely, ἐν ἀρχῇ, *in principio* of all that is ; πρὸς τὸν θεόν, pertaining to God, therefore itself θεός, God in kind (John 1¹), identical with the Word by which—πάντα δι αὐτοῦ ἐγένετο—God called all that is into being and into existence (John 1³). No more and no less than God Himself is there, in that this Word, οὗτος, i.e. Jesus whose story the Gospel wishes to tell, is there as the light in the darkness which comprehendeth not the light (John 1, 2⁴⁻⁵). Then that θεὸς ἦν ὁ λόγος is (John 1¹⁸) (according to the proper reading) expressly repeated : μονογενὴς θεὸς ὁ ὢν εἰς τὸν κόλπον τοῦ πατρός, He hath revealed the invisible God. The same equation between the seen, heard, touched object of Christian proclamation and the ὁ ἦν ἀπ᾽ ἀρχῆς is also found in 1 John 1. And so Paul also says, Θεὸς ἦν ἐν Χριστῷ καταλλάσσων (2 Cor. 5¹⁹) and ἐν αὐτῷ κατοικεῖ πᾶν τὸ πλήρωμα τῆς θεότητος σωματικῶς (Col. 2⁹). The passage Heb. 1⁵ᶠ·, in which the exaltation of the Son of God is fixed even above the angel world, is remarkable because there, in the words cited from the Psalms, even the distinction between θεός, which must perhaps still always be improperly interpreted as an adjective, and ὁ θεός disappears, and the Son is expressly described as ὁ θεός. Jesus may be called ὁ μέγας θεός (Titus 2¹³), ἴσος τῷ θεῷ (John 5¹⁸ ; Phil. 2⁶), ἐν μορφῇ θεοῦ ὑπάρχων (Phil. 2⁶), the ἴδιος υἱός of His Father (Rom. 8³²), the υἱὸς τῆς ἀγαπῆς αὐτοῦ (Col. 1¹³), the υἱὸς ὁ μονογενής (John 3¹⁶·¹⁸ ; 1 John 4⁹), ὁ ἐκ τοῦ οὐρανοῦ καταβάς (John 3¹³·³¹). He can say of Himself. ἐγὼ καὶ ὁ πατὴρ ἕν ἐσμεν (John 10³⁰). He is come from the Father (John 16²⁸). He has already worked hitherto, as His Father hath worked (John 5¹⁷). He hath life in Himself, as the Father hath life in Himself (John 5²⁶). He that seeth Him seeth the Father (John 14⁹). He can say with the Father, Before Abraham was, I am (John 8⁵⁸), and to the Father, Thou lovedst me before the creation of the world (John 17²⁴). For He had glory before the existence of the world (John 17⁵). Ὁ θρόνος σου ὁ θεὸς εἰς τὸν αἰῶνα τοῦ αἰῶνος Heb. 1⁸ makes God say to His Son. He is Alpha and Omega, the first and the last, the ἀρχή and the τέλος (Rev. 22¹³, cf. 1⁸·¹⁷), He that is and was and is to come, ὁ παντοκράτωρ (Rev. 1⁸), the same yesterday, to-day, and for ever (Heb. 13⁸). And therefore it is to be said of Him, as the prologue of John already emphasises, that through Him God made the aeons (Heb. 1²), that He is the Word of power, by which He upholds all things (Heb. 1³), that in Him was everything made, that is in heaven and on earth (Col. 1¹⁶ ; 1 Cor. 8⁶). He is πάντων κύριος (Acts 10³⁶). He can say of Himself, All things are delivered unto me of my Father . . . ! and therefore, Come unto me, all ye that labour and are heavy-laden, and I will refresh you (Matt. 11²⁷·²⁸). Just as also the content of Peter's confession in Matt. 16¹⁶, " Thou art the Christ, the Son of the living God," subsequently (Matt. 26⁶³ᶠ·) appears as the blasphemy which leads Jesus to the Cross.

Alongside of the first line emphasised in the previous section, this is the second line of the NT tradition. There this means, " Jesus is the Lord," the divinity of Jesus Christ.

The NT statement about the unity of the Son with the Father, i.e. about the divinity of Christ, cannot possibly be interpreted on the assumption that the original outlook and declaration of the NT witnesses concerned a human being, who subsequently was either exalted as such to divinity, or appeared among us as the personification and symbol of a divine being.

The point of view essential here is at once menaced if with M. Dibelius (*RGG²* art. *Christologie* I) the problem of NT Christology is formulated as " how knowledge about the historical figure of Jesus comes to be transformed so swiftly into faith in the heavenly Son of God." The whole question is whether one can take for granted such a knowledge about an " historical figure " as the first thing, a transformation of this knowledge into faith in the heavenly Son of God as the second, and then ask, in the style of a philosophic historian, how such a reversal could have taken place. We see no possibility on this road of ending anywhere save in a blind alley.—If the question be put in this way, there are in the main two modernly historical attempts to explain the origin of the above formulation (cf. for a description of them K. L. Schmidt, *op. cit.* beginning and end of the article adduced ; but also so early as Schleiermacher, *Der chr. Gl.* § 22), two attempts which in substance coincide exactly in an astonishing way, as early as the 2nd century, with the two most important side-lines of Christological thought finally rejected by the Church.

The NT statement of the divinity of Christ may be regarded in the first place individualistically, as the apotheosis of a man, a "great man," who as such, by the mystery of his personality and his work, made such an impression upon his environment, that quite inevitably there arose the enthusiastic impression and idea, " He is a God." Such a man presumably Jesus of Nazareth was, the originator and proclaimer of an attitude to life— unheard of in his own time, and, more or less, in other later times—of child-likeness, freedom, obedience, love, and faithfulness unto death, the more or less voluntary or involuntary Founder of the Christian religion, and the Founder of the Christian Church. From the inspired and inspiring Galilæan country rabbi he was, and as which he was originally venerated by his followers, he rises in their eyes to the stature of a prophet of the standing of Elijah, from the political Messiah which originally he at least also was to the Son of David, who as such could also be called the Son of God, to a heavenly being of the same name, who attests his presence in visions even after his bodily death, lives on in his "spirit," and is therefore, of course, also pre-existent, till asseveration, growing constantly warmer in an inverse ratio to its remoteness from the historical object, overreaches itself, and the equation between Jesus and God ceases to be impossible. And here the idea that at a definite hour, at his birth, or in his baptism, or in the transfiguration on the mount, or actually in his resurrection from the dead, God raised this man Jesus to such dignity and adopted him as His Son, might be a good symbol of what, in the zeal of their Christ-enthusiasm, men had done themselves : a marvellous man, who once upon a time had been known as such and who also had always really been regarded as such, was elevated by idealisation in the " eye of faith " right up to God, as could be and actually has been the case with other heroes too. This is the Ebionite Christology, or the Christology historically recon-structed on the lines of Ebionitism.

But secondly the NT statement of the divinity of Christ may also be interpreted in exactly the opposite sense, collectivistically : in it, the theory runs, we are concerned with the personification of an idea other-wise very familiar, of a general truth : say the truth of the community of godhead and humanity, or the truth of the creation of the world by God's Word and Wisdom, or the truth of redemption by way of Die and Be born! or the truth of the existence together of holiness and loving-kindness, of forgive-ness and claim. The actual circumstance that it was Jesus of Nazareth, in whom this idea was first seen as a phenomenon, was more or less accidental and indifferent, so indifferent that the concrete humanity of his earthly existence or, finally, even of his historical reality could also be queried. As a theophany, as a myth, i.e. as a general truth taking form, he was believed in as the well-known Son of Man in Daniel, or as the well-known pre-existent Logos, or as the well-known world-Saviour, about whom all Hellenism thought it knew a little, or as an analogue of the divine hypostases, as the Rabbis taught them, when they spoke of the *Memra* (the Word), the *Shechina* (the glory), the *Metatron* (the senior archangel of God). Since and so far as actually in Jesus of Nazareth the symbol of this idea was contemplated and venerated, he was called Kyrios, God's Son, and lastly, with a full awareness of the dialectic involved in the equation, God Himself. The power of a Christ-enthusiasm with a capacity and a need for this equation, was the power of the idea, the power of the conception of God as such condescending and becoming manifest, which in its relation to Jesus of Nazareth in par-ticular merely found its special focus of crystallisation, exactly as, at that and other times, it has also and demonstrably found these concentration points elsewhere. The universal " eye of faith " had now fallen once for all exactly upon him. But it was of it, this idea, that people thought and not of the Rabbi of Nazareth, whom as such they might or might not be acquainted with, without thereby gaining or losing much, whom at all events they wished to know only for the sake of the idea. That is the Docetic Christology, the one historically reconstructed in the tracks of docetism.

These two conceptions or explanations of the statement about the divinity of Christ appear to be in greater contradiction to each other than is really the case. The first regards Jesus as the, or as a, peak of history soaring into superhistory. The second regards him as the sucker of super-history penetrating down into history. According to the first he is the highest phenomenon of human life, according to the second the most perfect symbol of divine presence. Obviously it should not be too difficult to relate these two conceptions dialectically to one another and to reconcile them with each other. They have at least the view in common, that in the NT statement of the divinity of Christ we are, strictly speaking, dealing with a manner of speaking loosely meant and loosely to be interpreted.

As early as the second century the Church rejected Ebionitism as well as Docetism, and with them by anticipation the corresponding explanations of modern history as well. And the NT statement of the divinity of Christ can, in fact, only be understood on the assumption that it has nothing to do either with the apotheosis of a man or with the personification of an idea of God or of a divine idea. It bars these alternatives. But that, of course, takes place upon a line in which the plane on which the Ebionite and the Docetic lines intersect is itself cut by another plane, and therefore in a third dimension, perpendicular to it and to those lines. By pursuing thought persistently upon the former plane with its two dimensions, one cannot escape beyond the dialectic of history and superhistory, superhistory and history, the conception of a Christ-enthusiasm, in which out of an historical form there arises an heavenly essence or out of an heavenly essence an historical form. Then one speaks persistently, not of the Christ of the NT, but of man the idealist and mythologist, and of Jesus as the object of such a man's thought. Then one is not speaking of God's revelation. But the NT statement about the divinity of Christ means anything, only as witnessing to God's revelation. To explain it otherwise can only be to explain it in notorious opposition to the intention of the originators of it and in dispute with them. Ebionitism and Docetism are misunderstandings of a dialectic at work, and inevitably at work, in the thought and language of the NT writers, as surely as it is just men—because it has pleased God to assume humanity—who here think and talk, as surely therefore as the first plane with its two dimensions is the area in which they think and speak. (We shall return to this dialectic, which is present in the NT itself, in connection with the doctrine of the incarnation of the Word.) But their thought and language even upon this plane has a different meaning from that which it appears to have from the point of view of Ebionite and Docetic thought. This other meaning is given in the fact that the thought and language of the NT witnesses, at work like all human thought upon the first plane, are connected with the second plane which falls upon it perpendicularly, and which is identical with God's revelation. It is therefore, of course, true, that there is also clearly recognisable and distinguishable in the thought and language of the NT something like an opposite movement. It is, of course, true that above all in the Synoptists as a whole we have before us a Christological thought which in Jesus finds God—and above all in the Fourth Gospel a Christological thought, on the whole different, which finds God in Jesus. But the first does not mean that once for all in a mere man, in the historical form of a " great man," in an impressive personality, in a hero; the Synoptists actually found God. And the second does not mean that John found an idea, a general truth of an intellectual, moral or religious nature once for all actually personified in Jesus. The awkward starting-point of Ebionite thought, personality, and the awkward starting-point of Docetic thought, the idea, will be sought for in vain in the NT documents; it can never be anything but a sort of arbitrary construction, behind the documents and contradicting them. But the starting-point of Synoptic thought which finds God in Jesus is the fact, disclosed to certain men, of the divine emissary as such, the unambiguous fact of the man, who was in their midst, teaching and healing, dying and rising again, as a reality which, as divine, did not first require to be opened up and interpreted and asserted, but which called to their lips the confession, Thou art the Christ, the Son of the living God ! (Matt. 16¹⁶) immediately, not as a synthetic but as an analytic statement. And the starting-point of Johannine thought, which finds God in Jesus, was the fact, disclosed to certain men, of the divine mission, message, and revelation, which they found in Jesus, " grace and truth," " resurrection and life," becoming events, the actual occurrence of their being fed with the " bread of life " (John 6³⁵) their actually being given to drink of the living water (John 4¹⁰). " We saw—his glory." Whence, once more, resulted Peter's confession, only in the reverse direction, not as a synthetic but as an analytic statement, which at this point had to run : Κύριε, πρὸς τίνα ἀπελευσόμεθα; ῥήματα ζωῆς αἰωνίου ἔχεις· καὶ ἡμεῖς πεπιστεύκαμεν, καὶ ἐγνώκαμεν ὅτι σὺ εἶ ὁ ἅγιος τοῦ θεοῦ (John 6⁶⁸). From the point of view of these real starting-points of NT thought and side by side with these real starting-points, the common aim is in both cases understandable, namely the statement of the divinity of Christ. It was simply not the case that here an historical form had first to be " transformed " into an heavenly essence, or an heavenly essence first into an historical form, and in both cases a knowledge first into a faith. It is not how their knowledge but how their want of faith had been changed into faith, that the NT witnesses recount for us, and it is within faith that the opposed movement of their thought takes place. It has really nothing to do with the dialectic of Ebionitism and Docetism. For what is the meaning of the first step on a way, at the end of which a man is made equal to God, and what is the meaning of the first step on the second way, at the end of which God is a man ? Can this be the end of a way, of which it was not already the beginning ? Can the decisive assertion in the corresponding statements, or in the corresponding statement with the same meaning both times, be regarded as a result of thought won in an ascending or descending consideration or interpretation ? Can this assertion be anything else than an explanation of this very assumption, taken straight from the assumption, a *petitio principii*, as a logician would here without question have to say ? The actual content in the NT texts is at least this, that in Jesus it is God who is found, because in fact Jesus himself cannot be discovered as any one else than God. And it is in Jesus that God is found, because in fact He is not found anywhere else save in Jesus, but in him He is in fact found. This factual element at the start of the two ways of NT thought is revelation, the point of connection, situated in another dimension, which distinguishes this thought from that of the Ebionites and Docetists and their modern successors. Upon the background of this state of matters, which is simply to be found in the NT texts, the following consideration also may certainly be insisted on. By their assumption that there is at the end of an ascending or descending reflection—reflection upon the man Jesus as such and reflection upon divinity in special connection with the man Jesus—simply a small or even a great exaggeration, as the case might be, by means of which the statement of the divinity of Christ would spring up, or could be made intelligible, the Ebionite and Docetic Christologies impute to the thought of the Biblical witnesses a performance which the latter themselves could, of course, only have condemned as the blasphemy of which Jesus himself was accused, but really falsely accused. If Jesus had designated himself, or the oldest Church had designated him the Son of God, in the sense presupposed by both these conceptions then he and his Church would have been rightly expelled from the community of the OT. For what else could such idealising of a man or mythologising of an idea be, but characteristically the thing regarded by the OT as setting up and worshipping an idol, one of those unworthy and null rivals of Yahweh. How little could the word " God " have been understood in the sense of the OT by one who could imagine, or even hyperbolically pretend to imagine, that a man could really become God, or that the real God could have His copy in a man! Even though we could only claim in a way the first generation of the witnesses of Jesus as genuine Israelites, i.e. as Palestinian Jews, if we could trust them to have understood the difference between God and man, not as a quantitative one and therefore capable of being bridged over, but as a qualitative one, then we should have to describe it as *a priori* impossible that they should have thought in the way they must have thought, if they regarded the statement of the divinity of Christ in the sense of these two conceptions. If as Palestinian Jews they were capable of this statement at all, if they were confident of not only rejecting the charge of blasphemy raised against Jesus as a frightful misunderstanding, but of proclaiming it as the end of the OT, as the event in which, by rejecting no more and no less than Yahweh, Israel finally abandoned its own birthright—then that statement on their lips could not be the result of a rise or fall in speculation, it could, in its twofold movement, only be the expression of a, so to speak, axiomatic assumption, the explanatory utterance about a pure beginning of their thought, previously supplied to their thought. The explanation of their statement, Jesus is the Lord, can only be sought in the fact that it was so for them, and was so in the same actual and therefore obvious and indisputable way in which Yahweh of old was Israel's God. The complete perplexity of an historical outlook, which on the one hand cannot conceal from itself that the statement " lies in essentials ready to hand in the oldest literary witnesses, the epistles of Paul," on the other hand refuses to take account of the assumption, comes to the surface in the words of Johannes Weiss: " The coincidence of hitherto incongruous ideational elements in such a centre presupposes a power of attraction, which we cannot strongly enough ponder. How powerful must the mediate or immediate effect of the personality of Jesus have been upon the souls of his followers, that they were ready to believe such a thing of him, and to die for their faith!" (*RGG*[1] *art. Christologie* I). What indeed is the meaning of " power of attraction " and " mediate or immediate effect " in this case, in view of this effect? We may ask whether the early Church, apart from anything else, had not perhaps even more sense for historical reality and possibility, when she left it to heretics to trail to and fro over the beaten tracks of apotheosis and hypostasis Christology, but held it more to the point to look for the meaning of the NT statement of the divinity of Christ in the factual assumption in accord with it, exactly as the NT itself presents it.

Therefore—in our opinion so must we regard this NT statement in accord with the ancient Church—Jesus is the Lord, because he has it from the God, whom he calls his Father, to be the Lord, because with this Father of his, as the Son of this Father, as " th' eternal Father's only child," he is the Lord—an " is " which, if we are not in a position, with those who at first uttered it, to affirm it, we just deny, but which cannot be derived or proved or discussed, but can only be affirmed in an analytic proposition, as the beginning of all thought about it. In distinction from the assertion of the deification of a man or of the humanisation of a divine idea, the statement of the divinity of Christ is to be understood in the sense that Christ reveals his Father. But this Father of his is God. Therefore to reveal Him is to reveal God. But who can reveal God but God Himself ? Certainly no exalted man and certainly no descended idea can do that. Both are creatures. Certainly the Christ who reveals the Father is also a creature and his work a creaturely work. But if he were only a creature, then neither could he reveal God, just as surely as the creature cannot take the place of God, or act in His place. If he reveals God, he must himself be God, whatever be the relation with his creatureliness. And in that case he must be—for this is a case of either/or—complete true God, without deduction or limitation, without more or less. He is not " all but " and he is not " somehow " God. By every such limitation his divine being would be not only weakened but denied. To confess him as the revelation of his Father, is to confess him a being essentially equal in divinity to this Father of his.

But what does it mean for us—here, too, this must be our startingpoint—to confess Jesus as the revelation of his Father and so as His true Son ? If we now concentrate and now lay the emphasis on the fact that Jesus as the Revealer of the Father, His will and His operation, not only proclaims to us our Lord, but, by so doing, is himself our Lord, that therefore as the Son of the Father he also reveals himself—then what therein becomes an event, so far as it is an act of God, signifies obviously something different from the act of God the Creator, which we regarded as the inner concept of the content of the revelation of the Father. I.e. it signifies, as to the reality of God's lordship above and beyond our existence,

30

God's Lordship in His turning to us, in fact coming to ι s, speaking
to us, wishing to be heard by us and to be the cause of our sense of
responsibility. It signifies an intercourse, established by God,
between Him and us. Not only does God will and operate, but—
this is what takes place in His revelation in Jesus—He opens up
His will and operation to us. He does not treat us as He does
dust or clay, although as His creatures that is what we are. He
does not leave us simply subjected to His creative power, controlled and moved by His creative power, in order to fulfil His
purpose in us. He seeks us as those who can let themselves be
found. He converses with us as those who are capable of hearing,
understanding, and obeying. He deals as the Creator with us, but
as a Person with persons, not as a force with things. " Th' eternal
Good's your brother." And that is exactly what is so far from
being obvious ; what is rather miraculous ; and not only and
primarily as a miracle of all power, as the mystery in which the
statement *finitum non capax infiniti* is dissolved. That, of course,
is also the case. But it is not the dissolution of this statement that
is the mystery of the revelation of God the Son, it is the dissolution
of the other, far more incisive statement, *homo peccator non capax
verbi divini*. God's power to establish intercourse with us is, of
course, also, though in the long run not decisively, called in question
by the fact that He is infinite while we are finite, that He is Lord
over life and death while we are alive as those bounded by death,
that He is the Creator while we are people called out of nothing into
being and existence. But then this possibility in God is decisively
called in question by our being God's enemies. How do we know
that ? Certainly not of ourselves. Certainly not because we are
aware of the problematic nature of our being and existence as men,
or of the conflict between the spiritual and the natural sides of our
existence, or of the conflict between our theoretical ideals and our
practical achievements, or, generally, of the antinomies, amid
which runs the course of our thought and our existence. That we
are God's enemies does not at all follow from these in themselves
incontestable facts, and could only be described as a misanthropic
exaggeration, if intended to be an expression of these familiar
facts. The knowledge that " I have sinned . . . and am no more
worthy to be called thy son " (Luke 15[18f.]) is not the discovery of
an abstract anthropology. Only the son who has already recalled
to mind the father's house is aware that he is a lost son. We are
first and only aware of being God's enemies, because God has

actually established intercourse with us. But on the very assumption of the actuality of this happening we can regard this happening itself as nothing short of miraculous. The Word of God, the revelation of which is attested in Scripture, tells man that he is a rebel, who has wantonly abandoned the communion between himself as creature and God as Creator, and has placed himself in a situation in which this communion is impossible. It tells him that he wanted to be his own master, and thereby has betaken himself off to the sphere of the wrath of God, to the state of rejection by God and so of being closed against God. It tells him that his existence, contrary to what was determined at his creation, is a contradiction of God, a contradiction which excludes listening to God. It thus strangely tells him that he cannot hear it at all, this Word which tells him it ; and he cannot hear it because he does not want to, because the fact of his life is disobedience, and thereby in practice, so far as concerns the use he makes of his life, is a refusal to listen to what God says to him. Nay more ; this content of the Word of God spoken to man also makes it quite inconceivable, that man should succeed even only in hearing the Word of God, that God should turn to him and address him at all. His being closed to what God can say to him is merely an expression of the wrath of God which lies upon him. Must not this wrath of God, if it is serious —and the Word of God will tell us nothing else than that it is truly serious—consist above all and decisively in the fact that God has turned away His countenance from us and therefore does not converse with us, that for fallen man in the objective sense there is also not a Word of God at all ? If then we hear it notwithstanding, and if this has the double significance, that in fact we can hear it and that in fact we succeed in hearing it—and only on this assumption shall this and no other be our verdict upon ourselves and our situation towards God—we cannot regard this " hearing of ours notwithstanding " as a possibility remaining over to us notwithstanding (" somehow "), or as one to be created by us notwithstanding. That, obviously, we could only do through gross absentmindedness and forgetfulness about what we are told by the Word of God concerning ourselves and our situation before God. This is the interpretation of our " hearing notwithstanding," which quite simply would mean that we still had not yet heard or had again ceased already to hear. If we have heard and heard again —our " self-interpretation " really depends upon our hearing and not upon our self apart from this hearing—then we can only regard this possibility of our hearing as a possibility gifted to us, subjectively and objectively, in an utterly miraculous way, as the " notwithstanding " of grace, which on our side has nothing to correspond to it or to precondition it.

Τὸ φρόνημα τῆς σαρκὸς ἔχθρα εἰς θεόν· τῷ γὰρ νόμῳ τοῦ θεοῦ οὐχ ὑποτάσσεται, οὐδὲ γὰρ δύναται (Rom. 8⁷). Ἐχθροὶ ὄντες κατηλλάγημεν τῷ θεῷ (Rom. 5¹⁰). Ἐν αὐτῷ ζωὴ ἦν, καὶ ἡ ζωὴ ἦν τὸ φῶς τῶν ἀνθρώπων, καὶ τὸ φῶς ἐν τῇ σκοτίᾳ φαίνει, καὶ ἡ σκοτία αὐτὸ οὐ κατέλαβεν (John 1⁵). Ὃ οἴδαμεν λαλοῦμεν καὶ ὃ ἑωράκαμεν μαρτυροῦμεν, καὶ τὴν μαρτυρίαν ἡμῶν οὐ λαμβάνετε (John 3¹¹). Εἰς τὰ ἴδια ἦλθεν καὶ οἱ ἴδιοι αὐτὸν οὐ παρέλαβον (John 1¹¹). Ὃ ἑώρακεν καὶ ἤκουσεν τοῦτο μαρτυρεῖ, καὶ τὴν μαρτυρίαν αὐτοῦ οὐδεὶς λαμβάνει (John 3³²).

Thus the self-interpretation of the real hearer is created in view of the possibility of his hearing. He regards himself as the sort of person who is always robbing himself of this possibility. He can only regard God as the one who gives him this possibility, and by whose initiative it is a possibility.

In the next section, in the doctrine of God the Holy Spirit, we shall have to speak of the subjective side of this possibility, i.e. of the possibility of our being able to hear what God tells us. That God can tell us anything at all beforehand, this prime inconceivability in view of His wrath with sinful man, is in God's revelation the work of the Son or Word of God. The work of the Son or Word is the presence and manifestation of God which, in view of the fact that it is a miraculous event amid human darkness and despite this darkness, we can only designate revelation. The word reconciliation is another word for the same thing. So far as God's revelation as such achieves, what only God can achieve, namely, the restoration of man's communion with God, destroyed, nay annihilated by us, so far as, in the fact of revelation, God's enemies are already His friends, revelation itself is reconciliation. Just as on the contrary reconciliation, the restoration of that communion, the mercy of God triumphant in wrath over wrath, can only take the form of the mystery, which we actually designate revelation.

Paul describes Christ as him δι' οὗ νῦν (i.e. in Paul, in the presence of the *regnum gratiae* characterised by revelation) τὴν καταλλαγὴν ἐλάβομεν (Rom. 5¹¹). To God's good pleasure to suffer His πλήρωμα to dwell in him, corresponds His will δι' αὐτοῦ ἀποκαταλλάξαι τὰ πάντα εἰς αὐτόν (Col. 1²⁰). God was καταλλάσσων τὸν κόσμον in him, it says also to the same effect in 2 Cor. 5¹⁹). And hence the apostolic service is the διακονία τῆς καταλλαγῆς (2 Cor. 5¹⁸) reaching fulfilment in the injunction καταλλάγητε τῷ θεῷ (2 Cor. 5²⁰).— Thus the concept reconciliation does coincide with that of revelation, but not with that of redemption (ἀπολύτρωσις, σωτηρία). " Redemption " should in the NT signify the act of God, which, from the point of view of revelation or reconciliation, is God's act still outstanding, future, consummating : νυνὶ δὲ ἀποκατήλλαξεν (ὑμᾶς) ἐν τῷ σώματι τῆς σαρκὸς αὐτοῦ (Col. 1²²). Καταλλαγέντες σωθησόμεθα, (Rom. 5¹⁰). Cf. for the eschatological use of ἀπολύτρωσις, Luke 21²⁸ ; Rom. 8²³ ; Eph. 4³⁰ ; Heb. 11³⁵—of σωτηρία, 1 Thess. 5⁸ᶠ· ; Rom. 13¹¹ ; Phil. 1¹⁹, 2¹² ; Heb. 1¹⁴, 9²⁸. Distinct from this, " reconciliation " is the act of God that gives rise to the expectation of this future, His act in Christ as the mediator between God and man (1 Tim. 2⁵) or of the " new covenant " (Heb. 9¹⁵, 12²⁴), the bearer and bringer of εἰρήνη, just as, especially in Paul, it is regarded as the fundamental meaning of God's gracious turning to man (cf. the juxtaposition of χάρις and εἰρήνη in the forms of greeting) and is explained in Eph. 2¹⁴⁻¹⁵ as a divine act.

The inconceivable element in revelation as such, revelation as reconciliation which can only be a reality from God's side, this inconceivable element is the fact of the Son of God, who is the Lord in our midst, that is, amid our enmity towards God. Because the love of God which is made manifest in this fact cannot be identical with the love of God for the world which He wished to make and did create—between this world and our world lie sin and death—because the love of God manifest in this fact is rather His actual love for the lost world of man become guilty before Him (John 3¹⁶), for the world whose continuity with the original one is completely hidden from us—for that reason we cannot confuse God's lordship in the one case with God's lordship in the other, or directly identify them ; for that reason we must in the former case (in view of creation) speak of a first mode of God's existence, in the latter (in view of reconciliation) speak of a second mode of God's existence. As surely as we must declare that reconciliation, or revelation, is not creation or a continuation of creation, but an inconceivably new work of God above and beyond creation, so surely we must assert that the Son is not the Father, but that the one God is here—in this work—not apart from the Father, but simply the Son or Word of the Father.

It is not clear how the difference between the mode of existence of the Son of God and that of the Father—the same difference must in that case also be asserted about the mode of existence of the Holy Spirit—can be denied, without speculatively changing the significance of the seriousness of the wrath of God against sin and of the opposition between original and fallen man, between the world of creation and our world of sin and death, and so weakening it into a mere tension within a whole known to us and reviewable by us. On this supposition the inconceivability of revelation as the divine deed of reconciliation must naturally be contested, it must be viewed as a logical second or third act in the same creation series which for us is such an obvious whole, and it will seem an easy thing to identify the Reconciler-God with the Creator-God. In this way Schleiermacher regarded sin quantitatively as a mere deficiency, and consequently reconciliation (" redemption ") as the crowning of creation, and again, consistently, he viewed the Trinity modalistically, that is, regarded the difference of the three modes of existence as one that was abrogated in the profundities of God. A corresponding doctrine of the Trinity would also have to underlie the still more unfettered gnosis of E. Hirsch regarding the synthesis of origin and fall (*Schöpfung und Sünde*, 1932). It may also be asserted, conversely, that such disasters must ensue upon a doctrine of creation and reconciliation in which the necessary obstacles are not interposed by means of an orderly doctrine of the Trinity.

Conversely we must say that, since in the revelation of God we are concerned with His lordship amid our enmity against Him i.e. with the miracle of reconciliation, this work cannot be the work of a superman or demigod. The unheard-of nature of the love of God for the world of fallen man, the power of reconciliation would be underestimated, were the true divinity of the Reconciler called in question. A superhuman or semi-divine event, one which strictly speaking is not miraculous but in the last resort self-evident, within the universe and so creaturely, does not answer to the seriousness of the problem to be solved, does not answer to the character of almighty grace actually inherent in the event which Holy Scripture describes as the event of reconciliation or revelation. The character of almighty grace which this event possesses, in the light of which the problem to which it is the answer becomes a problem of infinite seriousness, demands the acknowledgment that its Subject is identical with God in the full sense of the word.

It is just from this standpoint, in view of a reconciliation the Subject of which can be no less a person or fact than God Himself, if its power and the seriousness of the problem it answers be grasped, if it is not to be regarded as a merely apparent reconciliation, that the knowledge of the true divinity of Christ has rightly been asserted and proclaimed from time immemorial. The so-called Homily of Clement (I 1) begins with the declaration that we must think of Jesus Christ ὡς περὶ θεοῦ, and forthwith explains that by the words ὡς κριτοῦ ζώντων καὶ νεκρῶν. We should not μικρὰ φρονεῖν περὶ τῆς σωτηρίας ἡμῶν. By thinking meanly of Christ we should show directly that we had likewise but a mean hope. There was a necessary coherence and correspondence in the knowledge πόθεν ἐκλήθημεν καὶ ὑπὸ τίνος καὶ εἰς ὃν τόπον. Similarly Gregory of Nyssa claims that who the benefactor is may and must be disclosed by his benefits, that the nature possessed by the agent must be disclosed by the event of his act : Ἀφ᾽ ὧν γὰρ εὖ πάσχομεν, ἀπὸ τούτων εὐεργέτην ἐπιγινώσκομεν, πρὸς γὰρ τὰ γινόμενα βλέποντες, διὰ τούτων τὴν τοῦ ἐνεργοῦντος ἀναλογιζόμεθα φύσιν. He who ascribed creatureliness to Son and Spirit and thus subjected himself to a creature, was not setting his hope on God and was deceived in thinking that as a Christian he was translated into a better condition (*Or. cat.* 14 and 39). This very context was also one which Luther was constantly emphasising : *Vincere peccatum mundi, mortem, maledictionem et iram Dei*, are not works of a *humana aut angelica potestas*, but *mera opera divinae maiestatis Qua re cum docemus homines per Christum iustificari, Christum esse victorem peccati, mortis et aeternae maledictionis, testificamur simul eum esse natura Deum* (*on Gal.* 1^{3}, 1535 W. edn. 40^{I}, p. 81, l. 18; *on Gal* 14 *ib.* p. 96, l. 15; *on Gal.* 3^{13} *ib.* p. 441, l. 16, 25, 31) . . . " for if sin is thus a big thing and its purification therefore costeth so much, that such a lofty person, as Christ is here praised, must himself set to it and purify it through himself, what then in such great matters could avail our poor and helpless action, for we are creatures, nay sinful and wicked perishing creatures? that were as if one were to undertake with an extinguished torch to inflame heaven and earth. There must here be as great a payment for sin as God Himself is, who is outraged by sin" (*Sermon on Heb.* $1^{1f.}$, 1522 W. edn. 10^{II}, p. 161, l. 21). " Now God maketh none a king who is not God, for He will not let the reins out of His own hands, will alone be lord over heaven and earth, death, hell, devil, and over all creatures. Since then he maketh him a lord over all that is made, he must already be God" (*Sermon on John* $3^{1f.}$, 1526 W. edn. $10^{I,2}$, p. 296, l. 37). " For where the person who offered himself for us was not God, it would help and avail nothing for God, that he was born of a virgin and likewise endured a thousand deaths. But it bringeth blessing and victory over all sin and death, that the seed of Abraham is also the true God, who giveth Himself for us" (*Sermon on Phil.* $2^{5f.}$; 1525 W. edn. 17^{II}, p. 236, l. 25). "We men are all sinners and lost. If then we are to become righteous and blessed, it must take place through Christ. But because through Christ alone we are righteous and blessed, He must be more than a pure and simple man. For man's hand and power can make no one righteous and blessed. God must do it Himself" *Serman on the Passion, How Christ was buried; and on Isa.* 53, E. edn. 3, 276). So, too, runs the answer to question 17 in the Heidelberg Catechism: the Mediator must be true God, " so that by virtue of his godhead he might bear the burden of the wrath of God in his humanity, and acquire and restore to us righteousness and life."

Thus Jesus is the Lord as the Son of God come to us, or the Word of God spoken to us. We thereby assert something which goes beyond the statement that God is the Creator or " Our Father in heaven." Jesus reveals the God who is the Creator and who is " our Father in heaven." But in so doing, in the unheard-of thing becoming an event, namely, that this God becomes manifest in him, that He reveals to us Himself, so surely the fact of revelation has a fresh significance regarding its content, so surely reconciliation is to be regarded not as the completion of creation, but only as a miracle in and upon the fallen world. In the previous section we heard that in the context of the NT witness, this revelation of the Creator and our Father cannot be abstracted from the Person of the Revealer. From this unity of the content of the revelation with the Person of the Revealer we there inferred the original and peculiar meaning of the Fatherhood of God, that He is the Father, because He is the Father of the only-begotten Son. From the same unity we at once have the further result of Jesus Christ's sonship to God: there is no abstract Person who reveals, but the Person who reveals is the Person Jesus Christ, subordinate to the Creator revealed by it (the Person), yet indissolubly co-ordinate with Him, existing with Him, in whom the revelation in question is a reality. To express it differently, there is no Jesus *per se*, who might perhaps later acquire the additional predicate of a bearer of the revelation of his Father. Just as there is also no revelation of the Father *per se*, which later might also be apprehended in Jesus, by way of an instance and in a pre-eminent form. But Jesus is the revelation of the Father, and the revelation of the Father is Jesus. And actually it is in virtue of this " is " that he is the Son or the Word of the Father.

Our criticism of Ebionite and Docetic Christology has shown us that in the NT witness the Person and the thing really constitute this unity, that the apostles' thought about Jesus Christ, whether starting with the Person or with the thing, invariably failed to express itself in the form of a syllogism, but ceased with the knowledge of the divinity of Christ, because that was where it had begun. From this side also we can fail to assert the unity of the content of the revelation with the Person of the Revealer, only if we decline to receive the NT witness, if we fail to attend to the prohibition and command set up therein.

And now in view of our exposition of creation and reconciliation we may further add that Jesus Christ's sonship to God also results from the fact that creation (the content of his revelation of the Father) and reconciliation (the content of his own self-revelation), while utterly different from each other in their signifi ance for us, also coalesce completely in their origin. In fact already, because of our wish to follow in the tracks of Holy Scripture itself, we were unable to grasp the concept of the Creator otherwise, than by the apparent detour *via* the knowledge of God as the Lord over life and death, as the God of Good Friday and Easter. And in our attempt to grasp the concept of the Reconciler we had to assume that there is a world created by God, although fallen and lost, a mankind created by God, although actually living in enmity towards God. Only in him who acts on us as Reconciler through cross and resurrection could we recognise the Creator, and only in the Creator who remains the Lord of our existence in spite of our enmity could we recognise the Reconciler.

Τῷ γὰρ ἐξ ἀρχῆς τὴν ζωὴν δεδωκότι μόνον δυνατὸν ἦν καὶ πρέπον ἅμα καὶ ἀπολομένην ἀνακαλέσασθαι (Gregory of Nyssa, *Or. cat.* 8).

We must distinguish them, these two, and obviously we must also distinguish them in such a way as to perceive and acknowledge the relation of subordination here existing. We must therefore say, that the Reconciler is not the Creator and that as Reconciler he follows the Creator, that he, so to speak, consummates a second divine act—not such an one as we might derive from the first, the following of which from the first we might review and realise to be necessary, but a second act related to the first in its complete novelty and inconceivability. God reconciles us to Himself, He comes to us, He speaks with us—that is what follows, and we must just say that it follows from the fact that He is first of all the Creator. We may also say that it follows from the fact that He is " Our Father in heaven." Were He not first of all the Creator and Father, who is the Lord of our existence, against whom we have sinned, whose wrath therefore lies upon us, but whose wrath is but the reverse of His love as Creator and Father, how in that case could He be the Reconciler, the Founder of peace? To this order of creation and reconciliation corresponds Christologically the order of Father and Son or Father and Word: Jesus Christ as the Reconciler cannot precede the Creator, or " the Father in heaven." He stands to Him in the irreversible relation of following upon Him and from Him, as the Son follows upon the father or from the father, as the word follows upon the speaker or from the speaker. But again this subordination and following cannot signify any difference in being, but merely a difference in the mode of existence. For reconciliation is not more easily conceivable or less divine than creation. It is not as if reconciliation as distinct from creation could be made intelligible as a creaturely event. But as creation is *creatio ex nihilo*, so reconciliation is the raising of the dead. As we owe life to God the Creator, we owe eternal life to God the Reconciler.

Ipse est autem creator ejus, qui salvator ejus. Non ergo debemus sic laudare creatorem, ut cogamur, imo vere · convincamur dicere superfluum salvatorem (Augustine, *De nat. et grat.* 33, 39). *Creasti me, cum non essem, redemisti me cum perditus essem. Sed conditionis quidem meae et redemptionis causa sola fuit dilectio tua* (Anselm of Canterbury, *Medit.* 12). " This fleeting temporal life we have through God, who, as we confess in the first article of our Christian faith, is the almighty Creator of heaven and earth. But changeless eternal life we have through our Lord Jesus Christ's passion and resurrection, who hath sat down at the right hand of God, as we confess in the second article of our Christian faith " (Luther, *Sermon on Matt.* 22[34f.], 1532 E, edn. 5, 151). How should the second act be less great and miraculous than the first ? We might rather on the contrary dispute the point and wish to see in the second, in reconciliation, the far greater miracle. As God is addressed in the offertory of the Roman Mass : *Deus, qui humanae substantiae dignitatem mirabiliter condidisti et mirabilius reformasti.* . . . But controversy would be aimless. *Intelligant redempti tui, non fuisse excellentius, quod initio factus est mundus, quam quod in fine saeculorum Pascha nostrum immolatus est Christus (Oratio nach der 9. Prophetie in der Vigil der Osternacht).*

Here genuine miracle stands side by side with genuine miracle, here neither one way nor the other can there be any question of a more or a less in miracle, or yet a more or less in divinity. Here in both cases what we have is merely an either/or. Here, then, sonship as well as Fatherhood, within and including the super- and sub-ordination of the modes of existence thereby expressed, is to be regarded as illimitably genuine divinity.

2. THE ETERNAL SON

Who is the Son of God? We have heard the preliminary answer: Jesus Christ, as him who reveals the Father and reconciles us with the Father, is the Son of God. For by being that, he reveals himself as the Son who has come to us or as the Word of God spoken to us. To this realisation derived from the Scripture witness to revelation, the only new thing added by the dogma of the Trinity is the interpretation to the effect, that Jesus Christ is able to reveal the Father to us and to reconcile us to the Father, because he reveals himself as the person he is. He does not first become God's Son or Word in the event of revelation. On the contrary, the event of revelation possesses divine truth and reality, because in it the specific nature of God becomes manifest, because Jesus Christ reveals himself as the person he already is antecedently, even apart from this event, actually in himself. His sonship, on the ground of which he is able to be the Revealer, the Mediator, the Reconciler, is not a mere conformation of God, behind which, in some higher essence of God that remains a mystery, there would be no Sonship, no Wordness, but possibly an inexpressible and speechless Itness, something divine, a θεῖον with a different or unknown name. No, revelation has eternal content and eternal validity. Throughout all the depths of deity, not as the penultimate but as the ultimate thing to be said about God, God is God the Son just as He is God the Father. Jesus Christ, the Son of God, is God Himself, as God his Father is God Himself.

How does this interpretation of the Biblical witness to revelation come about? Even here we can only give the very simple but momentous answer, that it comes about because we allow the equal, inconceivable divinity of the work of creation and of the work of reconciliation, and therefore the unity of Father and Son, as it confronts us in this witness with a significance for the revelation it attests, to stand and rank as the last word. The Church dogma of the divinity of Christ, as distinguished from the NT statements about the divinity of Christ, asserts nothing else but this, that in the simple assumption upon which this NT statement rests, the assumption that Jesus Christ is the Son of God because he is so (not because he makes this impression upon us, not because he fulfils what we fancy we should expect from a god, but because he is so)—in this simple assumption we must participate. With it, all thought about Jesus, and that must at once mean all thought about God, must begin and end. No reflection can claim to be the basis of this assumption, no reflection can call this assumption in question. Any reflection can but start from it and return to it. From this realisation arose the Church dogma of the divinity of Christ, and to it this realisation gives expression. For if it expressly regards the divinity of Christ as eternal divinity, when we assert that the Son come to us, the Word spoken to us, is antecedently the Son or Word of God *per se*, we thereby assert practically nothing else than simply that the statement about the divinity of Christ is to be regarded not as a derivative, but as a fundamental statement. Thus, declares the dogma, the apostles regarded it, and so must we also regard it, if we wish to understand the apostles. So must we therefore also understand the apostles and the statement, unless our own understanding should have led us more or less astray from the understanding of the early Church, which expressed and deposited this very understanding in the dogma. Our own understanding of it, as attempted by us here, has not so far led us away from the dogma of the early Church, but guided us to it. It might actually have been otherwise—for us the dogma has not a divine but only a human, pedagogic dignity. We might have turned our backs upon it, but we have no cause to do this. We may, and moreover we must, to express our own understanding of the NT, say what the dogma says. We cannot understand the NT statement about the divinity of Christ otherwise or better, than by retracing our thought of it in harmony with the early Church, i.e. by directly confronting it with the dogma of the eternal divinity of Christ. The dogma as such is not to be found in the Biblical texts. The dogma is an interpretation. But we can convince ourselves that it is a good, relevant interpretation of these texts. Therefore we throw in our lot with it in declaring that the divinity of Christ is true, eternal divinity. We recognise that divinity in his action in revelation and reconciliation. But it is not revelation and reconciliation that creates his divinity, but his divinity that creates revelation and reconciliation.

Κύριος ὢν κατὰ ἀλήθειαν, οὐκ ἐξ προκοπῆς τὸ κυριεύειν λαβών, ἀλλ' ἐκ φύσεως τὸ τῆς κυριότητος ἔχων ἀξίωμα. Καὶ οὐ καταχρηστικῶς ὡς ἡμεῖς κύριος καλούμενος ἀλλὰ τῇ ἀληθείᾳ κύριος ὤν (Cyril of Jerusalem, *Cat.* 10, 5).

Jesus Christ is therefore the real and active Revealer of God and Reconciler with God, because in him, His Son or Word, God sets and gives to be known, not some thing, be it the greatest and most significant, but Himself exactly as He posits and knows Himself from eternity and in eternity. He is the Son or the Word of God for us, because he was so previously in himself.

It is one of the many optical illusions of modernist Protestantism to have deemed it a possible duty to interpret and discredit this "antecedently in himself," i.e. the confession of the true eternal divinity of Christ, by pointing to a supposedly changed attitude, as compared with the early and mediæval Church, of the Reformers to this matter, as the exponents of an untheological, metaphysical speculation.—What is usually adduced from the utterances of the Reformers with this intention, is far from adequate to prove that they had ever thought of attacking, or even merely touching, the dogma of the divinity of Christ.

Above all there is a passage in the first edition of Melanchthon's *Loci* (1521), which is relevant here. In the introduction to this oldest evangelical dogmatics Melanchthon distinguishes among *Loci theologici* those which are *prorsus incomprehensibiles*, and those which according to the will of Christ would have to be *compertissimi* to all Christian people. Of the former it had to be said that *mysteria divinitatis rectius adoraverimus, quam vestigaverimus*. For the latter course was involved in great danger, and God had veiled His Son in flesh, *ut a contemplatione maiestatis suae ad carnis adeoque fragilitatis nostrae contemplationem invitaret*. Melanchthon therefore declares that he sees no reason to waste much trouble on those *loci supremi de Deo, de unitate, de trinitate Dei, de mysterio creationis, de modo incarnationis*. The Scholastics had been fools in the investigation of these things and the *beneficia Christi* had thereby been obscured. For the arguments (*e philosophia*, says the second edition 1522) which they had brought forward here had frequently been more worthy of an heretical than of a catholic dogma. On the contrary the other *loci* were vital ; on the power of sin, on law, on grace. *Nam ex his proprie Christus cognoscitur, siquidem hoc est Christum cognoscere, beneficia eius cognoscere, non quod isti docent eius naturas, modos incarnationis contueri. Ni scias, in quem usum carnem induerit et cruci affixus sit Christus, quid proderit eius historiam novisse ?* As a doctor must know more about plants than their nature, namely, their *vis nativa*, so Christ must be recognised as *salutare*, as this is clearly given in precisely those other *loci*, of which the Scholastics did not speak. One should follow the example of Paul in Romans where, as if he had anticipated the *disputationes frigidae et alienae a Christo*, he speaks not about the Trinity, the Incarnation, *creatio activa et passiva*, but just of the Law, sin, grace, i.e. of the *loci, qui Christum tibi commendent, qui conscientiam confirment, qui animum adversus satanam erigant*. It was the Rationalists of the 18th and the beginning of the 19th centuries (cf. e.g. Joh. Joach. Spaldin'g, *Über die Nützbarkeit des Predigtamtes*, 1772 p. 138 f.; K. G. Bretschneider, *Handbuch der Dogmatik*, vol. I 4th edn. 1838 p. 553) and in the more recent period it was especially A. Ritschl (cf. *Rechtf. u. Versöhnung* [4], vol. III p. 374 *Theologie und Metaphysik*, 1874 p. 60) and his pupils (cf. e.g., M. Rade, *Glaubenslehre*, vol. I 1924 p. 53; H. Stephan, *Glaubenslehre*, 2nd edn. 1928 pp. 166, 240) who thought they should rejoice in this passage. But the fact should not be concealed, that this passage does not assert what people would be glad to find in it. It betrays a transient mood but not a theological attitude which became theologically significant, even in Melanchthon himself. Even this mood was not directed against the content but against the importance of the Trinitarian dogma relatively to the other dogmas which lay nearer to Melanchthon's heart. Moreover it was not caused by Melanchthon's own, perhaps critical, preoccupation with the dogma of the Trinity, but on the one hand by his intensive preoccupation with those other dogmas, caused by Luther's instigation, on the other hand by indignation at the unchurchly theoretical way, in which he found the "Scholastics," i.e. the theologians of the late Middle Ages first known to him, busied with the doctrine of the Trinity. It was a passing mood : it needed subsequently only the emergence of an anti-Trinitarian to change his tone at once and to make room in his *Loci* for the dogma of the Trinity in spite of the utterance quoted. That mood in no wise became significant for Reformed confessional work or for any theological school.

If Calvin were more familiar to the friends of the Melanchthon passage, they would naturally also appeal to him. In 1537, at the time of his first stay in Geneva, the theological Church adventurer, Petrus Caroli, could charge him publicly with anti-Trinitarianism and not without gaining to some extent the ear even of serious people. The circumstances relating to this charge were these. The *Confession de la foy*, so authoritative for the beginning of the Geneva Reformation (in K. Müller, p. 111 f.), the contents of which are, of course, more significant for W. Farel, who at that time stood quite in the foreground, than for Calvin, is silent about the doctrine of the Trinity, alike in its doctrine of God and in its Christology. But in addition the first draft of the *Institutio* of Calvin himself, which appeared somewhat earlier in the same year (*cap.* 2 *De fide*, beginning), gives indeed a thoroughly correct and respectful exposition of the doctrine of the Trinity : there was not a vestige of truth in Caroli's objection, that Calvin avoided the expressions *trinitas* and *persona* ; but it is noteworthy that the author's interest in this matter is not exactly burning. · Further, in his apologetic pamphlet against Caroli, published in 1545, Calvin himself writes that the true knowledge of the divinity of Christ consists in placing all confidence and all hope in him and in calling on his name. *Quae practica notitia certior haud dubie est qualibet otiosa speculatione. Illic enim pius animus Deum praesentissimum conspicit et paene attrectat, ubi se vivificari, illuminari, salvari, justificari et sanctificari sentit (Adv. P. Caroli calumnias, C.R. 7, 312 f.).* Over and above this Calvin seems at that time to have had all sorts of objections to the authority and authenticity of the

Early Church symbols (*C.R.* 5, 337 ; 10², 84, 86 ; 7, 311 f.). And it is a fact that he energetically declined to yield to the demand of Caroli that to accredit his orthodoxy he should subscribe to these symbols, because of the " tyranny " of such a demand (*C.R.* 7, 315 ; 10², 120 f.). The whole dispute, theologically and humanly, is thoroughly obscure. But so much arises clearly from the passage adduced and above all from the first draft of the *Institutio* : at that time Calvin, like Melanchthon sixteen years earlier, was busied with other things, namely, like the latter, with the problems of the appropriation of salvation, and not with their objective presuppositions. In the case of W. Farel we may seriously ask whether at the outset he had not perhaps really lost sight of these latter points and to that extent stood, like so many of his contemporaries, at the beginning of the road which was bound to lead to anti-Trinitarianism. Of Calvin himself this cannot be said, even in view of that earlier time. Rather he had these presuppositions, even at this early date, more clearly in view than the Melanchthon of the utterances of 1521, In addition to the lack of a proper characteristic doctrine of the Trinity, which he actually sought to attribute to "Arianism," Caroli, who seems to have been pretty brainless, made it a reproach against him that he attributed to Christ the OT name of *Jehovah*. Of course Calvin meant that for an *elogium divinitatis* (*C.R.* 7, 312 ; 10², 121 ; 9, 708). To repeat—even of the Calvin of that date we cannot speak of anything else than of a somewhat peevish mood, strengthened by Caroli's malicious charge, but directed not against the objective presuppositions, but merely against their doctrinal formulation by the early church. How far removed he was from drawing anti-Trinitarian conclusions from this mood, is unambiguously attested by the completion of his *Institutio*, as well as by his attitude, say, in the case of Servetus.

The core of the matter comes clearly into view in Luther, to whom in this matter appeal is also wont to be made. It is his views which decisively underlie Melanchthon's utterances and also, of course, indirectly, those of Calvin. From his knowledge of man's justification in Christ alone and therefore by faith alone, he rightly drew the conclusion, that any human theology at all can only be the theology of revelation. So self-willed is it and therefore deadly dangerous, in the question as to man's justification, to aline oneself with the preconceived concept of the divine law, or the one arbitrarily abstracted from the pronouncements of Scripture, so self-willed and dangerous is it generally to proceed in theology from a preconceived concept of God or one arbitrarily abstracted from the pronouncements of Scripture. But as with the question of justification in particular, so with the entire theological question; it can only be answered by looking to the God who reveals Himself in Christ. As early as 1519 Luther calls it a thought already frequently repeated by him, that this is the *unicus et solus modus cognoscendi Deum* (disgracefully neglected by the *doctores sentientiarum* with their *absolutae divinitatis speculationes*) that *quicumque velit salubriter de Deo cogitare aut speculari, prorsus omnia postponat praeter humanitatem Christi* (*Letter to Spalatin of 12th Feb. 1519* W. edn. Letter 1, p. 328 f.). About the same time we have Luther's polemic to this effect : *Proinde, qui vult Deum cognoscere, schalam terrae infixam contueatur : cadit hic tota ratio hominum. Natura quidem docet, ut simus propensiores ad contemplanda magna quam abjecta. Hinc collige, quam inique, ne dicam impie, agant et speculantur, sua confisi industria, summa Trinitatis misteria : quo loco sedeant angeli, quid loquantur sancti, Cum tamen in carnem natus est Christus atque in carne mansurus sit. Vide autem, quid continget illis. Primo :* " if with their head they should push through to

heaven and look around heaven, and there should find no one but Christ laid
in the crib and in the woman's bosom, they would fall down again and break
their neck." *Et ii sunt scriptores super primum librum sententiarum. Deinde
adeo nihil consequuntur istis suis speculationibus, ut neque sibi neque aliis
prodesse aut consulere possunt.* " Begin sublimely down below, Thomas and
Philip, and not above" *(Schol. in libr. Gen.* on Gen. 28, W. edn. 9, p. 406, l. 11).
And still better known is the following passage : " For I have often said and
continue to say that men should remember when I am dead, and guard against
all teachers, as men ridden and led by the Devil, who aloft in highest position
begin to teach and preach God nakedly and separately from Christ, as hitherto
in high schools they have speculated and played with His works above in
heaven, what He is, thinks, and does by Himself, etc. But if thou wilt fare
securely and rightly touch on or grasp God, that thou mayst find grace and
help with Him, so let thyself not be persuaded to seek Him elsewhere than in
the Lord Christ, nor go round about with other thoughts and trouble thyself,
or ask anent another work, than as He hath sent Christ. Upon Christ set
thy knowledge and study, there let them also bide and take hold ; and where
thine own thought and reason or any one else leadeth and directeth otherwise,
but close thine eyes and say : I should and will be aware of no other God save
in my Lord Christ " *(Sermon on John* 17³, 1528 W. edn. 28, p. 100, l. 33 ;
cf. also *Comm. Gal.* 1³, 1535 W. edn. 40ᴵ, p. 75 f. ; W. edn. *Ti.* 6, p. 28). But
we should not fail to note that, so far as they are polemical in content, these
utterances of Luther's do not touch the doctrine of the divinity of Christ.
And so far as they are concerned with the divinity of Christ, they have no
polemical content. Luther's wish—that is his trend in this line of thought—
is, that divinity in general, and the divinity of Christ in particular, should
be made known, not by way of self-willed speculation but by way of knowledge of God's revelation, that is in fact by way of knowledge of the *beneficia
Christi,* and so of the *humanitas Christi,* i.e. of his human reality attested in
Scripture, by which his benefit reaches us. But he wants it fully known—
and that should never have been kept quiet or even merely put in the background. More prudent than the Melanchthon of 1521, Luther lost no opportunity of indicating, that in Jacob's dream it was a matter of the angels
passing up and down : *angeli ascendentes et descendentes : doctores precones
verbi Dei.* The way leads first from below upwards, from the *natura humana
Christi* to *cognitio Dei.* But it really leads upwards and then, therefore,
downwards again as well. Then *cum Χριστός in sic humilibus formis cognitus
est, tum ascenditur et videtur, quod est Deus. Et tunc cognoscitur quod Deus
benigne, misericorditer despectat (Sermon on Gen.* 28¹²ᶠ·, 1520 W. edn. 9, p.
494, l. 17 f.). Thus knowledge of the loving-kindness of God once more
depends directly upon the way leading from above downwards. " *Nos
Christiani* have not enough about how a *Creator* is to be reckoned compared
with a creature. *Sed docemus postea ex scriptura,* what God is in Himself . . .
quid est deus in seipso ? . . . *quid* is He in Himself, where He hath His divine
being by Himself ? *Ibi Christiani : Is unicus dominus, rex et creator, per
filium sic depinxit se, quod in deitate* He so existeth. . . . *Non solum inspici-
endus deus ab extra in operibus. Sed deus vult etiam, ut agnoscamus eum etiam
ab intra.* What is He inwardly ? " *(Sermon on John* 1¹ᶠ·, 1541 W. edn. 49,
p. 238, l. 5).

What remains of the whole appeal to the Reformation in this matter is,
finally, just the fact that the burning problem of the Reformers was a different
one from that of the 4th century, and that in the rough and tumble of the

struggle about this problem of their own they served themselves, perhaps had to, by incidentally putting the 4th century problem aside into its place with a somewhat impatient movement. No one could ever seriously maintain that for them it did not stand in this place, or that they were not aware of it as the inevitable presupposition of their problem or at all events did not at latest recognise it in the discussion with their adversary of the Left who was already emerging at that time. It may be explained in them (with Stephan, *op. cit.* p. 140) as a lack of theological consistency, that they not only did not attack the early Church doctrine, but in its place affirmed it as solemnly as possible ; or (with A. Ritschl, *Rechfert. u. Versöhnung⁴*, vol. I p. 145 f.) there may be seen in this attitude an outcome of their *ecclesiastico*-political consideration for the mediæval *corpus christianum* : the facts as such are clear and we are entitled to stick to them. The Reformers never dreamed of letting Christology resolve or dissolve into a doctrine of the *beneficia Christi*. Can it not be agreed that once for all and finally we have two different things, when Melanchthon (*Loci* 1535 *C.R.* 21, 366) says : *scriptura docet nos de filii divinitate non tantum speculative sed practice, hoc est iubet nos, ut Christum invocemus, ut confidamus Christo*—and when, as Ritschl and his school wished, *speculative* is simply scored out, i.e. simply transformed into *practice* ?

But the objection that in the dogma of the divinity of Christ an untheological speculation is involved, is also substantially foolish and untenable, and must in the end rebound against the originator of it.

J. J. Spalding, who was perhaps the first to attempt using the Melanchthon passage in this sense, argues, in a manner typical of all that is usually said along these lines down to our own times, as follows : " It is not what the son of God is in himself, in his nature impervious to our understanding, that belongs to our Christianity proper, to the generally necessary and fruitful knowledge of religion ; but it is what he is for us, that for which he was given to us, what we have to thank him for, the way in which we should accept and use him, in order to gain the bliss to which he would lead us. And how surely we can thereby dispense with all those hard phrases and still harder concepts ! " (*op. cit.* p. 142). " If there exists a clear divine declaration, that after my transgressions a conversion is once more granted to me, and an access to my bliss stands open ; if in this declaration I am told that this is mediated and applied to me through Jesus Christ, I do not see why this basis for my peace of mind should not be sufficiently reliable for me. To regard so universally declared an assurance as insufficient, to refuse to trust in it with complete composure, until I myself had first perceived how God could have made this gift of grace possible, or whether He was even entitled to forgive sin, would mean the assumption on my part of a sort of judgment upon God's holy laws of government, which could not possibly belong to me. He promises me forgiveness through Christ : more I need not. What my Redeemer was forced to do, forced to be, in order to be able to do that, belongs not to my religion, as regards either my virtue or my peace of mind ; that I leave purely to Him who has given me so clearly His word about my being accepted again. This declaration and assurance by the true God, that He will forgive me, it is incomparably more necessary for me to know, than the way in which He contrives to be able to forgive me ; and it would be difficult to find adequate grounds for making out of both of them something equally essential and important in the knowledge of religion " (p. 144 f.). In short, awareness of what the dogma asserts gives Christians " not the slightest addition to their blessedness and to their solace, but a correspondingly greater one to the vain burdening of their understanding " (p. 147). This line of argument, so significant for Enlightenment theology (in the broadest sense of the word), completely fails to see, that in the dogma it is by no means a question of enriching, or making difficult, the simple and in itself adequate " knowledge of religion," by an explanation of the possibility of its content as subtle as it is superfluous, but that in this " knowledge of religion " it certainly is—whatever " burdening of the understanding " that may imply, and in whatever sense it may " belong " to my religion, virtue, and peace of mind—a question of the mystery of the Word of God, i.e. that the truth of what Christ is for us, the truth of his *beneficia* is once for all the truth of the event of divine manifestation, and not the truth of a " universally declared assurance " detachable from this event. That the true God has forgiven me—that, and not merely that He wills to forgive me, is after all the content of the " knowledge of religion " under review here !— can only be heard and understood as truth in the mystery of God's Way, proceeding from His divine majesty into my sin-destroyed creatureliness. What has the general truth that there is forgiveness (as truth that may be seen and understood apart from the mystery of this way) to do with the truth of the grace of God ? The dogma of the divinity of Christ has to do with this truth, and therefore with the mystery of this Way, and therefore with the differences between the whence and the whither of this Way, and therefore with the difference between the Son of God in himself and for us. Upon the difference between the " in himself " and the " for us " depends the acknowledgment of the freedom and unindebtedness of the grace of God, i.e. of the very thing which really makes it grace. It is this acknowledgment which is consummated in the Church dogma, whereas Englightenment theology (in the broadest sense of the concept) is obviously in a state of war against it.

It is strange enough but it is true, that the Church dogma of the eternal, true divinity of Christ with its " antecedently in himself," actually denies and prohibits an untheologically speculative way of regarding the " for us." And it is perfectly certain that if we think we ought to reject the Church dogma, we surely do so because we are in the grip of an untheologically speculative way of regarding the " for us." That may be shown in three respects.

1. To refuse to hear of Christ being God antecedently in himself, in order thus and thereupon to become our God, is to turn the latter, his being God for us, into a necessary attribute of God. In that case God's being is essentially bound up with and conditioned as being manifest, i.e. as a relationship of God to man. In that case man is thought of as indispensable to God. In that case it is all over with the freedom of God in the act of revelation and reconciliation, i.e. with the character of this act as of grace. It then belongs to God's nature—*C'est son métier !* (Voltaire)—

31

to be bound to forgive us. And it belongs to the nature of man to have a God from whom he receives forgiveness. That, and not the Church dogma which forbids this thought, is untheological speculation.

2. If we confine ourselves to the Son of God for us, without remembering that he is the Son of God antecedently in himself, we at least must not call that knowledge by faith. That is, if knowledge by faith is knowledge of a divine act, of an unveiling of the veiled God, therefore of a coming forward, of a way of God ; if knowledge by faith is distinguished from any other kind of knowledge by being knowledge of the mystery of the speech of God— the speech of God which is contrasted with a silence of God, which as an actual event is truth between a *terminus a quo* and a *terminus ad quem* and not otherwise ! If we think we can understand the *beneficia Christi* apart from this event, then it is we, and not the Church dogma which reminds us of this event, who are carrying on untheological speculation.

3. If the task of theological reflection be confined to understanding Christ in his revelation, but only in his revelation in itself and as such, what in that case can be the measure and criterion of this understanding, this highly commended *beneficia Christi cognoscere* ? Obviously it will have to be something brought in by man. This measure may therefore be either the valuation, within our capacity, of human fact or the valuation, within our capacity, of the idea of God or of something divine. Because Christ is to be estimated highly according to this capacity of ours for valuation, therefore and to that extent, on the basis of our " value-judgment," we call him the Son of God. Once more we are face to face with the two Christological types, which we have learned to know as the Ebionite and the Docetic.

A. Ritschl—according to our classification his Christology belongs (as distinguished from that of the religio-historic school which follows him) undoubtedly to the " Docetic " type—has described as follows the event in which on this assumption knowledge of the divinity of Christ can be attained : " If the grace and faithfulness and the lordship over the world, visible alike in Christ's mode of action and in his bearing of suffering, are the essential attributes of God that are decisive for the Christian religion, it was consistent, upon certain historical occasions, to fix the proper valuation of the perfection of God's revelation through Christ in the predicate of his divinity " (*Unterricht in der. chr. Rel.* 1875 §24; cf. *Rechtfertigung und Versöhnung,*[4] vol. III p. 370 f.).

Must not all this interpretation, estimating, and valuation by means of a measure cocksurely imported and applied to Christ by the theologian (even if it seem to arrive back in result and phraseology at the content of the Church dogma) be the properly untheological speculation ? Whereas the Church dogma with its " antecedently in himself " is obviously meant to strike this very measure out of our hands, by telling us that knowledge of the divinity of Christ is but the beginning and not the result of our thought !

Undoubtedly the dogma of the divinity of Christ snaps the connection of mutuality between divine revelation and human faith. With the religio-psychological circle, with the theory of two elements of truth in a " unity of tension," which are accessible to us, or whatever these well-meant inventions may be called, we certainly do not arrive at what this dogma claims to assert. And if anything that cannot be gripped by this bag of tools is thereby, automatically, prohibited metaphysics, then, of course, this dogma is such metaphysics. But on the basis of the three points named, we must simply turn the tables and say that really prohibited metaphysics, in which the Reformers patently did not indulge, consists in absolutising that relation of mutuality, alleged to be accessible to us, reviewable and comprehensible by us, in regarding it as the reality in which God has so to speak handed Himself over to human thought and language, instead of remembering that our being in this relation may be pure illusion every time, and our thought while in it and our language about it be pure ideology, unless both are grounded in God Himself and continually being reconfirmed by God Himself. Because and so far as there is truth in what the dogma states, that God's word is the Word of God, for that reason and to that extent the relation of mutuality is true. The truth of it hangs, as on a nail, upon the truth of which the dogma speaks. And therefore, too, any truth there is in our thought and language about it depends upon knowledge of the truth of the dogma. Without it it is dreams and babble, though it may long have been called the theology of revelation and faith. For the very reason that Christ is the Son of God antecedently in himself, both the elements of truth to be found in mutual tension really exist (the elements of truth in Ebionite and Docetic thought) in which we know that he is God's Son for us, and not *vice versa*. How could a theology which was unaware of the freedom of the grace of God, unaware of the mystery of His way, unaware that the fear of the Lord is the beginning of wisdom—how could it come to call itself the theology of revelation and faith ? How should it be the knowledge of the *beneficia Christi* ? Is not all that just arrogant will-worship, all the worse because it behaves ever so humbly ? But there is no sense here in abuse. We are faced here, in particularly painful clarity, with the rift which bisects the Evangelical Church. Those who are here at loggerheads can neither understand nor convince each other. They not only speak another language ; they speak out of a different knowledge. They have not only a different knowledge, but also a different faith. In the last resort we can only protest at this point, as in other contexts we can only protest against the positions of Roman Catholic theology.

The document of most importance for dogmatic science, dealing with the Church dogma of the divinity of Christ, is the part relating to this problem of article 2 of the so-called *Symb. Nicaeno-Constantinopolitanum.*

The *Symb. Nic. Const.* is a baptismal symbol belonging to the last third of the 4th century, perhaps the baptismal symbol of the Church of Constantinople (or that of Jerusalem ?), into which were taken up the decisive determinations on the theology of the Trinity made by the Council of Nicæa in 325, and which, according to no more certain tradition, is supposed to have achieved recognition by the Council of Constantinople in 381. It has been a fixed part of the Eastern liturgy since 565, of the Western since 1014. We call it the document of most importance here for the dogma of the divinity of Christ,

1. because, of the three early Church symbols formally received by the Churches of the Reformation, its determinations in particular are in this respect at once the most trenchant and the most succinct ;

2. because, in reproducing in this respect in the main nothing but the ancient Nicene Creed proper, it gives us conclusively the result of early Church discussion on the divinity of Christ ;

3. because, on account of its liturgical significance in the Eastern and Roman Catholic Churches, it is fitted to remind us that over and above ecclesiastical severances, there was an œcumenical agreement on the Christian confession, although of course it was repeatedly altogether obscured from time to time ;

4. because it asserts unambiguously, what liberal Protestantism refuses to listen to, and what for that very reason must be restored to an unconditional validity in an evangelical dogmatics.

The relevant passage, with a short commentary on which we conclude our consideration of the problem engaging us, runs thus :

(Πιστεύομεν . . .)

1. εἰς ἕνα κύριον Ἰησοῦν Χριστόν
2. τὸν υἱὸν τοῦ θεοῦ τὸν μονογενῆ
3. τὸν ἐκ τοῦ πατρὸς γεννηθέντα πρὸ πάντων αἰώνων
4. φῶς ἐκ φωτός, θεὸν ἀληθινὸν ἐκ θεοῦ ἀληθινοῦ, γεννηθέντα οὐ ποιηθέντα

(Credo . . .)

1. *in unum Dominum Jesum Christum*
2. *filium Dei unigenitum*
3. *et ex Patre natum ante omnia saecula*
4. *Deum de Deo, lumen de lumine, Deum verum de Deo vero, genitum non factum*

5. ὁμοούσιον τῷ πατρί   5. *Consubstantialem Patri*
6. δι οὗ τὰ πάντα ἐγένετο   6. *per quem omnia facta sunt*
    (Text, *Denzinger* Mr 86)   (Text, *Missale Romanum*)

1. We believe in the one Lord Jesus Christ.—The concept " Lord " indicates to us first of all the significance of Jesus Christ for us. Compared with us he is the bearer of authority and power. He has a claim upon us and has us at his disposal. He commands and rules. But he does not do that in an accidental or preliminary way, in a partial or limited way, like other lords. His lordship is not of the derivative type, or based upon a higher lordship. It is lordship in the final, conclusive sense of the concept. It is lordship grounded in itself. That is the assertion of the stipulation " one " Lord. It means to assert that the statement of faith, " Jesus Christ is the Lord," is no mere analysis of the significance of Jesus Christ for us, manifest to us in faith. Rather it claims that, grounded upon himself apart from what he signifies for us, Jesus Christ is the actual thing he signifies for us, and that he can signify that for us, because, even irrespectively of that, he is that antecedently in himself.

How could faith (as the apprehension of what Jesus signifies for us) manage to regard itself as the justification for that statement of faith ? Rather, faith will only regard itself as justified by the fact that previously, preceding all our apprehension, Jesus Christ is in himself the very person he purports to be in giving himself to our apprehension. *Christus quamquam sit coelestis et sempiternae conditor civitatis, non tamen eam, quoniam ab illo condita est, Deum credidit, sed ideo potius est condenda, quia credidit . . . Roma Romulum amando esse Deum credidit, ista istum Deum esse credendo amavit* (Augustine, *De civ. Dei* XXII 6, 1).

The phrase " the one " Lord unites Jesus Christ immediately to the Father, of whom the confession in the first article had said emphatically, He is one God. If there can be no rivalry between the two concepts " God " and " Lord," if they refer to the one Being, to the one Being in the way in which the statements about creation and reconciliation refer to the one operation of this one Being, then by means of this stipulation the decisive statement is already made, that Jesus Christ is himself this Being, not His legate or plenipotentiary merely, but identical with Him. Therefore because he is the one Lord, because in this strictest sense he is the Lord, his lordship for us in his revelation has no beginning and no end, it breaks over us with the unheard-of and incomparable fall of eternal truth and reality itself, it cannot be realised or inferred from any standpoint whatsoever, knowledge of it begins with the acknowledgment of it. Only if he were a different Lord, one of the lords within our world, could it be otherwise. But he is this Lord, the " Lord of all lords " (Deut. 10¹⁷ ; 1 Tim. 6¹⁵). He possesses that significance for us, because it is the analogue of what his Being is " antecedently in himself."

2. We believe in Jesus Christ as in the only-begotten Son of God.—The concept " Son " will occupy as under point 4. The phrase " the only-begotten " emphasises in the first place the unity, i.e. the exclusiveness, the uniqueness of the revelation and reconciliation that took place in Jesus Christ. To believe in him as the Son of God, is to be aware of no other Son of God alongside of him, i.e. of no other revelations which might also be the revelation of God Himself, of no other reconciliations in which likewise one might be aware of being reconciled to God. There are indeed other immanent revelations and reconciliations as well, which operate within the created world : there are revelations of the Spirit and revelations of nature. One man can reveal himself to another. And a man can be reconciled to his fate, he can be reconciled indeed to death, and—which should be the greatest thing—reconciled to his fellow-man. But none of all that is the act of the Son of God. At all events, if a man believes in Jesus Christ the Son of God, if God is manifest for him in Him, and if he is reconciled to God through Him, in all these revelations and reconciliations he will not see the works of other sons of God. If they were to be genuine revelations and reconciliations, they could only be identical with the revelation and reconciliation through the Son of God. In that case it would be Jesus Christ who would have to be recognised as living and acting in them. The one revelation and reconciliation would not thereby become one among many.—But that is not all that the confession means to assert by the stipulation about the only-begotten Son of God.

Were this all, it might still just mean, that the NT υἱὸς μονογενής would have to be interpreted by the phrase which also occurs in the NT, υἱὸς ἀγαπητός. And that might be meant in the sense that a being distinct from God was the object of the special good pleasure, preference, choice, adoption of God, that he, this unique person, was called by God, Son, and installed as His Son, with the dignity and rights of sonship. And then that would mean for us that as such he would have to be acknowledged, as such he would have to be the object of faith. In that case it would be the exclusiveness of this belief, the so-called " absoluteness of Christianity," that would constitute the content of the confession. But if the confession with μονογενής confesses the unity, the uniqueness of the revelation that took place in Jesus Christ, that is something very different from the absoluteness of Christianity. The

confession does not state that in faith, at any rate in a faith regarded as a
" decision," one could or must choose, label and assert one possibility among
many, as the absolute one over against the many others. How should such
an exaltation of Jesus Christ attach itself to faith, where already the meaning
of his exaltation by his heavenly Father is quite a different one, being not an
innovation but the confirmation of something original and peculiar to him ?
The uniqueness of Jesus Christ as the Son of God, and therefore the uniqueness of the revelation and reconciliation which took place in him, is not a
predicate lent him subsequently by God. It is to be regarded, not as the
content of a synthetic proposition, but as the content of an analytical one.
Μονογενής is certainly not to be explained by ἀγαπητός, but on the contrary,
Non ideo μονογενής dicitur, quia ἀγαπητός, sed ideo est ἀγαπητός quia μονογενής
(Quenstedt, *Theol. did. pol.* 1685 I *cap.* 9 *sect.* 1 *th.* 34).

The only-begotten Son is according to John 1[18] God by nature.
God Himself, God in Himself, is in the mode of existence of the
only begotten of the Father. Therefore this only begotten is the
object of the Father's love, therefore he may become the object
of our faith. Antecedently to all revelation and all faith,
antecedently to the fact that the glory of this only begotten is
given to men to look upon (John 1[14]), it is the glory of God Himself. And therefore in its revelation it is " grace and truth."
Therefore the revelation of it can only be a single one. The
uniqueness [1] of its revelation and reconciliation for us is the analogue
of what God is in His Being antecedently in Himself, the Son of
the Father, beside whom there can as little be a second, as there
can be a second God alongside of the one God.

3. We believe in Jesus Christ as in the begotten of the
Father before all time.—Here too we must start from the
fact that this is said of Jesus Christ as the Revealer of God, therefore altogether of the God who acts in time on us and for us. The
pronouncement about God as such does not stand abstractedly
as a second alongside a first utterance about God as the Lord of
our history. But the pronouncement about God as the Lord of
our history is underlined by the pronouncement, that He is God
as such, not a mere analogy, even the highest, of God Himself in
a sphere of reality distinct from God. He does not signify but
he is God Himself. Thus the phrase " before all time " does not
exclude time, either the *illic et tunc* of revelation as it is attested
in Scripture, or the *hic et nunc* in which it is to become revelation
for us. It does not exclude, it includes time (concretely, this time,
the time of revelation) ; and so with history. But this very fact
that time (time of our time, the sinful creature's time and history

---

[1] [" Only-ness," *Einzigkeit;* so frequently—TR.]

—which is also the time and history of revelation) is included in a divine "before all time,"—this does not go without saying, this is a grace, a mystery, a foundation to be recognised in the fear of God. Therefore the pronouncement about God as such, about God Himself, must follow in set terms, for fear of the misunderstanding that here we might speak without revelation and faith, as though here we might speak "non-historically," where the whole point is to speak correctly about revelation and faith, correctly about history. Even the pronouncement about God as the Lord of our history is not insusceptible of misunderstanding. Taken by itself, even it might be a proposition in anthropological metaphysics. Rather, even it may and must be regarded merely as an underlining of the pronouncement about God as such. True, the statement about the pre-existence of Jesus Christ is only an explication of the statement about his existence as the Revealer and Reconciler, as of the God who acts on us and for us in time. But just as truly the statement about his existence is only an explication of the statement about his pre-existence. This person, the Son of God who exists for us, is the pre-existent. But only this person, the pre-existent Son of God, is the one who exists for us. The dogma of the incarnation of the Son of God will elucidate the first statement. The dogma of the divinity of Christ, which is occupying us here, emphasises the second.

The second article of the *Nic. Const.* distinguishes very clearly between these two spheres of knowledge. The dogma of the incarnation is stated in detail, not in the *Nic. Const.* but in the *Ephesinum* of 431 and in the *Chalcedonense* of 451.

"Begotten by the Father before all time" means, did not come into being in time as such, did not come into being in an event within the created world. The Son of God's becoming man and the recognition of him in his humanity as the Son of God by other men, are, although absolutely marked events in time, events within the created world. But this marked nature which they have does not itself originate and proceed from time. Otherwise they would only be relatively marked events, of which there are many others of the kind. Just because they have divine power, because the power of the temporal is here the power of the eternal, the power of the immanence of God here the power of His transcendence, the Subject of it must be regarded as existing before all time, as the eternal Subject, as eternal as God Himself, himself eternal as God. Jesus Christ does not first become the Son of

God by being so for us. He becomes so from all eternity, he becomes so as the eternal Son of the eternal Father.

" Before all time " should therefore not be regarded by itself again as a temporal determination. *Absque initio, semper ac sine fine : Pater generans, Filius nascens et Spiritus sanctus procedens*, says the *Conc. Later.* IV 1215 of all the three modes of existence of God. Upon the passage often quoted in this context, Ps. 2[7], " Thou art my Son, this day have I begotten thee! " Cyril of Jerusalem makes the pertinent comment: Τὸ δὲ σήμερον, οὐ πρόσφατον, ἀλλ' ἀΐδιον· τὸ σήμερον ἄχρονον, πρὸ πάντων τῶν αἰώνων (*Cat.* II 5). *Vox " hodie " notat diem immutabilis aeternitatis* is Quenstedt's rendering (*op. cit. th.* 15) and he therefore interprets (*op. cit. th.* 28) the concept of the generation of the Son from the Father in view of its relation to time, as follows : *Haec generatio Filii Dei non fit derivatione aut transfusione, nec actione, quae incipiat aut desinat, sed fit indesinente emanatione, cui simile nihil habetur in rerum natura. Deus Pater enim filium suum ab aeterno genuit et semper gignit, nec unquam desinet gignere. Si enim generatio filii finem haberet, haberet etiam initium et sic aeterna non esset.* We therefore may and must equally well say of this divine " antecedently " (decisive for the temporal event which impinges upon us to-day), that it takes place to-day as it took place yesterday and will take place to-morrow. *Nec tamen propterea generatio haec dici potest imperfecta et successiva. Actus namque generationis in Patre et Filio consideratur in opere perfectus, in operatione perpetuus.* Implying that the transcendence of this " antecedently " over against all time cannot signify any emptying of the temporal event founded upon this " antecedently," because it is genuine, eternal transcendence. What is real in God, must, precisely because it is real in God (not in the manner of created being), constantly be becoming real again. But this very becoming (because it is this becoming!) excludes all need for completion in that Being. This becoming, rather, simply confirms the perfection of that Being.

4. We believe in Jesus Christ as light of light, true God of true God, begotten, not made.—In this phrase we have to do with the characteristic and decisive determination of the divinity of Christ in the theology of the Trinity. It makes two assertions : One, that in the essence and operation of God we have to distinguish light and light, God and God, to distinguish, in the way in which within the created world we have to distinguish a source of light and a beam of light proceeding from it, a light that kindles and a light that is kindled, Father and Son, the Speaker and the spoken word. Next, that this distinction is to be regarded as a distinction in God Himself. Therefore it is not to be understood as if on the one side God was to be found, on the other side a creature, but so that on both sides equally the one God is to be found. Our effort is to interpret both the series here visible together, in their mutual relationship to each other.

The statements about the distinction and the unity in God are in the first instance simply statements about revelation, as the Church has found it attested in Holy Scripture. Here, in this revelation, God is in the one place and God in the other, God in one way and God in a different way, God the Creator and God the Reconciler, and yet but the one and same God. Here is the hidden and the manifest God, and yet the hidden God is none other than the manifest, the manifest none other than the hidden. The dogma in the first instance simply repeats this dialectic of revelation as such. It repeats the distinction and the unification. But according to the preceding phrase there can now no longer be any question but that, in relation to the revelation that took place in Jesus Christ, in order to interpret the revelation as such, something transcending revelation should be asserted, arising out of revelation something about a beyond and above revelation should be asserted. It should be asserted that as Christ is in revelation, exactly so is he antecedently in himself. Thus he is antecedently in himself light of light, true God of true God, the begotten of God, not His creature. We have to take revelation so utterly seriously that in it as the act of God we have to recognise immediately His being as well.

But by the fact that what is in question is the distinction and unity of two modes of existence of God Himself, we are already committed to the assertion, that while we may and must attempt to describe this distinction and unity, we should not expect to conceive it by these descriptions. We may and must think and express them. For should we renounce that, that would mean that we were withdrawing from the knowledge of them. But with the Biblical witness to God's revelation as we felt we must regard it, the knowledge of them is laid upon us, at least as a task for dogmatics. But we have cause to remind ourselves, that knowledge of the Word of God can only be knowledge of it in faith, and so decisively ac-knowledgment, man's responsibility towards the question set us by this object. This responsibility of ours cannot be fulfilled by a conceiving of this object or by any control over it. It will remain an object over against our thought and speech. Our thought and speech will never succeed in being appropriate to it, but only inappropriate (inadequate). Content of knowledge can become the possession of our thought and speech—even though we reproduce the dogma, nay the very expressions of Holy Scripture, in thought and speech—only by God's grace, not in itself. Regarded immanently it will in itself be and remain an inadequate, fragile thought and language.

(a) Relatively the most unassailable of the three formulæ in our phrase is the middle one, " Very God of Very God." The ἐκ describes most briefly the distinction between the two modes of being : true God, grounded on, proceeding from true God, that is Jesus Christ. That is God in this form only in this mode of existence. The distinction of the mode of existence in which Jesus Christ is God, thus consists in the relation to another mode of God's existence, a relation described by the ἐκ as " grounding in," as " proceeding from." On the other hand the unity of the two modes of existence, as modes of the existence of an absolutely identical Being, is described by the repetition of the substantive θεός, together with the adjective ἀληθινός, repeated with like emphasis.

In the Latin text which has become official we have the gradation *Deum de Deo, lumen de lumine, Deum verum de Deo vero* clearly kept in view. In the dispute with Caroli, Calvin called the passage a *battologia*, a *carmen magis cantillando aptum quam formula confessionis, in qua syllaba una redundare absurdum est* (*Adv. P. Caroli calumnias C.R.* 7, 315 f.). But it is better to regard it as intended to bring out the intensification of the thought from a lesser to a more exalted determination, *in actu* as it were.

The difficulty of even this very simple formula consists in the fact that, as soon as we attempt to interpret the ἐκ in this way, or in a way similar to that just employed, it inevitably arouses the idea of two independent essences, standing to one another in a definite relation of dependence, or, if we abstain from such an illustration, becomes meaningless, so that nothing more is said of a distinction in the *Deus verus*. The truth described actually lies beyond even these descriptive expressions. *Deus verus* and *Deus verus* do not confront each other as independent essences, but they exist in two ways in the same independent essence. It is this that here no language can reproduce appropriately, that even the language of dogma can only reproduce inappropriately.

(b) In the first formula " light of light," we have to do with an exalted but all the more parlous attempt at clearness. The concrete intention probably is, in the first instance, the simile of the sun and the sun's light which the Fathers were specially fond of applying. Jesus Christ as the one mode of God's existence is related to the first one in which he is grounded, from which he proceeds, as the light of the sun is related to the sun.

Ὤν ἀπαύγασμα τῆς δόξης αὐτοῦ, we read in Heb. 1³ of the Son of God. *Cum radius ex sole porrigitur . . . sol erit in radio, quia solis est radius, nec separatur substantia, sed extenditur. Ita de Spiritu Spiritus, et de Deo Deus, ut lumen de lumine accensum* (Tertullian, *Apolog.* 21).

We can but rejoice in the really lofty and beautiful figurative value of this formula ; yet we must confess that it not only presupposes the existence in space and time of the thing described by it, but also exposes it to a great variety of physical interpretations, of which probably not a single one would state what should here be stated by it. We incur similar difficulties if we understand *lumen de lumine* of a light that kindles and one that is kindled. Of course, confession in this figurative language is certainly not intended to indicate a *vestigium trinitatis* in the created world, or to make a pronouncement on the hypostatical character or on the *homousia* of light and light in such a twofold possibility of signification. But just because, strictly speaking, neither is it able to do so, the figure remains inadequate as a pronouncement upon Jesus Christ, while the Object remains clear beyond the expression used.

(c) Naturally, the decisive formula is the third, " Begotten, not created."

In its negative part, which should be taken first, it states that Jesus Christ as a mode of God's existence is of course of God, but not of God in the way in which the creatures are of God, from the highest angel to the tiniest particle of sun-dust, namely by creation, i.e. in such a way that he would have his existence as one different from God's existence, by the will and word of God. Of the human " nature " of Christ, of his existence as man, in which according to Scripture he meets us as the Revealer of God and the Reconciler with God, that will of course have to be said, but not of Him who here assumes human nature, i.e. who here exists as man—(" for us men," as the *Nic. Const.* later says)—so as not to let His existence and essence be exhausted or imprisoned by His human existence, so that in this human existence He may also be out and out not human, so that precisely in virtue of that wherein He is not human, in His human existence He may be the Revealer and Reconciler. He who here becomes man in order to become the Revealer and Reconciler, is not created. Otherwise revelation and reconciliation would be an event within creation, and, because creation is the world of fallen man, an event in vain. Because he who here became man is God, God in this mode of existence, therefore (and not otherwise) His human being is effective as revelation and reconciliation.

But now for the positive side of this formula ! Surprisingly enough it describes the real becoming of Jesus Christ, his eternal becoming appropriate to him as God, his original and dependent relationship as God in his determinate mode of existence, actually by means of a figure from the creaturely realm. And it might be added, by means of the figure which is significant for this sphere as no other is! "Begotten," that of course means emphatically, become in the same way as everything living in creation becomes, on the basis and presupposition of the divine creative word, become in the connection of sex in the twofold meaning of the word, become in the way in which the worm also becomes, become in the way in which man becomes, in the event in which creation and sin, in perhaps the most enigmatic manner, are not in each other but over against each other, by being together with each other. We should never shut our eyes to this stumbling-block, in order to understand things here.

Thomas Aquinas considers the distinctive point expressed by the metaphor of generation to be the *processio verbi* (*S. Theol.* I *qu.* 27 *art.* 2). On that point it must be said, that assuredly *generatio* and *processio verbi* must be regarded as describing the same material content. But not in such a way that one of these concepts may simply be reduced to the other. *Processio verbi* also must be apprehended as an important figure of speech, but likewise inadequate in its own way. The two figures, that of the Son and that of the Word of God, point to an object for which they are not appropriate. But for that very reason each of them must be taken seriously for itself, and neither of them should be dispensed with because the other is suggested.

In the first place, and obviously, the naturalness of the figure of generation makes it clear that here also, and therefore in all our language about Father and Son, we have, as a description of the two modes of God's existence, to do with a fragile, disputable figure. We describe God by this language, but we do not conceive Him.

The early Church, which did not invent this figure of speech but had discovered it there in Holy Scripture, and discovered it to be the most outstanding figure for this fact, was by no means in the dark as to its inadequacy, and often gave open expression to this. *Est in hoc mysterio generationis vocabulum ab omnibus imperfectionibus generationi physicae adhaerentibus purgandum* (Quenstedt, *op. cit. th.* 47). And already Cyril of Jerusalem expressly demands, that not only the most patent physical sense of the concept generation, but also that of generation in spirit (say, in the teacher-pupil relationship), or that of spiritual generation (as found in believers becoming children of God) must here remain absolutely barred.

But what then does the figure of speech mean?

In place of the intellectual categories which he was right in rejecting, Quenstedt laid down a new one, invented for this purpose, when (*op. cit. th.*

47) he spoke of a *generatio hyperphysica, quae fit ab aeterno, sine omni temporis successione, materia et mutatione et in sola essentiae communicatione consistit.* But the same thing was put more luminously when Irenaeus explained that: *Si quis itaque nobis dixerit, " Quomodo ergo Filius prolatus a Patre est ? " dicimus ei, quia prolationem istam, sive generationem, sive nuncupationem, sive adapertionem, aut quolibet quis nomine vocaverit generationem eius inennarrabilem exsistentem, nemo novit, non Valentinus, non Marcion, neque Saturninus, neque Basilides, neque angeli, neque archangeli, neque principes, neque potestates, nisi solus qui generavit Pater et qui natus est Filius* (*C. o. h.* II 28, 6) ; and when once more Cyril of Jerusalem declared, that the Father begets the Son ὡς οἶδεν αὐτὸς μόνος ; of this generation we could literally only say how at least it did not take place (*Cat.* 11, 11). Μὴ ἐπαισχυνθῇς ὁμολογῆσαι τὴν ἄγνοιαν, ἐπειδὴ μετ᾽ ἀγγέλων ἀγνοεῖς (*ib.* 11, 12). Εἰπέ μοι πρῶτον, τίς ἐστιν ὁ γεννήσας, καὶ τότε μάνθανε ὃ ἐγέννησεν (*ib.* 11, 14). Even the concept of *communicatio essentiae*, if taken strictly, actually asserts something which cannot be said without denying the unity of the essence of God. It does not lead us beyond the limit which in another passage (*op. cit.* I *cap.* 9 *sect.* 2 *qu.* 8 *font. sol.* 5) Quenstedt also must grant : *Satis est, nos hic τὸ ὄν tenere, quod scriptura docet, τὸ ποῖον vero reservare isti statui, qui mera lux erit.*

The figure of Father and Son asserts, and that by its entire worldliness and imperfection which cannot be overlooked, that the kind of—not the same but quite a different, an inconceivably and unspeakably other—but the kind of variety and the kind of continuity that exists in the created world between the person of a father and the person of a son, the kind of existence of the first for the second and the kind of existence of the second for the first —that that kind of twoness and oneness in the same existence exists between the mode of God's existence in which He becomes manifest to us in Jesus Christ, and the other one from which He is He who is manifest in Jesus Christ. The thing which, veiled in a mysterious intermingling of creation and sin, we only know as the generation of a son by a father, that same thing—not conceived but only described in its proper How by this figure, in its proper How as unsearchable to us as the essence of God in general—is God's self-positing, in which at the same time, and yet through Himself in indissoluble distinctness, He is the Father of Jesus Christ and Jesus Christ is the Son of the Father. Indeed this most powerful figure thus can and is meant merely to summon us to knowledge, so as never to keep us tied to itself alone, rather to lead our view at once onwards beyond itself to the Object, in presence of which, powerless though it is in itself, it might vindicate itself, to lead on to the ac-knowledgement, in which alone knowledge can here consist. Any association which may be sensibly suggested by this figure is legitimate, and no such association is legitimate. Anything that may be relevantly mooted here, the fecundity of the Father, the love that does not admit the possibility of Him wanting to remain alone, the dependence of the Son's existence upon the Father, the love which together with his existence he owes to the Father, the indissoluble fellowship of these two, based not on any choice, but on their two-sided existence—all of that may find u t t e r a n c e here, but all of it must also be able to relapse into s i l e n c e again. It is a n o n - k n o w i n g knowledge which is expressed in this figure. It should regard itself as a k n o w i n g non-knowledge. Like any word of man—but, of course, there are few places where it becomes so clear as here—it should merely be the s e r v a n t of the Word, which God Himself speaks about Himself. In this figure, which as such and in itself is already in fact a description of the deepest mystery of creaturely life, we may and should think of everything that can be sensibly thought of here regarding the Father-Son relationship in God : and then we should say, We are unprofitable servants, we have only thought and spoken in figures, as we were bound to do, but without being able to claim "rightness" for what we have there thought and spoken. The " rightness " belongs exclusively to that a b o u t w h i c h, not to that w h i c h, we have thought and spoken.

That " begotten," together with the whole figure of Father and Son in itself, asserts nothing, or that it does not assert the truth respecting God, by no means follows from all that. It asserts something inappropriate, but it asserts something, and it asserts the truth. If we describe the language of Father and Son as figurative, it is still just as well to recollect, that that can only refer to our human language as such, but not to the Object of it. It is therefore not as if the Father-Son relationship were itself a reality originally and properly creaturely, as if God in some hidden source of His essence were nevertheless something other than Father and Son, and as if therefore these names were optional and ultimately meaningless symbols, symbols the original and proper, non-symbolic content of which consisted in the said creaturely reality. On the contrary, it is precisely in God that the Father-Son relationship, like all creaturely relationships, has its original and proper reality. The mystery of the generation is originally and properly not a creaturely but a divine mystery, perhaps we ought to say outright, t h e divine mystery.

The *generatio ipsa* is *in divinis propriissima et longe verior et perfectior quam ullius creaturae* (Q u e n s t e d t, *op. cit. qu. 8 ekth.* 5).

But we only know the figure of this reality in its twofold inappropriateness as a creaturely, and as a sinful-creaturely figure. We can only speak of the truth in untruth. We know not what we say, when we call God Father and Son. We can only say it in such a way, that on our lips and in our concepts it is an untruth. For us the truth which we express, in calling God Father and Son is hidden and unsearchable.

The *modus generationis ipsae* is *in Deo longe alius quam in nobis estque nobis incognitus et ineffabilis* (Quenstedt, *op. cit.*).

But in thus naming God, we express the truth, His truth. In this sense " begotten " sufficiently asserts what a confession of faith at its necessary distance from, but also in its necessary relationship to its object, can and should say, in that it declares the mode of God's existence in Jesus Christ to be a real " from thence " and "thither" in God Himself, because it is the bringing forth from an origin which is real in God Himself. That is the proper and original Father-Son relationship, which as such we of course cannot realise, God's Father-and-Son existence. And now we must further state that in any case the impressiveness as well as the clarity of " begotten " lies also in its opposition to the discarded " created." To generate is less than to create, so far as the former denotes the reproduction of creature from creature, the latter the production of the creature in general by the Creator. But to generate is more than to create, so far as it denotes—the closed circle of creature and creature, as it is visible to us in what we know as generation, now becomes the figure—the reproduction of God from God, creation on the contrary denoting merely the production of the creature by God.

Quenstedt distinguishes as follows : *Generatio est entis similis secundum substantiam ex substantia gignentis productio. Creatio est entis dissimilis secundum substantiam ex nihilo extra essentiam creantis productio* (*op. cit. qu* 8 *font. sol.* 16).

In this feature of reproduction from God in God, as opposed to production by God, in the feature of the freedom in which God posits His own reality, compared with the freedom in which He posits a reality distinct from Him, in the feature of the love in which He is His own object, compared with the love, the object of which is an existent by His will, distinct from Him—in this feature lies the full meaning of " begotten, not created."

From this standpoint a controversial proposition of Scholasticism is understandable, which at this stage is significant for explaining the intention of the dogma. (J. Kuhn, *Kath. Dogmatik* vol. II 1857 p. 464, calls it outright "the supreme dogmatic definition, as it were the peak into which Nicene belief tapers.") Johannes Damascenus (*Ekdosis* I 8) has—in the footsteps of Athanasius (*Or. c. Ar.* 2, 29)—distinguished generation as the ἔργον φύσεως, creation as the ἔργον θελήσεως of God. Then Thomas Aquinas (*S. theol.* I *qu.* 41 *art.* 2) attaching himself to Hilarius (*Lib. de Synod. can.* 24 f.), has explained this to the effect that the generation of the Son is certainly to be regarded as a divine act of will, but only as the act of will in which *Deus vult se esse Deum* : as the act of will in which, in freedom of course, God wills Himself, and in virtue of this will of His is Himself. In this sense, in a manner indeed identical with this being Himself of God, the generation of the Son is also an ἔργον θελήσεως, because in that case θέλησις and φύσις are one and the same thing. But the generation of the Son is not an act of will in God, so far as there is supposed to be expressed in the concept of will freedom to will one way or the other. This freedom God possesses in respect of creation —God is free to will it or not to will it—and therefore creation is an ἔργον θελήσεως. But He does not possess this freedom in respect of His Godness. God cannot not be God. So also—which is the same thing—He cannot not be the Father and, therefore, can not be without the Son. His freedom, His aseity in respect of Himself, consists in the freedom to be God, and that means to be the Father of the Son, determined by nothing but by Himself. A freedom to be able not to be this would be an abrogation of His freedom. Thus the generation of the Son is an ἔργον φύσεως. It could not not take place, as surely as God could not not be God, whereas creation is an ἔργον θελήσεως, in the sense that it could also not take place, without God thereby being less than God. Quenstedt formulates it concisely : *Filius Dei est objectum volitum et amatum ipsius voluntatis divinae, non tamen per illam productus.* The Father begets the Son *volens*, but not *quia voluit* (*op. cit. qu.* 8 *font. sol.* 13). He does not beget him *necessitate coactionis*, but of course *necessitate immutabilitatis* (Hollaz, *Ex. Theol. acroam.* 1706 I 2, 37).

At this stage it is in place, for completeness' sake, to interpose a reminder, which is lacking in the *Nic. Const.* The figure of Father and of Son, to the express interpretation of which the *Nic. Const.* has been confined, is not the only one by which we have to make clear to ourselves the concept of the divinity of Christ. Alongside of it in the NT itself and in the language of the Church there stands the other one, that Jesus Christ is the Word of God. According to this figure he is, as a second mode of God's existence, distinct from a first mode, and once more essentially at one with it, just as the Word which Someone speaks is a thing distinct from Himself, and yet as His Word essentially no whit different from Himself. We say the same thing, whether we say the "Son of God" or the "Word of God"—*Verbum suum qui est Filius eius* (Irenaeus *C. o. h.* II 30, 9). We may perhaps say that the first figure is nearer the mark, when we regard the action of God in Jesus Christ materially as reconciliation, the second as nearer the mark, when we look at the action formally as revelation. Moreover, at least in the

32

first instance, the statement of the divinity of Jesus Christ as that of the Word of God is connected simply with the action of God upon us in Jesus Christ, attested in Scripture. Thus primarily and simply we also understand by this figure the *beneficia Christi*, that the Word of God spoken to us in His truth and reality can be (as the Son interceding with us for God and with God for us) nothing else and no less than God Himself.

When God speaks, then *Nus* and *Logos* participate in equal truth and dignity. *Deus totus existens mens et totus existens logos, quod cogitat, hoc et loquitur et quod loquitur, hoc et cogitat* (Irenaeus, *C. o. h.* II 13, 8 and 28, 5). *Non enim se ipsum integre perfecteque dixisset, si aliquid minus aut amplius esset in eius Verbo quam in ipso* (Augustine, *De trin.* XV 14). *Etenim non potest aliud quam quod es aut aliquid maius vel minus te esse in verbo, quo teipsum dicis, quoniam verbum tuum sic est verum quomodo tu es verax* (Anselm of Canterbury, *Prosl.* 23). " When Moses saith, in the beginning God made heaven and earth, no Person is yet specially named or expressed, But as soon as he saith further, And God said : Let there be light, he expresseth that with God there was a word before the light came into being, Now the same word that God speaketh there could not be the thing which was there created, neither heaven nor earth, since God, just by the speaking that He did, maketh heaven and earth together with the light and all other creatures, so He hath nothing more to create with than His word, therefore it must have existed before all creatures. If therefore it existed previously, before time and the creatures began, it must be eternal and another and higher being than all creatures, whereupon it followeth that it is God " (Luther, *Sermon on Gen.* 1¹ 1527 W. edn. 24 p. 29 l. 4).

Jesus Christ, the Word of God, meets us as nothing other than God, but in another way, in a different mode of being compared with God, so far as God speaks the Word, so far as the Word· goes forth from Him.

" But if God speaketh and the Word falleth, He is not alone, nor can He personally be the Word Himself that He speaketh, Therefore because the Word is also God, it must be another person, So the two persons are expressed : the Father who speaketh the Word and hath essence of Himself, the Son who is the Word and cometh from the Father and is eternally with Him " (Luther *op. cit.* 1 14, cf. W. edn. 10 I p. 183, l. 13).

The same revelation thus compels us to separate God and His Word and to combine them in one.

" Who cannot here gather from these words of Moses, how in the Godhead there must be two persons and yet but one godhead ? then he wisheth to deny the clear scripture. Again, who here is so acute as may here contradict ? He must allow the Word to be somewhat other than God the speaker of it, and must yet confess, it was before all creatures and by it the creature was made : so must he certainly allow it also to be God, for apart from the creatures there is naught but God. So must he also confess, there is but one God. And so this scripture constraineth and concludeth that these two persons are one complete God, and each is the true, one, perfect, natural God, who hath made all things, and that the speaker hath not his being from the Word, but the Word its being from the Speaker, yet all eternally and in eternity, beyond all creatures " (Luther, *Sermon on John* 1 [1f.] 1522 W. edn. 10 I p. 184 l. 6).

This variety and unity in God, presented to us inescapably in revelation itself, is acknowledged and underlined by the dogma, when it regards Jesus Christ, the Word of God, as the eternal Word. The Word of God in which He gives Himself to our knowledge, is no other than that in which He knows Himself. Therefore and thus it is God's own Word, the Word of truth to us in His revelation. According to the immediately preceding development in the history of dogma at that date, there can be no question that, in speaking of the Son of God, the *Nic. Const.* throughout intends the Word of God to be included in the meaning. The Word is the one Lord. The Word is spoken by the Father before all time. The Word is light of light, very God of very God. The Word is spoken by God, not made. The statement " Jesus Christ is the eternal Son of the eternal Father " must therefore have put beside it the statement that he is the eternal Word of the Father who speaks from all eternity, or the eternal thought of the Father who thinks from all eternity, the Word in which God thinks Himself, or expresses Himself by Himself.

Jesus Christ is God's eternal *emanatio intelligibilis utpote verbi intelligibilis a dicente quod manet in ipso* (Thomas Aquinas, *S. theol.* I *qu.* 27, *art.* 1).

As this Word, which God Himself thinks or speaks eternally by himself, the content of which, therefore, can be naught other than God Himself—Jesus Christ, as the second mode of God's existence, is God Himself.

But here too we shall not need to be blind to the fact that this language also in our mouths and in our concepts is inappropriate language. We know not what we say when we call Jesus Christ the eternal Word of God. We indeed know no such Word as, being distinct from the speaker, should yet contain and reproduce the entire essence of the speaker, no *Logos* with an adequate complement of *Nus*, and no *Nus* that could be expressed exhaustively in one *Logos*, no thought or language which should leave behind it the contrast between knowing and being, overcoming it by a synthesis. In short, we know no true word. And therefore neither do we know the true Word above the true word, the Word of God! Once more we must say what we said about the Father-Son relationship : that the true Word is, for us who think and speak in the doubly veiled sphere of creatureliness and sinfulness, strictly and exclusively the eternal Word hidden in God, Jesus Christ Himself. It is not the case that our creaturely thought and language, in relation to the creaturely reason that produces such a creaturely *logos*, should in itself have a command of allegory to justify us in a claim to think and speak the truth, when we call Jesus Christ the Word of God. But it requires revelation and faith, it requires the continuous gracious event of the incarnation of the eternal Word and the outpouring of the Holy Spirit, ever and again to arouse and lift up what we know as the Word to such a command of allegory, that it may become the truth when we call Jesus Christ the Word of God.

" Now must we open wide the heart and understanding, that we regard not such a word as a man's petty stumbling word, but as he is great that speaketh there, so great must we consider his word. 'Tis a word he speaketh in himself, and it abideth in him and is never sundered from him. Therefore according to the Apostle's thought we must so think as God speaketh with himself to himself and leaveth a word about himself in himself, but the same word is not a pure wind or noise, but bringeth with itself the whole essence of divine nature, and as it is said above in the Epistle about the appearance and likeness, the divine nature is so depicted that it completely coincideth with the likeness and it becometh and is itself the likeness, and so the clarity also omitteth the appearance, that it essentially entereth into the appearance. Accordingly also God so speaketh his word about himself, that his whole godhead followeth the word and naturally abideth in the word and is essential. Lo, there we see whence the Apostle hath his language, that he calleth Christ an image of divine being and an appearance of divine honour, namely from this text of Moses, who there teacheth, that God speaketh a word about himself, which may not be other than an image which indicateth him. Since each word is a sign that signifieth somewhat. But here that is signified, naturally in sign or word, which is not in other signs : therefore calleth he it rightly an essential image or sign of his nature " (Luther, *op. cit.* p. 186 l. 9).

Just on account of the inappropriateness of even this figure it would not be advisable to think of bringing the concept of the divinity of Christ right down to the same denominator as the metaphor " Word."

There appears to be at least a strong tendency in this direction in Thomas Aquinas—cf. *S. theol.* I, apart from *qu.* 27 *art.* 2 also *qu.* 24—and that not because of a special appreciation of the " Word " as the root concept of revelation, Scripture, or Church proclamation, but because of his anthropology, i.e. because of his estimate of the event of knowledge as the *similitudo supremarum creaturarum* (*qu.* 27, *art.* 1). On that we must say that the *emanatio verbi manentis in dicente* does not command allegory because such a *similitudo* is supposed to be immanent in it, but because in the event of revelation and faith it is aroused and elevated to a *similitudo*, to an allegory and thereby also to a capacity for allegory. The same thing must obviously be urged against the earlier mentioned doctrine of Augustine's of the *vestigium* or *imago trinitatis* in the three powers of the soul—*memoria, intellectus,* and *amor.* There is no *analogia entis,* there is only an *analogia fidei.* But it is instructive to see how the advantage which on his own theory even Augustine gives to the concept of the " Word "—*Eo quippe filius quo verbum*— is immediately reversed by him again in the words, *et eo verbum quo filius* (*De trin.* VII 2). He, of course, knows perfectly well that by " Son " something is said about Jesus Christ, which cannot be said with " Word," which must always be added in thought to what we know as "Word," namely, the continuity, the equality of essence between Speaker and Spoken. So he must combine the images : *Verbo quod genuit dicens est, non verbo quod profertur et sonat et transit, sed. . . . Verbo aequali sibi quo semper et immutabiliter dicit seipsum* (*ib.* VII 1). *Seipsum dicens genuit Verbum sibi aequale per omnia. . . . Et ideo Verbum hoc vere veritas est* (*ib.* XV 14). And likewise Thomas Aquinas does not omit to concede, that we require several *nomina* to express the perfection of the divine origin of Christ : *Filius, splendor, imago, verbum. Non autem potuit unum nomen inveniri, per quod omnia ista* (namely everything that ought to be signified by one or other of these names) *designarentur* (*S. theol.* I *qu.* 34 *art.* 2 *ad.* 3). F. Diekamp's *conclusio theologica,* that " the generation of the Son from the Father is an intellectual one " (*Kath. Dogm.* vol. I 6th edn. 1930 p. 329 f.) should be described as an unwarranted systematisation even of the view of Thomas. Cf. thereon the more cautious attitude of B. Bartmann, *Lehrb. d. Dogm.* vol. I 4th edn. 1928 p. 198 f., especially also the references to Thomas there given on p. 200.

It is just in a use of all figures, that is aware of its limits, even of the figure of the " Word," that the more confidently, in view of the event of revelation and faith, we shall all do our duty of always, in our human untruth, uttering the divine truth, *peccatores iusti* !

5. We believe in Jesus Christ as being "of one substance with the Father."—The incorporation of this particular stipulation in the original Nicaenum signified historically a bold anticipation, in most respects doubtful, but finally justified both historically and materially.

Ecclesiastically it was considered more than serious, that Constantine I should have dared formally to enjoin upon the Council of 325 this ὁμοούσιος, and that the majority of this Council, against their deliberate and contrary conviction, allowed the imposition of this imperial theology : from the standpoint of human ethics one's sympathies might well be ranged, not on the side of the orthodox minority led to victory in such a way, or still less on the side of the Eusebian middle party which presumably gave way for the sake of peace, but really only on the side of the annoying Arius and his handful of friends, who preferred suffering suspension and exile to the abandonment of their resistance. (An analogous scandal to the detriment of the Nicene faith took place in 355 at Milan !) The meaning and purpose with which the ὁμοούσιος clause was carried through was however far from clear : before Nicæa and for long after it, it was anything but manifest, whether in the concept of *homousia* (according to Irenaeus, *C. o. h.* I 5, 1 also familiar, for that matter, to Valentinian Gnosis) one was not subscribing to Sabellianism or even to a form of tritheism. In the 3rd and 4th centuries one could actually be an opponent of this formula on good grounds : as early as 269 it was expressly rejected by a Council at Antioch in justifiable self-defence against Paul of Samosata ! And the very group of theologians, which finally led the doctrine of the eternal divinity to victory, the so-called Neo-Nicenes (Basil and the Gregorys) finally sanctioned it only upon a very limited interpretation, in the sense of equality of essence with distinction of the persons. Conceivably it was dogmatism upon the hitherto relatively little discussed ὁμοούσιος that first really became the standard in the struggle for and against, a struggle which occupied the whole period between 325 and 381, and in which by large detours and with frequent reverses the Church was subsequently forced to learn what she had meant and decided upon in 325, *hominum confusione et Dei providentia*. It may indeed be questioned whether the authoritative theologians at the time of the Council of Constantinople, especially the Cappadocians, would of themselves have devised this formula. Even the West, with its greater capacity for resisting Arianism, which at certain moments was the salvation of the Nicene faith, did not ultimately produce the ὁμοούσιος, but accepted it as a *fait accompli*.

As a matter of fact it is only in a supplementary way that it can be understood and acknowledged, by relentlessly admitting that its origin is a puzzle. But in a supplementary way it may and must be acknowledged. And historically at that, because, along with ἀληθινὸν θεὸν and along with γεννηθέντα οὐ ποιηθέντα but still more unmistakably, for the thought of the time, than either of these determinations, it actually proved itself to be the formula, on which the resistance of the Arians was bound to be shown up as such and in the end to be broken—Hilarius (*De Syn.* c. 83) once wrote, not without humour : *Homousia si cui displicet, placeat necesse est, quod ab Arianis sit negatum.* And materially, because the Church's positive meaning (she must of course have had business enough breaking through to the knowledge of what she meant, and for all the dogmatising of 325 she was still far from this knowledge !) in connection with the other formulæ of the symbol has come clearly enough to expression, at all events in this following-up of ours.

" Of one essence," i.e. of identical essence, is the meaning of ὁμοούσιος, *consubstantialis*, become dogma.

So it was understood by Athanasius, virtually the leading man of the Church in the whole business : ἀνάγκη γὰρ . . . τὴν ταυτότητα πρὸς τὸν ἑαυτοῦ πατέρα σώζειν (*De decr. nic. syn.* 23) ; ἵνα μὴ μόνον ὅμοιον τὸν υἱόν, ἀλλὰ ταὐτὸν τῇ ὁμοιώσει ἐκ τοῦ πατρὸς εἶναι σημαίνωσιν (*ib.* 20) ; ἔχων ἐκ τοῦ πατρὸς τὴν ταυτότητα (*Or. c. Ar.* I 22) ; and frequently. And next in the West it was thus looked upon in a way decisive for the further development by Augustine. " In uniform essence," was the way in which Luther also and the authors of the Book of Concord translated the formula.

The interpretation " of equal essence," is involved in the interpretation that, if the Son is of one essence with the Father, he is also of equal essence with Him. On the other hand, " of equal essence " does not necessarily include the meaning " of one essence," but might be taken in a polytheistic sense.

The Neo-Nicenes, for whom the interpretation equality of essence was the predominant one, wished by it to call attention to the problem, under-emphasised by Athanasius, of the distinction and independence of the Persons. From that standpoint polytheism became a standing danger to Eastern theology. On the other hand, it must be granted that it was the premier place given to the unity of essence, that made modalism the standing danger to Western theology. But we may say that in the complete context of the confession, in which indeed the ὁμοούσιος is alone comprehensible, it is clear enough that unity of essence is not to be thought of apart from equality of essence (although it is not explicitly expressed in the concept itself) ; in other words, that the distinction between the modes of existence is not to be for-gotten nor their independence to be surrendered. On the other hand, the opposite is not the case, the security against polytheism is not so obvious. On this ground we vote for Athanasius' ταυτότης, i.e. for the Augustinian and Western interpretation of the ὁμοούσιος.

" Of one essence " means firstly and obviously a safeguard against the Arian view of Jesus Christ, as of a " demigod from below," a superman, similar indeed to God, but because similar, ultimately and in the last resort distinct from Him ; it underlines and intensifies the γεννηθέντα οὐ ποιηθέντα, it puts Jesus Christ over against every creature, even the highest, on the side of the Creator.

But " of one essence " also means secondly a safeguard against the idea of Jesus Christ, so current from the time of Origen, as of a lower degree, a lesser quantity within the godhead itself, as a " demigod from above " : it underlines and accentuates the ἀληθινὸν θεόν.

" Of one essence " thus faces up to the two sides which, in view of the situation in the 2nd century, we described as the Ebionite and the Docetic.

But " of one essence " also means thirdly a safeguard against the differentiation or multiplication of the essence of God by the distinction of the modes of existence, i.e. a safeguard against polytheism. It forces us really to regard the " Persons " as modes of existence, i.e. not as two subjects, but as the same subject twice (in indissoluble twiceness, of course ; that follows from the context of the symbol !), as two who are two, only in their mutual relation-ships and not in themselves, not in their essence. Ὁμοούσιος τῷ πατρί means " I and the Father are one "—I and the Father, only with this distinction does the " One " hold—but " one," only in this unity is there the I and the Father.

Of this most famous and, technically considered, most central concept of the dogma we must also say what we have said of all formulations of the preceding stipulations, that we are very far from conceiving the object, with regard to which we are trying to justify ourselves by means of this concept. Precisely when we take the concept of *homousia* non-polytheistically as well as non-modalistically, precisely when we regard it on the one hand, with Athanasius and Augustine, as identity of essence, and also, adopting the attitude of the Neo-Nicenes, let it speak of two distinct equal modes of existence of the one essence, it is then that it is obviously speaking of an essence of which we have no sort of an idea, it is then that it becomes a concept of the kind described in philosophy as " empty concepts." We have often enough asserted distinction in unity and unity in distinction as the meaning of the whole theology of the Trinity. It is precisely in view of the concept of *homousia* which claims to assert both, that it is in place for us to admit to ourselves, that ultimately we are only acquainted with unities without distinction, distinctions without unity. Upon these limits of our thinking and speaking, all figures of speech go to pieces : the figure of Father and Son, the figure of Speaker and Word, the figure of light and light, the figure—even that is a mere figure—of original and copy. There we never have the one essence in really two modes of existence, nor are there two modes of existence of really one essence, but we always have either one essence in what are only apparently, only in passing, two modes of existence. Or we have two modes of existence, to which actually two essences correspond—according to our interpretation of the figures, and all these figures can be interpreted in two ways. The really one essence in really two modes of existence is God Himself and God alone. He Himself, He alone is also Father and Son, Speaker and Word, light and light, original and copy. From Him the created, sinful creature receives the truth of its circumstances by His revelation. Him they must know, not independently and arbitrarily, but through His revelation in faith—in order to know their own truth. The concept of *homousia* is not an attempt at independent, arbitrary, so-called natural Knowledge of God. It is meant to be the servant of Knowledge of God through His revelation in faith. We have not made a secret of the historical and material doubtfulness of this very concept. We cannot, nor do we wish to conceal from ourselves, that considered in itself it is a very bad servant to Knowledge of God. Philosophers and philosophising theologians have made easy game of it from time immemorial. But now suppose so very much did not depend upon its innate goodness or the reverse. Suppose that for all its manifest raggedness it was the necessary standard which had of necessity to be raised at that time in the 4th century, and which since that time, to-day as well as frequently before, had to be kept aloft to spite the Arians, not the standard of a foolhardy speculative intuition on the Church's part, but certainly the standard of an unheard-of encounter, confronting the Church in Holy Scripture. What in that case would be the effect of anything that could be said against it ? Would she not have to be acquainted with it all and yet to recognise the concept as the dogma which, once she has come to know it, the Church can no longer let go ? Because in its entire foolishness it is always truer than all the wisdom which has proclaimed aloud its opposition to it ? We have no cause to take any other view of it. We are under no illusion as to the fact, that we do not know what we are saying, when we take this concept upon our lips. Still less can we be under an illusion, about all the lines of our deliberations on the divinity of Christ converging upon the one point at which we must agree with the dogma, that Jesus Christ is ὁμοούσιος τῷ πατρί, *consubstantialis Patri.*

It is in place to listen once more to L u t h e r, who by means of the contrast and unity of original and copy has also made the decisive statement regarding the concept of *homousia*. " Thus in these words 'tis powerfully taught, that Christ with the Father is a single true God, in all things like him, without distinction, except that he is from the Father and not the Father from him, like as the brightness is from the glory of the Divine essence, and not the glory of the Divine essence from the brightness."—" So too when he says that he is the image of His substance, he likewise attesteth powerfully, that Christ must be proper, natural God, and yet is not therefore many, but a single God. 'Tis said it is a counterfeit, when a picture is made exactly like that of which it is a picture. But it is a lack in all pictures that they have not nor are the same single essence or nature of the depicted, but are of another nature or essence. As if a painter, carver, or stone-mason should depict a King or prince upon a canvas, block, or stone, as exact and like as ever can be, so that all eyes must say : Lo, that is this or that King, prince, or man, etc. Such is, of course, an image or counterfeit. But it is not the essence or nature of the King, prince, or man, etc., but a bad picture, figure, or form of the same, and hath another essence, for its nature or essence is stone, wood, canvas, or paper, and who so looketh at or graspeth it, doth not behold nor grasp the essence, nature, or substance of the man, and every one saith, 'Tis a wooden, stone, canvas likeness. But it is not the living, essential, likeness of men. . . . But here Christ is the image of the Father, so that he is the likeness of His Divine essence and not made of another nature, but is (if one may so speak) a likeness of gods, which is of God and hath divinity in itself or of itself, as a Crucifix is called a wooden likeness of Christ, being made of wood. And all men and angels are made in the likeness of God, but they are not likenesses of his Essence or nature, nor made or arising out of his Divine nature, but Christ hath arisen out of his Divine nature from eternity, his essential Likeness, *substantialis imago, non artificialis aut facta vel creata*, which hath his Divine nature completely in itself and is also itself it, not made nor fashioned of somewhat else, like as the divine essence itself is not made nor fashioned of somewhat else. For if he had not the entire Godhead of the Father in himself and was not complete God, he could not be nor be called the likeness of his essence because the Father would have something over, wherein the Son was not equal or like unto him, so he would in the last resort be quite unlike and in no wise his Image according to the essence. For the Divine essence is the most individual of all, indivisible, so that it must be entirely where it is, or must not be at all " (Luther, *Die drei Symbola oder Bekenntnis des Glaubens Christi*, 1538 W. edn. 50 p. 276 l. 30 and p. 277 l. 19).

6. We believe in Jesus Christ as him "through whom all things were made."

We have to do with an almost literal quotation from John 1³ : πάντα δι' αὐτοῦ ἐγένετο καὶ χωρὶς αὐτοῦ ἐγένετο οὐδὲ ἕν ὃ γέγονεν it says there, even more stringently than in the symbol itself. Correspondingly John 1¹⁰, ὁ κόσμος δι' αὐτοῦ ἐγένετο ; 1 Cor. 8⁶, δι' οὗ τὰ πάντα. Col. 1¹⁵ᶠ·, he is the πρωτότοκος πάσης κτίσεως, ὅτι ἐν αὐτῷ ἐκτίσθη τὰ πάντα . . . τὰ πάντα δι' αὐτοῦ καὶ εἰς αὐτὸν ἔκτισται. Heb. 1², δι' οὗ καὶ ἐποίησεν τοὺς αἰῶνας.

It may be asked whether in the context of the symbol this statement should still belong to the determinations concerning the divinity of Christ, or whether, as a pronouncement upon his work as mediator already of creation, it should not rather constitute the transition to the succeeding formulæ on the incarnation and the work of reconciliation. Yet the syntactical form seems to point in another direction. But even were that the case—the content of this statement is at least also to be understood strictly in the sense of Trinitarian theology, and so understood signifies, that the Son of God too has part in the work which is ascribed in the first article of the symbol to God the Father, the work of creation. So regarded it is an indirect but all the more expressive confirmation of the ὁμοούσιος and thereby of all preceding stipulations. If the Son participates in what was described as the special work of the Father, if he works with the Father in the work of creation, that means, at least in the sense of Athanasius and of the theology which finally held the field in the 4th century, that he is of one essence with Him. Thereby " through him " all things are made, thereby he could be the mediator of creation, for that he had to be God Himself in kind.

The rejection of the Arian view of John 1³ and parallels is not expressly voiced in the symbol. According to Arius the Son is the personal creaturely instrument of the divine Creator. That is unconditionally barred by the ὁμοούσιος and the γεννηθεὶς οὐ ποιηθείς. Our stipulation thus only interprets the ὁμοούσιος to the extent of securing its own interpretation by the context of the symbol.

Once again we have to remember here the principle, *opera trinitatis ad extra sunt indivisa*. On our passage it declares that it means an appropriation when the Son (as is the case in the continuation of the symbol) has revelation and reconciliation ascribed to him. This appropriation is right and necessary, because itself grounded in revelation. But revelation cannot be properly understood unless we continue, that as this appropriation cannot debar the Father also from being the subject of this event (so far as the Father also is present and active, in and with the Son, in revelation and reconciliation), so neither can it debar the Son from also being the subject of the event of which the first article speaks, that is, the subject of creation. We follow John 1 and follow the earlier quoted expositions of Luther upon Gen. 1 and John 1, when we explain that Jesus Christ is the Word by which God has created the world out of nothing. It is as this Word of the Father that, in distinction from everything created by him, he is equal to the Father, true God from all eternity.

Where did God create the world ? Augustine asks himself. In heaven ? on earth ? in the air ? in the water ? in the universe ? But they themselves are all created ! Did He create them out of an existent, that He had previously taken in His hand for the purpose ? But *unde tibi hoc quod non feceras, unde aliquid faceres ? Quid enim est, nisi quia tu es ? Ergo dixisti et facta sunt atque in verbo tuo fecisti ea (Conf. XI 5, 7). Eo sempiterne dicuntur omnia (ib. XI 7, 9).* Therefore *Fecit omnia per verbum suum et verbum eius ipse Christus, in quo requiescunt angeli et omnes caelestes mundissimi spiritus in sancto silentio (De cat. rud.* 17, 28). *Constat . ∴. summam substantiam prius in se quasi dixisse cunctam creaturam quam eam secundum eandem et per eandem suam intimam locutionem conderet* (Anselm of Canterbury, *Monol.* 11). *Cum ipse summus spiritus dicit se ipsum, dicit omnia, quae facta sunt. . . . Semper in ipso sunt, non quod sunt in se ipsis sed quod est idem ipse (ib.* 34). In the same sense Thomas Aquinas has said yes to the question : *Utrum in nomine verbi importetur respectus ad creaturam ? Deus enim cognoscendo se, cognoscit omnem creaturam. Uno actu* God knows Himself and everything that is outside Him ; and so His word is not only the image of the Father, but also the original of the world (*S. theol.* I *qu.* 34 *art.* 3). So Luther: *Filius enim in se habet exemplar non solum maiestatis divinae, sed etiam exemplar omnium rerum creatarum (Comm. Gen.* 1²⁰ᶠ. 1535 f. W. edn. 42 p. 37 l. 30). Also the warmth of love with which a hen hatches her eggs, is according to Luther *ex verbo divino, quia, si absque verbo esset, calor ille esset inutilis et inefficax (Gen.* 1²² *ib.* p. 40, l. 9). But in contrast it is somewhat paltry and lacking in humour for K. G. Bretschneider (*Handb. d. Dogm.* vol. I 4th edn. 1838 p. 659) to assure us . . . we should have " to regard the whole idea of the creation of the world by the Son, as one belonging not to religion but to Johannine and Pauline theology," and for A. Ritschl, here too on the trail of early rationalism, to think he should note on the NT passages in question that " this combination leads over into the department of theology proper (!) and has no direct and practical significance for religious belief in Jesus Christ" (*Unterricht in. d. chr. Religion*, 1875 § 24). In view of the Bible passages and in view of the exposition of them by the Early Church, we can and must assuredly utter a warning against the inference (not excluded beyond cavil in Augustine or even in Anselm) that the creation of the world was as essentially necessary to God as the generation of the Son, that it did not result from a *nova voluntas* (so Augustine states it, *Conf.* XII 15, 18), that the existence of the world was necessarily included in God's Word (so it might appear, perhaps, according to the Anselmic expressions adduced), that therefore the world is an essential predicate of God. But we cannot possibly cast suspicion upon the thought as such, as an unnecessary theologoumenon.

The thought indeed has not only to make clear the meaning, for the abstract theology of the Trinity, of the fact that the work and therefore the essence as well of the Father and of the Son are one and the same. But in so doing, it illumines and makes plain once again, who and what Jesus Christ is in his revelation : not a stranger whom we might meet as a stranger, interpreting and choosing him according to our own thought and estimate, nor yet as a semi-stranger whom we had to judge according to our otherwise-derived knowledge of the God who sent him. But " he came to his own " (John 1[11]), into the world, to us whom he himself created, who from the start are his and he theirs. The Word which we hear in revelation, the Word by which we are called to the undeserved and, from our standpoint, impossible communion of God with sinners—this Word is none other than that by which we who should hear it, together with the whole reality that is distinct from God, are called into existence, without which we would be neither sinners nor righteous, without which we would not be at all. He who in revelation calls us from our enmity towards him unto himself, from death to life, by so doing, also gives himself to be known as him who previously called us out of nothing into existence—into existence as pardoned sinners, yet into existence as pardoned sinners. We cannot hear the Word of justifiction and sanctification, without it reminding us that it is just through this Word, in no other way and from no other cause, that we even exist, we who are justified and sanctified through this Word. This Word is the ground of our existence beyond our existence, it is just in virtue of its superlative existence, whether we hear it or not, whether we are obedient to it or disobedient, that our existence is a reality. This Word reached us, or ever we came or failed to come, by our coming or failure to come. Our coming or not coming is itself only possible, because this Word is real. The same Jesus Christ, through whom God binds us to Himself while yet enemies, the same has already bound himself to us, as those who belong to him, because he alone has called us out of nothingness, because he alone upholds us over nothingness. And by this our first bond with him, as it becomes manifest to us in the second and through the second, through his revelation, is measured the meaning which this second bond itself must have for us. That means being a sinner, as it is discovered to us as our existence in the revelation of Jesus Christ, separating ourselves from him, without whom we should not exist even in this separation—but separated from whom we cannot properly exist at all. To be a sinner means to have come to a place, where our existence is absolutely beyond conception, because there it really could not be anything but a downfall into nothingness, a place where our existence can only be understandable as an event of inconceivable kindness—or just ununderstandable. And that means to obtain grace, as it is once more discovered to us as our existence, in the revelation of Jesus Christ, in that he without whom he would not be, and from whom we have yet separated ourselves, not only does not, in spite of our separation, let us drop into the nothingness from which he called us, but, by accosting us as sinners and laying claim to us, presents us over and above existence with no less than himself, with communion and intercourse with himself. What does that mean ? It means that Jesus Christ the Word of God does not in his revelation require first of all to get the authority from somewhere or other, but he already has it antecedently in himself, authority to address us and to claim us. It is not a question of whether we wish to vindicate ourselves to him : we are responsible to him, and our whole existence, one way or the other, is responsibility towards him. There is no possibility of us appealing against him or withdrawing to some domain of our own, where to begin with we once lived by ourselves, where he does not yet touch us at all or has ceased to do so, to a so-to-speak neutral human existence, where for a start it is left to us to submit or not submit to the judgment and grace which he announces to us, from which we might treat with him at our ease. We are in fact aware of our human existence in no other way, than by the same Word which announces to us judgment and grace. Thereby it tells us that it itself is the ground of our human existence : upon this ground we are men and not otherwise. It reaches us, because already it always reaches, before it reaches us. It is the hand which already holds us by grasping us. It is the official act of the king, who was already king previously, and who has the strength and the right to perform this act. It surrounds us on all sides (Ps. 139⁵). It is the Word that has power, the Word of the Lord. And it is the Word of the Lord, by being the Word of the Reconciler, who is also the Creator.

In our inquiry into the NT doctrine of the divinity of Christ we ended with the tautology, that for the men of the NT Jesus Christ is the Lord, because he is the Lord. We cannot set this tautology aside, but we can now describe it in this way : To them he is the Reconciler-God, by being the Creator-God. His judgment and his grace touch them, because he touches their existence. Of course the reverse statement must also be made forthwith, that he touches their existence, by touching them with his judgment and his grace. The meaning thus cannot be that in their existence, in their creaturely humanness, they possessed a canon given them previously, were pleased upon the application of this canon to accept his judgment and his grace, and on that score believed in Him as the Lord and the Son of God. Rather by his judgment and his grace the way out, the way of escape into such a previously given and assured humanness is actually barred, every private canon wrested from our grasp and every private measurement spoiled. There and there only did they find themselves, their existence and so also the possibility of private judgment, on the very spot where they touched his wrath and his loving-kindness. But there they did find their existence and at the same time the possibility of a private judgment. They exist by being judged by him. And as men judged by him they now form their own judgment, they even form one about him. Therefore and thus their judgment about him is that he is God's Son. They assert thereby that he is our Reconciler, by being our Creator. They might as well surrender the judgment " We are," as the judgment " He is the Son of God." The two for them are inseparable, because their knowledge of themselves, their existence, their creatureliness, the Creator is from the same source as their knowledge of their reconciliation, because for them there is thus no gap to be taken account of, between a known Creator-God and Jesus Christ as a Redeemer and Saviour perhaps standing in some sort of connection with God. Because they owe their knowledge of their reconciliation to Jesus Christ, they are aware of themselves, their existence, their creatureliness, the Creator. So the ground is taken away from under their feet, on which they would have to stand, in order to inquire, to investigate, to get behind the question whether Jesus Christ is the Lord and God's Son. So they can only start with this knowledge, this confession. We must once more be guilty of an abstraction as between Creator and Reconciler, of making two expressions out of what was one for the men of the NT, if we are to read Ebionite or Docetic Christology into the NT

In this sense our statement also illuminates and explains, who and what Jesus Christ is in his revelation. It says of him, that in his revelation he has the immediate power of the Creator over men. But in making this acknowledgment we shall not in any way limit his power as Creator to this revelation.

As early as the 2nd century it was a favourite trick to contrast the δι' οὗ τὰ πάντα with the discovery, that the Church is the first creature of God, made earlier than sun and moon, καὶ διὰ ταύτην ὁ κόσμος κατηρτίσθη (Hermae Pastor, *Vis.* II 4, 1 ; *Clem. Hom.* 14, 1). And in the 20th century R. Seeberg has interpreted that Biblical thought thus : " If God created the world with the provision that the Church should come into being in it, then the will of God—and that means simply Christ—was already active at the creation and formation of the world. . . ." So far as the natural world " was to be the theatre of a spiritual and historical world, the divine will that there should be a history leading to the Church . . . was already active in such a way at the creative formation of the world, that the natural possibility was provided for the existence and continuity of a spiritual world " (*Chr. Dogmatik*, Vol. I 1924 p.463 f.). Even if we are ready to ignore the fact that " Church " should still be something different from " spiritual, historical world "—it still remains to be said that certainly Jesus Christ, as he through whom God· made everything, is also the κεφαλὴ τοῦ σώματος, τῆς ἐκκλησίας (Col. 1¹⁸). As the former he may be the latter and is so. But not as the latter is he the former ; not as Head of the Church, and so not first and not only in his revelation is he he through whom God made all things. Assuredly he is thus mighty in his revelation, because he is already the Creator. But he is not primarily or only the Creator, because he is so mighty in his revelation. If we allow ourselves converses here, if we are not content to recognise the Creator in the revelation, but proceed to derive creation as such from revelation and to make that its basis, that is just as forbidden a speculation as the attempt criticised earlier, to look upon revelation as *creatio continuata*. To attribute the Church, or revelation, straight off to creation or the creative will of God as such, is to forget or suppress the fact, that Church or revelation can only become an event as the answer to the sin of man, or else we must take it upon ourselves to include the sin of man in creation. And, moreover, we must in that case have forgotten the free loving-kindness of God which gives this answer, or be reducing it to a necessary member of a dialectical process. In that case, this speculative synthesis of the works of God (which is as inevitable a happening in Seeberg as in Scheiermacher !), by dissolving the distinction between the divine Persons, will find its fitting expression in a modalistic doctrine of the Trinity. Otherwise it cannot be asserted that the world was made for the sake of the Church, of revelation, and that this purpose is the meaning of the participation of the Son of God in creation. Such syntheses are not to be had at any other price than that of those inferences. If we do not wish to pay this price—and we have reasons for not wishing to pay it—we must renounce such syntheses.

The truth of the knowledge that Christ in his revelation has the power of the Creator, depends upon it being the acknowledgment of a fact and not an arbitrary combination. Where this power is experienced, there is literally nothing to combine, creation and revelation are not two truths to be held side by side, compared with each other and put into touch with each other, but the one reality of Jesus Christ, as the Revealer with the power of the Creator. And in that case this power of the Creator cannot be thought of as one specially related and limited to revelation.

Augustine, therefore, is right when he lets even the angels, and Luther, therefore, is right when he lets even the broody hen, be created by the Word.

Creation then means just divinity in its originality, above and beyond all creatureliness. It is that—we must, then, look back again to the theology of the Trinity—which the symbol means to assert with its δι' οὗ τὰ πάντα. By the δι' οὗ it distinguishes the Son completely from the Father. By the τὰ πάντα it wholly combines the Son with the Father here as well. In that way it is the first and last word in dogma, the first and last word as to who and what Jesus Christ is, " antecedently in himself "—yet also but the first and last word in the account of the reality of revelation, as it is plainly to be seen in the mirror of the witness of Holy Scripture.

§ 12

GOD THE HOLY SPIRIT

The one God reveals Himself according to Scripture as the Redeemer, i.e. as the Lord who sets us free. As such He is the Holy Spirit, by receiving whom we become the children of God, because, as the Spirit of the love of God the Father and God the Son, He is so previously in Himself.

I. GOD AS THE REDEEMER

For a third time we begin with the NT witness, that " Jesus is the Lord." But this time adding the query, How do men come to make that assertion ? We now assume that they believe, therefore they speak. They are to be taken seriously in what they assert. They are to be held liable for it. Which means that they say so, not as the result of arbitrary reflection, but in recognition of a fact. They say so, not from a desire to give the man an office or the office a man, but because the man has and fulfils the office. They say so, not as the aim but as the start of their thought about him. They say so because he is the Lord. Thus they do not say that he is a demigod from above or from below, the incarnation of a divine idea, or a superman—they say that he is God. Right on the basis of this assumption we necessarily come up against the question, How come they to make that assertion ? How come they to this start of their thought about him ? How is it that they believe in the Father through the Son, in the Son through the Father ? How come these contents into this vessel ? How comes this predicate, this faith, to this subject, the subject man ? How can this faith be anything at all ? Can men believe ? If faith means meeting the Lord who is God, meeting him as the NT witnesses met Jesus, that is, in hard objectivity, in the world which is the world of man, in which everything is problematical, everything must first be tested, and certainly nothing is to be tested with the result that it is identical with God—and yet meeting him in such a way, that nothing is problematical at all, nothing has first to be

33

discovered by way of testing, but in such a way that meeting with him as such is meeting with God ? That is the meaning of revelation in the NT. But even in the NT does not the man whom such a thing encounters belong to the revelation ? And how can such a thing befall a man ? Might it not be said that the whole concept of revelation at this point becomes problematic, if the assumption is that faith in revelation consists in such utterly unproblematic knowledge of God in Christ ?—It is not as if no new question existed at this point for the NT requiring a new answer.

Even in the NT and particularly there, the possibility of faith does not go automatically with the fact that Jesus takes the stage as the revelation of the Father, or as the person he is, namely the Son or the Word of God. It is always, and only then rightly, when in contrast with him, that man too is the person he is. How does he manage to see and to hear at this point ? When 1 John begins with the declaration, we attest and announce to you ὃ ἀκηκόαμεν, ὃ ἑωράκαμεν τοῖς ὀφθαλμοῖς ἡμῶν, ὃ ἐθεασάμεθα καὶ αἱ χεῖρες ἡμῶν ἐψηλάφησαν (1 John 1¹ᶠ·), that is the indication of a reality, the possibility of which in the NT is by no means to be taken for granted. Οὐχ ἀφ᾿ ἑαυτῶν ἱκανοί ἐσμεν λογίσασθαί τι ὡς ἐξ ἑαυτῶν (2 Cor. 3⁵). " He that hath ears to hear, let him hear ! " says the Synoptic Jesus about his proclamation. " Flesh and blood hath not revealed it to thee ! " is his answer to Peter upon his confession (Matt. 16¹⁷). In view of the incarnate Word, in the midst of revelation, it seems to be giving something like a postponement, setting a problem, a limitation, to revelation. Will revelation, particularly this, the real revelation, reach its goal after all ? Will it get at man ? Will it become manifest to him ? That does not appear to lie solely with the good or bad will of man. For if this manifestation takes place, if there are ears there that hear, that means that, Unto you it is given to know the mystery of the kingdom of God. Ἐκείνοις δὲ τοῖς ἔξω ἐν παραβολαῖς τὰ πάντα γίνεται. Seeing they are to see and not realise, hearing to hear and not understand, so that they cannot convert and it be forgiven them (Mark 4¹¹⁻¹²). In virtue of supreme material necessity that must be so, where such givenness does not take place.

Manifestation must be added as something special, as a special act of the Father or the Son or both, to the givenness of the revelation of the Father in the Son.

The Father must reveal it to man (Matt. 16¹⁷), the Father must draw him (John 6⁴⁴), the Father must give it to him (John 6⁶⁵), man must be given to the Son by the Father (John 10²⁹), he must hear and learn it of the Father (John 6⁴⁵). But it may also mean that it is the Incarnate Word of God Himself, who gives to them who accept it ἐξουσία to be children of God and as such to believe in his name, who therefore as such are what they are, not in virtue their first natural generation and birth but in virtue of a second divine one (John 1¹²⁻¹³, 3³). And they can also speak of a stream of living water proceeding from the throne of God and of the Lamb, clear as crystal (Rev. 22¹). That is the additional speciality of the manifestation in revelation. The riches of grace are not there for us in Jesus Christ, but ἐπερίσσευσεν εἰς ἡμᾶς ἐν πάσῃ σοφίᾳ καὶ φρονήσει γνωρίσας ἡμῖν τὸ μυστήριον τοῦ θελήματος αὐτοῦ (Eph. 1$^{8.9}$).

This special element then in revelation is undoubtedly identical with what the NT usually calls the Holy Spirit, as the subjective side in the event of revelation.

Jesus breathed on them, it says in John 20^{22} of the disciples, while he said to them, λάβετε πνεῦμα ἅγιον, and by this λαμβάνειν they become (substantially in complete agreement with Acts 2) what they are, his apostles, his envoys. The πνεῦμα is that which maketh alive (John 6^{63} ; 2 Cor. 3^{6}). " No man can say that Jesus is the Lord, but by the Holy Πνεῦμα (1 Cor. 12^{3}). Because we have received the πνεῦμα, which is of God, we know the things that are freely given us of God for what they are (1 Cor. 2^{12}). Sealed with the holy πνεῦμα of promise ye heard the Word of truth, the gospel of your salvation, and ye came to believe (Eph. 1^{13}). God must give us the πνεῦμα of wisdom and revelation unto the knowledge of Himself (Eph. 1^{17}). Except a man be born of water and πνεῦμα, he cannot · enter into the kingdom of God (John 3^{5}). Εἰ δέ τις πνεῦμα Χριστοῦ οὐκ ἔχει, οὗτος οὐκ ἔστιν αὐτοῦ (Rom. 8^{9}), Therefore in Acts 19$^{2f.}$ it is called the most striking sign of those who are baptised only in the name of John, but not in the name of Jesus, that they know nothing of the Holy Πνεῦμα.

Πνεῦμα θεοῦ or Χριστοῦ, like υἱὸς θεοῦ, is a figure of speech. According to John 3^{8}, Acts 2^{2} πνεῦμα means wind, as, coming from here, it goes mysteriously there, and of course still more definitely according to 2 Thess. 2^{8}, John 20^{22} breath, as it goes from the mouth of a living creature and can reach another living creature : invisibly and without removing the spatial distance between them. This little, movable paradox becomes in the NT, as already in the OT, the parable of the great irremovable paradox of the divine revelation. To say that God gives man His πνεῦμα, or that man receives this πνεῦμα, is now a claim that God comes to man, that He discloses Himself to man and man to Himself, gives Himself to man in experience, arouses man to faith, illumines him and equips him as a prophet or apostle, makes to Himself a community of faith and proclamation, to which He imparts His salvation together with his promise, in which He binds men to Himself and claims them for Himself, in short, in which He becomes theirs and makes them His. As this incomparable thing the πνεῦμα is τὸ πνεῦμα τὸ ἅγιον. Holy, because only God's πνεῦμα is so. And because His intention is the sanctification, i.e. the setting apart, the seizure, the appropriation, the marking out of the men who receive it, the marking out by which they become, what by themselves and of themselves they can neither be nor become, men who belong to God, who are in real communion with God, who live before God and with God. As the prototype of all Biblical uses of language about the divine πνεῦμα, the passage Gen. 2^{7} should be considered, in which it says of God that He breathed into man's face the breath of life, and that thus, and for the first time, man became living : *et inspiravit in faciem eius spiraculum vitae et factus est homo anima vivens* (*Vulg.*).

In the OT and NT the general expression for God's spirit, the Holy Spirit, is God Himself, in so far as He is able, in an inconceivably real way, without therefore being less God, to be present to the creature, and in virtue of this presence of His to realise the relation of the creature towards Himself, and in virtue of this relation to Himself to vouchsafe life to the creature. The creature indeed requires the Creator in order to live. He thus requires relation to Him. But this relation he cannot create. God creates it through His own presence in the creature, i.e. in the form of the relation of Himself to Himself. The Spirit of God is God in His freedom to be present to the creature, and so to create this relation, and thereby to be the life of the creature. And God's Spirit, the Holy Spirit, particularly in revelation, is God Himself, so far as He can not only come to man, but be in man, and so open up man for Himself, make him ready and capable, and so achieve His revelation in him. Man needs revelation, as surely as he is lost without it. He thus requires that revelation should become manifest to him, i.e. that he should become open to revelation. But that is not a thing within the power of man. It can only be God's own reality if it does happen, and it is therefore a thing only in God's power, that it can happen. It is God's reality, by God being subjectively present to men not only from without, not only from above, but also from within, from beneath. It is reality, therefore, by God not only coming to man, but meeting Himself from man's end. God's freedom to be thus present to man and hence to introduce this meeting—that is the Spirit of God, the Holy Spirit in God's revelation.

The work of the Holy Spirit consists in *nos aptare Deo* (Irenaeus, *C. o. h.* III 17, 2). He is the *doctor veritatis* (Tertullian, *De praescr.* 28). He is the *digitus Dei, per quem sanctificemur* (Augustine, *Se spir. et lit.* 16, 28). *Intelligo spiritum Dei, dum in cordibus nostris habitat, efficere, ut Christi virtutem sentiamus. Nam ut Christi beneficia mente concipiamus, hoc fit Spiritus sancti illuminatione : eius persuasione fit, ut cordibus nostris obsignentur. Denique, solus ipse dat illis in nobis locum. Regenerat nos, facitque ut simus novae creaturae. Proinde, quaecunque nobis offerantur in Christo dona, ea Spiritus virtute recipimus* (Calvin, *Catech. Genev.* 1545 in K. Müller, p. 125, 16). He is the *applicator, illuminator, sanctificator* (*Syn. pur. Theol.*, Leiden, 1624 *Disp.* 9, 21).

The Holy Spirit is not identical with Jesus Christ, with the Son or Word of God.

Even in the sentence in 2 Cor. 3[17], ὁ δὲ κύριος τὸ πνεῦμα, it is not a case of identifying Jesus Christ with the Spirit, but of asserting that to the Spirit belongs the κυριότης, the divinity of the Lord, of whom the apostle was speaking in v. 16. Where this Spirit is who is the Lord, who is God, there is freedom, so runs the continuation, freedom from that masking of the heart, such as makes the reading of Moses in the service of the Jews always unfruitful to this day : freedom to see and to hear. And in v. 18 there is mirrored in us—our face is uncovered—the glory of the Lord, and so we become transformed into his image, from His glory to a glory of our own—to wit, ἀπὸ κυρίου πνεύματος, through the Lord who is the Spirit. We are forbidden, not only by the linguistic usage elsewhere, but also by the meaning and context of this passage itself, even here not to identify the Spirit with Jesus Christ. The other passages where the Spirit is clearly named (so 1 Cor. 12⁴ᶠ·; 2 Cor. 13¹⁴; 1 Peter 1², etc.) along with the Father and Christ, or (so 1 Cor. 6¹¹) along with Christ alone, may simply be recalled here.

This non-identity between Christ and the Holy Spirit appears in the context of the NT witness to be as necessarily grounded as possible. That is to say, there is a Holy Spirit only after the death and resurrection of Jesus Christ, say in the form of knowledge of the crucified and risen One, i.e. on the assumption of the conclusion and completion of the objective revelation. Indeed, we saw earlier that in his passage through death into life he is the revelation of the Father. Those who believe in and confess him, believe in and confess Him as the exalted Lord. Therefore they stand—the Spirit in whom they believe and confess, and he who is the object of this faith and confession—confronting one another, as it were on two different levels. Therefore that which comes over, drops down from above, from the Exalted, is the Spirit.

This " descent " of the Holy Spirit is an idea of the Acts in particular (cf. Acts 2², 10⁴⁴, 11¹⁵). Therefore " Receive ye the Holy Ghost ! " (John 20²²) can only be a saying of the risen Christ. Therefore the outpouring of the Holy Spirit in Acts 2 is depicted as a work, supervening upon the completed *Kerygma* of the life, death, and resurrection of Jesus, of him of whom this *kerygma* speaks. Wherefore the peculiar doctrine of the Gospel of St. John, yet one assuredly significant for the understanding of the whole NT, is that Jesus (as distinct from John the Baptist) is ὁ βαπτίζων ἐν πνεύματι ἁγίῳ (John 1³³). Streams of living water are to flow from the body of him who believes in him, it says in the difficult passage John 7³⁸ᶠ·, with the addition that this Jesus spake of the Spirit, which they that believed on him should receive, and with the important explanation, οὔπω γὰρ ἦν πνεῦμα, ὅτι Ἰησοῦς οὐδέπω ἐδοξάσθη. Next, John 14¹⁶, the Spirit looks like the (once more, future) gift of the Father to the disciples, the gift for which Jesus will ask the Father on their behalf. The Father will send him in his, Jesus' name (John 14²⁶). On the other hand, John 15²⁶, he himself, Jesus, will send from the Father, him that proceedeth from the Father (ὁ παρὰ τοῦ πατρὸς ἐκπορεύεται). But for that, according to John 16⁷, Jesus on his part must first go away from the disciples : συμφέρει ὑμῖν ἵνα ἐγὼ ἀπέλθω. ἐὰν γὰρ μὴ ἀπέλθω, ὁ παράκλητος οὐ μὴ ἐλθῇ πρὸς ὑμᾶς. ἐὰν δὲ πορευθῶ, πέμψω αὐτὸν πρὸς ὑμᾶς. Finally, John 16¹³ simply and generally deals with his (the Spirit's) coming. It is obviously the fulfilment of this repeated promise, that we have before us in John 20²².

For all that it is scarcely the idea of the NT, that chronologically it was not till after Good Friday and Easter, that there were men who had received the Holy Spirit. In that case what can be the meaning of so frequently ascribing faith, in all seriousness, to disciples and non-disciples, even before Good Friday and Easter ? What was meant by Jesus' reply to Peter's confession (Matt. 16[17]) ? The story of the transfiguration (Mark 9[2f.] and parallels) shows that at all events the Synoptists counted on the possibility of anticipations of the conclusion and completion of revelation, the possibility of revelations of the exalted Christ, at a time antecedent to his appearing. And it may well be asked whether also the whole of the miracles of Jesus are not to be regarded, so to speak, as backward-striking rays of the glory of the Risen One, in fact whether in short the entire life of Jesus is not meant to be considered in this retrospective illumination. But even in John, where the chronological schematism seems more consciously and strictly carried out, the temporal relationship between him who lived as a man with the disciples and the exalted Christ, and therefore also between the Spirit promised and the Spirit given, is certainly more complicated than it looks at first sight. How ever are we to take John 2[11], if the future is not also here thought of as future, and likewise as already present ? And John 20[22] and the Pentecost account in Acts 2 must of course be regarded as the express and solemn testimony to an event, which chronologically was not limited, either forwards or backwards, to the precise day of Pentecost.

We must immediately add that, while the Spirit is the element in revelation that is different from Christ *qua* exalted, revelation so far as it is a happening to us and in us, he is still to be regarded completely as the Spirit of Christ, of the Son, of the Word of God. Therefore precisely not as a revelation of independent content, not as a new instruction, illumination, stirring up of man proceeding beyond Christ, beyond the Word, but simply as the instruction, illumination, stirring up of man by means of the Word, on behalf of the Word.

The Holy Spirit, it is true, is expressly called the " Spirit of Christ" in relatively few passages (Gal. 4[6]; Rom. 8[9]; Phil. 1[19]; 1 Peter 1[11]). As a rule he is simply called the "Spirit of God"; which in a series of passages must be regarded as the " Spirit of the Father." But we may take it that no incongruity between Christ and the Spirit is anywhere demonstrable, but once more the Gospel according to St. John reproduces the sense of the whole NT, when it makes Jesus say of the Spirit, ἐκεῖνος μαρτυρήσει περὶ ἐμοῦ (John 15[26]), οὐ γὰρ λαλήσει ἀφ' ἑαυτοῦ ἀλλὰ ὅσα ἀκούει λαλήσει καὶ τὰ ἐρχόμενα ἀναγγελεῖ ὑμῖν. ἐκεῖνος ἐμὲ δοξάσει, ὅτι ἐκ τοῦ ἐμοῦ λήμψεται καὶ ἀναγγελεῖ ὑμῖν (John 16[13f.]).

The statements as to the meaning and operation of the Holy Spirit in the event called revelation in the NT may be arranged in three groups.

1. The Spirit guarantees man, what the latter cannot guarantee himself, his personal participation in revelation. The act of the Holy Spirit in revelation is the Yea to God's Word, spoken through God Himself on our behalf, yet not only to us but in us. This yea spoken by God is the ground of the confidence

with which a man may regard the revelation as meant for him. This yea is the mystery of faith, the mystery of knowledge of the Word of God, but also the mystery of willing obedience, well-pleasing to God. All of it exists for man " in the Holy Spirit," to wit, faith, knowledge, obedience.

Ἐν τούτῳ γινώσκομεν ὅτι ἐν αὐτῷ μένομεν καὶ αὐτὸς ἐν ἡμῖν, ὅτι ἐκ τοῦ πνεύματος αὐτοῦ δέδωκεν ἡμῖν (1 John 4¹³). Here it is above all the specifically Pauline idea of the Holy Spirit that we have to consider here. The Spirit " dwelleth in us " (Rom. 8⁹·¹¹), and so he is the ἀπαρχή (Rom. 8²³) or the ἀρραβών (2 Cor. 1²², 5⁵ ; Eph. 1¹⁴), as it were the light, thrown out in advance, of the salvation which belongs to us from God. To participate in the Holy Spirit is to have " tasted the good word of God, and the powers of the world to come " (Heb. 6⁵). Together with Christ or the Word, the Holy Spirit beareth witness with our spirit, that we are the children of God : αὐτὸ τὸ πνεῦμα συμμαρτυρεῖ τῷ πνεύματι ἡμῶν (Rom. 8¹⁶). God reveals to us διὰ τοῦ πνεύματος what He wishes to reveal to us, because the Spirit " searcheth all things," even τὰ βάθη τοῦ θεοῦ, and because he, the Spirit, does so on our behalf, in us (1 Cor. 2¹⁰). He " helpeth our infirmities " (συναντιλαμβάνεται) ; we know not what we should pray for as we ought, but he maketh intercession for us (ὑπερεντυγχάνει) with his groanings which cannot be uttered (ἀλαλήτοις) by us : and so because here, quite apart from our being weak or strong, our being able or unable to pray, something appropriate to God (κατὰ θεόν) takes place in us, God hears and grants our prayer (Rom. 8²⁶f·). By the Holy Spirit the love of God (or, love to God) is poured forth in our hearts (Rom. 5⁵). In short, because and so far as he receives the Holy Spirit, man is a temple of God (1 Cor. 3¹⁶, 6¹⁹ ; 2 Cor. 6¹⁶), because and so far as he has received the Holy Spirit, we may tell him to his face that the word is nigh thee, *even* in thy mouth and in thy heart (Rom. 10⁸). The formula ἐν πνεύματι, so frequent in Paul, signifies the thought, action, and language of man, as taking place by participation in God's revelation. It is pretty much the subjective correlate to ἐν Χριστῷ, which objectively signifies the same material content.

2. The Spirit gives man the instruction and guidance which he cannot give himself. Here it becomes clear, what should also be remembered in our preceding pronouncement, that the Spirit is not, and does not become, identical with ourselves.

As a concept of Pauline anthropology πνεῦμα does not assert that the Holy Spirit, wholly or partially, originally or subsequently, belongs to the essence of man, but at best it denotes the place (beyond σῶμα and ψυχή), where reception of the Holy Spirit may become an actuality (1 Thess. 5²³).

He remains the purely other, the superior. We can only note what his yea is to the Word of God, this yea of his we can only repeat after him. As our teacher and leader he is in us, not as a power of which we might become the lords. He remains himself the Lord.

This is in the main the place to which the Johannine doctrine of the Paraclete belongs. The concept recalls the concept of *paraclesis*, so important to Paul. The latter signifies, what cannot be reproduced in German [or English ?], the combination of reminding and consoling which the apostle had so to speak to take up and pass on, which God brings His children to experience (cf. e.g. 2 Cor. 1³ᶠ·) It is this that Jesus according to the Fourth Gospel holds out as the special work of the Holy Spirit. The Spirit as the Paraclete is the " Spirit of Truth " (John 14¹⁷, 15²⁶, 16¹³). Ἐκεῖνος ὑμᾶς διδάξει πάντα καὶ ὑπομνήσει ὑμᾶς πάντα ἅ εἶπον ὑμῖν ἐγώ (John 14²⁶). Ὁδηγήσει ὑμᾶς εἰς τὴν ἀλήθειαν πᾶσαν (John 16¹³). Also of course identical with the Paraclete and so with the Holy Spirit is what in 1 John (also 2 Cor. 1²¹) is called the chrisma, of which it is also said, Ἔχετε ἀπὸ τοῦ ἁγίου καὶ οἴδατε πάντες (1 John 2²⁰). " . . . ye need not that any man should teach you : but as the same anointing teacheth you of all things, it is in truth and is no lie " (*ib.* 2, 27). But this is also the place for the fact that Paul ascribes to the Spirit an ἄγειν, or to believers an ἄγεσθαι by the Spirit (Gal. 5¹⁸ ; Rom. 8¹⁴), with which are to be compared the wonderfully direct instructions under which, especially according to the Acts (cf. e.g. Acts 8²⁹, 10¹⁹, 13², 16⁶ and often) this ἄγειν might materialise.

Along this entire line the Spirit is obviously less the reality in which God makes us sure of Him, as on the contrary the reality in which He makes Himself sure of us, in which by His immediate presence He makes good and executes His claim as Lord upon us.

3. Exegetically very obscure but, materially, certainly of most central importance is this fact, that the Spirit is the great, the only possibility, in virtue of which men can so speak of Christ, that their language becomes testimony, therefore that the revelation of God in Christ becomes actual anew by their speaking. Has that entry of God into us on His own behalf, in the twofold sense in which we have just been visualising it, an independent significance *qua* operation of the Holy Spirit, alongside the fact that man by the Holy Spirit should and may become a real speaker and proclaimer of real testimony, and so of the real Word of God ? Does not the NT doctrine of the Holy Spirit point right beyond all that the Spirit can mean for the believer in his relation to God, to what should happen in the believer and through the believer in the power of the Spirit for God, i.e. in the service of God ? Is not the relation between Spirit and Church, or the relation between the Spirit and the will of the Church's Lord that must be accomplished, the dominating and generally determinative relation ?

A Whitsun sermon is at all events not an exposition of Acts 2¹⁻¹⁴ unless it considers and enforces the fact that the outpouring of the Holy Spirit, which is the subject of this text, consists extremely concretely in the cloven tongues becoming visible and the disciples upon whom " it " rested beginning to speak " in other tongues," καθὼς τὸ πνεῦμα ἐδίδου ἀποφθέγγεσθαι αὐτοῖς. (Repetitions of this latter event are recounted in Acts 10⁴⁶ and 19⁶.) And the second effect of this Whitsun miracle consists in the fact that, γενομένης τῆς φωνῆς ταύτης the present adherents of all possible distant and neighbouring nations hear the disciples express in their own languages τὰ μεγαλεῖα τοῦ θεοῦ (Acts 2⁷ᶠ·). Of this speaking by the disciples and of this hearing by Parthians, Medes, and Elamites, etc., a Whitsun sermon would have to speak, if it claimed to be an exposition of Acts 2¹ᶠ·; also the impression of Peter's speech which follows, Acts 2¹⁴ᶠ·, so far as it does not consist in the exposition of the *kerygma* itself, lies entirely in the event being explained as the fulfilment of the Joel prophecy of the outpouring of the Spirit upon all flesh, which will consist in men—men and women, is the strikingly strong emphasis—beginning to "prophecy." It is that that is fulfilled at Pentecost. There is now over against the Lord Jesus, completely subordinate to him, of course, but constituting an element in the reality of his revelation, distinct from himself, an apostolate, men commissioned, empowered, and authorised by him to testify, whose human words may be taken by all sorts of nations as the proclamation of the "wonderful works of God." That is the doing of the Holy Spirit. The difficult exegetical question at this stage consists in how this gift of "tongues" at Pentecost is related to what, in 1 Cor. 12 and 14 under the same name, is very solemnly regarded and valued by Paul as a special gift of individual members of the Christian Church, although it is discussed with extreme reserve, not to say criticism. We do not have to pursue this question here. It is certain, that what Paul is acquainted with there under this name, has not the central significance for himself, or in his opinion for the Church either, which belongs to what is narrated in Acts 2. But it is just as certain, that what gives central significance to the narrative of Acts 2, the commissioning, empowering, and equipment of the apostolate, is for him too—and for him too, as the work of the Holy Spirit—the presupposition of its activity and message. Πρὸς φωτισμὸν τῆς γνώσεως τῆς δόξης τοῦ θεοῦ ἐν προσώπῳ χριστοῦ God let it shine in our hearts as on the first day of creation (2 Cor. 4⁶). "Ye shall receive the power of the Holy Ghost that is come upon you; and ye shall be my witnesses" says the risen Lord to his disciples, Acts 1⁸. We find the same juxtaposition of πνεῦμα and μαρτυρεῖν in John 15²⁶: the Spirit shall testify to you of me, and ye also shall bear witness! Again there is the saying of Jesus, to the effect that the disciples were not to be anxious what they should say in self-defence in the hour of impeachment: they were to say exactly what was given them in that hour. Οὐ γάρ ἐστε ὑμεῖς οἱ λαλοῦνες ἀλλὰ τὸ πνεῦμα τὸ ἅγιον (Mark 13¹¹ and parallels; in Luke 12¹² with the variation, the Holy Spirit διδάξει ὑμᾶς . . . ἃ δεῖ εἰπεῖν).

The Holy Spirit is the empowering to speak of Christ: he is the equipment of the prophet and the apostle, he is the call to the Church to serve the Word. So far as everything in which this qualification, equipment and call consists—we discussed this under points 1 and 2—is directed towards this goal, so far as it cannot be a private matter, but only a matter of the Church, or rather of the Lord of the Church, if there exist individuals to whom the Spirit guarantees that God's revelation lays hold of them, individuals whom the Spirit drives—to that extent we shall have to call this operation of the Spirit, mentioned in the third place, the decisive one. If we ask about the "mind" of the Spirit (τὸ φρόνημα τοῦ πνεύματος, Rom. 8²⁷), we shall have to reply, that it consists in him being the gift of speaking about the " wonderful works of God." But if we ask what it means to receive and to possess this gift, then we shall always have to be reading off the answer again from the first two determinations of our concept.

In the opening paragraph the nature and operation of the Holy Spirit in revelation is described by the two expressions with a play on Biblical utterances : he is " the Lord who sets us free," and " by reception of whom we become children of God." We may claim these actual two expressions as a summary of what we have to abstract from the witness of Holy Scripture to the nature of the Spirit, as an element in the revelation of God in Jesus Christ.

In the first place and formally, the concept of f r e e d o m declares, that when Scripture speaks of the Holy Spirit as the driving power in revelation, what is involved is an a b i l i t y or capability or capacity added to man as the addressee of revelation, which makes him the real recipient of revelation. That indeed is the problem with which we saw ourselves faced, how man can have faith. How does *homo peccator* become *capax verbi divini* ? The answer of the NT is to the effect that it is the Holy Spirit who sets him free for that and for the service to which he is thereby put.

Christ, we read in Gal. 5¹, has " set us free for freedom." Both there and all along the line the concept undoubtedly stands in contrast with the concept of the slavery conquered in Christ. This slavery consists in the first place— but only in the first place—in man's being bound to a law of God, misunderstood and misused by man, a law to which man ascribes divine authority and with which he is at pains to stand right, although in practice he does not recognise in it the voice of the God who commands, although he is far removed from letting it serve him as real revelation. But the nature and the curse of this slavery lies deeper : because man is thus bound, he is not able, not free to apprehend real revelation. The opposite of course must also be said, that because he is not free for real revelation, he is therefore thus bound. At all events he stands, in appearance but likewise only in appearance, believing in God, listening to Him, and diligent in serving Him, powerless in face of the living God, powerless to know Him as He is and to obey Him in the way He desires. Thus the freedom with which Christ makes us free may therefore not only consist in freedom from that bondage, it must also and it must decisively consist in freedom from the non-ability, the powerlessness mentioned, in freedom to receive the real revelation of God. That is confirmed for us by a glance at the important context of John 8³¹⁻⁵⁹. The Jews claim to be free as Abraham's people (v. 33). Jesus positively declares to them, "Whosoever committeth sin, is the servant of sin " (v. 34), and so not free. Why and to what extent ? " If the Son therefore shall make you free, ye shall be free indeed " (³⁶). But it is just that that is impossible ! Their sin is, that the Word of Jesus can have no place in them

(οὐ χωρεῖ ἐν ὑμῖν, v. 37), that they cannot hear it (οὐ δύνασθε ἀκούειν v. 43).
" He that is of God heareth God's words : ye therefore hear them not, because
ye are not of God " (v. 47). The freedom therefore with which the Son (v. 36),
with which the truth (v. 32) makes men free cannot possibly mean the mere
negation of the false bondage (scarcely mentioned in this context). So understood freedom would at once have to serve for an " occasion for the flesh to
have its head " (Gal. 5¹³), for a " cloke of maliciousness " (1 Peter 2¹⁶). So
understood it would obviously be nothing else but a new sort of un-freedom.
The really free are rather free as the servants of God (1 Peter 2¹⁶). There is
nothing to preclude the paradox of 1 Cor. 7²² about the Christian slave who
is the Lord's freedman because of his calling, and the Christian freeman who is
likewise a slave of Christ because of his calling, from pointing in this direction
too, according to its most natural meaning. One thing is certain : the freedom
which, according to 2 Cor. 3¹⁷, is where the Lord the Spirit is, signifies exclusively
the freedom to turn to the Lord, to God, as distinguished from the Jews for
whom, although and because they read the sacred texts, the face of God
remains hidden. And equally unmistakably the " law of liberty " spoken of
in James 1²⁵, 2¹², is the order directly contrasted, but quite positively contrasted, with the law of the Jews, the order under which stands the man
who is not only a hearer but a doer of the Word of God—and in James that
means not a forgetful, not a merely reputed hearer, but a real hearer, a
hearer in the action of his life, a hearer whom the Word claims in his existence.
If a man is capable of that, of being such a doer, i.e. such a real hearer of
the Word, he is free in the NT sense of this concept. It is not a matter of any
kind of freedom, any sort of ability one way or another. It is a matter—
answering to the freedom of God Himself, which we spoke of, His freedom
to be Himself, to be God—of man's freedom for God, of the " glorious liberty
of the children of God " (Rom. 8²¹), the *analogia fidei* of that divine liberty,
which alone really deserves to be called liberty. Such is the formal summary
of the operation of the Spirit in God's revelation : His operation consists in
freedom, freedom to have a Lord, this Lord, God, as Lord.

On the other hand the concept of being children of God
declares materially, that when Scripture speaks of the Holy Spirit
as the force in revelation, it is a matter of a being of that man,
to whom such freedom, such ability belongs. Such men are
what they are able for. They are able for the thing they are.
Thus and therefore they are real recipients of revelation, they can
have faith. Once again, how does *homo peccator* become *capax
verbi divini* ? The second (the first comprehensive) answer must
now be to the effect that he does not first become so, in order
next to be so, but he is so, and in that way, because of this being,
he becomes so. He is God's child. As such he is free, able to have
faith. And he is God's child, by receiving the Holy Spirit. But on
the contrary it may and must also be said, that he receives the
Holy Spirit by being God's child. At all events, in this receiving
of the Holy Spirit, he is, what in himself and of himself he cannot
be, one who belongs to God, as a child to its father, one who knows

God as a child knows its father, one who exists for God as a child exists for its father. Such is the second or material summary of the operations of the Holy Spirit in God's revelation.

Freedom for God, we repeat first of all so as to connect up with our formal determination of the content, is the freedom of the children of God (Rom. 8²¹). Clearly the NT concept of being a child of God can in no sense compete with the concept of Jesus Christ's being the Son of God. It is rather absolutely dependent upon the latter. The Fathers made the distinction that Jesus Christ is *Filius Dei natura*, believers are *filii Dei adoptione*. They are able to be so *adoptione*, because Jesus Christ is so *natura*. Because the Reconciler is the Son of God, reconciliation, revelation consists for the recipients of it in the fact that they, even they, are sons of God in the irremovable distinction between the pardoned and Him who pardons them, in God existing even for them, as a father exists for his child. " A man can receive nothing, except it be given him from heaven " (John 3²⁷). That does not hold of Jesus Christ's sonship to God, but it does hold of believers in God being His children. " By faith, in Christ Jesus, ye are the sons of God, because ye have been baptised into Christ and have (as such) put on Christ " (Gal. 3²⁶ᶠ·). In order to be God's child, a man must be called to the κοινωνία τοῦ υἱοῦ αὐτοῦ Ἰησοῦ Χριστοῦ (1 Cor. 1⁹). He must be begotten with the Word of truth " (Jas. 1¹⁸) ; and it is the " good gift " which comes to him altogether " from above," when the thing happens (Jas. 1¹⁷). It is emphatically a " birth from above " (John 3³), absolutely different from his natural birth, resting upon the ἐξουσία which the *Logos* himself must give him, in virtue of which he is God's child. But all that does not mean a limitation, but rather an underlining, of the constantly recurring indicatives, in which the NT says of believers that they are (Rom. 8¹⁴), we are (Rom. 8¹⁶), we are called and are (1 John 3¹ᶠ·), now are we (1 John 3²), ye are (Gal. 4⁶), in fact ye all are (Gal. 3²⁶)—sons, children of God, and therefore not servants (Gal. 4⁷) who only belong to the house for a time (John 8³⁵), but heirs (Rom. 8¹⁷ ; Gal. 4⁷), not Ishmael but Isaac (Gal. 4³⁰ᶠ·), not " strangers and foreigners " but " fellow-citizens with the saints and of the household of God " (Eph. 2¹⁹). To be such a child of God and to receive the Holy Spirit is one and the same thing. The Holy Spirit is τὸ πνεῦμα τοῦ υἱοῦ (Gal. 4⁶) and therefore the πνεῦμα υἱοθεσίας (Rom. 8¹⁵).

In what does he show himself to be such ? In a decisive passage Paul mentions only one thing, in which for him everything is obviously contained : in the Holy Spirit, and so as children of God, we cry, κράζομεν, Ἀββά, ὁ πατήρ (Rom. 8¹⁵ ; Gal. 4⁶). It is marvellously, but of a surety not accidentally, the same cry which the Gospel narrative (Mark 14³⁶) puts in the mouth of Jesus in Gethsemane as he prays. So then, in this form, the Son of God is the prototype of the sonship of believers. This Christ the children of God have " put on." This child, sinful man, can meet this Father, the holy God, as a child its father, nowhere else than at the place where the only-begotten Son of God bore and bore away his sins. Man's being set there does not exactly constitute his reconciliation—reconciliation consists in what the Son of God did and suffered for us—but in it the reconciliation is completed in him, it constitutes his participation in the reconciliation that came to pass in Christ. That is having the Holy Spirit. Having the Holy Spirit is being set together with Christ in that turn from death unto life. The likeness of a real recipient of the revelation of God, the likeness which gives the law to his thought, will, and speech, will thus always be the likeness of the death of Christ (Rom. 6^5; Phil. 3^{10}). And so too his freedom, his ability, his capability for God will not have to be regarded otherwise than as the power of Christ's resurrection, not as a freedom proper to and immanent in him but as a freedom accruing to him from God, one he can as little dispose of as realise, one that can only be regarded in its factuality, and as a fact of God at that. In this fact God assures us of Himself and He assures Himself of us and He teaches us what we should say as his witnesses. All pronouncements about the Holy Spirit, like all pronouncements about the Son of God, can only be connected with this divine fact. From the standpoint of it alone, alike in the NT as for ourselves, are they comprehensible or else incomprehensible.

Compare with what has been expounded here Luther's utterances in *Gal.* $4^{6f.}$ (W. edn. 40^1, p. 579–597). He calls "Abba, Father" the cry of the Holy Spirit in our hearts amid the very severe, the complete powerlessness and despair of this heart of ours in view of its radical sinfulness, in view of its doubt of even God's graciousness, in view of the Devil's accusation, *Tu es peccator!*, in view of the wrath of God who threatens us with eternal damnation, in the temptation in which there is no experience of the presence and help of Christ, where rather even Christ seems to be angry with us, where all we have to cling to is the *nudum verbum*. Then that cry rings out, pierces the clouds, fills heaven and earth, rings so clearly, that when they hear it, the angels think they have never heard anything at all before, in fact that in the whole world God Himself hears nothing else but this sound, and yet, *quantum ad sensum nostrum attinet* it is a trifling groan, in which we ourselves completely fail to hear this cry of the Spirit. What we experience is the temptation, what we hear are the voices, what we see is the face, of hell. Were we now content to trust our experience, we might just give ourselves up for lost. There and then—which of course none understand who speak *speculative tantum* of the Holy Spirit, such as Papists and fanatics—Christ is almighty, regnant, and triumphant in us. The word, that obscure "groanlet" (*gemitulus*), that *affectus* in which, in spite of all and without having any ground in experience, we can say, Father!—this word now becomes more eloquent than any Cicero or Virgil. Curiously enough, in this very passage (*op. cit.* p. 586, l. 13, 29) Luther lifts his hand for his mightiest blow at the *pestilens error* of Catholic doctrine, that in this life there is no real, inexpugnable certainty of the grace of God. When and where is there such certainty? Certainly not as regards ourselves, but as regards the *promissio et veritas Dei, quae fallere non potest. Aversis oculis a lege, operibus, sensu et conscientia*, this certainty becomes an event, as the grasping of the divine promise. The promise brings us this certainty, so far as it brings us the power to utter that cry of Abba, Father ! which in our mouth and heart is the smallest, before God the greatest, the one thing, because it is the cry of His own Spirit in us. *Tum certo definitum est in caelo, quod non sit amplius servitus sed mera libertas, adoptio et filiatio. Quis parit eam ? Iste gemitus.* But that comes to pass through my accepting God's promise. And as for my accepting God's promise, *hoc fit, cum isto gemitu clamo et respondeo corde filiali isti voci, Pater. Ibi tum conveniunt pater et filius* (p. 593, l. 18). But *quanta magnitudo et gloria hujus doni sit, humana mens ne quidem concipere potest in hac vita, multo minus eloqui. Interim in aenigmate cernimus hoc, Habemus istum gemitulum et exiguam fidem, quae solo auditu et sono vocis promittentis Christi nititur. Ideo quoad sensum nostrum res ista centrum, in se autem maxima et infinita sphera*

est. Sic Christianus habet rem in se maximam et infinitam, in suo autem con-
spectu et sensu minimam et finitissimam, Ideo istam rem metiri debemus non
humana ratione et sensu, sed alio circulo, scilicet promissione dei, Qui ut infinitus
est, ita et promissio ipsius infinita est, utcumque interim in has augustias et,
ut ita dicam, in verbum centrale inclusa sit.' Videmus igitur iam centrum, olim
videbimus etiam circumferentiam (p. 596, l. 16).

In what has been said so far the fact has already been expressed,
that the Holy Spirit is according to the evidence of Scripture no
less and nothing else than God Himself—distinct from Him
whom Jesus calls his Father, distinct also from Jesus himself, but,
no less than the Father and no less than Jesus, God Himself,
altogether God.

Again we recall 2 Cor. 3[17], ὁ κύριος τὸ πνεῦμα, the Lord is the Spirit.
We think of the famous πνεῦμα ὁ θεός, God is (the) Spirit (John 4[24]). In
both passages the reverse, that the Spirit is the Lord, the Spirit is God, is
not only permitted but enjoined, not indeed in the contexts in question, but
as a conclusion from what is said. The same equation is presupposed in
Acts 5[3f.], where Ananias is reproached with having lied to the Holy Spirit,
and where immediately thereupon it says, οὐκ ἐψεύσω ἀνθρώποις ἀλλὰ τῷ θεῷ;
just as also according to Mark 3[28f.]—whatever is meant by it—there could
not possibly be a blasphemy against the Holy Spirit which makes man guilty
of an unforgivable, eternal sin, if the Spirit were less, if he were something else
than God Himself.

That not only these and similar passages, but that the whole
NT doctrine of the operation of the Spirit implies the divinity
of his essence, can only be properly disputed, if we have first explained away the fact that the NT Church did confess, by Ἰησοῦς
κύριος, its faith in Jesus Christ as in God Himself. If the Christ of
the NT is a demi-god from above or from below, then of course
faith in him becomes a human possibility. However unusual he
may be as a phenomenon, he can be explained as having arisen out
of certain manageable and clear grounds and presuppositions. In
that case, as a matter of fact, there is likewise no need for the
divinity of the Holy Spirit who creates this faith. The name
" Holy Spirit " may very well be a mere name for a specially deep,
serious, and living conviction of truth or experience of conscience,
and we may as well keep calm silence altogether in the matter of
describing what according to the NT is the foundation of faith.

In that case we may, with Karl Holl, describe thus the experience and
reflection of the heathen contemporaries of the early Church who attained to
faith: " This thought of Jesus' about God (meaning, the thought of the God
who first of all and fundamentally forgives and then and thereupon begins to
make demands) which ran so sharply counter to all natural religious feeling,
nevertheless possessed its hidden, its irresistible power. It worked its way in
more deeply than any other concept of God. For it spoke to the conscience.

Was it not convincing that he who strove upwards to God should have had to take his standard not by human respectability or heroism, but by the unconditioned, by God's own moral nature, by His loving-kindness ? But the man who made an earnest attempt at it, lost against his will the distinction between right and wrong, between pure and impure. The solemn word of entrance into the mysteries, " whoso hath lived well and righteously," became a superficiality. For such an aim γνῶθι σεαυτόν now acquired its full mordancy. . . . From the depths of such introspection there grew up an understanding of Jesus' thought of God. Was it not really the case that the God by whose gifts man lived always bore man up with forgiving loving-kindness ? Only that man had become unconscious of Him ! And was not the God who sought the heart of man, who knew how to win back even the lost, greater, holier, mightier in such love than all the gods of high Olympus ? Thus everything fitted into a compact meaning. If a man grasped it, he had the feeling of having been wakened up from a dream. The boldness, the utter novelty, or whatever is meant to-day by that overdone slogan, the irrational element, in the preaching of Jesus alone would not have done it. What is merely irrational, exercises at best the limited and transitory attraction of forceful arbitrariness. But the victorious factor in Christianity is, that in this case the irrational produced an illuminating meaning, that what hit sound human intellect on the head proclaimed itself to the meditative as the revelation of a deeper, a convincing t r u t h about God and man (*Urchristentum u. Religionsgesch. Ges. Aufs. z. KGesch.* vol. II 1928 p. 18). Compare this analysis of Holl's, which purports to be NT exegesis, with Rom. 8[16f.], Gal. 4[6f.], and Luther's explanation thereof. Surely no one would wish to assert that in both cases the same thing is being said in different words. No, obviously here there has entered right into the place of the Holy Spirit man's capacity to distinguish and decide, by means of which Jesus' thought of God may " work its way into" him like any other concept of God, however more deeply it penetrates than any other—in virtue of which, like waking from a dream, he can by deep introspection become conscious of what hitherto he had not been conscious, in virtue of which he can establish as illuminatingly sensible, what at first offended him, in virtue of which he can, in one word, convince himself of the " truth about God and man," expressed in Jesus' thought of God. Here the measurement is not by the infinite circle of the divine promise, but altogether *humana ratione et sensu.* Here " the victorious factor in Christianity " does not consist in Christ being powerful in the powerlessness of man, or in the centre without a visible or inexperienceable circumference, but in Christ, or rather in Jesus' " thought of God," having a " compact meaning," illuminating to man or at least to the " meditative." Here the expression " Holy Spirit " need not be heard, and at last the doctrine of the divinity of the Spirit certainly need not be presented. Obviously the NT must be thus read here, because even where it speaks of Christ, it is taken to be speaking of the bearer of a special thought of God, of which man is indeed unaware, but properly able to take hold, the bearer of the deep convincing truth, that the relation between forgiveness and claim, contrary to healthy human understanding of it (i.e. to the superficial Greek self-knowledge !) is the exact opposite of what is usually assumed.

If we may now assume that this is not a tenable exegesis of NT Christology, then the transformation of the NT doctrine of the

Spirit into a doctrine of a very deep, very conscientious conviction of truth is also untenable. For if the case with the men of the NT is such that the divinity of Christ became clear to them, not on the ground of their knowledge and choice, but on the ground of their being known and chosen (not as the result but as the start of their thought about him), then the faith, or the basis of the faith, of these men cannot be regarded as a faculty unfortunately hidden from themselves, nor the occurrence of their faith be regarded, formally, as waking up from a dream or, materially, as a recollection of what was the case already at bottom. There is in that case no category of faith within history of religion, nor yet can conscience be dragged in as the δός μοι ποῦ στῶ, to explain the possibility of faith. Faith, the NT πίστις, is rather to be regarded as a possibility coming from a mode of God's existence, a mode of existence which is on a level, in essential unity, with Him who in the NT is described as Father and Son.

In faith an " anointing " or " sealing " is presupposed, which can have no resemblance to the creature " anointed " or " sealed " (Athanasius, *Ep. ad. Serap.* I 23 ; III 3). Were this presupposition, the Holy Spirit, a creature, he would not mediate to us any μετουσία θεοῦ. We should then once more have to do, ourselves creatures, with a mere creature, and would remain remote from the θεία φύσις. But if it is true that by the Holy Spirit we are deemed worthy of that μετουσία, would we not be mad to dream of denying his divinity ? (*ib.* I 24). We may certainly have doubts about the conceivability here indicated. But may we therefore doubt that here we have the correct exegesis of the NT doctrine of the Spirit, as distinguished from the modernistically Protestant theologian cited just previously ? If we look back upon the results of our analysis of the NT doctrine of the Spirit, i.e. upon the predicates which we have seen ascribed to the Spirit and his operation in revelation, what else can we say than that *Spiritus vox hic a creaturae notione plane submovenda est* ? (*Syn. pur. Theol.*, Leiden, 1624 *Disp.* 9, 2).

But now that also means, that the creature to whom the Holy Spirit is imparted in revelation, by no means loses thereby his nature and his kind as a creature, so as to become himself a sort of Holy Spirit. Even in receiving the Holy Spirit the man remains a man, the sinner a sinner. And likewise in the outpouring of the Holy Spirit God remains God. The statements about the operations of the Holy Spirit are statements the Subject of which is God and not man, and under no circumstances could they be transformed into statements about men. They speak of the relation of God to man, to his knowledge, will and feeling, to his experience active and passive, to his heart and conscience, to his soul-and-body existence, but they cannot be reversed and regarded as statements about the existence of man. To say that God the Holy Spirit is the Redeemer who makes us free, is a statement of knowledge and praise of God. We are, we are ourselves in virtue of this statement, redeemed, set free, children of God in faith, in the faith which we confess by this very statement ; but it means, in the act of God of which this statement speaks. This existence of ours is thus enclosed within the act of God. By confessing this faith in the Holy Spirit, we cannot so to speak look back and abstractly consider and establish our existence, enclosed as it is in the act of God, as redeemed, liberated children of God. We may, of course, be strong and sure in faith—that we are so, is just the act of God we are here confessing, the work of the Holy Spirit—but we cannot, by contemplation of ourselves as the strong and sure, dream of specially strengthening and assuring ourselves a second time. To have the Holy Spirit means to let God be one's confidence, and not one's own possession of God. It lies in the nature of God's revelation and reconciliation in time, it lies in the nature of the *regnum gratiae*, that " having God " and our " having God " are two different things, that our redemption is not a relation such as we can review, i.e. such as we can understand both ways, from God's side and from our own. Paradoxically enough we can only understand it from God's side, i.e. we can only understand it in faith as posited by God. Faith is, that we look upon it as posited and fulfilled and completed from that side. But not as fulfilled and completed from our side, not in such a way as though we were at once visible to ourselves in the existence which corresponds to this fulfilment and completion from God's side, i.e. in our state of redemption or blessedness or eternal being-alive. Even if we could take it so, that would mean that all need for faith would be left behind. It would have to stop being a " Nevertheless ! " It would have to stop being obedience and adventure. It would have to stop being faith at all. It would be sight. For it would mean sight if we could review, take a *conspectus* of how what is true from God's side is also true from ours. That would be more than God's revelation and reconciliation in time, that would be our existence with Him in eternity, in the *regnum gloriae*. If we cannot resolve this distinction, or anticipate this beyondness of revelation and faith, then that must mean that we can only regard redemption, so far as thereby more than the act of God, so far as thereby our own existence is to be asserted,

34

as future, i.e. as accruing to us from the side of God. We possess it in faith.

But our possessing it in faith means that we possess it as a promise. We believe that we are redeemed, set free, children of God, i.e. we take up as such the promise promulgated in the Word of God in Jesus Christ, although and while we do not in the least understand it in regard to our present, or in the least see it as fulfilled and completed ; we take it up, because it speaks of an act of God upon us, although and while we only see our empty hands, which we thereupon stretch out to God. We believe in our future existence, we believe in an eternal life in the midst of the valley of death. It is thus, in this futurity, that we have and possess it. The certainty with which we are aware of this possession is just the certainty of faith, and certainty of faith means concretely certainty of hope.

'Ελπιζομένων ὑπόστασις, πραγμάτων ἔλεγχος οὐ βλεπομένων (Heb. 11¹). Therefore the concept of being God's children, so important, as we saw, is gladly explained, especially by Paul, by the concept of the inheritance (κληρονομία), not indeed yet entered upon, but legitimately within view, and as such certain (Rom. 8¹⁷ ; Gal. 3²⁹ ; Tit. 3⁷ ; also Jas. 2⁵). Therefore it says in Gal. 5⁵ that we in the Spirit by faith wait for the hoped-for righteousness (and precisely as hoped-for, present in Jesus Christ !)—ἐλπίδα δικαιοσύνης ἀπεκδεχόμεθα—therefore it says in 2 Cor. 5⁷ that we walk by faith and not by sight, and in a passage that cannot be over-pondered, Rom. 8⁵·³ᶠ·, that we, the same (note the double καὶ αὐτοί) who have the ἀπαρχὴ τοῦ πνεύματος, with the whole creation do groan in the expectation of sonship, so far as by sonship is to be understood the fulfilment and completion of the promise, the ἀπολύτρωσις τοῦ σώματος. Τῇ γὰρ ἐλπίδι ἐσώθημεν· ἐλπὶς δὲ βλεπομένη οὐκ ἔστιν ἐλπίς· ὃ γὰρ βλέπει τις, τί καὶ ἐλπίζει; εἰ δὲ ὃ οὐ βλέπομεν ἐλπίζομεν, δι' ὑπομονῆς ἀπεκδεχόμεθα. God hath begotten you again. How? Through the resurrection of Jesus Christ from the dead! To what? To a living hope, namely, to the inheritance incorruptible, undefiled, that fadeth not away, reserved in heaven for you (1 Pet. 1³ᶠ·). We are called and are the children of God, we are so now . . . and it doth not yet appear what we shall be. We know that when he shall appear, we shall be like him (1 John 3¹ᶠ·). Your life (i.e. your salvation) is hid with Christ in God. When Christ our life shall appear, then shall ye also appear with him in glory (Col. 3³ᶠ·). Abraham is the father of all believers, because he considered not his own body now dead, nor that of Sarah, but gave the glory to God, in the certainty that what He promises, He is able also to perform ! (Rom. 4¹⁹ᶠ·). Therefore the Holy Spirit Himself is called the πνεῦμα τῆς ἐπαγγελίας (Eph. 1¹³), therefore his office upon us is our sealing εἰς ἡμέραν ἀπολυτρώσεως (Eph. 4³⁰, cf. 1¹⁴).

Everything that is to be said about the man who receives the Holy Spirit, is driven and filled by the Holy Spirit, is in the NT sense an eschatological pronouncement. Eschatological means, not " with an improper or unreal intent," but " related to the ἔσχατον," i.e. to what from our point of view is still in arrears for our experience and thought, to the eternal reality of the divine fulfilment and completion. Precisely and only eschatological pronouncements, i.e. pronouncements related to this eternal reality, may, as pronouncements upon temporal circumstances, claim to have a real and proper intention. Or how could man be able to intend anything more real and more proper than the truth in this particular relation.

The NT speaks eschatologically, when it speaks of man's being called, reconciled, justified, sanctified, redeemed. That is the precise way in which it speaks really and properly. We must understand that God is the measure of all reality and propriety, understand that eternity exists first and then time, and therefore the future first and then the present, as surely as the Creator exists first and then the creature. He who understands that need take no offence here.

We can only speak non-eschatologically, i.e. without any such relation to an Other, a beyond, a future, about God Himself ; in this case, about the Holy Spirit and his work as such. It may of course be said that even our language about God and His work is so far eschatological, as our thoughts and words as such, the whole lot of them, cannot grasp this object, but can only point beyond themselves to it. But what is there pointed to, if we are speaking of God, His nature and work, has itself no bound and no limit, is not related to an ἔσχατον, is itself the ἔσχατον. That is the thing we cannot say of the man we know, even and above all in faith. He does not live an eternal life. That is and remains the predicate of God, of the Holy Spirit.

He is Lord over every creature but is not lorded over ; He deifies but is not deified. He fulfils but is not fulfilled ; he permits participation but does not participate : He sanctifies but is not sanctified (Joh. Damasc., *Ekdos.* I 8).

But of ourselves we must say, that God so presents Himself to us in His revelation, that we are and remain, in fact only then properly begin to be, rich in Him, poor in ourselves. Both things become our experience ; that we are rich in God ; and that, in consequence and for the first time properly, we become poor in ourselves. But it is not in what we experience that we possess divine, spiritual riches, divine, spiritual poverty. What we experience, what changes in us in quantity and quality, expands, develops, moves up and down, perhaps even forwards in a straight line or in spirals, what may become the object of an anthropology, psychology, or biography of the believing individual, is, as a human sign of the fact that God has presented Himself to us by His revelation in faith, certainly not to be treated lightly. We would be intromitting with extraordinary things, if such signs were not to become visible at all. But it also holds true, that " the things which are seen are temporal, but the things which are unseen are eternal " (2 Cor. 4¹⁸). Man remains man, who can deceive himself and others ; sign remains sign, which may fade again and disappear ; but the Holy Spirit remains the Holy Spirit in every respect, the spirit of promise. Even and precisely the child of God in the NT sense will not for one moment or in any respect cease to confess, " I believe that I cannot of my own reason or power believe in Jesus Christ my Lord or come to him ! " God remains the Lord even and precisely when He Himself enters our hearts as His own gift, even and precisely when He " fills " us. No other intervenes for us with Him save Himself. Nor does any other intervene for Him with us save, once more, Himself. No one else speaks from us, when He speaks through us, save, once again, Himself. " In thy light we see the light " (Ps. 36¹⁰). So it requires the divinity of the Holy Spirit. So it requires the essentiality, the directness of the work of the Holy Spirit. We are grasping, not at a more but at a less, and ultimately at nothing, if, in addition to the security which is identical with God Himself, we imagine we must grasp at an active and positive experience unambiguous in itself, at a guarantee of the guarantee so to speak, in order thereby to make up our minds about the certainty of faith. As if a certainty, about which a man must first make up his mind, could be the certainty of faith. " If I have but thee, I ask naught of heaven and earth," and further, " Though body and soul languish within me, yet thou, God, art for ever my heart's comfort and my portion " (Ps. 73²⁵ᶠ·). Thus we think and speak ἐν πνεύματι. Whereas by grasping at something else, at oneself, by looking for comfort and confirmation in ourselves, we but betray the fact that we are still far from thinking and speaking ἐν πνεύματι, or have long since ceased to do so. We can only conceive of God in ourselves, by conceiving of ourselves in God. Just as we can, of course, only conceive of ourselves in God by conceiving of God in ourselves ! It is only ἐν πνεύματι that we can and shall wish, one way or the other, to turn from ourselves to God, to pray to God, but not to consider God or dispose of God. But once more he alone prays who looks for everything at God's hand. And once more he alone looks for everything at God's hand who looks for nothing at his own.

Μακρόθεν ἑστώς, not daring to lift up his eyes to heaven, " God be merciful to me a sinner ! " prays the publican in the temple. And this man went down justified to his house (Luke 18[10f.]). Did Jesus go into the ship to Simon or not ? Did he fill his ship with abundance or not ? But what has Simon to say to that ? " Depart from me, for I am a sinful man ! " (Luke 5[1f.]). " It should be understood, that . . . all that is not Christ is altogether unclean and damned including birth and all life, And no purity or holiness cometh into us or out of us, But over and above us and far beyond us, yea above all our sense, wit, and comprehension, in Christ alone by faith 'tis found and attained " (Luther, *Sermon at Torgau* 1533 W. edn. 37, p. 57, l. 32). Thus we think and speak ἐν πνεύματι.

What we have to offer, to sacrifice to God in order to pray rightly, is ourselves, with this complete lack of claim.

We have to sacrifice a " broken spirit," a " broken and a contrite heart " (Ps. 51[19]), a heart that knows that it must be created in us by God as a new heart—a spirit that knows that it must be created in us by God as a new, certain spirit—and that that is what it must pray for (Ps. 51[12]).

Upon this lack of claim depends the rightness of all prayer and its chance of being answered.

Rom. 8 is unthinkable without Rom. 7 (and including Rom. 7[24]) and in such a way that Rom. 7 is not interpreted as a glance back at a past of the Christian man, but as a finding about his present and about his whole future in time, and just because he is a Christian. *Veni creator Spiritus !* is true and gets through, if it is persistently a weeping, if no present or perfect *venit* comes in to spoil everything. It is just because it is in God and of God, that simple *venit* is the truth !

That faith has an immovable basis, that there is certainty of faith through God's revelation, depends upon this basis being sought in God, not only at the beginning but also in the middle and at the end, in God and nowhere else, not in ourselves. Grace is also the Holy Spirit received, but we ourselves are sinners —that is true. To say anything else is to be unaware of the divinity of the Holy Spirit in God's revelation.

2. THE ETERNAL SPIRIT

The Holy Spirit does not first become Holy Spirit, God's Spirit, in the event of revelation. But the event of revelation has clearness and reality on its subjective side, because the Holy Spirit, the subjective element in this event, is also what is essential in God Himself. What He is in revelation He is antecedently in Himself. And what He is antecedently in Himself He is in revelation. Right within the deepest depths of deity, as the final thing to be said of Him, God is God the Spirit as He is God the Father and God the Son. The Spirit outpoured at Pentecost is the Lord, God Himself, just as the Father, just as Jesus Christ is the Lord, God Himself.—Once more, if we are asked how this assertion comes to be made, we can only reply, that for the making of this assertion no special dialectical towering is required : what is rather needed is to take the thing as it stands at its own value, just to take seriously the Biblical assertions themselves. According to these assertions, the work of the Holy Spirit in revelation is a work which can only be ascribed to God Himself, and which is therefore actually and expressly ascribed to God. Beyond this the d o g m a of the Holy Spirit, to which we now turn, has nothing new to say. Here, too, the dogma invents nothing, it merely discovers what of course was and is not obviously discoverable in the NT, what is only more or less clearly hinted at in the NT. It is thus not itself to be found in Scripture, but in the exegesis of Scripture. It does not speak of a divinity of the Holy Spirit different from that in which He reveals Himself to us according to Scripture. But it fixes the fact that this divinity is true, essential, eternal divinity. The Spirit is holy in u s, because He is so antecedently in H i m s e l f.

The doctrine of the divinity and of the independence of the Spirit's divine mode of existence, achieved general understanding and recognition in the Church at a period considerably later than the corresponding doctrine of the Son.   In the primitive tripartition of the Symbol, one can of course see it making itself known from the start.   But the Fathers of the second and as late as the third century confined themselves as a whole to speaking of the operations and gifts of the Holy Spirit ; the consequence of which was that the subordination view on the one hand, that He was a creature or a creaturely force, and the modalistic view on the other, of His identity with the Son or Logos, were frequently encroached upon, at all events were nowhere exactly barred.   One point was relatively clear and unambiguous, which later spread to both sides, but was at that time represented only by T e r t u l l i a n (in his pamphlet against Praxeas), in a manner perhaps not unconnected with his Montanist valuation of the Spirit in particular.   Even the Nicene Creed with its ὁμοούσιος for the Son remains content, like the older forms of symbol, with mentioning the Holy Spirit as the object of faith, without even at this stage setting its face against Arianism.   It was A t h a n a s i u s who then (in his letter to Serapion directed against Macedonius of Constantinople) saw the connections here as well and spoke the decisive words. He was followed (not without tardiness) by the Neo-Nicenes and the Council of 381.   The perfectly clear formulation, corresponding plainly with the definitions of the *Nic. Const.* about the Son, the dogma first received in the 5th century (the *Quicumque vult*).   For the closure of the doctrine we shall have to look as late as the assumption of the *filioque* into the Creed of the Western liturgy (finally achieved in 1014) and the schism of the Eastern Church, caused by the rejection of this addition.

The difficulty and the slowness with which Christian knowledge about the Holy Spirit permeated the Church is deeply grounded in the nature of the case. To admit that the Holy Spirit is the Lord, wholly and utterly God, the divine Subject, in the sense in which the Father of Jesus Christ is, in which Jesus Christ Himself is, is certainly the far harder and more exacting demand; not only and not at all mostly for formal thought, but in face of what man might once and for all think about himself in actual relation to God. In the problem of the Spirit within the concept of revelation the issue is man himself and his being present at God's revelation. Even though man lets himself say, that the fountain of revelation, the Father, is God wholly and utterly, and perhaps also that the Revealer too, the Son, is God wholly and utterly, just so as to be able to be God's Revealer in that way, the question still remains open, whether God should have said, that even his, man's, presence at revelation, the reality of his meeting with the Revealer is not his, man's, work, but once again wholly and utterly God's own work. Were the Spirit, the mediator of revelation to the subject, a creature or a creaturely force, we would be asserting and maintaining, that in virtue of his presence with God and over against God man in his own way is also a lord in revelation. For our relation to creatures and creaturely forces, even in circumstances most unfavourable to us, is after all a reciprocal one, a co-operation of freedom and necessity, a relation between one pole and its opposite. Even modalism regarding the Spirit, the identification of the Spirit with Christ, would mean that man confronts revelation as an object. If it gains control over him, he also must and can get control over it. Moreover, as the recipient of the fulness of grace, man might then regard his faith for good as an " instrument of action " (so A. Ritschl, *Rechtf. u. Vers.* vol. I 1900 p. 157). By the doctrine of the divinity and the independence of the Spirit's divine mode of existence man is as it were called in question within his own house. It now becomes clear for the first time that his presence at revelation cannot be the presence of a partner or opposite, that from his presence no claims or privileges can arise for him as against God, that it can only be a factual, inconceivable, miraculous presence, factual because God is there ; as we already stated, not only objectively but also subjectively, not only from above but also from below, not only from without but also from within. The dogma of the Holy Spirit means the knowledge, that in every respect man can only be present at God's revelation, as a servant is present at his master's action, i.e. following, obeying, imitating, serving ; and that this relation—which makes it different from any human relation between master and servant—is in no wise and at no point reversed. It is this knowledge in detail of the unconditionality, i.e. of the irreversibility of the lordship of God in His revelation, that makes the dogma of the Holy Spirit difficult ; difficult of course, intellectually also, but certainly with this added intellectual difficulty, only because man flatly refuses to admit what it implies.

It follows that this particular doctrine must constitute the last stage in the development of the Trinitarian dogma. It had to be achieved, ere the doctrine of grace, which then became the special theme of the Church in the West, could become the burning question, ere the struggle and victory of Augustine over Pelagius could take place. Even the Reformation with its doctrine of justification by faith alone can only be understood against the background of this particular dogma. Of course its real and full importance was never understood in Catholicism (not even in Augustine !) and only very partially even in post-Reformation Protestantism. Modernist Protestantism in its entirety has largely been, quite simply, a reversion to the obscurities and ambiguities of the Ante-Nicenes regarding the Spirit.

In this case also we now turn, for a closer exposition of the dogma, to the Nicaeno-Constantinopolitan Symbol.

The relevant passage from the third article of the Creed runs

(Πιστεύομεν . . .)	(Credo . . .)
1. εἰς τὸ πνεῦμα τὸ ἅγιον, τὸ κύριον	1. *in Spiritum sanctum Dominum*
2. τὸ ζωοποιοῦν	2. *et vivificantem*
3. τὸ ἐκ τοῦ πατρὸς ἐκπορευόμενον	3. *qui ex Patre Filioque procedit*
4. τὸ σὺν πατρὶ καὶ υἱῷ συνπροσ-κυνούμενον καὶ συνδοξαζόμενον	4. *qui cum Patre et Filio simul adoratur et conglorificatur*

1. We believe in the Holy Spirit, the Lord. The foundation Greek text here uses κύριον adjectivally. This does not signify any limitation of the assertion, as implied in the Latin *Dominus* and the German " Herr."—As little as the Father and the Son is the Spirit *Dominus*, Herr, as one alongside of other two Lords. He is so in inseparable unity with them. What must be said here first of all, with a back reference to the ἕνα κύριον of the second article, is that the Holy Spirit, together with the Father and the Son, is the bearer of the Lordship of God, which is not based on any higher lordship. He is, with the Father and the Son, the one sovereign, divine Subject, the Subject who is not liable to any disposal or inspection by another subject, who derives His being and His existence from Himself. But the adjectival use of κύριος, together with the fact, so far not yet evaluated by us (and likewise not obvious in Latin or German), that πνεῦμα itself is a neuter,

must at once draw our attention to the special way in which the Holy Spirit in particular is all that we have said. Both circumstances hint to us that He is all that in a neutral way, neutral in the sense of distinct, namely distinct from Father and Son, whose mode of existence is always a reciprocal one, but neutral also in the sense of related, namely related to Father and Son, whose reciprocity is not an opposition (Gegeneinander) but an approximation (Zueinander), a distinction (Auseinander), and a participation (Miteinander). This participation of the Father and the Son is the Holy Spirit. Thus the special feature of the Holy Spirit's divine mode of existence consists, paradoxically enough, in Him being the common factor between the mode of existence of God the Father and that of God the Son. Not what is common to them, so far as they are the one God, but what is common to them so far as they are the Father and the Son.

Spiritus sanctus commune aliquid est Patris et Filii (Augustine, *De trin.* VI 5, 7). He stands " midway between the Begotten and the Unbegotten " (Johannes Damasc. *Ekdos.* I 13). *Nomen Spiritus sancti non est alienum a Patre et Filio, quia uterque est et spiritus et sanctus* (Anselm of Canterbury, *Ep. de incarn.* 2).

The Holy Spirit in particular, then, even were that possible in the case of Father and Son, could under no circumstances be regarded as a third " person," in the modern sense of the concept. The Holy Spirit in particular is in a specially clear way what Father and Son also are, not a third spiritual subject, a third I, a third Lord alongside two others, but a third mode of existence of the one divine Subject or Lord.

In this respect it is noteworthy that the Church has forbidden the portrayal of the Holy Spirit in human form (Bartmann, *Lehrb. d. Dogmatik*[7], vol. I 1928, p. 194).

He is the common factor, or better, he is the communion, He is the act of the " communityness " of the Father and the Son. He is the act in which the Father is the Father of the Son or the Speaker of the Word, and the Son is the Son of the Father, the Word of the Speaker.

He is *communio quaedam consubstantialis* (Augustine, *De trin.* XV 27, 50) ; He is the *vinculum pacis* (Eph. 4[3]), the *amor*, the *caritas*, the reciprocal *donum* between Father and Son ; such is the favourite line of expression, especially in the Augustinian succession. He is thus that love with which God (loves Himself i.e. loves Himself in each case as Father and Son, and so) as Father loves the Son, and as Son loves the Father. *Si charitas qua Pater diligit Filium et Patrem diligit Filius, ineffabiliter communionem demon-*

strat amborum, quid convenientius quam ut ille dicatur charitas proprie, qui Spiritus est communis ambobus (Augustine, *De trin.* XV 19, 37). To that extent—the figurative nature of this usage need not be emphasised—He is the result of their common " breathing," *spiratio.*

How far is this act to be regarded as a special divine mode of existence ? It is obviously to be regarded as a special divine mode of existence, because this common being and operation of the Father and the Son, alongside that of the Father and the Son separately, is a special mode of divine existence, distinct from the other. It is obviously to be regarded as a divine mode of existence, because in this act of His God-being as Father and Son, in this reciprocal love of His, God can be and effect nothing else and no less than somewhat equal to Himself. In fact, there cannot be any higher principle, from which and in which Father and Son must first find themselves together, they can find themselves together only in their own principle. But this principle is the breathing of the Holy Spirit, that is, the Holy Spirit Himself. Once more, the effect of this love is not the created world, it is the reciprocal love of the Father and the Son ; their effect must therefore be somewhat equal to them, and this equal somewhat is just the Holy Spirit.

Father and Son are *non participatione, sed essentia sua, neque dono superioris alicuius, sed suo proprio servantes unitatem Spiritus in vinculo pacis* (Augustine, *De trin.* VI 5, 7): *Nam ideo amor non est impar tibi aut Filio tuo, quia tantum amas te et illum et ille te et seipsum, quantus es tu et ille, nec est aliud a te et ab illo* (Anselm of Canterbury, *Prosl.* 23). *Si nulla umquam creatura, id est si nihil umquam aliud esset quam summus spiritus Pater et Filius : nihilo-minus seipsos et invicem Pater et Filius diligerent. Consequitur igitur hunc amorem non esse aliud quam quod est Pater et Filius, quod est summa essentia* (*Monol.* 53).

God is thus—and to that extent He is God the Holy Spirit— " antecedently in Himself " the act of communion, of impartation, He is love, gift. For that reason and in that way and on that basis He is so in His revelation. Not *vice versa* ! We know Him in that way in His revelation. But He is not so, because He is so in His revelation ; but because He is so antecedently in Himself, He is so also in His revelation.

In His revelation He is the *donator doni*, because in Himself, as the Spirit of the Father and the Son, He is the *donum donatoris* (Augustine, *De trin.* V 11). *Donum vero dicitur non ex eo tantum, quod donetur, sed ex proprietate, quam habuit ab aeterno. Unde et ab aeterno fuit donum. Sempiterne enim donum fuit, non quia daretur, sed quia processit a Patre et Filio . . . temporaliter autem donatum est* (Petrus Lombardus, *Sent.* I dist. 18 D). *Donum non*

dicitur ex eo quod actu datur, sed in quantum habet aptitudinem ut possit dari.
Unde ab aeterno divina persona dicitur donum, licet ex tempore detur (Thomas
Aquinas, *S. th.* I *qu.* 38 *art.* 1 *ad.* 4). *Amor habet rationem primi doni, per*
quod omnia dona gratuita donantur. Unde cum Spiritus sanctus procedat ut
amor . . . procedit in ratione doni primi (ib. art. 2 *c.*).

Therefore, says the dogma with its τὸ κύριον, the Holy Spirit
is the Lord (acting upon us in revelation as the Redeemer)
who makes us really free, really children of God, who really gives
His Church utterance to speak the Word of God, because in this
work of His upon us He does nothing else temporally than what
He does eternally in God, because this mode of His existence in
God's revelation is at the same time a mode of existence of the
hidden essence of God, so that it is really the hidden essence of
God Himself, and therefore the Lord in the most unrestricted
sense of the concept, who—in His utter unsearchableness—becomes
manifest in revelation in this respect also.

2. We believe in the Holy Spirit, the life-creating. This
statement also teaches the divinity of the Holy Spirit. It does
so, in a manner analogous to the *per quem omnia facta sunt* of the
second article, by pointing to the fact that the Holy Spirit, with
the Father (and the Son), is the subject of creation. He is not
only the Redeemer, as surely as redemption stands in indissoluble
correlation with reconciliation, as surely as reconciliation reaches
achievement in redemption. He is thus also the Reconciler together
with the Son and as the Spirit of the Son. And just as in reconciliation and as its presupposition God the Father becomes manifest
through the Son, i.e. God the Creator, and as the work of creation
becomes manifest as having taken place through the same Word
that became flesh in Jesus Christ—so too the Holy Spirit now
becomes manifest, as He who also co-operates in creation in His
own way.

In the first instance, no doubt, we have to regard the ζωοποιοῦν (which
reminds us of the already cited NT passages John 6[63] ; 2 Cor. 3[6]) soteriologic-
ally. But behind these passages themselves stands the recollection of the
significance for the *regnum naturae* assigned in the OT to *ruah* and *neshamah*
of Gen. 2[7] where Adam does not, like Christ the second Adam according to
1 Cor. 15[45], himself become the πνεῦμα ζωοποιοῦν but rather a " living soul "
through the " living breath " of God. And from there we pass at once to
the " spirit," which according to Gen. 1[2] swayed (" brooded ") above the
" ocean " of a creation still formless, still unfilled and uninformed by any life,
by which according to Ps. 33[6] the " host of heaven " is made, which according
to Gen. 7[15] is in all flesh, which according to Ps. 139[7] is in every place whither
man can go, to that " breath " in every creature, which according to Ps. 150[6]
makes it bound to praise the Lord, because according to Ps. 109[29f.] it is

His, the Lord's breath, by which the creature is created, and without which it would have forthwith to vanish away.

We have already at the beginning of our section given thought to this general and, in order, primary meaning of the concept spirit. In the order of knowledge it can only be the second. For as only through revelation (and so through the Spirit in the soteriological sense of the concept) we recognise ourselves and all that exists as the creation of God at all, so too in particular with their creation by the Word and the Spirit (this time in the first and general significance of the concept). This general significance of the Spirit, His significance as the Creator Spirit, should however consist in the fact that the creature not only exists in its own existence, distinct from the existence of God, according to the will of the Father achieved through the Word, but also is and remains, in itself and of itself, capable of such an existence of its own, just as it must also remain sustained objectively in its existence by the Word of God. The Holy Spirit is the Creator God along with the Father and the Son, so far as God, as Creator, creates not only existence but life. From this point of view we cannot avoid speaking of a presence and operation of the Holy Spirit, presupposed in revelation, primary, universal, related as such to the creaturely existence of man and the world. As little as the *per quem omnia facta sunt* of the second article, as little as the dogma of creation in general, can it be the object of a universal, independent knowledge, preceding the knowledge of revelation. Neither, therefore, can it become the object of a natural theology. It can only be known and confessed on the basis of revelation and in faith. But on the basis of revelation and faith, confessed it must be—at once as the necessary consequence of the divinity of the Holy Spirit, at once with reference to the statement, *opera trinitatis ad extra sunt indivisa*, but also because of its pregnant content.

Ἡ δὲ τοῦ ἁγίου πνεύματος μεγαλωσύνη ἀδιάλυτος, ἀπέραντος καὶ πανταχοῦ καὶ διὰ πάντων καὶ ἐν πᾶσιν ἀεί ἐστιν, πληροῦσα μὲν τὸν κόσμον καὶ συνέχουσα κατὰ τὴν θεότητα, ἀχώρητος δὲ κατὰ τὴν δύναμιν, καὶ μετροῦσα μέν, οὐ μετρουμένη δὲ (Didymus of Alexandria, *De trin.* II 6, 2). *Spiritui sancto . . . attribuitur quod dominando gubernet et vivificet quae sunt creata a Patre per Filium.* He is the *bonitas*, and so the goal, and so the *primum movens* of creation (Thomas Aquinas, *S. theol.* I qu. 45 art. 6 ad 2). Therefore in the *Offertorium* of the vigil before Pentecost, with a clear recollection of the fact that the Holy Spirit in baptism is also the Holy Spirit in Creation, the Roman Church prays according to Ps. 104[30]—*Emitte Spiritum tuum et creabuntur et renovabis faciem terrae.* And in the *Introitus* for Whitsunday—*Spiritus Domini replevit orbem terrarum, allelujah : et hoc quod continet omnia scientiam habet vocis.* And in the well-known Whitsuntide hymn :

> *Veni creator spiritus,*
> *mentes tuorum visita,*
> *imple superna gratia*
> *quae tu creasti pectora.*

And in the *Oratio* for Ember-day (Saturday) in Whitsun week—*Mentibus nostris . . . spiritum sanctum infunde cuius et sapientia conditi sumus et providentia gubernamur.* But Luther, too, is aware of a *duplex Spiritus quem Deus donat hominibus : animans et sanctificans.* By the *Spiritus animans,* e.g. all *homines ingeniosi prudentes, eruditi, fortes, magnanimi* are impelled. *Soli autem christiani ac pii habent Spiritum sanctum sanctificantem* (W. edn. *T.T.* 5, p. 367, l. 12). And Calvin was able to describe the Holy Spirit, according to the general definition of the three modes of God's existence, as God's *virtus per omnia quidem diffusa, quae tamen perpetuo in ipso resideat* (*Cat. Genev.* 1545 ; in K. Müller p. 118 l. 28). Gen. 1² he interpreted in this way, that the existence of things—created in the first place as chaos (*inordinata moles, massa indisposita*)—quite as much as their nature or their form (*pulcher et distinctus ordo*), had required—in order not only to become but to be created, in order to have the stability of an *arcana Dei inspiratio*—a *vigor* accruing to them from God (*Comm. on Gen.* 1², 1544 *C.R.* 23, 16). And it was Calvin who regarded the thought which follows as an important expression of the doctrine of the divinity of the Holy Spirit—*ille enim est, qui ubique diffusus omnia sustinet, vegetat et vivificat in coelo et in terra. Iam hoc ipso creaturarum numero eximitur, quod nullis circumscribitur finibus ; sed suum in omnia vigorem transfundendo essentiam vitam et motionem illis inspirare, id vero plane divinum est* (*Instit.* I 13, 14). Again J. Gerhard teaches that *Quemadmodum in prima creatione Spiritus sanctus aquas fovendo iisque incubando fuit efficax, ita in rerum creatarum conservatione idem cum Patre et Filio efficaciter agit :* in springtime *qua cuncta revirescere ac frondescere incipiunt, postquam per hiemem fuerunt emortua ;* but also in the growth of each new individual in which its species is renewed (*Loci* 1610 Bk. III 10, 132). And Paul Gerhardt in the Whitsun hymn " Enter thy Gates " :

> In thine own hands thou holdest,
> Lord God, the whole vast world ;
> The hearts of men thou turnest
> According to Thy will.
> Thy grace, then, O vouchsafe us
> · · · · ·

3. We believe in the Holy Spirit, who proceedeth from the Father and the Son.

This phrase corresponds to the *genitum non factum* of the second article. First of all then it ought to express the negation, that the Holy Spirit is not a creature. It cannot be said of any creature that it " proceeded " from God, i.e. that it is an emanation of the divine essence. The creation of the world and of man is not a ' procession," not an emanation from God, but the institution of a reality distinct from God, with an essence of its own, not a divine essence. What proceeds from God can, we repeat, only be God. And because the essence of God cannot be divisible, a thing that proceeds from God—and the dogma describes the Holy Spirit as such a thing—cannot be something that goes outside of God, and so in particular not an emanation in the usual sense of the concept, but only a mode of existence of the one essence of God, which remains in itself and is homogeneous ; in this case, obviously, proceeding not from the one essence of God as such, but from another mode or from the other modes of existence of this essence. The phrase is thus, in the first place, the description of the divinity of the Holy Spirit, in this case not in respect of the *opus ad extra* common to the three modes of existence, but in respect of its reality as a divine mode of existence, i.e. of its reality in its relation to the other divine modes of existence. This reality is of the kind that marks it out as being of the divine essence along with the Father and the Son. That is the one assertion made by the *qui procedit*.

Processionis vox accipienda est . . . juxta actionem Dei ad intra . . . id est qua ita agit Deus in essentia sua, ut reflexus in seipsum, divinae essentiae communione relationem realem constituat (Syn. Theol. pur. Leiden, 1624 Disp. 9, 10).

The other is a delimitation towards the Son or Word of God. The operation of the Holy Spirit in revelation is in fact a different one compared with the Son or Word of God. While never at any point separated from the latter and only to be distinguished from the latter *per appropriationem*, it is still never at any point to be confused with the latter. Particularly if we are resolved and bound to refrain from thinking to a finish about revelation, we shall venture to unify for thought the objective element of the Word and the subject element of the Spirit in revelation, in the essence of God yes, but not as modes of His existence ; rather we shall acknowledge that the Holy Spirit, alike in His revelation and antecedently in Himself, is not only God, but in God independently, like the Father and like the Son. But once more there is not a second, special revelation of the Spirit alongside that of the Son and so there are not two Sons or Words of God, but in the one revelation the Son or Word represents the element of God being assigned to man, the Spirit the element of God being appropriated by man. But by analogy, if we do not wish in our thinking to abandon the basis of revelation, we must obviously acknowledge a distinction in reality between what the Son and what the Spirit are antecedently in themselves. Thus the *qui procedit* has in the second place the meaning of distinguishing the divine mode of existence of the Spirit from that of the Son, described by the *genitus* (and so by implication from that of the Father also).

It is an isolated oddity that the Shepherd of Hermas (*Sim.* V 5, 2; 6, 5 f. ; IX 1) calls the Holy Spirit the Son. The need for distinguishing the Spirit not only from the creature, but also from the Son or Word of God, follows at once, within the dogma itself, from the *unigenitus* of the second article. Both distinctions are comprised in the statement of Gregory Nazianzene—ὃ καθ' ὅσον μὲν ἐκεῖθεν ἐκπορεύεται, οὐ κτίσμα· καθ' ὅσον δὲ οὐ γεννητόν, οὐχ υἱός (*Or.* 31, 8), and the statement of the *Quicumque vult—Spiritus sanctus a Patre et Filio, non factus nec creatus nec genitus, sed procedens.*

But what is the meaning here of " procession," *processio*, ἐκπόρευσις ? It is not accident or carelessness that the concept is one which in itself might also be applied to the origin of the Son from the Father, that therefore it actually does not indicate the differentia of the origin of the Holy Spirit in particular, but really and strictly just asserts that alongside of the generation of the Son or the speaking of the Word the Holy Spirit possesses in God this " somehow " different procession of its own. The peculiarity of this procession compared with the first may be indicated by the concept of " breathing," *spiratio*, but, strictly speaking, merely indicated. For how is breathing to be distinguished from generation, if by both is to be indicated with equal unconditionality the eternal genesis of an eternal mode of God's existence ? Would not every thinkable and assignable distinction inevitably lead to the denial once more, either of the divinity or of the independence of the divine mode of existence of the Holy Spirit ? The difficulty with which we are here faced is indeed insuperable.

Distinguere inter illam generationem et hanc processionem nescio, non valeo, non sufficio (Augustine, *C. Maxim.* II 14, 1). The same declaration has also been made by Joh. Damascenus (*Ekdos.* I 8), and it is also frequently repeated later. *Quo modo a generatione differat, explicabit nullus* (M. Leydecker, *De veritate rel. reform.* 1688 p. 28, quoted from H. Heppe, *Dogm. der. ev. ref. Kirche*, 1861 p. 94). Frequently with the specific warning that *istud discrimen tutius ignoratur quam inquiritur* (so F. Turretini, *Inst. Theol. el.* I 1679 Bk. III qu. 30, 3). And a Church definition of the more accurate meaning of the *processio* has never been reached on good grounds.

The feeling which involuntarily arises here, that the difficulty with which we are faced here might have a more than accidental significance, reaching beyond this special question, is correct. Why can we not specify the difference between the generation of the Son and the breathing of the Spirit, although—once more on the supposition, that is, that in our thinking we are not for abandoning the basis of revelation, that we are for regarding the manifest God as the eternal God—we are forced to assert it ? The moment we would measure, for purposes of definition, what we call the *spiratio Spiritus*, by what we term the *generatio Filii*, there obviously becomes visible and operative what in our discussion of that *generatio* we clearly established, that that *generatio* or *loquutio* is also an attempt to express what man cannot express essentially, what he cannot attain to by his language. How is the Son of God begotten ? How is His Word spoken ? We do not know, either when we are speaking of the eternal reality or when we are speaking of the temporal reality, which can be indicated by these figures—for both of them are but figures ! Our knowledge can only be acknowledgment of the fact. For that reason we are now embarrassed to know at what point, in order to realise what *spiratio* is, we can compare *spiratio* with *generatio*.

Augustine (*op. cit.*) had his reasons for his definite *nescio*, and they were, *quia et illa (generatio) et ista (processio) est ineffabilis*. In the last chapter but one of his work on the Trinity (*De trin.* XV 27, 50) he did indeed come back once more to the question, and now appears, at least by suggestion, able to give a positive answer to it. In short, by means of his familiar doctrine of the *imago trinitatis* in the human soul he makes us consider whether the genesis of the Spirit might not be related to that of the Son, as will or love to knowledge in the soul. Will issues from knowledge without being a figure of knowledge (*voluntatem de cogitatione procedere nemo enim vult, quod omnino quid vel quale sit nescit—non tamen esse cogitationis imaginem*). So the Spirit from the Son ! This suggestion is next taken up by Thomas Aquinas and expanded (*S. theol.* I *qu.* 27 *art.* 3 and 4). The procession of the Holy Spirit is the *processio secundum rationem voluntatis*, distinguished from the *processio secundum rationem intellectus*, because it issues from the latter and is related to the latter by presupposing it. *Ideo quod procedit in divinis per modum amoris, non procedit ut genitum, vel ut filius, sed magis procedit ut spiritus (art. 4 c)*. Modern Catholic dogmatics seems (cf. e.g. F. Diekamp, *Kath. Dogm.*[6] vol. I 1930 p. 345 f.) to consider this declaration a real answer to the question, and therefore makes no further use of the Augustinian *nescio*. On the other hand it should be remembered, that as distinct from Thomas Augustine did not neglect, with regard to that suggestion, to point out that the light which is thrown by the *imago trinitatis*, which we ourselves are, upon this question, is always being met by our *infirmitas*, which is caused by our *iniquitas* and can only be healed by God Himself, and so he would rather close his book *precatione quam disputatione*. We were unable to take over the entire theory of the *imago trinitatis* and shall therefore have to say that we cannot regard the question in respect of the Spirit as being answered by means of it either. To look upon *generatio* as knowledge, i.e. of the Son as the Word of God, is, as we saw, a true and significant, yet an inadequate way of looking at it, the real import of which remains hidden from us by our thinking we understand it, and by our really understanding it as well as we can. And therefore the explanation, relative thereto, of the Holy Spirit as will proceeding from knowledge, cannot help us at all to anything but a further analogy somewhat arbitrarily constructed. Rather the impossibility, conceded in Augustine's first saying, of suggesting the difference, when we should have forgotten it, must remind us that the *processio* of the Spirit and of the Son may indeed be described but not conceived.

That means no more and no less than that we cannot establish the How of the divine " processions " and therefore of the divine modes of existence. We cannot define the Father, the Son and the Holy Spirit, i.e. we cannot delimit them one from the other. We can only establish, that in revelation there are before us three that mutually delimit each other, and if we do not wish to think beyond revelation, we must hold to it that these three who mutually delimit themselves are also reality antecedently in God Himself. We can establish the That of the divine processions and modes of existence. All so-called establishings, on our part, of the How of this delimitation should prove themselves impracticable. In our hands the concepts presented to us through Holy Scripture prove also incapable of grasping what they should grasp. What would have to be said, will obviously be said definitely and exclusively by God Himself, by the three in the one God who mutually delimit each other in revelation, without it ever coming down to a repetition on our part, or even merely to a repetition such that we should have to remain conscious of our Incapacity, in which we continue to be directed to the truth of God beyond the utterly questionable truth of our thoughts and words. The *ignoramus* which we must admit regarding the distinction between generation and breathing which has got to be asserted, is thus the *ignoramus* which we must admit regarding the whole doctrine of the Trinity, i.e. regarding the mystery of revelation, regarding the mystery of God in general. If we could define that distinction, we could proceed to define the Son and the Spirit and then the Father also and in that way God Himself. For God Himself is just the Father, the Son and the Spirit. Only if they were not God could a definition be given at this point, such a definition as would be more than a description of the fact that God Himself is to the fore in His revelation. But what is to the fore in God's revelation is the Father, the Son and the Spirit. A first-class definition of these three could thus only be given if the Father, the Son and the Spirit are not God. Thus for the very sake of what the doctrine of the Trinity has to say, namely that the Father, the Son, and the Spirit are God, it may not at this particular juncture claim to say more, it

35

may not at this particular juncture end up in a definition. It is this that in Trinitarian theology should be the significance of the *qui procedit*.

Τίς οὖν ἡ ἐκπόρευσις; Εἰπὲ σὺ τὴν ἀγεννησίαν τοῦ πατρός, κἀγὼ τὴν γέννησιν τοῦ υἱοῦ φυσιολογήσω καὶ τὴν ἐκπόρευσιν τοῦ πνεύματος, καὶ παραπληκτίσωμεν ἄμφω εἰς θεοῦ μυστήρια παρακύπτοντες (Gregory Nazianzene, *Or.* 31, 8).

But according to the Latin text of the creed to which we adhere at this point (*ex Patre Filioque*), the procession of the Holy Spirit is His procession from the Father and from the Son.

The Creed, which in the original text has only ἐκ τοῦ πατρός, is not, as is here above all to be noticed, as yet involved in the famous dispute which arose on this point. According to John 15²⁶ it says "from the Father," without implying "not from the Son." It might refrain from saying that, in the first place because there was at that time, even among Greek theologians, no opposition to the material content of that addition. Just as unreservedly as is the case in this addition, Epiphanius, e.g. could say—Πατὴρ ἦν ἀεί, καὶ τὸ πνεῦμα ἐκ πατρὸς καὶ υἱοῦ πνέει (*Ancoratus* 75) ; or Ephraem—"the Father is the Begetter, the Son the Begotten from the bosom of the Father, the Holy Spirit He that proceedeth from the Father and from the Son (*Hymnus de defunctis et trinitate* 11) ; and as late as the 5th century Cyril of Alexandria— Τὸ πνεῦμα τὸ ἅγιον . . . πρόεισι δὲ καὶ ἐκ πατρὸς καὶ υἱοῦ (*Thes. de trin.* 34). But at the same time the Creed could not dream of excluding the *Filioque*, because one could not fail to see what heresy it was against which they had to take measures. The opponents against whom the phrase is directed are once more those deniers of the divinity of the Holy Spirit, the Macedonians, who of course asserted the procession of the Spirit from the Son also, but in the Arian sense, as the procession of one creature from another creature. By excluding the ἐκ τοῦ υἱοῦ the Creed would obviously have been conceding, in crying contradiction to its second article, that less is involved in the ἐκ τοῦ υἱοῦ than in the ἐκ τοῦ πατρός. But it was also in this opposition to these *Pneumato-machi* that the Creed had to and could avoid teaching the *Filioque* in so many words. It wished, with retrospect to the γεννηθέντα ἐκ τοῦ πατρός in the second article, to place the origin of the Spirit as regards consubstantiality with the Father on a parallel with the origin of the Son. That was expressed by the ἐκ τοῦ πατρός and by it alone (the ἐκ τοῦ υἱοῦ was in fact likewise confessed by the opponents in their Arian fashion). We must therefore say that there exists no necessary reason—the reason in fact just adduced is not a necessary one—why the *Filioque* might not have stood in the original Creed.

The fact that the *Nic. Const.* for centuries did not possess in the West a sacrosanct character and even subsequently never acquired it to the degree in which at a very early date it was assigned to it in the East, was the formal possibility—and the fact that in the West Augustine's doctrine of the Trinity continued to spread universally as the expression of common knowledge, was the positive reason why there and then at this point (it started, so far as is known, at the beginning of the 6th century in Spain) the *Filioque* was primarily adopted in the liturgical use of the Creed. Approval of this usage by the Roman Curia had to wait for fully five hundred years. Almost contemporaneously with a dispute between the Frankish and the Greek monks in Jerusalem (808) because of the singing of the *Filioque* in the Mass by the former, in which Pope Leo III supported the orthodoxy of the addition objected to, the same Pope, at a Synod in Rome (810), disapproved of the insertion as such in the Creed and (809) expressed to Charlemagne, who by a Synod at Aachen pleaded for it, the wish that the *Filioque* should cease to be sung in his Chapel Royal. The.general tendency of thought in the West, however, was and remained different. But it was the opposition of the Eastern Church, gradually becoming clearer, to the doctrine contained in the addition, i.e. it was the negation in content not yet included in the creed itself and not to be explained on the basis of the Creed, that first led to the *Filioque* being officially permitted. The Creed which in 1014 became an acknowledged part of the Roman Mass includes the *Filioque*. In that way it became a dogma in the Western Church. But even in the Union negotiations of the later centuries the Popes (so expressly Benedict XIV in the Bull *Etsi pastoralis*, 1742) took up the position that the addition to the liturgical text, as far as the Greeks were concerned, was not to be taken as the *conditio sine qua non* for setting aside the schism, but only confession of the truth expressed in the addition. In the theology of the Trinity, the Reformation was also strongly enough alined on Augustine to range itself obviously and without ado on the basis of the universal Western confession, and so, implicitly or explicitly, the addition also became part of the Evangelical confessional writings. True, one might incidentally decide, within the bounds of Old Protestant theology (so J. Coccejus, *S. theol.* 1662 12, 8) that it was a mistake for the Roman Church to have altered at that time the Symbol solemnly established in its ancient form by Leo III—as a matter of fact the business is not exactly a shining testimonial to the Roman Catholic theory of the certainty of the Church's doctrinal power, united in the hands of the Pope—one might (like Quenstedt, *Theol. did. pol.* 1685 I *c.* 9 *sect.* 2 *qu.* 12 *object. dial.* 16) declare that in this matter the orthodox decision belonged *non ad simplicem fidem sed ad peritiam theologicam*, and should only not be altogether denied by any one ; one might indeed broadmindedly (like F. Turretini, *Inst. theol. el.* I 1679 Bk. III *qu.* 31, 6) declare in so many words, that the Greek view of the matter was not to be regarded as heresy, only the Western view to be regarded as the better one—still, among Lutherans and Reformed there was complete unanimity, that substantially one had to adhere to the decision taken once upon a time so surprisingly, irrespective of Council and Pope.

In the whole affair the struggle was always really only waged with sharpness and seriousness from the side of the East, while the West in the main confined itself to the defensive. (Cf. for this the formula of the *Conc. Lugd.* II 1274, *Denz. Nr.* 460: *Damnamus et reprobamus qui negare praesumpserint, aeternaliter Spiritum sanctum ex Patre et Filio procedere*.) Whereon it should yet be noted that the opposition, even from the side of the East, was strictly speaking first keenly felt and expressed after the time of Photius (9th century), who was still interested in the schism from quite other motives, and strictly speaking always and pre-eminently from the standpoint of the formal complaint as to the illegitimate and loveless way in which the West took the lead in this alteration of the Symbol. (Cf. for this the moving complaints of A. St. Chomjakowin *Ostl. Christentum. Dokumente*, edited by H. Ehrenberg, vol. I p. 156 f.). As for the theological interpretation of the conflict at least in modern Russian orthodoxy, alongside of the contemporary L. P. Karsavin —who of course is not to be taken too utterly seriously—who in obscure language makes the *Filioque* responsible for the doctrine of the immaculate conception and of Papal infallibility, as well as for Kantianism, the belief in progress and many other evils of Western civilisation (*Ostl. Christentum*, vol. II p. 356 f.), there stands at the time of the union negotiations between Orthodox and Old Catholics the Archimandrite Sylvester of Kieff, who was perfectly satisfied with concluding, upon grounds of history of dogma, that the *Filioque* in any possible sense could only be asserted of the *opus trinitatis ad extra*, but not of the inner life of God (*Answer to the Note on the Holy Spirit contained in the Old-Catholic Scheme*, 1875) ; but also the incomparably saner V. Bolotow in St. Petersburg, who indeed represented the Augustinian *Filioque* as a private opinion wrongly erected into dogma, but who held the thesis of Sylvester to be impracticable, rather indicating that even the negation of the *Filioque* was not contained in the Symbol, and finally reaching the conclusion that the whole question had not been the cause of the separation and could not constitute an *impedimentum dirimens* to intercommunion between Orthodox and Old-Catholics (*Thesen über das " Filioque," Revue intern. de théol.* 1898 p. 681 f.). This last standpoint must be the one to which we should hold, as the prevalent view to-day in Eastern Orthodoxy.

We have reasons for adhering to the Western tradition concerning the *Filioque*, and since ecclesiastical separation of West from East is now a fact and is to be regarded as such (whether rightly or wrongly, is a question by itself), we have cause to take account of it.

It is no less than the entire statement of our view, here essayed, of the doctrine of the Holy Spirit and of the Trinity in general, which in the first instance brings us fundamentally to this side. Even supporters of the Eastern doctrine do not dispute that the Holy Spirit in the *opus ad extra*, and so in revelation (and from there, looking backwards, in creation) is to be regarded as the Spirit of the Father and of the Son. But we are completely tied to the rule—and regard this rule as fundamental—that pronouncements upon the reality of the divine modes of existence, " antecedently in themselves " could not in content be any different from those that have to be made about their reality in revelation. The whole of our statements on the so-called immanent Trinity proved very simply for us to be confirmations and underlinings, or, materially, the indispensable major premises of the economic Trinity. They could not and were not meant to state anything else than that one had to abide by the distinction and unity of the modes of existence in God, as they meet us, according to the testimony of Scripture, in the reality of God in His revelation. The reality of God in His revelation is not to be bracketed with an " only," as though somewhere behind His revelation there stood another reality of God, but the reality of God which meets us in revelation is His reality in all the depths of eternity. We have to take it as seriously as that, particularly in His revelation. In connection with the special doctrine of the Holy Spirit, that means that He is not only the Spirit of the Father and of the Son in His operation outwardly and upon us, but that He is to all eternity—no limit or reservation is here possible—none other than the Spirit of the Father and of the Son. " And of the Son " means that there exists not only for us, but exists in God Himself no possibility of an opening and readiness and capacity in man for God—that of course is the work of the Holy Spirit in revelation—for it would come from Him, from the Father who reveals Himself in His Word, in Jesus Christ —and at the same time and just as necessarily from him who is his Word, from the Son, from Jesus Christ who reveals the Father. As the Giver of the Holy Spirit Jesus Christ is not apart from the Father from whom he, Jesus Christ, derives. But as the Giver of the Holy Spirit the Father is also not apart from Jesus Christ, to whom He Himself is the Father. The Eastern doctrine does not dispute that such is the case with revelation. But it reads off its pronouncements upon the being of God " antecedently in Himself " not from revelation, it does not adhere to the order of the divine modes of existence, which according to its own admission is valid in the realm of revelation, but it reaches out beyond revelation, in order to arrive at a quite different picture of God, " antecedently in Himself." At this point, quite apart from the result, we must at once record dissent. Whence do we get the right to isolate passages like John 15²⁶, which speak of the procession of the Spirit from the Father, in face of the many others which just as clearly describe Him as the Spirit of the Son ? Is it not much more appropriate to regard such opposite pronouncements in the light of the mutual supplementing which admittedly is found in the reality of revelation, and to acknowledge the content thus brought to view as also the one which is valid to all eternity, as being the content in the essence of God Himself ? For us then the Eastern rejection of the *Filioque* is already formally suspect, because it is openly a speculation which interprets a separate passage of the Bible in isolation, because it is unrelated to the reality of God in His revelation and for faith.

But this formal defect at once involves a material significance. The *Filioque* is the expression of the knowledge of the communion between Father and Son, knowledge that the Holy Spirit is the love, which is the essence of the relation between these two modes of existence of God. And the knowledge of this communion is nothing else than the knowledge of the ground and confirmation of the communion between God and man, as a divine, eternal truth, as created in revelation by the Holy Spirit. On the intradivine, two-sided communion of the Spirit, which proceeds from the Father and from the Son, is founded the fact that in revelation there is a communion, in which not only is God there for man, but in reality—that is the *donum Spiritus sancti*—man is also there for God. Just as on the other hand in this communion in revelation, created between God and man by the Holy Ghost, the communion in God Himself, the eternal love of God becomes knowable, knowable as the mystery, surpassing all understanding, of the possibility of such reality in revelation, knowable as the one God in the mode of existence of the Holy Spirit.

Missio haec temporalis (Spiritus sancti) praesupponit aeternum illum Spiritus sancti (aeque a Filio atque Patre) processum estque eius declaratio et manifestatio (Quenstedt, *Theol. did. pol.* 1685 ch. 9 sect. 2 qu. 12 beb. 3).

This whole insight and outlook is lost by denying the immanent *Filioque*. If the Spirit is also the Spirit of the Son only in revelation and for faith, if in eternity, which means in his proper and original reality, he is only the Spirit of the Father, then the communion of the Spirit between God and man lacks objective content and ground. However revealed and believed in, it stands as a merely temporal truth without eternal ground, upon itself so to speak Whatever in that case may be said of the communion between God and man, in that case it at least lacks warranty in the communion between God the Father and God the Son, as the eternal content of its temporal reality. Would that not mean an emptying of revelation ?

Everything would look still worse if the denial of the *Filioque* were not merely confined to the immanent Trinity, but were also to be countenanced in the interpretation of revelation, if, that is, the Holy Spirit in his *opus ad extra* also were to be regarded one-sidedly or over-emphatically as the Spirit of the Father. Here we must be very careful, because in theory that is actually a point in dispute. Yet we cannot avoid asking whether, if the denial, if the exclusive *ex Patre* is to hold as eternal truth, we can avoid the conclusion, first, that the relation of man to God is to be regarded decisively from the viewpoint of Creator and creature, and in that case acquires a more or less expressly naturalistic, unethical character ; secondly, that this relation after we set aside the Mediator of revelation, the Son or Word, as the ground from which it springs, will assume the nature of an immediate, direct relation, of a process of mystical union with the *principium et fons Deitatis*.

Even if the peculiarly unrestrained manner of thought and speech, characteristic of the Russian theologians and philosophers of religion as it meets us in Ehrenberg's documents, though it does obliterate every boundary between philosophy and theology, reason and revelation, Scripture, tradition and immediate illumination, Spirit and Nature, *Pistis* and *Gnosis* (as well as the distinction between the economic and the immanent Trinity !), were held to be irrelevant to the omission of the *Filioque*, we should at least have to remark upon an extraordinary coincidence between this omission and such phenomena as are only too easily regardable as results or as necessary parallel phenomena of this omission.

But be that as it may, in the Eastern conception of the relation between the divine modes of existence, we cannot recognise their reality, as we think we know them from the divine revelation according to the witness of Scripture.

Nor yet in the conception, in which it excludes the ἐκ τοῦ υἱοῦ, but is willing to concede a διὰ τοῦ υἱοῦ as a possible exegesis of the ἐκ τοῦ πατρός. For even this διὰ τοῦ υἱοῦ does not lead and is not, according to the purpose of Eastern theology, supposed to lead to the thing upon which everything seems to us to depend, namely, to the thought of the complete consubstantial communion between Father and Son as the essence of the Spirit, originally answering to the communion between God as the Father and man as His child, the creation of which is the work of the Holy Spirit in revelation.

The διὰ τοῦ υἱοῦ, *per filium*, has the usage of most Greek and Latin Fathers before the schism on its side. Moreover, neither can it be contested that, so far as the Son Himself is the Son of the Father, the procession of the Spirit from the Son is ultimately referable to the Father. But neither did the Latin Fathers contest this. A u g u s t i n e himself has unambiguously declared that *principaliter* the Spirit proceeds from the Father, and the Son has it from the Father, *ut et de illo procedat Spiritus sanctus* (*De trin.* XV 26, 47, cf. 17, 49 ; In *Joann. tract.* 99, 8). But Eastern doctrine since the schism, and also the older Eastern doctrine so far as later interpreted in a schismatic sense, says more than this : it takes the ἐκ τοῦ πατρός in the sense of ἐκ μόνου τοῦ πατρός ; it therefore takes the διὰ τοῦ υἱοῦ, not as a description of what is, on the supposition of the generation of the Son, the immediate procession of the Spirit from the latter also, but as the transmission or extension or prolongation of the procession of the Spirit from the Father. It found itself classically represented in Gregory of Nyssa's figure of the three torches, the second of which is kindled at the first, and the third at the second (*De Spir. s.* 13). It is expressed (according to Bolotow *op. cit.* p. 692) in the other figure according to which the Father is to be compared with the mouth, the Son with the word, but the Spirit with the breath which gives sound to the word : so far as the breath is breathed forth for the sake of the Word, so far as the expression of the Word inevitably implies the breathing, the Word is the logical *prius* of the breathing, and to that extent the διὰ τοῦ υἱοῦ holds good. But so far as the Word does not bring forth the breath, and the breath does not come from the Word but from the Mouth, the ἐκ τοῦ πατρός holds good but not the ἐκ τοῦ υἱοῦ. Says a likewise gladly adduced phrase from Athanasius (*Ad. Serap.* I 20) the secondary source of the Spirit in the Logos is not to be an ἐκπορεύεσθαι, but only an ἐκλάμπειν παρὰ τοῦ λόγου τοῦ ἐκ πατρός. Generation and breathing thus appear, according to this view of the διά τοῦ υἱοῦ " as a movement continuing in a straight line, in which the second movement issues from the first" (M. J. Scheeben, *Handbuch der Kath. Dogmatik*, new impression, 1925 vol. I p. 820). The Son is a mediating principle, the Father alone is the αἰτία, a principle in the strict sense of the Word.

In this interpretation we must obviously also reject the διὰ τοῦ υἱοῦ, though it goes without saying by itself. And in contrast to it the adherence of the West to the ἐκ τοῦ υἱοῦ must appear comprehensible and necessary. If the διὰ τοῦ υἱοῦ thus understood really excludes the proper origin of the Spirit from the Son also, that means that there is no *relatio originis* between Son and Spirit, i.e. that the Spirit can only improperly be called the Spirit of the Son, certainly not in the sense in which the Son means the Son of the Father. But further, in that case, if the Son is not also the proper origin of the Spirit, Father and Son have not everything in common, but their origination in respect of the Spirit falls apart into a primary and a merely secondary. But even the unity of God the Father ought to be questioned, if, instead of Him being already, as the Father of the Son, also by implication the origin of the Spirit, the origin of the Spirit from Him appears as a second function alongside His fatherhood. Finally and above all, in this conception the Spirit loses His mediating position between Father and Son, and Father and Son lose the mutual connection in the Spirit.

Possibly an unsubdued remnant of Origenist sub-ordinationism is to be claimed among others as the source of error in the Eastern conception. But above all it is the unity of the Trinity which throughout we must hold to be endangered by the denial of the *Filioque*. We saw in another place that tritheism has always been the special danger of Eastern theology, and in view of the Trinity constructed by denial of the *Filioque* we cannot moreover avoid the impression, that here the *trinitas in unitate* is being in most threatening fashion overemphasised, compared with the *unitas in trinitate*. For the sake of this *unitas* the *Filioque* impressed itself upon Augustine and permeated the West. Our decisive reason for adhering to this view we discover in the fact, that only in this *unitas*, and not in the curious juxtaposition of Father and Son with respect to the Spirit, as it is manifest in the Eastern doctrine, do we find anything to correspond with what we know in revelation as the work of the Holy Spirit. If the rule holds, that God in His eternity is none other than He who discloses Himself to us in His revelation, then in the one case as in the other the Holy Spirit is the Spirit of the love of the Father and of the Son, and so *procedens ex Patre Filioque*.

The positive meaning of the Western conception of the dogma may, according to what has been said, be summarised as follows :

By being the Father in Himself from eternity, God brings Himself forth from eternity as the Son. By being the Son from eternity, He comes forth from eternity from Himself as Father. In this eternal bringing forth of Himself and coming forth from Himself, He posits Himself a third time as the Holy Spirit, i.e. as the love which unifies Him in Himself. By being the Father who brings forth the Son, He brings forth the Spirit of love; for, by bringing forth the Son, God already negates in Himself, from all eternity, in His utter simplicity, existence in loneliness, self-sufficiency, self-dependence. Also and precisely in Himself, from all eternity, in His utter simplicity, God is directed towards the Other, refuses to be without the Other, will only possess Himself, by possessing Himself along with the Other, in fact in the Other. He is the Father of the Son in such a way, that with the Son he brings forth the Spirit, Love, and thus is in Himself the Spirit, Love. Of course He had not to be the Father of the Son in order to satisfy a law of Love, because Love was the reality which even God had to obey. "The Son is the first, the Spirit the second in God," means that by being the Father of the Son, by, as Father, bringing forth the Son, He brings forth the Spirit and so the negation of existence in loneliness, the law and the reality of Love. Love is God, the highest law and the ultimate reality, because God is Love and not *vice versa*. And God is Love, Love goes forth out from Him as His Love, as the Spirit which He Himself is, because He posits Himself as the Father and so posits Himself as the Son. In the Son of His Love, i.e. in the Son in and with whom he brings Himself forth as Love, He then brings forth also in the *opus ad extra*; in creation the creaturely reality distinct from Himself, and in revelation reconciliation and peace for the creature that has fallen away from Him. The Love which meets us in reconciliation and, looking backwards from that, in creation, is therefore and thereby Love, the highest law and the ultimate reality, because God is Love antecedently in Himself; not merely a supreme principle of the connection of separation and communion, but Love which wills and affirms, seeks and finds in separation the other thing, the Other Person in communion also, in order to will and to affirm, to seek and to find communion with it (Him) in separation also. Because God is Love antecedently in Himself, therefore love exists and holds good as the reality of God in the work of revelation and in the work of creation. But He is Love antecedently in Himself, by positing Himself as the Father of the Son. That is the interpretation and proof of the *qui procedit ex Patre*.

Just because we thus interpret and prove it, we must now continue, that likewise, by being the Son who comes forth from the Father, God brings forth the Spirit, He brings forth Love. In this mode of existence also He negates loneliness in His utter simplicity, He is turned towards the Other, refuses to be without the Other from whom He is. How could He be the Son otherwise than as the Son of the Father ? How should God be less the origin of Love by the fact that He is the Son, than by the fact that He is the Father ? Different as Father and Son, God is at one in the fact that His variety is that of the Father and of the Son ; there-fore, once more, not variety as it might also occur in a supreme principle of separation and communion, not a loveless variety, but that variety which affirms separation in communion and com-munion in separation. How then should the breathing of the Spirit belong less essentially, less really and originally to the Son than to the Father ? And in view of the *opus ad extra* we must further ask : if it is true that God reveals Himself to us through His only-begotten Son, if it is further true that God's only-begotten Son is no less and nothing else than God the Father, if it is further true that God's revelation is at least also the revelation of His Love, if revelation would not be revelation without the outpouring and impartation of the Spirit, by which man becomes God's child, should not this Spirit be directly the Spirit of the Son as well ? Is the Son here just mediately, just derivatively the Giver of the Spirit, the Revealer of Love ? But if he is so here immediately and directly, how can He be so, if He is not so in reality, in the reality of God antecedently in Himself ? If Love is here, and if from this standpoint it is already a reality in God's creation, in the Son and through the Son, we have no reason and no warrant for thinking beyond what holds good here ; and in that case it is the Love of the Son also antecedently in Himself, also in eternity. As the Son of the Father He is in that case also the *spirator Spiritus*. Of course, as the Son of the Father. To that extent the *per Filium* holds good. But *per Filium* cannot now mean *per causam instru-mentalem*. This Son of this Father is and has all that His Father is and has. He is and has it as the Son. But He is and has it. So He is also the *spirator Spiritus*. So He has also the possibility of being so. In this way we interpret and prove the *qui procedit ex Patre Filioque*.

At this point the question might arise whether, to correspond with the procession of the Spirit from the Father and from the Son, there ought not also to be asserted a procession of the Son from the Father and from the Spirit. In favour of that, on the one hand, the exegetical point might be made good, that the work of the Holy Spirit appears in revelation in more than one respect as one of creating or of begetting. Above all the birth from the Spirit which conditions insight and entry into the kingdom of God, in John 3⁵ᶠ·, might be adduced here. If, so we might ask, the children of God are Spirit-begotten, is something corresponding not also to be said of the Son of God? And is something corresponding not actually said of the Son of God in revelation? In the story of the baptism at the Jordan (Mark 1⁹ᶠ· and parallels) does not His Sonship to God appear as caused by the Spirit descending upon Him? Does not Rom. 1³ also speak of Jesus Christ being appointed Son of God with power κατὰ πνεῦμα ἁγιωσύνης ἐξ ἀναστάσεως νεκρῶν? And what should we say to Luke 1³⁵ at first sight, .where in the angel's prophecy of the Virgin Mary's impending conception it says, πνεῦμα ἅγιον ἐπελεύσεται ἐπὶ σέ, καὶ δύναμις ὑψίστου ἐπισκιάσει σοι, διὸ καὶ τό γεννώμενον ἅγιον κληθήσεται υἱὸς θεοῦ, and to Matt. 1¹⁸, where it is likewise said of Mary, εὑρέθη ἐν γαστρὶ ἔχουσα ἐκ πνεύματος ἁγίου, and to Matt. 1²⁰ where we read, τὸ γὰρ ἐν αὐτῇ γεννηθὲν ἐκ πνεύματός ἐστιν ἁγίου? If we apply our rule here also, that dogmatic pronouncements upon the immanent Trinity can and must be read off according to content from the determinations about God's modes of existence in revelation, are we not in that case forced to assume also between the Spirit and the Son an original relationship, which in that case would be neither generation nor breathing but a third thing? And one might wish to say, that only then is the circle of mutual relations, in which God is One in three modes of existence, a complete and self-enclosed one, and that already for that reason such an origin of the Son from the Father and the Spirit is to be postulated.

This second, systematic argument may at once be dismissed. If the circle, the Perichoresis, between God's three modes of existence must really be a circle of mutual origins, and must as such be perfect, then in the first place an origin of the Father from the Son and from the Spirit would also have to be discovered. The Perichoresis, being of course a complete and mutual one, is not one of the origins as such, but one of the modes of existence, as the modes of existence of the one God. It is a further description of the *homousia* of Father, Son, and Spirit, but with begetting and breathing in themselves it has nothing to do, and so moreover does not require any completions in this direction, so that the postulate in question cannot for a moment be described as having, formally, a legitimate basis.

It is more difficult to set aside the first exegetical objection. For that we must observe throughout, that the work of the Holy Spirit regarding the Son in revelation, which is the subject of discourse in all these passages, is not the sort of thing that might be described as commensurable with the eternal generation of the Son through the Father or with the eternal breathing of the Spirit through Father and Son, so that from it a further eternal relation of origin might possibly or necessarily be read off. This commensurability completely lacks this element; for generation and breathing are productions from the essence of God the Father, or of Father and Son, but not productions from another essence. The productions of the Holy Ghost, on the other hand, described in the passages named, are altogether productions of another essence presupposed as existing. This can be shown very clearly in John 3 : birth of the Spirit is a new birth, a rebirth, and the man to be born of the Spirit to be the child of God is already there, by the fact that this happens to him. He is born of the Spirit to be the child of God. But clearly it cannot be said, that the child of God which this man becomes is created or begotten by the Spirit. It (the child of God) is what it is, in communion with Jesus

Christ, the eternal Son of God. The same is the case with the story of the baptism in Jordan, which is certainly to be conceived as a parallel to the story of the Virgin Birth. It is this man Jesus of Nazareth, not the Son of God, who becomes the Son of God by the descent of the Spirit. Again, the appointment of Jesus Christ to be the Son of God by the Holy Spirit, Rom. 1, is expressly related to the resurrection. The ὁρισμός is the exaltation and revelation of the Crucified and Dead to the glory of the Son of God. It describes the participation of the Jesus Christ, hitherto described according to his humanity, in the majesty of the eternal Son. This Son of God as such does not derive His existence from this ὁρισμός, or from the Holy Spirit. But it is of the Holy Spirit that the Jesus Christ who is described according to His humanity has it to be this Son of God. But it is pretty much the same also with the Virgin Birth passages here under consideration. The incarnation of the Son of God out of Mary cannot indeed consist of the origination for the first time, here and now, of the Son of God, but it consists in the Son of God taking to Himself here and now this other thing which already exists previously in Mary, namely flesh, humanity, human nature, human-ness. And now the dogma of the Virgin Birth by no means specially claims that the Holy Spirit is the Father of the man Jesus and so, when the Son of God becomes man, becomes also the Father of the Son of God. But it claims that the man Jesus has no Father (exactly in the way in which as the Son of God He has no mother). What is ascribed to the Holy Spirit in the birth of Christ, is the assumption of human-ness in the Virgin Mary into unity with God in the Logos mode of existence. It is the work of the Holy Spirit in the birth of Christ that this is possible, that this other thing, this human-ness, this flesh exists for God, for communion, in fact unity with God, that flesh can be the Word by the Word becoming flesh. This work of the Spirit is prototypical of the work of the Spirit in the *becoming* of the children of God ; thus in fact we *become*, only not directly but indirectly, *per adoptionem*, in faith in Christ, what we are not by nature, namely, children of God. But that work of the Spirit is not ectypical of a work of the Spirit upon the Son of God Himself. What the Son has to " thank " the Spirit for in revelation is his human-ness, the possibility that flesh can become his, and so he, the Word, become flesh. How could we read off from that he had him (the Spirit) to thank for his eternal Son-ness ? He is the eternal Son, of the essence of the eternal Father which is also His own, and so not by the assumption of another essence. So that what is to be inferred from these passages for the understanding of the eternal Trinity, has nothing to do with an origin in God ; it should rather be the confirmation of what has already been said, that as the Holy Spirit in revelation binds together God and man, Creator and creature, the Holy One and sinners, so that they might become Father and child, so he is in himself the communion, the Love which binds Father to Son, and Son to Father.

But now with this interpretation and this proof we have already said the final word, which has always been said and must necessarily be said to explain the Western conception, namely, that the *ex Patre Filioque* does not signify a double, but it signifies a common origin of the Spirit from the Father and the Son. The fact that the Father is the Father, the Son the Son, the former bringing forth, the latter brought forth, is not common to them ; in that respect they are distinct modes of God's existence. But what they have in common is, that between them and from them, as God's third mode of existence, is the Spirit, Love. This third mode of existence cannot result from the first alone or from the second alone nor yet from a co-operation of the two, but only from their one being as God the Father and God the Son, who are not two " persons " either for themselves or in co-operation, but two modes of existence of the one being of God. Thus the one Godness of the Father and of the Son is, or the Father and the Son in their one Godness are, the origin of the Spirit. What is between them, what binds them together is therefore not a mere relation, is therefore not exhausted in the truth of their juxtaposition and association, is therefore, as an independent divine mode of existence over against them, the active approximation and interpenetration of Love, because these twain, Father and Son, are of one essence and that a divine essence, because God's Fatherhood and Sonship as such must be related to each other in this active approximation and interpenetration. That the Father and the Son are the one God is the reason why they are not only bound together, but bound together in the Spirit, in Love, why therefore God is love and why Love is God.

In revelation it is true, so says Augustine, that *Spiritus et Dei est qui dedit, et noster qui accepimus*, it is true that the Spirit of God can also be called the spirit of Elijah or the spirit of Moses, and therefore the spirit of a man. This miraculous truth has its ground in God Himself, in the fact that Father and Son (although the Son derives from the Father, who thus exists *principaliter*) are the *principium* of the Holy Spirit. *Non dua principia, sed sicut Pater et Filius unus deus et ad creaturam relative unus creator et unus dominus, sic relative ad Spiritum sanctum unum principium (De trin.* XV 14, 15). This unity in the origin of the Spirit was exalted to dogma in the *Conc. Lugd.* II 1274 : *Non tanquam ex duobus principiis, sed tanquam ex uno principio, non duabus spirationibus, sed unica spiratione procedit (Denz. Nr.* 460). And the *Conc. Florent.* in 1439, in adopting the Augustinian exposition of the *per Filium* quoted earlier, added : *Quoniam omnia quae Patris sunt, Pater ipse unigenito Filio suo gignendo dedit praeter esse Patrem, hoc ipsum quod Spiritus sanctus procedit ex Filio, ipse Filius a Patre aeternaliter habet a quo etiam aeternaliter genitus est.* In this sense, it was held, the *Filioque* was added to the Symbol *veritatis declarandae gratia et imminente necessitate (Denz. Nr.* 691).

4. We believe in the Holy Spirit, "who with the Father and the Son together is worshipped and glorified." This phrase of the Symbol also, the last to be considered here, defines the divinity of the Holy Spirit. To a certain extent it reaches back to the first one. There it said that as the Father, as the Son is the

one Lord, so too is the Spirit ; and now, as the one Lord is to be worshipped and glorified as the Father and as the Son, so also as the Spirit. Note how in the Latin text by the addition of the *simul* the tritheistic appearance, which would not be completely avoided by the bare *cum* and is perhaps also not completely avoided in the two Greek compounds, is excluded. " With " cannot here mean " alongside of "—the divine modes of existence are not alongside of one another—but " together with " or " in and with " ; but again not in such a way that the Spirit would be a mere attribute or relation of the Father or of the Son, but in such a way that it can be said equally well of the Father or of the Son or of both, that together with the Holy Spirit they are to be worshipped and glorified. That is, " exactly as " the Father and the Son are.

Hence in the Roman Mass and also in the Evangelical liturgy the *Gloria Patri et Filio et Spiritui sancto.* Hence in Luther's *Hymn of the Trinity*:

> " We believe in Holy Ghost,
>   God with Father and the Son."

Hence in M. Rinckart's " Now thank ye all our God " v. 3 :

> " Praise, honour, glory be to God
>   The Father and the Son.
>   And unto Him, equal of both,
>   On heaven's highest throne."

Obviously it is the divinity of the Spirit, as it must now be fixed from the human standpoint also, that must here be stressed. It might be asked, why it should be stressed with precisely this indication of a so to speak liturgical character. Why does it not say, who with the Father and the Son is to be believed in or loved ? Whatever the historical explanation may be, we shall at least have to say, that the indication in this precise form signifies in fact a twofold assurance. By the designation of it as the object of worship (*proskynesis*) and glorification the, abstractedly considered, neuter πνεῦμα is brought into relation with the personality of God, guaranteed by the designations πατήρ and υἱός. Not in Itself (that does not hold of Father or Son either) but because it is identical with the one God, the Spirit also is not a neuter, not an It but a He, the great, original, incomparable He, over whom man has no power, but who has all power over man. And by designating It as the object of worship and glorification the Spirit, which is, particularly in revelation, the Spirit of God and of man (*Spiritus Dei et noster*), the consummation of the communion between God and man, is also once more and emphatically withdrawn from the realm of man. His dwelling in us, the fact that there is a being of man " in the Spirit," must not for a moment deceive us as to the fact that the not only quantitative but qualitative difference between God and man is not removed even or actually in revelation, but is actually set up in revelation, in order that on the supposition of this difference God and man might have communion. Only that spirit (in distinction from all created spirits) s the Holy Spirit, who is, remains, and always becomes again transcendent over man, by being immanent in him. " Worship and glorification " means approach on the understanding and consideration of remoteness, not any sort of remoteness, not the bald, mathematical remoteness of the finite from the infinite, but the remoteness of man as a creature from God as the Creator, of man as a sinner from God as the Judge, of man as pardoned from God as the freely and causelessly merciful. Hence *proskynesis*, hence glory to God in the highest ! Nowhere, it is clear, could confusion between believer and the object of belief, between Lover and Beloved, be so imminent, as just in connection with this third mode of God's existence in His revelation. " Who together with the Father and the Son is to be worshipped and glorified," that must cut across the confusion. This gift, the *donum Spiritus sancti*, refuses to be abstracted from the Giver of it. But the Giver is God. We can only have the gift by having God and in the way in which we have God. At this point only one more reference must be made to the significance of this phrase in particular for the whole doctrine of the operations of the Spirit, and especially for the whole doctrine of faith. One would think that a blind man would be forced to see here that if man's presence at God's revelation, the *Deus in nobis* is to be expressed in full content, it can only be understood from the standpoint of the divine Subject, the irremovable Subject as such. Moreover, and emphatically, the doctrine of the *gratia Spiritus sancti applicatrix* cannot lead to an independent anthropology. Justification and sanctification are acts of that divine Subject, precisely because the Latter. gives Itself to us to possess. It gives itself to us to possess as the *Spiritus sanctus, qui cum Patre et Filio simul adoratur et conglorificatur.* Thus It becomes our salvation, and not otherwise. We have held this phrase continually before our eyes in all that had to be said anent appropriation of grace and salvation in our contexts up to date, and we shall also have to keep it before us in future. So we may forbear underlining it specially once again at this point,

A discussion of the three-in-oneness of God cannot better be closed than in the way Augustine did so at the conclusion of his work on this subject (*De trin.* XV 28, 51). There he explains once again in simple words, that he believes in God the Father, Son, and Holy Spirit, because God has so revealed Himself in Scripture. The " Truth " had not been so expressed, *nisi trinitas esses. Ad hanc regulam fidei dirigens intentionem meam, quantum potui, quantum me posse dedisti, quaesivi te, et desideravi intellectu videre quod credidi et multum disputavi et laboravi.* And now he sees himself impelled to pray, *Libera me, Deus, a multiloquio quod patior intus in anima mea, misera in conspectu tuo et confugiente ad misericordiam tuam.* He is aware in fact of the parlousness not only of his language but also of his thinking. He therefore prays not to fall asleep over or persist in what he has thought and said merely by human much-speaking. He is aware that God Himself alone can be the consummation of what man says and thinks of Him. R. Seeberg (*Lehrb. d. Dogmengesch.* vol. II 1923 p. 163) concludes from these words of Augustine's, that at the end he is worried about the " fulness of visions." Now that might very well be. There are theologies whose authors at the end have no need to worry, because the " fulness of visions " has for good reasons been consistently spared them. Augustine was not in this happy position. He had run the risk, the " fulness of visions " had in fact come upon him. In such danger one may come to grief. And a theologian who runs the risk may not only come to grief himself, but also bring others to destruction. Hence the tenor of Augustine's last petition and at the same time the closing words of his book, *Domine Deus une, Deus Trinitas, quaecumque dixi in his libris de tuo, agnoscant et tui : si qua de meo, et tu ignosce, et tui. Amen.*

INDEXES

I. BIBLE QUOTATIONS

II. NAMES

III. SUBJECTS

Holy Scripture (*continued*)—
 Inspiration, 126 f., 139.
 Jesus Christ, 121 f., 129 f.
 Prophecy, 57, 115 f., 120 f., 125 f.,
  128 f., 164, 169, 301 f., 370.
 Written-ness, 117.
 cf. Church, Revelation, Word of
  God.
Holy Spirit, 171 ff., 207 f., 373 f.,
  513 f.
 Deity, 513 f., 515 f., 525 f., 534 f.,
  558 f.
 Creator, 539.
 Lordship, 536.
 Proceeding from Father and
  Son (*spiratio, Filioque*), 541 f.
 Stipulations of Nicene Creed,
  536 ff.
 Worshipped with Father and
  Son, 557.
 and Jesus Christ, 516 f., 542.
 Work, 373 f., 518 f.
  Children of God, 444, 514, 523 f.,
   529 f., 555.
  Freedom for God, 516, 522.
  Instruction and Guidance, 519.
  Knowledge and Obedience,
   207 f., 519, 528 f.
  Service, 520.
  cf. Doctrine of Trinity, Three-
   in-Oneness.

Jesus Christ—
 beneficia Christi, 476, 480, 484.
 Christology, 47, 105, 144 f., 197,
  335, 358, 371, 405.
 and the Church, 3, 11, 16, 44, 53,
  62, 106, 113, 235, 299, 380,
  432.
 Divinity, 332 f., 371, 442 f., 460,
  462 f., 469 f., 474 f.
  Begotten of the Father, 487.
  Begotten, not created, 492.
  Creator, 506 f., cf. 447.
  the one Lord, 485.
  the Only-begotten, 486.
  Stipulations of Nicene Creed,
   484.
  of one Substance with the
   Father, 501 f.
  Very God of Very God, etc.,
   491.
 and the Father, 361 f., 368 f.,
  494 f., 503 f., 512, 553 f.,
  556 f.
 and Holy Spirit, 517.
 Humanity, 151, 179 f., 197, 371,
  442, 492.
  Suffering and Death, 464.
  Word and Deed, 458.
 Resurrection, 371, 444.

Jesus Christ (*continued*)—
 Revelation, 133 f., 433 f., 442,
  448, 468 f.
 Second Coming, 135, 155.
 Virgin Birth, 556.
 Word of God, 121, 127, 155 f.,
  174, 282 f., 442, 497.
 cf. Doctrine of Trinity, Three-in-
  Oneness.
Judgment, 184, 204 f., 229, 509 f.
Justification, 200, 262 ff., 276, 508,
  513.

Knowledge, 214.
 cf. Word of God.

Language about God, 1 f., 16, 51 f.
Law, 204.
Life, eternal, 446, 531.
Lord's Supper, 98.
 Transubstantiation, 99, 105.

Man—
 Conscience, 230, 232, 235.
 Existence, 19 f., 39 f., 142 f., 233,
  240, 250 f., 445 f., 508.
 Feeling, 230, 232, 235.
 imago Dei, 273 f.
 Intellect, Reason, 152, 231, 234,
  262.
 Self-determination, 228 f., 237, 280.
 status integritatis et corruptionis, 148.
 Subsidiary departments of Psycho-
  logy, 232.
 Will, 230 f., 235.
 cf. Theology (Natural; Anthro-
  pology).
 cf. Word of God.
Modernism, 36 f.
 Dogmatics, 39, 287, 289 f.
 Enlightenment, 39, 288, 377, 378,
  481.
 Holy Scripture, 118, 140, 295 f.
 Proclamation, 68 f.
 cf. Theology (Natural).

" Piety " (" Religion "), 38, 232, 243,
  245, 248 f., 252, 333, 434.
Prayer, 25, 54, 83, 84, 111, 265,
  532 f., 560.
Preaching, 56, 61 f., 77 f.
 cf. Church Proclamation.
Predestination, cf. Election, God
  (Freedom), Revelation (God
  as Subject).

Rebirth, 19, 99, 168, 254, 444 f., 514,
  523 f., 555.
Reconciliation, 134, 161, 465 f., 471,
  485, 524.
 cf. Creation, Jesus Christ, Revelation.

PRINTED BY
MORRISON AND GIBB LIMITED
EDINBURGH AND LONDON